Eric M. Moormann
Pompeii's Ashes

Eric M. Moormann
Pompeii's Ashes

The Reception of the Cities Buried by Vesuvius
in Literature, Music, and Drama

DE GRUYTER

Cover image: Luigi Bazzani (1836–1927), Woman in a Peristyle. Signed and dated ("Luigi Bazzani, Roma 1879"). Oil on canvas. Private collection, Bologna. The peristyle is not one known from Pompeii. It has been invented by the artist.

ISBN 978-1-5015-1583-5
e-ISBN (PDF) 978-1-61451-873-0
e-ISBN (EPUB) 978-1-61451-918-8

Library of Congress Cataloging-in-Publication Data
A CIP catalog record for this book has been applied for at the Library of Congress.

Bibliographic information published by the Deutsche Nationalbibliothek
The Deutsche Nationalbibliothek lists this publication in the Deutsche Nationalbibliografie; detailed bibliographic data are available in the Internet at http://dnb.dnb.de.

© 2017 Walter de Gruyter Inc., Boston/Berlin/Munich
This volume is text- and page-identical with the hardback published in 2015.
Typesetting: eScriptum GmbH & Co. KG, Berlin
Printing and binding: Hubert & Co. GmbH & Co. KG, Göttingen

♾ Printed on acid-free paper
Printed in Germany

www.degruyter.com

Preface

This book is the result of my wide-ranging interests in various fields. My archaeological love for Pompeii, Herculaneum and Vesuvius dates back to a visit to the Pompeii exhibition in The Hague (The Netherlands) in 1973 as a first-year undergraduate. Professor Willem Peters introduced me to Pompeii and Herculaneum in person in 1975, and many visits have since followed. A second fondness – literature and the study of the fortune of the classical world, commonly described with the German term *Nachleben* – has lead to various publications in that field.

Yet, love need not always result in publications, let alone books. The concretization of what had always been a dormant *rêverie* started when in 1998, I was invited by Pietro Giovanni Guzzo, the Superintendent of Pompeii, to give the opening speech at "Pompei, scienza e società," an international scientific congress organized on the occasion of the 250th anniversary of Pompeiian excavations and research. An edited version of that speech appeared in various languages in the exhibition catalogue for "Ercolano. Storie da un'eruzione." In the years between that first essay and the book you have in your hands, various articles have come off the presses, and although they have been further altered and added to, they form the basis of the chapters herein.

Not all works presented here are masterpieces. In fact, only a handful of poems and a single novel are worth reading as literary masterworks. The interest of all works treated here, however, is their common topic – the cities buried by Vesuvius and the emotions they have evoked and continue to evoke in the authors and their readers, and, hence, the ways in which Pompeii and Herculaneum are recreated. The testimonies discussed in this book are, for the most part, prose text (travelogues, novels, novellas, short stories), whereas poetry is mostly limited to narrative evocations of Pompeii and Herculaneum, "epic" poetry. Lyrical poetry has been included only in a few instances, and could easily serve as fodder for another study separate from this one.

I do not claim to give a complete overview of all fictitious evocations of the Vesuvian cities. Such a task would, frankly, be impossible, given the simple prospect of finding all of these works, most of which were – and are – published by obscure presses in remote places and remote times. My capacity to read these texts is another point of interest, since the authors write in their own languages, many of which I cannot read. This implies a domination herein of evocations written in Europe and North America – especially in French, German, English, and Italian. Indispensable is the 1998 *Nova bibliotheca pompeiana. 250 anni di bibliografia archeologica* and its first supplement published in 2012 by Laurentino García y García, who included all sorts of evocations, including written and stage works, paintings and pieces of music. When, in the notes, I remark "Not in

García y García," I do not mean this critically; rather, my hope is to encourage a future supplement to his invaluable compilation that includes a mention of the given work.

Even in the time of the Internet and digitized sources, paper books are the principal sources for this study. All of the works that I include herein, I read in their original editions or subsequent translations and/or the editions indicated; I did not form any of my opinions based merely on a reading of secondary sources. I was able to do research in a large number of libraries, and profited much from the large collections in the national libraries in The Hague, London, Paris, Washington D.C., Berlin, Naples, and Rome, as well as university libraries in Amsterdam, Nijmegen, Ann Arbor (Michigan), Austin (Texas), Cambridge (Massachusetts), Oxford, and the libraries of various institutions in Rome. As a true library addict, I have undoubtedly forgotten some of the collections I consulted. In all of these places, I received the kind assistance of the librarians, to whom I give my sincere thanks. The Universities of Amsterdam and Nijmegen financed some of my bibliographical errands.

Friends surely have suffered over the years due to my long discussions on this topic and yet, they have given immeasurable assistance. I am deeply grateful to many of them and to colleagues who helped me by searching for (and through) texts, providing photocopies and translations, and critically reading parts of this book. I want to name a few of them: Stephan Mols, Alessandra Corda, Pietro Giovanni Guzzo, Gemma Jansen, Robert Kragting, Pieter Muijsken, Paul Hulsenboom, Adrian Stähli, Giuseppe Pucci, and Miguel John Versluys. John R. Clarke, Cathleen Coleman, Nathalie de Haan, and Ann Olga Koloski-Ostrow read (parts of) the text in various stages of development, gave critical assessments, and helped considerably to improve the text's structure and style. Aaron Ostrow was the most critical reader of all: he critically edited the text and offered countless alternatives for my sometimes-opaque formulas and thoughts. Finally, I thank Pietro Giovanni Guzzo, who, as I have said, pushed me to realize this project and warmly welcomed the manuscript so that it has now been transformed into this book. It is for this reason that I want to dedicate this work to him as a *spiritus rector*, a stimulating friend and colleague, with an extremely warm heart for all things Pompeian.

Stephan Mols and Riccardo Helg have provided illustrations. Helg was so kind to procure the cover illustration, a painting from a Milanse private collector. All other images come from my own collection.

Two general remarks should be made. First, in the descriptions of the works I discuss, I maintain the original spelling of the names throughout the text of this book. Generally, each author adapted ancient names to the rules of his or her own language, which sometimes will appear to be misspellings. Herculaneum appears as "Herculanum," "Ercolano," and "Herculane," to list some, and Pompeii becomes "Pompeya," "Pompei," "Pompéi," or "Pompeï." As for personal names, Vettius, for example, becomes "Vezio," "Vettio," and "Vette," among other variations, depending on the original language of a given work. This is also true in elaborations of works like Bulwer-Lytton's *The Last Days of Pompeii*: Glaucus can appear as "Glauco" or "Gláuco," and Ione as "Yone" or "Jone."

Second, this book thanks its existence to innumerable literary and documentary publications. Sometimes, I have decided to offer descriptions of particularly captivating passages or plot points to my readers. In order not to burden the text, I have chosen to include characteristic quotations, mostly from English sources, to be presented in the running text, while paraphrasing and sometimes translating others. For the most part, the translations and some additional quotations from English and non-English contributions are included in the notes, which therefore may look terrifying due to size and number, and are not necessary for a full understanding of the text, but do, I think, provide additional flavor.

Amsterdam/Nijmegen, Spring 2014

Contents

Introduction —— 1

I   From Treasure Hunting to Archaeological Dig.
          History of the Excavations of Herculaneum and Pompeii —— 7

II   Travelers to the Vesuvian Cities —— 95

III   Pagan Pompeii in Fiction —— 165

IV   Jews and Christians in Pompeii Novels —— 215

V   Modern and Contemporary Visits to Pompeii in Fiction:
          A Perilous Affair —— 257

VI   Time Traveling to Ancient Pompeii —— 307

VII   Real and Fictional Manuscripts from Pompeii and Herculaneum —— 333

VIII   Pompeii on Stage and Screen —— 359

IX   Herculaneum Under Vesuvius —— 391

X   Intimations of Pompeii: By Way of Envoy —— 413

Bibliography —— 429

Index of Names, Places, and Subjects —— 469

Introduction

Pompeii: dead and alive, beautiful and ugly, complete and broken, grand and humble, drunk and sober, pious and licentious... All of these epithets – and more – have been given to Pompeii, even the contradictory ones, often in the same texts, and by the same men and women who dedicated their writing talents to the topic of awaking the sleeping city Pompeii once was. Poor Pompeii – how many poetasters and botchers, how many hysterical devotees, how many people have misunderstood and misused you to create a Pompeii of their own? Find solace in the good products of skillful pens and divert yourself from the bad. In the following, all of these expressions will be highlighted.

From their discovery in the middle of the eighteenth century onwards, Herculaneum, Stabiae and Pompeii have attracted throngs of visitors to southern Italy. Here, one can catch a glimpse of life in ancient society, life that was abruptly cut short in A.D. 79, when Vesuvius erupted after a centuries-long period of peace and rest. The contact with first century Roman society that these southern Italian cities allowed not only inspired students of ancient cultures, but also gave rise to numerous fictional representations in the form of poems, novels and short stories, as well as plays, operas, and movies. These intimations are the subject of this book. They will be analyzed according to a number of aspects, including the role of Pompeii and Herculaneum within the text, the reason(s) authors chose Pompeii or Herculaneum as a topic in the first place (if this is known or can be gleaned from the texts), and ways in which authors represented the ancient towns and their inhabitants. My goal is not to judge each work's artistic quality, although better writing usually means a more original story. The discovery of the cities also influenced the world of visual arts, but this will not be the subject of this book, although examples shown in the illustrations offer a good sample of their variety.

Each chapter in this book can be read independently, as each discusses a topic from a specifically defined point of view. Chapter I overviews the excavations and research carried out since the first excavations began. The first objects from Herculaneum were brought to light in ca. 1710, and digs began at Pompeii in 1748. Stabiae was explored some years later. For readers familiar with Pompeian archaeology, this story will contain a lot of common knowledge, but since in the following chapters I often refer to historical facts and ideas, I cannot do without this overview. One of my goals is to place the results of the excavations in relation to descriptions given and stories told in travel literature and fiction.

Especially during the first hundred years, the literature kept pace with the scientific explorations and therefore, a good understanding of travelogues and fiction from this period relies on at least some knowledge of a number of relevant contemporary archaeological publications, which frequently contain the tesserae used by fiction writers to compose their mosaics of the old cities. As time passed, authors began to depend more on the works of their colleagues and on travel guides and manuals, and the public's demand for fantasy writing with a scientific basis became less common.

Travel literature, the topic of Chapter II, is a fertile source for knowledge about personal experiences in the excavations. The late eighteenth and the early nineteenth centuries provide hundreds of travel journals in the form of monographs. Visits to Herculaneum, Pompeii and the archaeological collections in the Royal Palace at Portici and (later) Naples were essential. I give an extensive presentation of the most original impressions – which were often wordily repeated by later authors – to illustrate the emotions people had upon experiencing these places. By way of explaining the differences between the many points of view, it is useful to keep in mind the provenance and background of the visitor at hand and the ever-changing times during which these reflections were written.

Many travel accounts repeat notions taken from older travel accounts without mentioning the source. This is important, because "original" views or observations are often the result of those already recorded by other people. Travelogues also offer an overview of the metamorphosis of Herculaneum and Pompeii. What began as ruins from which one could learn history, transformed, as the literature evolved, first into romantic ruins personally experienced by countless travelers, and then into idealizations of ancient towns which are contrasted with modern cities and urban concepts.

Chapter III again recalls impressions of travelers, and begins with an overview of various responses to encounters with victims (found as skeletons, cavities in the volcanic material, or preserved as plaster casts). It then focuses on fictional and tenacious motifs like the story of the brave sentinel at the Herculanean Gate. More space is dedicated to works of fiction that play out in ancient Pompeii from the first century B.C until A.D. 79, in which more or (often much) less famous people live through a wide variety of fortunes and misfortunes, including political intrigue, love affairs and murders. The greater share of them ends with the eruption of Vesuvius, a disaster caused either by nature or by the gods.

When instead authors interpret the eruption as a punishment by God, we deal with Christian novels, which suggest that the Pompeians are erased for their licentiousness; they are the theme of Chapter IV. Bulwer-Lytton's 1834 *The Last Days of Pompeii* has been the most influential such novel to date. Bulwer-Lytton does not address the question of whether Christians actually lived in Pompeii, but after his work became widely known, signs of their presence were apparently found in the excavations, and consequently, a subgroup of Christian novels popped up after the 1850s. The institutionalization of Christian archaeology as a special branch of archaeology may have played a role in this surge of interest.

In Chapter V I discuss fiction in which Pompeii plays a role in the lives of modern people. Travelers become the protagonists of stories that – partially or completely – take place in and around the excavations. We will primarily encounter foreign tourists, but also Italian locals and archaeologists. Some visitors even come into contact with ancient citizens. Chapter VI concerns the motif of time traveling. The emerging interest in psychology and psychiatry during the nineteenth century stimulated writers to trespass the borders of the dead and to venture into an extinct reality. Among the fascinating personalities we will encounter are local tour guides who tell clichéd stories, leave their own domain and become former Pompeians. Some more recent works feature time travel to the future, and reflect on the buried cities from there.

A curious group of works is that of alleged manuscripts found in the ashes of Pompeii and Herculaneum, which are dealt with in Chapter VII. The discovery of the charred papyrus scrolls in the Villa of the Papyri at Herculaneum stimulated the genre of "lost manuscripts." We will see short stories, novels, diaries, epics – even political pamphlets – all masquerading as ancient texts. The excitement of finding a previously unknown or long-lost masterpiece is what continues to drive this concept. In the 1990s, new excavations that were carried out at the Villa of the Papyri rekindled the public's interest in such lost masterpieces.

Chapter VIII presents examples of operas, stage plays, pieces of music, and songs, all of which were inspired by Pompeii. Some of these works are adaptations of existing works of fiction, while others are original inventions. Reenacting the drama of A.D. 79 must have been a challenge for stage artists. Chapter IX gives the floor to Herculaneum, Pompeii's oft-disregarded smaller sister, and examines some fictitious works and poems, which are dedicated to this site. Works of fiction dedicated to Vesuvius itself are also briefly presented in this chapter.

Finally, in Chapter X, I hope to synthesize all of these impressions in order to make clear the impact all of these intimations have had on the image of Pompeii, as created by the various categories of artists, dramatists, authors, scholars and amateurs, and hope to conclude that Pompeii is and always will be a construct both of fantasy and archaeological research. Much like the archaeologists who had exposed an ancient civilization to the post-ancient world, the primary challenge for writers, stage producers, and other artists, was to re-create Pompeii – that is, create a version of Pompeii they could call their own – and present it to a hungry public.

Previous Studies

I am not the first to study intimations of Pompeii and Herculaneum; although the number of studies on this topic has grown in the last decade, examples of previous scholarship are rather few. Unfortunately, many older studies are superficial or inaccurate. The bibliographical documentation in most cases is weak and – as the reader will observe – finding a mentioned poem, story or novel is often a difficult task, even in the age of Internet searches and online databases. In most cases these studies deal with specific topics and thus yield a fragmentary image. Many earlier studies are further limited by a certain linguistic chauvinism, such that works only from a given language are included.

On May 6, 1888, the archaeologist Antonio Sogliano gave a lecture in the "Circolo Filologico" in Naples on *Pompei nella letteratura*, in which he wanted to engage the audience with literary texts and not bore them to death with archaeology (p. 5: "noja mortale"). The old city became a new Ariadne, first abandoned and then woken up after a long sleep to start a new life.[1] For that reason one can re-create Pompeii in one of two ways: as a buried city and as a discovered city. This distinction, I think, is fundamental, as it defines the two main streams of inspiration for literary writers. Sogliano's essay contains several briefly but elegantly discussed examples, and is a good introduction to the older texts. After Sogliano, there were no publications on this matter for a very long time.

A short essay by Jean Seznec was also the result of a lecture, which Seznec presented in 1948 on the occasion of the second centenary of the Pompeian excavations. In his paper, the great literary historian dealt especially with French authors of the Age of Enlightenment, like Diderot. Curtis Dahl, an archaeologist and literary historian wrote a similar text in 1956, which gives examples of literary evocations of Pompeii in various languages. Seznec's and Dahl's papers are pleasant enough to read, but it is difficult to check their sources, as references are missing. L. Goldstein had a similar scope in his 1979 paper "The Impact of Pompeii on the Literary Imagination." Egon Caesar Corti's 1940 *Untergang und Auferstehung von Pompeji und Herculaneum* was an extremely popular work about the history of Pompeii and its cultural impact, and was reprinted and translated into many languages continuously until the late 1970s.[2] Some of his untrue assertions have become fact in later scholarship; we will encounter them throughout this

---

[1] Sogliano 1888, 8: "nuova Arianna abbandonata e ridestasi, dopo un lungo sonno, ad una nuova vita."
[2] Corti 1940. For all these editions, see García y García 1998, nos. 3318–3327. On Corti, see Wallisch 1957. A similar, updated and very informative narrative is Harris 2007, which unfortunately contains many misspelled names and terms.

book. In his 1966 *Pompeji. Eine Stadt in Literatur und Leben*, Wolfgang Leppmann stresses the lack of quality in most literary evocations of Pompeii, and claims that the best authors are Pliny, Leopardi and Bulwer-Lytton. Leppmann claims that later generations of authors do not pay much attention to the theme of Pompeii, although he observes a revival in the 1950s and 1960s. In all of the works discussed by Leppmann, a fascination with the apocalypse is patent.

Christiane Zintzen dedicated her 1998 dissertation to archaeological themes eternized in literature: Schliemann's Mycenae and Pompeii are the main topics. As far as I know, her pages on Pompeii are the first serious attempts at analyzing the literature vis-à-vis the monument. Victoria Zimmerman, in her 2008 *Excavating Victorians*, has a similar approach to the use of archaeology as a motif in fiction in the nineteenth century. Another German study, Thorsten Fitzon's 2004 *Reisen in das befremdliche Pompeji*, contains many new insights about the way both classicist and romantic writers adopted Pompeii as a theme in their works, and demonstrates Fitzon's profound knowledge of literary texts about Pompeii. Zimmerman and Fitzon both concentrate on German literary works. Marie-France David's 2001 study of French decadent literature, *Antiquité latine et Décadence* and Göran Blix' 2009 *From Paris to Pompeii* are both valuable sources and analyses of French evocations of Pompeii. Hans-Joachim Glücklich's 2008 *Pompeji lebt* and Béatrice Robert-Boissier's 2011 *Pompéi. Les doubles vies de la cité du Vésuve* bring together a rich number of evocations from mediums like fiction and cinema. Stefano Rocchi's 2006–2007 essay "Gialli storici ambientati a Pompei" offers a narratological analysis of some sixteen thrillers concentrating on Pompeii, among the thousands of crime novels that play out in Antiquity. Ingrid Rowland's 2014 *From Pompeii* presents the reader with well- and less well-known evocations, like Sannazzaro's 1504 *Arcadia*, Bartolo Longo's 1872 creation of modern Pompeii, not far from the ancient excavations, and Renoir's 1881 trip to the excavations. Two good recent volumes of collected papers about the fortune of Pompeii in literature and arts are those edited by Victoria Gardner Coates and Jon Seydl (2007), and by Shelley Hales and Joanne Paul (2011).

In an attractive 1992 volume of the French Bouquin series, Claude Aziza assembles three complete novels (Bulwer-Lytton, Bertheroy and Llewellyn), two novellas (Gautier and Jensen), and fragments of other works, which serves as an excellent anthology of intimations of Pompeii and Herculaneum. The foreign texts have been translated into French. A similar volume is Dieter Richter's 2005 *Pompeji und Herculaneum*, which also presents fragments of known and unknown authors, presented in chapters, each of which focus on a specific topic, like traveling, street life, and erotica.

Travel accounts as a genre have been studied extensively. There are a number of studies that discuss Pompeii in more or less detail. Especially worth mentioning here are Elisabeth and Raymond Chevallier's lucid 1984 book about eighteenth-century travelers to Italy and the travelogues they produced. In 1980 the Chevalliers produced a French edition of Friedrich Johann Lorenz Meyer's beautiful 1798 travel book *Darstellungen aus Italien*. Other important monographs on this topic are Chantal Grell's 1983 *Herculanum et Pompéi dans les récits des voyageurs français du XVIII*^{e} *siècle* and Mirella Romero Recio's 2012 *Ecos de un descubrimiento*. Still other works will be discussed or quoted in relevant places throughout this book, especially in Chapter II.

I hope that this summary confirms for the reader that *Pompeii's Ashes* has been a project worth undertaking. To my knowledge, it is, to date, the most comprehensive one-volume collection of the widest variety of Pompeian works. Its primary goal is to illustrate the massive impact Pompeii has had on the world's collective imagination and creativity during the past several centuries.

I From Treasure Hunting to Archaeological Dig. History of the Excavations of Herculaneum and Pompeii

In Antiquity, the region at the foot of Vesuvius was renowned for its healthy climate, fertility and beauty. There were good ports in ancient Herculaneum and Pompeii, and navigable rivers flanked Pompeii. The area was rather densely inhabited by people living in farmsteads, villages and small cities. Pompeii, Herculaneum and Stabiae, lying around Vesuvius, were to be singled out in history because of their unhappy fortune in A.D. 79, not thanks to specific features that placed the towns above other average settlements in the Roman world.

Undoubtedly, many eruptions had happened before – some of them are also known from stratigraphic excavations – but Vesuvius seemed dead, or had been sleeping for ages, when it exploded in 79.[3] This eruption was so powerful that the fill of the wide caldara – which looked like a plain top next to the ridge of Monte Somma – was blown up, crumbled by the heat and the gases coming from inside the earth. Thanks to a long description of the event in two letters by the younger Pliny, seventeen years old at the time, written some twenty years later to his friend, the historian Tacitus, volcanologists are able to reconstruct the event. Many people were able to save themselves, but a great number died on this day of hell.[4]

The small towns had no particular importance within the Roman Empire. They are barely mentioned in the written sources we possess,[5] and many questions remain open: when were they founded and who were their first inhabitants? How did they develop? Herculaneum was said to have been founded by Hercules; the other places do not have a foundation myth, but the same Hercules would also be the founder of Pompeii.

No famous men are reported in the sources as originating in these towns. Cicero possessed a villa on the outskirts of Pompeii called Pompeianum, and

---

[3] See i.a. G. Mastrolorenzo in Mühlenbrock/Richter 2005, 29–40; G. Corsi et al. in Meller/Dickmann 2011, 24–34; M. Barth, ibidem, 73–80.
[4] *Epistulae* 6.16 and 6.20. They are included in numerous books on the cities of Vesuvius, e.g. García y García 1998, 44–49; Mühlenbrock/Richter 2005, 41–43; Richter 2007, 24–33. Travel writers and even fiction authors sometimes insert fragments from the letters, probably to enhance the veracity of their texts. Modern insights are collected in Scarth 2009, 39–88. For volcanological research in the seventeenth and eighteenth century see Cocco 2013.
[5] All relevant ancient literary sources in García y García 1998, 30–59. Cooley/Cooley 2004 give these and other texts from Pompeii itself.

another nobleman, Calpurnius Piso had a villa near Herculaneum. Many think that the Villa of the Papyri must have been his property.⁶ In the time of Augustus there were other rich people with fancy villas nearby, e.g. M. Vipsanius Agrippa, married to Augustus' daughter Julia. Their last son, M. Agrippa Postumus, so called because of his birth after his father's death in 12 B.C., is associated with a villa unearthed and destroyed around 1900 at Boscotrecase. The family of Nero's second wife, Poppaea, originated in this region and possessed some houses and villas; she herself has been associated with 'Villa A' at Torre Annunziata, ancient Oplontis.

The main event mentioned in the written sources – and verified during the excavations – was a very strong earthquake on February 5 A.D. 62. Writing in the early second century, Tacitus describes this occurrence in his *Annals* (15.22) under that year, whereas the philosopher Lucius Annaeus Seneca, in an essay on the origin of earthquakes, gives the names of the two consuls of the year 63, Regulus and Virginius. Although Seneca's treatise came out only a few years after the event, most scholars think that this mention is an interpolation of a later date and that we should follow Tacitus.⁷

Like Pliny the Younger at around A.D. 100, Dio Cassius described the eruption of 79 a hundred years later. According to him, the inhabitants of Pompeii were sitting in the theater at midday when disaster struck. The cataclysm would have been so enormous that rescue was barely possible.⁸ People returned afterwards to Pompeii, where the ashes and lapilli were easier to remove, but the epigram written some ten years later by Martial only speaks about a former time (see Chapter IX, note 1442). A disaster of this kind was also described in the Antonine or later *Oracula Sibyllina*. The Jewish prophecy is about a pseudo-Nero, who will come from the East to the West:⁹

---

6 Most recently Mattusch 2005, 20–23; M. Capasso in Zarmakoupi 2010, 89–113.
7 63: i.a. Gross 1989, 246, 255, 269; Brok 1995, 341, 344–345. 62: i.a. Vottero 1989, 178–179, 576 (with extensive bibliography); A. Varone in Mols/Moormann 2005, 315–324. In this book I use the year 62, unless in quotations or paraphrases of 63 adepts. An interesting thesis is Kurt Wallat's proposal (2005), to surmise two earthquakes, in both 62 and 63.
8 Dio Cassius, *Roman History* 66.23, quoted at p. 393. An anonymous author in the *Philosophical Transactions* 47 (1753) 150–159, esp. 155, observes that this was not true, since no skeletal remains had been found.
9 *Oracula Sibyllina* 4.130–136: ἀλλ' ὁπόταν χθονίης ἀπὸ ῥωγάδος Ἰταλίδος γῆς / πυρσὸς ἀποστραφθεὶς εἰς οὐρανὸν εὐρὺν ἵκηται, / πολλὰς δὲ φλέξῃ πόλιας καὶ ἄνδρας ὀλέσσῃ, / πολλὴ δ' αἰθαλόεσσα τέφρη μέγαν αἰθέρα πλήσῃ, / καὶ ψεκάδες πίπτωσιν ἀπ' οὐρανοῦ οἷά τε μίλτος, / γινώσκειν τότε μῆνιν ἐπουρανίοιο θεοῖο, / εὐσεβέων ὅτι φῦλον ἀναίτιον ἐξολέσουσιν. It might also refer to Etna or Stromboli. I owe this reference to Prof. Daniël den Hengst. I also found it quoted as early as in Capacius 1607, 454. See now i.a. García y García 1998, 51; Cooley/Cooley 2004, 42–43;

> But when from a crevice in the Italian earth
> A fire will escape and reach wide heaven,
> And will burn many towns and kill men,
> And when many glowing ashes will fill the large heaven
> And drops will fall out of heaven like blood,
> Then know that it is the scorn of God in heaven,
> Since they will ruin the people of pious guiltless.

This *vaticinium eventu* can be compared to Seneca's rationale of the description of the earthquake of 62:[10]

> It will also be profitable to keep in mind that the gods do nothing like that, and that neither heaven nor earth are shaken by the ire of deities: these thing have their own causes and do not rage upon order but, exactly as our bodies are disturbed by certain vices they are disturbed, and then, when they seem to do damage, they suffer it.

As to the exact day of the eruption, most generally August 24, around midday, has been assumed. New research, however, seems to indicate a date in the fall, e.g. October 24. For our topic, this is not so relevant, but I think that the latter date seems to correspond with various facts, like the victims' clothing, fruit harvested, and the discovery of a coin dated September 79.[11]

What Happened Before 1738

In some medieval and Renaissance Italian texts Pompeii is mentioned as an example of a lost culture.[12] To my knowledge, the oldest mention in prose in which the buried cities are evoked is Giovanni Boccaccio's *Comedia delle Ninfe*

Richter 2007, 36–37. Marcus Aurelius, *In semet* 4.48, sees the disaster as a warning to concentrate yourself on your life here: "How many towns entirely died, to say it this way, Helike, Pompeii, Herculaneum and others." García y García 1998, 40; Richter 2007, 36.

10 Seneca, *Quaestiones Naturales* 6.3.1: "*Illud quoque proderit praesumere animo, nihil horum deos facere, nec ira numinum aut caelum concuti aut terram: suas ista causas habent nec ex imperio saeuiunt sed quibusdam uitiis ut corpora nostra turbantur et tunc, cum facere uidentur iniuriam, accipiunt.*"

11 Pliny clearly gives August 24 (see Ciarallo/De Carolis 1989). But for the October thesis, that was already put forward by Carlo Maria Rosini in 1797, see G. Stefani in Meller/Dickmann 2011, 81–84, with bibliography.

12 Collected in García y García 1998, 61–62. See also Carotenuto 1980, 171–173. Oplontis (modern Torre Annunziata) is indicated on the famous *Tabula Peutingeriana* in Vienna, which relies on a late-antique Roman map.

fiorentine from 1341–1342.¹³ Ameto listens to stories told by nymphs. In one of them, the nymph Lia recounts her trip as a bride from Sicily to Rome to meet her groom. On her way north the vessel passes Capri, Sorrento, the cliffs of Stabiae, Pompeii and Vesuvius, imitator of Etna.¹⁴ Then she sees Pozzuoli, Cumae and Baiae. This list of names adds an exotic touch to the Nymph's tale, and does not focus on the fatal events. Quite extensively Flavio Biondo discusses the location of Herculaneum and Pompeii in his *Italia Illustrata* in the middle of the fifteenth century: the first should be near Torre del Greco, the latter in the surroundings of Castellammare di Stabia, but nothing is extant. Pliny died during the study of the eruption.¹⁵ Niccolò Perotti's dictionary of the mid-fifteenth century highlights Herculaneum among five towns called Heraclea:¹⁶

> The fifth Heraclea is in Campania, Italy, and is also named Herculaneum. It lies by the sea near Pompeii and has a promontory that enjoys marvellous breezes from winds they call Etesiae, which is why it is true that the air is very healthy over there. This town used to be the domain of the Oscans, as well as Pompeii that is irrigated by the river Sarnus. Then it was held by the Thusci and Pelasgi, followed by the Samnites. It was also the market town of Nola and Nuceria, not far from Mount Vesuvius that is cultivated with excellent fields except for its peak. It is largely covered by a plain, but this is barren and abounds with ashes, having in front of it hollow caves full of burnt stones. So, it is easy to conjecture that these places were once ablaze with fire, but that the flames were extinguished when their fuel ran out.

This long silence upon Campania and its buried cities remained almost undisturbed until the beginning of the eighteenth century. One of the few post–79 activ-

---

13 Boccaccio 1964, 761. Mentioned in Sogliano 1888, 13; Leppmann 1966, 59; García y García 1998, 61. Boccaccio lived at Naples from 1328 onwards and probably saw volcanic activities (Richter 2007, 47).
14 "e le rocche di Stabia e la già grande Pompea e Veseo, imitatore de' fuochi d'Enna."
15 Biondo 2010, 332–333: "*Herculaneum [...] nullas habet vetustatis reliquias praeter superioris Plinii mortis locum quem ibi fuisse necessarium tenemus.*" On Pompeii p. 340–341. García y García 1998, 61; nos 5359–5360 (First edition, Verona 1482).
16 Perotti 1994, 250 (Lib. I, Epigr. IV, 353): "*Quinta in Campania Italia, quae et Herculaneum dicta est, incumbens mari iuxta Pompeios et promuntorium habens mirum in modum uentis afflatum, quos uocant Etesias, propter quod saluberrimum ibi esse aerem constat. Hanc urbem tenuerunt Osci, sicut Pompeios, quos Sarnus amnis abluit, postmodum Thusci et Pelasgi, deinde Samnites, erat que Nolae et Nuceriae emporium, non longe á monte Vesuvio, qui amoenissimis agris incolitur excepto cacumine. Id magna ex parte planiciem habet, sed infructuosum est et cinere scatens, cauernos prae se ferens, antra plena adustis lapidibus, ut facilis coniectura sit ea loca quondam arsisse, sed defecisse flammas cessante materia.*" First print in 1489 and conceived as a commentary to Martial's epigrams. Gacía y García 1998, 61; no. 10.493. I thank my colleague Bé Breij for a check of my translation. Cf. Sannazzaro around 1500, here Chapter III, pp. 170–171.

ities at Pompeii known formed works for the construction of irrigation canals in the years 1594–1600, when Domenico Fontana hit ancient houses; a memorial slab in the street between insulae I 6 and I 7 marks this fact.[17] Some inscriptions came to light[18] and the toponym Civita in the area of Pompeii recorded the earlier presence of a *civitas*, a city, as stated by Lucas Holstenius.[19] But apart from some brief notices like Holstenius' and that in *Neapolitana Historia* by Giulio Cesare Capaccio nothing happened until 1689.[20] This and other publications did not try to link

---

17 Most recently Rowland 2014, 31–32. Woldemar Kaden's *Eine pompejanische Nike* (in Kaden 1892, 229–257) plays out in this era. The Neapolitan nobleman Antonio Falangola receives Don Juan of Austria after his victory at Lepanto in 1571. The general falls in love with Falangola's daughter Diana. A bronze statuette of a Nike found in a Roman house under Falangola's villa in the region of Pompeii and Stabiae, cities nobody remembers any longer, serves as a symbol of their lucky bond. Their daughter Johanna, who enters the monastery of S. Chiara at Naples, becomes the founder of the Church of S. Maria della Vittoria in that town. The addition "Vittoria" obviously refers to Lepanto, but is that also true for the statuette? This love story, based on a local legend, is similar to romantic stories told by authors like Stendhal and Gregorovius on palaces and churches in Rome. It illustrates a certain continuing assessment of the presence of the antique cities in the Renaissance and Baroque. As far as I know, Kaden is unique in recalling the Vesuvian towns in an early setting.
18 *CIL* X.938: a slab in the Church of the Madonna at Scafati, and other texts found by Fontana: Bowersock 1978, 462–463.
19 Holstenius 1666 (In Ortelium), 156 remains fundamental, since he states that he saw remains: "[...] *sed ejus uestigia uidi paulo supra turrem Graecorum.*" Winckelmann 1997a, 145 gives another quotation from this work. Cf. Bowersock 1978 on Holstenius and Bianchini 1697, 1747. For a map of the area before the excavations see Longobardi 2002, 39, fig. 22. Brief mentions also in Alberti 1568, 190–191 (García y García 1998, no. 97 for other editions).
20 Capacius 1607, 461, in Chapter IX of Book II on Pompeii and Herculaneum: "*Vbi ea urbs posita fuerit, multos annos ignorauimus. Hac tamen aetate dum rustici agrum colerent, & foederent, inuentae sunt concamerationes, tum uero pauimenta parietesque, marmore tecti, & multae inscriptiones, quae plurimum lucis attulerunt.*" At p. 417, in Chapter X on Stabiae, he dismisses the finds at Civita as remains of Stabiae: "*Placuit plerisque ibi aedificatum fuisse, ubi hoc tempore ad Vesuuium ruinas cernimus, quas Ciuitatem uulgus appellat, quibus ipse qui ea loca accurate consideraui, non assentior, & intercedesse ibi Tauraniam affirmarem. Vera asserunt qui ibi Stabias extructas dicunt, ubi noua hac aetate ciuitas posita est quam Castrum maris appellant.*" Referred to in Bowersock 1978, 463. A similar notice in Baudrand 1682, I, s.v. Herculaneum (near Torre del Greco in the Terra del Lavoro); II, s.v. Pompeianum (property Cicero near Torre Annunziata) and s.v. Pompeii (near Torre Annunziata according to Flavio Biondo, next to Scafati following Cluverius): " [...] *Sed Lucas Holstenius pro certo affirmauit Pompeios fuisse, ubi nunc maxima visuntur rudera, loco qui Civita uulgo dicitur in uicinis, ubi Ambrosius Notanus Stabias olim fuisse extimauit, sed lapides nuper hic effossi, & Stabias translate Pompeios fuisse certo ostendunt, tum nomen ipsum Civita hoc confirmat, tum etiam interuallum inter Pompeios & Nuceriam 12 mill. pass. ostendit circa Scafati ponendum esse, sub Nerone Terrae motu concidit.*" S.v. Stabile he refers to modern Castellammare di Stabia. Johann Caspar Goethe (1932, 181–183) refers to Cellarius and probably means Capaccio. On Capaccio, see Cocco 2013, 43–44, 121–122.

fortuitous finds with the ancient towns hidden under the feet of modern people. Instead, they convey a greater perspicacity about the topography of ancient Campania than the first generation of excavators at Pompeii, who would not know its name before 1756, when inscriptions were found recording the name Pompeii (see note 76). A late example of this kind of antiquarian scholarship before the first explorations is that of the learned priest Niccolò Partenio Giannettasio SJ. In 1704 he published *Ver Herculanum*, a history of Campania. He mentioned the ancient cities destroyed by Vesuvius, but did not hint at explorations or even fortuitous finds. The book is a clear example of research relying on written sources only, both ancient and later texts.[21]

One of the first stratigraphic soundings in archaeology was carried out in the area of Vesuvius, as early as 1689.[22] The astronomer Francesco Bianchini described a small dig by the Neapolitan architect Francesco Picchetti next to the volcano. To establish the chronology of the period between the Diluvium and our time, this excavation was very important for him. In an area 1,500 meters from the sea, they encountered at a certain depth some layers of earth that seemed to be systematized in order, one horizontally upon the other.[23] They found after the fourth "suolo" inscriptions from the Roman era, and at 100 *palmi* in depth there were other traces. Picchetti's account gives a precise stratigraphy of what is called by him the Villa of Pompey: nine layers. The layer that interests us, labeled A, contains inscriptions and pieces of iron. Bianchini ascribes the Roman objects to the "Città di Pompej," not far from Scafati, where traces were found previously. Bianchini was not only familiar with astronomy, but he also had a good command of ancient sources, and might have had, as Giuseppe Pucci has suggested, a keen eye for these still largely unknown phenomena.[24]

Andrew Wallace-Hadrill and his colleagues at the Herculaneum Conservation Project made new finds concerning early discoveries in the towns buried by Vesuvius. When they cleaned some of the Bourbon tunnels (see below), they found shards from Medieval and Baroque pottery, dating from before the eighteenth

---

21 There is a second edition of 1715. This *Ver Herculanum* was expanded with *Aestates Surrentinae*, *Autumni Surrentini* and *Hyemes Puteolanae* (Giannettasio 1722, 2vols). McIlwayne 1988, no 3.66; García y García 1998, no. 5939.
22 Pucci 1989. On Bianchini, see Schnapp 1996, 185–188 (but nothing on this project).
23 Bianchini 1697 and 1747, 246: "alcune striscie di terra, che parevano disposte con ordine, quasi fossero suoli, o pavimenti, collocate orizontalmente l'un sull'altro" (in "Deca Terzo. Ovvero del Tempo Eroico"). The following is discussed on pages 246–251. At p. 249 he distinguishes two more strata, viz. of eruptions in 472 and 1631.
24 Pucci 1989, 47; 1993, 126–127. Several authors have made mention of this research in their works, e.g. Venuti 1748, 52–53; Martini 1779, 80–88; Russel 1750, II, 202 ("about sixty years ago"); Castellan 1819, 357. See Borrelli 1992, 52 note 60 for other old references.

century. Wallace-Hadrill suggests that previous work had been carried out here, but with no written record. The lack of official interest might even be explained by the superstition reigning in the area of Naples that these impious remains would bring misfortune.[25]

Discoveries in the Early Eighteenth Century

The precise date of the "first" finds of Herculaneum remains an enigma.[26] The area was occupied by the houses of the village of Resina. As is well known, the discovery is connected with the French Prince or Count of Elbeuf who started to construct a villa around 1710, when he was in the service of Austrian troops occupying Naples and environments in the Wars of Succession.[27] This is situated in the harbor of Resina, Granatello, and not – as is often suggested – on the spot where a deep well was dug in the hard lava during the preparations for the construction. Workers found antiquities in this pit, as had apparently happened previously in other deep excavations.[28] Gennaro Borrelli has made clear that Elbeuf had acquired other properties and that the pit could have been sunk there for the sake of antiquities.[29] Officially, it was said that Elbeuf was looking for water, but following rumors spread by local workers, others thought that he was searching for marble. The marble in this case would be reworked into plaster of Paris, which should serve as the basic material for the rococo stuccoes in the new properties, or was even sent to Naples for some churches.[30] The presence of this material reminded the people of the existence of the

---

25 Wallace-Hadrill 2011, 45–47. More extensively Camardo 2013, 326–336.
26 "First" meant as the traditional discovery, but see above and Wallace-Hadrill 2011, 47–48.
27 On Elbeuf (also spelled Elboeuf), see Borrelli 1992, 39–41; Papaccio 1995; Rowland 2014, 52–55. Because of his sharing foreign military troops King Louis XIV had virtually executed him, so that in fact he was exiled from France. Elbeuf had come to Naples in 1707 and would become rich thanks to his marriage with the Princess of Salsa in 1712.
28 Borrelli 1992, 40 records informative tips by Niccolò Amenta about previous finds (on him p. 52 note 25). Breton 1855, 20 gives 1684 as the first year, when "un boulanger, creusant un puits à Portici, rencontra quelques ruines romaines; ce puits, qui existe encore aujourd'hui, descendait précisément au milieu du théâtre d'Herculanum!" See also Camardo 2013 for pre-1738 finds of antiquities in Herculaneum.
29 See Borrelli 1992, 41–42 on the two pits in the "bosco pietroso". Cf. Papaccio 1995.
30 Among the earliest references is D'Arthenay 1748, 1, who gives the search for water as the reason for sinking a pit (idem Volkmann 1777–1778, 296–297). De Lalande 1769 and 1786, VII, letter XV, suggests plaster production, as do Miller 1776, 285, Starke 1802, II, 112 and Castellan 1819, 356. Venuti 1748, 99 and De Brosses 1991, 599 tell about columns in S. Gennaro at Naples.

buried cities Herculaneum and Pompeii. The years 1706,[31] 1708,[32] 1709,[33] 1711,[34] 1712,[35] and 1713[36] are most frequently mentioned in the early accounts, but one even finds 1720.[37] Some years are surely incorrect, as Elbeuf arrived in 1707 and left Naples in 1716 after having sold all his properties.[38] In a meticulous reconstruction of this period Francesca Longo Auricchio has argued that 1711 was the most plausible year of the discovery, and Jens Daehner has reached the same conclusion.[39] A conclusive reason might be the brief announcement in the *Giornale de' letterati d'Italia* of that year in which the discovery of marble objects by the Prince of Elbeuf in a temple in ancient Herculaneum is made public.[40] Columns in various sorts of marble were found as well as an architrave with the inscription: *Appius. Pulcher. C. f. Cos. MP. VIIvir. Epulonum.* (Appius Pulcher, son of Claudius, imperator, consul, seven-man of meals). It was argued at length

---

31 Cochin/Bellicard 1757, 9.
32 Carotenuto 1932, 75.
33 Most recently Wallace-Hadrill 2011, 347.
34 Venuti 1748, 54–55; Russel 1750, II, 203; Palermo 1792, 36. In modern times i.a. Herbig 1960; De Seta 1982, 85–91.
35 Gori 1748, IX: 1711 or 1712, probably in a Temple of Hercules.
36 E.g. D'Arthenay 1748, 13; Fougeroux de Bondaroy 1770, 11; C. [= Chevalier de Jaucourt] in *Encyclopédie*, Supplément 3 (1777) 349–358 s.v. Herculanum; Starke 1802, II, 112; Castellan 1819, 356; Breton 1855, 41.
37 Chevalier de Jaucourt in *Encyclopédie* 8 (1765) 150–154 s.v. Herculanum, esp. p. 150: "Il n'y a près de dix ans que l'on parle toûjours avec admiration de cette découverte." English translation in Seznec 1949, 150. Micheletti (1846, 41, 292) writes that Elbeuf "dalle nostre maraviglie, con violata fede e contumaci traffichi, arricchiva i musei di Savoia e di Polonia, miseri di proprie celebrità ed avidi delle nostre [...]." But on p. 321 he gives 1711, when Stendardo (see note 40) stopped "lo sciagurato traffico dell'Elbuf." Galignani 1819, 477–480 is vague with some 30 years after 1689. On him Gori 1748, 1–2. This late year also in Saint-Non 1782; D'Ancora 1803, 29–30.
38 Longo Auricchio 1997, 178; Borrelli 1992, 43. Winckelmann 1997a, 156, therefore has "spätestens 1716." Coyer 1775, 229 narrates that he met him, but he gives the year 1736. Caylus must have heard about the work by Elbeuf in 1715: he succinctly concludes: "Il [E.] a peu creusé, cependant il a beaucoup tiré." Mentioned by Kimball 1953, 1254 and Chevalier/Chevalier 1984, 21.
39 Longo Auricchio 1997, 176–177, note 10; Daehner 2007, 1–11. Cf. Parslow 1995, 22–24. De Caro 2013, 16 has 1710.
40 *Giornale de' letterati d'Italia* 5 (1711) 309–311 "Di Napoli"; quotation p. 309: "Nel casale di Resina, con l'occasione di racconciare una cisterna s'incontrarono alcuni marmi, il che diede impulso al Sig. Principe d'Elbeuf di farvi scavare a sue spese; e si crede esservi stato un Tempio dell'antica città detta Herculaneum, mentovata da Plinio, Cicerone, Mela, e Strabone." The notice was probably compiled by Giuseppe Stendardo (on him Borrelli 1992, 42), but Minico Imperato is also mentioned (Parslow 1995, 22). The *Giornale* was a sort of yearbook edited at Venice under the protection of the Principe di Toscana by great scholars like Apostolo Zeno and Scipione Maffei. Cf. Stendardo's report from 1711 reproduced in Gori 1748, 1 and partially quoted in Borrelli 1992, 53 note 92.

Discoveries in the Early Eighteenth Century — 15

Fig. 1: Theater at Herculaneum: view from within an eighteenth century Bourbon tunnel through hard volcanic material, with stage (*proscenium*) in the center, stage wall (*scaenae frons*) on the left, and a narrower tunnel visible on the right (photo Stephan Mols)

that he was Cicero's friend known from his letters. Moreover there was the statue of a woman that might be a portrait of the Vestal Claudia, mentioned by Valerius Maximus.[41] The finds included statues of Hercules and some women. Contemporary descriptions of the pit and of the finds pulled out from it are almost completely lacking.[42] As late as 1740 Charles De Brosses (see Chapter II) visits the old soldier at Florence.[43]

Clearly, the count had had great luck by hitting the stage building of the Roman theater of Herculaneum, where he came across marble columns and revetments of its sumptuous façade (fig. 1). Three female statues, which were brought to light in good shape, had adorned niches of the stage façade and represented Muses or local elite women. In 1713, Elbeuf gave them to Eugene, prince of Savoy, commander of the Austrian troops, lover of culture and a distant relative. His heirs sold the statues to Frederick Augustus II, Elector of Saxony in 1736, and they are still on display in the art collection of the former Saxonian court at Dresden, the Albertinum.[44] Borrelli's investigations about the properties have made clear that Elbeuf's enterprise was a rather nasty business, kept as secret as possible and only aiming at his personal interests.

Luckily we know the pit itself, because King Charles started new investigations there in 1738. Presumably, the King ordered the old pit to be reopened after hearing rumors about the earlier finds.[45] The story that the King's wife Maria

---

41 *Giornale*, p. 311 "... che potrebbe essere di Claudia Vestale nominata da Valerio Massimo." The brief notice finishes by saying: "Se vi accaderà qualche altra scoperta, non lasceremo di ragguagliare la Repubblica letteraria." But there are no more volumes to do so. The text hints at the daughter of Appius Claudius, described in Valerius Maximus 5.4.6, who helped her father during a triumph, when he was attacked by a plebeian tribune.

42 Some accounts quoted in Venuti 1748 and Gori 1748 as well as those listed by Longo Auricchio 1997.

43 De Brosses 1991, Letter 25, p. 447–448: "[Elbeuf] tâche, autant qu'il peut, par ses manières polies, de réparer celles des Lorrains, dont il convient le premier sans aucune peine. Il joue à merveille le bonhomme et l'affidable; et ce que j'y trouve le mieux, il nous fait trez bonne chère, sans aucune façon qui sent le prince." The whereabouts of Elbeuf after his departure from Naples in 1719 remain unclear. Some marbles were used to decorate the St. Stephen's in his native village Elbeuf-sur-Seine (Papaccio 1995, figs 40–49).

44 They are known as the "Grosse Herkulanerin" and [two] "Kleine Herkulanerinnen". See Longo Auricchio 1997, 178–179, figs. 1–2; Mühlenbrock/Richter 2005, 274; Daehner 2007, 1–17; Müller 2012, 183–185, 193, figs 39–41 on these finds and their adventures before their final destination Dresden. Between 1711 and 1713 they were restored at Rome.

45 Borrelli 1992, 47. See, for instance, a letter of William Hammond mistakenly dated March 7, 1731, in *Philosophical Transactions* 41 (1744, for the year 1739–1740) I, 345–346: he records at Resina a "Well in a poor Man's Yard." Here remains of ancient buildings were found, possibly belonging to the town Aretina, destroyed by Vesuvius. Briefly discussed in Michel 1984, 106, who

Amalia Christina, a daughter of the King of Saxony, knew the statues at Dresden from her infancy has turned out to be a romantic fantasy on the basis of these data.[46] Local informers and experts like Amenta and Stendardo could have encouraged the King to reopen the old pits. This enterprise proved to be so productive that real excavations started below the streets of Resina.

Very soon the discovery of an ancient city, more than twenty meters under the modern city of Resina, became known outside the inner circles of the court and visitors from abroad came to see the treasures found. Their impressions will be discussed further in Chapter II.

A New King Has His Own Ambitions

At the beginning of the eighteenth century, southern Italy formed part of the Spanish Empire and was governed by a Spanish viceroy. Partly due to the problems of hereditary succession in Spain itself, conflicts rose across the whole of Europe and, after too many battles and conferences, the south of Italy became an independent kingdom. The new King was chosen from the Spanish Bourbon dynasty that had reigned over the area from 1500 onwards. He was the eighteen year old Charles – Carlos in Spanish, Carlo in Italian – who would become a very ambitious sovereign who wanted to put his newly-formed state definitively on the map of Europe. He believed that the old city of Naples should acquire an illustrious court and become an important center of power and culture, in order to attract both noble and intellectual visitors. Great architectural projects included the enlargement of the old residence of the viceroys (Royal Palace), the erection of summer palaces in Naples (Capodimonte), Caserta (Reggia) and Portici, the construction of useful buildings for the population like the enormous Hospital of the Poor (Albergo dei Poveri), and theaters for drama and opera, especially San Carlo theater, which still exists as an annex of the Royal Palace. The court members could not do less than build their own palazzi and country houses in the shadow of the royal premises.[47]

---

argues that Britain was much earlier informed than France about the finds at Herculaneum. Also reproduced in Zani 1993, 74, note 37.
46 Corti 1940, beginning of Chapter VI. His version is retold in many publications, up to Wallace-Hadrill 2011, 48 (with some irony). Harris 2007, 58, 67, does not draw this conclusion. See Mafrici 2010, 31–49.
47 Acton 1956; *Civiltà* 1979–1980; *Golden Age* 1981; De Seta 1981; 1982; 1988, 165–208; Imbroglia 2000.

Both foreigners and Neapolitans praised these eager construction activities. Naples always possessed a court, but the main impression of a visitor entering the city formerly had been that of a community dominated by the catholic clerical orders; numerous churches (like Rome), but even larger monasteries (unlike Rome) such as Santa Chiara and San Gregorio Armeno occupied the main part of the old center.

For one of his summer residences the King chose Portici-Resina, a village some eight kilometers south of Naples along the new road constructed by the government, to Calabria. Along the coast stood a number of 'Vesuvian villas' belonging to members of the court where even on a hot summer day an agreeable breeze tempered the sticky atmosphere. The area chosen by the King contained the villa Caramanico, begun by Elbeuf.

The Bourbon Exploration of Herculaneum[48]

In order to penetrate down to the Roman stratum, some 25 to 27 meters under the actual street level, workers made vertical and horizontal tunnels in the concrete-like volcanic mass and followed the walls of the ancient buildings they encountered to give them a sort of orientation (fig. 1). The miners operated like moles under the smoky and feeble light of torches and had to beware of gases escaping from the volcanic material. The removal of the debris was complicated and slowed the progress. Convicts did the hardest work: no free local man dared to go down into the dangerous galleries for miserable payments. The workers were forced to creep through the tunnels dragging heavy iron balls attached to their ankles – the fear that they would attempt to steal things or flee the scene was very strong – and many of them died underground.[49] The number of workers varied, depend-

---

48 Among the numerous accounts I single out Venuti 1748; Gori 1748; D'Arthenay 1748; Corti 1940, Chapter VI; Herbig 1960; Leppmann 1966; Trevelyan 1976, 39–73; Zevi 1979; Strazzullo 1980 and 1982; Guerrieri 1982; Pannuti 1983; Allroggen-Bedel 1986; Fernández Murga 1986; A. Allroggen-Bedel in Franchi dell'Orto 1993, 35–40 (political implications); Pagano 1993; Schnapp 1996, 242–247; Strazzullo 1997; Pace 2000, 21–33; Mattusch 2005, 33–75; M.P. Guidobaldi in Mühlenbrock/Richter 2005, 17–26; Harris 2007, 25–43; Blix 2009, 9–15; Jacobelli 2011, 11–19; A. Wallace-Hadrill in Hales/Paul 2011, 367–379; De Caro 2013.
49 *Philosophical Transactions* 47 (1753) 156, anonymous letter of April 18, 1751: "The labours of cleaning the place is performed by slaves, who work chained together, two and two." This is apparently no problem for Mr. Freeman, who writes on May 2, 1750 from Naples to Lady Mary Capel about the refusal to unearth Herculaneum instead of making tunnels (ibidem, 133): "But I have been told, it was impossible, seeing the vast depth of earth and Stone they must have been obliged to have made way thro'. That reason does not satisfy me; they having slaves enough, of the rascally and villainous sort, to complete such a work. What a fine thing would it have been to come

ing on the availability of money and convicts. Once tunnels no longer provided items to be carried off, they were backfilled with material from the ongoing work in newly-made tunnels, so the area visible at Herculaneum always remained very restricted. Some spots were even excavated two times, like the alleged palaestra, where excavators stripped the walls of the large exedra in 1743 and again in 1761.[50] The theater remained the only monument constantly explored and on view.[51]

The first soundings were made on the instigation of Marcello Venuti, who would be knighted by the King in 1740. He had come to Naples on the bequest of the court and was serving simultaneously as the director of the Farnese collection at Capodimonte and as royal librarian when in the fall of 1738 he suggested excavating at Herculaneum.[52] According to him, the finds in Elbeuf's property stemmed from ancient Herculaneum. Daily supervision was entrusted to Roque Joaquin de Alcubierre, who had training as a mine engineer. He would lead the excavations until his death in 1780. The Minister of Interior Affairs, Bernardo Tanucci (who held this position from 1754 to 1776), would coordinate the work.[53]

---

directly down to the roof of the building, instead of digging round, and to have found all things in their first situation!" Tanucci XVI, 237 (September 25, 1765) reports King Charles: "Mi affligge Paderni dicendomi aver poco fa saputo che una slamatura in Pompei aveva oppressi 4 cavatori, tre dei quali si sono estratti vivi e uno morto." Freeman is also quoted in Rowland 2014, 80–81.
50 Allroggen-Bedel 1983b.
51 On the theater, see Pagano 1993; 2000, 75–78 and A. Allroggen-Bedel in *Ercolano* 2008, 24–33. The actual entrance was constructed in 1865 by Fiorelli.
52 Venuti and his brother Ridolfino feature in a novel by the Dutch author Arthur Japin about the first lover of Giacomo Casanova, Lucia, who visits with her mistress and teacher Zélide the excavations carried out by them and a third brother Filippo. In *Een schitterend gebrek* (Japin 2003, 2005, part II, Chapter 4), Marcello is a dusty scholar, the others are nice young playmates for the ladies. Zélide takes the excavation – where they see the theater and the "Basilica" with its statues – as a starting point for a discourse about the balance between reason and emotion: the city lies covered under the thick layer put there by Vesuvius like our souls under the flesh and the weight of knowledge. It is a typical Enlightenment topic put forward with verve. Venuti would be praised by Bayardi (1752, I, XVIII): "Tra tante Relazioni, ne sono uscite però alcune che anno il loro merito. Se l'Autore di una di esse, Accademico Etrusco, il quale insieme co' suoi dotti fratelli è stato anche il restauratore dell'Accademia, dopo aver veduti i primi scavi, si fosse trovato in Napoli, allorchè si fecero i maggiori, e che avesse avuto il campo d'esaminare pel minuto ogni monumento, sarebbe indubitatamente dalla sua penna uscita in vista una Storia incomparabile d'Ercolano, e ne avrebbe posti nel loro vero lume i monumenti. Egli era uomo da farlo, come da quel poco che à dato alle stampe può agevolmente dedursi. Avrebbe scritto in maniera, che dopo di lui, nè a me, nè ad altri, sarebbe rimasto da scrivere."
53 See *Tanucci* 1986; García y García 1998, 82, with bibliography; Parslow 1995, 19–22, 27–31, and passim; John E. Moore in Mattusch 2013, 89–122. After Charles' departure to Spain, Tanucci wrote long letters in which the excavations formed a continuing subject matter, partly formulated in the form of quotations from the weekly reports, partly in personal remarks some of which will be cited in due order.

The oldest excavation reports derive from the last months of 1738. Fortunately, a large number of these reports were sent weekly to the Ministry of the Interior and have been preserved in the National Archives in Naples. As a result, we know many precise details about the progress of the work from the outset.[54] These texts were written in Spanish during the first decades of the explorations.

Unfortunately, like most people involved in this and other archaeological enterprises, Alcubierre had not the faintest idea about proper archaeological method. His orders from the Court were to find as many spectacular objects as possible[55] and meticulously make note of unusual finds in the weekly reports. The brief descriptions of the work carried out and the discoveries made helped authorities decide what to transport to the royal palace at Portici. Alcubierre's ultimate failure was not only the result of his total lack of knowledge and experience, but also of the scope of the project, which extended radically beyond the skills and expertise of everyone involved. The finds were rich and the methods of excavating and extracting the treasures hidden under thick layers of volcanic material had to be developed on the spot. There were no advisers available, although foreigners did suggest that experts from Britain, France or Germany would do better.

An early collaborator was the French engineer Pierre Bardet de Villeneuve, who had already worked in the area since 1737. He was in charge of the excavations from 1741 to 1745, when Alcubierre was apparently removed for bad conduct or illness. He made an accurate map of the explorations; only the orientation of the theater is wrong.[56]

In 1749 Karl Weber became an assistant to Alcubierre, taking over the main responsibilities in 1750, although Alcubierre remained the head of the organization. Weber was a Swiss engineer and a military man, and kept the works going steadily until his death. The sensible biography Christopher Parslow dedicated to him reveals his noble feelings for the antiquities and his wish to form a sound set of documentation that would enable a better understanding of the treasures dug up from under Resina. Even in the Herculaneum tunnels he sought a systematic procedure in which the outlines of the buildings explored might be understood.[57] Among his most significant work was the excavation of the Villa of the Papyri. The

---

54 Most of them were published in the nineteenth century thanks to the work of Giuseppe Fiorelli (*PAH* I–III) and Michele Ruggiero (1885). Additions in Pannuti 1983.
55 See the harsh criticism, collected in Parslow 1995, 32–38.
56 Parslow 1995, 38–41, 49–60. A brief interruption of the work apparently was caused by a war, finished with the Battle of Velletri in 1744 (Palermo 1792, 39, 49).
57 Parslow 1995. E.g. plans of the *Praedia* of Julia Felix at Pompeii, the Villa of the Papyri and, again, the theater at Herculaneum. Cf. Grell 1995, 210–211.

numerous Greek and Latin text scrolls that were found would evoke enthusiastic reactions among travelers and scholars alike (see Chapter VII). When making sketches and plans of parts of the excavations, Weber was foolishly blamed for slowing the progress, but fortunately, we still possess some of these accurate and highly valuable documents. The plan and the accompanying commentary on the Villa of the Papyri is a striking example of his skills. Volkmann apparently knew about the plans, stored as big secrets in Naples.[58] We know that he wrote Tanucci about his map of Herculaneum in 1765, but never saw it published, although in 1796 it finally was. Weber's map differs from Bardet's, for example, in that its palaestra is too small.

The King and his wife showed some interest, but were probably not fully conscious of the importance of these finds. They presumed that the antiquities could serve as excellent decoration for the new palace at Portici. After a short time, however, it became clear that the steady stream of paintings, statues, bronze objects and ceramics would occupy a much larger space and that a special accommodation should be created to store all of them. The staff was enlarged with a curator and restorers, and gradually a more or less professional museum, the *Herculanense Museum*, was growing in volume and importance, systematized on two floors of the palace at Portici (see below, pp. 30–33).

All these activities stimulated locals and foreigners to praise King Charles in prose and poetry. One example is a lavish eulogy by Pietro d'Onofri from 1789, which mentions the excavations of the towns destroyed by Vesuvius as one of Charles' beneficent works.[59] The Spanish author Juan Andrés hailed the King when he was in Pompeii in 1786.[60] Charles' prestige was further enhanced by

---

58 Volkmann 1777–1778, III, 303: "welche als ein großes Geheimniß in Neapel aufbewahret werden."

59 D'Onofri 1789, XVII: "... e mette in luce le tre vetuste Città, Stabia, Pompei, ed Ercolano, coverte dalle ceneri del ignivomo Vesuvio, e forma di esse imprezzabili Gallerie." D'Onofri 1789, C: "O Vesuvio, o Vesuvio, tu ora sei celebre per il Re di Napoli Carlo III; per questo Re ti sentiam sempre nominare nelle nostre parti, e questo buon Re ti ha anche santificato, perchè per esso tutti ti visitano, e tutti ritornano nelle lor Patrie con delle tue reliquie." McIlwayne 1988, no 3.89; García y García 1998, no. 4651. Similar words in *Encyclopédie* 8, 1765, 150–154 s.v. Herculanum (Chevalier de Jaucourt). Cf. still Micheletti 1846, 292: the excavations were "apportando alla più che sofferente Archeologia. Gli avi nostri furono rivendicati dalle onte che la superba posterità loro apponeva, come ignoranti di chimica e di costumi agiati ed eleganti."

60 Andrés 2004, 205: "El nombre de Carlos III sera inmortal en los fastos de la Literatura y mientras dure el estudio de la Anticuaria vivrá en las bocas y plumas de los eruditos el restaurador de Herculano y Pompeya, enterradas por tantos siglos." On him and his popular works about Italy, see M. Gigante, *Cronache Ercolanesi* 30 (2000) 128 (with bibliography); Arbillaga 2005, 317–347; Romero Recio 2012, 35–39.

visits of monarchs and other important persons like Joseph II of Austria[61] and Gustav of Sweden, and the King even got praise from strangers who transmitted his fame to their countries. As to Gustav, his great interest is evinced in a letter to count Von Creutz about the great importance of the site and the little effort made to reveal its treasuries.[62]

The commitment of the King went so far that he joined the restorers in the museum at Portici to clean the finds. As he was cleaning some cameos, someone suggested that he should make a chain for himself, but the King refused, saying that the finds should remain in royal Neapolitan property. Inside what had at first looked like an ostrich shell but was just a lump of lava, a ring with a bearded head was found, which the King would bear for several years.[63] The King also looked after the moral elevation of his people, preventing the exhibition of an obscene bronze statue, that of Pan mating a goat (p. 118, fig. 4). His confessor would have told him that it should not be put on display.[64]

---

61 The emperor was on the spot on April 6, 1769 and house VIII 2, 39 was called after him. La Vega's description in the weekly reports is very long and detailed (*PAH* I, 228–231). He appears on the drawing of people next to the skeleton of the victim in a cellar.

62 Von Prochwitz 1986, 251 (letter from February 14, 1784): "J'ai été avant-hier voir Pompéi. Rien n'est plus intéressant que cette découverte, et il est bien triste que l'on ne travaille pas avec plus d'ardeur à découvrir ces restes précieux de l'Antiquité." He orders a model of the Temple of Isis at Pompeii (*Napoli e la Svezia in età gustaviana*, Naples 1985, 29).

63 D'Onofri 1789, CII: "Egli stesso il Re Carlo alle volte si divertiva a certe ore a ripulire le cose rinvenute sotto terra. Un giorno nel ripulirsi una gran quantità di Cammei, (che son gemme figurate) ci fu chi disse, che già ne erano tanti da poter formarne due intere catenelle di Oriuoli, potendo solamente un Sovrano portar in dosso tai cose. Ma il buon Re subito rispose: 'Oibò, voglio che tutto il pubblico si goda quelle cose che si son trovate, e si ritroveranno.' Ed in tanto s'indusse a portar nel ditto un'anello ritrovato nello scavo, per il fatto accaduto nel suo ritrovamento, narratomi dal Sig. D. Camillo Paderni." Similar story in Palermo 1792, 59–60. On the ring, see P.G. Guzzo in Mols/Moormann 2005, 331–333.

64 D'Onofri 1789, CV: "Fu trovato una volta negli scavi un Satiro di bronzo dell'altezza di tre palmi, in atto con una capra sì sconscio e brutto, ch'egli è bello il tacere, e gli fu portato in Napoli a vedere: avendolo il Re osservato, subito ben chiuso lo rimandò in Portici a D. Giuseppe Canart, con ordine di non farlo vedere a nessuno; e quando poi col medesimo s'incontro gli domandò anzioso, se aveva subito ricevuto il Satiro, e gli soggiunse: 'Il mio confessore mi ha detto, che quel gruppo è degno di essere posto ben bene in un mortajo; onde ti raccomando a non farlo vedere:' e non volle affatto, che fosse situato fra le cose nel Museo a vista di tutto. Questo fatto ci porge un forte motivo da ammirare la gran virtù, e la gran religione del sempre glorioso fu nostro Re l'invitto Carlo III di Borbone." Similarly, Palermo 1792, 59–60: "Ma di tutte le più sorprendenti cose, che si ammirano in questo Musèo, Io credo che niuna vinca, anzi nemmeno pareggi, l'inarrivibil statua di un Satiro, in atto assai sconcio con una Capra. La bellezza di questo picciol gruppo non può esprimersi, vieppiù perchè volendo descriverla, comunque si possa, troppo di danno ne risentirebbe il costume. Ella è tale, che qualunque più serio Socratico ne resterebbe

A new advantage for the court became clear: the collection at Portici formed an extra attraction for foreign visitors, who came to admire these curiosities and works of art found just twenty meters under their feet, and thanks to the explorations, the young kingdom saw its prestige grow considerably both within and outside Italy.

The court tried to prevent publications about the excavations and the finds in its desire for a monopoly on the revelation of excavation news. Nevertheless, Venuti published an account of the first results in Spanish for the King (1740), which he enlarged after his withdrawal to Cortona.[65] The latter booklet – in Italian – soon became known abroad thanks to translations into German and English. Venuti dedicated it to Frederick Christian, Royal Prince of Poland and Elector of Saxonia, and defended its publication with enthusiasm.[66] A similar anthology was published by Antonio Francesco Gori, who like Venuti was one of the founders of the *Accademia di Cortona*. He gives excerpts and synopses of newsletters

---

commosso; ed Io, per avventura non ne accettuerei lo stesso Senocrate che vinse con poca pena le irresistibili carezze di Frine. Il Re Cattolico ordinò, che si tenesse coverto, ordine, che fin oggi con sommo rigore fa osservarsi dal suo gran Figlio, nè si mostra ad alcuno di quei che ottengono il permesso di vedere il Musèo, se non con ispeciale ordine di S. M. Gran male, che il suo Autore avesse impiegato i suoi modelli in un oggetto sì laido: se avesse cangiate le sue idee, niun più di lui sarebbe oggi celebrato: ma in quella Città, che il Vesuvio distrusse, sembra, che la principal cura fosse di darsi bel tempo, regnandovi, per quanto ne apparisce da' monumenti, una sfrenata licenza. Così gli uomini si abusano de' doni divini! Esse Città dotate di tanti pregi, e riunendo quanto di più leggiadro, e giocondo sa compartir la natura, si abbandonarono alle loro passioni, onde cercaron soddisfarle anco col renderle perenni nell'opre d'arte: Gran scuola per ogni un di noi a tener sempre in freno strettissimo i nostri affetti, se non vogliam piombare in quell'opre, che recano scorno all umanità." These are very lengthy descriptions of things that must remain unseen... We do not know this bronze statue, but it must be similar to the famous marble group found in the Villa of the Papyri (p. 118, fig. 4; on this statue, see Chapter II, pp. 117–119). This text is more laudatory than factual and stems from the pen of a court member.

65 Tanucci II, 411–412 (17 September 1748) to Ridolfino Venuti, about this edition, starting as follows: "La voce di una stampa delle anticaglie di Resina che si mediti e sia prossima alla lite, è la cagione dell'incomodo ch'io do a V.S. illustrissima. Questa voce ha disgustato il Re mio Signore per più motivi." Later, he liked the work (see note 144). Other criticism came from Giacomo Martorelli, see Trombetta 1984, 153–154.

66 Venuti 1748, VII: "La fama di tal fortunato avvenimento, degno solo di un Re, cui è desiderabile ogni più brillante fortuna, ha eccitato per tutto il mondo tanta, e così gran maraviglia, che reca non solo invidia alle più belle raccolte, e alle più culte nazioni, ma ancora una lodevole curiosità a tutti coloro, che della storia, e delle Antichità si dilettano, voglio dire a tutti coloro, che hanno fiore di senno." McIlwayne 1988, no 3.162; García y García 1998, nos 13.900–13.902 (including a short biography and various editions and translations into German and English).

and accounts in letter books.⁶⁷ A French overview of the discoveries was provided in an anonymously published booklet attributed to Moussinot or D'Arthenay.⁶⁸

Some monuments caused a particular impression, e.g. two marble equestrian statues. The statues were discovered "avanti del tempio sul Foro de' Ercolano," not far from the "Basilica," according to La Vega's explanation on his map. Twenty-eight normal and thirty-eight forced workmen were employed to transport these marbles to Portici on May 23, 1743. The persons depicted were a youth and an elderly gentleman, and both were called Marcus Nonius Balbus; that they were a father and son was a logical thought, but thanks to thorough research by Stefania Adamo Muscettola, we know that the statues represent one and the same person, gifted two times in his life with such special monuments.⁶⁹ One of these statues was erected in the courtyard of the Portici palace,⁷⁰ and the other inside. Both were copied in the shape of ceramic statuettes by the royal manufacture in Naples. The younger equestrian lost his head to a cannon ball in the revolutionary year 1798. Both figures earned high praise from travelers, like Lumisden, who wrote that the "son" was better than the Marcus Aurelius on the Capitoline Hill in Rome.⁷¹

A truly major discovery was made when excavations in a new shaft, dug around 19 October 1752, produced very high quality bronzes and, slightly later that year, some 1,860 carbonized papyri, not at first recognized as such, but rather soon discovered to be Greek texts from antiquity (p. 41, fig. 2). All efforts

---

67 Gori 1748. McIlwayne 1988, no. 3.158–159; García y García 1998, no. 6240. Latin versions nos 6242–6244. Venuti also published English reports in *Philosophical Transactions* of 1748 (see Mullett 1957). Other early publications are briefly discussed in Zevi 1979 (with bibliography in vol. II).
68 D'Arthenay 1748. There are no references to other publications. See García y García 1998, 362 and 841 on D'Arthenay and Moussinot. McIlwayne 1988, no 3.146 (under Arthenay, Moussinot d'). C. Grell and C. Michel (in Franchi dell'Orto 1993, 138) and E. Framarion and C. Volpilhac-Auger (in Cochin/Bellicard 1996, 9) see it as a publication by D'Arthenay; Bertrand 2008, 563, 589 assumes two authors, D'Arthenay and Moussinot. The anonymous reviewer in *Journal des Sçavants* of July 1748, 323–328 suggest that the text was written on behalf of the French ambassador in Naples, the Marquis de l'Hôpital.
69 Adamo Muscettola 1982; Allroggen-Bedel 2010, 368–370.
70 Apparently originally covered by a sort of glass house, as we read in the guide to Naples by Palermo (1792, 28): "Ella [the statue] vien situata in mezzo ad un recinto di ferri e stava tutta riparata da grandi cristalli, che la defendevano dall'umido, che potea portarle i venti del vicin mare, e dalla polvere, che l'immenso numero delle vetture, che vi passava potean cagionarle; ma oggi si son tolti i cristalli, si osserva interamente scoperta."
71 Lumisden 1797, 471–472 (letter of 18 April 1750): "Some connoisseurs say that this statue is preferable, in point of execution, to the so justly celebrated one at the Capitol, of Marcus Aurelius Antoninus, of Corinthian brass. The former is indeed more ancient, and perhaps the work of a more eminent master: but, – 'Non nostrum inter vos tantas componere lites.'" Same judgment is that of Barthélemy (p. 84). On the vicissitudes mentioned, Adamo Muscettola 1982.

were focused on this structure and for nearly two years all interest was turned to the Villa of the Papyri (see here Chapter VII).[72]

Gradually, however, the stream of spectacular finds at Herculaneum diminished and, as Pompeii proved to be a more convenient place to work, the authorities decided to stop work at Herculaneum in 1766 and to concentrate entirely on the nearby dig.

The Bourbon Explorations at Pompeii and Stabiae

As we have seen, some twenty kilometers south of Portici-Resina, the area named Civita was known for a long time as a spot where antiquities could be found.[73] No description of it prior to the excavations is at hand, except for those of the late seventeenth century, but presumably some indications were available: the oval shape of the amphitheater was well discernible in the landscape and parts of columns were probably scattered over the fields.[74] These fertile grounds were intensively used as vineyards and vegetable gardens and peasants frequently found antiquities digging holes for planting vines or trees.

The notices of stray finds at Civita stimulated the court to do some soundings at this spot, and on 30 March 1748, work started after the report of occasional finds of column pieces and paintings in "un paraje llamado la Civita," not far from Torre Annunziata and immediately recognized as Pompeii.[75] The find of this second town aroused curiosity about which town was where. The first finds at Herculaneum had led to the speculation that here was the famous Pompeii of Pliny's letters, but Stabiae was suggested as well.[76]

---

72 See Mattusch 2005; Zarmakoupi 2010.
73 See already Capasius 1607, 461. On these excavations Parslow 1995, 44–46, 107–115; *idem* in Guzzo 2001, 19–27; Longobardi 2002, 39–44.
74 *PAH* I, 5, under 26 October 1748, here is the reference to "un lugar que llaman el amphiteatro". As far as I know, Micheletti (1846, 328) is the first who wonders why no one initiated excavations earlier, since local farmers constantly dug up pieces of lava and there was "un [Fontana's] canale sotterraneo, tagliato dal fiume Sarno (che l'attraversava, e che scorre tacitamente sotto le basi del Tempio d'Iside)."
75 *PAH* I, 1, under March 23, 1748. Pietro Lasena was one of the first to mention these new excavations (Gori 1748, 62–63; letter of April 23, 1748): "Adesso il Re, sapete? ha cominciato lo Scavamento a Pompei, ed ha trovato tre Camerini bene intonacati, e un bel Quadro dipinto con festoni di frutti, una maschera in mezzo, e alcuni uccelletti intorno a' frutti. Questo l'ho inteso da altri, ma non l'ho veduto." Martini 1779, 90–91 notices confusion about the starting date.
76 E.g. *PAH* I, 1, 6. In November 1756 the name Pompeana appears two times in the reports, when they find sepulchral inscriptions (*PAH* I, 46). The inscription of Vespasian mentioning

The area investigated first was what we now call the *Praedia* ("properties") of Julia Felix, which Amedeo Maiuri would re-excavate in the early 1950s.⁷⁷ At Pompeii it was much easier to clear away the debris than dig the painstaking tunnels under Resina: the ruins at Pompeii were covered with a considerably thinner layer (to a maximum of seven meters) of volcanic material – mainly lapilli and dust – which was rather loosely packed. It soon became clear that the method of tunneling was inadequate for Pompeii, since the galleries could easily collapse. It was here, therefore, that the first real open-air excavations began.

These excavations of Pompeii did not follow any methodical rules.⁷⁸ After clearing away the upper layers, workers explored the rooms they encountered. Remains of roofing tiles and sections of upper walls, which included holes where wooden roofing beams would have rested, and many other chunks of fallen walls were carelessly removed. The goal was to assemble removable loose objects, wall paintings and floor mosaics, as was the practice at Herculaneum. Upon inspection by one of the museum custodians or, by most historical accounts, the leader of the excavation, Camillo Paderni or Giuseppe Canart, they decided whether to strip the mosaics and (parts of) the paintings.⁷⁹ One advantage became clear in relation to the paintings. Able to see the whole wall instead of only a small part, the excavators could chose larger fragments or even entire walls to cut out. The latter practice is seen for the first time with a wall from the *Praedia* of Julia Felix with the immensely popular still lifes in the upper register.⁸⁰

The earliest excavations apparently were not rewarding enough, for in October 1750 the work stopped, only to be taken up again in March 1755.⁸¹ It is clear from the stoppage that the excavators had not yet seen the potential for an

---

Pompeii was registered in the report of August 20, 1758 (*PAH* I, 153; *CIL* X 1018). Another inscription announcing gladiatorial games by the troop of Ampliatus in which Pompeii is mentioned was found on July, 23, 1768 (*PAH* I, 219–220; *CIL* IV 1184). La Vega tells Joseph II in 1769 that they know since six years that here is Pompeii (*PAH* I, 231). In the famous *Encyclopédie* we find in vol. 13 (1765) 13 s.v. Pompeii that the town, devastated in A.D. 79, has not yet been rediscovered (signed D.J.= Chevalier de Jaucourt).

77 See Parslow 1995, 118–122; C. Parslow in Mattusch 2013, 47–72.

78 See the harsh evaluation in Zimmerman 2008, 106. This part of her book gives important insights into the relation between archaeology and fiction (Zimmerman 2008, 105–126).

79 The first suggestion to strip mural decorations seems to have been given by Stefano Moriconi, who had arrived at Herculaneum in July 1739 to treat paintings with a varnish (Ruggiero 1885, XIV, referring to the report of 11 July 1739 at p. 37; cf. Rossignani 1967, 36).

80 *PAH* I, 25, under 13 July 1755: "una fachada de un muro pinada 17 pal. y 9 on larga y 8 pal, alta." Canart asks to make a drawing before removing the decorations from the wall. Now Museo Nazionale, Naples, inv. 8598: *PPM* III, 289. See *PPM Disegnatori* 31–139 for various examples.

81 *PAH* I, 12. Some notices in November 1754 (*PAH* I, 11–12) suggest a reconnoiter of the spot.

interesting monument for visitors, let alone an object of scientific archaeological studies. The remarks by travelers were doing their work in a certain way. The year 1755 is often mentioned in travel accounts as that of the discovery of Pompeii, an error explained by the fact that from this date onwards the explorations would no longer be interrupted.[82] Now that the opened trenches were no longer being backfilled, the open-air museum would rapidly become a reality, but it would still take some years before noteworthy areas became visible, namely, what is now called Insula Occidentalis VI and VII, the properties of Filippo Irace, Domenico Cuoco and others.[83] Francesco La Vega took over Weber's job after the Swiss' sad death in 1764, and worked for many decades at Pompeii. One of his major accomplishments was the systematic cleaning of the area around the Herculanean Gate, so that visitors could walk a stretch of the street inside and outside the city wall.[84]

There must have been some reluctance at the Court to leave the excavations open out of the fear that visitors would take souvenirs home with them. The risk of losing valuable and unique finds to tourists and robbers impeded the Neapolitan court to change its policies. In other parts of the Reign, supervisors were called to protect the monuments in the same way as in Pompeii.[85] This hesitation proves how strong the interest in objects was. The fervid sale of ancient objects to foreigners in Rome might have been another reason the Court wanted to keep them for itself. The meaning of the finds did not concern the King or his workers and the excavations encountered – as we will see – heavy criticism from scholars and other travelers.

Regardless of whether or not buildings were backfilled after the dig, the excavators normally did not make written or drawn documentation of the remains. However, Paderni had sketches made that enabled him to reset pieces of painting and mosaic into their original shape. The ruins primarily served as a mine of murals, mosaics and movable objects. No one really asked what he or she was excavating. Rummaging around, the excavators did not even recognize the difference between interior and exterior walls[86] and the streets were seldom mentioned

---

82 E.g. C. [= Chevalier de Jaucourt] in *Encyclopédie*, Supplément 4 (1777) 502 s.v. Pompeii; Latapie 1953, 245; Palermo 1792, 71, who reports as one of the first finds a relief of a phallus, "segno impressovi, ch'era consegrato alla lascivia."
83 See C. Parslow in Guzzo 2001, 19–27. And see the original reports in *PAH* I. Interestingly Joseph II asked for the reasons, when he saw buildings indicated on La Vega's map they had not visited (*PAH* I, 230): in the first years the excavators would not have recognized a town here!
84 *PAH* I, 236 (November 11, 1769). On La Vega, García y García 1998, 701 (with bibliography); Parslow 1995, 268–281. His diaries have been edited in Pagano 1997a.
85 Grell 1995, 193–195.
86 E.g. *PAH* I, 40, 116, 117. Karl Weber would understand it (cf. *PAH* I, 162). Paderni even wrote an account to be sent to Charles in Spain in 1768–1769, but remained as a manuscript in the Ecole Française de Rome and edited by U. Pannuti (Paderni 2000).

in the weekly reports.[87] Restorations were limited to the covering of the upper layer of walls, the addition of small roofs to "protect" the paintings left *in situ* and the like.[88] The Marquis de Sade saw a room in the House of the Surgeon covered with a refurbished roof, so that he got an impression of the house's original splendor.[89]

After the tombs, mainly explored in 1758, one of the first buildings to become visible was the city gate at the northwest corner of Pompeii known as the Herculanean Gate.[90] It was a "lucky" find, as it was one of the original entrances to the old city, and it led to intensive research which resulted in the discovery of houses inside the city walls, along a street paved with huge basalt blocks and provided with sidewalks, similar to those seen in the galleries at Herculaneum and – without the sidewalks – in the streets of Naples (p. 154, fig. 5). The houses were painted both inside and outside. Shops and signs of owners came to light. Outside the gate a series of tombs amidst suburban villas lined the same street. An inscription mentioning the *Pagus Augustus Felix Suburbanus* made an interpretation of living quarters *extra muros* plausible. As this street was to become a logical entrance for more than a century, the image of the city as a society where the living and the dead stayed next to each other, especially in the *pagus*, was soon created. In the visitors' perception, the inhabitants seemed to be absent only for a brief appointment, but the skeletal remains on the streets and in the houses were the silent testimony to the disaster. One villa, covered after having been researched, was assigned to the famous politician Cicero, whose *Pompeianum* is known from his correspondence.[91] All these buildings were stripped, where possible, of the most precious elements, like figural scenes in the wall paintings and floors.

On a slope in the southern area of the town, a series of public monuments came to light in the 1750s. First of all, there was a badly ruined temple with columns of

---

87 The first time I found one such mention is that of the Street of Tombs on September 17, 1758 (*PAH* I, 153): "la calle basolada."

88 E.g. Hamilton 1777, 170, plate XIV: "A.A.A. Shops. The tiled sheds, represented in the plate, are modern, and placed there to preserve the paintings on the walls, which are very lively." These shops are the façades of insula VI 1.

89 Sade 2008, 276: "On a couvert cette dernière pièce pour en conserver les peintures qui vraiment méritent de l'être, tant par leur mérite réel que par la singularité de leur conservation." He probably saw room 19 of the house, excavated in 1770–1771, of which only a small central figure panel was removed and one complete wall was illustrated in *Pitture d'Ercolano* V, pl. 83 and Piranesi 1804 (*PPM* IV (1993) 72–80).

90 The "puerta de la ciudad" is used as topographic indication from January 1764 onwards (*PAH* I, 154).

91 E.g. Cicero, *Letters to Atticus* 2.1.11, 10.15.4, 16.11.6. Famous are the mosaics of Dioskourides, showing scenes from Menander's plays and fine black wall decorations of the early first century A.D., associated with the "Villa of Cicero," found in June 1758 (*PAH* I, 152).

the Doric order, laid out on a triangular open space, soon called Foro Triangolare. These remains were immediately associated with the well-preserved Greek temples at Paestum discovered almost simultaneously, and they proved, according to many people, that Pompeii had once been a Greek city.[92] Adjacent to it a courtyard and two theaters were found. Small rooms flanking the courtyard (which must have served as foyers for the theater guests and as training grounds for youth) contained skeletons of chained persons, probably slaves, and bronze helmets adorned with sumptuous relief and apparently used in parades and gladiator fights in the amphitheater. The founders of the small theater (*theatrum tectum*: covered theater) were mentioned on a slab: Gaius Quinctius Valgus and Marcus Porcius. Two brothers Holconius had paid for reconstruction works in the big theater, according to a pair of inscriptions, and the architect of these works, Marcus Artorius Primus was eternalized in another inscription. Furthermore, there was another training center, a palaestra where a beautiful statue of a standing nude athlete had stood, fragments of which had been collected by La Vega in 1797.[93] Perhaps the most spectacular find was a temple dedicated to the Egyptian goddess Isis: the objects found and the decorations on the walls proved the exceptional nature of this arcane figure (see Chapter II, pp. 141–144).

The same excavation method was used at a beautifully located spot along the edge of a hill, in a seashore village called Castellammare ("di Stabia" was added at the end of the nineteenth century), some ten kilometers south of Pompeii. At ancient Stabiae some Roman villas were found and re-covered after the explorations. They were to be rediscovered in 1950 by a local headmaster and dilettante archaeologist, Libero d'Orsi, who would become subject of a novel himself (see Chapter V, pp. 282–283). Fortunately, in the last decades the interest in these monuments has increased.

In 1759 King Charles was called to Spain to succeed Ferdinand VI who had died. He left the throne to his nine year old son Ferdinand, who was placed under the custody of Tanucci. Charles did not take finds with him to his new reign and even gave back the afore-mentioned finger ring. Paderni was asked to be a dealer for the acquisition of antiquities from Rome for the royal collections.[94] Whereas Charles continued to follow the progression of discoveries from Madrid as we know from the letters dispatched by Tanucci, Ferdinand did not demonstrate

---

92 De Waele 2001. For Paestum, Raspi Serra 1986 and 1990; De Jong 2010. For Pompeii as a Greek town, see Moormann 2003b; De Haan 2014a, and below, pp. 71–74.
93 Pagano 1997a, 144–145 (statue of Doryphorus, copy of a creation by Polyclitus, not recognized by Pagano). Cf. *PAH* I, 65–69 on work in the palaestra in 1797, with mentioning parts of the Doryphorus on April 13 and August 17 and 31.
94 Alonso Rodríguez 2003. On Tanucci and Charles and their contacts after the King's departure, see G. Anes in *Tanucci* 1986, 57–81.

a strong commitment to the archaeological project. This contrasted with the genuine interest of his future wife, Maria Carolina, the daughter of the Austrian emperor Joseph II and Maria Theresia.[95]

The Museum at Portici

Herculae exuvias Urbis traxisse Vesevi ex
Faucibus una vide regia vis potuit[96]

Some twenty years after the start of the explorations at Herculaneum, the storerooms in the Palace at Portici were full of material and could no longer be shown to guests. Therefore, it was decided to devote a special wing of the palace to exposing the treasures, and the *Herculanense Museum* officially opened its doors in 1758.[97] It was by no means a public museum. Like access to the excavations, access to the collection was possible only with a special permit. This had to be obtained from Tanucci, and a request was made via the ambassador in Naples. For most guests this was no problem, since they belonged to the elite of society, but even they could not go without such a letter.[98]

As for the arrangement of the objects, we must rely on descriptions of visitors, the note by Franceso Piranesi from 1806 and later accounts. These sources sometimes contradict each other, which is understandable given that it was strictly forbidden to make notes and sketches. A visitor's every movement was meticulously controlled by a guard; objects could be stolen, copied in a drawing or simply touched, all of which had to be prevented. As a matter of fact, guests

---

[95] This Queen was instrumental in the government, since her husband spent most of his time hunting. She practically ruled the state, assisted by John Acton in a position like Tanucci's in the previous decades. Mafrici 2010, 51–82.

[96] "Only one, i.e. royal force was able to extract the remains of Hercules' town from the mouth of Vesuvius." Distich written by the local scholar Alessio Simmaco Mazzocchi and applied at the entrance of the rooms with the paintings. Tanucci wrote a reaction: *Herculae monumenta Urbis quo reddita fatis /Esse Tito credas, reddita sunt Carlo* ("You would belief that the monuments of Hercules' town were given back to Titus by fate, but they were given back to Charles"). See Pullo 1792, 52–53.

[97] For Paderni's reports in the *Philosophical Transactions*, see note 106. Cf. Ramage 1992, 656–658; Zani 1993. Regarding the museum, the best study is Allroggen-Bedel/Kammerer-Grothaus 1980, 1983. See also Represa Fernández 1988; M. Borriello in Piccioli 1998, 23–27; Cantilena/Porzio 2008 (here Chapter II).

[98] See De La Roche 1783, 59: "Ces permissions ne se refusent guères, mais elles ne sont point prodiguées."

could be terribly impertinent, like Anna Miller. She wanted to touch a piece of paper with her finger, to take some tiny "atom" with her, but even that was seen as a theft of the King's unique possessions.[99] Despite the severe rules, sometimes people succeeded in making notes and drawings. It was because of this that the Comte de Caylus was able to publish some objects at Portici drawn by a friend, but he stressed that he was not permitted to betray his source, whose reputation he wanted to protect. It is even said that Winckelmann (see p. 44–45) entered, looked in utmost concentration trying to learn some inscriptions by heart, left after several minutes to write down a note, and entered again to continue the visit. The guards found it suspicious, but apparently he succeeded in misleading them, so that his two publications on the excavations contain a number of correctly copied texts.

Descriptions of this sort and a map by Francesco Piranesi enabled Agnes Allroggen-Bedel and Helke Kammerer-Grothaus to present a trustworthy "guide" to the old museum.[100] Winckelmann saw five rooms in 1758, Fougeroux de Bondaroy described nine rooms in 1763, and from 1799 there were eighteen rooms on the first floor. The fifth room contained the papyri and the device Piaggio had made to unfold them, room 6 showed the reconstruction of a kitchen, room 7 had bronze statuary and in room 8 there were imprints and body parts of victims, like the famous woman's breast (see Chapter III). In room 18 the "obscene objects" like the famous tripod with the ithyphallic satyrs[101] were on display. Wall cases contained the smaller pieces: lamps with erotic scenes, phalli et cetera. Apparently everyone could see this room, as the accounts of both ladies and gentlemen testify. The lower floor displayed hundreds of paintings and large statues. On the second floor store rooms and studios were arranged. Mariana Starke described the situation in the museum around 1800: the minister's permit was valid for a whole year and the museum was open every day from 9 to 1 and from 3 to 6, excluding holidays. She warned that the lower rooms with the paintings were chilly.[102]

---

99 Miller 1776, 263–264: "I wished to have been permitted to rub my finger (as a little remained on it) upon a piece of paper, just to bring with me an idea of the colour; but besides a sharp, though civil reprimand, for my curiosity, he [the guard] insisted peremptorily on my not carrying off an atom; 'for,' said he, 'it is a curiosity no monarch upon earth can boast the possession of, besides my master, the King of Naples.'"
100 Allroggen-Bedel/Kammerer-Grothaus 1980 and 1983; Kammerer-Grothaus 1981.
101 From the *Praedia* of Julia Felix, see here infra and Chapter II, p. 117.
102 Starke 1802, II, 117: "The lower-rooms of the Museum, which contain the Paintings, are damp and cold – the upper apartments, which contain the bronze Statues, Vases &c. are tolerably warm." Because of the prohibition against making notes she gives a long synopsis of the objects, partly based on the *Antichità d'Ercolano* (see below, p. 35). Fernández Murga 1989, 18 maintains that this interdict was abolished in 1775, the one against making drawings never officially expired.

The arrangement of the objects according to categories corresponded with the taxonomy used in antiquarian studies of the seventeenth and eighteenth centuries that would be criticized by Winckelmann. From our point of view, a modern museum aspect was the reconstruction of the kitchen – a rather peculiar conception compared to the purely aesthetic approach of the rest of the finds, which was criticized by no less than Diderot, who found the interest for common objects out of place.[103]

The staff was small, yet two individuals should be singled out. The already mentioned French sculptor Giuseppe (originally Joseph) Canart, was at the museum from 1739.[104] Paderni was trained as a painter and came into the King's service in 1749.[105] He had been at Herculaneum with Canart as early as 1739–1740 and reported the find of the theater to his friend and artistic colleague, the English painter Allan Ramsey.[106] Remains had been found of an amphitheater, a chariot and a broken equestrian statue, which were under Canart's custody.[107] According to one letter, Paderni thought that the excavations at Herculaneum were like those at the Roman catacombs and that it was a shame no documentation was being made:[108]

---

103 Vivant Denon reports that La Vega reconstructed an oil press in Pompeii, which he described in D. Grimaldi, *Memoria sulla economia olearia antica e moderna e sull'antico frantojo da olio trovato negli scavi di Stabia*, Naples 1783, esp. 53–71 (non vidi). See Janin 2007, 169, letter from June 7, 1783. Not in *PAH* I.
104 For more about Canart, see Scatozza Höricht 1982.
105 Forcellino 1999, 9–36. The "delineatore di Sua Maestà" (p. 18) might already have been Paderni. For Paderni, see Forcellino 1993; 1999; M. de Vos in Franchi dell'Orto 1993, 99–116. On the difficult relationship between Paderni and D'Alcubierre, see Fernández Murga 1986, who stresses Paderni's good bond with Tanucci. Tanucci incessantly and quite irritatedly reports these conflict to King Charles, e.g. Tanucci X, 391–392, letter from 22 January 1761: "Gran discordia è tra Veber, Alcuvier, Paterni circa le escavazioni; mi fanno relazioni sopra relazioni tutte animose; son queste derivate dalle mie querele sulla sterilita di esse scavazioni." Tanucci XI, 490, 514, 556, letter from November 23, 1762: "Querulo Paterni che nulla è riuscito nelle sue speranze sul nuovo scavo [Stabiae]. Alcuvier continua a gridare."
106 *Philosophical Transactions* 41 (1744) II, 484–489, letter by Paderni to Ramsey of November 20, 1739, also in Zani 1993. But considering what he says, it may have been written somewhat later. Ramsey translated this and other letters into English. In the same letter he gives the date of February 20, 1740 for a visit to Portici. Other letters by him in the same *Philosophical Transactions* 48 (1755) II, 634–648 (Resina is not Herculaneum; bust of Epicurus found in Villa of the Papyri); 821–825 (statues of drunk satyr and "Seneca" found in the Villa of the Papyri); 49 (1756) 109–112 (discovery of statues of boys and Silenus in the same villa); 490–508 (Pompeii, amphitheater; tripod with ithyphallic satyrs; Stabiae); 50 (1758) 49–50 (two scrolls deciphered, on rhetoric and music); 619–623 (inscription temple Mater Deum, writing utensils etc. from Herculaneum; restoration bronze statue).
107 Ibidem, p. 485: "SigGioseppe Couart, as Sculptor to the King, had the Care of the Statues found there, with Order to restore them, where they are damaged."
108 Ibidem, p. 488 and 489.

> The First Mistake those Men they call Intendants have committed is, their having dug out the Pictures, without drawing the Situation of the Place, that is, the Niches, where they stood: For they were all adorned with Grotesques, composed of most elegant Masques, Figures, and Animals: which, not being copied, are gone to Destruction, and the like will happen to the rest. [...] I left then a Paper of Directions how to manage. If they do not observe them, the greater Misfortune will be ours, to hear that what Time, Earthquakes, and the Ravages of the Volcano have spared, are now destroyed by those who pretend to have the Case of them.

Notwithstanding this criticism, Paderni was a good person for the job of custodian of the collection at Portici. He would be active in this function until his death and never left the area but for a year in Spain (1765–1766). His education as a painter was useful, because he made drawings of the objects that became the basis of several engravings for the *Antichità d'Ercolano*. His diary and *Monumenti* provide extremely useful data regarding the excavations and the finds made at Herculaneum.[109] His work, however, was not easy, as he struggled with the methods of restoration and often received too many pieces at one time to work on. He wrote to his friend, the painter Thomas Hollis:[110]

> At present my time is much taken up, in a work extremely difficult and tedious; which is this: When the theatre was first discovered, there were found in it, among other things, several horses in bronze, larger than life; but all of them bruised, and broken into many pieces. From this sad condition they are not yet restored. But his majesty having expressed a particular desire to see that effected, if possible, with regard to one of them, I resolved to attempt it; and accordingly have set about it.

During a brief period around 1760, Paderni assumed the supervision of the excavations at Pompeii, but this came to an end in 1763 when the Court accused him of destroying wall paintings. His work resulted, for the first time, in buildings and streets being opened to the public, and included drawings of buildings in his *Monumenti*. In that respect, he is among the first to present documentation of the antique urban remains rather than of the objects in the museum.[111] The reconstruction of the kitchen in the museum and the illustration of every-day utensils, like vessels and bronze utensils, make him a forerunner in the study of daily life.[112]

---

109 The texts are reproduced in Forcellino 1999, who also illustrates the half of the forty-three plates of *Monumenti*. This document is in the Ecole Française de Rome, whereas the *Diario* is in the Archivio di Stato at Naples.
110 *Philosophical Transactions* 50 (1758) 50. The horses mentioned are those found in the theater, belonging to a quadriga. See also Winckelmann 1762, 24; 1997, 81–82 (wih commentary at pp. 167–168).
111 Forcellino 1999, 32. See *Monumenti*, plates XXVII (Porta d'Ercolano), XXVIII (schola of Mammia), unfortunately not reproduced in Forcellino.
112 Forcellino 1999, 22, 27. Cf. Fougeroux de Bondaroy 1770. As late as 1792, volume VIII of the *Antichità* would contain these sorts of objects.

Publications in Eighteenth-Century Naples

As the number of unearthed treasures grew, the court was called upon to publish accounts of the excavations. Naples had little fame in the field of antiquarian studies, whereas it was famous for modern approaches of sciences like economy and agriculture.[113] Delphine Burlot had recently discovered that the court envisaged an illustrated publication of the finds as early as 1746, but the few remaining copies of this work demonstrate such rough craftsmanship that they were most likely not ready for distribution.[114] Apparently, this project was aborted in favor of one put forward by the Roman priest Ottavio Antonio Bayardi, whose first work was a never completed multi-volume *Prodromo delle antichità d'Ercolano*, of which the first volume opens with a dedication to the King.[115]

Bayardi's research gained some momentum with the publication of a catalogue, which was long expected by the Court.[116] Bayardi decided to use Montfaucon's method of classification and, because of his weak health, begged for understanding.[117] In 1755 Tanucci founded a scientific academy, and included Bayardi among its twenty-seven members, among which Mazzocchi, Martorelli,

---

113 García y García 1998, 799; publications nos 9079–9083. See his museum's distich, above p. 30. On intellectual life in Naples, see various essays in Imbroglia 2000: G. Imbroglia, pp. 70–94, on Enlightenment, E. Ciosi, pp. 118–134, on academies, A. Schnapp, pp. 154–166, on antiquarian studies. Special issue of *Journal of the History of Collections* 19, fascicle 2 (2007), partly by the same authors.
114 Burlot 2011. She knows three copies of *Disegni tagliati in rame di pitture antiche ritrovate nelle scavazioni di Resina*, Naples 1746, which consist of ninety rather primitive copper plates. There is a preface listing the objects without any indication of context or provenance.
115 Bayardi 1752, I, I (preface). See García y García 1998, 177. *Prodomo*, ibidem no. 1412. His name is also spelled as Bajardi. L. Moretti, *Dizionario Biografio degli Italiani* 5 (1963) 284–285 s.v. Baiardi, Ottaviano Antonio: a very informative brief article. See also Trombetta 1984, 155–156.
116 Bayardi 1755, I (preface): "Sire, Ella è così, o SIGNORE, troppo indugio porta seco la necessità d'un Prodromo, che non può tampoco, come mi figuravo, in pochi mesi ancora giungere al bramato suo termine. Per quanto mi vado immaginando ve n'è ancora per un pajo d'anni, e forse di più." McIlwayne 1988, no 8.30; García y García 1998, no. 1414.
117 Bayardi 1755, XXI: "sanità di cui non abbondo." The catalogue provides very brief descriptions, with Roman inventory numbers referring to the objects. These were cancelled later, for which reason we cannot consult Bayardi's catalog with ease (cfr. Allroggen-Bedel in various contributions): 738 paintings (pp. 1–140), 350 bronze and marble statues (pp. 141–183), 915 vessels (pp. 184–293), 24 tripods (pp. 293–295), 163 lamps (pp. 295–315), 40 candelabra (pp. 315–323), 732 varia, like phalli nos 295–316 and, at pp. 420–422 no. 709, the tripod with the satyrs "alcuni giorni sono discoperto" (p. 444) who have (p. 420) "il priapismo notabile." As to mosaics and inscriptions Bayardi announces another volume. Tanucci felt a great annoyance: Tanucci III, 36 (September 20, 1752 to Nefetti): "Baiardi è stato letto da tutti fino a dieci carte; dopo quello ognuno ha desertato."

and Tanucci himself.¹¹⁸ This *Accademia Ercolanese* asked Bayardi to prepare a proposal for a series of publications and started to publish the huge luxury volumes of the *Antichità di Ercolano*.¹¹⁹ They did not include any documentation about the excavation or where objects were found; objects were merely described and illustrated, and classified by their physical status (painting, bronze) and without records about the context of their discovery. Tanucci asked the *Accademia*'s members to write comments and descriptions of the objects illustrated on the plates. These contributions remained anonymous.¹²⁰

Bayardi fell ill and wished to return to Rome.¹²¹ The government granted him this wish,¹²² and in 1756 he went back to Rome without bitterness. Volkmann quoted an epigram about Bayardi:¹²³

---

118 De La Condamine 1762, 382–383 reports the new start of the excavations in Pompeii in 1755. Cf. also Barthélemy (Sérieys 1801, 123). See Trombetta 1984, 157–161. Parslow 1995, 153–198 describes the vicissitudes around Weber's failed application for a membership in this academy.
119 1757–1792, twelve volumes published. Illustrations are already announced in Gori 1748, XI–XII: "[...] e attualmente s'incidono bravamente in Rame a spese del Re, per darsi prontamente in luce, ornati di erudite illustrazioni." Franceschini made engravings of the equestrian statues of the Balbi. On the edition of the *Antichità* see Praz 1979; Trombetta 1984; Pannuti 2000. On the academy E. Chiosi in *Tanucci* 1986, 493–517; La Rosa 2010.
120 Tanucci IX, 124 (letter from November 18, 1760): Finally "tutte [le spiegazioni] si riducono ad uno stile semplice, facile, e breve." Cf. Tanucci XVI, 115–6 (letter from September 10, 1765 to Cantanti): he is praised by La Ligneville for his preface to volume II, but should have signed this text.
121 Barthélemy saw him in Naples (Sérieys 1801, 53): "Sans son Prodrome, il seroit plus estimé; car il sait et fait beaucoup [...]." Sérieys 1801, 71–72; 137: "Il a grande envie de quitter cette ville, et il me paroît qu'on ne sera pas trop difficile sur le congé qu'il demande. Au fond, c'est un galant homme, qui jouit d'une érudition immense, mais qui ne sait pas s'en faire honneur." García y García 1998, nos 1330–1332. On his departure, Tanucci IV, 87 (July 6, 1756), short letter to Bayardi; 252 (October 29, 1756 to Guglielmo de Lulof).
122 Strazzullo 1980, 273. Tanucci was happy anyway and had a very negative opinion of Bayardi, see *Tanucci* 1986, 89–90 and his letters, e.g. Tanucci II, 356–357 (letter from February 10, 1748 to Giacomelli in Rome): "Le anticaglie di Portici occuperebbono almeno tre dotti antiquari, per ben dieci anni. E venuto da cotesto paese il vostro mons. Bajardi, e in pochi mesi dice che ha finito due grandi tomi in foglio, che tuttte spiegano ed illustrano le cose trovate finora. [=*Prodromo*] Pensate voi che saranno questi due tomi. Due o tre volte ch'io mi son trovato a parlare con esso alla presenza del Re sopra qualche pezo d'antichità ho dovuto dissentire, e con mio dispiacere scoprire ch'ei ne sapeva meno di me che non ho fatto alcuno studio d'antichità figurata e ne so soltanto quanto la conversazione di Buonaroti ne aveva nel mio capo inserita a quella che già vi era di storia scritta."
123 Volkmann 1777–1778, III, 297–298, second stanza: "*Herculea urbs, quondam saevis oppressa ruinis /Et terrae vastis abdita visceribus, /Magnanimi regis jussu jam prodit in auras, /Raraque tot profert quae latuere prius: /Miramur signa ac pictas spirare figuras, /Priscorum doctas artificumque manus. /Sed quam non motus terrae valuere, nec ignes /Perdere, Scriptoris pagina dira valet. /En iterum tetris misere tot mersa tenebris, /Bayardi in libro tota sepulta iacet.*" The whole poem in R. Paolini et al., *Memorie sui monumenti di antichità e di belle arti: ch'esistono in Miseno* [etc.], Napoli 1812, 283, and Maizony de Lauréal 1837, XXI. Trombetta 1984, 156 cites it from another source of 1840.

> The town of Hercules, once oppressed by cruel ruins and hidden in the vast innards of earth, now comes to light on command of the magnanimous King and brings so many rare things to the fore that were hidden before: we admire how statues and painted figures take breath as well as the learned hands of old artists. But, while neither earthquakes nor fires were able to destroy her, the horrible page of an Author is. Look, she is again drowned in so much black darkness and lies completely entombed in Bayardi's book.

Hollis told the following anecdote:[124]

> In the summer 1752, when the two first volumes of a work related to Herculaneum, Stabiae, Pompeii, and the antiquities discovered in those cities of late years, were ready for publication, Mons. Baiardi, the author of them, a learned good prelate from the Romish communion, though it hath been said of a genius not altogether suitable to that work, waited on the King of Naples, now King of Spain, to receive his directions for the distribution of those volumes, which had been printed by his own special command, in order to be scattered, as other volumes have been since, among the learned every where; the King said to him immediately, without noticing Neapolitan, Spanjard, or any other people, Give five hundred copies to the English. Bajardi, who was by no means disinclined to that nation, replied bowing, I fear, in that case, the rest of Europe will fail of their proportion. – LET THE PRESS BE SET ANEW.
> COUNTRYMEN,
> Applaud the munificence of the Monarch, and believe him to be, what in fact he is, though sometimes misled by bad servants, a friendly, honest man.
> An English Traveller. But while neither earthquakes nor fires could ruin the town, a dire page of an Author can. Look, again they sent so many merged into black darkness, in Baiardi's book she lies, entirely buried.

The opulent volumes of the *Antichità* served as gifts to royal colleagues and noblemen who got access to the court.[125] Their failure was their limited distribution: even though they were not rare, since printed in some hundred copies, they did not arrive on the desks of people who had a real interest in the excavations.[126]

---

124 Blackburne 1780, 485. On Hollis (1720–1770 [Ingamells: 1774]): Ingamells 1997, 512–513. He was among Paderni's correspondents (cf. notes 97, 106).
125 Even Tanucci was not free to give them away, for instance, to his friend Nefetti, see Tanucci V, 637 (letter of February 7, 1758 to Nefetti): "Il libro delle Pitture d'Ercolano si dà dal re a chi lo chiede. Tengo ordine di mandarne uno a Botta, uno a milady Oxford [=Orford], uno a Narvaez, uno a Viviani, uno a Albizi, uno a Torigiani. Dunque, che volete che io possa fare? Se si vendessero tali libri ne comprerei uno per voi. Ma il Re non li vuol vendere." In the same vein he writes to the Marchess of Lignville (p. 766, March 2, 1758): "Non si vende, ma non obtusa adeo gestamus pectora Poeni [Virgil, *Aeneis* 1.567: but let us, Phoenicians, not be insensible]." On the *Antichità*, see Trombetta 1984; Allroggen-Bedel 1986; Pannuti 2000.
126 Tanucci XV, 284 (April 9, 1765 to Squillace): 2000 copies of *Antichità* IV. Björnståhl 1777, 277: "Der Preis von diesen Werken ist nicht so hoch, als man sich vorstellen sollte; anfangs, so lange

That Winckelmann struggled to get a copy gives us an idea of this imbalance, in that scholars were apparently deemed unworthy of these volumes.

The genius behind the curtains was Tanucci, the only professor who succeeded in becoming a minister. Jacob Jonas Björnståhl observes that he refused to be mentioned among the authors and asked his interviewer not to write about this topic, since the *Antichità* was supposed to be a team effort.[127] According to the mineralogist Johann Jacob Ferber it was Ferdinando Galiani who made the decisive suggestion for two important changes: the open-air excavations at Pompeii and the wider diffusion of the *Antichità*.[128]

Dupaty made a strong comparison between Winckelmann and the *Antichità*: one man, Winckelmann, had reached more than the entire group of Neapolitan scholars.[129] The *Accademia Ercolanese* got tired of the incessant criticisms about the slow progress made and decided to publish a series of engravings made for the *Antichità*: *Gli ornati delle pareti ed in pavimenti delle stanze dell'antica Pompei incise in rame* but also as "fogli volanti, distributi con poc'ordine in vero."[130] Each painting was presented without any comments, and only sometimes with an indication of its provenance.[131] A great difference from the *Antichità* is that we see complete wall and floor decorations, and no cut-out fragments, which makes them still precious. Among the artists are those of the *Antichità*, like Raffaello Morghen, Gio-

---

sich der König vorbehalten hatte, sie nach Belieben zu verschenken, waren sie kaum für Geld zu bekommen. Se. Majestät fährt noch fort, Monarchen, Prinzen und Minister damit zu beschenken, hat aber nun Erlaubnis gegeben, daß andre es kaufen dürfen." He gives the price of 12 ducats and stresses the costs of production, mentioning the numerous artists involved.

127 Björnståhl 1777, 281: "Dadurch, sagte er, verliert das Werk von seinem Ansehen, wenn man weiß, daß eine einzige Person von unbekannten, und nichts weniger, als schimmernden Namen, Verfasser davon ist, anstatt, daß es sich in weit grösserer Achtung erhält, wenn man glaubt, es sey von einer ganzen Gesellschaft abgefaßt. Mein Vorsehen ist, setzte er hinzu, unbekannt zu leben, und ich hoffe, daß mir niemand dies Glück rauben wird." Cf. note 120.

128 Ferber 1773, 121–122: "Seinen Vorstellungen ist es auch zu verdanken, daß die Ausgrabungen zu Pompeja nicht, wie im Herculano, wieder verschüttet werden, und daß man jetzo in der königl. Bibliothek die Beschreibung und Abbildung der Alterthümer im Cabinette zu Portici kaufen kann, wovon ehemals der König nur an gekrönte Häupter Geschenke machte."

129 Duclos n.y., 125: "On a beaucoup écrit sur Herculane; mais personne n'a rien donné de si savant et de si instructif, que l'abbé Winkelmann, le plus habile antiquaire que j'aie connu. Il étoit, en cette qualité, attaché au pape, et fort communicatif; je prenois, à Rome, grand plaisir à converser avec lui. Il avoit consenti à une correspondence avec moi; et j'ai appris, avec le plus vive douleur le crime qui nous l'a enlevé." He refers to Winckelmann's assassination at Trieste. There are no such letters in Rehm, who reproduces this passage (Winckelmann 1952–1957, IV, 257, with commentary on p. 511).

130 Naples, I, 1796; II, 1798.

131 E.g. "Casa Pseudourbana" = Villa of Diomedes: I, 1–24 and II 17, 21.

vanni Casanova and Francesco Morelli. Research into the documentation of the Temple of Isis has made clear that many engravings were never even published.[132]

All these publications encountered heavy criticism. Caylus was very skeptical about the choice of paintings made for the first volume of the *Antichità*, which included tiny and insignificant figures as well as ugly arabesques. He also believed that the texts were too long and repetitive.[133] His negative judgment of Volume II reflected that of cardinal Paciaudi, but he studied it with his friend Galiani.[134] That did not hinder Caylus, however, from inserting illustrations into his work copied from or already made for the *Antichità*, together with works of a "pensionnaire" of the French Academy in Rome.[135]

A cheap edition of the *Antichità* by Thomas Martyn and John Lettice was important for the diffusion of Herculanean motifs in neo-classical art and handcraft.[136] Loved and reviled alike, these decorations would conquer Europe.[137]

---

132 *Alla ricerca di Iside*, Naples 1992.
133 Caylus I (1752) 42–43: "Les petites femmes en l'air et les Centaures [from the Villa of Cicero] seront toujours très-agréables, et j'avoue que je n'aurais pas placé dans un ouvrage de cette importance, et surtout dans le premier volume, des prétendues architectures, qui ne sont que des arabesques des plus mauvais et qu'on ne peut regarder que comme des opérations chinoises. L'explication ne me plaît guère; elle est allongée et remplie de choses inutiles et répétées partout. D'ailleurs aucun de ceux qui y ont travaillé n'entend les arts et ne dit rien qui puisse y avoir du rapport. Cependant cette partie était assez importante et trouvait sa place dans un pareil ouvrage." On Caylus see the necrology in the posthumous volume VII of 1767; Seznec 1949, 151, 154 (sarcastic remarks by Diderot); Ridley 1992. The other volumes: II, 1756; III, 1759; IV, 1761; V, 1762; VI, 1764 e VII, 1767. The importance is reflected in the immediate translation into German: *Des Herrn Grafen Caylus Sammlung von Aegyptischen, Hetrurischen, Griechischen und Römischen Alterthümern*, Nürnberg 1766 (348 pages with 106 plates).
134 Caylus I (1752) 243: "Ce n'était pas la peine de nous tenir si longtemps le bec dans l'eau pour le IIe tome d'Herculanum, puisqu'il est si mal executé."
135 Caylus II, 130–132. He dares not give his sources (Caylus III, 1759, 143): "La crainte d'attirer des dégoûts à l'haute Artiste qui m'a comuniqué ces desseins, m'oblige à cacher son nom; car l'Antiquité à Naples est une affaire d'Etat, & c'est avec une sorte d'inquiétude que je comunique les monumens de ce pays. Je crains de rendre leur approche encore plus difficile; mais les difficultés ne pouvant être plus grandes, la réflexion fait sentir qu'on n'a rien à ménager, & que par conséquens on peut se livrer à la jouissance du moment." Tanucci asked Paderni about this question, who suggested Piaggio or his assistant Vincenzo Merli (Tanucci X, 51, August 25, 1761 to Charles): "Mi ha dopo molto detto che non è responsabile, perché sta e passa per quelle stanze il padre Antonio e il Merlo [Piaggio and Merli] suo aiutante; di quest'ultimo mi ha parlato poco vantaggiosamente. Stimerei che quei due si potessero passare ad altro quarto, perché conviene che Paderni sia responsabile." Münter meets Merli in 1785 (Andreasen 1937, 9)
136 *Antiquities of Herculaneum*, London 1773. Cfr. Dobai 1975, 1205–1206; Trombetta 1984, 162.
137 Nisard (1877, 243 note 2) observes: "S'il [Paciaudi] faisait pitié sous le rapport du dessin, c'était aussi un peu la faute des monuments originaux. L'influence que les Pitture d'Ercolano

In the late eighteenth century, general guides to Naples started to include some pages on the excavations and on the museum at Portici. Apparently, the court was no longer making objections. The local revolution and the French occupation are probably what caused this change in the old politics of monopolizing all sorts of publications.[138]

Publications in Learned Circles in Europe

Among the first important works about the excavations at Herculaneum – and unique thanks to its illustrations – is a booklet by Nicolas Cochin and Charles Bellicard, *Observations sur les antiquités d'Herculanum* from 1754.[139] Cochin was a draughtsman who would become the most important print maker in France. He was in Rome in 1749–1750 as one of the guides of the brother of Madame de Pompadour, the marquess Abel-François de Vandières and was accompanied by the architect Bellicard on his trip to the South.[140] In Naples, they were guests of D'Arthenay, secretary of the French ambassador and possibly author of an early account (see p. 24). Their story delivers a positive image of the excavations, that matches the ideas of the *Anciens* in the discussion on the importance of Antiquity for the *Querelle des Anciens et des Modernes*.[141] From Cochin's point of view as an artist, the study of Roman wall paintings was important.[142] His judgment of the wall paintings was not very positive, apart from the praise of the Theseus and the Minotaur from the "Basilica" at Herculaneum. The architectural paintings

---

ont exercée sur l'école européenne à la fin du XVIIIe siècle et au commencement du XIXe a été pernicieuse. Elles ont fini par dégoûter quantité de gens qui, par réaction, se sont mis à étudier une antiquité moins saturée de pavots."
138 E.g. Palermo 1792. García y García 1998, no. 10.146. As the title indicates, it was a sequel to Carlo Celano's *Notizie del bello, dell'antico, e del curioso della Città di Napoli per i Signori Forastieri*, Naples 1692. Cf. also Cassini 1778, 646–654 (Herculaneum), 654–657 (museum), 657–660 (Pompeii). McIlwayne 1988, nos 2.416, 2.63; García y García 1998, no. 2702.
139 Cochin/Bellicard 1754. This booklet had first come out in English under the name of Bellicard: *Observations upon the Antiquities of the Town of Herculaneum, Discovered at the Foot of Mount Vesuvius*, London 1753. On this work Michel 1984, 108–109; Michel 1991, 3 (editions); De Seta 1992, 126–128.
140 Michel 1991, 1–67; 1993, 67–70; E. Flamarion and C. Volpilhac-Auger in Cochin/Bellicard 1996, 11–12. See Gordon 1990 on Bellicard's manuscript notebook in the Metropolitan Museum.
141 On this debate in the eighteenth century, see Michel 1984, 106–107.
142 Already before his return he published an essay on the paintings: Cochin 1751. See Michel 1984, 1991 and 1993; E. Flamarion and C. Volpilhac-Auger in Cochin/Bellicard 1996, 14–17. Michel underlines the importance of the trip for Cochin's career (Michel 1993, 67–70).

were considered the worst of all.¹⁴³ Strikingly, the images of paintings and objects found at Herculaneum in this publication are rather primitive, when compared with those of the Campi Flegrei and considering Cochin's skills as a draughtsman. Since the authors refer to the severe rules about drawing and writing in Naples, they probably drew these images from memory, intentionally making them extra 'primitive' to bolster their criticism of these prohibitions.¹⁴⁴

Caylus' afore-mentioned *Antiquités* was a vast work about the old cultures of the Mediterranean, the Near East and Northwest Europe. It contains various reflections on objects found in Herculaneum and Pompeii.¹⁴⁵ Caylus never visited the sites, but was well informed, despite the never-answered demand for "éclairissemens" from the King about the prohibitions from making notes.¹⁴⁶ He gleaned notes from his correspondence with Cardinal Paciaudi and travelers, hoping to learn about the Herculanean antiquities.¹⁴⁷ He believed that the paintings were of low quality, apart from the Theseus and the Minotaur.

Caylus' method, like that of the Encyclopédistes, concentrates on the function of the objects in ancient society. His point of view, in contrast with Cochin and Bellicard, was that of the *Modernes*. Classical antiquity, he believed, is an excellent culture to imitate and emulate, but it is not insuperable,¹⁴⁸ and Pompeii and Herculaneum are ideal for a reconstruction of antique life, since they offer incredible information that surpasses what a mere object, like an incense burner, can offer.¹⁴⁹ As in the *Antichità*, Caylus arranged the items according to formal criteria, like format and material (similar to the taxonomy of Pliny the Elder and that of the seventeenth and eighteenth century, see p. 32, 115).

---

143 See the account of his voyage to Naples in 1758 (Michel 1991, 209): "absolument mauvais; non seulement il n'y a pas de perspective, mais même l'architecture en est de mauvais goût: il semble qu'elle soit gothique par anticipation." Even the Theseus was now seen as weak (Michel 1991, 203-204): "Ce n'est qu'une ébauche avancée."
144 Tanucci found the work a "bagatelle," not being based on autopsy, while Venuti 1748 was fine: Tanucci V, 13 (letter May 24, 1757).
145 Regarding the towns, he only mentions the sidewalks and the relatively low number of dead people found in the ruins (Caylus I, 1752, 3). See also note 133.
146 Caylus II, 1756, 120. Kimball (1953, 1254) records that in 1715, Caylus was at Elbeuf's pit, but he did not enter.
147 Caylus I (1752) 49-51: "Il faut espérer qu'après une si longue attente [viz. from 79 onwards] nous serons instruits de toutes ces découvertes, qui doivent répandre un si grand jour sur l'antiquité [...]." Nisard 1877.
148 On his dispute with Cochin, see Michel 1993, 112-115, 242-244.
149 Caylus VI (1764) 21: "On peut avancer hardiment que les monumens d'Herculanum instruiront nos neveux d'un nombre infini d'usages, de procédés & de détails dont nous ne faisons encore que soupçonner les Anciens, & même faiblement. Les ruines de cette Ville infortunée, peuvent seules réparer le plus grand nombre de pertes causées par la négligence, l'avarice ou la barbarie. Cette bagatelle que l'on voit sous ce numéro [a lamp on plate LXVI.5] en est une preuve."

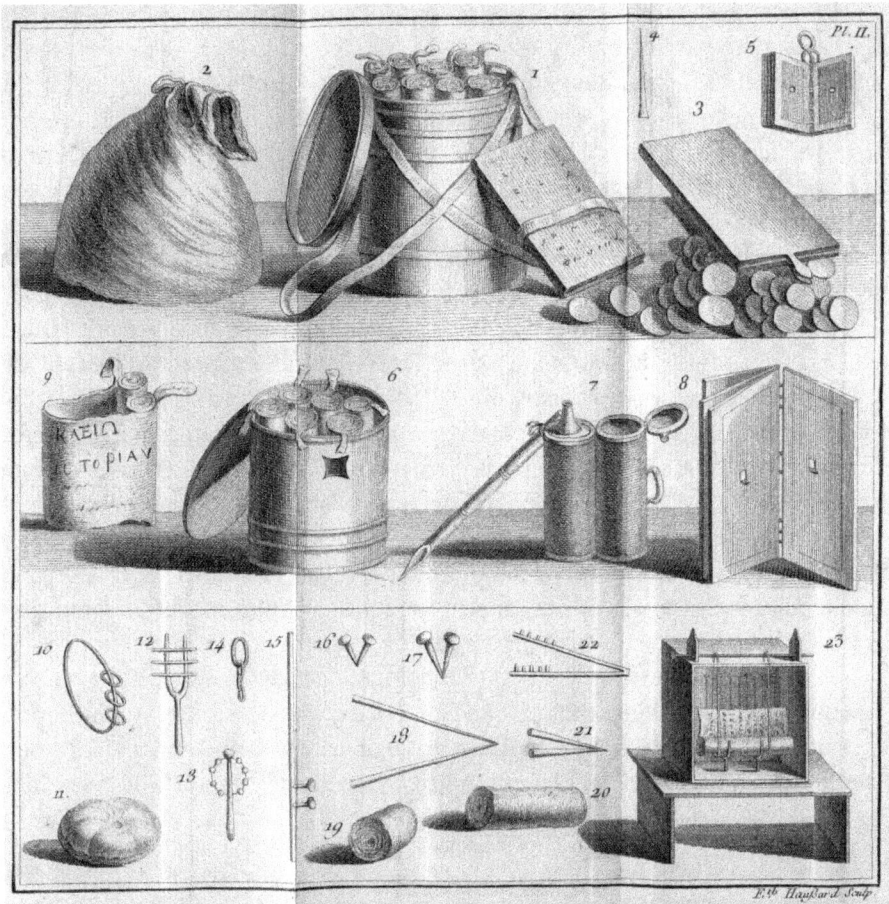

Fig. 2: August Denis Fougeroux de Bondaroy, *Recherches sur les ruines d'Herculanum* (1770), plate 2. Upper and middle row: still lifes of writing utensils and a coin box. Lower row: writing utensils, sistrum, tibiae, nails, a charred loaf, and charred papyrus scrolls, and Piaggio's papyrus unroller.

Like many others, Caylus wished to buy an original object from the excavations, like an unpublished papyrus, even by means of a clandestine dig. It would have been a great pleasure to unroll his own ancient text, which, of course, he was never able to do.[150]

---

150 Caylus I (1752) 112; 128, etc.; 101: "Je répondrais bien de parvenir à le dérouler. Que de plaisir! Quel événement dans la république des lettres? Je ne serais pas injuste; j'en ferais tout l'honneur au roi d'Espagne et à notre Académie. Un tel usage mériterait-il le nom de vol?" Other examples of suggested theft in Caylus I (1752) 86 etc.

Household utensils form the central item of a book by August Denis Fougeroux de Bondaroy, based on his visit in 1763.[151] At length he speaks about the volcanic material in Herculaneum and its stratigraphy. Despite the low visibility in the tunnels, he regards a daylight exploration as unfeasible because of the thick masses of lava.[152] Household items are of high interest, showing how people lived. An essay on "Fabriques des mosaïques" concludes the booklet.[153] Fougeroux's work betrays an attention to the objects used in daily life, a characteristic of his book which goes well with science. Paintings serve to illustrate aspects of ancient life like religion, writing, music, and making wine (fig. 2).[154]

The fact that Fougeroux paid so much attention to utensils and illustrated them on as many as three plates was the reason for which Diderot attacked him. In his view, a book dealing with ordinary objects as opposed to the arts was not worthy of being in the luggage of a traveler to the south.[155] It sounds strange that the editor of the *Encyclopédie*, who was so interested in the arts and crafts of his own time that there should be extensive descriptions and lavish illustrations of these topics in this work, did not recognize the relevance of ancient forerunners. But entirely in accordance with the views of his time, Diderot saw Antiquity as an example of high culture and the daily-life aspects were irrelevant for modern people. The finds at Herculaneum and Pompeii, interesting since they made known aspects of common life, apparently did not trigger Diderot to change his mind.[156]

Fougeroux knew Winckelmann's *Sendschreiben*, which also stressed the importance of studying old "Geräthe" that had grace and showed ancient peoples' good taste. Modern artists would gain profit from copying them.[157] One of Winckelmann's

---

151 Fougeroux 1770. McIlwayne 1988, no. 3.230; García y García 1998, no. 5430.
152 Fougeroux 1770, 23–24: "J'avoue qu'il semble qu'on pourroit conduire ces travaux différemment, en les prenant par petites parties, & examinant avec plus de soin les édifices que l'on soupçonneroit avoir appartenu à quelques riches ou curieux. On en retireroit probablement plus de connoissances sur la batisse des anciens. Mais il est toujours certain que les travaux tels qu'on les exécute, ont donné lieu à des découvertes, non seulement curieuses, mais très-utiles."
153 Fougeroux 1770, 149–227.
154 Fougeroux 1770, 143: "Il est certain que les peintures & les autres morceaux tirés d'Herculanum pourroient jetter un grand jour sur l'Histoire & l'état des Art dans ces temps si éloignés de nous."
155 "Il y a aussi de ce gens qui vont à Herculanum et qui s'ébahissent sottement d'y trouver des objets usuels, par exemple ce M. Fougeroux qui a rapporté de là-bas un catalogue fort sec d'articles de ménage." From "Recherches sur les ruines d'Herculanum par M. Fougeroux de Bondaroy" in Diderot 1875–1877, X, 257; Diderot 1971, VIII, 321–322. Cf. Pucci 1989, 48 and his note 9.
156 Cf. Seznec 1949, 154; Blix 2009, 18.
157 Winckelmann 1762, 61–62; 1997a, 109–110: "Die vornehmste Betrachtung über alte Geräthe und sonderlich über die Gefäße, sollte auf die Zierlichkeit derselben gerichtet seyn, in welcher alle unsere Künstler den Alten nachstehen müssen. Alle ihre Formen sind auf Grundsätze des guten Geschmacks gebauet, und gleichen einem schönen jungen Menschen, in dessen

reviewers, Christian Gottlob Heyne, would single out this point and quote Winckelmann extensively.[158]

François de Paule Latapie was among the first to describe the excavations at Pompeii carried out in the light of the day. In a presentation in 1776 in the Académie Royale des Sciences, Lettres et Arts de Bordeaux, he gave a clear definition of Pompeii's importance in respect to Rome: its mediocrity guarantees other forms of information than Rome's grandiose ruins. Therefore, it is no problem that houses are small, since even in the smallest ones there are novelties to discover.[159] A striking detail is the presence of glass in the windows, while bones are the remains of the victims, often collected by the visitors as souvenirs (cf. Chapter III, p. 182). Latapie was the first to record names of houses formed on the basis of graffiti on their façades.[160] He suggested the excavation of, or at least the full discovery of the walls of the town in order to obtain a notion of its size. In Latapie's view, farmers ruined the archaeological site with their agricultural activities.[161] This concern might have its origin in Latapie's profession as a student of gardening, which was evidenced in the detailed depiction of planted trees and shrubs on his plan. In many respects, his plan, the first known plan of the excavations – Esquisse du Plan de Pompeii faite de mémoire pour donner une idée des positions respectives des fouilles en Fevrier 1776 – gives a distorted view of the ancient city but offers insight into the primary monuments known at that time.[162] Francesco Piranesi would publish a plan in 1785, whereas Latapie's sketch remained hidden in the archives of his academy.[163]

Gebährden, ohne sein Zuthun oder Denken, sich die Gratie bildet; diese erstrecket sich hier bis auf die Handheben der Gefäße. [etc.]" See also the excellent remarks in Winckelmann 1997a, 238–240 on his terminology. Fougeroux 1770, IX quotes this text. Like Winckelmann he devotes many words to ink and writing.
158 Reproduced in Winckelmann 2001b, 112.
159 Latapie 1953, 225. The year 1755 given as the moment of rediscovery may be due to the commencement of the daylight excavations, see pp. 26–27.
160 So A. Maiuri in Latapie 1953, 247 note 26, commenting on Latapie 1953, 233.
161 Latapie 1953, 233–234: "Les paysans en fesant des fosses pour planter leurs vignes ont détruit avec la bêche et quelquefois à la sappe tout ce qu'ils ont trouvé de batimens qui fesoient résistance et se sont servis des pierres soit pour batir des maisons soit pour séparer leurs possessions par des murailles sèches." Indeed, Hamilton 1777 shows modern plantations in the garden of the Villa of Diomedes and several travelers record gardens, providing food and drinks for the tourists.
162 Latapie 1953. Guzzo (2008, 12) sees Latapie's pioneering work as proof of his intellectual liberty.
163 On Piranesi, see Allroggen-Bedel 1983a and Kockel 2000.

Latapie's main critic was of course Winckelmann, who – justly – boasted to have studied at Portici for many months, much more than any passing traveler. He hoped to escape the court's vengeance with the publication of his 1762 and 1764 libels in German instead of one of the learned languages: *Sendschreiben von den Herculanischen Entdeckungen* and *Nachrichten von den neuesten Herculanischen Entdeckungen*.[164] Caylus' French translation of the *Sendschreiben* had the effect Winckelmann feared: the Neapolitans soon took notice of Winckelmann's caustic remarks.[165]

Winckelmann's criticism concerned three cardinal points: (1) the prohibition against publishing anything about the discoveries, (2) the incompetence of the personnel involved, and (3) the management of the finds. His first book championed the effort to abolish the prohibitions, train the personnel and more properly manage the finds. After Cochin and Bellicard, Winckelmann was the first to offer extensive descriptions as well as comments on finds themselves rather than on the excavations, which had been the norm in the work of others before him. Inscriptions are often quoted correctly, which suggests that he must have learned them by heart. Among the people involved, diplomatically, he did not hit Tanucci, but Alcubierre, who according to him, and as an Italian saying went, knew as little of the excavation as crabs knew of the moon.[166] Bayardi, Martorelli, and Mazzocchi got their share of criticism, too, as omniscient but stupid authors, without insight or understanding, writing books that were too thick. The only praise was for Weber and Piaggio. Winckelmann's succinct style contrasts with the pompous publication of the Neapolitan academics. It is especially worth noticing that he always associates the finds with other antique objects or written sources, trying to illustrate their relevance for archaeology on a broader scale than Naples.

---

164 Winckelmann 1762 and 1997a; 1764 and 1997b. For his original sketches and reactions see Winckelmann 2001b. On Winckelmann and Naples, see Leppmann 1966, 77–97; De Franciscis 1975; Allroggen-Bedel 1990; F.-W. von Hase in Meller/Dickmann 2011, 328–335, and contributions quoted in the following notes. Fundamental: M. Gross, M. Kunze, and A. Rügler in Winckelmann 1997a, 9–57.
165 *Lettre de M. l'Abbé Winckelmann, Antiquaire de Sa Sainteté, à Monsieur le Comte de Brühl, Chambellain du Roi de Pologne, Electeur de Saxe, sur les Découvertes d'Herculanum*, Dresden/Paris 1764. The "Avis de l'imprimeur" – by Caylus? – expresses the hope: "Je crois qu'il [the reader] ne lira pas sans plaisir un Ouvrage, qui contient des détails plus circonstanciés qu'aucuns de ceux dans lesquels on étoit encore entré, & un récit fidele de tout ce qui s'est fait & passé avant que de parvenir à l'importance découverte d'Herculanum, & de plusieurs autres lieux importans des environs. Personne assurément ne les a mieux vûs, ni mieux expliqués que l'Auteur dont je donne l'ouvrage." See also Zevi 1979, 59; Winckelmann 1997a, 37.
166 Winckelmann 1762, 19; 1997a, 78: "Dieser Mann, welcher mit den Alterthümern so wenig zu thun gehabt hatte, als der Mond mit den Krebsen, nach dem Welschen [i.e. italienischen] Sprichworte, war durch seine Unerfahrenheit Schuld an vielem Schaden und an dem Verluste vieler schönen Sachen."

He did not criticize the excavation methods or the extraction of objects: it would be too burdensome to lay open Herculaneum. At Pompeii the open-air dig was easy, but developed too slowly and with too few workmen.[167] Despite his hitting the core of the excavations' problems, nothing changed and nobody attempted to revise any methods. Even internal criticism to more extensively divulge the results of the research failed.[168]

The answer to Winckelmann's *Sendschreiben* was an anonymous booklet attributed to Mattia Zarillo (or Zarrilli), a member of the *Accademia Ercolanese*. For him, Winckelmann was a Goth who wrote for other Goths, lazy (if learned) linguists who did not want to travel to the South, and who like moles, were running in the mines of dark knowledge.[169] It is true, the author admits, that the excavators destroyed some bronzes and other objects, but otherwise the King would need still more showcases. He defends his colleagues Martorelli and Mazzocchi; the latter wrote a beautiful epigraph about the base of the equestrian statue of Balbus and, besides, he was internationally famous.[170] As to Alcubierre: he never wanted to be an Antiquarian, but was a good military architect and for that reason was chosen to direct the complicated subterranean excavations.[171]

---

167 Winckelmann 1762, 21–22; 1997a, 79–80. He did not yet understand the enormous value of excavations and left them to curious English travelers. In contrast, the *Nachrichten* devote more space to the Pompeian excavations (Winckelmann 1764, 5; 1997b, 10).
168 E.g. by Fernando Galiani expressed to minister Tanucci in the form of a true cri de coeur. See Knight 1995, 213; Allroggen-Bedel 1996.
169 *Giudizio* 1765, 4; Winckelmann 2001b, 4: "quella razza di Dotti, che non escono dallo studio delle lingue, e sono come gli scavatori delle miniere, gente così avvezza al bujo, ed alla dura fatica delle sole braccia, che la luce le nuoce, e 'l pensare non trova come penetrare nell'ottuso, ed oppresso spirito." Leopardi would describe the members of the academy as blind moles (see p. 53).
170 *Giudizio* 1765, 9–13, text on p. 13; 19; Winckelmann 2001b, 141–144, esp. 143; 146.
171 *Giudizio* 1765, 22; Winckelmann 2001b, 147, even refers to Winckelmann's crab comparison: "[Alcubierre] non si è vantato mai di essere dotto Antiquario. Egli professa l'Architettura militare: e se da sua Maestà Cattolica fu scelto a dirigere gli scavi, fu scelto nel concetto di saper dirigere uno scavo sotterraneo in modo, che non pericolasse, e di saper prendere le piante degli Uffiziale, che ha ben disimpegnata la sua incombenza, dicendo, che ha tanto, che far'esso coll'antichità, quanto la Luna co' granchi? Sarebbe bella se io dicessi, che l'Abbate ha tanto, che fare esso co' Camei, e Corniole del Museo di Stosch, quanto la Luna co' granchi, perchè l'Abbate non è esso incisore di pietre? Gli incisori porgono all'Abbate materia di far pompa del suo vasto profondo sapere, e l'Alcobierre estrae dal fondo della terra i monumenti preziosi, vasta materia per l'erudizione." The booklet was sold together with a pamphlet by Berardo Galiani from 1765, in which the same defense – even in similar formulas – is made in a succinct manner (Galiani 1765, 7; Winckelmann 2001b, 154).

One of the major scholars in Naples was the English ambassador Sir William Hamilton, who stayed from 1764 until 1800, surely a longer period than he wished, but thanks to his publications, made himself unforgettable.[172] Although volcanology was his primary field of interest, he also published about Herculaneum and Pompeii. He guided many visitors to the excavations and to Vesuvius and had a small collection of Pompeian objects.[173] This was a wonder, since almost nothing Pompeian was on the art market. One of the first illustrated accounts of the excavations in Pompeii is Hamilton's paper in the still existing periodical *Archaeologia*.[174] The text mainly is a brief commentary on a set of plates,[175] and focuses – for the first time in the excavation history – on architecture. Plate VI, for instance, shows the "Barracks of the gladiators." On a shelf there are some skulls seen as the remains of "soldiers".[176] The plates are very "dry," in that they do not contain additions that create a romantic or other particular atmosphere. There are no people, and "dramatic" situations, with skeletons, lack, although the description contains emotional remarks. Hamilton wanted to record the situation and avoided inserting private feelings. The fact that his publications are in a scientific periodical and the product of a scientific presentation may have been important factors. This publication and the lavish *Campi Phlegraei* would be cited by many scholars. In the latter work he tried to explain the different layers of vol-

---

172 E.g. Hamilton 1776 on volcanology. See i.a. Constantine 2001 and Knight 2003. His first wife Catherine Barlow died in 1783 and his second marriage, to Emma Hart, provoked a scandal, as she was below his social status. For more on her, see Russell 1972 and Ittershagen 1999. Cf. the forgery of documents by Donatone 2000 (see Knight 2003, 7–8) and the splendid novel *The Volcano Lover* by Susan Sontag (1992). On Hamilton's collections Jenkins/Sloan 1996. On Hamilton as a volcanologist, Scarth 2009, 185–226; Cocco 2013, 206–207, 218–223. Ramage 1992 has precious unpublished documents of Hamilton's interest as an archaeologist.
173 See the witty description of Goethe's disembarrassment on seeing these things, when he visited Hamilton: Goethe 1988, 331 (May 27, 1787), quoted in Chapter II, pp. 150–151, note 577.
174 Hamilton 1777: "Read at the Society of Antiquaries, Jan. 26, Feb. 2–9, 1774." The paper was also published as a monograph. Martini 1779, 103–162 follows Hamilton's descriptions and illustrations.
175 Plates VI–XVIII. These are anonymous, with "Basire sc" written underneath. Hamilton's regular painter, Pietro Fabris, is probably responsible for them. He made the splendid illustrations for *Campi Phlegraei* (Hamilton 1776).
176 Hamilton 1777, 161: "In the prison of this barrack, the skeletons of several soldiers were found, and some with iron fetters on their leg-bones; their sculls are now placed on the shelves D. for the inspection of the curious. It is certain, that in these sculls, and in many others, that have been found at Pompeii, the teeth are remarkably found; perhaps among the Ancients, who did not make use of sugar, they might not be so subject to decay as ours." The letter D on the plate refers to this explanation. Modern research has shown that all ancient inhabitants suffered from tooth diseases (e.g. Lazer 2009)!

canic material covering Herculaneum (volcanic mud hardened like concrete by water) and Pompeii (showers of pumice, fragmented volcanic material).[177]

Among the most influential illustrated books of the eighteenth century is Saint-Non's *Voyage pittoresque*, with its 450 high-quality illustrations by skilled artists. It would be translated into English and the term picturesque formed a basic element in the titles of many works to follow. Saint-Non visited Naples in December 1759 and April 1760 on his Grand Tour, and was encouraged by Caylus to study the antiquities from the Vesuvian cities.[178] He undertook the publication of the *Voyage* many years after and involved Vivant Denon (see Chapter II, p. 140) and some members of the French Academy in Rome; Petra Lamers has reconstructed this rather complicated project. The Vesuvian cities are the subject of the second volume.[179] Saint-Non argues that while Herculaneum was rather famous, Pompeii ran the risk of remaining unknown because of the lack of publications including descriptions and illustrations.[180] This is why his artists have taken the liberty of suggesting a more dramatic, "picturesque" atmosphere – e.g. Hubert Robert's illustrations of the excavations of Herculaneum in a wild, rocky landscape, with small people laboring and impressive finds scattered over the place, and that of the skeleton in a (fantasy) subterranean room. Such an exaggeration seemed necessary to evoke emotions in the readers, because in reality, nothing was visible above the ground except for the unspectacular entrance into the subterranean galleries.[181]

---

177 Hamilton 1776, 34–35, 55, 57–60, pl. XLI (Temple of Isis, with stratigraphy of ash layers at right side).
178 Cf. Chevallier/Chevallier 1984, 72–90; De Seta 1992, 164–168; Lamers 1995; Denon 2009. On the word "picturesque," see E. Williamson in Denon 2009, 17–49; cf. De Jong 2010.
179 Saint-Non 1782. The work guaranteed a vast diffusion of various works of painting and statuary like the satyrs from the Villa of Cicero (II, 18–19, pl. 68: Lamers 1995, 33–36; cfr. Knight 1995, 214), "vendor of amorini" and a woman on a marine monster drawn by Charles Monnet (Lamers 1995, 309, no. 321–322 = II 11–12, pl. 30). Other artists are Pierre-Adrien Pâris (Lamers 1995, 312–323 no. 328–353), Jean-Augustin Renard (Lamers 1995, 335–339 no. 377–386) and Louis-Jean Desprez (Lamers 1995, 201–204: temple of Isis and Villa of Diomedes).
180 Hamilton 1777 formed the principal source (Saint-Non 1782, II).
181 Saint-Non 1782, XIII–XIV: "La jolie Composition que l'on voit à la tête de ce Chapitre, & qui est destinée à représenter les fouilles d'Herculanum, est absolument d'invention. [...] Voulant donc donner ici une idée des fouilles qui ont été faites à Herculanum dans l'intérieur des terres, le Peintre [Robert] a été contraint de laisser prendre un peu l'essor à son imagination. Ce en qoi il s'est seulement conformé à la vérité, est d'avoir représenté sur les devants de sa Composition une partie des différentes Curiosités que l'on a retiré de cette ancienne & malheureuse Ville, soit en Vases, soit en Peintures antiques: on en distinguera facilement parmi ces dernières, deux des plus connues & des plus considérables, dont l'une est le Centaure Chiron qui enseigne au jeune Achille à jouer la Lyre, & l'autre une Composition allégorique à la naissance de Telephe, fils d'Hercule, qui fut nourri & allaité par une Biche." On Saint-Non's influence on ideas about ancient paintings, see E. Chevallier in Franchi dell'Orto 1993, 57–72.

Almost all the publications briefly presented here focus on objects and paintings, the things brought to the museum at Portici. Hamilton and Saint-Non were the first to illustrate the houses and other edifices and also changed the approach among travelers, who began to concentrate more on the urban landscape. This early lack of interest contrasted greatly with the study of the temples of Paestum, which resulted in lavishly illustrated publications from the first years after discovery. The monumentality of these temples and, still more importantly, the liberty to study them in their remote position without any royal proviso considerably stimulated research.[182]

The Years 1800–1860

In 1799 King Ferdinand and the court fled to Palermo, the second capital of the kingdom, because of local revolts and the fact that French troops guided by general Championnet occupied Naples. The revolutionary dream of a republic, the Repubblica Partenopea, lead by local intellectuals, turned out to be a failure and Ferdinand returned. He fled again in 1806 to Palermo, taking with him many crates of artifacts and papyri. The French occupation from 1806 to 1815 onwards had rewarding consequences for the excavations at Pompeii after a time of lesser activities[183] Napoleon's substitute, the general Joaquin (or locally: Gioacchino) Murat, successor of Joseph Bonaparte in 1808 as King of Naples, and his wife Caroline, one of Napoleon's sisters, showed a great interest in the ancient city.[184] Caroline paid many visits to the site and personally influenced the work being done.[185]

---

[182] See Raspi Serra 19986 and 1990; De Jong 2010, 129–133.

[183] In 1799, Master Pasquale Scognamiglio and Francesco La Vega wrote a comprehensive report for the first seven months, followed by some notes on the remainder of that year. Apparently work was interrupted several times (*PAH* I, 72–74). The reports for 1800–1805 are extremely brief or completely missing (there is nothing for 1802, 1804 and 1805); reports for subsequent years are again longer and more detailed. There is a report by Arditi to minister Miot about the works to be carried out (*PAH* I, 177–187).

[184] See S. Adamo Muscettola in Guzzo 2001, 29–49; S. De Caro in *Vesuvio* 1998, 225–240; Jacobelli 2008, 145–149; Mafrici 2010, 111–132. Joseph visited the spot around March 2, 1806, when they had started work in the House of Sallustius (*PAH* I, 77).

[185] Cf. *PAH* I, 4 (15/5/1808): King; 73 (18/11/1811): Queen; 24 (3/10/1809): Queen; 54 (5/4/1811) and 57 (4/5/1811): Queen with cousin of Tsar of Russia; 95 (30/9/1811): Queen, arrived without previous notice, to see tombs of Umbricius Scaurus and Ampliatus, but she is shown an atrium prepared in July; 98 (21/11/1811) and 99 (29/11): Queen, accompanied by the Count of Clarac; 107 (17/3/1813): Queen with Clarac and Canova; 110 (8/5/1813): Queen; 111, 114 (21/5/1813): Queen;

A positive element for the local people was the continuity of the personnel working in the excavations, because they were not replaced by French employees. Ferdinand appointed Felice Nicolas as a director of the excavations and museum collections in 1805. Nicolas remained in charge under the French rule, whereas Francesco La Vega's brother Pietro was responsible for the excavations themselves. Nicolas would be succeeded by Michele Arditi in 1807, who remained responsible until his death in 1838.[186] Arditi had been a member of the *Accademia Ercolanese* from 1787 onwards, and was one of the last real antiquarians in the style of Mazzocchi.

The number of workers increased with totals as high as 600 people reported. The method of excavating changed, too. Workers first explored the top layers of volcanic material and unearthed the uppermost parts or contours of the buildings. They could then decide which buildings to excavate entirely.[187] Another major innovation was better documentation, which resulted in clearer plans of the excavation area. The city walls were explored on the uppermost layer and the area of the forum and its surrounding buildings was cleared, the first coherent plot of public buildings in the city, and connected with the Herculanean gate by the also unearthed "Via Consolare." From now on, people really walked through the streets of an ancient town (cf. pp. 318–319, fig. 14). The French architect François Mazois was in charge of publishing the architecture of the town, while Aubin-Louis Millin and the German painter Friedrich Catel simultaneously produced a splendid publication about some tombs outside Herculanean Gate, which marked the start of scientific publications. Millin's book was dedicated to the Queen.[188]

The excavation policy did not change under the French and the practice of cutting out paintings and mosaics was maintained throughout the nineteenth

---

24/6/1813: Queen with Clarac; 123 (18/8/1813): Queen at House of Sallustius; 139 (14/12/1813): King and Queen, find of silver vase; 150 (15/5/1814): Queen gives a coin to one of her guests. Clarac 1813 gives the account of an excavation carried out in the presence of the Queen outside the Herculanean Gate.

186 Bonucci 1830. His frontispiece shows a portrait of Arditi depicted on a shield that is carried by a flying Victoria on a painting from Pompeii (S. Reinach, *Répertoire des Peintures*, Paris 1922, 146 no. 1 on the right; Helbig 1868, no 908; *Museo Borbonico* VIII 54). Cf. García y Gacía 1998, 127 (with fig. and bibliography). See the anonymous article in *Dizionario biografico degli Italiani* 4 (1962) 38–39; S. Adamo Muscettola in Guzzo 2001, 29–34; De Haan 2014a.

187 *PAH* I, 66 (21 September 1811): "Con tale sterramento si vanno scoprendo le parti superiori degli edifizj, fra le quali si osservano più colonne che formano un peristilio. Si prosiegue la ricerca del muro della città, e nello stesso tempo si va formando la strada che lo deve seguire."

188 See Millin 1813: tombs of Umbricius Scaurus, with the lost stucco reliefs of gladiators (p. 7–70, pls. II–III), of Calventius Quietus (p. 70–84, pls. IV–V) and of Naevoleia Tyche (p. 85–97, pl. VI–VII). Also in Clarac 1813. On Millin, see D'Achille et al. 2011 on his contacts with Naples.

and even greater part of the twentieth century. Material belonging to upper floors was rarely recognized as such. Repairs of the ruins themselves were carried out on a very limited scale.

The road from the Herculanean Gate to the center of town became fully free (p. 154, fig. 5) and the discovery of the forum with its public and sacred buildings further boosted Pompeii's popularity. One of the major finds was the Temple of Jupiter, where a skeleton was found in a subterranean room under the high podium. At first thought to be the municipal prison, it would soon become a locus of drama in novels. The temple in a courtyard at the Westside of the forum became the "Temple of Venus" and got its correct name, Temple of Apollo, when in 1860 a Venus temple was found near Porta Marina. Other prestigious monuments were the macellum, a market place called Pantheon, the Temple for the Fortuna of Augustus, a public latrine and the public measuring table.

The main private dwelling unearthed during the French occupation was the House of Sallustius, outstanding for its lavish display of luxury. The excavators found a garden with a series of separate rooms, which they interpreted as a "motel" for love affairs, called *venereum* after an adjective of the goddess of love.[189] One of the garden walls showed a huge representation of Actaeon and Artemis, and another, a painted garden and a marble fountain in the shape of a sphinx.

Under Ferdinand, who was reinstalled in 1815, the employees who had worked under the Murat regime continued, including Arditi and Antonio Bonucci.[190] The latter would have a successor in Carlo Bonucci, who was in charge of various ranks as architect and director of Pompeii between 1828 and 1849.[191] The possibilities granted to foreigners to carry out research in Pompeii also continued. The Russian A. Brulloff published a monograph on the then recently discovered public baths near the forum.

The King made an important decision regarding the museum. The Palazzo degli studi, "the Studi" for short, the former seat of the university, became the

---

[189] Mazois 1824, II, 75–79, pls XXXV–XXXIX: esp. p. 76–77: "un appartement secret, consacré au plaisir et à l'amour; sa distribution et les peintures qui le décorent ne permettent pas de douter que ce fut un venereum privé." For an insertion of this topic into his novel, see Mazois 1819, 1820, 1822. On the origin of the term "venereum", see C. Parslow in Mattusch 2013, 58–59 (inscription from the *Praedia* of Julia Felix, *CIL* IV 1136).

[190] A. Venditti collected the very few things known on Bonucci in his brief portrait in *Dizionario biografico degli Italiani* 12 (1971) 452–453.

[191] Carlo is often seen as a cousin or grandson of Antonio. Contra: A. Venditti in *Dizionario biografico degli Italiani* 12 (1971) 455–456; García y García 1998, 216–217; S. Adamo Muscettola in Guzzo 2001, 35; Blix 2009, 70–71, 72.

Real Museo Borbonico. Next to the paintings and the sculptures from the Farnese collection, inherited by Charles as the last – remote – member of that illustrious family, the antiquities of Vesuvius were to be installed.[192] This transport was carried out in phases between 1816 and 1822. The contemporary arrangement of the objects according to material categories like paintings, bronzes, glass objects, still reflects the way these items had been on display at Portici. The excavation context played no role, even when the location of a painting's discovery was known.[193]

New discoveries of private houses in the post-Napoleonic period included the House of Pansa, which occupied an entire block, and was named after a painted name on the façade. It included a brothel and a shop with a painting of a peacock, which represented good luck. The House of the Tragic Poet was small, but luxuriously furnished, and named after a mosaic with an old man dressing actors for a stage play. The mosaic of a watch dog with the inscription *Cave canem* near the front door recalled Trimalchio's painted dog in the first-century Latin novel *Satyrica* by Petronius. During the 1830s, director Pietro Bianchi concentrated on the area of the Via della Fortuna.[194] In 1832, he oversaw the lucky find of the House of the Faun, named after the bronze statuette of a dancing satyr. An extremely rich set of floor mosaics was explored, the most famous of which depicts a battle between Alexander the Great and Darius. Its precise interpretation provoked a hot debate in which Goethe, shortly before his death in 1832, made an interesting suggestion on the basis of a drawing sent to Weimar by Zahn.[195] The mosaic was protected by a glass roof, and reproductions were produced in Naples. Details appeared on vases and

---

192 See De Franciscis 1963, 11–56; Sampaolo 2013. For the Farnese collection, see Gasparri 2007. An engraving in the *Voyage pittoresque* of Saint-Non (1782, plate next to p. 54; cf. Lamers 1995, 196–198 no 169) showing the transport of these objects is fancy: it refers to the first plans to bring together the various collections, made in the late 1770s by the Marquese della Sambucca. The original is a drawing by Louis-Jean Desprez in Stockholm (Denon 2009, 63). On the artist, see Denon 2009, 68–72.
193 Alfonso De Franciscis only reached the ultimate goal of incorporating the excavation context in the 1970s with the three rooms dedicated to the Villa of the Papyri and in 1989 Stefano De Caro coordinated the recomposition of the finds from the Temple of Isis. But as a whole, the museum still displays the order invented in the eighteenth century and based on taxonomy.
194 A. Venditti highlights his architectural work, namely the piazza in front of the Royal Palace at Naples, in *Dizionario biografico degli Italiani* 10 (1968) 166–168. See also Ossanna Cavadini 1995.
195 See Chapter II, pp. 155. In his *Corricolo*, Dumas (1842; 2001, Chapter 26) gives a hilarious description of a learned discussion.

fabric.[196] This and other figural pieces were lifted and brought to the museum in Naples in 1843.[197]

In the nineteenth century Pompeii became a crucial scholarly stop. The digs transmitted real life from the past directly to the present, and invited visitors to Pompeii and readers of publications concerning it to reflect on the destiny of this ancient town and of their own cities. Studies about urbanization in an urbanizing society like that of the nineteenth century often referred to Pompeii.[198] Its value clearly surpassed that of the old curiosity shop it had been in the previous century. According to the American historian Virginia Zimmerman, Danish ancient historian Barthold Niebuhr's work was instrumental, for he stressed that reenacting the past could essentially fill the gap between that past and the present. Pompeii could play a paramount role in this process, as we will see throughout many works discussed in this book.[199]

This was less the case for Herculaneum, although the authorities started new excavations there. They hoped to explore the town by daylight, removing many meters of volcanic material, and satisfying the demands travelers had already expressed in the eighteenth century. Between 1828 and 1835 the House of Argus, the House of the Skeleton – for a long time the only place where remains of a victim of the A.D. 79 eruption were found – and the House of Aristides came to light (p. 398, fig. 17). The finds were evidently not sufficient compensation for the

---

196 Viardot 1842, 262: "[...] aujourd'hui bien abritée sous un toit et des vitrages que supportent les débris de l'antique maison romaine, et protégée ainsi contre les entreprises des voyageurs non moins que contre les injuries du ciel. Elle est devenue à Naples un véritable objet de mode. On la grave, on la lithographie, on la reproduit, en proportions réduites, sur des plaques de porcelaine, sur des vases de terre cuite faits en imitation des vases étrusques; on la brode sur des canevas, on l'imprime sur des étoffes." García y García 1998, no. 13.934.
197 Unfortunately nothing is known about the date and process of lifting and transport to Naples, let alone about the restoration and installation in the museum. Undoubtedly, the Alexander mosaic was cut into small manageable pieces, but the restoration must have been so radical that no traces of such a treatment can be seen. The enormous mosaic was originally at ground level, but later was moved to the mosaic room on the first floor, together with the other mosaics from the House of the Faun.
198 E.g. Clarac 1813, 1: "Les ruines si curieuses et si instructives se multiplient pour nous relever des secrets ou des énigmes que la lecture seule des auteurs anciens ne pouvoit nous expliquer." Cf. Taine 1910 (here Chapter II, pp. 133–134). In a novel by Michael Georg Conrad (1888, II, 19–25, quotation p. 23) on building speculation in Munich in the late nineteenth century, Pompeii is seen as an ideal dwelling place: "Hier traf sich eine geistreiche, elegante Bürgerschaft ihres Daseins und das künstlerisch schöpferische Talent wurde seines Lebens und Schaffens froh. Eine Welt der Schönheit und der Freude nicht grösser, als eine Münchener Vorstadt."
199 Cf. Zimmerman 2008, 109–111.

difficult task, and the work stopped in 1835.²⁰⁰ Giacomo Leopardi was very critical of the slow progress of the work, as he wrote in his *Paralipomeni della Batracomiomachia*. This epic – a sort of continuation of the pseudo-Homeric *Batrachomyomachia* ("War between frogs and mice") from the Hellenistic era – describes the residence of the mice under the earth, called Topaia. It features palaces, statues and columns like every big city, but it does not need light.²⁰¹ Topaia, therefore, is like the hidden treasures at Herculaneum²⁰² and might be the tunnel from Naples to Pozzuoli or even, I want to suggest, the one described in Sannazaro's Arcadia (see Chapter III, pp. 170–171).²⁰³ Behind this metaphor hides Leopardi's

---

200 See Pace 2000, 109–117 and Camardo 2013, 307, fig. 1, who gives the years 1825–1860. These works are rarely referred to in travel books. E.g. Nicolai 1835, I, 268–269: "Mit unaussprechlichem Gefühl traten wir in die ausgegrabene, freiliegende Straße. Allein diese Rührung sollte nicht erhebende Begeisterung werden; die Enttäuschung griff abermals mit scharfen Krallen in unsere Brust. Wer mit den Klassikern in der Hand erzogen worden, wer die Alten aus ihren Büchern und ihren Thaten liebgewonnen, der macht sich ein glänzendes Bild von ihrer Größe. Wer aber außerdem die Trümmer des Koliseums gesehen, der wähnt, eine aufgegrabene Stadt des Alterthums müsse überall den Stempel der Größe an sich tragen, oder doch überall einen vorgerückten Culturzustand seiner Bewohner bekunden! Was sahen wir dagegen? Eine mit Lava gepflasterte, an der Seite mit schmalen Trottoirs versehene Straße, so eng, daß wir nicht begreifen, wie sich hier zwei Wagen ausweichen konnten, und etwa zwanzig einstöckige, dach- und fensterlose Häuser von Backsteinen, deren Wände und Fußböden vollkommen erhalten sind, so klein und unbedeutend, daß man sie eher für Wohnungen der Liliputaner, als für die der Alten halten würde!" McIlwayne 1988, no 2.319; García y García 1998, no. 9864. Richter 2005a, 91–92 correctly sees Nicolai's as a critical, anti-Italian travel book.
201 Not finished upon Leopardi's death, it was published in Paris in 1842 by his friend Ranieri. Leopardi 1987, I, 207–310, canto III, 2, 6–10. Cf. Sogliano 1888, 30 and the following notes, and see Moormann 2001 and 2003c. García y García 1998, no. 7927. On Leopardi in Naples see Damiani 1998; Cacciapuoti 1998; Gigante 2003.
202 Canto III, 2, 11–14. "[11] D'Ercolano così sotto Resina, / Che d'ignobil case e di taverne / Copre la nobilissima ruina, / Al tremolar di pallide lucerne / Scende a veder la gente pellegrina / Le membra afflitte e pur di fama eterne, / Magioni e scene e templi e colonnati / Allo splendor del giorno ancor negati. [12] Certo se un suol germanico o britanno / Queste ruine nostre ricoprisse, / Di faci a visitar l'antico danno / Più non bisogneria ch'uom si servisse, / E d'ogni spesa in onta e d'ogni affanno / Pompei, ch'ad ugual sorte il fato addisse, / All'aspetto del Sol tornata ancora / Tutta, e non pur sì poca parte fora. [13] Vergogna sempiterna e vituperio, / D'Italia non dirò, ma di chi prezza / Disonesto tesor più che il mistero / Dell'aurea antichità porre in chiarezza, / E riscossa di terra allo straniero / Mostrare ancor l'italica grandezza. / Lor sia data dal ciel giusta mercede, / Se pur ciò non indarno al ciel si chiede. [14] E mercè s'abbia non di riso e d'ira, / Di ch'ebbe sempre assai, ma d'altri danni / L'ipocrita canaglia, onde sospira / L'Europa tutta invan tanti e tanti anni / I papiri ove cauta ella delira, / Scacciando ognun, sui mercenari scanni; / Razza a cagion di cui mi dorrebb'anco / Se boia e forche ci venisser manco."
203 Leopardi knew Sannazaro's work very well, as shown in his analyses in *Zibaldone* (Leopardi 1991, III, 1458 s.v. Sannazaro). Bracco 1982, 316–318 suggests that Leopardi may have visited Pompeii by night, which is unlikely, considering his poor health. Cf. Moormann 2001, 16. There

fight against the Neapolitan intelligentsia, and their dreamer's mentality. Leopardi attacked Francesco Maria Avellino, director of the excavations and a central figure in the Neapolitan academic circles, together with his friends as a "hypocrite mob."[204] Leopardi may have been exaggerating, since Avellino and other academics were very active in the study of antiquity.[205] As in *La ginestra*, Leopardi sees people working at Herculaneum moved by private vanity and not by eagerness to expand science.[206] Leopardi portrays strangers going down to the dark remains of Herculaneum under Resina, and seeing monuments hidden from the light of day. He argues that if these ruins were in Germany or Britain, the visitor would not need torches, since they would be visible, like those at Pompeii, and asserts that Italy should unearth these treasures to prove its greatness.

A third, short burst of activities at Herculaneum happened in 1869–1875, when parts of the public baths were found, but the rest of the "Sleeping Beauty" of Herculaneum was to remain undisturbed until 1927 (see Chapter IX). Therefore, we return to Pompeii.

Despite the progress made in the first decades of the nineteenth century, and the increasing number of scientific publications, excavators still lacked much interest for the architectural remains themselves, which were rapidly falling into decay. One such example was the amphitheater, already documented in 1748 and excavated at the beginning of the nineteenth century. The excavators were excited to find the names of the same magistrates who had been responsible for its construction carved in the stone benches, but paintings adorning the walls of the arena fell off after one cold and rainy winter in 1816 and were lost. Fortunately, watercolors and drawings had been made, or else they would have been forgotten

---

is a Dutch tragedy by Wanda Reisel on the death of Leopardi, but it lacks Pompeian recordings (Reisel 1992; production of 1989).
204 P. Treves sketches the portrait of an erudite, but uncreative historian who did not take advantage of his contact with the visiting scholars from abroad, especially Germany (*Dizionario biografico degli Italiani* 4 (1962) 652–655). Cf. Cerasuolo 1987, 61–63; García y García 1998, 140; A. Fraschetti in De Caro/Guzzo 1999, 43–50. But see Carl Ottfried Müller, who could work rather freely, as he writes on 3 January 1840 (Müller 1908, 305): "Zwar soll nichts noch ineditrtes gezeichnet werden; doch auch dies Verbot wird nicht streng genommen. Avellino spricht viel von meinen Meriten; auch erfahre ich, daß ich seit Jahren Mitglied der Herculanischen Academie und also hier so zu sagen literarisch accreditirt bin; das Diplom muß unterwegs wo liegen geblieben sein. Sehr förderlich ist mir auch die Bekanntschaft mit unserm Landsmann Zahn, der hier ganz einheimisch ist, Nachgrabungen macht, Kunsthandel treibt und mit aller Welt in Verbindung steht." The membership of the Academy was renewed in a session assisted by Müller (1908, 308). On Müller, see Calder/Schlesier 1998.
205 Bracco 1982, 307. Idem Gigante 2003, 30–31; see previous notes.
206 See also Rothemann 1996, 74, 77–78 and Gigante 2003, 38–42.

forever.[207] Like those in the amphitheater, paintings and mosaics in houses also suffered from exposure to the weather. Objects and decorations were ripped off, leaving the houses bereft of their souls, and transforming them into empty boxes, and there was little substantive information available for visitors, who were subjected to the whims of local guides. Nevertheless, most visitors did not care that the excavators had haphazardly unearthed one house after another and failed to keep the area tidy, but instead heaped up the debris close by. Thousands of roof tiles encountered by every excavator in the first place had simply been thrown away.

Monographs and Guide Books for the Learned and General Public in the Nineteenth and Early Twentieth Century

François Mazois' four great folios of the 1820s, which were the first to include all aspects of Pompeian architecture, are still a masterpiece of scholarship. For twelve years, Mazois lived amidst the ruins at Pompeii, with their "air de jeunesse qui charme."[208] He only lived to see the first two completed, but all four were eventually edited by François-Charles Gau.[209] The first volume features streets, city walls and tombs, and the second focuses on private houses.[210] One plate shows an excavation, with women and children carrying away baskets of lapilli.[211] The third and fourth volumes both open with obituaries for Mazois by Artaude, which reveal that King Joachin Murat and Queen Caroline encouraged Mazois in the Napoleonic era to carry out thorough research, as did King Ferdinand after his return to power. Volume III is about the portico behind the theater, the theaters themselves and the forum; Volume IV is about temples.[212]

The first Pompeii guidebooks were published in the same period as Mazois' folios. Sir William Gell's *Pompeiana* were particularly influential for the earliest fiction authors. Gell moved definitively to Naples in 1816 due to gout. The architect John Peter Gandy contributed the lavish illustrations to Gell's text of

---

207 *Pompei 1748–1980*, 36, 133; *PPM Disegnatori* 105–111; Hufschmid 2009, 259–262, figs 291–293; appendix 50. These paintings are trustworthily represented in the 2014 film *Pompeii* (here p. 385).
208 Mazois 1824, I, 3.
209 Gau is known from the *Antiquités de la Nubie, ou Monuments inédits des bords du Nil, situées entre la première et la seconde cataracte dessinés et mesurés en 1819*, Paris 1822–1827.
210 Mazois 1824, II, 2; long section on houses on pp. 3–29.
211 Mazois 1824, II, pl. XLI, fig. 1. He mentions 500 workers in the Napoleonic era, yet with "peu de respect pour les monuments" (p. 81).
212 The text of this volume was edited by Barré. An appendix by Quatremère de Quincy presents the mosaic of Alexander.

his seminal first set of *Pompeiana* of 1819.[213] These were made with the help of a lanterna magica. *Pompeiana* had a large readership, and in 1832 Gell published a supplement under the same title. It is curious to see that the 1853 edition of *Pompeiana* I contain the same plates as the first edition. Clearly, this and other publications were often not updated in reprints. The images of later editions still show the people in 1832 dress.[214]

According to various testimonies, Gell was a mild and sweet man, an affectionate companion.[215] He figured as an amiable guide of English tourists who, like Hamilton in the 1770s and 1780s, never refused such a job despite his gout. In Naples, his inseparable friend was Keppel Craven, with whom he had once taken up residence in London in 1803 after a mission to Greece and Asia Minor.[216] Craven would survive Gell for sixteen years and died in 1852.

The architect Thomas Leverton Donaldson is known for his 1827 lavish folio volumes. These presented a trustworthy image to people who did not go to Pompeii.[217] The interest in the town was not defined by works of arts like paintings, but by its density of information about daily life:[218]

> The dreadful catastrophe which involved in one common ruin Herculaneum, Pompeii, and Stabia, lamentable as it is to contemplate in all its horrors and desolation, offers a field for the indulgence of that laudable curiosity which had been so long unsatisfied, that a general despair prevailed of such a gratification as it now enjoys.

---

213 Gell/Gandy 1852, IX. According to this preface, Gandy also wrote the first chapter.

214 As to the plans there is some confusion. Gell/Gandy 1852, XVI has a "Plan of the City, as excavated to April, 1819." Next to p. X, however, there is an updated plan without explanation, whereas plate I next to p. 11 described the situation in 1817, with the "newest" monument being the Temple of Jupiter on the Forum.

215 Clay 1976, 3–4; Harris 2007, 161–163. Sir Walter Scott was fond of him (ibidem, 14–15, here p. 124).

216 Craven is a son of Elisabeth Berkeley, who led an adventurous life. After an unhappy marriage with Craven, she fled to Germany, to escape her tyrannical and cruel husband. Here she first became a mistress, then, after her husband's death, the wife of the Markgrave of Ansbach. After his death, she returned to England, but decided finally to take residence in Naples with her son. See her *Mémoires de la Margrave d'Anspach*, Paris 1826, 294, in which there are some remarks on Hamilton and the paintings of Herculaneum. On Gell's drawing activities in Athens, simultaneously with Elgin's looting of the Acropolis, see D. Williams in Tsingarida/Kurtz 2002, 103–164. Craven published books about southern Italy (Craven 1821 and 1837). Cf. García y García 1998, nos. 3383–3385.

217 Donaldson 1827, 1: "My object was to represent Pompeii at large, and in its detailed parts, in their actual, existing state, after the lapse of so many ages, and as the eye of the traveler will now behold them." The book is for those who have not visited the site (p. 19). García y García 1998, nos. 4629–4630.

218 Donaldson 1827, 2.

The architect William Barnard Clarke produced a richly illustrated, nearly 600 page volume that compiled authors like Mazois, Gell, and Donaldson.[219] It was a book to read at home. He catalogued eighty houses and described extensively those of Meleager, the Tragic Poet, Pansa, Regina Carolina, and Bacchus, as well as the Villa of Diomedes. Italian counterparts, but with fewer or no illustrations, were Bonucci's and Vinci's guides of the 1820s.[220]

Almost all written guides use a structure that seems based on the pioneering works of Mazois and Gell. After a brief history of the discovery and the excavations, the author sketches Pompeii's history, explaining the city's name, geomorphology and the classical sources. The descriptions of the monuments follow functional categories: squares and streets, fortifications, tombs, sacral and thermal buildings, and houses, and differ merely in the length of the general explanations of the various aspects (e.g. the lay-out of the Roman house, the structure of baths).

On the French market, people had to wait for an original contribution until the mid 1850s. Ernest Breton intended to offer a cheap and handy guide, to be used on site or read at home. Although it had a large format, two editions came out within one year. By reading his book, travellers and other readers got a realistic depiction of the ancient life at Pompeii, focusing on private matters.[221]

In the 1850s, ongoing research rendered Gell's 1819 and 1832 books out of date, and with Breton's 1855 book too thick to be practical, the publication of smaller guides became popular. Marc Monnier enjoyed great success with his elegant and vivid 1864 guidebook, translated into many languages and republished in many editions in French.[222] His preface is written as a dialogue between a bookseller in

---

219 Clarke 1847. The 1831–1832 first edition consisted of two volumes in pocket format and was published anonymously, and at p. 1 (introduction) Clarke is introduced, "by whom the materials for this work have been collected, and the drawings made, either from the originals or from the plates in the above works." Cf. García y García 1998, nos. 3055–3060, about this attribution.

220 Bonucci 1827 (first edition 1825; García y García 1998, nos 1871–1874, 1876, 1886–1887, 1891, 1907–1908). Vinci 1827 copied (to put it mildly) numerous data from Bonucci 1827 (García y García 1998, nos 13.953–13.962). A German monograph of that period is Von Agyagfalva 1825.

221 Breton 1855, 2: "Notre but principal est de populariser la connaissance de ces ruines célèbres en présentant, dans un seul volume de format portatif, et d'un prix peu élevé, le résumé des grands travaux qu'elles ont fait naître; de servir de guide au voyageur lorsqu'il parcourra le Forum, le temple d'Isis ou la voie des Tombeaux; de lui permettre d'en emporter avec lui un souvenir fidèle et durable; enfin de donner à celui auquel un tel bonheur est refusé une idée exacte de ce tableau palpitant de la vie publique et privée des Romains. Nous nous adressons principalement aux gens du monde... " Nevertheless, Chapter VIII only "est destiné à servir d'itinéraire pour visiter Pompéi" (p. 4). McIlwayne 1988, no 3.301; García y García 1998, nos. 2096–2099.

222 I use the second edition (Monnier 1865). García y García 1998, nos 9544–9549 lists many editions.

Naples and a tourist, and lays out what a visitor to Pompeii would need for a meaningful tour. First of all, a guidebook should be affordable, slim and accessible,[223] but according to the bookseller, such a book did not exist, so he suggests the traveler write one himself. In the following, Monnier directly addresses the reader, and says that Pompeii was a small town of 30,000 inhabitants whose monuments were not like the Pantheon in Rome or the Maison Carrée in Nîmes. Its streets were narrow and its houses were small, and it looked as if it were the day after the fire.[224] The brothel demonstrated that Pompeii was a small Sodom, punished by Heaven like the biblical town.[225] According to Monnier, Fiorelli's archaeological work was paramount (p. 76, fig. 3; see below, pp. 74–81), for he had rekindled the fire of research started by people like Mazois and Zahn in the 1820s. Monnier's book is full not only of passion, but even of sentimentalism, with its longing for contact with and re-enacting of the past. In his own book, Johannes Overbeck advised visitors to Pompeii to bring Monnier's book with them.[226]

Overbeck, an esteemed professor of archaeology and ancient art, had been asked by his editor to write a handbook like Gell's, which would illustrate Roman life and history based on the excavations at Pompeii. But, as he confessed in his preface, he had no occasion to do research in Italy.[227] The result was a learned work, based on the study of available literature, but full of mistakes. Because it was too thick, Overbeck's book was meant to be studied at home.[228] He would notably improve the later editions (1866, 1875) and wrote a still authoritative fourth edition in collaboration with August Mau. In Overbeck's eyes, the importance of Pompeii was that history displayed itself in the streets and the houses (p. 154, fig. 5).[229] Monuments like the Temple of Isis and the amphitheater serve as

---

223 He gives the following characteristics: D'Aloë 1857 is dry, Mazois 1824–1839 is heavy, Niccolini 1854–1896 is expensive, and Dumas 1842, 2001 is too light.
224 Monnier 1865, 17: "Ne vous attendez à trouver des maisons ou des monuments qui soient debout et couverts, comme le Panthéon à Rome et la Maison carrée à Nîmes. Vous seriez tristement déçus. Figurez-vous plutôt une petite ville à constructions basses, à rues étroites, qui aurait brûlé tout entière dans une nuit."
225 Monnier 1865, 59: "Pompéi fut une petite Sodome châtiée comme l'autre par le feu du ciel."
226 Overbeck 1866, X: "Büchelchen wie das allerliebst geschriebene von Marc Monnier." He criticizes it for sentimentalism concerning the drama in the Villa of Diomedes (p. 34).
227 Overbeck 1866, I, VII. García y García 1989, 878 mistakenly says that Overbeck was at Pompeii for the first time in 1873 with Mau. Overbeck 1873, VI, mentions a visit in that year, to update the previous edition. Mau was instrumental for the fourth edition (see Overbeck/Mau 1884, Preface). For editions and criticisms see García y García 1989, no. 10.021–10.024.
228 Overbeck 1866, I, IX ("Periegese"), in response to his critics.
229 Overbeck 1856 and 1866, I, 4: "derjenige Ort, welcher am Vollkommensten und Klarsten ein Stück der antiken Welt mitten in unsere moderne stellt" And, on p. 5 in both editions: "hier trieb

testimony for the decline of paganism.[230] The baths are proof of the bright side of Pompeian life, and the town's architecture was modest, with technical flaws in the structures erected after the earthquake of 62. Pompeian society stood at the brink of decline, for things were made for practical use and not for the sake of mere art.[231] Overbeck evidently saw Pompeii as a mix of good Greek taste and Roman pragmatism, in a long development that would lead to the inevitable fall of the Roman Empire.[232] His aestheticism clearly matched the German common opinion formed by Winckelmann's aesthetics, in which Greece was the cradle of art, and Rome represented the genius of practical commodities to improve daily life.

The growing demand for slimmer guidebooks did not preclude a new generation of thick handbooks. Similar to Breton's book were two publications by public servant and amateur archaeologist Gustave-Bascle de Lagrèze and the archaeologist Henri Thédenat.[233] To Lagrèze, Pompeii was not an ideal example of an ancient city simply thanks to its architecture, inscriptions, or artifacts (all of which had been studied by more learned authors than him). Instead, he viewed it as a series of material testimonies of ancient daily life matching the written sources, and so yielding a realistic reconstruction of the past.[234] Pompeii was a

---

sich der lebhafte Verkehr eines sorglosen Völkchens durch die Strassen und Gassen, ja hier lag die Gedanke an Untergang und Zerstörung so fern, dass am Tage des Verhängnisses das Amphitheater von Pompeji von einer schaulustigen Menge erfüllt war."

230 As for the Temple of Isis, Overbeck (1856, 28; 1866, I, 31) concluded "dass der neueste, fremdeste und abstruseste Aberglauben des sinkenden Heidenthums der zäheste gewesen sei." The amphitheater provoked the following observation (Overbeck 1856, 135; 1866, II, 161): "Von den Schauplätzen edler musischer Kunst führt uns unser Weg zu dem Schauplatze jener blutigen und grausamen Spiele, vor denen selbst das abgehärtetste moderne Gemüth schaudernd zurückbebt, und in ihrer Ausbildung eine der dunkelsten Nachtseiten des sinkenden Heidenthums zeigen, zum Amphitheater, in welchem die Thierhetzen und die Gladiatorenkämpfe stattfanden."

231 Overbeck 1856, 340; 1866, II, 116: "III. Zweiter oder artistischer Haupttheil." Art made "nicht Unnützes", whereas we live "in unkünstlerischen, in rein praktischen Zeitaltern" (Overbeck 1856, 341; 1866, II, 116–117): "Noch ist die Trennung nicht erfolgt, aber sie ist vorbereitet und hat begonnen, schon hat das rein praktische Handwerk die Kunst aus dem Gebiete der gewönlichen Bedürfnisse des Lebens verdrängt. "

232 Overbeck 1866, I, 6–8.

233 As explained in the subtitle of the work: Étude à l'aide des monuments de la vie païenne à son déclin, de la vie chrétienne à son aurore, de la vie musulmane à son apogée. Lagrèze 1872 (here quoted from the third edition of 1889); 1887. García y García 1998, nos. 7643–7644. I did not see his *Rome et Naples, simples notes* of 1864 (García y García 1998, no. 7642), which gives an approximate date of his visit to the excavations.

234 Lagrèze 1889, 2: "Je ne me suis pas servi de l'archéologie comme architecte ou comme érudit pour mesurer un édifice et fixer son style, pour déchiffrer une inscription et déterminer son âge. Ce travail avait été déjà mieux fait que je n'aurais su le faire; mais jamais l'archéologie n'avait eu pour moi plus de charme et d'utilité. Je l'ai consultée comme le meilleur commentaire des do-

gay town of no less than 40,000 inhabitants, Lagrèze writes, whose streets bristled with life. The city was dedicated to Venus and the Pompeians, "these noble lusts of intelligence" ("les nobles voluptés de l'intelligence!"), watched masterpieces by Aeschylus and Plautus in the theaters, and to satisfy their emotions liked to view cruel scenes in the amphitheater.[235] Despite his stressing of moral decline, Lagrèze did not judge Pompeii a sinful city rightly punished by Destiny, and ends with his assertion that Pompeii did not fall by the hand of God, but that Roman civilization was self-destructive.[236]

The French archaeologist Henri Thédenat attempted to give a complete panorama of the history of the excavations and art of Pompeii.[237] The illustrations are both modern photos and old engravings. Regarding the history, the French and Fiorelli get a place of pride. Fiorelli's plaster casts of the victims are trustworthy portraits of the city's inhabitants a visitor cannot contemplate being overcome with emotion, (p. 314, fig. 13).[238]

---

cuments écrits; je l'ai prise pour guide dans la recherche des usages d'autrefois, et elle m'a aidé dans mon travail de reconstruction du passé."

235 Lagrèze 1889, 5: "Les rues, animées jadis par une population de quarante mille âmes, sont aujourd'hui muettes et tristes comme le silence des ruines; mais le même soleil splendide les éclaire, et les souvenirs peuplent la solitude. [...] Pompéi, dédiée à Vénus, était une ville de plaisir. [...] Comme ils appréciaient, ces Pompéiens, les nobles voluptés de l'intelligence! et comme ils applaudissaient Eschyle, Plaute, et tous les chefs-d'œuvre de la Grèce et de Rome! Mais aussi comme les émotions violentes convenaient à ce peuple voluptueux et cruel, qui mettait son bonheur à assister au spectacle des agonies humaines, et qui sourd aux prières du gladiateur vaincu, le condamnait sans pitié pour le voir mourir avec grâce!" Lagrèze includes many "romantic" stories about a town that is for him the emblem of Roman gaiety, luxury and license (e.g. Lagrèze 1892, 120–127 on dinner parties, 182 on paintings, 204 on love, 215 "Ville de Vénus").

236 Lagrèze 1889, 526 "Nous n'avons pas besoin de dire que si la religion du Christ a assisté à la décadence et à la ruine de la grandeur romaine, elle est restée étrangère aux causes qui ont entraîné cette épouvantable catastrophe, qu'il n'a pas dépendu d'elle d'arrêter. Rome, en s'imposant au monde entier par la violence, en employant la corruption comme moyen de gouverner, en donnant à son empire des proportions illimitées, a conspiré contre elle-même et travaillé à la destruction de sa puissance."

237 Thédenat 1906, here quoted from the third edition of 1928. García y García 1998, nos. 13.533 (various editions).

238 Thédenat 1928, 37: "Fiorelli, après avoir enlevé les ossements, fit couler, dans ces moules, du plâtre liquide; il obtint ainsi ces fidèles portraits de Pompéiens que l'on ne peut, sans émotion, contempler au petit Musée de Pompéi, si instructif. Ce ne sont pas de vaines images plus ou moins fidèles, mais l'empreinte prise sur les Pompéiens eux-mêmes, au moment où, il y a près de deux mille ans, ils venaient de rendre le dernier soupir." There also is Jules Monod's book that forms part of a long series of "Guides Monod" (Monod n.y.) of the same time. García y García 1998, no. 9552 (various editions). This is no guide, but a general account of all aspects of Pompeii as a source for knowledge of ancient culture.

Mau made major contributions to a better understanding and chronology of the wall paintings. He would have been happy about the growing number of books documenting wall paintings, many of which were rapidly decaying, often unprotected by roofs. Large folio plate volumes by the Niccolini brothers and smaller editions by Presuhn and D'Amelio, which contained color illustrations of lost murals, still have value today.[239] Felice Niccolini followed an administrative career and was briefly Director of the Archaeological Museum in 1882, whereas his brother Fausto worked as an architect, among other things, redesigning this museum.[240] Fausto's son Antonio, who would be instrumental in the debate about the restoration of the House of the Vettii, continued the project after the death of his father and uncle.

There was also a growing interest in the inscriptions as a primary source of historical relevance.[241] Pompeii was, and is, a rich treasure for texts written on the walls, discovered *in situ*, that could illustrate in an immediate way the lifestyle of its inhabitants, which was largely lacking in the classical sources. These inscriptions were met with the interest of a large number of visitors, who had been trained in Latin during their school days. As a matter of fact, epigraphy greatly helped the process of bringing the dead town and, consequently, ancient society, to life. Scientific editions by Theodor Mommsen, Karl Zangemeister and others in the *Corpus Inscriptionum Latinarum* series were among the first great results of new research, which was mainly carried out by German scholars. Scribbles on walls would also feed the imagination of many fiction authors, especially in the creation of living citizens as protagonists of their books.

In the following section, two scientific problems will be highlighted as examples of the archaeological debate in the nineteenth century, that is Pompeii's chronology and its purported Greek character.

---

239 Niccolini 1854–1896 and 1997 (facsimile of a number of plates, with a good introduction by Stefano De Caro); Presuhn 1877 and 1882; D'Amelio 1888 (who found his own plates more accurate than Niccolini's).

240 Their father Antonio, architect, had worked for the Real Museo Borbonico and designed the stage of Pacini's *L'ultimo giorno di Pompei* (see Chapter VIII, pp. 362–364).

241 That was less so in previous times, when travelers merely copied inscriptions they saw during their excursions. Several travel books, therefore, look like collections of texts written on stone, like that of Caspar Goethe (see Chapter II, pp. 145–147).

The Sense of Time in Early Studies on Pompeii

It is debatable whether students of Pompeii's antiquities during the first century after its discovery paid attention to the chronological development of the living city until 79.[242] The archaeologist Kurt Wallat believes that they did and that Pompeii's advantage was that it possessed numerous data that helped researchers arrive at sound dating proposals.[243] Wallat's statement begs verification: did publications during the first hundred years of Pompeii's excavation even enter into the discussion of time and history of the archaeological remains, or did they merely rely on literary sources which lacked a sense of time? Since "scholars" of that time were mostly interested in traditional antiquarianism (they preferred the study of objects without bothering with the find context), they did not critically use sources and their publications were purely descriptive. Pompeii was an ideal object for antiquarian descriptions, presenting itself to both tourists and scholars in that era as the exemplary antique town, showing all aspects of Greek and/or Roman society, of undetermined antiquity simultaneously. Renato Fucini's impression epitomizes the emotions of visitors and studiosi in those years:[244]

> Pompeii is the town that was able to die better than all her beautiful sisters of Magna Graecia, because violent death by asphyxia is the only death that befits her beauty. Concerning the colossal ruins of Agrigento and Syracuse, their skeletons corroded by time, the archaeologist cannot study osteology, while the cadaver of Pompeii has all her limbs intact; her blood stands still but has not lost the rosy color apparent under the smooth skin. The spirit has left and the body has not been corrupted.

---

242 See Moormann 2005.
243 K. Wallat, *Gnomon* 74 (2002) 714: "Seit dem Beginn der Ausgrabungen in Pompeji im späten 18. Jh. und schon während der systematischen Freilegung im 19. Jh. waren Wissenschaftler bestrebt, die jeweiligen Befunde in einen chronologischen Kontext einzubinden. Pompeji bot und bietet bis heute eine große Anzahl an Kriterien, die für Datierungen überaus hilfreich sind."
244 Fucini 1997, 93: "Pompei è la città che ha saputo morir meglio di tutte le altre sue bellissime sorelle della Magna Grecia, poiché la morte violenta per asfissia è l'unica morte che si addice alla bellezza. Sui giganteschi ruderi di Agrigento e di Siracusa, sui loro scheletri corrosi dal tempo, l'archeologo non può studiare che osteologia, mentre il cadavere di Pompei ha tutte le sue membra intatte; il suo sangue è fermo, ma non ha perduto il roseo colore che trasparisce sotto la pelle gentile. L'anima è partita ed il corpo non si è corrotto." This page forms part of Chapter III on Amalfi, Sorrento and Pompeii; the first edition was published in Florence in 1878, one year after the trip (cf. García y García 1998, no. 5565–5567 for various editions). Fucini was known as a poet under the anagram-pseudonym of Neri Tanfucio. His Naples book was praised by Benedetto Croce for its realistic and severe judgment of the poverty-struck capital of southern Italy.

When going through early publications to look for glimpses of chronological insight, it becomes clear that they generally deliver a Pompeii which, despite its myth and its history, has no historical stratigraphy in the archaeological remains. Enlightenment-era studies about the origins and early days of Pompeii were purely based on the interpretation of scarce mentions in ancient written sources. Hercules had founded Herculaneum, and Pompeii probably had the same origins.[245] Cochin and Bellicard argued that the year of Herculaneum's foundation was 1238 B.C., as calculated from the chronology in the *Antiquitates Romanae* of Dionysius of Halicarnassus.[246] If this were correct, Herculaneum would have been one of the oldest cities in Italy. Oscans lived there before Greeks arrived in Cumae, although the exact date of this influx of new inhabitants was not yet known, and to date, still isn't today. Although ancient texts refer to considerably later moments in Pompeian history, chronological hallmarks like the Second Punic War, the Social War of 91 B.C., Sulla's installation of the *Colonia Veneria Pompeiana*, the A.D. 59 riot in the amphitheater, and the earthquake of 62 were not seen as indicators of urban, architectural or artistic changes in the town. Consequently, the inhabitants, from Oscans to Romans, always lived in the same types of houses, worshipped the identical gods, and strolled the same streets that visitors have strolled in modern times.

As for the old Oscan inhabitants, bizarre etymology enticed odd theories. Henri Sass noted "obscenities" in the excavations and in the collections at Portici and explained them in a peculiar way by connecting the term "obscene" with the Oscans, the first inhabitants of Herculaneum:[247]

> From the indecent tendency of their [viz. the Oscans'] manners, the word obscoenum (quasi oscenum) is supposed to be derived.

---

245 As a result of this desire to discover Pompeii's roots, there was – and is – a lot of speculation about its name, associated with such Greek words as *pompe* (procession or track of cattle, especially that of Hercules), *pente* (five), a local term meaning "port," to name a few. To this day, this problem remains unsolved. For more on the term *pompe*, interpreted as the cattle of Geryoneus with which Heracles was wandering through Italy, see Isidorus from Sevilla, *Etymologiae* 15.1.51: "*Ab Hercule in Campania Pompeia, qui victor ex Hispaniam pompam duxerat*" ("Pompeii in Campania is named for Hercules who, as a victor, had led cattle from Spain"). Pompeii's Greek name is Pompeïa (Dionysius of Halicarnassus 1.44.1), Pompaia (Strabo 5.4.8.13) or – like the Latin form – Pompeïoi (Dio Cassius 64.23.3).
246 Cochin/Bellicard 1757, XVI, after Dionysius of Halicarnassus 1.44.1 (also quoted in García y García 1998, 37).
247 Sass 1818, 195. McIlwayne 1988, no 2.240; García y García 1998, no. 11.949.

In the 1850s Alphonse D'Augerot published a fictitious correspondence between "Valmer" and "Fanny D." written at Pompeii in "Septembre 185*." The correspondents suggest that Pompeii's name stems either from Syrian or Oscan *pum* (mouth of a burning furnace) or from the Greek *pompeion* (interpreted as warehouse).[248] In the letter, Pompeii was an Oscan city with old walls from that period, pure and simple. It would become rich, which was not entirely beneficial, since together with opulence, corruption penetrated the town's walls and affected the inhabitants.[249]

These claims stand next to those about the Doric Temple on the Foro Triangolare, which was seen as the oldest part of town. It was a happy coincidence that its discovery in 1767 and subsequent excavation ran contemporaneously with the first explorations of the Doric temples of Paestum in the 1750s. Winckelmann dated these sanctuaries to the archaic period, and all subsequent scholars followed his lead.[250]

Friedrich Leopold Graf zu Stolberg, when he wrote about the remains of Pompeii as testimonies to ancient Greek art, was fully inspired both by Winckelmann's view of classical antiquity and by Romantic fascination for landscape. Roughly worked, he writes, the column drums were noble and strong, not corrupted by weakness, and really Doric in spirit. It was the same spirit one found in the poems of Pindar and Theocritus, in the records of the ancients, and the Doric music.[251]

Bonucci ranked the Doric temple under the Etruscan monuments,[252] whereas Donaldson compared the temple to those at Paestum and attributed it to Hercules himself. Donaldson believed that the Foro Triangolare should be called the

---

248 D'Augerot 1877, 19: "Pum, Peah, bouche d'un fourneau ardent." McIlwayne 1988, no 2.471; García y García 1998, no. 3642.
249 D'Augerot 1877, 22: "Mais avec l'opulence, la corruption a pénétré dans son enceinte." This idea might have been inspired by Livy's Preface 8–12 to Book 1 of his *Ab urbe condita*, in which *luxuria* is seen as a decaying force (I owe this suggestion to Nathalie de Haan).
250 Winckelmann 1762 and 2001. First illustration in Hamilton 1777, 162, pl. VII. See the rich collection of recordings in De Waele 2001, 13–42.
251 Stolberg 1822, 69: "Von weit höherem Alterthum als alle andre Gebäude, die aus Pompeji's Schutt bisher aufgehüllet worden, sind Trümmer eines Tempels, dessen große dorische Säulenknäufe von früher Zeit altgriechischer Kunst zeugen, da sie in halb roher Einfalt noch nicht ausgebildet, aber voll Adels und Stärke war, und im wahren dorischen Geiste jede Zier als Tändelei verschmähte. Eben dieser Geist athmet aus dem dorischen Dialekt des Pindars und des Theokritos; er athmete, nach den Zeugnissen der Alten, aus der dorischen Musik." This fragment stems from Letter 71, March 1, 1792, p. 62–80.
252 Bonucci 1827, 178.

Forum Nundinarium or vegetable market.²⁵³ In Gell's work the Doric Temple got a very brief description, apparently being a less attractive monument than the adjacent theater area, which was amply illustrated. Gell believed that too little was preserved to make an adequate drawing and simply claimed that it was a "Greek temple."²⁵⁴ Breton stressed the antiquity of the temple, arguing that the Foro Triangolare had probably not been open to everybody, and had been closed under Sulla, and repeated Mazois' claim that it had originally formed the town's acropolis.²⁵⁵ Breton explained its bad state of conservation by the result of continuous spoliation after 79, when parts of the monument were still jutting out above the lapilli.²⁵⁶

An interesting early observation on chronology can be found in a letter of Björnståhl. He suggested that all Pompeian wall paintings dated from after the earthquake of 62 when the city was fully restored. The inscription in the Temple of Isis, which mentions the restoration financed by Popidius Celsinus, formed his proof.²⁵⁷ Mazois suggested that the paintings at Pompeii followed Roman trends initiated under Augustus and therefore, without saying it explicitly, the French scholar attributed all of them to the imperial period.²⁵⁸

Mazois focused on various aspects that could help date specific buildings. In general, he considered Pompeii's architecture as Greek. Some influences from other nations, albeit "très légères," were also noticeable.²⁵⁹ Houses were simple and only grew in size and luxury at the end of the Republic, when Roman influences increased.²⁶⁰ In the volume on public buildings Mazois argues that cisterns might be an older system for the collection of water than the pipes one saw above the ground. This new theory would be generally accepted, as was the following. The forum showed restorations from after the earthquake and its layout had odd-

---

253 Donaldson 1827, I, 41–42. This idea was taken from Mazois.
254 Gell/Gandy 1852, 178–179, 190–191, plate LXVII; quoted in De Waele 2001, 22.
255 Mazois 1829, 18, with a reference to Cicero, *Pro Sulla* 22. As to its location, Gell 1832, II, 203: Mazois' thesis about the acropolis on this spot (Mazois 1829, 18) cannot be accepted.
256 Breton 1855, 38, 39, 129. D'Augerot 1877, 94 sees the temple's ruinous state as an indication of its antiquity.
257 Björnståhl 1777, 258–259 (in Letter 17, dated July 30, 1771, pp. 246–264 on Herculaneum): "von neuem in Stand gesetzt." Björnståhl 1777, 259: "Also sieht man, von welcher Zeit man die Malereyen zu Pompeji rechnen kann."
258 Mazois 1824, II, 62.
259 Mazois 1824, I, 21.
260 Mazois 1824, II, 7, 63 (Etruscan influence). The presentation of the Forum Baths leads Mazois (1829, 68) to a comparison with the simple baths of Scipio, described by Seneca: the baths of Pompeii, therefore, must be of the last years of Pompeii and offer an example of the degeneration of Roman society.

ities due to the succession of phases. The "Temple of Venus" (actually that of Apollo) would be older than the forum, as well as some streets that lead to the forum. Moreover, the capitals of this temple and the Temple of Jupiter were Greek. Mazois also noted that the theater quarter must have been the oldest part of town; here he had the Foro Triangolare and the Doric temple in mind again.[261]

Gell has little on chronology. In early times there had been Oscans, followed by Etruscans and Campanians. From the Sulla revolts onwards, the city was Roman. The state of the buildings explicitly mentioned was the result of restorations from after the 62 earthquake. Gell's descriptions of the monuments themselves are illustrated with indiscriminate text sources from different periods: Plautus, Livy, Vitruvius, Virgil and the satirists of the first century A.D., to record a few only, served to instruct readers about names and functions of parts of temples, houses and public buildings. The uncritical use of various genres of texts, works from the Republican to late Imperial periods, and phrases quoted out of context remained common and would continue until very recently. Learned novels like Mazois' *Le palais de Scaurus* and Böttiger's *Sabina* are the "best" examples of this custom (see Chapter III, pp. 190–192).

With a few exceptions, like the city wall of Pompeii, there is no timeline running through Gell's description. He makes remarks about the Greek architectural orders, which are all present in various Forum buildings. Pompeii, unfortunately, is not a good example of their use and development: the custom of covering columns and capitals with stucco layers obscures the pure forms.[262] A sense of chronology comes to the fore in the description of the two triumphal arches that flank the Temple of Jupiter. In his explanation of the beautiful plan of the Forum area, Gell states that the arch at the west side might be younger as it was composed of brick and rubble. The other one is called the "Old Triumph Arch."[263]

---

[261] Mazois 1829, 17, 34, 35.
[262] Gell/Gandy 1852, 145. This objection returns in the travel book of Gell's friend Lady Blessington (1839, 277; Clay 1979, 62): "For example, in the Temple of Venus, several Grecian entablatures, in tolerable taste, have been barbarously plastered over and painted, transforming them from a pure Grecian to a bad Roman style."
[263] Gell/Gandy 1852, 150 no. 2 and 158 no. 33, explanations to the map on plate XLIV. Gell remarks at no. 2 that his idea that this arch had a pendant at the other side now has to be rejected, viewing the results of later excavations, but his first supposition should be maintained (see V. Kockel in Müller 2011, 21, fig. 8). This correction in the second and third editions is not taken into account in the description of the gate and the reconstruction of the Forum at p. 167, pl. LI. As to the "Old Arch," Gell 1832, I, 81 and II, 78 connects this arch with Tiberius or Caligula. De Maria 1988, 253 nos. 36–37 has the "old" theory about a couple of arches, dated to A.D. 18 De Maria 1988, 254–255 discusses the other arch, attributed to Germanicus' sons Nero and Drusus, dated to 23 A.D. or a little later. For new proposals, see Müller 2011, 82–92, who also publishes drawings by Gell (p. 26–27, fig. 16).

In the second series of *Pompeiana*, Gell discusses the Temple of Fortuna Augusta. The excavators found inscriptions mentioning a Marcus Tullius, son of Marcus, as builder of this marble temple on private land. This temple for the imperial cult of the Fortuna Augusta was erected at the beginning of the first century A.D. in honor of the emperor Augustus. The fact that Gell merely called the shrine "Temple of Fortuna" implies that he did not understand the importance of the adjective *augusta* as a reference to the emperor. Gell shared the general opinion which suggested that this Tullius might have been the great orator Cicero himself, or his son.[264]

Mazois also neglects the information given by *augusta*.[265] In his view, the lack of a *cognomen* (surname) would be an indication for the attribution of the temple to the father or grandfather of Cicero. Like other authors, he was spellbound by the idea that Rome's most famous orator was tangible via his relatives.[266] Nevertheless, while discussing the relief in which a priest makes an offering at the altar in the Temple of the Genius Augusti at the east side of the Forum, Mazois criticized those who want to see a portrait of Cicero in that priest: nonsense, we must not try to find Cicero everywhere![267]

Breton agreed with Gell on the Fortuna temple[268] and did not include many observations concerning chronology. He stated that the buildings of Pompeii were constructed in a Greek style, albeit with some Roman flair. Breton reinforced Mazois' argument that the paintings were all the product of one group of painters directed by one single master.[269] He mentioned some cases of damage caused by the 62 earthquake, including the Temple of Apollo (in his time still thought to be of Venus), which showed signs of that disaster, whereas the absence of the Temple of Jupiter's columns was the result of a restoration project. The same was true for the Forum. The restoration of the columns in the portico behind the grand theatre gets no precise date.[270] A vague time period is given for the theater: in Rome, the first permanent theater was that of Pompey, and other theaters were

---

264 Gell 1832, I, 69, 74–75. See i.a. Castrén 1975, 76; Franklin 2001, 27–29.
265 Mazois 1838, 35 (text Gau on the basis of Mazois' work). In contrast, an inscription mentioning an *augustalis*, found elsewhere is correctly interpreted as naming a priest of the emperor's cult (Mazois 1829, 61).
266 That fascination for Cicero as living in Pompeii can be found in fiction and poetry, e.g. Bianco 1833, third "colloquio;" Dix 1848, 33–38; Vecchi 1864, Chapter III. Cf. here Chapter III, pp. 171, 192–193.
267 Mazois 1838, 35 (text by Gau on the basis of Mazois' work).
268 Breton 1855, 63.
269 Breton 1855, 27: "Quant à leur décoration, c'est avec raison que Mazois dit qu'elle est d'un goût tellement uniforme, qu'on serait tenté de croire au premier moment que toute la ville fut ornée par les mêmes artistes et sous la direction d'un seul homme." See Mazois 1824, I, 21.
270 Breton 1855, 48, 52 (temples), 136 (portico).

constructed consequently, like that of Pompeii.²⁷¹ Another proposal concerns the Basilica, whose Ionic capitals, Breton claimed, dated it to the first century B.C.

The City Walls of Pompeii

Even on the earliest maps, the walls' circuit was recognized in the landscape, but they were easier to study after the French excavation in the early nineteenth century, which was followed by a complete unveiling in the 1850s. Letters of the Oscan alphabet carved into the walls served as proof of their antiquity and got various labels: Oscan, Etruscan, and old Greek. According to Mariana Starke they were Hebrew characters.²⁷²

Mazois argued that as a necessary protection of a city's inhabitants, the walls were the oldest parts of any town. The earliest settlers would have needed adequate shelter and went to great lengths to ensure the safety of their growing city.²⁷³ Mazois claimed that although the ramparts of Pompeii were not built using the "Cyclopic" technique (with large worked blocks put together in dry masonry) known from city walls in central Italy, and were therefore not extremely old, they were most likely archaic, because the dry masonry consisted of trapezium-shaped blocks with oblique sides, and Oscan or Greek characters were carved into their surfaces, proving the Oscan or Greek origin of the town.²⁷⁴ Mazois observed repairs made during the Social Wars, recognizable by their careless technique.

Gell admired the masonry technique and the stucco decoration of the wall's façades:²⁷⁵

> The walls of Pompeii are, perhaps, the only part of the city at all calculated to resist that rapid decay, which seems to hasten the disappearance of every other remain within their circuit.

In his *Pompeiana* from 1819, Gell believed that Oscan marks on the masonry blocks and the Oscan inscription in the Nolan Gate were signs of lower class

---

271 Breton 1855, 172.
272 Starke 1802, II, 105.
273 Mazois 1824, I, 33: "Les plus anciens monuments d'une ville sont ordinairement ses murailles; car le premier besoin des hommes qui s'y rassemblèrent dans l'origine, étant d'y trouver la sécurité, ils durent réunir leurs efforts pour élever autour d'eux quelque enceinte capable de défendre leur cité naissante."
274 Mazois 1824, I, 34–35, plate XII.
275 Gell/Gandy 1852, 87: opening sentence of the chapter on the city walls.

people, probably to be understood as the workmen's tokens.[276] In this way the strange spelling of the gate's inscription could be explained as the consequence of the corruption of language, like the corruption of pure Italian clearly observed in the Neapolitan dialect.[277] Gell compared Pompeii's walls to the Etruscan walls at Volterra, and the shape of the Nolan Gate to that of the Lion Gate at Mycenae. These comparisons, however, did not lead him even to venture a tentative date for the walls. The reader remains a little puzzled as to the meaning of the quoted sentence about decay: did Gell mean that the city walls could survive contemporary elements of decay – a development he observed in the excavations given the lack of protective measures – or was he alluding to their durability in antiquity?[278] In his book of 1832, however, Gell concluded: "[The walls] are of a very remote time, if we may judge from the appearance of the masonry." The construction technique represented another argument for an early date.[279] He had probably read Mazois' notes on this topic, when he wrote this new opinion.

Bonucci also believed that the walls were very old, mentioning the presence of "Etruscan letters" and observing that the walls were repaired after the siege of Sulla.[280] According to Breton, the city walls are the oldest parts of the town; the reader gets references to Mycenae and Praeneste and other fortified sites. The walls were Oscan and the shape of the inscriptions was identical to those of the Wall of Servius Tullius in Rome. Therefore, the Pompeian fortifications are dated to the middle of the sixth century. In Breton's view, the walls between the towers near Mercury Street and the Vesuvian Gate were newer (maybe constructed in 91 B.C., the Social War), as deduced from the technique. He observes their disuse after the entrance of Sulla's troops and their clumsy repair during the Civil War of Pompey.[281] In the third edition of his work (1870), Breton compared the presence of column drums in the ramparts of Pompeii to those in the northern walls of the Acropolis of Athens, which he had described in his 1862 book about Athens.[282]

---

276 Gell/Gandy 1852, 87: "Oscan is supposed to have been the language of the lower orders." Same opinion: Clarac 1813, 3; Bonucci 1827, 82.
277 Gell/Gandy 1852, 92 note 1; 92–93 note 3 (corruption). Gell gives the text on p. 92 and an illustration can be found on p. 98 (vignette). Mazois 1824, I, 52–53 expressed great doubts as to the relationship between the Nolan Gate and its inscription, according to him placed there by a work man.
278 Gell/Gandy 1852, 18.
279 Gell 1832, II, 162–163, quotation at p. 163. Ibid., 163–164 and 203, Gell also includes remarks about the Nolan Gate and adds the beautiful plate LXXXV showing its inside. On the basis of the Oscan inscription with the dedication to Isis, he prefers to call it the Gate of Isis.
280 Bonucci 1827, 79–82.
281 Breton 1855, 9.
282 Breton 1862.

Why Disregard Time?

The reason not to reflect upon the antiquity of the city itself stems from the dominating impression most visitors maintained after their tour: the idea of a city not quite dead, or one awaiting new inhabitants, pervaded a lot of travel accounts and memoirs (see Chapter II). The German Romantic poet August von Kotzebue waited for a drink in one of ancient Pompeii's bars, in which ring stains from cups were still visible, and whose bartender seemed to have left momentarily to do some shopping (p. 160, fig. 6). Finally, he exclaimed to a friend that, if no bartender showed up, they would just go to another bar.[283] Louise Demont first expected to encounter the proprietor of a house, when she walked around in its rooms but concluded that the town was dead:[284]

> While you are wandering through the abandoned rooms, you may, without any great effort of imagination, expect to meet some of the former inhabitants, or perhaps the master of the house himself, and almost feel like intruders, dreading the appearance of anyone in the family. In the streets you are afraid of turning a corner, lest you should jostle a passerby; and on entering a house the smallest sound startles, as if the proprietor were coming out of the back apartments. The traveller may long indulge the illusion, for not a voice is heard, not even the sound of a foot to disturb the loneliness of the place, or interrupt his reflections. All around is silence, not the silence of solitude and repose, but of death and devastation, the silence of a great city without one single inhabitant!

For Breton, the fact that modern man had entered a city described by Pliny and Tacitus was more satisfying than it was eerie. Educated with the texts of ancient writers, including Cicero, another "inhabitant" of Pompeii, he considered it irrelevant to research Pompeii's history, for – as Breton says at the end of his book – every visitor simply wants to meditate upon the things they have just seen in the company of the contemporaries of Pliny and Titus.[285]

---

[283] Von Kotzebue 1805, I, 363: "Wir möchten den Hausherrn bei Namen rufen, er scheint nur, um eines kleinen Geschäftes willen, sich auf kurze Zeit entfernt zu haben, vielleicht um die Gefäße wieder zu füllen, die in diesen Vertiefungen standen, denn seht, der Marmortisch trägt ja noch die geringelten Spuren der Tassen, welche von Trinkern, die eben weggegangen sind, hier niedergesetzt wurden. Wird niemand erscheinen? wohlan, wir gehen in das nächste Haus."
[284] Demont 1821, 292–293. Her party was at Pompeii in 1814.
[285] Breton 1855, 366, last words of the long last phrase: "... et pourtant, quel est celui d'entre nous qui au retour de Pompéi et d'Herculanum n'éprouverait le besoin de se recueillir et de vivre encore quelque temps dans la solitude et de la méditation avec les contemporains de Pline et de Titus?"

There is one chronological reference based on the basalt of the streets. The geologist John Phillips argued:[286]

> Of all that meets the eye in the interior of Pompeii nothing appears so old in style as the pavement, which, except by occasional mendings, may be readily believed to have been laid by Pelasgian hands at the building of the city. This polygonal pavement – its hard solid block worn by the traffic of a thousand years before the beginning of our era, especially planned for the passage of the bigae, between raised footways with convenient stepping-stones – excites, and deserves to excite, more wonder than all the bright columns, and baths, and grottoes, and flesh-coloured frescoes, of this gay and luxurious city.

These reflections testify to the vivid interest in Pompeii's history, and show that some authors really did contemplate the various historical phases of the town's history as expressed in the archaeological remains. However, no writer ever tried to reconstruct the archaeological development of the town and its architectural and art-historical phases. In a certain way this quest for history is connected with another problem: was Pompeii a Greek town?

Pompeii's Greek Mask

"Pompeii you know was a Greek city."[287] Not only Shelley, but many others fostered the idea of Herculaneum and Pompeii as Greek communities, mixed up with elements from Roman society. The question is why this Greek notion emerged. As we have seen in the previous section, three arguments related to a possible Greekness prevailed in the early years: Hercules as a founder of the city, the Doric temple on the Foro Triangolare, and both the serious and semi-scholarly etymology of the name "Pompeii" as a Greek word.[288] The earliest writers on Pompeii, namely Venuti, Bayardi, and Cochin and Bellicard, simply presented it as Greek

---

286 Phillips 1869, 33.
287 Shelley 1964, 70–76, no. 491, letter from January 23–24, 1819 to Thomas Peacock. This section is a reworked version of Moormann 2003b. Shelley could have gleaned the idea from Forsyth 1813, 305 who associated Pompeii's history with Homer: "There is no impropriety, I hope, in applying Homer's description to Pompeii. The domestic simplicity of Homer's age subsisted in some parts of Greece down to the Persian invasion. During that period this part of Italy was colonized by Greeks. Colonies generally simplify the accommodations of their mother-country, and their long struggle for subsistence debars them from innovations of more polished life. Hence Pompeii may have retained the modes which it derived from Greece, after Greece itself had relinquished them. Pompeii had been a Greek city, before the Romans came, and bears more marks of it, rather than from its mistress."
288 See here note 245. On the notion of Pompeii as a Greek city, see also De Haan 2014a.

and argued that, in the early days of the city's existence, Oscans and Greeks lived there together.[289] Thanks to his influential *Geschichte der Kunst des Alterthums* from 1764 and his two pamphlets about Herculaneum, discussed above, Winckelmann was the most influential author to underline the Greek character of the Vesuvian cities.[290] In general, he firmly believed that the Greeks had brought civilization to the Mediterranean and that modern societies should continue to develop its best elements. His opinion that all things Greek were vastly superior to other cultures, including the Romans, would become a standard belief among scholars and amateurs of Greek art and literature during the following century. In Campania, Winckelmann argued, Greek influences could still be seen in the artifacts, rather than in magnificent buildings and statues. His student Volkmann fervidly advocated the idea of Greekness in his highly influential travel guide, stating that everything in these towns was Greek, notwithstanding the fact that Latin was the language spoken there.[291] Simultaneously, the admiration for the beauty of specific objects found in the excavations was another excuse to see Herculaneum and Pompeii as bearers of Greek culture.

Winckelmann's claim that the Greeks were "superior" would also influence romantic authors. In this vein Jean Paul sketched the region's romantic spell in *Titan*. Campania was permeated by an epic Greek combination of horror and bliss, nature and people, eternity and minutia. Local people danced amidst columns, ruins, rocks made by Vesuvius, and in vineyards on top of dead Herculaneum.[292] Shelley similarly claimed that it was the atmosphere that made Pompeii Greek:[293]

> Every now & then we heard the subterranean thunder of Vesuvius; its distant deep peals seemed to shake the very air & light of day which interpenetrated our frames with the sullen & tremendous sound. This scene was what the Greeks beheld. (Pompeii you know was a Greek city.) They lived in harmony with nature, & the interstices of their incomparable columns were portals as it were to admit the spirit of beauty, which animates this glori-

---

289 Venuti 1748, 35; Bayardi 1752; Cochin/Bellicard 1757, XVIII–XXIV.
290 Especially in his *Sendschreiben* and *Nachrichten* (Winckelmann 1997a–b). Cf. Leppmann 1966, 77–97; De Franciscis 1975; Allroggen-Bedel 1990.
291 Volkmann 1771, 1777–1778.
292 Jean Paul 1961, 645, "114. Zykel" in "29. Jobelperiode": "Immer dieselbe große, durch dieß erhabene Land ziehende epische griechische Verschmelzung des Ungeheuern mit dem Heitern, der Natur mit den Menschen, der Ewigkeit mit der Minute. – Landhäuser und eine lachende Ebene gegenüber der ewigen Todesfackel – zwischen alten heiligen Tempelsäulen geht ein lustiger Tanz, der gemeine Mönch und der Fischer – die Gluth-Blöcke des Bergs thürmen sich als Schutzwehr und Weingärten, und unter dem lebendigen Portici wohnt das hole todte Herkulanum – im Meer sind Lavaklippen gewachsen, und in die Blumen schwarze Sturmbocken geworfen." Cf. Jean Paul 1933, 280–281.
293 Brett-Smith 1909, 167; Shelley 1964, 73–74, 75.

ous universe to visit those whom it inspired. If such is Pompeii, what was Athens? what scene was exhibited from its Acropolis? (...) O, but for that series of wretched wars which terminated in the Roman conquest of the world, but for the Christian religion which put a finishing stroke to the ancient system; but for those changes which conducted Athens to its ruin, to what an eminence might not humanity have arrived!

Overbeck defined the House of the Tragic Poet as an expression of the purest Greek spirit, with a display of Greek education and taste.[294]

Another Greek feature – at least as experienced by the travelers – was erotic art. Diderot's *Encyclopédie* typified the Vesuvius cities as places dedicated to Venus, the most venerated goddess in the Greek world. After a discussion of bronze phalli found there, Jaucourt remarked that Campania, Capua, and Baiae were regarded as hot spots or areas of debauchery, which was proved by these objects. The most obscene objects were not displayed in the Palace of Portici.[295] Jaucourt's and similar texts formed the basis of the lustful image of Pompeii and Herculaneum that became popular throughout Europe. As late as 1907, Édouard Schuré wrote that Pompeii was "a Greek hetaera who played the cither, sang like the Muses, and danced like the three Graces. She knew lust, literature, and art."[296] In his own words, he repeated the notion of the city of Venus from the *Encyclopédie*. The turn from debauchery to Greek (sexual) freedom was easily made.

Greekness could also exert negative influences. Henry Swinburne, who was critical about the artistic level of the Herculanean paintings, saw them as a severe defect of a Greek town:[297]

> It is remarkable that in the representations of porticoes and temples, the style is as barbarous as that of the Gothic ages; the columns are slender to excess, the entablatures heavy and crowded with fantastic ornaments, which I was surprised and shocked to find in a city where the Greek taste in arts ought to have been more religiously adhered to. I saw no landscape in which the artist has discovered any thorough knowledge of perspective.

---

[294] Overbeck 1856, 206; 1866, I, 263 (here quoted): "(...) jedenfalls treten uns in diesem wenig ausgedehnten Domicil die meisten Spuren reingriechischen Geistes uns entgegen und bezeugen, dass der Besitzer ein Mann von Bildung und Geschmack und beiher auch von Wohlhabenheit gewesen ist."
[295] C. [= Chevalier de Jaucourt], *Encyclopédie* Supplément 3 (1777) 349–358 s.v. Herculanum, esp. 352: "Au reste, les villes de la Campanie, Capoue & Baies, étoient regardées, plus que tout autre endroit en Italie, comme des lieux de volupté et de licence, Vénus étoit spécialement honorée à Herculanum; & l'on trouve les attributs de ce culte obscène sur beaucoup de lampes de bronze, où l'imagination s'est épuisée dans les formes les plus bizarres; mais on ne les a point exposées dans le cabinet de Portici."
[296] Schuré 1907, 5:"une hétaïre grecque, qui joue de la cithare, qui chante comme les Muses et danse comme les Grâces. Elle sait les voluptés, les lettres et les arts."
[297] Swinburne 1783, II, 102; 1790, III, 151.

Dr. Thomas Arnold, the famous "headmaster of Rugby," argued that corruption had affected Pompeii:[298]

> ... it is a place utterly unpoetical. An Osco-Roman town, with some touches of Greek corruption – a town of the eighth century of Rome, marked by no single noble recollection, nor having – like the polygonal walls of Cicolano – the marks of a remote antiquity and a pure state of society. There is only the same sort of interest with which one would see the ruins of Sodom and Gomorrah, but indeed there is less. One is not authorized to ascribe so solemn a character to the destruction of Pompeii; it is not a peculiar monument of God's judgements, it is the mummy of a man of no worth or dignity – solemn, no doubt, as everything is which brings life and death into such close connexion, but with no proper and peculiar solemnity, like places, rich in their own proper interest, or sharing in the general interest of a remote antiquity, or an uncorrupted state of society.

Giuseppe Fiorelli's Revolution in Research and Administration

The revolutionary events around 1860 brought the end of the Bourbon monarchy. Garibaldi – whose own interest in Pompeii is unclear[299] – gave the honorary directorship of the museum, without any real authority or responsibilities, to the French writer Alexandre Dumas, who had accompanied Garibaldi's unification expedition in Sicily and wrote propaganda pamphlets in support of Garibaldi's mission in France. Dumas dreamed of divulging knowledge about ancient Pompeii among all social classes.[300] His appointment offended the Neapolitans who remembered Dumas' unflattering sketches of Naples in *Le corricolo* of 1842.[301] Moreover, Garibaldi decided that the Museo Borbonico would become a national

---

298 Stanley 1904, 743–744.
299 Schwegman 2008, 10; Esposito 2008; Avvisati 2010; De Haan 2014a. Garibaldi visited Pompeii on October 22, 1860, while he was briefly in Naples (Esposito 2008, 70; Avvisati 2010, 11–20, fig. 9, 14–15; Jacobelli 2011, 36–39, fig. 48).
300 Ridley 1983; L. García y García in Jacobelli 2008, 73–83; Schwegman 2008; Esposito 2008, 73–74; Avvisati 2010, 49–55; Jacobelli 2011, 39–54. The poet had hoped to get a real position, but in fact Spinelli and his colleague Giulio Minervini remained in function. Dyer 1868, 50 suggested that Dumas "lived at Naples in princely magnificence; but he was totally unfit for the office assigned to him, and is said to have visited Pompeii only once." Similar doubts in Schwegman 2008, 11. This would contradict Dumas' vivid descriptions in *Le corricolo* of some decades before (Dumas 2001), when he was severely limited in his movements and had to escape like a spy (see J.-N. Schifano in Dumas 2001, 8–10). A strange fact is that Louise Colet does not mention Dumas or his excursions to Pompeii in her recordings of her encounters with Garibaldi in 1860 (Colet 1861).
301 Esposito 2008, 74 note 9 quotes a letter of Felice Niccolini to Garibaldi, in which this book is seen as a "ritratto ne lusinghiero ne benigno degl'Italiani di Napoli."

museum, and that the closed cabinet of "obscene" objects should be opened for everyone. This must have been a blow to Domenico Spinelli, the principe di San Giorgio, who in 1852, in his function as museum director, had removed works of arts like Titian's Danae from the rooms accessible to the general public.[302]

Among the local archaeologists involved with this political change, the most outstanding personality was Giuseppe Fiorelli. He had acquired a good name for himself as early as the 1840s in numismatics and starting working at Pompeii in 1847. He had made rather caustic comments about the reigning directors Avellino and Bonucci and the disorganization of both museum and excavations. He ran into even more trouble given his involvement in the political debate on the future of the kingdom and the unification of Italy, for which he was jailed in 1849. Shortly before 1860 he became the personal secretary of the Bourbon Prince Leopold, the brother of King Ferdinand II, who held more progressive opinions on Italian unity than his brother. In prison, Fiorelli started compiling a huge collection of archival materials on the excavations, which would result in his *Pompeianarum antiquitatum historia*. Clearly, Fiorelli must have been a man of enormous energy and efficiency, and gifted with the talent of making contacts with Italian and foreign scholars.[303]

Fiorelli's stardom rose steadily in and outside Naples. He was appointed Chief Inspector of the excavations and Professor of Archaeology in 1860, and in 1863, after Spinelli's death, he became Director of the museum and Superintendent. This combination of roles remained the responsibility of one person at a time until the 1970s, when a restructuration of the administration of archaeological monuments led to a new organizational model. Fiorelli's career signifies the turning point between more than a hundred years of treasure hunting and scholarly archaeological study of the buried cities. Among his main concerns were the improvement of the scientific approach to excavating, and, consequently, new directions in research. He was the first active excavator who considered Pompeii as a source of its own. Pompeii's remains, he believed, should be explored with special attention to the urban workings of the city itself.[304]

He was also instrumental in improving both the tourist's experience and the security at the archaeological sites. At Herculaneum, for example, he made visit-

---

302 This suggestion is mine, based on the documents collected in Esposito 2008, 71–73. Cf. Avvisati 2010, 52–53 (Spinelli), 57–63 (closed rooms).
303 There is a great bulk of literature about Fiorelli: Genovese 1992; S. De Caro in Fiorelli 1994, 5–51 (with bibliography); G. Kannes in *Dizionario biografico degli Italiani* 48 (1997) 137–142; Barbanera 1998, passim; De Caro/Guzzo 1999; U. Pappalardo in Fiorelli 1875 (re-edition 2001), 9–18; Schwegman 2008; Jacobelli 2011, 55–70.
304 Blix 2009, 72–73 interprets this new focus as a result of an increasing general interest in towns and city life. In Chapter II, pp. 133–134, I discuss Taine's observations on this topic.

Fouilles récentes faites à Pompéi sous la direction de M. l'inspecteur Fiorelli, en 1860.

Fig. 3: Marc Monnier, *Pompéi et les Pompéiens* (second edition, 1867, abridged and adapted for young people), plate opposite p. 16: "Fouilles récentes à Pompéi sous la direction de M. l'inspecteur Fiorelli, en 1860," recent excavations in Pompeii under the direction of inspector Fiorelli. A tourist (in foreground, with top hat) is guided through the area between the atrium and peristyle of the House of the Small Bull, named after the bronze statuette of a bull, which is visible on the marble table in the center of the atrium. The guide is pointing at another ancient object, which excavators "happen to find" amidst the debris at the very moment of the tour.

ing the famous theater possible by constructing a spacious brand new entrance. At Pompeii, the excavation resembled a piece of Emmenthal cheese rather than an urban site (pp. 318–319, fig. 14). He ordered workmen first to remove the large piles of lapilli and excavation debris from the ancient city's streets before starting new digs to unearth the areas between the formerly excavated complexes (fig. 3). In his Pompeii guidebook of 1875, he explained that the town had to be excavated systematically on the basis of the layout of streets and house blocks. Finally, the recognition of the victims, "preserved" as cavities in the volcanic fill, added a significant element of knowledge, populating the city, as it where, with its former inhabitants.[305] Fiorelli

---

[305] Fiorelli 1875, 22: "A me parve di dover tenere un modo diverso nella scoperta della città. Essendone l'area, rinchiusa dal muro di cinta, spartita in nove segmenti da due cardini e due

also built a site museum, next to the Porta Marina,[306] where he exposed the gypsum casts and other new finds (p. 314, fig. 13).

All these works took some ten years and rarely yielded important new discoveries, at least in the eyes of the old-fashioned treasure hunters and tourists who wanted merely to be impressed by shiny new objects. The criticism of Fiorelli's "dull" work was easily warded off by his clearly written explanations of the new methodology. After a certain while, therefore, he was met with esteem as the general public's mentality changed radically, even in the most common tourist books, and it became an honor to shake the hand of Fiorelli himself.

Thanks to his revolutionary excavation process, the excavators became aware that the city was subdivided into house blocks, surrounded by streets. These blocks, called *insulae*, received numbers, as did every entrance to a building from the street, which corresponded with the Italian practice of those days. Clusters of house blocks together formed urban districts, called *regiones*. Today, every building at Pompeii has an address composed of three numbers, according to this system introduced by Fiorelli.[307]

The excavation practice simultaneously improved by employing a technically superior stratigraphic method, probably first utilized in the House of Siricus in 1852.[308] The horizontal layers of lapilli were more carefully removed, and finds

---

decumani, che s'incrociano mettendo capo alle porte, opiniai che giovasse scavare successivamente ognuno di questi segmenti, e completarne lo sgombro, prima di passare oltre alla ricerca di località adiacenti, solo così potendosi ottenere la continuità degli edifizi scoperti, ed evitare lo accumulamento di terreni interposti.

Laonde mi diedi a distruggere i monticelli di pomici e ceneri, che trovansi disseminati nell'ambito degli scavi anteriori, ed a completare la scoperta di taluni edifizi in parte rimasti inesplorati, perchè creduti poco fruttuosi in oggetti di qualche importanza. Nel quale ingrato lavoro di dodici anni, se non rinvenni moltissimi preziosi monumenti, ebbi però a constatare più volte il modo diverso con cui i Pompeiani perirono: altri trovandone schiacciati nelle case, dalla caduta dei soffitti o delle mura; altri sopraffitti nelle vie da esalazioni mefitiche, che togliendo loro il respiro, ne fecero venir meno la vita, per cui distesi in terra sembrano trapassati in placido sonno; altri finalmente affogati nei lapilli, che penetrando da pertutto con le acque, e ricolmando ogni vuoto, avevano impedita la fuga a chi pure avrebbe potuto altrimenti salvarsi."

306 Fiorelli 1875, 121; Longobardi 2002, 45, figs. 30–32, 49–50; Stefani 2010; Dwyer 2010, 69, 82–94.
307 So, the House of Sallustius has the "administrative address" VI 2, 4, viz. regio 6, insula 4, house door 2. The idea was already proposed in a five-pages leaflet (Fiorelli 1858). Cf. Fiorelli 1875, 23–25: The successive numbers are "a fin di mantenere la serietà scientifica, e di evitare gli errori invalsi per un sistema fallace di nomenclature, che toccò il suo apogeo con la romantica consacrazione della casa di Diomede." There had been some attempts at a systematization by Bonucci and Spinelli, and alterations and criticism would follow: Borriello 2008.
308 I. Bragantini, *PPM* VI (1996) 229. Cf. Castiglione Morelli 2008, 526 on similar work described in old periodicals. On Fiorelli's innovations, Barbanera 1989, 32.

were registered in their context. For the first time, the roofs could be studied and reconstructed. An important discovery was that atrium roofs had a square opening in the middle (compluvium) and were inclined inwards; so rain water could pour into a basin (impluvium) that was installed in the floor. The illustrations in most books from before the 1870s depict flat and entirely closed roofs.

Fiorelli correctly recognized cavities encountered from the very start of the excavations as vacuums caused by the gradual putrefaction of organic material like wood and flesh. Among these negative "voids" human skeletal remains sometimes came to light. Skeletal remains had been found even during the early excavations, but their imprints in the surrounding lapilli had seldom been recorded.[309] By filling these hollow spaces with fluid plaster – a technique used for the first time in February 1863 in the House of the Skeletons – a new attraction was born. The plaster dried and was cleared of lapilli, and from the resulting cast, the shapes of wooden objects, trees, animals and people became tangible. These casts aroused sentimental feelings in the hearts of visitors, who were now able to stand shoulder to shoulder with the victims of the eruption (p. 314, fig. 13). The Neapolitan writer Luigi Settembrini even stated that Fiorelli had "discovered human pain."[310]

Fiorelli also brought about other major changes. The personal permit needed to get access to the excavations disappeared in the early 1860s. Visitors were required to pay an entrance fee and respect official opening hours. Despite the fact that visitors now needed to pay, this change was democratizing: persons of every nationality, age, and gender could enter the site, as long as they obeyed the regulations formulated by law. Visitors hired guides or guards to visit the monuments, and many of the old, unqualified ciceroni were licensed. It was forbidden to tip the guides, who suddenly saw a sharp decrease in their income, and Fiorelli soon had to increase their wages from one and one and a half to two lire, and from two to two and a half lire.[311] Unfortunately, the new guides were not tested

---

309 See Chapter III, pp. 180–185 on the famous skeletal remains in the Villa of Diomedes that inspired various authors of fiction.
310 Dwyer 2010, 56 (long quote). Dwyer 2010, 72: Fiorelli remarked that these people were "stolen from death," which returns in Dwyer's book title. Cf. Stefani 2010.
311 Fiorelli 1873, 173: "A costoro venne assegnato lira una e cent. cinquanta per giorno, estensibile a due; e poichè i custodi ottenevano dai curiosi retribuzioni più o meno volontarie a titolo di mance, per la cura che prendevano di essi nella visita ai monumenti, e con la istituzione della tassa d'ingresso veniva loro vietata qualsiasi regalia, fu mestieri dare a tutti un supplemento di paga, proporzionato al servigio renduto da ciascuno, anche in vista dei larghi guadagni perduti, e dello aggravio di fatica per la guardia notturna, e per la nettezza di Pompei, che prima pagavasi separatamente ad operai, destinati a svellere le erbe in tutto l'anno." Cf. Staats Evers 1872, 105–106, quoted in Chapter V, pp. 299–300. On this tip i.a. Howells 1988, 58. In guide books this news was included immediately, e.g. in Murray 1873 and 1883, 209–210: guides "are forbidden to

to check what they really knew, and remained largely ignorant about the monuments themselves. The number of guards grew from 16 in 1861 to 41 in 1872, and night visits to Pompeii were no longer permitted under the new rule.

In 1866, Fiorelli founded a small archaeological school for Italian students from the whole country who would become the future leaders of the new archaeological regime.[312] This school functioned until the beginning of the twentieth century in the appropriately-named Vicolo dei Soprastanti in Pompeii, and some important archaeologists conducted their first studies there. The accent on the "whole" of Italy stemmed from an idealism that the treasures belonged to the new, unified Italy, and that people from the entire country could study here and work at Pompeii. Even so, many successive directors and staff members originated from the former Bourbon kingdom. Fiorelli simultaneously encouraged the work of foreign students, especially Germans like Wolfgang Helbig, Heinrich Nissen, Theodor Mommsen, and August Mau.[313] The classicist Theodor Gomperz stayed for the first time in Naples in 1871 to study the papyri, and wrote to his wife about his work and his curious "encounter" with erotic paintings at Pompeii.[314] Shortly

---

accept any gratuity, but if the visitor wishes to mark his sense of any extra attention he may do so by purchasing some of the photographic views of the ruins which they are permitted to sell." De Séranon 1877, 61, pegs the number of visitors to Pompeii at 40,000 in 1869, and to Herculaneum at 2,000. The excavations were free on Sundays and many local people in traditional attire could be seen (De Séranon 1877, 68–69). Lagrèze 1892, 52: fee is 2 francs, Sunday free entrance.

312 See Barbanera 1998, 21–34; M.L. Sagù in De Caro/Guzzo 1999, 173–194. One of the first longer descriptions of Fiorelli's activities is Breton 1870, 271–273. Breton mentions two students, Eduardo Brizio from Turin and Salvatore Dino from Naples. Brizio is spokesman of his schoolmate Sacchetti in his charming 1876 Pompeii sketch (Sacchetti 1979, 45 note 4).

313 During his first visit to Pompeii, Mommsen wrote to Hensen about how interesting and moving it was to see the Roman domestic atmosphere after some thousand years: "Es ist doch höchst interessant, ergreifend möchte ich sagen, die häusliche Heimlichkeit nach ein paar tausend Jahr wieder ans Licht gekommen zu sehen." The excavations went on rather well, according to the young scholar; he met here the poet Friedrich Hebbel. See Wickert 1964, 142. On Helbig and Naples, see Voci 2007.

314 Kahn 1974, 62–63 on the 1871 visit. Kahn 1974, 206 (letter of April 3, 1889): "Am meisten Eindruck machten mich gestern einige neu ausgegrabene Darstellungen stark obscönen Inhalts, die Communion der Geschlechter in allen möglichen und unmöglichen Variationen darstellend und dabei mit einem wahren Zauber der Schönheit übergossen. Das gibt gar viel zu denken. Eine liegende weibliche Figur, die linke Hand hinter dem Haupt, vor der ein Jüngling kniet, aber nicht wie bei einer Liebeserklärung auf dem Theater, sondern ganz anders! u.s.w. u.s.w. Ein ganzes Gemach mit solchen Darstellungen, eine schöner als die Andere, 100 Meilen weit entfernt von der Art, in der unsere schmutzigen Witzblätter Derartiges abbilden möchten, wenn sie dürften – das gehört, wie gesagt, zu dem allermerkwürdigsten, was man sehen kann. Kaum weniger charakteristisch ist ein kleinwinziger Gassenladen, in welchem nur ein gemauertes Bett steht, und draußen auf der Gasse als Aushängeschild ein Phallus! Dies ist nicht für Harry, wohl aber

after, in 1873, the German classicist Ulrich von Wilamowitz-Moellendorf arrived to assist Mommsen, his father-in-law, and to work on his own projects. He met Mau, stayed in the primitive Albergo Sole at Pompeii and got special permission from Fiorelli to work day and night.[315] Heinrich Schliemann, the future excavator of Troy and Mycenae, visited the excavations in 1868. He was interested in aspects such as the ancient residents' daily life, and met Fiorelli, and his young assistants Giulio De Petra (see p. 82), Francesco Salvatore Dino and Eduardo Brizio, but did not study the excavation methods. He would return to Naples and die there on December 26, 1890.[316] His house in Athens, the Iliou Melathron was adorned with Pompeian frescoes.[317]

Fiorelli took the first steps towards a program of restoration and conservation of the ancient city, but it would not be until around 1895, under De Petra's leadership, that the first houses were reconstructed, using original materials found *in situ* as much as possible. The house of two freedmen, the Vettii brothers, and that of the Silver Wedding (named for the silver wedding of King Umberto I and his wife Margherita in 1893) are among the oldest examples of reconstructed Pom-

---

das Folgende. Über einem sehr lebhaft dargestellten Trinkgelage stehen die Worte: Facitis vobis suaviter etc., ein unglaubliches Latein, das wie eine schlechte Übersetzung des deutschen: Ihr thut Euch gütlich klingt und für welches jeder Gymnasiast jetzt beim Ohr genommen würde." Harry is his son Heinrich, a classicist like his father. The inscription is *CIL* IV 3442b, found in V 2, 4, whereas the group of erotic paintings might be those in room f of house IX 5, 14–16, House of the Restaurant, excavated in 1878–1879 (*PPM* IX, 1999, 660–669; Clarke 1998, 178–187). John Clarke added the following remark (email from February 25, 2010): "Too bad Gompertz apparently didn't see the painted phallus with *hanc ego cacavi*. It was found up on the east wall of the vicolo between this house and the Casa del Centenario, but it must have been removed to the Collezione Pornografica by the time of Gompertz's visit. He might have enjoyed puzzling out that inscription, solved only by Housman in Praefanda."

315 Von Wilamowitz-Moellendorf 1928, 161: "Wir waren im Besuche ganz unbehindert, denn durch Mommsen waren wir Fiorelli vorgestellt, zu dessen großzügiger Verwaltung es stimmte, uns bei Tag und Nacht in Pompei jede erdenkliche Freiheit zu gewähren, so daß uns die Wächter beinahe als Vorgesetzte betrachteten. Es stand damals ein Haus für wissenschaftliche Arbeit in der Stadt, auch mit einigen Büchern. Dort liebten wir bei Nacht zu sitzen oder durch die Gassen zu schlendern, wenn der Mondschein auf die Ruinen so belebend wirkte wie auf die Burg von Athen oder wie die Fackelbeleuchtung der Statuen im kapitolinischen Museum. Wenn eins gespenstisch genannt werden durfte, war es nur das Letzte." García y García 1998, nos 14.297–14.303. In Nietzsche 1975–2004, II.7.1 (1998) 602, there is a letter from the classicist Erwin Rohde to his mother about his Pompeii visit with the archaeologist Karl Dilthey. Rohde and Dilthey also stayed in Sole ("Zur Sonne") and loved the place very much.

316 Bloedow 2001.

317 Bloedow 2001. On the house see C. Reinsberg and H.J. Kienast in Reinsberg/Meynersen 2012, 74–88.

peian monuments.[318] Fiorelli also attempted to place statues and pottery in glass cases in the houses, but these displays would not last long, since numerous thefts forced the objects to be moved back to the museum. Apparently, the idea of substituting casts and copies was seldom seriously considered until recently.

After Carlo Bonucci's 1828 "pocket companion," Fiorelli's 1875 guide was the first of a long series of guides to the excavations at Pompeii published by the Superintendents.[319] *La descrizione di Pompei* gives an excellent overview of his fifteen years of work, including the aspects I have briefly laid out here. It is the first of a new type of guide: rational, severe, and systematic. In a way, it is an inventory and not a real guide, systematically describing each building in the topographical order of regiones and insulae. No words are wasted on jokes, anecdotes, or discussions. The lack of systematic chapters – apart from a brief introduction on Pompeii's history – makes the book unattractive for general readers, but it remains a rich sourcebook for students of Pompeii.

Obtaining a high administrative function in the state administration in Rome, Fiorelli designed a bureaucratic system for the administration of archaeological and other kinds of monuments in the whole of Italy. An important means of recording the results of the excavations taking place under the aegis of these new archaeological services was the *Giornali degli scavi di Pompei* (edited between 1869 and 1879), which formed the example for the *Notizie degli scavi di antichità*, a national gazette in which the results of excavations became public. It is no wonder that Fiorelli's name was on the lips of every person interested in Pompeii in the last four decades of the nineteenth century.[320]

Despite all of Fiorelli's revolutionary accomplishments, which were continued by Michele Ruggiero, we lack a clear policy of excavation and conservation. What was the goal for unearthing house after house in Pompeii? How was Pompeii thought to function in the public space, both as an ancient city and as a modern tourist attraction? For Fiorelli, Ruggiero and their successors – De Petra (1893–1900, 1906–1910), Spinazzola (1911–1923), and Maiuri (1924–1961) – the aim apparently remained a complete excavation of Pompeii without ever answering

---

318 See i.a. Longobardi 2002, 52. He mentions Salvatore Cozzi as the chief architect of these restorations. Harris 2007, 183, mistakenly considers Fiorelli as the house's excavator.
319 "Pocket companion," term used by Gell 1832, I, XI. Fiorelli 1875; 2001 (García y García 1998, no 5292).
320 To give one example, Breton (1870, 2, 25) thanks Fiorelli for "la nouvelle organisation" and sees how a new era of prosperity has begun for Pompeii; we see some 500 workers in the excavations during the first months of 1861. "une nouvelle ère de prospérité s'est ouverte pour Pompéi et nous trouvons dans les premiers mois de 1861 jusqu'à 500 ouvriers employés aux fouilles." Cf. Dyer 1868, 50–53. Overbeck dedicated the second edition of his *Pompeji* (1865) to Fiorelli.

these (and other) questions. The increasing call for a slower pace and a more intense scientific program did not find ready acceptance in local Neapolitan circles. It is as if each director wanted to make his own spectacular discovery.[321] Today, scholars agree that it would have been more beneficial for the long term preservation of Pompeii to leave more undisturbed rather than mindlessly excavating countless houses, since the maintenance of the ruins gradually became more complex and expensive, and the chance of unearthing ground breaking objects or buildings smaller. Pompeii and Herculaneum were the "lucky survivors" thanks to their relatively good preservation, a paradox used in comparisons between Rome and the small Vesuvian towns, but even these treasures needed care. Whereas Rome had huge surviving public monuments, Pompeii and Herculaneum demonstrated what ancient life was really like, in the shape of less notable constructions like houses and modest public buildings.

The excellent conservation under the volcanic material even evoked reflections about how "our" culture would be preserved for future generations. Frederic Harrison proposed an underground museum of the nineteenth century, when this era was coming to its end:[322]

> It is the duty of an age to be self-conscious, and to reflect how its acts and its thoughts will appear in the eyes of a distant posterity. It is mere affectation to deny that our doings and our lives will be as interesting to the men of the twenty-ninth century as the doings and the lives of the ninth century are to us…

De Petra stood on the brink of a new century.[323] He had assisted Fiorelli in the Archaeological School and worked as director of the museum in Naples since 1875, while he was also chair of Archaeology at the University of Naples. After Ruggiero's retirement in 1893, De Petra became Director of the Vesuvian excavations. He fostered great concerns about the enormous export of objects which had been found during legally allowed but for him intolerable excavations by private landowners like Vincenzo De Prisco at Boscoreale. Especially the acquisition of Boscoreale's famous silver treasury by Baron Edmond de Rothschild and donated to the Musée du Louvre in Paris frustrated him to the point of sending letters to the Minister of the Interior requesting to change the laws about excavations on private land. Instead of being heard, he was dismissed in 1900, clearly a political scapegoat. He was able to return in 1906 under a new government, and was no longer deemed

---

321 Harris 2007, 225–226 stresses Maiuri's eagerness to discover something great.
322 Harrison 1890, 606. García y García 1998, no. 676.
323 A. Gabucci, in *Dizionario biografico degli Italiani* 39 (1991) 23–25; Barbanera 1998, 59–61; Cerasuolo 2005, 8–21; Dwyer 2010, 118; A. Argento in *Soprintendenti* 2012, 276–285. On the excavations at Boscoreale, see Oettel 1996, 30–38; Jacobelli 2011, 70–77; Barbet/Verbanck-Piérard 2013.

guilty of anti-loyalist activities. Only in 1909 were better laws passed concerning the archaeological excavations on private grounds. Ettore Pais, the first non-Neapolitan high official, served as Director from 1901–1905, during which time he encountered a high degree of hostility for not belonging to the Neapolitan elite.[324]

The Early Twentieth Century

Vittorio Spinazzola's excavations became the new state of the art, given his reuse of building materials collected in the excavations for the reconstruction and restoration of the monuments. Another main point of interest was archaeological stratigraphy, a constant weakness in Pompeian archaeology.[325] The "new excavations" along the Via dell'Abbondanza led to discoveries of grand houses like the House of the Cryptoporticus and the House of the Ephebe or of Cornelius Tages. As in former times, scientific information remained scarce, if we look for publications other than the reports in the *Notizie degli scavi*.[326] Spinazzola, however, was fired in 1923 for vaguely formulated political reasons, before he ever could publish extensively.[327] Afterwards, he worked for many years on his *Pompei alla luce degli scavi nuovi di via dell'Abbondanza (1910–1923)*, a large publication on these excavations, but never saw it printed. The type and already printed parts were lost during World War II, but thanks to the efforts of his son-in-law, the archaeologist Salvatore Aurigemma, it would finally come off the presses ten years after Spinazzola's death, in 1953.[328] It includes a box of plates with numerous scientific reconstruction drawings of building facades, upper stories, and interiors, which was quite a novelty. The two huge text volumes are still a hallmark of extensive

---

324 Dwyer 2010, 116 mentions the Neapolitan philosopher Benedetto Croce as an active opponent.
325 Cf. Barbanera 1998, 153–154. See also F. Delpino in Guzzo 2001, 51–61; J. Hartnett in Hales/Paul 2011, 246–269; Dwyer 2010, 118–120 (about the decision to leave the casts in the houses instead of bringing them to the museum; all subsequent excavators would adhere to this decision); F. Delpino in *Soprintendenti* 2012, 718–725.
326 Critical note expressed by Alfred Ippel, who claims that the treasures of these sites are the possessions of all nations (Ippel 1924, 44): "Alle diese Schätze sind geistiger Besitz aller Völker; dieses Pfund vergraben hieße es verkommen lassen." He says this in a lecture on the "Casa Omerica" or House of the Cryptoporticus.
327 S. Aurigemma in Spinazzola 1953, XI note 1, interprets this licensing as a political act of the upcoming fascists against Spinazzola, a liberal. Cf. bibliography in note 325.
328 Spinazzola 1953. Aurigemma had also worked in the Pompeii excavations and was sent off with his father-in-law in 1923. For more on him, see A. Gabucci, *Dizionario biografico degli Italiani* 34 (1988) 205–207, esp. 206; Barbanera 1998, 98–100; S. Bruni and P. Desantis in *Soprintendenti* 2012, 92–104. Aurigemma's introduction in Spinazzola 1953, I–XXXI is full of important data.

and detailed documentation and interpretation. Spinazzola's biggest fault was his failure to communicate his finds and his insistence on keeping the excavations surrounded by high fences, so that Italian and foreign colleagues alike did not get full insight into his activities until the 1953 publication.[329]

Herculaneum remained silent during the nineteenth century. Apart from the two small open-air excavations and Fiorelli's construction of a new entrance to the theater, nothing happened to attract visitors and scholars to Resina (p. 398, fig. 17). At the beginning of the twentieth century, however, there were calls to recommence work at Herculaneum. Charles Waldstein, the former director of the American School of Classical Studies at Athens and excavator at Argos, started a worldwide movement hoping to create a positive attitude about starting a major dig at Herculaneum. He tried to get archaeologists, politicians, sponsors and the general public together on the same page, and attempted to form an international research team composed of specialists in various fields who were to unveil Herculaneum from under the lava.[330] The reception of Waldstein's idea was favorable and his stimulating 1908 book, written together with the politician Leonard Shoobridge, was published to great acclaim, even in Italy. A growing chauvinism in Italy and perhaps the celebration of the fifty years of independent Italy, however, interrupted Waldstein's progress. King Victor Emanuel III withdrew his support, as did other Italians, and the nation defended the refusal as an act of national interest.[331] Almost two decades would pass before the excavations really started again, when the same King hammered the first blow with a pickaxe on March 15, 1927.

The Era of Amedeo Maiuri

Amedeo Maiuri was working on Rhodes for the Italian Archaeological Service, when, in 1924, at the age of 38, he took up the task of guiding the enormous Superintendency of his native area, Campania and Molise.[332] Throughout his

---

329 See Ippel 1924, 43 "Auf keinen Fall darf er [der Besucher] es versäumen, sich die Erlaubnis zum Besuch der nuovi scavi, der neuesten Ausgrabungen zu verschaffen, die wie ein Heiligtum hinter hohen Brettwänden bewacht werden. ... Zum ersten Mal seit 200 Jahren macht man diese Ausgrabungen jetzt unter Anwendung aller modernen Künste der Erhaltung..." These methods were, according to him, introduced by his compatriot Wilhelm Dörpfeld in Greek archaeology.
330 See Waldstein/Shoobridge 1908. For Herculaneum in the twentieth century, see Pace 2000, 121–129.
331 See, e.g., Carotenuto 1980, 358: "menomazione della dignità nazionale" ("impairment of national dignity"). Cf. Wallace-Hadrill 2011, 62–63.
332 There is a lot of literature about Maiuri, which often presents him as an idealized figure, but a serious biography is lacking. The most notable writings on Maiuri include: De Franciscis et al.

career, he carried out an incredible multitude of Roman projects in Herculaneum, Pompeii, Capri, as well as excavations in Greek sites like Velia and Cumae. He had a good and rapid pen and published a steady stream of books, booklets, scientific essays, impressions and journal articles.[333] Even in his popular works he stressed his scientific program of laying open antique towns in all their aspects. Pompeii and Herculaneum formed the best examples for both the learned and tourist world.[334] It has recently been said adroitly that Maiuri "invented Herculaneum" thanks to his special attention paid to this site after the first axe's blow made by the King in 1927.[335]

A topic not studied before by the local archaeologists was the history of Pompeii before 79. From the middle of the nineteenth century, attempts were made to develop a chronology of the city's building history and the emergence of its arts. Previously, foreigners like Nissen and Mau had carried out most of these path-breaking studies, for example on the chronology of architectural structures.[336] Maiuri understood that modern times called for more than the discovery of "new" houses. Therefore, Maiuri's stratigraphic soundings below the level of A.D. 79 were a major innovation. He argued that stratigraphic research beneath the upper layer of ancient Pompeii would reveal new data about Pompeii's history. His work on the Forum, around the Temple of Apollo and within the House of the Surgeon, along the city walls and in the Doric Temple was revolutionary.[337] Although Maiuri could not answer every question about the development of Pompeii, he formulated the agenda that would and will continue to occupy many generations of archaeologists. This sort of work, however, was not done at Herculaneum, where the hard ground level made this sort of research difficult.

1990; Barbanera 1998, 142–143, 153–154; Parisi 2000, 261–267; F. Zevi in Guzzo 2001, 73–79; P.G. Guzzo, *Dizionario biografico degli Italiani* 67 (2006) 682–687; Harris 2007, 211–230; Cotugno/Lucignano 2009; Monteix 2010, 1–36; Wallace-Hadrill 2011, 63, 73–83; P.G. Guzzo in *Soprintendenti* 2012, 442–448; De Haan 2014b. Cotugno and Lucignano, significantly, call Maiuri "grande" in the title, and definitely show hagiographic features.
333 García y García 1998, nos 8376–8649; Cotugno/Lucignano 2009, 235–244 nos 135–299.
334 Maiuri 1931, 6: "Lo scavo è inteso ormai al fine essenziale della visione integrale degli edifici scoperti: vengono salvati e ricollocati al loro posto tutti gli strumenti superstiti delle strutture superiori di una abitazione." The eleventh edition of 1964 has the same text on p. 8.
335 Monteix 2010, 1: "Inventio Herculanei" (title of the chapter); 35.
336 A fine analysis of wall techniques and structures yielded data for a better chronology. See, for instance, Carrington 1936, Preface. The author himself "interprets [the ruins] on historical lines."
337 For example, *Alla ricerca sulla Pompei preromana*, edited only in 1973, but containing older texts published between 1930 and 1953: García y García 1998, n. 8644.

Maiuri was favored by time and by politics, in terms of financial possibilities and administrative power to undertake all of his excavations. He had the support of the fascist regime in Rome, which was of the opinion that these projects were very valuable for Italy, in that they would present a positive image to the world. Some authors have argued that Maiuri was not much interested in politics unless he could get support for his many "children," the excavations around Naples.[338] He might have been more obliged than willing to include the following quotation of the Duce in the first of his popular guidebooks, dated October 24, 1931, in which Mussolini underlines the uniqueness of the Vesuvian cities:[339]

> You can offer to the world enchanting prospects and unpeeled towns that are unequalled on the surface of the Earth.

To promote his successes and to get support, Maiuri gave numerous lectures, both for uniformed fascists and other audiences. Several times he endorsed the idea of archaeology as an active form of research that favored the state's ideology to get strength and historical foundation. Publicizing the results was an important means to secure a wide awareness of Maiuri's efforts. The continuation of the archaeological projects was his main goal.

---

338 Umberto Pappalardo explains in Cotugno/Lucignano 2009, 15 that the fascist era has been left out of Cotugno/Lucignano's book for reasons of delicacy. Moreover, Pappalardo argues, Maiuri was declared innocent after the war. Cotugno and Lucignano (2009, 225–226) dismiss any form of filofascism on Maiuri's part. But see the endless lists of public performances of high members of the party (pp. 106–112, 117–120). For other voices on the topic, see Manacorda 1982, 454–455; Bracco 1983, 50–52 (in a sort of neo-fascist book); Manacorda/Tamassia 1985, 29; Barbanera 1998, 149–150; Harris 2007, 211–230, esp. 212 ("Under Fascism and Maiuri Pompeii became a hostage of politics."); Fröhlich 2008, 204 (the latter two publications give one quotation illustrating Maiuri's vision on Roman and German cultures as the basis for the modern Italian and German states); Guzzo 2010 (example of a fascist lecture); Monteix 2010, 15–16. Without more research having been carried out, one should read the balanced short biography by Guzzo, mentioned in note 332.

339 A. Maiuri, *Ercolano*, Rome, Novara, Paris 1932 (volume in the series "Visioni italiche"), first page: "potete offrire al mondo panorami incantevoli e città dissepolte che non hanno uguali sulla faccia della terra." Cf. studies mentioned in note 332. Cf. Carotenuto 1932, 13: "Dopo duemila anni, scuote il capo dal lungo torpore una delle più graziose e fiorenti città pagane, a riconfermare ancora una volta quella millenaria civiltà di che, a giusto titolo, va orgogliosa la nostra stirpe." Despite these patriotic words he regretted the abortion of Waldstein's plans (Carotenuto 1932, 77; M. Capasso in De Franciscis et al. 1990, 60–61). As far as I know, Maiuri's was the first guidebook entirely devoted to Herculaneum. A famous photograph shows Maiuri showing Mussolini around the excavations of Pompeii in 1940 (Guzzo 2001, 72; Harris 2007, 226, fig. 41). See on Mussolini and Herculaneum also Monteix 2010, 14–15.

After 1945, Maiuri was briefly submitted to a critical evaluation of his work during the war by the allies, but he was not punished and continued his work as passionately as ever, and rather successfully until his official retirement in 1961 at the age of 75. His projects were largely financed the Cassa del Mezzogiorno, the special finance institute for the economic development of southern Italy. Thanks to his more popular publications for the general public, Maiuri became the absolute prince of Campanian archaeology, much like Fiorelli had been in his age. He reigned Neapolitan archaeological society as a sort of independent ruler, and was (and still is) named "Don Amedeo" by his compatriots. His zeal was nationalistic and patriotic, and not very open to the international scholarly community.[340]

His zeal did not, however, keep foreign scholars completely out of the picture. International projects were carried out, but they were mostly based on already-excavated material, and did not interfere with the excavation projects of the local archaeologists. The chronology of wall painting, for instance, was a field that saw a prolific production of foreign publications, especially in Germany and the Netherlands, until the end of the twentieth century.[341] Especially in the first decades of the twentieth century, foreign students of Roman archaeology would complain about the poor quality of data available, and what little academic profit that could be had by studying them given their unreliable nature. That is likely explained by the scarcity of professional publications of excavation records.[342] The stream of preliminary reports by the Superintendent and his assistants seldom got sequels in the shape of extensive monographs or analytic articles by the same excavators. Maiuri was a splendid exception to that rule.

---

340 When Karl Schefold wrote his still valuable catalog of paintings in the houses of Pompeii (*Die Wände Pompejis*, Basel 1957), he got no access to large parts of Maiuri's excavations in the regions I and II, for Maiuri claimed the publication of these finds.
341 E.g. Ippel 1924 198–199, who recalls the names of – already dead – important German scholars: "Auch wir Deutschen können mit Freude feststellen, in der Pompejiforschung mit an erster Stelle zu stehen. Die Namen von Schöne, Nissen und Mau kann man nicht vergessen."
342 Pernice 1926, 1–4 discusses "Pompejis Bedeutung für die Altertumswissenschaft und Kunstgeschichte". He states at p. 1: "... So sehr man den Trieb nach Belehrung und Vertiefung des eigenen Wissens anerkennen muß, den meisten Besuchern bleibt Pompeji eben doch nur eine Kuriosität." Information would help: "Man darf wohl sagen, daß an diesem, schwerlich zu grau geschilderten Zustand die archäologische Wissenschaft selbst einen nicht geringen Teil der Schuld trägt." In these years Erich Pernice would publish various important scholarly works on arts and crafts (mosaics, bronzes), see García y García 1998, nos 10.474–10.490, whereas Karl Lehmann-Hartleben executed pioneering research on domestic architecture with Friedrich Noack. He was expelled from the Third Reich and emigrated to the USA, for which reason the book remained rather obscure (see F. Seiler in Guzzo 2001, 63–71; titles in García y García 1998, 7431, 7875–7884, 9902).

Like Spinazzola, Maiuri enthusiastically practiced restoration. He used ancient techniques to re-erect walls and columns, and to restore roofs, but forgot to take into account the fact that future generations of scholars would want to distinguish between the surviving ruins and the reconstructions. This is a great handicap for scholars who study the genuine antique remains, especially at Herculaneum, where the weathering of antique and modern materials has produced identical wall faces.

A bad stroke of luck for Pompeii was the heavy bombardment on August 24, 1943, which in an ironic twist, was the same day as Vesuvius' 79 eruption. The southwestern part of the city was afflicted with 250 bombs, which completely devastated Fiorelli's site museum, the Porta Marina and some nearby houses.[343] Fortunately, Maiuri had sent most materials exposed in the museum to the monastery of Monte Cassino in June 1943, so that these objects were safe. From there they were brought to other depositories, just before this venerated old sanctuary was quasi-annihilated itself under Ally bombs. The Allies defended the attack by recording the presence of German officers near the excavations, and continued to attack both ancient and modern Pompeii in September, hoping to hit the Germans, who were withdrawing to the north. Maiuri did not make a big deal of these barbarous attacks, because he found himself on the brink between the fascist government and the allied troops' temporary government.[344] Despite the fact that Maiuri's leg was broken due to a hit during the bombardment (he remained slightly incapacitated for the remainder of his life),[345] neither he nor other authorities dared to protest loudly, as would happen after the destruction of Monte Cassino. Therefore, the event fell into almost complete oblivion. A

---

343 For a discussion about the effects of World War II, see García y García 2006, 19–36. A new site museum was built after the war: Longobardi 2002, 56, figs 49–51.

344 García y García 2006, 28, recalls the fascist sympathy of Maiuri's colleague Della Corte. The director of the German Archaeological Institute at Rome, Reinhard Herbig, refers to Aurigemma's description of the bombardment (in Spinazzola 1953, XIX–XXIX, figs. II–XVI) to make clear that the Germans were not guilty (Herbig 1956, 169–170): "Er [Aurigemma] verzichtet auch nicht – und dafür dürfen wir Deutsche dankbar sein, denen in jeder 'Guida' die von uns verursachten Kriegsschäden da und dort vorgerechnet zu werden pflegen – auf die höchst eindrucksvolle Darstellung der Bombardierung Pompejis durch die alliierten Verbände im Jahr 1943. Diese militärische Großtat wird unter Heranziehung bildlichen und anderen Dokumentmaterials in erfreulich rücksichtloser Deutlichkeit gebrandmarkt." But Herbig was not fully innocent, since he made an impeccable academic career in the Nazi period (see G. Badder, *Neue Deutsche Biographie* 8 (1969) 584–585). Maria J. Sergejenko (1953, 23) however, ascribes the bombardment to the Germans – maybe meant as a critique against western Germany on behalf of the Soviets?

345 Cotugno/Lucignano 2009, 13, 89, 223. Lowry 1961 and Peyrefitte 1976 (see Chapter V) would refer to the bombardments. On the bar-restaurant (see below), see Longobardi 2002, 64–65.

long-lasting effect was the installation of the bar-restaurant in the section of the Forum Baths, which had been destroyed.

Among the collaborators in the archaeological service, Olga Elia deserves to be mentioned.[346] She was one of the very few women to hold important positions; her last such position was Archaeological Superintendent of Liguria. Between 1929 and 1961 she worked in Pompeii, Stabiae, and Torre Annunziata-Oplontis and carried out many projects.

The Last Fifty Years: Consolidation of the Monuments and Intensification of Research

From 1961 to 1976, Alfonso De Franciscis, a modest man and a good scholar, ended the ongoing excavations and paid more attention to restoration and maintenance.[347] His only large excavation in Pompeii was the House of Julius Polybius along the Via dell'Abbondanza. At Herculaneum he completed Maiuri's excavation of Insula VI with the exploration of the club house of the Augustales. The discovery of a huge villa under a former pasta factory at Torre Annunziata led to the large excavation of a complex attributed by him and others to the family of Nero's wife Poppaea, and the recognition of ancient Oplontis. Maria Giuseppina Cerulli Irelli initiated the excavation in the so-called Insula Occidentalis at Pompeii, which had been partially explored in the eighteenth century, and where up to recent years various groups of scholars have been working. She also conducted research on the old excavations at Herculaneum. Her successors, Fausto Zevi (1976–1982) and Stefano De Caro (1982–1984), were extremely severe about granting permission to begin new digs. They forbade nearly all forms of excavation except rescue projects and trial digs in already ruined complexes. Scientific publications about these projects by the excavators are unfortunately almost entirely nonexistent, apart from several papers by De Caro on Pompeii and on a villa near Boscoreale.

In the post-Maiuri era, large worldwide exhibitions became increasingly popular. Pompeii became an export article of "Made in Italy." The first exhibition, with treasures from the Museum at Naples and the storerooms at Pompeii, traveled around the globe in 1972–1974. Italy was proud of its past, and Pompeii served

---

346 L. Gervasini & G. Stefani in *Soprintendenti* 2012, 297–303. Gervasini and Stefani note how Elia was harshly dismitted by Maiuri in 1960 for unclear reasons (p. 298).
347 V. Castiglione Morelli, *Rivista di Studi Pompeiani* 20 (2009) 15–18; S. De Caro in *Soprintendenti* 2012, 247–259. For his publications, see García y García 1998, nos 3792–3878.

as a gift to all people interested in archaeology. Cerulli Irelli made great efforts to spread Pompeii fever in Japan, where she lived and worked for several years. The former provincialism gave way, and the door opened to international activities. There was suddenly room for research projects by foreign archaeologists, like the study and documentation of entire house blocks, and stratigraphic soundings in the gardens of formerly excavated houses. The number of monographs dedicated to old and new excavations has exploded in the last couple of decades, with authors from all over the world. The superintendency launched series of monographic publications that include works by both Italian and foreign scholars.[348]

When a heavy earthquake devastated many structures in the Vesuvian area on November 23, 1980, a photo campaign started in the late 1970s by the Istituto Centrale di Restauro e del Catalogo proved invaluable, for the damaged buildings were already at least partially catalogued. The ten huge volumes of *Pompei, Pitture e Mosaici*, edited by the institute of the Enciclopedia Italiana, are a sound scholarly product, which unfortunately came too late to document a great number of structures, which makes frequent consultation of old publications imperative.[349] Unfortunately, the buildings extra muros are not featured in this compendium, whereas for Herculaneum and the other Vesuvian sites no similar project has ever been envisaged.

In 1982, the large superintendency of Naples and Caserta was split into two. Pompeii, Herculaneum and Stabiae formed one part, guided by Baldassare Conticello until 1994. The rest of Naples' surroundings formed the other, and fell under Enrica Pozzi's and De Caro's care (1990–2003). This separation is understandable if one considers the extreme archaeological richness of the vast area, but it meant that the collection in the National Museum in Naples was rudely cut off from its old links to Pompeii. It depended on a willingness to collaborate, although the relationship between the new Superintendents was rather hostile. Conticello started a huge excavation project in the House of the Chaste Lovers, named after "chaste" depictions of banqueting lovers, while he also organized

---

348 Monografie 1–16 between 1986 and 1998, Studi 1– from 2001 onwards. Moreover there are periodicals: *Cronache Pompeiane* 1–5 (1975–1979), *Pompeii Herculaneum Stabiae* 1 (1983), *Rivista di Studi Pompeiani* 1– (1987–), all edited under the aegis of the Amici di Pompei. Among the foreign projects I only mention Volker Michael Strocka's series *Häuser in Pompeji*, twelve volumes in grand folio published between 1984 and 2004.
349 *PPM* I–X. An eleventh volume, *PPM Disegnatori*, contains watercolors, drawings and other historical documents. The series was preceded by three volumes of lists of photos made in the campaigns of the late 1970s: *Pitture e pavimenti di Pompei*, edited by the Gabinetto Fotografico Nazionale in Rome in 1981, 1983, and 1986.

numerous exhibitions.³⁵⁰ Since these failed to include the material in the Naples museum, they provided a distorted picture of ancient reality. Superintendent Pier Giovanni Guzzo (1994–2009), who started as a relative freshman in Pompeian matters, reestablished contact with the Naples superintendency. The intensive exhibition policy has been continued, but the shows now again contain material from both Pompeii and Naples. In 2008 the two superintendencies were combined again in the form of the Soprintendenza Speciale per i Beni Archeologici di Napoli e Pompei, which was placed under the aegis of Guzzo.³⁵¹ Since 2009, this large superintendency has had various directors, about whom I do not write, keeping Guzzo's directorship as the end of the history recounted here. I only mention Teresa Elena Cinquantaquattro who has been succeeded in 20214 by Massimo Osanna.

The works at Herculaneum follow a similar policy as Pompeii: restoration and consolidation are the key words of the directors over the last decade. This caution came after the bad experience of conducting open-air excavations at the Villa of the Papyri in the 1990s. Supported by politics and institutions, Marcello Gigante succeeded in realizing grand-scale works, aiming to find a supposed Latin counterpart of the Greek papyri known up to now (see Chapter VII). This project was carried out in an inadequate way, and failed to produce the results desired by the famous papyrologists. The site was severely damaged and the superintendency was forced to continue archaeological work and restorations, yet on a more modest scale.³⁵² A new approach to research was the clearing of the eighteenth-century tunnels, which was started recently by the director of the excavations, Maria Paola Guidobaldi, in charge since 1998. The large-scale "Herculaneum Conservation Project" was successfully launched thanks to financial supports of the Packard Humanities Institute. Andrew Wallace-Hadrill, former director of the British School at Rome and now professor in Cambridge, leads this project together with Guidobaldi and other local archaeologists.³⁵³

---

350 Unfortunately, no academic publication has been made of this important building. On the inappropriateness of this name, see Guzzo/Scarano Ussani 2011: it might have been a brothel. On Conticello, who was not unanimously appreciated by both Italian and foreign archaeologists, see the very laudatory obituary by A. Varone, *Rivista di Studi Pompeiani* 22 (2011) 7–10.
351 For more on this matter, see Guzzo 2003a and 2007, and his professional memoirs in Guzzo 2011.
352 Apart from some insufficient excavation reports by Antonio De Simone, some recent publications have shed better light on this work and its results. See A. de Simone and M.P. Guidobaldi in Zarmakoupi 2010, 1–62. On the practical vicissitudes Guzzo 2011.
353 See Wallace-Hadrill 2011.

Today, all archaeologists working in and on Pompeii admit that one of the biggest challenges is the preservation of the vast ruins that have come to light in the past 250 years. All understand that it is far too late to rescue every monument; too much has already been definitively ruined in the course of time. The ever-increasing number of tourists – some two million per year to Pompeii alone – causes plenty of erosion in itself, and rigid management is compulsory. Archaeologists have to make room for managers and restorers, who manage and restore the excavations as tourist attractions.

These matters, however, are not the topic of this book, although already the earliest accounts of the excavations contained lamentations about the rapid loss of archaeological evidence. We will encounter some of these voices in the following chapters.

Conclusion: From Tunnels to Trenches

The first tentative excavation at Herculaneum followed previous haphazardly-made finds under the village of Resina, which is in the area of ancient Herculaneum. By means of tunneling down through the thick layer of over twenty-five meters of volcanic material, miners sought treasures that could illuminate the young Kingdom, founded in 1734. The court and the elite of Naples remained rather stoic about these discoveries, whereas the discovery of this subterranean town prompted foreigners to write enthusiastically to relatives and friends about their encounters with the underground remains. Gradually, Neapolitans became aware of the value not only of artifacts, but of the sites themselves, so that open-air excavations in Pompeii after 1755 brought to light the houses and streets of an ancient Roman town, which was unparalleled in Europe. Scientific research did not keep pace with these discoveries. At first, in order to keep the secrets unique, nothing was published at all, and later, travel accounts urged the court to take steps, which resulted in the *Antichità d'Ercolano*. Intellectual discourse, however, was almost uniquely a matter of foreign students and interested laymen.

The unsystematic excavation methods and the simple-minded desire to enrich the royal collections remained more or less unchanged until 1860, and led to the extraction of all moveable finds, as well as mosaics and paintings being stripped from floors and walls. The urban aspect of Pompeii – a unique point in comparison with other archaeological monuments in the Mediterranean – was scarcely even considered relevant. Studies failed to reflect upon the town as an example of ancient society, for the lion's share of the increasing number of publications concentrated on single buildings or building categories, and works of art.

The nineteenth-century approach developed from the antiquarianism of the previous century, and moved towards the study of Pompeii as a monument of ancient daily life, focusing on houses and the artifacts found there alongside well-studied Greek and Roman texts. The Vesuvian material became an independent source for knowledge of antiquity.

In this discourse two questions come to the fore: did Pompeii's chronological development stimulate scholars to write about Pompeii's history rather than only about its monuments and its last days, and why did so many people see the town as an expression of Greek rather than of Roman culture? Most early authors did not question Pompeii's chronology, and assumed all monuments had simply been there forever. Greekness or Romanness had to do with a personal preference for things Greek or Roman. The mythical figure of Hercules was instrumental in defining Herculaneum and Pompeii as Greek, and the luxury evident in both cities and free sexual morale enhanced this impression.

In the second half of the nineteenth century we observe an increasing professionalization of archaeology in general, and of Pompeian archaeology in particular. Officials were professionally trained, which increased their effectiveness at managing the newly installed superintendencies. Thanks to Fiorelli's school, Pompeii formed the educational cradle of many Italian archaeologists. For Pompeii itself it implied better excavation and restoration methods. The sites were seen as monuments of the living past, to be cared after by modern men. The professionalization of archaeology profited from the developments made at Pompeii and so did Pompeii from better-trained archaeologists.

A drawback was the gradual closure of research in and around the excavations for foreigners, especially under Maiuri. Many Italian archaeologists of the early and mid twentieth century believed that they could properly execute the digs and the publication of the results simultaneously. Despite the good work followed by reports in the *Notizie degli scavi*, the final documentation of the still-rapid digs remained superficial. Spinazzola and Maiuri were the only officials to publish monographs on important projects, while the rest of the excavations remained neglected like those of the previous 150 years.

The last two decades present another image altogether. Local archaeologists have become aware of the gigantic problems of research and maintenance, and have realized the necessity of involving colleagues from academic institutions within and outside of Italy. As for the restoration, former officials were less interested than modern ones. The aid of non-Italian sponsors is now welcomed and no longer seen, like it was in former times, as an intrusion.

The enormous number of discoveries made during 250 years of excavating has attracted increasing numbers of tourists. The publication of books and booklets about old and new finds grew in a similar way. All superintendents and excavation directors contributed and continue to contribute to this genre, which fulfills its goal of making Pompeii and her sister city known around the world.

Pompeii and Herculaneum are no longer mysterious places. Publications, TV documentaries, and exhibitions, as well as exploding numbers of tourists to the sites, have brought them among the most famous historical places in the world. Especially Pompeii has become a brand name that must be experienced. In the literary evocations we will encounter in the following chapters, the town becomes the image of ancient Roman daily life, in which all sorts of adventures took place, and where all layers of Roman society intermingled.

II Travelers to the Vesuvian Cities

> "A man who has not been in Italy, is always conscious of an inferiority, from his not having seen what it is expected a man should see. The Grand object of travelling is to see the shores of the Mediterranean."[354]

Introduction: Grand-Tourists Going South

The visitors to Pompeii and Herculanum who are presented in this chapter typically saw Italy as the apogee of ancient culture and the cradle of all expressions of art. They visit(ed) cities and monuments, which illustrate at least one of these aspects.[355] Starting in 1500, various "categories" of visitors, each with their own goals, made the journey south to Italy. Artists, the first category, traveled across the Alps in order to better know the art of Italian Renaissance masters and Antiquity, both of which were increasingly growing in importance in the eyes of both the learned and non-learned public. They seldom wrote travel diaries; at least, we possess very few such records. Another category consisted of young noblemen from

---

[354] Dr. Johnson on the Grand Tour (citation in Chaney 1998, 113). Johnson never visited Italy.
[355] The bibliography on this theme is vast. Here I present several titles and their primary focus: Brooks 1958 (Americans); Menichelli 1962 (French nineteenth century); Wright 1965 (American writers); Lo Gatto 1970 (Russians); Fussell 1980 (British, twentieth century); Frank-van Westrienen 1983 (Dutch); Grell 1983 and 1995, 204–222 (French); Chevallier/Chevallier 1984 (French); Reinhold 1984, 265–275 (Americans); Del Litto/Kanceff 1986 (Stendhal and other travelers); Pemble 1987 (English, 1830–1914); Kanceff/Lewanski 1988 (Polish); *Edele eenvoud* 1989 (Dutch); Hentschel 1991 (learned travelers); Brilli 1991 (car travels), 1992 (general), 1995 (general); De Seta 1992 (British, French and Germans); Mozzillo 1992 (travelers at Naples); Kanceff/Rampone 1992; Knight 1995 (mainly British at Naples); Martinet 1996 (European travelogues); Risaliti 1996 (Russian and other Slavic travelers); *Grand Tour* 1997 [English edition 1996]; Ingamells 1997; Chaney 1998; Black 1999; Bertrand/Pichetto 2001; Moe 2002 (view on the "South"); Martin/Person 2002 (Americans, nineteenth century); Tammisto 2002 (Finnish travelers); Chapman/Stabler 2003 (British women); Brilli 2003 (clichéd images of Italians); N. Büttner, Tourismus, *Der Neue Pauly* 15/3 (2003) 523–533; Leibetseder 2004 (Germany seventeenth and eighteenth century); Arbillaga 2005, 139–252 (Britain, France, Germany and USA), 253–477 (Spain); Brilli 2006; Vautier 2007 (artists; anthology); Bertrand 2008 (French); A. Bendixen and W.M. Decker in Bendixen/Hamera 2009, 103–144 (Americans); Mullen/Munson 2009 (British, nineteenth century); Boulton/McLoughin 2012 (Brits); Müller 2012, 113–465 (Germany); Romero Recio 2012 (Spanish travelers to Pompeii). For some anthologies, see: Fasulo 1938 (nothing on Pompeii or Herculaneum); Hersant 1988 (some fragments on Pompeii); Pfister 1996 (nothing on our areas, but good short biographies and historical details on our travelers).

England, Germany, France and other Northern European countries who, upon finishing their university studies, decided to experience the world. Some such noblemen chose to continue their studies in Paris, Leiden, Padua, or other cities, but most decided to tour Europe, and trained in fighting, horseback riding, dancing, and sports after their obligatory daily visit to a noteworthy church, palazzo or ruin. While the grand tour might have included Switzerland, France, Germany, and the Republic of the Seventeen Provinces, the culmination was always a long visit to Italy. A third category of visitors included students and scholars, who wanted to expand their knowledge and their network by visiting colleagues and institutions. Antiquity formed one of the main topics of their studies and the choice of Italy, therefore, was compulsory.

Visitor numbers remain unknown, but the greatest share of them during the eighteenth century was English, until the Napoleonic wars caused a blockade on the Continent. After them were the French, followed by the Germans, and, at a considerable distance, individuals from other countries. Since Italians wrote few travel books, they seem to be absent in this story, but we may nonetheless assume a steady number of Italian visitors.[356] Almost no one traveled alone; most traveled in parties, which were sometimes composed of members of the various categories. The young noblemen engaged teachers and/or guides, who helped them with everything from making practical arrangements at resting places to enlightening them about the places they were visiting. In her 1789 book *Thraliana*, Hester Lynch Piozzi summarizes what a trip to Italy should offer:[357]

> I have been diverted with Folly, & shocked by Vice, pained by Incredulity, and sicken'd with silly Implicitness of Belief. Entertained extremely well upon the whole though, and enriched with many new Ideas, among which those excited by Vesuvius Pompeia &c. will be the last to forsake me. The Works of Man may be great & lovely: Apollo de Belvedere however, or Venus de Medici soon fade from one's Remembrance, & leave the Cascade of Terni, and Gloom of Pozzuoli indelibly impressed. Of all I have seen – Venice most pleased, & Naples most astonished me: Rome is dazzling without Sublimity in its *Materiale*, and Splendid without being Majestic in its Religious Functions. Gold & Glare, Pomp & Pageantry soon sicken the Observers of Life & Manners, who seek for Images that will not tarnish, and Truths which will never decay.

---

356 Grell 1995, 215 note 46 gives the following numbers of admission documents for Pompeii through December 1775 – December 1776: 20 French, 20 English, 6 Germans, some 40 Italians and a few other persons. Bertrand 2008, 80–84 gives the number of travelers who wrote travel accounts. On French travelers see also C. Grell/C. Michel in Franchi dell'Orto 1993, 133–144.
357 Balderston 1951, II, 638–639. For more on Piozzi, see Balderston's introduction and Ingamells 1997, 770–771. The title of Piozzi's book about her 1785–1786 trip to Italy stems from the name of her first husband, the brewer Henry Thrale, who died in 1781. There are remarkably few references to Pompeii in her letters (Bloom/Bloom 1989).

Besides diaries and journals, the literary form travel books usually take is of a bundle of letters sent home to family members, colleagues or even fictitious persons. Authors often do not conceal that these are not real pieces of correspondence, as we read in an observation in the preface of Gabriel-François Coyer's 1775 "letters to Aspaise."[358] And if instead, the author claims that a letter really is private correspondence, why would he publish it?[359] The printed versions surely do not exactly reproduce either the actual experiences the authors had, or their impressions of them in original drafts thrown onto paper in hotels, pensions or coaches, but these final printed editions are often the only versions that survive.[360] The travel book genre has a long history; for Campania, we must go back to the earliest grand tourist writings in the sixteenth century.[361]

A survey of hundreds of travel books has made it clear to me that some include extremely personal, fascinating statements and dull copies of previous descriptions all at once. The advantage of this survey is that one becomes aware of the fact that many travelers wrote the same "personal" experiences. A written record of a trip often served as a prestigious gift to friends or family members, and gave the author a higher status in society. Hence, written accounts range from simple descriptions of the places, monuments and landscapes, to individual impressions of Italy's past and present, the decay of antiquity, the power of nature and encounters with local people. Especially the earliest travelers were able to break new ground, and wrote both thorough descriptions of and personal reflections upon the wonders in Italy. Third and fourth generation voyagers felt the burden of these first impressions, and as a result, it was more difficult for them to maintain a fresh and open mind towards these places. They often abandoned the heavy travel guide books and stuck to writing down their personal experiences or making rapid sketches of their daily activities. New discoveries at Pompeii got thorough attention. In many late-eighteenth and early nineteenth-century records, there is an obvious fascinating with morbidness, as we will see in Chapter III. The emotions ventured in romanticism matched perfectly

---

358 Coyer 1775, 8. Aspaise is Aspasia, the famous learned friend of Pericles in fifth-century Athens.
359 E.g. Sharp 1766, Preface. His letters are very lively, indeed, but contain little about the Vesuvian cities. Baretti 1768 found it a work full of lies (for more on him, see García y García 1998, 161 and nos 1268–1271; McIlwayne 1988, no 2.155).
360 In the scope of this book, the critical comparison between first and final draft is not very important. Bertrand 2008 studied both published and unpublished French travelogues. A famous case is that of Goethe's *Italienische Reise*, published in parts shortly after his return in 1788-1789, but for the greater part in book form in 1816–1817 and 1829 (see p. 151 and Florack-Kröll 1986).
361 See Arbillaga 2005, 17–41, 57–117; for Naples and Pompeii, see pp. 135–136.

with descriptions of experiences of visits to the excavations, which we can glean from records in literature.

After a relatively meager season of traveling during the Napoleonic era, British tourism soared during the nineteenth century, especially when group visits became the rule thanks to professional travel agencies. No longer did only members of the upper class elite travel to the continent. Around 1850, Thomas Cook, the first travel agent, introduced the idea of mass tourism and made visiting the south less time-consuming and less expensive, given the efficient use of modern means like steam ships and trains.[362] Together with the higher speed of travel, site visits became shorter, and travel accounts suggest a certain degree of haste that led to more superficial observations. To get an impression of such nineteenth-century parties, one might read Dickens' complaints about vulgar travel groups in his 1845 *Travels to Italy*, and the hilarious description of an American Mediterranean cruise in Mark Twain's 1869 *The Innocents Abroad*.

During the Romantic period, the Italian South became an idealized area of bliss, and many people made their grand tour in order to flee from ordinary northern life rather than to acquire knowledge about the Greek or Roman past. In written accounts, personal emotions became more prominent than the record of obligatory highlights. Writers could get acquainted with Pompeii's original inhabitants by strolling through the streets and visiting the now empty houses where the spirits of the old Pompeians still seemed to live.

The introduction of cars around 1900 prompted a new, albeit small, boom of travel accounts, which sometimes included technical information about the roads and the maintenance of the automobiles.[363] Today, "tourism for the millions" has rendered a trip to southern Italy far from exclusive, and almost no one boasts about having been abroad. The need for publishing travel accounts on European destinations has become less compulsory and travelers focus on less known spots or on individual encounters. Nevertheless, Campania has played a considerable role in the continuous flow of travel books from 1740 until today.

As for the gender of travelers to Campania, it is clear from the outset that men formed the majority in the first century. Women usually traveled in the company of their relatives – fathers, brothers, husbands – or as the *dames de rôbe* or *dames de chambre* of other elitist ladies. Some women would publish travel books and, as we will see, these accounts are among the best. Nowadays, the distinction between men and women authors is no longer relevant.[364]

---

362 A railway station was built at Pompeii in 1844.
363 See Brilli 1991.
364 See A. Neri in Kancef 2003, 409–417 about British traveling ladies; Müller 2012, 123–125 and

Foreign Impressions of Campania

In the sixteenth and seventeenth centuries, Naples was, despite its long history and prestige as one of the greatest capitals of Europe, not considered a necessary stop on the grand tour, but after the establishment of the new kingdom in 1734, and the spread of rumors about newly excavated cities, it became increasingly popular.[365] In Naples itself, visitors paid most attention to the court, theater (especially opera), and the *lazzaroni*, the extremely poor lower class that more or less lived in the streets, without adequate shelter. In the city's surroundings, there were various other attractions, like the Reggia of Caserta to the north, and the old city of Pozzuoli, with its amphitheater and the Solfatara to the west. The ascent up Vesuvius was often combined with an inspection of the King's summer residence at Portici and the Pompeian collections. Herculaneum and Pompeii were among the most important monuments, and some people went to Salerno for the well-known monastery (or *certosa*) of Cava dei Tirreni and nearby Paestum to see its three Greek archaic and classical temples.

Goethe's *Italienische Reise* (see pp. 148–152) greatly influenced many authors. He did not hide behind descriptions of landscapes and monuments, and formulated his own feelings. Another fascinating traveler was Friedrich Johann Lorenz Meyer, whose *Darstellungen* are neither precise descriptions nor a journal as usual, but spontaneous impressions penned down on the spot and inspired by what he saw. Some of these he would develop into finished prose, when he had the energy to do so.[366] Meyer hoped to deliver the very emotions he had felt traveling in Italy for five months. Since dates were not relevant to him, we must deduce that the year of his writing was 1783 from his mention of "the last eruption of four years ago," by which he must be referring to the eruption of 1779.[367] His description of the ascent up Vesuvius after a visit to the Teatro di San Carlo has all the drama of the archetypical savage and the sublime, "erhaben" landscape. Silent vapors, moved by subterranean winds, take the shape of columns, and the

---

passim (learned women).
365 *Civiltà* 1979; *Golden Age* 1981. For Naples, see Moe 2002, 37–81.
366 Meyer 1792, V–VI: "Ich entwarf sie in meinem Tagebuch an den Orten selbst, und führte diese Entwürfe nachher, hier mehr dort weniger, aus, je nachdem die Stimmung des Augenblicks jenen Entwurf und diese Ausführung mehr oder wenig begünstigte." McIlwayne 1988, nos 2.175–2.176; García y García 1998, nos 9171–9173. For more about the interesting early romantic Meyer, who believed that his grand tour had changed him mentally, see Chevallier 1980, XI–LII.
367 Meyer 1792, 372. Cf. Chevallier 1980, XVII, XLIII–XLV. On the 1779 eruption, see Scarth 2009, 204–212.

inside of the crater remains almost completely invisible.[368] The power of the earth apparently also captivated the excavators of Herculaneum, where the tunnels offered no hint of an ancient town whatsoever. Meyer describes these tunnels as a labyrinth, impossible to comprehend, and refers to an old story about collecting single bronze letters from inscriptions without writing down the texts, forcing later antiquarians to spend many hours trying to reconstruct them.[369] Finally, when Meyer visited Pompeii, a city abandoned after a battle came to his mind, and here again we read about the drama he sensed in Campania: "The silence of a tomb seemed to have arrived after the rattling of weapons, and emptiness without people after the rumor of assailants."[370]

The travelers in the nineteenth and twentieth centuries often compared their countries with Italy, and Pompeii's history and their own. Hippolyte Taine, for instance, looked at Pompeii as a sort of model for the modern urbanization of Paris.[371] The British, who formed the largest and for a long time the wealthiest contingent of travelers, were preoccupied by social class, the superiority of

---

368 Meyer 1792, 374–375, 380 (part of a very long description: 364–385): "Ein schwarzgrauer Dampf stieg ohne Geräusch herauf; bald wirbelte er heftig, wie von unterirdischen Winden getrieben; bald richtete er sich in ungeheurer Säulenform gerade auf; bald ward er von der oberen Luft zurück gedrängt, verweilte einige Sekunden in der Tiefe, und stürmte dann plötzlich wieder herauf. Von dem Wind zerstreuet, strömte er an der entgegengesetzten Bergseite herab. – Die inneren Seiten der Bokka zu sehen, ward mir nur in den Augenblicken vergönnt, wenn der zurückgehaltne Rauch etwas verzog. Hingestreckt an dem äussersten Rand, bog ich mich dann, von meinen Begleitern gehalten, mit dem halben Leib hinein, und sah grosse aus dem tiefen Schlund heraufgebirgte Felsen, überzogen mit einer feuerfarbigen Schwefelrinde, die von mehrern, durch ihre erhitzte Phantasie betrogenen Reisenden schon oft für glühende Feuermassen angesehen und dafür ausgegeben worden sind. (...) Nach einigen Stunden vollen Genusses dieser erhabenen Szene, ward der Rückweg angetreten." Similar impressions were recorded by other travelers, see Richter 2007, 80–82. Like Winckelmann had before him, he drinks a bottle of Lacryma Christi at the summit.

369 Meyer 1792, 421: "Ohne allen Plan, und mit einer alle Gränzen des gesunden Menschenverstandes überschreitenden Unwissenheit, irrte man, ohne eine bestimmte Direkzion anzunehmen, beim Sprengen der Gänge unter der Erde umher, füllte, um die Transportkosten zu ersparen, die alten Gänge mit dem Schutt der neuen wieder aus, gerieth darüber mit diesen wieder in jene, und hatte so eine Jahrlange Arbeit oft vergebens gethan. Vermuthlich um die Alterthumsforscher mit recht schweren Problemen zu beschäftigen, wurden die an den Mauern der alten Gebäude gefundenen Inschriften in Tragkörben nach *Neapel* überbracht, nachdem man die Buchstaben an dem Ort selbst, ohne auch nur einen Punkt zu verlieren, einzeln aus dem Stein heraus gebrochen hatte." He concludes that the slow progression of the excavations is regrettable, but a mercy for the future (p. 416).

370 Meyer 1792, 424: "Grabesstille schien dem Geräusch der Waffen, menschenleere Öde dem Tumult der Belagerer gefolgt zu sein."

371 See pp. 133–134 on Taine. Well analyzed in Mullen/Munson 2009.

English society over all others, and the Anglican Church, so their written work reveals a certain amount of arrogance.[372] The Germans wanted to learn a lot and checked the veracity of printed guidebooks,[373] raved about Winckelmann and Goethe, and liked to include a certain degree of sentimentalism in their writing. The French, whose writing demonstrated a clear and rarely abandoned intolerance of the Neapolitans, were analytical and critical of the social and political situation and considered themselves worthy successors to the old Romans.[374] At the beginning of the nineteenth century, when Americans began to arrive – late – they often showed an almost childish enthusiasm for, or on the contrary, a tendency to underestimate the values of the old world.[375] The Italians themselves played a peculiar role. Until 1860, northern Italians, although they spoke the same language, were formally considered foreigners, and looked upon the southerners with great contempt. That changed little over the years after the unification of the country in 1860, and even now some view the *meridionali* with disdain, although others are more diplomatic, and refer to the South's economic and social problems. Some Italian travel accounts could easily have been written by actual foreigners. I do not know of any travelogues written by southern people, although there are literary impressions of local people like the popular Neapolitan writer Salvatore Di Giacomo at the end of the nineteenth century.[376]

In this chapter, I will discuss impressions of visits to Portici, Herculaneum, and Pompeii in chronological order, following the development of the excavations. The earliest decades have a disproportionate number of repetitive impressions, although some of these travelogues became standard works that needed to be included in the luggage of every gentleman. Several travel books were translated into various languages and enjoyed especially large readerships.[377] Some of the facts and fictions mentioned in travel accounts would provide material for fiction writers, and therefore get major attention herein.[378]

---

372 For eighteenth-century British travelers, see Ingamells 1997. For the nineteenth century, see Mullen/Munson 2009.
373 A good example of a control freak is Johann Caspar Goethe (see p. 146).
374 Bertrand 2008, 235–247 discusses the French perception of Neapolitans; 491–544 (Naples). See also F. Brizay and M. Cuaz in Bertrand/Pichetto 2001, 125–139; 140–159.
375 See Reinhold 1984, 265–275.
376 See Casale 1985 and A Pellegrino, *Dizionario Biografico degli Italiani* 40 (1991) 24–29. A nice view is that from 1876 by a northerner, Roberto Sacchetti from Turin (Sacchetti 1979, 41–73).
377 García y García 1998 provides good overviews of editions and translations.
378 Unfortunately not all travelers recorded their impressions. So we lack those of famous people like Laurence Sterne, John Wilkes, James Boswell, and Edward Gibbon, who all visited Naples in 1765 (cf. Sterne 1930; Boswell 1955; Gibbon 1956, I, 190–191; Gibbon 1984, 182, where he portrays the "boy-king" Ferdinand and Lord Hamilton, "who, wisely diverting his correspondence

Before going to Herculaneum and Pompeii with our travelers, let me recall Heinrich Heine, who never ventured south of Rome. Sitting in the amphitheater of Verona and attending a popular comedy, he reflects on antiquity and Italy. Although the subject matter in the modern play Heine sees is "innocent," this is not a characteristic shared by Roman plays. Heine argues that this is the case, since the Romans' high self-esteem led them to build gigantic monuments for theatrical performances and games, like those we still see in Rome. In order to gain an understanding of Roman private life, as low-profile as his own, or that of anyone of his generation, Heine claims that nothing is more important than the study of Pompeii's architecture, "der alte Steintext." While the Greeks were masters of arts and Jews possessed God, the Romans dominated the world thanks to their grand idea of Rome.[379]

Herculaneum in Eighteenth-Century Accounts

The oldest accounts on the discovery of an ancient subterranean city were spread throughout Europe via newspapers and scholarly letters, like the small pamphlets of Venuti and Gori of 1748.[380] As we have seen in Chapter I, the court tried to prevent every form of publication but could not obstruct distribution of the news via travel accounts. Even the prohibition from making notes in the excavations

---

from the Secretary of State to the Royal Society and British Museum, has elucidated a country of such inestimable value to the naturalist and antiquarian"). A brief account of their stays in Naples are in Bowersock 1978, 468–470; cf. Ingamells 1997.
379 Heine 1956, 302–303: "Das ganze Spiel hatte keinen Tropfen Blut gekostet. Es war aber nur ein Spiel. Die Spiele der Römer hingegen waren keine Spiele, diese Männer konnten sich nimmermehr am blossen Schein ergötzen, es fehlte ihnen dazu die kindliche Seelenheiterkeit, und ernsthaft, wie sie waren, zeigte sich auch in ihren Spielen der barste, blutigste Ernst. Sie waren keine grosse Menschen, aber durch ihre Stellung waren sie grösser als andre Erdenkinder, denn sie standen auf Rom. Sowie sie von den sieben Hügeln herabstiegen, waren sie klein. Daher die Kleinlichkeit, die wir da entdecken, wo ihr Privatleben sich ausspricht; und Herkulaneum und Pompeji, jene Palimpsesten der Natur, wo jetzt wieder der alte Steintext hervorgegraben wird, zeigen dem Reisenden das römische Privatleben in kleinen Häuschen mit winzigen Stübchen, welche so auffallend kontrastieren gegen jene kolossale Bauwerke, die das öffentliche Leben aussprachen, jene Theater, Wasserleitungen, Brunnen, Landstraßen, Brücken, deren Ruinen noch jetzt unser Staunen erregen. Aber das ist es ja eben; wie der Grieche gross ist durch die Idee der Kunst, der Hebräer durch die Idee eines heiligsten Gottes, so sind die Römer gross durch die Idee ihrer ewigen Roma, gross überall, wo sie in der Begeisterung dieser Idee gefochten, geschrieben und gebaut haben." His *Reisebilder. Italien* are from 1828.
380 See, e.g. Michel 1984, 106–107; A. Wallace-Hadrill in Hales/Paul 2011, 367–379. Here pp. 23–24.

and the Portici museum, let alone from copying inscriptions and drawing paintings, was inadequate to prevent tourists from writing down memories in their notebooks and letters. These notes were especially important in the first decades, when printed travel guides did not yet include Herculaneum and Pompeii.[381] The following amusing words were written in Naples in 1740 by Horace Walpole, the son of the Prime Minister and future author of the *The Castle of Otranto*, to his friend Richard West,[382] while Walpole was in the South with his friend and study pal, the future poet Thomas Gray.[383]

> One hates descriptions that are to be found in every book of travels; but we have seen something today that I am sure you never read of, and perhaps never heard of. Have you ever heard of the subterraneous town? a whole Roman town with all its edifices remaining under the ground? Don't fancy the inhabitants buried it there to save it from the Goths: they were buried with it themselves; which is a caution we are not told they ever took. You may walk the compass of a mile; but by the misfortune of the modern town being overhead, they

---

381 Most travel books were re-edited and reused for ages and apparently remained functional. Updates were rare.

382 Walpole 1948, 222 (June 14, 1740, entire letter pp. 222–224). He describes the visit to Naples in his "Short Notes of the Life ..." (ibid. p. 8), but leaves out Herculaneum. Cf. Leppmann 1966, 71 (long quotation); McIlwayne 1988, no 3.315; García y García 1998, no. 14.083. Walpole's friendship with Gray dates from their time at Eton (1734) and failed at Reggio Emilia in 1741; it would be restored some years later.

383 Gray writes to his mother Dorothy during a visit to the ruins at Baiae, Pozzuoli, and Cumae, north of Naples (Gray 1935, 163–164, letter 88, June 14, 1740): "We have been in the Sybil's cave and many other strange holes under ground (I only name them because you may consult Sandy's travels); but the strangest hole I ever was in, has been to-day at a place called Portici, where his Sicilian Majesty has a country-seat. About a year ago, as they were digging, they discovered some parts of ancient buildings above thirty feet deep in the ground: curiosity led them on, and they have been digging ever since; the passage they have made, with all its turnings and windings, is now more than a mile long. As you walk you see parts of an amphitheatre, many houses adorned with marble columns and incrusted with the same; the front of a temple, several arched vaults of rooms painted in fresco. Some pieces of painting have been taken out from hence, finer than any thing of the kind before discovered and with these the King has adorned his palace: also a number of statues, medals, and gems; and more are dug out every day. This is known to be a Roman town, that in the Emperor Titus's time was overwhelmed by a furious eruption of Mount Vesuvius, which is hard by. The wood and beams remain so perfect that you may see the grain; but burnt to a coal, and dropping into dust upon the last touch." McIlwayne 1988, nos 3.113–3.114; García y García 1998, no. 6286. Cf. Gray 1890, 252–257, in almost the same formulation, He further remarks (1890, 253–254): "The work is unhappily under the direction of Spaniard people of no taste or erudition, so that the workmen dig, as chance directs them, wherever they find the ground easiest to work without any certain view." In letter 204 of 21 August 1755 (Gray 1935, I, 432) to Stonhewer he speaks on Bayardi's *Prodromo* and appears to follow the developments with great interest.

are obliged to proceed with great caution, lest they destroy both one and t'other. By this occasion the path is very narrow, just wide enough and high enough for one man to walk upright.

Walpole reports rumors on the find of an amphitheatre with paintings showing architectural elements, brought to Portici and unvisible, all still in 1740:

> There might certainly be collected great light from this reservoir of antiquities, if a man of learning had the inspection of it; if he directed the working, and would make a journal of the discoveries. But I believe there is no judicious choice made of directors. There is nothing of the kind known in the world; I mean a Roman city entirely of that age, and that has not been corrupted with modern repairs. Besides scrutinizing this very carefully, I should be inclined to search for the remains of the other towns that were partners with this in the general ruin. 'Tis certainly an advantage to the learned world, that this has been laid up so long. Most of the discoveries in Rome were made in a barbarous age, where they only ransacked the ruins in quest of treasure, and had no regard to the form and being of the building; or to any circumstances that might give light into its use and history.

Many of the critical observations expressed in this letter will return in later accounts. It was not easy for these first visitors to get down into the tunnels. The local people mistrusted these *Milordi* (a pluralized form of "My lord") and also lacked confidence about what was going on under their feet. George Knapton, an English portrait painter and a member of the Society of Dilettanti, wrote to his brother Charles how he had heard from an "old Man, living next Door to the Well" (that is, the access to the excavation) that digging had taken place there twenty-seven years before, that is in 1713. In the following he describes the difficulties with the inhabitants of Resina:[384]

> Having given you some Account of what is taken out of this subterraneous City, I shall now proceed to what remains in it, and our Journey down to it. At our coming to the Well, which is in a small Square, surrounded with miserable Houses, filled with miserable ugly old Women, they soon gathered about us wondering what brought us thither; but when the Men who were with us, broke away the paltry Machine with which they used to draw up small Buckets of Water, I thought we should have been stoned by them: Till, perceiving one more furious than the rest, whom we found to be *Padrona* of the Well, by applying a small Bit of Money to her, we made a Shift to quiet the Tumult. Our having all the Tackle for descending to seek, gave Time for all the Town to gather round us, which was very troublesome: For, when any one offered to go down, he was prevented either by a Wife or a Mother; so that

---

384 *Philosophical Transactions, giving some Account of the present Undertakings, Studies, and Labours, of the Ingenious in many considerable parts of the World* 41 (1744, for the years 1739–1740) 489–493. The Knapton quotation is from pp. 490–491. McIlwayne 1988, no 3.117; García y García 1998, no 7440. On Knapton see Redford 2008.

we were forced to seek a motherless Batchelor [sic] to go first. It being very difficult for the First to get in, the Well being very broad at that Part, so that they were obliged to swing him in, and the People above making such a Noise, that the Man in the Well could not be heard, obliged our Company to draw their swords, and threaten any who spoke with Death. This caused a Silence, after which our Guide was soon landed safe, who pulled us in by the Legs, as we came down. The Entrance is 82 Feet from the Top of the Well: It is large and branches out in many Ways, which they have cut. We were forced to mark with Chalk, when we came to any Turning, to prevent losing ourselves. It gives us a perfect Idea of a City destroyed in that Manner.

Visiting the underground galleries meant creeping through narrow horizontal tunnels on the level of the ancient floor. Artillery officer John Northall noted that there was little to see, but the excitement of standing in front of the remains of an entire city compensated the efforts. He was also thrilled by the view of artifacts revealed in the volcanic material. He even suspected there were multi-story houses among the ruins under his feet.[385]

Joseph Spence, professor of poetry and subsequently of modern history at Oxford, gave a telling description of the tunneling as early as 1741 in a letter to his mother:[386]

The King of Naples has had people continually at work there for some years, and they have wrought narrow passages, perhaps quite through it. We walked a line of near a mile in it, and they say one might go six, if one was to take all the turns of it. They have generally followed the line of a wall, wherever they met with one (and they met with them perpetually) sometimes the inside, and sometimes the out, just as it happened: so that the line goes zigzag. The insides are generally covered with stucco (a better kind of plaster) and painted red, of which I have a great many pieces to show you. In several places they have found pictures on it, and some very good ones. The best are conveyed to a house of the King's in that neighbourhood, in which they have already about 140 pieces of these old pictures, beside statues, columns, and other pieces of wrought marble; and they continually find something new, of one or other of these kinds. 'Tis all dark, and we walk all the way with torches,

---

385 Northall 1766, 260: "In entering this subterranean, first, there is a steep descent of seventy-two paces, strait forward; then, turning to the right, is another of seventeen ancient steps; after which is seen the appearance of the outsides of houses; bases of pillars of brick, some stuccoed and fluted, some standing upright, other overset. We went into several rooms, some circular like baths, all stuccoed in compartments, and painted. We walked upon marble floors worked in mosaic, in pretty taste. Here, stamping the foot, it sounded hollow; by which we conjectured we were in one of the upper rooms of a house. We saw some beams that were burnt to a coal, and crumbled to pieces when touched; others not burnt, and the wood of these is so hard and tough that a knife would scarce cut it." He was there in 1752 (Ingamells 1997, 713). McIlwayne 1988, no 2.140; García y García 1998, no. 9912.
386 Spence 1975, 374. McIlwayne 1988, no 3.121; García y García 1998, nos 13.113–13.114. For more about Spence, see Ingamells 1997, 881.

which makes it rather too hot than too cold, though you are so deep under the present surface of the earth. We mounted out of it by a staircase of sixty steps, and went thence to the King's house to see the curiosities that had been discovered in it. Among the pictures some were excellent, but the world will one day or other know more of them, because they design to publish prints of them.

The first woman to describe the discoveries was Katherine Dunford, the future Lady Fetherstonhaugh, who was there in February 1751. Parts of her letters were published a hundred years later and praised for their fresh spontaneity.[387] The subterranean visit clearly had its limits:

> I imagined that, having once got into the houses, I could have walked about them; but every place is filled with lava, and it adheres so closely as to have taken the impression of everything it surrounded; and is with difficulty separated, though it is of a much more sandy substance than the lava is in many other places over which it has run. We observed in some places pieces of burnt beams and rafters which looked as if they had supported a floor. In one passage we passed by a great number of pillars about three feet distant from one another, supposed to have been a portico; they are of brick, plastered over, fluted and painted red. They are broke off a little above the base, and thrown down, so that they now lie in a horizontal position in the midst of the lava.
> [... Having descended into the theatre] I must now take breath a little, for it is very close and hot underground, and not very agreeable among the galley-slaves who are employed to dig there. They are chained two and two, and have a guard over them. The smoke of the torches made us very near as black as they were, and we were glad to return to Naples, and change our dress.

Wilhelmine, the margravine of Bayreuth and the elder sister of Frederick the Great, who was known as a many-sided artist, was at Herculaneum with her husband Frederick III in 1755 and called it a mine ("Bergwerk").[388] With ashes and drops of water falling on his head, Pierre Jean Grosley, a French magistrate from Troyes, probably had the same mine-like association, and wrote about how frightening it

---

[387] Her letters were published by Chatterton (1861, 16: he discusses the character of her letters); 46, 50 for the quotations. See also Leppmann 1966, 75. According to Leppmann and García y García 1998, no. 5142, the quoted letter was published in the *Philosophical Transactions* of 1763, but I was unable to find it. Dunford, who must have been a good acquaintance of Gambier and Pitt (see Chatterton 1861), was traveling with her future husband Utrick Fetherstonhaugh and his group (for more about them, see Ingamells 1997, 354).

[388] Kammerer-Grothaus 1998, 17. The same word was used by Goethe some twenty years later. Cf. R.P. de Singlande, who in 1758 received permission to visit "cette précieuse mine" (de Singlande 1765, II, 136, 138, quotation).

could be under the earth.[389] Pierre Brussel, a French traveler, even described the rattling of the convicts' chains in this sort of Hades or Tartarus of the poets.[390]

Charles de Brosses, a magistrate and man of letters from Dijon,[391] attracted attention with his three letters on Herculaneum and Vesuvius, written in 1739–1740 and edited in 1750 after a 1749 presentation in the Académie Royale des Inscriptions et Belles-Lettres in Paris.[392] The third letter, based on Venuti's 1748 book, discusses the problems of the excavation method, the haphazard tunneling and the removal of the finds.[393] Important terms are *curieux* and *particulier*, as they underline the nature of the research the first visitors conducted.[394] De Brosses is much more enthusiastic as he describes Vesuvius; the prohibition on making notes might be the reason for the contrast.[395] In reading his lines, one wishes for open-air excavations, a wish also expressed by Andrew Lumisden, a

---

[389] Grosley 1769, II, 226: "In the part where the excavation was freshest, I perceived the ashes, which constitute the whole ground hereabouts, loosening from the upper part of the gut, dropping on my head, and run down along the wall like corn through a hopper: this alarmed me; and I communicating my apprehensions to the company, we all, without any long deliberation, made off faster than we had come in." McIlwayne 1988, no 2.149; García y García 1998, nos 6352–6355. Volkmann 1777–1778, XII criticized his letters for his sloppily composed stories, which were published anonymously for that reason: "Sie begreifen einige artige Anekdoten, die den Leser angenehm unterhalten, sind aber mehr flüchtig zusammengerafft als gründlich und zuverläßig. Vielleicht hat der Verfasser auch aus dieser Ursache seinen Namen verschwiegen."

[390] Brussel 1768, 281–282: "Le nombre des galériens qui travaillent dans ces souterrains obscurs, le bruit des chaines qu'ils traînent à leurs pieds, la lueur foible des torches fumantes, tout ne nous peignoit pas mal les enfers & le tartare des Poëtes, & nous fit désirer de quitter ce lieu de tristesse pour nous rendre à la lumiére des Cieux." Not in McIlwayne 1988 and García y García 1998.

[391] See De Brosses 1991, 71–81 for his itinerary. On De Brosses, see De Seta 1992, 123–126; Parisi 2000, 37–41; McIlwayne 1988, nos 3.102, 3.172; García y García 1998, nos 2185–2197.

[392] This letter is incomplete, see Capasso 1991, 563–620 for the history of the manuscript and the partial publications.

[393] De Brosses 1991, 567: "Il est aisé de juger qu'on ne peut voir que d'une manière fort imparfaite les restes d'une ville enterrée, quand on [n']a fait qu'y pousser au hazard quelques conduits bas et étroits. Il n'y a point de place un peu spatieuse, où l'on se soit donné du vuide; on ne fera jamais rien de bien utile, si on continue à travailler de la sorte et si on ne prend le parti d'enlever les terres dans un espace considérable depuis le sol extérieur jusqu'au rez-de-chaussée de la ville. Aprez avoir examiné cet espace et retiré ce qui s'y retrouveroit de curieux, on pouroit découvrir l'espace voisin, en rejettant les terres sur le précédent, et ainsi de proche en proche. Ce seroit un grand travail, mais dont on se trouveroit indemnisé par une quantité de raretez; surtout en sculpture et en peinture. Tout ce qu'on y a trouvé dans ce genre and fouillant à l'aveugle peut faire juger de ce que produiroit une recherche méthodologique."

[394] For this observation, see Bologna 1979, 389–391.

[395] According to Leppmann 1966, 75.

Scottish catholic advocate and Jacobite who lived in Rome for almost 20 years in exile.[396] Another negative opinion about the excavation method comes from Jérôme Gabriel Richard, an author who became influential thanks to numerous editions and translations of his *Description*, in which he points out the quality of buildings and objects, both of which teach us about the splendor and greatness of Greeks and Romans.[397]

Johann Wilhelm von Archenholz, a Prussisan officer and historian, whose *Rom und Neapel* was widely read in Germany, explained the excavation's flaws through a theological lens. According to him, the Neapolitans spent too little money on these excavations simply because they found no relics of saints – relics which he, as a Lutheran, could not but despise.[398]

Volkmann, the author of the most authoritative German travel guide of his time, argued against the plea for open-air excavations, which he said would be too expensive. Besides, Portici would vanish from the earth and the ruins would become prey

---

396 Lumisden 1797, Appendix VI, pp. 466–478, quotation p. 477: "I cannot help regretting the method they have taken to clear out this city. Had they laid it open from the top, we should have had the pleasure of seeing it as it formerly stood; we should have seen the disposition of the streets, houses, temples, &c.; we should have seen the interior of the houses, and a thousand curiosities we are now deprived of. But, as the city lies so far below ground, it would have been an immense expense to have wrought in this manner." The text had appeared before (note on p. 466) in the English version of Cochin/Bellicard 1754. Lumisden presents it again and hopes that it will still be useful to the reader despite the recent developments. On Lumisden, see Ingamells 1997, 616–617; McIlwayne 1988, 2.139; García y García 1998, no. 8221.

397 Richard 1769, 481–482: "Ce que l'on regrette véritablement, c'est que le roi des deux Siciles, lorsqu'on commença les excavations, n'ait pas ordonné que l'on découvrît ce théâtre par le dessus, & qu'on en débarasse de façon à le conserver en entier. Autant que j'ai pû en juger, il n'étoit chargé d'aucun édifice assez important pour que l'on regretât la perte; les jardins qui sont au-dessus sont un objet de peu de conséquence. Aussi on auroit conservé à peu de frais, un édifice antique, construit & décoré dans le temps que les beaux arts etoient à leur perfection dans l'empire Romain, & qui réunissoit dans sa construction les graces et le goût des Grecs, avec la magnificence Romaine. Il eut été fort aisé de le restaurer avec ses matériaux mêmes, & quand on n'eût conservé que ce qui étoit entier, ç'eût toujours été beaucoup, car c'étoit un édifice unique dans le monde." McIlwayne 1988, no 2.152; García y García 1998, no. 11.354. Richard does not ask for an excavation of ordinary houses (p. 483). Quoted in Grell 1995, 206 as an example of concern for the condition of Herculaneum itself.

398 Von Archenholz 1990, 265; 1993, 367–368: "Freilich, wären hier die Knochen eines großen Heiligen aufzusuchen gewesen, so hätte man keine Kosten gescheut, um sie aus der Tiefe der Erde herauszuholen, und man würde sie sodann nach Belieben küssen können. Es versteht sich, daß diese Ehre nur sehr vornehmen Personen zuteil geworden wäre, geringere hätten sich mit dem Glück begnügen müssen, bloß die Einfassung der Knochen zu belecken." McIlwayne 1988, no 2.165; García y García 1998, nos 838–842. Von Archenholz's book was heavily criticised by Goethe (1988, 145).

of decay.³⁹⁹ His defense of the Neapolitan excavation method made it clear that he understood the rules about visits and documentation, which were also clear to the painter James Russel, who states that permission to enter the excavation is difficult to obtain. The authorities had to prevent visitors from stealing objects and abusing the goodness of the liberal court.⁴⁰⁰

A few visitors racked their brains over the question of which city laid under Resina; most decided it was Pompeii. Christopher Hervey, a traveler only known for his criticism of the existence of so many small Italian states in those days, acknowledged the two cities mentioned by Dio Cassius and argued that a lost town mentioned in the sources need not necessarily be the one found by excavators. Besides, he claimed, theaters and amphitheaters were often features of an emperor's villa.⁴⁰¹ As a matter of fact, Venuti had already published the solution in 1748: a large inscription found in the theater firmly proved that Herculaneum was there, not Pompeii or Stabiae.

---

399 Volkmann 1777–1778, III, 304: "Sonderbar ist der Wunsch mancher Reisenden, welche wünschen, daß die ganze Stadt gleichsam aufgedeckt und die darauf liegende Erde abgetragen würde. Was für Kosten würden nicht erfordert, eine ungeheure vierzig Ellen tiefe Rinde über einen so großen Platz, als Herculanum eingenommen, abzutragen, und die verhärtete Lava zum Theil wegzusprengen? Portici mit allen seinen Häusern müßte abgetragen und ein neuer Berg von dem Schutte und der ausgegrabenen Erde aufgeführt werden. Und zu welchem Ende? Um verfallenes Mauerwerk, viele kleine elende Häuser, die in Ruinen liegen, und die kahlen Wände einiger größern, wovon man die Male[re]yen bereits sorgfältig abgenommen zu sehen, die Lage der Gassen wird genau aufgenommen, folglich kann man sich, wenn der ganze Platz durchwühlt ist, einen hinlänglichen Begriff daraus machen." McIlwayne 1988, no 2.413; García y García 1998, no. 14.014. On him W. Richter in *Pompeji 79–1979*, 126–137; *Goethe in Italien* 1986, passim, cat. no. 26

400 Russel 1750, II, 314–315 (15 September 1749): "Besides, it is with greater difficulty that strangers are now admitted to see these antiquities; and are observed with greater jealousy and watchfulness, since the scandalous behaviour of some sharpers, who have not scrupled to pocket any small rarity, upon which they could lay their hands. This pilfering curiosity is the greatest abuse of the generosity and good nature of the Prince of the country: and at the same time a very great injury to strangers, by drawing upon them a deprivation of that liberty, which had been allowed them in the fullest extent before." McIlwayne 1988, no 3.119; García y García 1998, no. 11.784 (erroneously: John Russel). Russel's book was originally published anonymously. For more on Russel, see Ingamells 1997, 830–832.

401 Hervey 1785, III, 30 (7 March 176 nos1): "Now as there has been a town lost, and a town found, people imagine that the town lost must be inevitably the same with that discovered, which I do not think a certain consequence. Nor do I hold it absolutely certain that what they have discovered under the ground was a town. I think they might have found as many things in a village, or even in a villa. They have discovered indeed a theatre I believe, or rather an amphitheatre, but some Roman emperors had amphitheatres in their villas." McIlwayne 1988, no 2.150; García y García 1998, no. 6779. Dio is quoted in Chapter IX. On Hervey, see Ingamells 1997, 489.

The Museum at Portici

> "The museum at Portici keeps the relics of the venerable old time, sanctified by their high antiquity, from the altar of the gods and their holy offering utensils to the humblest household goods."[402]

Albeit not always in the romantic style of Meyer, all journals contain a description of the collection in the palace at Portici, unless the author had no permit to enter.[403] For some visitors, the excavations, at least those in Herculaneum, were less interesting than this museum. Madame Du Bocage, a highly estemeed French poet and playwright, wished that the monuments were in a more amenable spot than this "house of gnomes," and was happy to go directly to Portici, where the finds were in a safer condition than they would have been in the ancient town. She even hoped that the objects would be brought to a still more distant and therefore safer place, far from Vesuvius.[404] For Ann Riggs, better known as Lady Miller, the wife of the military man John Miller, the museum was also the main reason to come to Portici.[405]

---

402 Meyer 1792, 414: "Von dem Altar der Götter und ihrem heiligen Opfergeräth, bis auf das geringste Hausgeräth herab, bewahrt das *Museum zu Portici* die durch das hohe Alterthum geheiligten Reliquien der ehrwürdigen Vorzeit dieses Landes."
403 E.g. Burney (Scholes 1959, I, 271): via Hamilton. Chevallier/Chevallier 1984, 27 give other examples. Hamilton wrote a complaint to Tanucci when a fellow Briton did not get access to the collection: Ramage 1992, 656. Allroggen-Bedel/Kammerer-Grothaus 1980, 1983 are fundamental for the reconstruction of the display of objects in this building. See also Chapter I, pp. 30–33; Represa Fernández 1988 and Cantilena/Porzio 2008.
404 Du Bocage 1771, 239–240 (October 15, 1757): "Ne croyez pas que j'aye vu ces précieuses reliques, où on les trouva. Vous connoissez mon aversion pour l'habitation des Gnômes: ma promenade dans cette ville souterraine fut courte, la fumée des flambeaux m'offusquoit, le froid me gagnoit & j'y cherchois en vain les morceaux remarquables qu'on en a enlevés. [...] Ne pouvant en découvrir que très peu de restes, je la quittai promptement de peur d'un rhume, & fus en admirer les débris dans les galeries de *Portici*. Il seroit à souhaiter qu'on les portât plus loin; j'ai peur qu'un jour le *Vésuve* ne rensévelisse ces trésors, tirés à grands frais du centre de la terre, où ce volcan les plongea." McIlwayne 1988, no 2.147; García y García 1998, no. 4751.
405 Miller 1776, 251 (Letter XXXVI, February 9, 1771): "Was there nothing beside the Cabinet of Portici and Pompeia curious or worth seeing in Italy, I think they would greatly overpay the traveller for all the inconveniences he must have suffered from bad roads, inns &c. if still more miserable than what we have experienced, and that that supposition was within the limits of possibility." For more about Miller, see Ingamells 1997, 660–661 and A. Trotta in Cantilena/Porzio 2008, 93–103.

Canart was not always present, and assistants like Filippo Castori, named by Volkmann, were deemed ignorant by many authors of the journals.[406] The presence of the assistants, however, was important, since visitors were not allowed to explore the sites on their own, let alone make sketches or notes. The simple explanation given for that rule was "It is the wish of the King!"[407]

Some authors record how the finds were displayed in the museum rooms. According to Richard, the artifacts were arranged in a sensible order.[408] He was permitted by the guide to make "une idée de la distribution." He praised Charles for not taking these treasures with him, when he became king of Spain in 1759. The king eventually sent back an ancient ring with a gemstone, which he had been wearing when he left for Spain. We now know that this ring is a fake.[409]

As we glean from testimonies, the largest class of artifacts were the ancient paintings displayed on the ground floor. Richard describes the procedure of removing the paintings from the walls of the Roman buildings. It consisted of cutting out the contours of the section to be stripped and loosening it, as cautiously as possible, by means of inserting long sharp iron rods behind the stucco. If the workmen succeeded, they mounted the fragments on a piece of slate,[410] framed them and covered them with windowpanes which could be opened to see the paintings better.[411] Sometimes the surface was treated with some cleaning fluid, a fixative, or even with wax, according to a method invented by Camuccini. The German poet Johann Heinrich Keerl recalls the same procedure for the

---

406 Volkmann 1777, 310.
407 Meyer 1792, 420: "Meine etwas voreilige Frage an den Aufseher des *Museums* nach der Ursache dieses strengen Verbotes, ward mit einem diktatorschen '*Vuole il Re!*' (So will es der *König*) beantwortet."
408 Richard 1769, 487: "les objets (…) y sont rangées avec beaucoup d'ordre, mais on n'en permet pas la vûe qu'avec de grandes précautions; car il paroît que l'on y est fort jaloux de tout ce que l'on y possède, & que l'on ne veut pas même pas souffrir que l'on en prenne des notices exactes." The brief quotation in the text is in Richard 1769, 488.
409 Richard 1769, 525. Cf. Chapter I, note 63.
410 Richard 1769, 524: "[O]n ouvre à petits coups de marteau la muraille autour du tableau que l'on veut enlever, & on fait ensorte que les quatre côtés soient, autant qu'il est possible, à ligne droite; après quoi on appuye dessus quatre morceaux de bois, contenus & resserrés avec de longues clefs de fer; cette opération faite, on scie la muraille par derriere, & on enleve le tableau que l'on garnit ensuite de tables d'une pierre mince & noire appellée *Lavagna*, que l'on unit au corps même de la muraille, sur lequel est la peinture à fresque, avec un fort mastic." For a description in almost the same wording, see Saint-Non 1782, 8, quoted in Siotto 2007, 120 note 2.
411 Volkmann 1777–1778, III, 329: "Die größeren haben Glasthüren, welche man öf[f]nen und die Gemälde genauer besehen kann." About preservation and exhibition techniques in the museum, see Moormann 1991; *Iside* 1992, 115–117; D'Alconzo 2002; Siotto 2007.

removal of precious paintings from the Temple of Ceres, as described by Varro.⁴¹² Like in previous periods in Rome, the workmen apparently tried to cut out the desired fragment, including the lower preparatory layers of the painting, leaving bare walls. In a few cases, the supporting wall itself was taken away as well, which obviously caused serious damage to the structure of the building, and caused the fragments to be very heavy. The workmen clearly thought that leaving the entire piece of wall intact would keep the painting in better condition, but the slate slabs actually provided much stronger support.⁴¹³

The importance of the paintings was their uniqueness; little of this kind was known at this time. The court, therefore, paid a lot of attention to them, but the reactions of travelers were not often encouraging. In the first accounts of the paintings, like those of Venuti and Paderni, the praise was great. They were called unique, and if not superior to contemporary works, at least as good, and were believed to match with descriptions of works by ancient painters only known from written sources. As more pieces came to light, however, and increasing numbers of travelers and scholars could study them in the museum, enthusiasm diminished. They were no masterworks by Zeuxis or Apelles, but rather ordinary house decorations, and in the case of figural scenes, they displayed an akward understanding of perspective and distorted proportions. Christian Michel, the biographer of Cochin (see Chapter I, pp. 39–40), sketched the changing appreciation of the paintings in relationship with the famous *Querelle des Anciens et des Modernes* and compared the French debate on the uniqueness of ancient

---

412 Keerl 1791, 10–11: "Man bediente sich daher der vom Varro beschriebenen Art, mit welcher man ehedem verschiedene kostbare Gemälde aus dem Tempel der Ceres heraus gebracht hatte, welcher sich im großen Cirkus zu Rom befand. Nachdem man die Mauer mit leichten Hammerschlägen rings um das Gemälde geöffnet hatte, so suchte man die vier Seiten, so viel es möglich war, in gerade Linien zu bringen, und schloß so das herausgenommene Gemälde vest zwischen einen Rahm von vier durch eiserne Klammern an einander bevestigten Hölzern; alsdann sägte man die hintere Mauer hinweg, und hob sodann das Gemälde von seiner Stelle, wobei man jedoch die Vorsorge brauchte, es mit einer Art Schiefer oder andern schwarzen dünnen Steines, den man Lavagna nennt, von hinten zu versehen, welcher mit einem gewissen starken Gummi an die Wand bevestigt wurde, auf welcher das Gemälde aufgetragen ist. Diese Art, Malereyen hinwegzunehmen, ist um so leichter, weil der Kalk, auf den man ehedem malte, so dick und vest ist, daß alle mittelmäßig große Stücke, ohne den geringsten Bruch heraus geschnitten worden sind. Man durfte sie nur mit Eisen beschlagen, und mit oben beschriebenen Steinen versehen." McIlwayne 1988, no 3.239; García y García 1998, no. 7304. The intervention by Varro is mentioned by Pliny the Elder in his *Naturales Historiae* 35.154 (*crustas parietum excisas tabulis marginatis inclusas* – "wall pieces cut out and held in framed panels"). Keerl translated Saint-Non's *Voyage pittoresque* into German (Fitzon 2004, 119 note 13).

413 See Siotto 2007, 124. The first method is called "distacco," the second one "stacco a massello."

civilization to international voices.[414] Later authors, however, offered their positive reactions to the paintings, admiring the decorations as if they were of very high quality. Moreover, as the German archaeologist Agnes Allroggen-Bedel has argued, the cut-out fragments often corresponded very well with the Rococo taste of that time.[415] Charles Burney, a British composer and music historian, was in Naples in 1770 collecting material for a history of music.[416] Upon seeing the paintings, he observed that they were the product of decorators rather than of famous artists. Therefore, like the work of contemporary house decorators, some were bad, and others were attractive.[417] At the same time Burney praised the Achilles and Chiron from the "Basilica" in Herculaneum for the exact reproduction of Achilles' lyre.

A reason for the negative judgment on these murals might be the earliest publication by Cochin and Bellicard, who had drawn from memory the most important scenes in Portici, like the paintings from the "Basilica."[418] De Brosses discussed the Theseus and the Minotaur at length; Francesco Solimena, the most venerable Neapolitan painter, had rightly observed that Theseus' arms were too long, "but ancient physiologists considered long arms as a proof of strength and

---

[414] Michel 1984, 107. He argues that the finds were not conclusive in the debate about the superiority of the Ancients. The paintings were too insignificant and the towns of Pompeii and Herculaneum too small to expect masterpieces from them. Cf. Chevallier/Chevallier 1984, 52–54.
[415] Allroggen-Bedel 2000; A. Allroggen-Bedel in Mühlenbrock/Richter 2005, 153–165. Michel 1984, 105, 115 refers to the long-lasting praise for the "Vendor of Erotes" from Stabiae, indeed a good example of Rococo-like genre painting (see Gardner Coates/Lapatin/Seydl 2012, 90–95). For some French reactions see Chevallier/Chevallier 1984, 40–60. Cf. also the debate between Caylus and Cochin on this topic, refered to previously.
[416] He observed in room 3, next to medical utensils and *phalli*, instruments like a bronze trumpet and some flutes. Scholes 1959, I, 272: "…a species of trumpet, found in Pompeii not a year ago […] There are still the remains of seven small bone or ivory pipes, which are inserted in as many of brass, all of the same length and diameter." Scholes 1959 contains C. Burney, *The Present State of Music in France and Italy; or, the journal of a Tour through these Countries, undertaken to collect Materials for a General History of Music* (London 1771, second edition 1773) and fragments of "Memoirs," which Burney intended to publish and in which his book plus other souvenirs were to be incorporated. McIlwayne 1988, no 2.159; García y García 1998, nos 2330–2334. The text is still a highly important source for the music practice in eighteenth-century Italy. For more on Burney, see De Seta 1992, 157–159; Ingamells 1997, 161–162; Melini 2007, 87–94.
[417] Scholes 1959, I, 275: "These pictures, in Fresco, or detrempe, and taken off the walls must not all be supposed of equal goodness – some one may imagine to be done by *house painters*, of no great reputation when alive – but amidst a great deal of bad and middling, are many elegant designs well executed."
[418] Cf. Michel 1984, 108, with reference to Cochin's defense in Cochin 1751, a publication that rapidly was made known in Europe. See Chapter I, pp. 39–40 for more information on this booklet.

courage."[419] Cochin himself critizised the poor perspective in the paintings and considered the finds of secondary rank, since Herculaneum, after all, was not Rome or Athens. On the other hand, the Scottish Jacobite Lumisden admired them as works possibly better than the lost paintings of Apelles.[420] Rather positive about the mural decorations was the Swedish orientalist Jacob Jonas Björnståhl, who in 1771 pegged the number of paintings in six rooms at 1,400. He compared some to Raphael, but concluded that in general, painting in ancient times was less developed than sculpture.[421]

An important aspect to keep in mind is that the travelers, at least before the start of the open-air excavations at Pompeii in 1755, never saw more than small bits and pieces out of context, chosen by the excavators only for their decorative value.[422] In general, the figural scenes were better appreciated than the partial decorative schemes as we have just seen in the example of the large figure paintings found in the "Basilica" at Herculaneum.

When the Catholic British scholar Henry Swinburne saw the paintings on the walls of Pompeii, he found them primitive, or even "Gothic," not matching his idea of Greek culture.[423] The rapidity of decay *in situ* did not help to obtain pos-

---

419 De Brosses 1991, 507–508, 570, 608: "mais les physiologistes anciens regardoient la longueur des bras comme une marque de force et de courage."

420 Lumisden 1797, 473: "And if such is the value of these pictures, what must have been the works of Apelles and the other masters of Greece, so renowned in story?" Similar praise in Richard 1769, 517–520.

421 Björnståhl 1777, 269–272: "Viele davon sind recht schön, und könnten mit Raphaels Malereyen verglichen werden. Doch scheint die Malerkunst nicht so hoch bey den Alten gestiegen zu seyn, als die Bildhauerkunst, worin man sowohl in Marmor als in Metall die unvergleichlichsten Meisterstücke hat. Doch nehme ich mich wohl in acht, eigne Urtheile über diese schöne Stücke der Kunst zu wagen, denn dazu wird eigne Kenntniß erfordert, um das auf mich anzuwenden, was der jüngere Plinius an den Sever im 3ten Buche schreibt: *De illis judico quantum ego capio, qui fortassis in omni re, in hac est, per quam exiguum sapio*." McIlwayne 1988, no 2.171; García y García 1998, nos1721–1723. The Latin quotation is a paraphrase of Pliny the Younger, *Letter* 3.6.1: *Ex hereditate quae mihi obvenit, emi proxime Corinthium signum, modicum quidem sed festivum et expressum, quantum ego sapio, qui fortasse in omni re, in hac certe perquam exiguum sapio: hoc tamen signum ego quoque intellego* ("Out of a sum of money I have inherited I have just bought a Corinthian bronze statue, only a small one, but an attractive and finished piece of work as far as I can judge – though in general maybe my judgment is limited, and very much so here" – translation B. Radice, Loeb Classical Library, Cambridge Mass. 1969, I, 181).

422 In contrast, see Goethe's essay *Von Arabesken*, in which fourth-style decorations were discussed in their complete form (Grumach 1949, 658–669; cf. Zintzen 1998, 114–121; here p. 151 and note 579).

423 Swinburne 1783, II, 102; 1790, III, 151: "It is remarkable that in the representations of porticoes and temples, the style is as barbarous as that of the Gothic ages; the columns are slender to excess, the entablatures heavy and crowded with fantastic ornaments, which I was surprised

itive opinions about the murals, since they lost their brightness and colours as soon as they were unearthed. According to Russel, they dated to just before the eruption of Vesuvius.[424]

Bronze statues, tripods (see p. 117), utensils and papyri were often highlighted. The French mathematician and geologist Charles Marie de La Condamine summarized what was visible, and accented the well-preserved metal objects as well as the silver cups, which looked like modern coffee cups.[425] He discussed some objects as if he were a modern-day Pliny according to the material from which they were made, since he viewed the entire situation professionally, having been sent on expedition by the *Académie Royale des sciences, Physique générale*. Despite this, he did not bring research tools to take away samples, since he traveled light for the "rétablissement de ma santé."

The reconstructed kitchen was also admired, as we know from the German poet Karl Philipp Moritz and other visitors. It would be reproduced in the Pompeianum of the Bavarian King Ludwig I at Aschaffenburg. The kitchen contained a portable stove, silver cups, a device to cook four eggs at a time, and cooking vessels.[426] Moritz was very critical about the decontextualisation – to use a modern

---

and shocked to find in a city where the Greek taste in arts ought to have been more religiously adhered to. I saw no landscape in which the artist has discovered any thorough knowledge of perspective." For more on Swinburne, see Ingamells 1997, 916–919; Mozzillo 1992, 201–252.

424 Russel 1750, II, 274: "Tho' it seems strange at first sight, that these paintings are so well preserved, yet the surprize will not long continue, if we consider that they could not have been long exposed to the injuries of the air. They must necessarily have been very new, when they were first buried under the ashes or the *lava* of Vesuvius…"

425 De La Condamine 1762, 367: "Après les manuscrits, ce qui m'a le plus frappé, c'est le grand nombre & la variété d'ustensiles de ménage & de petits meubles domestiques, dont plusiers ressemblent beaucoup aux nôtres; & il faut remarquer qu'il n'y a guère que ceux de métal qui aient pû se conserver si long-temps. J'ai vû entre autres choses de ce genre des tasses d'argent ciselées, avec leur soucoupe, de la forme de nos tasses à café. Mais ces détails ont déjà donné matière à beaucoup d'écrits; & les antiquités ne sont pas ici mon objet. Je me bornerai donc à quelques réflexions sur l'état de certains arts méchaniques chez les anciens, & sur leur progrès parmi nous." McIlwayne 1988, no 2.143; García y García 1998, no. 7625. Cf. *Histoire de l'Académie royale des sciences, Physique générale*, published in De La Condamine 1762, 10.

426 Moritz 1997, II, 578: "In das häusliche Leben der Alten, wird die Einbildungskraft bei dem Anblick ihres ganzen Hausrates versetzt, der sich in großer Vollständigkeit hier befindet; denn in dem einen Zimmer sieht man eine ganze antike Küche; einen tragbaren Ofen von Bronze; Tassen von Silber, die mit unseren Kaffeetassen viele Ähnlichkeit haben; Feuerzangen, Röster, einen vierfachen Löffel um vier Eier auf einmal darin zu sieden, vergoldete Gefäße, und versilbertes Küchengeschirr." McIlwayne 1988, no 2.184; García y García 1998, no. 9625. Cf. Miller 1776, 260–261. This reconstruction was a masterpiece by Paderni (cf. Chapter I, p. 31 and fig. 2). A similar installation was seen in the museum in Naples by Lady Blessington (1839, 284–285). On the Pompeianum, see Wanderer 1859; Von Roda 1988.

term – of the objects by bringing them to Portici. Out of context, they failed to conjure up the daily life of the ancient Romans.⁴²⁷

A consistent topic is that of paintings and objects with a sexual connotation – phallic-shaped amulets, statuettes and statues of men with big penises, scenes of love-making – which were on show either in the Portici Museum or *in situ*. All objects were categorized, so that lamps were put together as were the amulets, pots and pans, etc. Like those of the contemporary Neapolitans, the amulets served to ward off evil and, according to some travelers, to enhance a woman's fertility.⁴²⁸ Volkmann was shocked by all such "pornographic" items, and upon seeing the showcases with the statuettes of Priapus in the second room, explained their multitude as a consequence of the indecency of the modern people of Campania. Despite the vast number of artifacts on display, there were still those that were only visible with a special permit from the King.⁴²⁹ The lamps with erotic scenes brought Sain-Non to the same conclusion: the old inhabitants of Herculaneum were entirely depraved of good manners and only venerated Venus.⁴³⁰ Less prudish was Jakob Georg Christian Adler, a Lutheran theologian and future professor of eastern languages from Schleswig-Holstein, who early in 1781 stood in front of the same case in room 2, and singled out a bronze statuette in which Priapus is making obscene gestures which invite women to have intercourse with him (and which are still observable today in the streets of Naples).⁴³¹

---

427 Moritz 1997, 577: "Schade, daß diese herrliche Denkmäler des Altertums, wodurch man gleichsam ein paartausend Jahre älter, und in die vergangenen Zeiten zurückgestellt wird, nicht in den Gebäuden, wo man sie fand, an Ort und Stelle bleiben konnten, wo sie auf dem eigentlichen Fleck ihrer Bestimmung uns ganz in das häusliche Leben der Vorwelt würden hingezaubert haben." For more about Moritz, and complaints expressed by other travelers, see Blix 2009, 60–62.
428 E.g. Seigneux de Correvon 1770, I, 213: They give "espérance de devenir fécondes."
429 Volkmann 1777–1778, 316: "Da die Ausschweifungen zu Capua, Neapel, und an dieser ganzen Küste aufs Höchste getrieben wurden, so darf man sich nicht wundern, daß so viele unzüchtige Vorstellungen im Herculanum ausgegraben wurden. Viele derselben, welche die ärgste Laster vorstellen, sind nicht einmal öffentlich aufgestellet, und werden nicht ohne besondere königliche Erlaubnis gezeigt." On the Priapi: Volkmann 1777–1778, 322.
430 Saint-Non 1782, 35: "Un grand nombre de ces Lampes, par leur forme, ainsi que par les figures obscènes dont elles étoient ornées, paroissent avoir été consacrées au culte de Vénus. On ne peut douter que ce culte ne fût très en honneur dans toutes les villes de la *Campanie*, & spécialement à *Herculanum*. Pour s'en convaincre, on n'a qu'à jetter les yeux sur une suite de *Phallums*, en bronze ou en argent, que le Roi de Naples a fait graver à la fin du sixième Volume du Recueil de ces Antiquités d'Herculanum, & on verra jusqu'à quel point les Habitans de cette ancienne ville avoient porté la dépravation de l'esprit & des moeurs."
431 Adler 1783, 263: "Unter diesen ist eine kleine einen Finger lange Figur von Erz, das Kleinod dieser ganzen Samlung [sic], ein Priap in völliger Menschengestalt, so wohl gestaltet und mit solchem Fleiß bearbeitet, daß man alle Muskeln des kleinen Körpers entdeckt. Er hält die rechte

A famous obscene object was the bronze tripod supported by ithyphallic satyrs, found in the *Praedia* of Julia Felix at Pompeii.[432] Burney, the musicologist, reached the same conclusion as Volkmann and Saint-Non, the author of the *Voyage Pittoresque*:[433]

> One of the Tripods is of most beautiful sculpture in Bronze, supported by three satyrs – each holds out his right hand quite open, and has a droll, laughing countenance and each has only one ear, one leg, one arm, and one foot – but they are amazingly well carved or moulded. These were chiefly found in Herculaneum, which, as well as Capua and Baia, was frequented by the most licentious and voluptuous among the Romans, and Venus was in a particular manner honoured and worshipped at Herculaneum.

The *akme* of visitor-tittilating perversity was a marble statue from the Villa of the Papyri in Herculaneum of a she-goat and Pan making love, clearly enjoying themselves and smiling at each other (fig. 4). Not displayed in the museum, but in Canart's "private" house next door, one needed special permission to see this object of pleasure that once again proved Campania's sexual depravation.[434] Johann Heinrich Bartels, the future Mayor of Hamburg spent many words on it and concluded that the statue was of little artistic value.[435] In contrast, the phi-

---

Hand an den Kopf, und den vierten Finger an die Bakke, ein pantomimisches Zeichen, das noch zuweilen von den Italienern gebraucht wird, und bedeutet, *Capisco*, ich verstehe es schon! ich verstehe schon, was ihr guten Frauen von mir verlangt! Mit der Linken macht er die Figur, die die Italiener eine Feige, *fica*, nennen, (womit das *pudendum muliebre* bezeichnet wird,) oder hält den Daum zwischen den beiden nächsten Fingern, so, daß seine Spizze über denselben etwas hervorragt." Winckelmann 1762, 32; 1997a, 92 saw it as a figure equal to Michelangelo's sculpture. Illustration in Winckelmann 1997b, pl. 43.
432 According to *PAH* I, 21–22 (June 15, 1755), it was found in a tomb, but in reality was found in the *Praedia* of Julia Felix, as has been reconstructed by Christopher Parslow (in Mattusch 2013, 47–72; on the tripod esp. 56–57, 59–60, figs 7 and 12). Also in the *Epitome* of Aloys Riau (*PAH* I, Pars Secunda, 136): "Pregevole tripode con Satiri osceni, rinvenuto nel suddetto sacello." See also Hamilton 1777, 168, plate XII: "In a little room which you enter by the door D, was found the famous and beautiful Tripod of bronze supported by Priapi, Fauns, which now stands on a table in the first room of the Museum at Portici." Winckelmann 1762, 48–49; 1997a, 100 gives Herculaneum. Cf. Chapter I, p. 31. For more about this tripod, see García y García/Jacobelli 2001, 223 (after Barré 1872, 222–223, pl. 57, who wrongly thinks that there are two different tripods and suggests that they would be nice coffee tables if stripped of the *phalli*).
433 Scholes 1959, I, 272. It was depicted, without the *phalli*, on Le Gynécée by Jean-Léon Gêrome (Betzer 2010, 475, pl. 10) for whom the source might have been Saint-Non (see Betzer's note 35).
434 Bartels 1791, 98 mentions "Cannert." McIlwayne 1988, no 2.189; Garcia y Garcia 1998, no. 1321. See Chapter I, p. 22.
435 Bartels 1791, 98: "Daß man in dem Vaterlande der Priapen – denn das war Pompeji, wie die vielen Vorstellungen derselben zeigen, – auf eine solche Idee kommen konnte, nimmt mich nicht Wunder; aber wahr bleibt es immer, die Polissonnerie ist zu groß, und wenn es Scherz sein sollte,

Fig. 4: Pan mating a goat, now in Naples, Museo Nazionale, inv. 27709. This statue was kept apart from the other objects in the Herculanense Museum in Portici and later on in Naples, where it still makes up part of the Gabinetto Segreto. The carefully executed sculpture once adorned a garden in the Villa of the Papyri.

losopher Diderot liked it, but knew it from a plate; he never saw the statue in person.[436]

---

der Scherz zu plump, als daß man mit Vergnügen dabei verweilen könnte. Im Ernste scheint mir das ganze Stük [sic] es nicht zu verdienen, daß man so viel Wesen daraus macht, als geschehet."
436 Diderot 1970, 227: *Salon de 1767* [also in Diderot 1969, XXVI, with slight differences; Diderot 1963, 198–199]: "Et si ces pensées qui ne sont pas tout à fait ridicules, s'élèvent, je ne dis pas dans un bigot, mais dans un homme de bien; et dans un homme de bien, je ne dis pas religieux, mais esprit fort, mais athée, âgé, sur le point de descendre au tombeau, que deviennent le beau tableau, la belle statue, ce groupe du *Satyre qui jouit d'une chèvre*, ce petit *Priape* qu'on a tiré des ruines d'Herculanum, ces deux morceaux les plus précieux que l'Antiquité nous ait transmis, au jugement du baron de Gleichen et de l'abbé Galiani, qui s'y connaissent. Voilà donc en un

The group plays a prominent role in Marquis De Sade's 1797 novel *Histoire de Juliette*. The narrator recounts how Juliette, the protagonist, is guided through the collection of Portici by King Ferdinand in person, and is aware of the eroticizing power of this and other works of art that she sees with her friends in the Portici museum.[437] After observing how the lovemaking figures in the wall paintings are either very flexible or have a great imagination, Juliette finally sees Pan and the goat, which she thinks is surely the most beautiful and perfect piece. During their vivid conversation, the King tells her that this sex act is common in his country, and adds that he has personally and happily engaged in it many times. Juliette lets it be known that her friend and travel companion Clairwil has had the same experience. Moreover, the King continues, big dogs also know how to please women, including Queen Charlotte [Maria Carolina]. Juliette agrees and makes a political, anti-Austrian remark: if Austrians would only make love in this way, to dogs, there would not be so many of them.[438]

---

instant, le fruit des veilles du talent le plus rare brisé, mis en pièces." Diderot makes this observation in a discussion of a half-nude girl in "Le Coucher de la mariée" by Pierre-Antoine Baudouin, now in the Museum of Arts at Ottawa, and of the display of erotic art in the public atmosphere (Diderot 1970, 225–228; for engraving see Diderot 1963, pl. 42). Baudouin did no good job according to Diderot, being a master "d'un petit goût." Redford 2008, 11, fig. 5.4 shows a similar sculpture of a Pan and a goat. The Priapus is that of *Antichità d'Ercolano* II, 377. Diderot's enthusiasm contrasts with the disgust of Fougeroux de Bondaroy (1770, 75–76), who, despite writing down many words, never gives a real description of it (see Chapter I, p. 31). While in Portici, Winckelmann got no permission to see it (Winckelmann 1762, 34; 1997a, 89).

437 Rather dryly Juliette recalls fourteen rooms with objects, another section with paintings, and the house of Canart with the group of Pan mating the goat (Sade 1998, 1068). Sade personally met the king and described his way of living (Sade 2008, 33–34). He would even have been asked to stay at the king's court (C. Thomas in Sade 2008, 22).

438 Sade 1998, 1068–1069 (in 'Part V'): "On remarque, en général, dans toutes ces peintures, un luxe d'attitudes presque impossibles à la nature, et qui prouvent une grande souplesse dans les muscles des habitants de ces contrées, ou un grand dérèglement d'imagination je distinguai parfaitement, entre autres, un morceau superbe représentant un satyre jouissant d'une chèvre : il est impossible de rien voir de plus beau ... de mieux fini. 'Cette fantaisie est aussi agréable que l'on la trouve extraordinaire,' nous dit Ferdinand. 'Elle est, nous dit-il, encore fort en usage dans ce pays-ci; en qualité de Napolitain, j'ai voulu la connaître, et je ne vous cache pas qu'elle m'a donné le plus grand plaisir.' – 'Je le crois,' dit Clairwil; 'cette idée m'est venue mille fois dans la ville, et je n'ai jamais désiré d'être homme que pour l'éprouver.' – 'Mais une femme peut très bien se livrer à un gros chien,' dit le roi. – 'Assurément,' répondis-je, 'de manière à faire croire que je connaissais cette fantaisie.' – 'Charlotte,' poursuivit Ferdinand, 'a voulu l'essayer, et elle s'en est parfaitement trouvée...' – 'Sire,' dis-je bas à Ferdinand, avec ma franchise ordinaire, 'il serait bien à désirer que tous les princes de la maison d'Autriche n'eussent jamais foutu que des chèvres, et que les femmes de cette maison n'eussent connu que des dogues : la terre ne serait pas empestée de cette race maudite dont les peuples ne se déferont jamais que par une révolu-

Sade himself traveled through Italy in 1775–1776 and compiled a *Voyage en Italie*.[439] His fascination with the goat and the satyr goes back to his visit in the spring of 1776 to Portici, which he wrote about with some of the same sensibilities found in his novel.[440] Sade's long description of the collection at Portici[441] does not differ much from other memories, apart from this singling out the marble group from the Villa of the Papyri. He considers both ancient and modern people as slaves of debauchery. The area of Naples, he writes, is filthy and oversexed, and amounts to a rotten society, which he sharply criticizes in both his travel book and novel. The novel, therefore, is not simply displaying peculiar forms of sex, but really offers a critical view into the Kingdom and its vices. Sade's interest in sex is reflected not only in his remarks on some paintings in the museum, but also in his observations about prostitution in Naples, including local parents offering their children to tourists and the King's garden hut at Portici in which he received young girls.[442] Sade is certainly no simple "dirty mind," but a very critical viewer of Naples who reflects on both the ancient and modern situations with a sharp and well-defined spirit, which is lacking in other, more simplified reactions concerning the allegedly oversexed character of Campania's ancient inhabitants.

---

tion générale.'" Not in García y García 1998, who, at no. 11.832, gives *Daphnis and Chloe*, which I was unable to find. A partial quotation in German in Richter 2005, 93–94. For the statue of Pan and the goat, now National Museum inv. 27709, see Stähli 1999, 24–25, 389–393 cat. 12; figs 7–9 (with bibliography; the book is fundamental for a good understanding of the representation); Mattusch 2005, 155–156; Mühlenbrock/Richter 2005, 281–282; *Ercolano* 2008, 264 no 56. A crude terracotta copy in the British Museum reflects its popularity (Vout 2013, 20–21, fig. 17).

439 Sade 1973, XVI. On Sade and Naples: B. Didier in Kanceff/Rampone 1992, 351–378 [without the example cited here]; M. Delon in Sade 1998, 1367–1370; Sade 2008, with a good introduction by Chantal Thomas.

440 Sade 2008, 264–265: "Mais le morceau le plus secret et le plus singulier de toute cette collection nombreuse se conserve chez le sieur Canart, sculpteur du roi. C'est un groupe de marbre d'environ un pied et demi de hauteur dont le sujet est un satyre jouissant d'une chèvre. Il est difficile de mettre plus d'âme et d'expression que l'artiste n'en a mis tant dans tous les mouvements et les muscles du satyre, que dans ceux de la chèvre. Sa langue sur le bout de ses lèvres exprime tout le plaisir qu'elle sent, et la maniere vive dont le satyre la tient par sa petite barbe ne sert pas peu à lui donner de la chaleur. Tout est en action dans ce beau morceau, tout est en feu; la plus exacte pureté de style le caractérise. Mais on ne permet pas à tout le monde d'en juger, et la sévérité de moeurs du marquis Tanucci a obtenu du roi de n'en accorder que tres difficilement la permission." I owe this reference to my colleague Nathalie Roelens, who also pointed to the brief mention made by Barré 1872, 221–222, pl. 56.

441 Sade 2008, 243–265.

442 Sade 2008, 52, 53, 54–54 (venereal diseases, prostitution), 242 (king's cabin), 262 (bad graffiti in the museum), 263 (painting of satyrs with boy and girl).

Pompeii in the Eighteenth Century

After the government decided in 1755 to leave the excavated monuments open to visitors, travelers rapidly fixed almost all their attention on Pompeii. The general feeling about Pompeii's advantage, which was summed up by Björnståhl, was that visitors could walk around in daylight.[443] Policies governing the removal of virtually all objects, mosaics, and paintings, however, did not change. The latter left barbarous holes in the wall decorations, now more clearly visible at Pompeii than in the tunnels of Herculaneum. When he was in the Temple of Isis, Volkmann commented on his clear preference to view everything *in situ*. He argued that the paintings would have suffered less if they had been left on the walls, but we now know that by being preserved in the museum, they are in better shape, since the excavated houses were not regulated with an ideal and constant climate and were subject to robbers and unreliable tourists.[444]

There was a common cry from visitors that since the daylight excavations were so easy compared to the mining works necessary at Herculaneum, the work at Pompeii was progressing too slowly. This was blamed on the local mentality. Piozzi's remarks, for instance, betray no great respect for the hosts:[445]

> it is in the power, as a Venetian gentleman said angrily, of an English hen and chickens to scratch it open in a week, though these lazy Neapolitans will leave it not half dislodged, before a new eruption swallows all again.

It became a literary trope that the houses were small, almost like doll houses, as Goethe put it.[446] As a matter of fact, the first excavations did not bring to light

---

[443] Björnståhl 1777, 254: "Diese Stadt gefällt mir besser als Herculanum, weil sie ein größeres und angenehmeres Ansehen hat, und mehr entblößt ist; denn anstatt, daß man in das finstere Herculanum mit vielen Fackeln vor sich hinunter geht, um sich fortzuleuchten, geht man in Pompeji mit Sonnenschirmen, um sich vor der starken Sonnenhitze zu schützen."
[444] Volkmann 1777–1778, 369: "Es ist schade, daß man die anderen Malereien nicht an den Wänden gelassen, und das ganze Gebäude so zu unterhalten gesucht hat. Sie machten daselbst ein Ganzes aus, das man besser hätte beurtheilen können, und die Gemälde würden durch die Abnehmung von den Wänden und die Fortschaffung nicht so sehr gelitten haben." Similar critical notes are expressed by Pierre-Jacques-Onésyme Bergeret de Grancourt, a rich gentleman and maecenas of artists like Fragonard with whom he travelled to Italy (Bergeret 1895, 315): "Par leur ancienneté, on souhaiteroit, en voyant toutes ces maisons, qu'on eût laissé en place quelques-uns de ces ustansiles qui auroient touché et intéressé d'avantage à leur place." For more about him see the introduction of Tornézy, pp. 1–65.
[445] Piozzi 1789, II, 36–37.
[446] Goethe 1988, 198 (see p. 149). Cf. Swinburne 1783, II, 101; 1790, III, 150; Dupaty 1789, II, 189.

houses with large and spacious rooms, and because archaeologists were not yet familiar with the construction of ancient atria, with high roofs and grand surrounding areas, there was a very poor understanding of the actual shape of these houses. The contrast with a villa, like that of Diomedes along the Street of Tombs, was great indeed. William Beckford, the author of *Vathek*, writes:[447]

> On the whole, the plan and construction of this villa are extremely curious, and its situation very happily chosen. I could not, however, help feeling some regret, in not having had the good fortune to be present at the first discovery. It must have been highly interesting to see all its antient relics (the greater part of which are now removed) each in its proper place; or, at least, in the place they had possessed for so long a course of years. His Sicilian majesty has ordered a correct draught of this villa to be taken, which it is hoped, will one day be published, with a complete account of all the discoveries at Pompeii.

Beckford's travel account differs from ordinary travel books in that it switches back and forth between illusion and reality. He asserts that if people really wants to experience the past, they must give themselves alone time with ancient monuments. This makes one's encounter with the past feel like a dream that becomes a fictional vision.[448]

Some travelers described seeing treasures rise from the lapilli just as they approached a given spot. For a small tip, the workmen would surely have been willing to arrange such "discoveries," but traveler's dreams of taking home souvenirs were very rarely fulfilled. Some authors did not utter a word about these "spontaneous" finds, but in excavation reports and travelogues we find references to the visits of noblemen in relation to these kinds of discoveries (p. 76, fig. 3).[449] Emperor Joseph II of Austria, father of the Queen of Naples, was surprised to see in front of him so many found artifacts and asked if he was visiting a genuine dig rather than a trick prepared for special guests.[450] His visit on April 7, 1769 made a

---

[447] Beckford 1971, 221–222. Beckford destroyed the book almost immediately after publication, apparently because of his sharp criticism of the Netherlands (and therefore, of the English seeking a better relationship with the Dutch Republic), but there may have been other unknown reasons. Some five copies survived. This work was re-edited in a purged version as [William Beckford] *Italy; with Sketches of Spain and Portugal. By the Author of "Vathek"*, London 1834, 2 vols. McIlwayne 1988, no 2.185; García y García 1998, nos 1481–1483. See Ingamells 1997, 71–73. He met the Mozarts (see Chapter VIII, p. 360) in Sir William Hamilton's residence.
[448] See the good analysis of Beckford's book by Constanze Baum in Hales/Paul 2011, 34–47.
[449] Jacobelli 2008, 43–58 and Mary Beard in Mattusch 2013, 221–223 give accounts of some cases.
[450] *PAH* I, 229: "L'Imperatore fu sorpreso, e dubitò ancora che ad arte si fossero situate tutte quelle cose per adulare la loro fortuna; ma gli si fece conoscere da me [La Vega] per la situazione delle cose, per la qualità della terra che le conteneva, e per la relazione di quello che si era fatto, la verità." Cooley/Cooley 2004, 200–202 give an English translation of the entire passage on the

great impression, according to the lengthy description in the excavation report by the director, Francesco La Vega. His party included the King and Queen of Naples, Joseph's secretary of state Count Kaunitz, Sir William Hamilton and M. D'Ancrevil, an assistant, who together with La Vega, explained the miracles of the site.

When a prince from a Northern European nation was unable to travel to the South, he might have tried to bargain for an ancient object as compensation for his "loss." Frederick the Great did as much, in a 1753 letter to Francesco Algarotti, a connaisseur of art and author who had been in his court, in which he asked for a piece of marble from the excavations. Upon Algarotti's reply, in which he wrote that he would not go to Herculaneum at all, the king reacted with irritation, since that was the place to be![451]

Pompeii, "that paradise of emptiness," as seen from the Nineteenth Century

Nineteenth-century travel books on Italy often mention a greater speed of travel and, consequently, briefer stays, with fewer possibilites to deeply absorb impressions of the country and its monuments. This is also true for the sections about Pompeii, although the excavation remains a major destination.[452] Personal impressions are recorded more expressively than in earlier writing, and the prevailing topic tends to be the author's confrontation with the sudden death of Pompeii and Herculaneum. This is evinced from beautiful expressions like "cette momie de ville," written down by Alexandre Dumas père in his *Corricolo*.[453]

Emperor's visit. Our quotation at p. 200–201: "The Emperor was surprised, and even wondered whether all these things had been placed artificially in order to flatter their good fortune; but he came to realize the truth as I pointed out the position of the finds, the type of earth that contained them, and when I reported what had been done." A detailed analysis of Joseph's visit is given by Eugene Dwyer in Mattusch 2013, 253–258. See here p. 22.
451 Preuß 1846–1856, XVII, 101: "Vous n'allez donc point à Herculanum? J'en suis faché; c'est le phénomène de notre siècle; et si de si fortes entraves ne me retenaient ici, je ferais cent lieues pour voir une ville antique ressuscitée de dessous les cendres du Vésuve." I owe this reference to Ignace Bossuyt. In Algarotti's *Oeuvres* of 1772 I could not find anything referring to this peculiar question.
452 Mullen/Munson 2009, 83–101 (Italy), 99–101 (Pompeii); Kovacz 2013 (Pompeii). Mary Beard (in Mattusch 2013, 205–2281) gives an excellent account of travelers' experiences, in which she stresses the disappointment caused by the ruined state of the excavations. The quotation in the title is from James 2006, 231, quoted more extensively below, pp. 135–136.
453 Dumas 1842; 2001, chapter 26. Also in Aziza 1992, 440. Dumas might have taken it from a poem by Victor Hugo published in *Les orientales* of 1829, namely "Lui" (no. XL, section III, strofe 4, lines 94–96; many editions): "Qu'il éveille passant cette cité momie, / Pompéi, corps gisant d'une

Another frequently used label, "city of the dead" stems from the pen of Sir Walter Scott who, despite his sickness, visited the excavations on February 9, 1832.[454] These formulas illustrate the mentality many visitors had by this time. Arriving in a town that was a sepulcher for the victims of a great catastrophe, they were able to peer into the private lives of these people, which had so abruptly been interrupted by Vesuvius. During the first decades, this impression corresponded with the Romantic way of experiencing landscapes and towns. Later on, the increasing number of technical innovations and industralisation invited reflection on ancient society compared to the modern world. The importance of the excavation as a source for the knowledge of ancient society was no longer as urgent as it had been in the eighteenth century. As a result, Pompeii became a tourist attraction one went to experience rather than a monument of educating value.

The increasing number of guide books and informative flyers enabled visitors to prepare themselves at home and tour the site independently.[455] They no longer relied exclusively on the local ciceroni, although despite the new books, the ciceroni's jobs were by no means near extinction! Neither did visitors any longer need to pen down interesting facts, since they were recorded in books.[456] The travelogues contain more personal experiences and concentrate on the feelings of the authors themselves. The German traveler Carl Friedrich Benkovich gives an idea of the rather desolate state of the excavations after his visit on December 4, 1802: with little work underway, local people were living in excavated houses

---

ville endormie, / Saisie un jour par le volcan [...]" ("That he wakes up when he passes by this mummy town, Pompeii, the lying corpse of a sleeping town / one day taken by the volcano"). See Costa 1996, 104–106. Not in García y García 1998. Goethe has "mumisierte Stadt", here p. 149, note 572.

454 On Scott at Pompeii, see Gell 1957. Gell (1957, 8) describes how Scott had to be carried in a chair: "He thus was enabled to pass through the city without more fatigue, and I was sometimes enabled to call his attention to such objects as were the most worthy of remark. To these observations, however, he seemed generally nearly insensible, viewing the whole and not the parts, with the eye not of an antiquary but a poet, and exclaiming frequently 'The City of the Dead,' without any other remark. An excavation had been ordered for him, but it produced nothing more than a few bells, hinges and other objects of brass which are found every day. Sir Walter seemed to view, however, the splendid mosaic representing a combat of the Greeks and the Persians with more interest, and seated upon a table whence he could look upon it, he remained some time to examine it. We dined at a large table spread in the Forum, and Sir Walter seemed cheerful and pleased. In the evening he was a little tired, but felt no bad effects from his excursion to 'the City of the Dead.'" The mosaic is that of Alexander and Darius in the House of the Faun (see Chapter I, p. 51 and p. 155 on Goethe and this mosaic).

455 E.g. Bonucci 1827, 1828; Clarke 1832, 1847 (Garcia y Garcia 1998, nos 3056–3060); D'Aloë 1857 (and older eds); Donaldson 1827. Here Chapter I, pp. 55–57.

456 See Moormann 2003a. On written guides Mullen/Munson 2009, chapter 4.

and earned money by selling wine and food to tourists. Benkovich reports seeing a veteran being shaved and two women picking fleas from each other's heads.[457] He finishes his recollection of Pompeii with a description of a dinner party in the ancient town.[458] Dinner parties like these had already become a recurring theme in eighteenth-century travelogues.[459] The party of Mrs. Jameson, for example, had taken a bountiful lunch with them:[460]

> Where Englishmen are, there will be a good cheer if possible; and our banquet was in truth most luxurious. Besides more substantial plates, we had oysters from Lake Lucrine (or Acheron), and classically excellent they were; London bottled porter, and half a dozen different kinds of wine. Our dinner went off most gaily, but no order was kept afterwards: the purpose of our expedition seemed to be forgotten in general mirth: many witty things were said and done, and many merry ones, and not a few silly ones.

According to Lady Blessington, a great connoisseur of Italy and a central figure in British upper class circles, Gell endorsed this idea, noting that luxurious food of all nations and all seasons was served on lavish dishes. She quoted his observation that "Sight-seeing is proverbially an occupation that incites hunger; and they, above all other people, prepare for its indulgence."[461]

Tourism took its toll and spoiled the ruins by the bad behavior of travelers who graffitied their names. The Romantic German poet Johann Gottfried Seume

---

[457] Benkowitz 1806, 10: "Ich habe mitten in Pompeji einen alten Invaliden sitzen sehen, der sich von einem andern barbieren ließ; und auf der Schwelle eines antiken Hauses sah ich zwei Weiber, wovon die eine etwas auf dem Haupte der andern suchte, das man besser nicht nennt. Da diese Menschen auch betteln, sich schimpfen, schamlos sich in jeder Rücksicht betragen, so wird man durch diese unheiligen Scenen etwas in seinem Genusse und in der Illusion gestört."
[458] Benkowitz 1806, 17–18 on getting grapes: "Dies ist eine sehr angenehme Humanität, zumal da man in Pompeji in Absicht der Bewirthung nicht gut berathen ist. Denn die alten Pompejaner können nicht mehr gastfreundlich seyn; die neuen aber haben keine Anlage zu dieser Tugend, und es ist sehr gut, daß der König hier den Wirth macht." On dinner (Benkowitz 1806, 36): "Sie [the handicapped] stahlen uns die eine Hälfte davon, und die andere Hälfte verzehrten wir in dem Soldatenquartier dicht an den Saulen, welche den Haupttheil davon ausmachen, so daß ich behaupten kann, in einer antiken Stadt gegessen zu haben."
[459] See Chard 2007. The German architect Karl Friedrich Schinkel (1979, 194) describes a lunch in the Caserma dei gladiatori in September 1824: "Fremde Weine, Champagner in Eis fehlten dabei nicht. Das Frühstück reichte für den ganzen Tag aus." Cf. above Scott (note 454) and below Sedgwick (note 484).
[460] Jameson 1826, 245–246.
[461] Blessington 1839, 283. "They" are the British. Her party was composed of people from various nations. An Italian in her party found the English to be aloof. On Blessington's 1823–1826 sojourn in Naples, see Clay 1979.

cursed the tourists who scribled texts on the walls of the small houses.[462] He was a peculiar person who had come to the South from Germany on foot, without any company, and was more interested in nature than in towns and arts. His writing, therefore, hides his erudition, and marks the end of Romantic travelogues.[463]

The great novelist Stendhal was undoubtedly one of Italy's greatest admirers. His exalted love of Italy, the "Stendhal syndrome," which he incurred in Florence, would infect many travelers in the years to come.[464] His words on Pompeii are not clear as to the precise dates he visited the excavations. According to various references in his work, Stendhal seems to have been there many times.[465] His remarks often show the same formulas and reflections, so that I get the impression that a precise chronology was not very important for Stendhal, but merely recalled details fitting the story at hand. In contrast with Stendhal's editor Vittorio Del Litto, who refers only to a single visit in 1811, Leslek Slugocki has argued that the author returned in later years. Stendhal would have observed the smaller number of workmen under the Bourbons, 118, as opposed to the 500 under the French regime. His January 14, 1832 letter to Domenico Fiore mentions the Alexander mosaic in the House of the Faun, which Stendhal would have seen *in situ*. Slugocki found a graffito in the Temple of Isis that read, "M. HENRI BEYLE," and claimed that it dated to 1817.[466] His arguments are not very strong, since the existence of the graffito was never confirmed, and even if it had been there, Stendhal might have scribbled it on the wall on another date. He might have even made his "observations" about the number of workmen and about the Alexander mosaic using only written sources. All these doubts lead me to the

---

462 Seume 1879, III, 70, 70–71: "Ich lief eine Stunde in Pompeji herum und sah, was die Andern auch gesehen hatten, und lief in den ausgegrabenen Gassen und den zu Tage geförderten Häusern hin und her. Die Alten wohnten doch ziemlich enge. (...) Es ist etwas mehr als unartig, daß die alten, schönen Wände so durchaus mit Namen befleckt sind. Ich habe viele darunter gefunden, die diese kleine Eitelkeit wol nicht sollten gehabt haben." García y García nos. 12.385–12.386. The first part of this quotation also in Richter 2005, 67. Jane Waldie (1820, III, 111) copied following graffito by some British visitor: "He who writes here in hope of fame, / Discloses both his folly and his name."
463 De Seta 1992, 219–221.
464 See Del Litto/Kanceff 1986, and Mozzillo 1992, 125–158.
465 Slugocki 1977, 181 gives the following periods Stendhal was in Naples: October 5–10, 1811, February 28 – March 1, 1817, August 22 – September 23, 1827, December 31, 1831 – January 21, 1832, July 1833, April 30 – May 2, 1836, October 21 – November 9, 1839.
466 Slugocki 1977, 22 (seen in 1974). Stendhal's graffito would have been visible on the façade of the Nilometer, next to the temple itself. I have not been able to retrace it on any of my visits, but see the picture in *PPM* III (1991) 808.

conclusion that Stendhal's notes are so imprecise that it is likely he was never even there more than once.[467]

It seems likely that Stendhal's only visit, which he only recorded in three sentences, occurred on October 8, 1811.[468] In *Rome, Naples et Florence en 1817*, Stendhal defines Pompeii as the most curious thing he has seen during his travels.[469] An interesting addition, which detracts from some of his suggestions about Pompeii's uniqueness, is the distinction he makes several years later, deeming Pompeii still the most peculiar site in Italy, but only for someone who has been to Rome.[470] *Rome, Naples et Florence* of 1826 has remarks on the hermit of Vesuvius, probably a former dignitary.[471] In *Promenades*, under the entry for January 21, 1828 Stendhal discusses the famous inscription *Hic habitat felicitas* from the House of Pansa.[472] The evil eye or *jettatura*, a peculiarity of Naples that fascinated Dumas, Nerval, and Gautier, fed gossip about the director of the museum at Portici apparently possessing that vice.[473]

Stendhal's image of Italy, and therein of Pompeii, was similar to older impressions by French travelers like De Brosses, Joseph Jérôme de Lalande (an atheist like Stendhal), and Charles Pinot Duclos. According to Philippe Berthier, one of

---

467 Cf. Mozzillo 1992, 133–134. He so explains the insertion of a banality like "ce n'est pas le lieu d'en parler..." in the *Journal* of 1823 (Stendhal 1962, 535).
468 Stendhal 1981, 795.
469 Stendhal 1973, 51: "Ce que j'ai vu de plus curieux dans mon voyage, est Pompéi ; on se sent transporté dans l'antiquité ; j'y suis retourné aujourd'hui pour la septième fois." (February 26, 1817). Stendhal 1973, 56 (March 5) about the paintings at Portici: "Il y a beaucoup de simplicité noble, et rien de théâtral." He makes the same remarks under April 2, 1817 in *Rome, Naples et Florence* (1826): Stendhal 1973, 535, returning for the eleventh time. *Ibidem* on paintings (date April 5, 1817). Under the entry on March 5, 1817 he claims to have gone three times a week (Stendhal 1973, 524).
470 Stendhal 1973, 966: "Ce que nous avons vu de plus curieux en Italie, c'est Pompéi; mais sans les souvenirs de Rome, les restes encore vivants de Pompéi ne nous eussent guère touchés."
471 Stendhal 1973, 524 (March 5, 1817): "Le prétendu ermite est souvent un voleur converti ou non; bonne platitude écrite dans son livre et signée Bigot de Préameneu." Again, there is an older description of the ascent on October 10, 1810, with reference made to the same Bigot (Stendhal 1973, 1580–1581).
472 Stendhal 1973, 889: "Se figure-t-on une femme honnête habitant Pompéi, et lisant tous les jours cette inscription quand elle passe dans la rue ? La pudeur, cette mère de l'amour, est un des fruits du christianisme. Les louanges exagérées de l'état de virginité furent une des folies des premiers pamphlétaires chrétiens ; ils sentaient bien que ce qui fait la force d'un amour ou d'un culte, ce sont les sacrifices qu'il impose. Mais, par l'effet de leurs discours, une vierge chrétienne eut un genre de vie indépendant et libre ; elle put traiter de pair avec l'homme qui la sollicitait au mariage ; et l'émancipation des femmes fut accomplie."
473 Stendhal 1973, 565, on July 2, 1817, being an addendum of 1824: "Don Jo, directeur du musée de P***, et homme de mérite, a le malheur de passer pour *iettatore*." He is referring to Andrea De Jorio. See García y García 1998, 380–381 and here Chapter V, p. 293.

the editors of Stendhal's works, this leads to his descriptions as a sort of "palimpsest," in which his personal impressions were borrowed and not, in fact, novel experiences.[474]

In the English world, three early travelers had the greatest influence, since their descriptions formed the basis for British travel guides: Forsyth, Eustace, and Starke. The Scottish writer Joseph Forsyth observed the peculiar situation of war time in Portici, while the museum was almost empty and the most important objects had been transferred to Palermo. At Herculaneum, "[t]he theatre, indeed, remains in the state of a mine."[475] At Pompeii, he would have preferred to see objects *in situ*, and old houses inside the site inhabited.[476] "Here one step brought us into a state of existence two thousand years earlier than our own. I saw nothing admirable, but much that was curious …"

During his 1802–1803 stay in Italy, the Irish priest John Chetwode Eustace – whose book on Italy would become a bestseller – considered the French as "*figuranti* in the political drama, destined to occupy the attention for a time, and to disappear when the principal character shows himself upon the stage."[477] Eustace's esteem of Italy was not high. He refers to the locals' "characteristic stupidity resolved to cover [the resurrected Herculaneum] with a palace."[478] The empty museum, in which John Hayter was working on the papyri during his visit, was

---

[474] Ph. Berthier in Del Litto/Kanceff 1986, 35–58, esp. 49: "Et d'emblée, il la [Naples] découvre moins qu'il ne la reconnaît." In contrast, G. Bertrand in Kanceff 2003, 57–72, argues that Stendhal wrote independently.

[475] Forsyth 1813, 292. Museum: on papyri (pp. 292–294) and paintings (pp. 294–296) from a "town of secondary rank." Even Vesuvius (p. 299) is deluding: "*Vesuvius* is now an exhausted subject. Its fire and smoke, its glory and terrors, are vanished for the present. Ladies, as I read in the Hermit's Album, go down to the bottom of the crater. Naturalists, on comparing its latter eruptions, have pronounced the volcano to be now in its old age, and another Torre del Greco is rising on the lava of the last." McIlwayne 1988, no 2.210; García y García 1998, no. 5410. Cf. Keith Crook in Forsyth 2001, XI–LXIII; Mullen/Munson 2009, 108.

[476] Forsyth 1813, 306–313.

[477] Eustace 1817, VIII. McIlwayne 1988, no 2.209; García y García 1998, no. 5081 (many editions). The architect James Hakewill made the same trip as Eustace in order to make illustrations (sadly not of Pompeii) for his *A Picturesque Tour of Italy, from Drawings Made in 1816–1817* (London 1820). See Mullen/Munson 2009, 108. They recall how in Dickens' *Little Dorrit* (see below p. 132) this work still serves as the main source. Comparisons were made between Eustace's and Forsyth's travel books, see Keith Crook in Forsyth 2001, XI–LXIII

[478] Eustace 1817, III, 23. And he continues (p. 33–34): "More treasures, without doubt, might be extracted from this long forgotten mine of antiquity, but the almost inconceivable indifference of the Spanish court, and the indolence with which the excavations have been carried on: as well as the manner, which is more influenced by a regard of the safety of the heavy useless modern palace, than by any considerations of curiosity and interest in the ancient city, have hitherto in spite of public eagerness checked or rather suspended the undertaking."

"the most curious and most valuable [find]."[479] In contrast, Eustace gave Pompeii high praise, after criticizing visitors who believed everything guides told them.[480] He found the Villa of Diomedes a perfect building and attributed it to Arrius (see Chapter III, p. 176) and went on to suggest that if it had been better preserved, with its mobile objects still present, Pompeii would be even more meaningful:[481]

> But independent even of this advantage, and stripped as it is of almost all its moveable ornaments, *Pompeii* possesses a secret power that captivates, I had almost said, melts the soul. [...] All around is silence, not the silence of solitude and repose, but of death and devastation; the silence of a great city without one single inhabitant.

The third and most influential British author is Mariana Starke. Her 1800 book on Italy was reprinted several times, and became a guide used by visitors in the early nineteenth century. She had come as a reporter, probably imitating Mary Wollstonecraft, who had gone to Paris in 1789 to see the French Revolution. This is evinced from the title of her *Travels in Italy between the Years 1792 and 1798; containing a view of the late revolutions in that country.* It is a work full of fresh observations and useful advice for travelers. Starke writes in favor of the French and Napoleon, since Italy was now safe. People in Sorrento and its surroundings were able to meet her in the last years of her life, when she resided there.[482] In 1820, Starke's work was republished by John Murray II as the first of a successful series of travel handbooks, to be re-edited by his son John Murray III until c. 1900.[483] In various accounts people are mentioned walking around, first, with

---

[479] Eustace 1817, III, 37. Cf. chapter IX, p. 401. On Hayter, see also Drummond 1810.
[480] Regarding supposed oracles in the Temple of Isis. Eustace 1817, III, 43: "In the first place, it does not appear that oracles were ever given at *Pompeii*, as this was a privilege reserved to the ancient and more renowned temples; in the second place, oracles had ceased every where long before this temple or edicula (for it scarcely deserves the former appellation) was erected; thirdly, these entrances are too public, and the whole contrivance too gross to dupe the dullest peasant, much less the polished inhabitants of *Pompeii*." Eustace claims that Dio Cassius was mistaken as well (p. 49): "As for the circumstance of the inhabitants, of either Herculaneum or Pompeii, being surprised while in the theatre, it is so palpable an absurdity, that it is difficult to conceive how the historian above-mentioned [Dio] could relate it with so much gravity." He believes that all residents would have been able to escape.
[481] Eustace 1817, III, 47; 54, 55 (quotations). Cf. Valéry 1838, 517.
[482] McIlwayne 1988, no 2.195; García y García 1998, nos 13.200–13.205. See Ingamells 1997, 890–891; Mullen/Munson 2009, 109–114.
[483] Mączak 2003; Mullen/Munson 2009, 114–122 on Starke/Murray. Starke is often quoted in this book as an exemplary description of Europe and matters of traveling (see index at p. 377). García y García 1998, no. 1761 records some Murray editions under the name of Octavian Blewitt.

Starke and, later, Murray.⁴⁸⁴ Some quotations serve as testimony to the typical Starke interest in practical information. In September 1797, in Pompeii:⁴⁸⁵

> We hired a carriage for the whole day, took a cold dinner, bread, wine, knives, forks, and glasses, and set out at seven in the morning for Pompeii, bargaining, however, with our Voiturin to stop two or three hours at Portici on our return.

A four hour visit starts at "the soldiers' barracks" and finishes at lunchtime at the Villa of Diomedes. She feels as though Pompeii is still a living town:⁴⁸⁶

> To visit it even now is absolutely to live with the ancient Romans: and when we see houses, shops, furniture, fountains, streets, carriages, and implements of husbandry, exactly similar to those of the present day, we are apt to conclude that customs and manners have undergone but little variation for the last two thousand years.

Herculaneum, an hour and a half from Naples, is less rewarding:⁴⁸⁷

> The excavations at Herculaneum are now so much filled up, that it is scarcely worth a Traveller's while to descend into them; part of the Theatre, however, may still be seen; but as a model of the whole is placed in the Museum at Portici, and as the air of Herculaneum is heavy and damp almost to be dangerous, *Persons with weak lungs should on no consideration go down.*

Starke compares modern customs with ancient ones: like the ancients, modern people in Campania have one large meal a day at three o'clock, mourners can be seen all over, and streets are as busy as in ancient times.

One gleans many practicalities about traveling *en famille* in the middle of the nineteenth century in the amusing series of Rollo's travels, as described by

---

484 E.g. Sedgwick 1841, II, 250 "And, finally, my dear C., after going over the ruined temples of Isis and Hercules, we returned to our own actual life – all that was left of it unexhausted – and, sitting down on the steps of the temple of Venus, we ate buns, and drank our Capri, and sympathised with one of our friends, who feared he should outstay his Naples' dinner and his favourite omelette soufflé, and laughed at an unhappy English pair whom we had repeatedly encountered, the man swearing it was 'all a d-d bore, these old rattle-trap places,' and his consort, with Madame Starke open in her hands, learning where she was to give one, and where two notes of admiration!" Sedgwick was in Naples in February 1840. McIlwayne 1988, no 2.336; García y García 1998, no. 12.331. George Eliot hoped to escape people with Murray's handbook, when she strolled around Pompeii on May 4, 1860 (Eliot 1977, 291). On the "Murrays" and other travel guides, see Mączak 2003.
485 Starke 1802, II, 97. Quoted from Letter XXI, dated September 1797, dedicated to the area around Vesuvius and Paestum (pp. 96–142).
486 Starke 1802, II, 107–108.
487 Starke 1802, II, 116–117. Cf. her remark on the museum quoted in Chapter I, p. 31 (Starke 1802, II, 117).

the American author of children's books Jacob Abbott. Rollo, a well-educated American boy, has learned the main principles of behavior in public and while traveling.[488] Obviously, Rollo and his party have to prepare all sorts of things to realize their trips. A set of twelve slim volumes is dedicated to Europe; it is the sequel to travels in his home country. In *Rollo in Naples*, the party arrives in Naples from Florence, and plans to see Rome as the last stop before crossing the Atlantic Ocean. Naples is clearly described, as are Herculaneum and Pompeii.[489] Herculaneum is of little interest, but they do see the theatre, guided by a man who knows no English.[490] At Pompeii, next to the entrance, there are "immense heaps of this rubbish" – a detail described in few other books.[491] A visit to the museum in Naples is an obligatory stop, and again we read a detail not recorded elsewhere: signs above the doors of the exhibition rooms explain their contents. All over the museum there are things for sale.[492]

In 1844–1845, Charles Dickens resided in Genoa with his family, having earned enough money with his latest publications to take a sabbatical. The family also traveled throughout Italy during this year. Dickens collected his experiences in the very personal and outstanding *Pictures from Italy*, which cast new light on the misery of poor people in Italy, without forgetting the bright sides of the country.[493] Dickens was restless during his stay in Italy, often moving from one town to the other, mocking other British travelers, and criticizing written guides and organised travels.

In February 1846, Dickens visited Naples and its surroundings. As can be expected from this socially conscious author who had published unforgettable pages on the slums of London, Neapolitan life stimulated him to write some very moving pages.[494] Dickens criticized the Catholic Church as one of the causes of

---

488 Abbott 1858. García y García 1998, no. 9. To illustrate the practical side of these volumes, financial expenses get long descriptions in every volume.
489 Abbott 1858, 80–85. Then they go to Vesuvius (pp. 91–116). The Hermitage now is a ruin (pp. 80–81). Their guide Philippe is "… a very intelligent-looking young man, neatly dressed, and with frank and agreeable countenance" (p. 93).
490 Abbott 1858, 116–117.
491 Abbott 1858, 166. On Pompeii, Abbott 1858, 157–173. Fiorelli had these heaps removed in the 1860s.
492 Abbott 1858, 174–187. Cf. the story about De Jorio told by Hog 1824 (here Chapter V, p. 293).
493 Dickens 1846. I use the modern Penguin Classics edition (Dickens 1998). García y García 1998, nos 4479–4486 gives many editions and translations. He records a later visit of 1853. Cf. Leppmann 1966, 209–211 (evocations in a journalist style); Kate Flint in Dickens 1998, VII–XXX. Prein (2005, 163–170) does not discuss Dickens, but gives other examples of what he calls "Zeitreisen:" travels with interest for political and social circumstances. See also Rowland 2014, 151–157.
494 Flint in Dickens 1998, XX–XXI points at the misery recorded at Fondi and Naples.

the miserable state of things in Italy. Pompeii comes to the fore when Dickens describes a new cemetery at Poggioreale as worse than "the ghostly ruins of Herculaneum and Pompeii." Apart from the Colosseum, none of the ancient sites he sees impress Dickens very much for their archaeological value, but the Vesuvian towns do move him sentimentally.[495] He feels how near the ancient inhabitants are, since the traces of their activities are tangible. He records the skeletons in the Villa of Diomedes (see Chapter III, p. 180), and buildings with "fresh traces of remote antiquity." He visits the subterranean theater of Herculaneum in what seems a "disordered dream." The objects in the museum also transmit the living past.[496] As he looks upon Vesuvius and experiences a "strange and melancholy sensation of seeing the Destroyed and the Destroyer making this quiet picture in the sun," Dickens reflects on daily life and the untimeliness of the disaster.[497] The ubiquitous culprit is Vesuvius, "the genius of the scene."[498]

The Pompeii section apparently does not show a very profound interest in archaeology,[499] but rather a fascination for this monument of the living past. Nevertheless, archaeology and geology were among Dickens's fields of interest and he made metaphorical descents into the earth, for instance, the dark layers of London.[500] In his novel *Little Dorrit* of 1855–1857, the author would profit from his experiences in Italy to describe the travels of the Dorrit family and others to the South. Mr. Dorrit sees this move as a necessary step into high society after his long stay in prison on account of his debts. This party does not go further than Rome, in contrast with the amiable couple Mr. and Mrs. Meagle. Among their souvenirs in their crowded house, Arthur Clennam sees "archaeological" objects:[501]

> There were antiquities from Central Italy, made by the best modern houses in that department of industry; bits of mummy from Egypt (and perhaps from Birmingham); model gondolas from Venice; model villages from Switzerland; morsels of tesselated pavements from Herculaneum and Pompeii, like petrified minced veal; ashes out of tombs, and lava out of Vesuvius;

---

495 Dickens 1998, 169–171. See Zimmerman 2008, 120 on Dickens and the attraction of artifacts.
496 Dickens 1998, 171. This notion is similar to that of John George Francis (1847, 133), who considered the museum as a sort of "bazar, but with wares 2000 years old." Cf. on these artifacts Zimmerman 2008, 114–115.
497 Dickens 1998, 169–170 (all quotations). He might have thought of Leopardi's *La Ginestra*'s "sterminator Vesevo" (see p. 136).
498 Dickens 1998, 171. On subsequent pages, Dickens continues with a bewildering account of his ascent of Vesuvius.
499 My impression is substantiated by that of i.a. Zimmerman 2008, 160, who cites other studies on this topic.
500 Zimmerman 2008, 143–173: "Dickens among the Ruins."
501 Dickens 1991, 192–193 (i.e. Book I, chapter XI). It is briefly mentioned in Mullen/Munson 2009, 99.

Spanish fans, Spezzian straw hats, Moorish slippers, Tuscan hair-pins, Carrara sculptures, Trastaverini scarves, Genoese velvets and filagree, Neapolitan coral, Roman cameos, Geneva jewellery, Arab lanterns, rosaries blest all round by the Pope himself, and an infinite variety of lumber.

And the list of souvenirs continues. Among these objects, the Pompeian mosaic pieces are singled out as curiosities by the strange simile made to veal, apparently chopped into small square cubes.

As we have seen with Emperor Joseph, excavations were often arranged to coincide with the visits of special guests. Pius IX was the only Pope to visit the excavations in the nineteenth century (1849), and it has been documented that he received the objects unearthed in his presence as a gift for the Vatican Museum. Stanislao D'Aloë's lengthy description of October 22, 1849 does not betray a peculiar archaeological interest of the high pontiff, who sojourned outside the Papal State in temporary exile. But, in contrast with the Meagles, he could boast about having original *pompeiana*, probably stemming from the House of Marcus Lucretius.[502]

As discussed in the Introduction to this chapter, with the opening of the railway connection to Pompeii in 1844, visiting became cheaper and easier, and did no longer call for organizing coaches and personnel. The presence of this modern means of transport, however, also evoked feelings of irony and disappointment. Why did the corpse that was Pompeii need a modern, living device like a railway, asked the popular Spanish author Pedro Antonio de Alarcón when he came to Pompeii in January 1861.[503]

Comparisons between ancient Pompeii and modern towns are rare in travel books of this period, apart from the innumerable references to the basalt streets of Naples. The French historian Taine, after his visit to Pompeii in February 1864, is one of few authors who made such a comparison. While Pompeii flourished in Roman antiquity, he argued, the people in Gaul and Germany were living like beasts. Creating towns, he thought, brought mankind out of a state of barbarism and increased civilisation.[504] Economically, the town had no industrial activities,

---

502 On this visit and an extension description of the finds, see *Pio IX* 1987.
503 De Alarcón 1943, 336: "¡La ciudad-cadáver tiene su estación de ferrocarril! ¡La ciudad enterrada durante dieciocho siglos se coloca de un solo paso a la altura de nuestra civilización! ¡Espantosa ironía!" For more on Alarcón and Italy, see Arbillaga 2005, 375–390; Romero Recio 2012, 109–115.
504 Taine 1866, 72; 1910, 57–65, in chapter "Plusieurs journées à Herculanum et Pompéi": "Au contraire, les hommes ici faisaient de leur ville leur joyau et leur écrin; l'image de leur acropole, avec ses temples blancs dans la lumière, les suivait partout; les villages de notre Gaule, la Germanie, toute la barbarie du Nord, ne leur semblaient que cloaque et désordre. A leurs yeux, qui

since there were no steam engines, and profited from the handcraft of slaves. Pompeii was, to use a modern term, a consumer city.[505] Taine asserts that life was easy and people needed little. Their houses merely served as sleeping quarters, and daily activities took place outside.[506] They relaxed in their gardens, and had simple wall paintings which functioned as background decoration, and did not ask for special attention.[507] Figural topics, Taine continues, were banal, too, depicting divine or couples in love, landscapes, or still lifes. As with statuettes, when wall paintings included people, they were often represented as beautiful nudes trained by sports and outdoor living, like modern English gentlemen and the elite of old French families. Nudity symbolised their intimate and primitive relationship with nature. Sex also had its pure natural function and was not debauchery. Taine claims that art demonstrated how to be beautiful, which, he believes, people no longer were.[508] Taine even contends that Pompeii's tombs did not exhibit sadness or a melancholic character due to the fact that the ancients believed that death was simply the final moment of one's life, and not as dire as Hamlet would experience it.[509] Taine clearly sees Pompeii as the *locus classicus* of natural life, which is radically different from modern towns.[510]

---

n'avait pas de cité n'était pas véritablement un homme, mais une démi-brute, presque une bête, bête de proie dont on ne pouvait faire qu'une bête de somme. La cité est une institution unique, le fruit d'une idée souveraine qui a régi pendant douze siècles toutes les actions de l'homme; c'est la grande invention par laquelle il est sorti de la sauvagerie primitive. (...) Pompéi est un Saint-Germain, un Fontainebleau antique; on voit l'abîme qui sépare les deux mondes." Also in Aziza 1992, 535–541.

505 Taine 1866, 74–75; 1910, 60: "C'est l'esclave qui tournait la meule; l'homme s'était appliqué au beau, non à l'utile; ne produisant guère, il ne pouvait guère consommer."

506 Taine 1866, 76; 1910, 61: "l'essentiel était la vie publique."

507 Taine 1910, 66–73 in the section "Au musée de Naples." Quote on p. 66: paintings are "effacés, non pas seulement par le temps (j'ai vu des peintures fraîches), mais de parti-pris."

508 Taine 1910, 70: "Aujourd'hui nous ne faisons des nudités que par pédanterie ou par polissonnerie; chez eux, c'était pour exprimer leur conception intime et primitive de la nature humaine. Cette glorieuse conception les suit jusque dans leur débauche. Dans les peintures des mauvais lieux, aux lupanars de Pompéi, les corps sont grands, sains, sans fadeur voluptueuse ni mollesse engageante; l'amour n'y est point une infamie des sens ni une extase de l'âme: c'est une fonction." Also quoted in Aziza 1992, 535–541.

509 Taine 1866, 80; 1910, 64–65: "La mort n'était point troublée alors par la superstition ascétique, par l'idée de l'enfer: dans la pensée des anciens, elle était un des *offices* de l'homme, un simple terme de la vie, chose grave et non hideuse, qu'on envisageait en face sans le frissonnement d'Hamlet." This positive view was also applied in descriptions of the Street of Tombs, like in that by Bergeret (1895, 316, 317): "Il faut avoüer que cette rue bien entière fait impression. [...] Si on occupait beaucoup d'ouvriers, il est facile de remuer la matière qui a englouti cette ville. Et ce sera une jouissance singulière de pouvoir un jour se promener dans toutes les rües."

510 Cf. Blix 2009, 73–74.

Pompeii rarely had occasion to be compared with other large mid-nineteenth-century excavations in the Near East. One exception was the historian (and abolitionist) Joseph Beldam, who saw both Pompeii and Niniveh in 1845–1846. Pompeii's advantage was its seeming completeness and the attraction of being "alive." For that reason he concluded:[511]

> There is a strangeness in such a spectacle that makes it quite unique. The discoveries on the banks of the Euphrates and Tigris, wonderful as they are, do not, in these respects, at all equal it.

The view of a professional journalist, traveling on the expenses of the *Daily Alta California* and *New York Tribune*, is that of Mark Twain in 1867, when he joined a party on a cruise along the coasts of the Mediterranean.[512] Pompeii was a luxurious town, with streets "cleaner a hundred times than ever Pompeiian saw them in her prime."[513] However:[514]

> I wish I knew the name of the last one that held office in Pompeii so that I could give him a blast. I speak with feeling on this subject, because I caught my foot in one of those ruts, and the sadness that came over me when I saw the first poor skeleton, with ashes and lava sticking to it, was tempered by the reflection that may be that party was the Street Commissioner.

Another American, Henry James, described in his *Italian Hours* of 1909 a visit during a late and lazy Sunday afternoon six years later, in 1873, in an entirely different mood than Twain:[515]

> The impression remains ineffaceable – it was to supersede half-a-dozen other mixed memories, the sense that had remained with me, from far back, of a pilgrimage always here beset with traps and shocks and vulgar opportunities, achieved under fatal discouragements. Even Pompeii, in fine, haunt of *all* the cockneys of creation, burned itself in the warm still eventide, as clear as glass, or as the glow of a pale topaz, and the particular cockney who roamed about a plant and at his ease, but with his feet on Roman slabs, his hands on Roman

---

511 Beldam 1851, 43. Not in García y García 1998, who gives poems published in 1823. On the work by Dickens's friend Austen Henry Layard at Niniveh, interesting in this context, see Zimmerman 2008, 108, 134 and endnotes.
512 Twain 1869 and 1984, Chapter 31.
513 Twain 1869, 328; 1984, 259. Leppmann (1966, 211–215) rightly observes that Twain's originality lies in the fresh approach of the nineteenth-century "stemmberechtigter Bürger" (p. 212), who appreciates normal street cleaning and the like. See also Rowland 2014, 158–167.
514 Twain 1869, 329; 1984, 260.
515 James 1993, 613–614. See on James and Italy i.a. Wright 1965, 198–248; W.M. Becker in Bendixen/Hamera 2009, 128–130. After James' first trip in 1869–1870, which lead him as far as Paestum, he would be a correspondent of *The Nation* between 1872 and 1874. His preferred towns were Rome and, later, Venice.

stones, his eyes on the Roman void, his consciousness really at last of some good to him, could open himself as never before to the good curious fallacy of a close communion, a direct revelation.

This impression of a small, but perfect ambiente *sui generis* is characteristic and is already present in a letter James wrote to his mother of 1869, recording his first visit:[516]

> To Pompei [sic] I have made two good visits – having the 2d time, happily my one Sunny day. You can't know Pompei, I fancy, until you've seen the sunshine leading its silent march thro' that paradise of emptiness. That Pompei should be interesting I of course expected: it's a way so many things have! But I certainly wasn't prepared for that! What "that" is, mother dear, you must come some day & see. You can't paint a perfume & you can't write the feeling of Pompei. Truly, as dr. Arnold says – "that hard Roman world," &c. "But ok, its heart – /, its heart, was sore / And it could not thrive!" And so Vesuvius came down & buried it alive, Pompei is simply the great Roman world on a reduced scale & you get there in a deeply concentrated form the emotion you feel, diffused, diluted, in Rome.

The Spanish author and philosopher Miguel de Unamuno compared his impressions with literary predecessors when he was at Pompeii in July 1889 with the guide Gennaro. He did not experience Scott's sad "City of the Dead," but found an almost living and disordered town, full of corpses and extremely obscene paintings. He describes the sun shedding its light over the decay of paganism, its melancoly resigned and arrogant together, full of light and harmony. Leopardi touched a chord with his image of the broom on Vesuvius ("retama"; cf. Leopardi's poem "La ginestra"): it consoled the grey mountain with its fine smell, being mortal and immortal simultaneously. Looking at the ruins, one feels how death is an incident of life; it is as if one hears a cicada singing about the eternity of life and the vanity of glory, when one comes to the fields next to the ruins and the mountains.[517]

---

[516] James 2006, 231, letter from December 21, 1869.
[517] De Unamuno 1951, 839, 840: "En Pompeya topa el visitador curioso por todas partes huellas de la vida desenfrenada, simbolos de su perpetua renovación, desnudeces humanas, pinturas murales de una obscenidad extrema. Se ostentaba, con todo el soberano descaro que le daba el sol, la desvergüenza de la vida en aquel ocaso del paganismo. (...) Aun así y todo, se comprende la melancolía, pero una melancolía olímpica, a la vez resignada y arrogante, llena de luz y de armonía. A aquellas ruinas corresponde un cantor como Leopardi, que contemplando a través de las mochadas columnas del templo la bipartida cúspide del Vesubio, que aún amenaza a las esparcidas ruinas, la noche secreta en que corre el fulgor de funérea lava por los vacíos teatros, por los templos deformes, por las destrozadas casas, se vuelve a la olorosa retama contenta del desierto, al que consuela con su per-

But not all famous travelers were so positive or deemed it necessary to record their feelings upon seeing Pompeii. The composer Richard Wagner, for instance, a man who loved Italy and sojourned several times in Campania, remained mute. After the first Bayreuther Festspiele of 1876, he and his family made a long trip to the South. According to his wife Cosima, a visit to the museum in Naples conveyed a noble impression of the remains of the disaster.[518] In Sorrento in 1880, trying to regain his health in the mild climate, Wagner wrote the second act of *Parsifal*, inspired by the Villa Rufolo in Ravello as the setting of Klingsor's garden. Apparently, he did not go to Pompeii with Cosima and the children. Since Cosima eternized all deeds, observations, and emotions of the "Master," she would most likely have recorded any thoughts he might have had about the excavations, but there are none, except for a remark that Pompeii might also have been Cneius.[519]

Among Wagner's visitors during his first stay in this area were Friedrich Nietzsche, his friend Paul Rée, and Malwida von Meysenbug.[520] Nietzsche and Rée stayed in Sorrento for several months. In his extensive correspondence Nietzsche noted a lot, but nothing about the excavations.[521] Meysenbug regretted that Nietzsche's visit to the excavations was superficial, as she wrote to him on May 17, 1877.[522] Although originally a classicist, Nietzsche indeed made very few references to Pompeii, and these are not always flattering. In *Die fröhliche Wissenschaft* of 1882, he includes Pompeii among the expressions of simple taste in the South.[523] A similar remark concerns the small and simple buildings the ancients

---

fume, y le recuerda cómo morirá inclinando al hado su inocente cabeza sin creerse inmortal. Contemplando las ruinas de Pompeya y frente a ellas su verdugo que lanza bocanadas de aliento de la Madre Tierra, se siente que es la muerte un accidente de la vida, como en la desolada campiña romana, junto a las ruinas que se tienden al pie de los montes sabinios, se oye cantar a la cigarra la eternidad de la vida y lo vano de la gloria." On Unamuno in Pompeii, see Romero Recio 2012, 121–122 (with part of our quotation).

518 Wagner 1976–1977, I, 1005 (October 2, 1876): "Vom Museum habe ich heute nur die antiken Statuen und Wandmalereien angesehen; ernster erhabener Eindruck, wie Unsterblichkeitsruhe über dem Krampf des Daseins." They return several times. Pompeii is visited with the whole family on October 23 and makes all happy ("heiter", Wagner 1976–1977, I, 1009).

519 Wagner 1976–1977, II, 539 (June 2, 1880): "Die Kinder in Pompeji (Richard sagt: Es kann ebensogut Cneius heißen)." He clearly hints at Gnaeus Pompeius, or Pompey, the great Roman general of the first century B.C.

520 Wagner 1976–1977, I, 1011 (October 27, 1876). Cf. Nietzsche 1988, XV, 71–72 (Chronik zu Nietzsches Leben)

521 See Nietzsche 1975–2004, II.5 (1980).

522 In Nietzsche 1975–2004, II.6 (1980) 558: "Ich musste immer schmerzlich daran denken, wie wenig Sie und Rée davon gesehen haben."

523 Nietzsche 1988, III, 432–433 (Book 2, no 77): "Das Thier mit gutem Gewissen. – Das Gemeine in Alledem, was im Süden Europa's gefällt – sei diess nun die italienische Oper (zum Beispiel

were capable of constructing.⁵²⁴ This means that in a certain way, Nietzsche subscribed to Winckelmann's idea of noble simplicity ("Erhabenes") as a quality of ancient art and culture.

Herculaneum in the Nineteenth Century

As we have seen, Starke deemed Herculaneum much less interesting than Pompeii. Indeed, the theater, hidden under the masses of volcanic material, was for a long time the only visible proof of its existence (p. 15, fig. 1). Until a more decent flight of steps was constructed in the 1860s, the climb down was uncomfortable, proviking emotions of horror and fear, since its dismal and chilling aspect really horrified visitors who took pains to get down:⁵²⁵

> What a singular contrast does its present situation offer to the original character and situation of the edifice! This gloomy, subterraneous hollow, resembles a mine, or rather a sepulchral catacomb, where is entombed the corpse of a gigantic fabric. Once dedicated to popular festivity and amusement, now it is engulfed in utter darkness and horror.

This reaction by the Scottish traveler William Rae Wilson fits into the romantic and emotional approach, almost like the atmosphere evoked in nineteenth-century gothic novels. The German writer Fanny Lewald called the town a "Riesengrab" when she was there in 1846, a dark "giant grave" not hospitable to the living people, the "children of light." The descent provoked the idea of "Todesschauer," or "grim death" itself living here. These poor people had been forgotten for generations and had vanished with their entire civilization; yet, life went on...⁵²⁶

Rossini's und Bellini's) oder der spanische Abenteuer-Roman (uns in der französischen Verkleidung des Gil Blas am besten zugänglich) – bleibt mir nicht verborgen, aber es beleidigt mich nicht, ebensowenig als die Gemeinheit, der man bei einer Wanderung durch Pompeji und im Grunde selbst beim Lesen jedes antiken Buches begegnet: woher kommt dies?"
524 Nietzsche 1988, III, 151 (in *Morgenröthe* of 1881, Drittes Buch, no 109): "*Das Griechische uns sehr fremd.* – Orientalisch oder modern, Asiatisch oder Europäisch im Verhältniss zum Griechischen ist diesem Allem die Massenhaftigkeit und der Genuss an der grossen Qualität als der Sprache des Erhabenen zu eigen, während man in Pästum, Pompeji und Athen und vor der ganzen griechischen Architektur so erstaunt darüber wird, *mit welchen kleinen Massen* die Griechen etwas Erhabenes anzusprechen wissen und auszusprechen *lieben.*"
525 Wilson 1835, 230.
526 Lewald 1847, II, 184–185: "Der Eindruck, welchen das verschüttete Theater gewährt, ist einer der entsetzlichsten, die man sich zu denken vermag. Unsere Führer gingen uns die hohe Treppe herunter mit Fackeln voraus. Es war feucht und kalt in den Gewölben, Todesschauer schienen darin zu wohnen; immerfort wähnte ich, der Angstschrei der Menschen müsse ertönen, die hier, im Theater versammelt, ihr Ende fanden, als das Unheil hereinbrach. [...] Und diese ganze

The few parts of Herculaneum excavated in the nineteenth century were not very appealing, and the small size and slow progress of the work did nothing to ameliorate such impressions.[527] For some visitors, though, Herculaneum seemed grander than Pompeii due to its bigger houses (like the House of Argus, p. 398, fig. 17), and there was, perhaps, some strife between visitors who favored Pompeii and those who favored Herculaneum.[528]

Rampant with poverty, filth, and chaos, the modern village failed to improve the negative feelings. William Dean Howells, the American consul in Venice in the 1860s, made a comparison between old and new Herculaneum:[529]

> We had the aid of all the poverty and leisure of the modern town – there was a vast deal of both, we found – in our search of the staircase by which you descend to the classic plain, and it proved a discovery involving the outlay of all the copper con about us, while the sight of the famous theatre of Herculaneum was much more expensive than it would have been had we come there in the old time to see a play of Plautus or Terence.

This rather poor opinion would only change after 1927, the year Maiuri started large-scale open-air excavations, which facilitated visits and made the town more attractive (see Chapter I, p. 85).

Stadt war untergegangen, spurlos verschwunden mit all ihrem Luxus, mit all ihrer Lebensfülle, so gänzlich verschwunden, daß kaum ein Gedanke daran zurückblieb, daß man Jahrhunderte lang ihres Daseins sich kaum noch erinnerte. Tausende von Menschen, ganze Generationen sind verschüttet, verbrannt – und die Welt hat doch bestanden und es ist dadurch gar nichts anders geworden in der Allgemeinheit." McIlwayne 1988, no 2.360; García y García 1998, no 7972.

527 Nicolai 1835, I, 268–269: "Mit unaussprechlichem Gefühl traten wir in die ausgegrabene, freiliegende Straße. Allein diese Rührung sollte nicht erhebende Begeisterung werden; die Enttäuschung griff abermals mit scharfen Krallen in unsere Brust. Wer mit den Klassikern in der Hand erzogen worden, wer die Alten aus ihren Büchern und ihren Thaten liebegewonnen, der macht sich ein glänzendes Bild von ihrer Größe. Wer aber außerdem die Trümmer des Koliseums gesehen, der wähnt, eine aufgegrabene Stadt des Alterthums müsse überall den Stempel der Größe an sich tragen, oder doch überall einen vorgerückten Culturzustand seiner Bewohner bekunden! Was sahen wir dagegen? Eine mit Lava gepflasterte, an der Seite mit schmalen Trottoirs versehene Straße, so eng, daß wir nicht begreifen, wie sich hier zwei Wagen ausweichen konnten, und etwa zwanzig einstöckige, dach- und fensterlose Häuser von Backsteinen, deren Wände und Fußböden vollkommen erhalten sind, so klein und unbedeutend, daß man sie eher für Wohnungen der Liliputaner, als für die der Alten halten würde!" Other examples of disappointment in Lemercier 1835, II, 214; Wilson 1835, 232; Lewald 1847, II, 188; De Alarcón 1943 [on 1861], 353–355; Erskine 1894, 282. See also examples collected by Blix 2009, 60–62.

528 Howells 1988, 73: Even the local guards working in Herculaneum felt that "their" site was superior to Pompeii. For an illustration of the House of Argus, see Breton 1855, plate in face of p. 345, here p. 398, fig. 17.

529 Howells 1988, 71. Significant heading: "A Half-Hour at Herculaneum." Vance 1989, I–II, often refers to him (see his indexes).

Sex, Debauchery, and Superstition

In travel books and fiction, a relatively small number of monuments (out of hundreds) were continually highlighted. To the old favorites discovered in the eighteenth century, like the Villa of Diomedes and the Temple of Isis, other buildings were gradually added, namely the theaters, the amphitheater, the forum and its temples, the baths, and many residences. Newly excavated houses, with their floors and walls in all of their original splendor, were the most demanded. The chronology of the excavation, therefore, can be followed by looking at the houses and objects referred to in travel books and fiction. The names of these houses are often fanciful in both fiction books and scientific literature.[530] The excavators and guides attributed the houses to persons whose names were painted on the façade, which were – not illogically – interpreted as the proprietors. Other indications were found in texts on finger rings, potsherds or graffiti inside the houses. In the twentieth century, the local archaeologist Matteo Della Corte was prolific in inventing fake names and false attributions with his *Case ed abitanti di Pompei*.[531]

In 1770, on one of the first excavated exterior walls – namely on the western side of the street leading into the town's center from the Herculaneum Gate – a door post bearing a tuff-stone relief of an erect *phallus* was discovered.[532] Denon and many others assumed it to be a sign of a brothel or "Venereum." De la Roche put this hypothesis in a very chic way, by stressing the peculiar energy exhibited by the relief.[533] Jean-Marie Roland de La Platière, a French inspector of industry and future leader of the Girondins in the French Revolution, who visited Pompeii in 1776 or 1777, believed that the rough execution of the relief, which contrasted with the fine Roman style, was proof enough this was a place of debauchery.[534]

---

530 E.g. the modern name of House of the Chaste Lovers (see p. 91, note 350).
531 Della Corte 1965 (third edition). For a brief biography, see L. García y García, *Rivista di Studi Pompeiani* 20 (2009) 19–22. For his publications, see García y García 1998, nos 3965–4151. A critical assessment can be found in Mouritsen 1988, 13–27, esp. p. 23: "Della Corte is primarily interested in telling entertaining stories, and the identifications are therefore kept on a personal level and are often almost of an anecdotic nature." Similar criticism in Castrén 1975, 31–33. A good anthology of graffiti in Hunink 2014.
532 *PAH* I, 238 (May 5, 1770). See C.C. Parslow in Mattusch 2013, 59.
533 De la Roche 1783, III, 64: "On ne peut non plus se méprendre sur l'indication d'un *Lieu de debauche*, dont l'insigne sculptée en relief au-dessus de la porte, est d'une énergie singulière." On Denon, see De Seta 1992, 168–171; Mozzillo 1992, 325–436; Denon 2009; De Jong 2010, 129–133.
534 Roland 1780, II, 211: "Sur la porte d'une maison de cette rue, est une figure taillée sur pierre, qu'on croit être une enseigne, & qui tient quelque chose d'un *Priape*, d'où l'on n'a pas manqué d'inférer que c'étoit un lieu public: mais cette figure est assez mal faite, pour qu'on puisse la prendre pour toute autre chose; & il seroit bien étonnant que, dans un temps où l'art étoit à un

A German medical doctor, Hermann Friedländer, was also absolutely certain he was correct, when he recognized the apotropaic force of this *phallus*.[535] Dumas mocked the various learned interpretations, including those of the *Accademia Ercolanese*, and one which understood it as the sign of a jeweller.[536] Finally, there were also more basic interpretations like Hamilton's:[537]

> The Priapus, cut in stone, and placed in a niche on the outside wall of this house, is called here the sign of the Brothel, which they suppose to have been kept in the house; but it has more probably been placed there in the honour of the Deity so called, in the same manner as we see frequently now, against the houses of this country, a St. Francis, a St. Antony, &c. It is evident, from the very public situation, that such a representation did not in those days convey any indecent idea.

In the run of time, many more would be discovered, and this particular relief lost its special quality. Nevertheless, each new find rekindled Pompeii's "hotness." Moreover, these objects eventually fell into oblivion due to greater finds like temples.

In 1764, the first sacred building was found at Pompeii, the Temple of Isis.[538] It was easily identifiable thanks to the inscription above the main entrance (see Chapter I, p. 29), and both the objects found within and the decoration featured Egyptian style and iconography. The lengthy reports and the drawings made of the walls before the paintings were removed make it possible to reconstruct the sanctuary rather accurately. A back room contained an altar on which eggs and other food were placed as gifts for Isis. The skeletal remains were interpreted as the corpses of the Isis priests, one, at dinner in the temple at the moment Vesuvius erupted,[539] and another, fleeing with a purse of money. These holy men had no scruples about giving false oracles.[540] Hogg's guide, who had worked on a

---

aussi haut dégré de perfection, on eût si maussadement imité la nature; il n'est pas plus vraisemblable que, chez une nation polie, on ait affiché le vice aussi publiquement."
535 Friedländer 1819, II, 236: "Der Priap über einer Hausthüre dürfte indessen wohl nicht die niedriche Bedeutung haben, welche der Cynismus mancher Ausleger ihm beilegt. Man weiß, wie sehr dies Zeichen als Symbol geheimer Siegeskräfte bei den Alten verehrt ward!"
536 Dumas 2001, 414: "Apres cette maison s'élève un grand pilier dont la nature occupa fort l'académie d'Herculanum. Elle prétendit d'abord entre autre choses, que cette image était un talisman contre la jettatura, et puis elle y reconnut une enseigne de bijoutier. Comme cette opinion était la moins plausible, tout le monde s'y rallia." On *jettatura* see above p. 127 and Chapter V, p. 263.
537 Hamilton 1777, 169, plate XIII, as to letter D.
538 *Iside* 1992 gives an account of the eighteenth-century documentation.
539 E.g. Dupaty 1789, II, 280.
540 Fisk 1838, 208: "In this temple, too, you may see the secret staircase, and the passage through which, and the position to which, the priests ascended when they gave the oracles that were supposed to come from the god. Italy, it seems, commenced and has *grown old* in

British ship, told him that in this temple there had been human sacrifices, and that these priests ate human flesh, which made Hogg reflect very negatively on the morale of modern Catholic priests.[541]

The paintings, especially the large landscapes in the first court depicting Egyptian stories and decorative elements, were peculiar. Tanucci intended to leave them *in situ*, but their rapid deterioration due to bad weather made it necessary to remove them,[542] which displeased Volkmann, and led Swinburne to observe that the workers "have left disagreeable vacancies that disfigure the walls."[543] Augustin Creuzé de Lesser, a public servant under Napoleon who resigned when his travel book met no approval from the Emperor, even spoke of a profanation of the sanctuary: the deceased priests found here were bereft of their eternal rest, while the many objects brought to the museum at "insignificant" Portici.[544]

The readers of the classics applied their knowledge of Apuleius' *Golden Ass* to Pompeii and wondered whether the Temple of Isis served for the execution of secret mysteries dedicated to Isis. Some discussions took into account the found objects: Denon argued that the finds as such did not reveal anything hidden. For Starke the temple was[545]

---

holy frauds." Clarac 1813, 56, pls. 12–13 has these finds: "[...] il est probable que tous ces objets précieux ont été abandonnés par quelque prêtre d'Isis; il crut assurer sa vie en se débarassant de ses richesses qui retardoien sa fuite."

541 Hogg 1827, 83–84: "If these opinions become, as is to be desired, a little more general in this country, the lazy monks will be made useful, and, in spite of themselves, even respectable; they will be employed in scraping the roads and in cracking stones."

542 Other observations gleaned from Tanucci's letters to Charles. Tanucci XVI, 45 (August 13, 1765): drawings made; 79 (August 27, 1765): "[.] penso di farlo [the temple] rimanere incluso da una periferia di muraglia, acciò si possa conservare e vedere, tenendosi le chiavi dal custode del museo di Portici." P. 206 (October 15, 1765): "Non posso spiegare il piacere, che sabato ebbi, essendo andato a Pompei per vedere quel tempio d'Iside. È un tutto benché manchi il tetto o altro, che coprisse, e formasse la parte superiore del tempio. [...] Non fui in tempo di proibire che si trasportassero alcune pitture al museo. Penso se è possibile di farle rimettere ai luoghi loro. Il resto è per mia disposizione rimasto, perché sia veramente un tutto." An English tourist would have slept here and died! P. 279 (November 19, 1765): King Ferdinand and Hamilton have been in the temple for one hour. P. 352 (December 17, 1765): Morghen and Casanova have made drawings of all paintings, which were subsequently removed. He wrote much later still about a wall: Tanucci XVII, 216 (March 27, 1766).

543 Volkmann 1777–1778, 369; Swinburne 1783, II, 99; 1790, III, 146.

544 Creuzé de Lesser 1806, 190: "On a d'ailleurs déshonoré ce temple comme tout ce qu'on a trouvé là; on a enlevé et transporté dans l'insignifiant Portici des tables isiaques, des statues, des ustensiles nécessaires aux cérémonies ... On n'a pas même respecté les ossements des malheureux prêtres surpris, au milieu de leurs fonctions, dans ce temple qui fut jamais destiné à être couvert, et où, par conséquent, ils eurent le bonheur de périr sur-le-champ."

545 Denon 1997, 127; Starke 1802, II, 100. Waldie 1820, III, 111 has similar remarks.

especially worth notice; for, to contemplate those altars from whence so many oracles have issued, to trace the very hiding-place into which the Priests squeezed themselves when they spoke for the statue of the Goddess, nay, to discover the secret stairs by which they ascended into the *sancta sanctorum*; in short, to examine the construction of a Temple evidently built long before Pompeii was destroyed, is surely a most interesting speculation.

Starke had an opponent in Eustace, who strongly doubted the existence of an oracle at Pompeii, as it was too trivial in comparison with the great sanctuaries of Greece.[546]

The find of the Iseum stimulated the publication of both serious and ridiculous studies about the complex. Domenico Migliacci noted that the presence of roof tiles scattered around the site indicated that at least most of the complex was roofed, and that there were destructive holes made by farmers planting trees. He also claimed that the presence of Latin inscriptions proved that the people of Pompeii spoke Latin, although they were Greeks.[547] One inscription referred to the restoration of the building after the earthquake thanks to a gift by Popidius Celsinus.[548] The indication of Celsinus' age, *sexs*, provoked a hot debate about whether one should read the number as six or sixty. Migliacci fervidly defended the latter, since, he argued, no person would have been made member of the council of decurions at such a young age as six.[549] He concluded that Popidius obtained free entrance thanks to his old age. Others translated *sexs* simply and correctly as six.[550] Migliacci's booklet also contains a paper in which the further-

---

546 Eustace 1817, III, 43, quoted here, p. 129, note 480.
547 Migliacci 1765, 5: "segno evidente, che contuttochè quella fosse una città Greca, tuttavolta eras' ivi renduta comunale anche alla gente ordinaria la lingua latina." García y García 1998, no. 9229. The year A.D. 81, given in the title of his work is not explained.
548 *N. Popidius Celisinus aedem Isidis terrae motu conlapsam a fundamento p(ecunia) s(ua) restituit. Hunc decuriones ob liberalitatem cum esset annorum sexs ordini suo gratis adlegerunt (CIL X 846)*: "Numerius Popidius Celsinus rebuilt the temple of Isis, collapsed by the earthquake, from its foundations with his own money. Because of his liberality the councilors of the town made him member of the ordo although he was six years old only." On him i.a. Castrén 1975, 207–208.
549 Migliacci 1765, 21: "La difficoltà ella è, per qual motivo nella Iscrizione dicendosi, i Decurioni aver aggregato *Gratis* al loro ordine Numerio Popidio, per la sua liberalità, vi si apponga la circostanza dell'età di anni sessanta; essendo marcio sproposito sognarsi *anni sei* o *sedeci*, per esser la parola mozza e puntata, SEX. o SEXS. ricercandosi l'età d'anni 25 pel Decurionato." Similarly, in Denon, 1997, 126, whose opinion returns in Saint-Non 1782, 121 and *Encyclopédie, Supplément* 4 (1777) 502 s.v. Pompeii; De Bourke 1823, 236 (written in 1795): "Il me semble que l'inscription dit tout simplement que Popidius avait soixante ans lorsqu'il fut agrégé à cet ordre." The same in Vinci 1831, 182.
550 Martini (1779, 326) admonishes against reading the text according to our taste, and recommends reading it according to the Romans' customs. As he points out, fathers promoted often their children in order to give them good positions in the future. Popidius' father did not yet

more unspecified "A.G." defends this opinion: the boy could have been guided by his father, and the free entrance was a reward from the side of the Decurions.[551]

The Temple of Isis provoked a mixture of fantasy, horror, and realism that formed a sound basis for fiction. Many nineteenth-century novels or short stories on the last days of Pompeii had one or more Isis priests. "Archaeological" data adopted from the evidence *in situ* are the table or altar loaded with food, the staircase to a secret room, the temple building itself, and a great richness suggested by the lavish decoration. Apart from Bulwer-Lytton, whose character Arbaces had recently arrived from Egypt, most authors presumed the cult to be old.

To complete these impressions of the first hundred and fifty years, we now take a look at three travel books, each written by a different generation of the same family.

Three Generations of Goethes at Herculaneum and Pompeii

Documents from subsequent generations of the same family encompassing the developments of Italian travel and travelogue, over as long a period as hundred years covered by three generations, are extremely rare. Johann Caspar Goethe, Johann Wolfgang (von) Goethe and August von Goethe are fascinating exceptions.[552] Even apart from the paramount influence of Johann Wolfgang's travel book in the nineteenth century, the three Goethes are interesting on their own. Only Johann Wolfgang would be read – and was read – during his own lifetime, whereas the travel notes by his father Johann Caspar and his son August were not published until the twentieth century. The Goethes admired Italy and belong, in that sense, to the main stream of travelers. In contrast to the many young grand-tourists of the eighteenth century, all three Goethes were no longer young students or recent university graduates, but already more or less involved in society. On each of their respective trips, Johann Caspar was thirty, Johann Wolfgang was thirty-eight, and August was forty years old. Johann Caspar still traveled in the traditon of the German "Kavalierstour" after his studies of law, and wanted to learn as much as possible about both ancient and modern Italy. He looked at Italy's society with the mentality of a well-bred Lutheran from the north. For his son and grandson, the trips were merely escapes from the psychological stress of everyday life.

---

know the juridical implications of a freedman pushing his freeborn son. Martini's explanation was sound and proved a good understanding of the text.
551 A.G. n.y. García y García 1998, no. 9230 gives Naples 1766.
552 This section is a reworking of Moormann 2011b.

The routes chosen by the three Goethes were traditional, and covered many identical stretches of road and towns. In 1740, Johann Caspar crossed the Alps through Austria, visited Venice, then traveled to Bologna and Rome, which were the most important goals of his trip. After a detour via Rimini, Ancona and Loreto, he continued through Lazio down to Naples. On his way back, he traveled through Rome, Florence, Venice, and Milan, ending in Turin and Genoa. The first part of Johann Wolfgang's trip in 1787–1788 was identical. After Bologna he hit Florence and Assisi before reaching Rome, where he stayed for a couple of months. While in Naples, he decided to travel to Sicily, which was still rather exceptional in his days. Since he crossed the Tyrrhenian Sea by ship to reach Palermo, he did not go through Calabria. He had a second long stay in Rome, before returning to Weimar via Siena, Florence, Bologna, Milan, Como, and Constance. August started his 1830 trip in Milan, after crossing the Alps in Austria. From there, he went to Venice, Genoa, La Spezia, and Florence. From Leghorn he took a ship to Naples, and ultimately traveled by coach through the Pontine Marshes to Rome, where his death made an abrupt end to his Italian experience.

All three Goethes were continuously accompanied during their trips. Whereas Johann Caspar never alludes to his company or his servant, Johann Wolfgang often speaks about his (temporary) companions, mostly German artists living in Italy or taking a similar trip. August relied on a network of his father's acquaintances in most towns he visited, including bankers, diplomats and artists. Strikingly, all three Goethes barely came into direct contact with local people unless these men and women were providing services at hotels and restaurants, or as coach drivers and guides. As in other travelogues, the observations of the local way of living must be taken with a grain of salt, since they were made from a distance, and were hardly ever based on personal experiences.[553]

Johann Caspar's trip to Italy took eight months, but formed part of an extended tour of two years, with stays at Regensburg, Vienna, Paris and Strasbourg.[554] Italy was his favorite country, and Naples, his most beloved city. Johann Caspar wrote his text in Italian, in order to master this language as a proof of "Bildung." In this way he also demonstrated the utility of a long tour that should not be considered as a pleasure trip, since he acquired a good knowledge of Italian. He worked on the manuscript until 1764, but had no intentions of publishing it.[555] Wolfgang

---

553 See, e.g., the long letter of May 28, 1787 in Goethe's *Italienische Reise* (Goethe 1988, 332–338) on the Neapolitan mob.
554 See A. Meier in Goethe 1988, 487–499; Kopp 2010, 12–19.
555 Goethe 1932. The official title was *Viaggio per l'Italia fatto nel anno MDCCXL. ed in XLII. Lettere descritto da J. C. G.* In the following I quote from this edition and give references to the German edition (Goethe 1986).

received the text in 1794 after the death of his mother, and did not think of publishing it either. Johann Caspar was particularly attentive to inscriptions of all ages and sorts, meticulously copying and comparing them with previous collections: he added new texts, observed errors, and emended defective text versions.[556] The insertion of these data reveals a learned form of curiosity and the wish to discover novelties and the characteristics of a new country.[557] As a consequence of his Lutheran point of view, Italy and the Catholic Italians are often described negatively, remarks which belong to the most personal parts of his book. The church, according to Johann Caspar, had hardly developed after paganism, and even surpassed it in stupidity.[558] Nevertheless, Italy was valuable for the education Johann Caspar wanted, since it offered many things esteemed in this period of Enlightenment. He believed that it was only possible for a traveler to catalogue "important" things ("to be known") once he saw them with his own eye (see p. 147, note 563 for his remarks on the real existence of Herculaneum). Like other people in his era, Johann Caspar esteemed art for the skill of the artists, proper composition and realism, and not for its artistic value. Ancient Italy interested him less than the modern country, and for that reason, described antiquities only briefly, which is also true for the "barbarous" Middle Ages. Among his topics of interest were theatre, landscape and nature. Like his son would be later, he was fascinated by the problem of the genesis of the earth, and reflected upon the theories of Newton. Therefore, Vesuvius mattered and was described at length in a letter from Naples in April 1740,[559] in which it is characterized both as an object of study for scientists and as the scourge of Neapolitans.[560] He remembered the difficult ascent, and drank the local mediocre Lacryma Christi wine, but took time to observe phenomena of former recent eruptions. The view of the volcano was impressive and compensated his climbing efforts. Johann Caspar went down into the crater, saw a lot of sulfur, and contemplated volcanism, which, according to him, amounted

---

556 Goethe 1932: inscriptions collected in volume II; Goethe 1986: most inscriptions omitted.

557 A. Meier in Goethe 1986, 580, quotes the definition of "Reisen" in *Zedler's Universallexikon* (1742): "Das gemeine Absehen bey Reisen soll gemeiniglich darinnen bestehen, daß man die Welt kennen lerne, das ist, die Völcker in ihren Sitten, Gewohnheiten, Auffürung betrachtet, und alles gehöriger massen zu seinen Nutzen anwendet."

558 E.g. letters of March 2, 1740 on inquisition, March 4 on reliquaries, March 9 on citizens in the papal state, March 18 on the Madonna of Loreto, and all Rome letters. See on the Lutheran background I. Felber in *Goethe in Italien* 1986, 22–23.

559 Letter XXVII, April 10, 1740. Goethe 1932, 174–185; 1986, 194–207. Cf. Von der Thüsen 2008, 31–32.

560 Goethe 1932, 174 (1986, 195): "lo studio dei fisici, la sforza dei Napoletani e l'orrore d'ognuno che parlarne sente, massime di quelli che lo pigliano per la porta dell'ingresso, anzi per la residenza del Diavolo."

to the pushing up of volcanic material from cavities beneath the mountain. He felt sad about the dangers hidden in this mountain, which were constantly menacing this happy fertile countryside.[561]

Very brief are Johann Caspar's observations on Herculaneum, which he visited for fun. After a brief history of historical eruptions, he concluded that the actual excavations at Resina were revealing Herculaneum. Goethe had to show his travel permit and went down with difficulty. Among the first things he saw were carbonized pieces of wood and walls of buildings. Some walls were covered with rustic paintings in red and green, of "ethnic" gusto, showing gods and monsters.[562] Contemplating these remains, a visitor could dismiss the hesitation about the real existence of Herculaneum spread among people far from Naples.[563] Finds were collected in one room in the palace at Portici, where one could see them, but making notes was not allowed. Goethe doesn't single anything out, but optimistically suggests that the king would publish these finds.[564] He confesses to his imaginary correspondent in Germany that he had even taken away pieces of painted plaster, burnt wood and stones from the volcano, which would prove his descriptions. Even if one might raise doubts concerning the "impresa chimerica" carried out by the Neapolitans, the world could expect much greater results in the near future. Johann Caspar finished this letter with a description of a dinner with the King and his wife in Portici, and did not continue on the subject of Herculaneum. The simple observation of its existence apparently satisfied him.

---

[561] Goethe 1932, 181 (1986, 202): "È peccato veramente che questa fertilissima campagna sia, con tutta la vicinanza, soggetta a detto monte; o più tosto, che fortuna per una nazione, la quale, vivendo nel paradiso terrestre, perderebbe facilmente la rimembranza del celeste, se non fosse così vicina a questa bocca infernale."

[562] Goethe 1932, 182 (1986, 204–205): "[...] già adesso puonsi vedere le muraglie, pinte rusticamente di due colori, bigio e rosso, con varie figure, d'un gusto etnico e bizarro, rappresentanti Deastri e immagini orride, di forma spaventevole, come ordinariamente i libri che trattano di queste cose antiche ce le fanno vedere in istampa."

[563] Goethe 1932, 183 (1986, 205): "Sono tra le nazioni forastiere alcune che non vogliono dar fede a questa scoperta, chiamandola chimerica. Egli è vero che i dubbi intieramente spariscono, quando si vede con proprii occhi l'oggetto che li occasionava, ma, mi dica, di grazia, quante cose vi sono, che senza adocchiarle dobbiamo credere, quantunque da uomini di fede pur diligentemente sono state notate?" To see things with one's own eyes was an important aspect of positivism (Bertrand 2008, 507).

[564] Goethe 1932, 182 (1988, 204): "[...] cose di gran prezzo, le quali vengono esposte e conservate in un salone a Portici, ove ognuno può ammirarle, ma senza farne il nenomo disegno, poichè il re, ovvero il suo ministro, si riserba la gloria di farli scolpire dai più celebri maestri ed esibirli poi al pubblico, e particolarmente al mondo letterato d'ogni sorta."

Johann Wolfgang saw his Italian voyage as an escape from Weimar and the official duties he had to fulfill. In the first sentence of his book, he writes: "Early, at three o'clock I edged away from Carlsbad, since otherwise no one would have given me license."[565] At the same time, he also expresses that he would have no problem returning, if only after this therapeutic trip. Therefore, his voyage – and the book on it – was sentimental rather than rational, as his father's tour and book had been. Already famous, he traveled incognito as "Filippo Miller, Tedesco, Pittore," but he shed this alias in various circumstances. In the Neapolitan diaries he mentions that he was recognized as the author of *Die Leiden des jungen Werters*. His trip lasted eighteen months and included two long stays in Rome, the main goal of his travel. A couple of letters were published briefly after his return, but it was only in 1816–1817 that the first half of the *Italienische Reise*, including the first sojourn in Rome and the excursions to southern Italy and Sicily, was published as part two of his *Aus meinem Leben*, hence as a sequel to *Dichtung und Wahrheit*. An edition about the second stay in Rome followed in 1829.[566] The trip back from Rome to Weimar was completely left out, since the author wanted to end with a farewell to the eternal city like Ovid's, when this poet had to leave Rome to live in exile in Tomi. The entire work shows an eagerness to absorb all sorts of experiences, knowledge, skills (including drawing), and demonstrates the intention to analyze and understand the objects he describes, whether natural phenomena, works of arts, people or cityscapes. In this way the *Italienische Reise* strongly differs from all previous eighteenth-century travelogues which mostly recorded the experiences as a matter of learning and reflection with one's own eyes. It's an important part of Goethe's autobiographical works in that it marked his "emancipation" as an independent individual and his spiritual development concerning the arts and natural history.

Although Johann Wolfgang probably did not read his father's book before his departure, he had been inspired by his father's stories and by the presence at home in Frankfurt of engravings bought in Rome in 1740, showing *vedute* of

---

[565] Goethe 1988, 9: "Früh drei Uhr stahl ich mich aus Karlsbad, weil man mich sonst nicht fortgelassen hätte."

[566] Among the earliest publications of Goethe's Italian journey are *Römische Eligien* of 1795 and *Venezianische Epigramme* of 1796. On the edition of sections of the text, see H. von Einem in Goethe 1988, 574–578. There is a facsimile of the travel diary written for Charlotte von Stein, edited by K. Scheurmann and J. Golz (Frankfurt am Main 1997). Recent publications on Goethe's *Italienische Reise* include: *Goethe in Italien* 1986; Hoffmeister 1988; De Seta 1992, 205–219; Schulze 1994; Martinet 1996, 113–119; Scheurmann/Bongaerts-Schomer 1997; Von der Thüsen 1999; A. Beyer and G. Radecke in Goethe 1999, 278–283; Jacobs 2004; R. Melcher in Reinsberg/Meynersen 2012, 42–46. On the trip and its outcome, Boyle 1991, 413–530.

the eternal city.⁵⁶⁷ Much can be said about this remarkable travelogue, but in the context of this book I concentrate on Campania. Naples was visited twice: February 25 through March 29 and, after Sicily, May 17 through June 4, 1787; here his main company was the painter Johann Heinrich Wilhelm Tischbein, who had lived in Rome since 1783. Campania was considered entirely different from other Italian regions he had seen.⁵⁶⁸ When Johann Wolfgang went up Vesuvius for the first time on March 2, he saw the not yet hardened lava from an eruption of two months earlier. Other visits to the black, rough and impressive landscape followed. He tried to note the most important geological observations (March 6). On March 20, he ascended to see the beginning of a new eruption. Again the hellish landscape ("Höllengipfel") fascinated him, and he collected samples of volcanic material for his geological collection at home.⁵⁶⁹

In the passage about his first visit to Pompeii, on March 11, Johann Wolfgang observes the remarkable town, with its modest dimensions and narrow streets.⁵⁷⁰ The excavated public buildings and houses are small and show traces of plunder by the modern excavators. He compares the town's disappearance under the ashes with the covering of a mountain village by snow. On his way back to Naples, Goethe views the modern houses along the road as similar to the ancient dwellings. Even the Villa of Diomedes is a "scale model or dollhouse" more than a real building: "mehr Modell und Puppenschrank als Gebäude."⁵⁷¹ In general, he was slightly disappointed by "mummified" Pompeii.⁵⁷² He probably took rest on the

---

567 He mentions his father's influence in book I of *Dichtung und Wahrheit*. Cf. in *Goethe in Italien* 1986, 174, cat. 13–14; 218, cat. 91; Goethe 1999, 279.
568 I.a. entries of February 25 (Goethe 1988, 184: "und nun fanden wir uns wirklich in einem andern Lande.") and February 27, 1787. Cf. the ecstatic description of the last view of the Bay of Naples and Vesuvius, before departure to Sicily on July 2 (Goethe 1988, 345–347). Some German readers found Goethe's enthusiasm regarding the Italian landscape too great, and thought he preferred it to Germany (see Beebel 2002).
569 Goethe 1988, 645 (comment): Goethe wrote notes to Charlotte von Stein and made a watercolor of these volcanic activities. Specimens of objects stemming from Vesuvius in Goethe's collection are in Scheurmann/Bongaerts-Schomer 1997, II, 95. On Goethe and Vesuvius, see Von der Thüsen 2008, 96–110. The volcanic activities were not very big in Goethe's days (cf. Scarth 2009, 237–238, and his list of eighteenth-century eruptions on p. 231).
570 Goethe 1988, 198: "Pompeji setzt jedermann wegen seiner Enge und Kleinheit in Verwunderung." Boyle 1991, 461 mentions Domenico Venuti and his wife as Goethe's hosts, whereas of course Tischbein was with them, as well as Georg Hackert, a brother of the famous painter Philipp Hackert; cf. note 577.
571 Goethe 1988, 198.
572 Goethe 1988, 199: "Den wunderlichen, halb unangenehmen Eindruck dieser mumisierten Stadt wuschen wir wieder aus den Gemütern, als wir, in der Laube zunächst des Meeres in einem geringen Gasthof sitzend, ein frugales Mahl verzehrten und uns an der Himmelsbläue, an des

schola of Mamia, the half-round "Bank am Tor," where his patron Duchess Anna Amalia of Weimar would sit in 1789 to be painted by Tischbein (cf. p. 154, fig. 5).[573]

A couple of days later, Goethe defines Pompeii as a gift to mankind, due to the fact that much misery had occurred there.[574] The town pleased him, despite his earlier remarks, and together with Tischbein, he made sketches. At Herculaneum on March 18, 1787, he laments about the excavation method at this site, and expresses his wish that German miners had done the work.[575] As late as 1827, when, in a letter to Goethe, the German painter Wilhelm Zahn pointedly observed that only one eighth had been excavated, Goethe would reply that excavations needed to be done very slowly.[576]

Johann Wolfgang was well received in the museum at Portici. He related many of the numerous finds to the – in his eyes – small houses, and concluded that these objects attested to a merry life of the ancient inhabitants of Pompeii and Herculaneum. He highlighted some bronze objects (a bucket and lampstands), but did not describe the museum itself.

Goethe tells a curious story about a visit to the residence of the British ambassador in Naples, Sir William Hamilton, whose second wife Emma Hart played music while the host showed Goethe his collection of artifacts. Seeing two candelabra similar to those in Portici, Hackert urged him not to show any sign of recognition, given his questions: did Hamilton steal objects, or were they gifts of the King, as is more plausible? Or, were they nothing but modern copies?[577]

Meeres Glanz und Licht ergötzten, in Hoffnung, wenn dieses Fleckchen mit Weinlaub bedeckt sein würde, uns hier wiederzusehen und uns zusammen zu ergötzen."
573 Goethe 1988, 204 (March 13, 1787): "Das Grab einer Priesterin als Bank im Halbzirkel mit steinerner Lehne [...]. Ein herrlicher Platz, des schönen Gedenkens wert." The Duchess wrote a small travel account. The following sentences could have been conceived on this bank during her stay at Naples in 1789, although the final version dates to 1796–1797 (Hollmer 1999, 67): "Der Geist des Wanderers, welcher sich augenblicklich in ein so hohes Alterthum versetzt siehet, fühlt sich weit über seine Zeiten erhoben, und glaubt mitten unter den Schatten großer Männer des Alterthums zu wandeln." See also Cyprian Norwid using this *schola*, here Chapter VI, p. 308.
574 Goethe 1988, 204 (March 13, 1787): "Es ist viel Unheil in der Welt geschehen, aber wenig, das den Nachkommen so viel Freude gemacht hätte. Ich weiß nicht leicht etwas Interessanteres."
575 Goethe 1988, 211–212: "Jammerschade, daß die Ausgrabung nicht durch deutsche Bergleute recht planmäßig geschehen; denn gewiß ist bei einem zufällig räuberischen Nachwühlen manches edle Alterthum vergeudet worden."
576 Grumach 1949, 447 quotes a remark noted by F. von Müller on September 13, 1827 (=*Gespräche* 3, 446 in the Sophienausgabe), that finishes with "Ei nun, um verständig und klug zu werden, haben wir schon jetzt genug." On Goethe and Zahn, see Zintzen 1998, 116–117; Th. Fitzon in Hales/Paul 2011, 15–33.
577 Goethe 1988, 331 (May 27, 1787): "... zwei ganz herrliche Kandelaber von Bronze. Mit einem Wink machte ich Hackerten aufmerksam und lispelte ihm die Frage zu, ob diese nicht ganz

Johann Wolfgang's sections on Pompeii and Herculaneum differ from most travel books in that he barely describes monuments or objects, but records his feelings upon seeing them, which also occurs in other travelogues, though in a less clear way. The lack of descriptions of mural paintings and figural scenes can be explained by the transport of the paintings to the Palazzo Caramarico in 1787–1788, as was suggested by the German scholar Thorsten Fitzon. In his 1789 essay, *Von Arabesken*, Goethe describes wall systems, most of which would now be called Fourth-Style paintings: monochrome panels, adorned with figural scenes and adorned with "arabesques."[578] As late as the 1820s he would occupy himself intensively with paintings, especially thanks to his contacts with Zahn, who was copying newly excavated wall paintings for his lavish publication *Die schönsten Ornamente und merkwürdigsten Gemälde aus Pompeji, Herculanum und Stabiä*. In his review of the first part of the *Ornamente*, Goethe reversed his previous negative opinions about the Pompeian paintings.[579] Goethe's account is a mix of classicism and romanticism.[580]

The *Italienische Reise* as a whole is the result of a reworking as late as 1816–1817 and 1829. At the very day of *Parilia*, the mythical foundation of Rome, viz. April 21, in 1817, Friedrich Heinrich von der Hagen received the first volume and immediately read it in its entirety.[581] For Hans Christian Andersen, *Italienische Reise* was

---

denen in Portici ähnlich seien. Er winkte mir dagegen Stillschweigen; sie mochten sich freilich aus den pompejischen Grüften seitwärts hierher verloren haben. Wegen solcher und ähnlicher glücklicher Erwerbnisse mag der Ritter diese verborgenen Schätze nur wohl seinen vertrautesten Freunden sehen lassen." I was not able to find these candelabra, but there is a bronze tripod from Hamilton's collection in the British Museum (Jenkins/Sloan 1996, 111 cat. 3). Goethe had also been at Hamilton's during his first stay (note on March 22, 1787; Goethe 1988, 217). Hamilton 1776, 59, pl. XLV: fragment of painting from Herculaneum with volcanic material still sticking to it in Hamilton's collection. This and specimens of volcanic stone were sent to the British Museum.
578 See quotation in Grumach 1949, 674–675. Fitzon 2004, 296–297 note 259.
579 Grumach 1949, 658–669: Goethe's texts on Pompeian paintings, all from 1816 and later. On Goethe and Zahn, see Leppmann 1966, 112–116; *Goethe in Italien* 1986, 253–254. See texts on this matter collected in Grumach 1949, 447–452. Zahn would review Goethe's *Farbenlehre* in 1830.
580 Cf. Th. Fitzon in Hales/Paul 2011, 15–33.
581 Von der Hagen 1818–1819, IV, 3–4: "Ich wollte eben auf den Vatikan gehen, da ward Goethe's Italienische Reise, der erste Band, von Reinholds gebracht. Ich dachte geschwinde noch einen Blick hinein zu thun: aber ich ward bald festgebannt und von Blatt zu Blatt gezogen, und fast auf einem Fuße stehend habe ich das Buch, nicht so wohl durchgelesen, aber verschlungen: es machte mir jedoch kein Bauchgrimmen. Vorn ergötzte sich ähnliches Reiseschicksal und die Regenverfolgung: auch wir fuhren ja von Kaltwasser über Regensburg und Wasserburg nach Italien. Dann aber reizte auch der völlige Widerspruch, hauptsächlich in Verona und über Palladio, der uns ganz und gar nicht imponirte; und wie wir in Italien überhaupt immer der Heimat gedachten und noch gedenken, und nur allmälig so in diese Herrlichkeiten hinein gezogen

a source of inspiration, which is also featured in Andersen's *Improvisatoren* of 1835.[582] Many considered the work as the best introduction into the evocation and experience of the most beautiful country of the world. Goethe's quest for spiritual freedom also greatly impressed nineteenth-century readers.

This was even true for Goethe's son, August, whose life more or less took place in the shadow of his father. He was the only son of Johann Wolfgang and Christiane Vulpius to reach adulthood. August married Ottilie von Pogwisch, who bore him three children, and lived in Weimar, working in the court as *Kammerjunker*, or court dignitary. Apparently, he sought a separation from his father to improve his spirit and to learn. His trip had, like his father's, the character of a psychological liberation and personal development ("Selbstbildung").[583] In April 1830, August went to Italy in the company of his father's inseparable assistant Johann Peter Eckermann, who returned to Weimar after their visit to Genoa in July.

August's diary, letters, and some other documents have been carefully edited, so that the reader can form a good image of his tour. Everything had been collected in special files in Johann Wolfgang's archive, and the editors suggest that he might have planned to publish them.[584] After a long stay at La Spezia, handicapped by a broken arm, August sailed from Leghorn to Naples, where he arrived at the evening of September 11, 1830. Zahn took care of him, organising a place to lodge, and trips in and around Naples. The description of this stay, which lasted until October 15, is rather lengthy in comparison to those of other famous towns like Milan, Venice, and Genoa, and within this section, Pompeii takes pride of

---

wurden. Goethe hatte dagegen Heimweh nach den hesperischen Garten, und war förmlich krank an Italien: er wäre ganz gestorben, wenn er nicht hinein gekommen wäre. In dieser Leidenschaft ergriff er auch schon in Verona das nächste als das höchste, und ward ungerecht gegen die Heimat: so wie es uns vielleicht manchmal umgekehrt widerfahren ist. Wie ist ihm nun aber Italien auch erschienen! So viele sind hier, und hin und her gereiset und haben davon gemeldet, aber so hat es noch keiner angeschauet und abgespiegelt: nämlich, wie ein Italiener selber, und doch mit dem Deutschen in tiefsten Hintergrunde. Es gehören freilich auch solche Augen dazu; und ein anderer kann und soll sie nicht zur Brille gebrauchen, das gibt nur optische Täuschung. – Wie leicht ist es Goethe's 'Kennst Du das Land?' zu parodiren, wenn man es kennt! wir haben uns schon manchmal, bei zu häufig sich aufdringenden Anlässen damit ergötzt: Land und Lied parodiren sich aber schon selber." On the reception of this work, see H. von Einem in Goethe 1988, 580–581, and Beebel 2002 (esp. Tieck on landscape).

582 Cf. Mozzillo 1992, 159–194 on Andersen and Italy. See also D. Maurer in *Goethe in Italien* 1986, 154–167.

583 See A. Beyer and G. Radecke in Goethe 1999, 283–284, who quote a poem of August illustrating his wish to escape from the leash, the "Gängelbande." On August von Goethe, see also Völker 1992.

584 See A. Beyer and G. Radecke in Goethe 1999, 278–289.

place. He felt happy and relaxed in Naples,[585] and was lucky to climb an active Vesuvius and experience a (modest) eruption, a thing his father and grandfather had not witnessed.

One of August's first excursions in Naples, September 30, brought him to the museum, where he recognised many paintings from reproductions made by Zahn and Ternite in his father's home, collected in the previous years by Johann Wolfgang.[586] He liked the Hercules and Telephus from the "Basilica" at Herculaneum, as well as still lifes. The next day, August hastened[587] to arrive at Pompeii, where he was happy to stand on "classical" grounds and to see buildings and other things recognizable from prints at home. The Street of Tombs (fig. 5) made a notable impression and the tombs were worthy of attentive contemplation. He also saw the Villa of Diomedes, the forum, the theaters, and some houses (Tragic Poet, Sallustius, Meleager, which was just being excavated). All these empty monuments did not fill him with sadness, since past and present shake hands in this town.[588] After a hearty lunch, Zahn and August went to Resina to see the theater of Herculaneum, and the small part of town open to the light of day. The remainder of their day was spent on Vesuvius, where they saw a minor eruption, and from which they returned to Naples after midnight. During a second visit to the museum, August studied sculpture, vases, and utensils, and saw the cabinet of obscene objects, about which he hoped to report orally upon his return home.[589]

August returned to Pompeii in the late afternoon of September 24, 1830. With a permit from director Bonucci, he saw the progress made in the excavation of the House of Meleager, where a painting of the Judgment of Paris had just been completely uncovered. He observed how tourists' every wish could be fullfilled by tipping, and how nothing happened without. August stayed in a small inn next to the excavation, which was often used by Zahn, and visited Pompeii again the following morning, but only to "rescue" a small terracotta statuette and to have breakfast in the Building of Eumachia. He dedicated October 7–10 entirely to visiting Pompeii. Bonucci personally welcomed the son of the great Johann Wolf-

---

585 Goethe 1999, 170, 176.
586 Goethe 1999, 163: "Wie fühlte ich den Vortheil gerade in diesen Dingen so vorbereitet zu seyn und wie herrlich kommt mir zustatten, daß ich die Zahnschen und Ternitschen Copien kannte. Ich fand manches bekannte liebe Bild, so auch das Original des Köpfchens was Sie lieber Vater mir in meine Stube gegeben haben." Ternischen Copien: plates by Wilhelm Ternite in his series *Wandgemälde* (1839–1858).
587 Goethe 1999, 164: "wir aber eilten vor der Hand..."
588 Goethe 1999, 165: "Es ist wunderbar, bei mir machte alles dieses keinen traurigen Eindruk, es war mir als wenn Vergangenheit und Gegenwart sich freundlich die Hand reichten."
589 Goethe 1999, 169: "Das Cabinet der Obscönen Gegenstände wurde ebenfalls gesehen, mündl. mehr darüber."

Figur 18. Aussenansicht des herculaner Thores.

Fig. 5: Johannes Overbeck, *Pompeji in seinen Gebäuden, Alterthümern und Kunstwerken für Kunst- und Alterthumsfreunde* (second edition, 1866), fig. 18: "Aussenansicht des herculaner Thores," external view of the Herculanean Gate. Stray dogs, goats, and two people (possibly tourists) are the only living creatures apart from two tiny persons at the end of the so-called Consular Road inside the gate. On the right hand side, the *Schola* of Mamia and the Tomb of Cerrinius Restitutus are visible. The Tomb was interpreted as the guardhouse of a sentinel, whereas the *Schola* served as a resting place for many tourists.

gang Goethe, and showed him the new excavations as if he were a royal guest. On October 8, August experienced his moment of fame, when the House of the Faun was dedicated to his father under the name Casa di Goethe, with the idea of celebrating his visit of 1786.[590] The ceremony's memory lived longer than August;

---

590 Goethe 1999, 185: " Pompeji den 8October 1830 wurde angefangen an Goethes Haus die durch Asche verschüttete Pforte zu öffnen, nach einigen Stunden bemerkte man schon daß es eines der schönsten und wichtigsten zeither an das Licht geförderten Häuser seyn würde, denn man fand gleich eine Schale auswendig mit Gold belegt inwendig von Blei. Die Architektur gleich beym Eingange war ebenfals so prachtvoll as merkwürdig, denn der gewöhnliche Sims machte schon ein Coridor mit neten korinthischen Säulchen, das ganze wurde getragen von vergoldeten Sfingsen, die Wände von gewöhnlich mit brillanten bunten Farben zeugten sich." Butterworth/ Laurence 2005, 3–4 suggest that Johann Wolfgang personally attended the excavation of this

later travelers such as the Dutch public servant Johan Hendrik Beucker Andreae, who was in Pompeii in 1840–1841 referred to it.[591] The famous mosaic of Alexander and Darius, found on October 24, 1831, would not be unearthed, when August was in Naples. Even the statuette of the faun, which gave the house its current name, had not yet been discovered, and August probably only saw the section of the entrance and the beginning of the atrium. After the mosaic was uncovered, Johann Wolfgang received a drawing and a letter from Zahn; Johann Wolfgang acutely suggested the interpretation of a Battle of Alexander and Darius, in which Darius was forced to flee and to leave his soldiers without their general.[592]

August's voyage would finish with his death in Rome on October 27, 1830. August Kestner, a son of Johann Wolfgang's former friend Charlotte Buff, buried him in the Cimitero Acattolico next to the Pyramid of Cestius, and placed a stela with a tondo head by Thorvaldsen, and bearing the inscription *Goethe filius patri antevertens obiit annor. XL MDCCCXXX*.[593] In Rome, poor August even lost his own name. His death was caused by his unhealthy way of life, especially his excessive drinking, examples of which abound in his travelogue.

August does not describe, let alone interpret, the monuments he saw. His manuscripts portray a man who roamed the streets of Pompeii and felt happiness, increased by the pure beauty of the ruins, the paintings and the mosaics. He frequently mentions how at home he feels, as though he were in his father's house, while seeing familiar things. The sensation recalls Johann Wolfgang's confrontation with Rome after seeing the city in his father's engraving in Frankfurt as a young boy. August's *Ruinenfaszination* was a common form of loving antiquity in the first half of the nineteenth century.[594]

The three Goethe travel accounts are excellent examples of the different ways grandtourists made records of their voyages to Italy, the main destination on their educational excursions. The fact that they correspond to three generations of one family is, as far as I know, unique. Johann Caspar Goethe meticulously documented every building and object he saw, while comparing it with previous travel books.

---

house. Guzzo/Scarano Ussani 2011, 63 suggest Zahn as the initiator of it being named for Goethe.
591 Beucker Andreae 1856, 210.
592 See Grumach 1949, 670–672. Interpretation in a letter from March 10, 1832 to Zahn (Grumach 1949, 671): "Nun ist mein Wünsch erfüllt, und es möchte wohl keine Frage seyn, daß jenes Mosaik den Alexander als Überwinder, den Darius in dem Seinigsten überwunden und persönlich zur Flucht hingerissen vorstellt." See also Andreae 1977, 29–36 and B. Andreae in Scheurmann/Bongaerts-Schomer 1997, I, 135–138, on Goethe and this mosaic. Dumas 2001, 420–438, chapters XXXIX–XL, gives a hilarious account of various mostly nonsense interpretations of the mosaic.
593 "Preceding his father, Goethe the son died in 1830, forty years old."
594 Cf. J. Elsner in Tsingarida/Kurtz 2002, 190–206.

Since Herculaneum was new and not yet included in such guides and travelogues, his impressions of this town are more personal than those of other places. Johann Wolfgang, on the other hand, recorded his personal feelings after seeing and experiencing Italy and its beauties. He did not refrain from emotional outbursts, even when he was in Pompeii. Finally, August traveled for his personal pleasure on a sort of sabbatical leave, and put down personal notes that reflect a way of looking and thinking typical of the second quarter of the nineteenth century.

The Twentieth Century

As tourism continued to increase, Pompeii lost its position as a unique monument. Nevertheless, the less numerous recollections of Pompeii in twentieth-century travelogues are often very interesting, because the authors of these travel accounts or diaries tried to find original and personal approaches to the traditional genres.

The introduction of the automobile provoked the description of motorized trips through the rough South, which lacked good roads, roadside assistance or gas stations. The journeys described in these early twentieth-century travel accounts reinvent the voyages of the pioneers in previous centuries, as they lacked truly modern comforts (i.e. new roads) and required travelers to cope with never experienced technical (i.e. fuel) problems.[595] The interest in the ancient cities in these accounts is rather scarce, probably because the travelers sought modern experiences instead of antiquities. A few examples illustrate this new fashion.

Otto Julius Bierbaum was a well-known poet, novelist and journalist in the Germany of the late nineteenth century.[596] In 1902, during a period of illness and stress, he gladly accepted the invitation to make a long car trip and to publish articles in two Austrian journals – *Die Woche* and *Der Lokal-Anzeiger* – which would also pay all his expences. He boasted that he was the first German traveling to the South by motorcar. His writing conveys the sense that Bierbaum himself did the driving, but, like others, he had a professional chauffeur who was capable of doing repairs and changing tires. The small company also included his Italian wife Gemma. In Naples he saw the paintings from Pompeii, which he deemed not very artistic, but skillfully executed, and unfortunately important sources of

---

595 See Brilli 1991; Mullen/Munson 2009, 200–203.
596 See Wilkening 1977; von Pilar 1995, 1–50 (heavily criticizing Wilkening on p. 17). Briefly Brilli 1991, 24–28; Richter 2007, 94–95.

inspiration for modern house decorators.⁵⁹⁷ Bierbaum went to Vesuvius, but not with a party organised by Cook. Being part of such a group would have been too cheap and would have made him feel like part of a flock of sheep ("billig und herdenweise"). According to Cook's German assistant, Bierbaum's was the fourth private car on the slopes of the volcano. Thoughts of death might come up here, Bierbaum argues, but he found it better to reflect upon that topic at Pompeii, where the visitor would be more struck by the image of ancient life than by the gruesome end of the inhabitants.⁵⁹⁸

The archaeologist and art critic Dan Fellows Platt was a man of the world, who, thanks to his wealth, became a collector of Italian art. His *Through Italy with Car and Camera*, which describes a trip in Autumn 1907, contains many photographs of his car and Italian admirers.⁵⁹⁹ He presents himself as an old friend of August Mau, "the German expert, to whom all at Pompeii bow down." From the "Director" (perhaps De Petra), he received a permit to see running excavations.

Francis Miltoun was an author specialized and successful with books about trips in motorcars in Europe, Africa and Asia. He wrote about Pompeii quite traditionally:⁶⁰⁰

> Pompeii is remarkable, but it is disappointing. All that is of real interest has been removed to the Naples museum. Without its Forum and its magnificent temples and Vesuvius as a *toile de fond* Pompeii would be a dreary place indeed to any but an archaeologist. It is a waste of time to view any restored historic monument where modern house painters have refurbished the half-obliterated frescoes.

---

597 Bierbaum n.y., 392: "Die rein dekorativen Sachen: Ornamente, Frucht- und Blumengewinde, Darstellungen von Tieren u. dgl. haben den Renaissancedekorateuren zum Vorbilde gedient und leben heute noch auf den Schablonen unserer Anstreicher – soweit man das ein Weiterleben nennen darf. Sie sind in dieser uns hier vors Auge tretenden frühesten Form sehr reizend, aber man sagt sich doch: nun endlich fort damit aus unseren Häusern." Partly reproduced in Richter 2005, 77. Not in García y García 1998. Other works by Bierbaum bearing titles with cars are *Das röthliche Automobil* from 1905 (an autobiography) and *Mit der Kraft-Automobilia* from 1906. See also N. Vismara in Jacobelli 2008, 86.
598 Bierbaum n.y., 405: "Gewiß, das ist sehr schrecklich gewesen, aber es ist nur natürlich, daß uns heute das Schicksal der vor achtzehnhundert Jahren auf grausame Weise ums Leben Gekommenen weniger interessant ist, als der Einblick in antikes Leben, den wir diesem traurigen Ereignis verdanken." On Cook and Vesuvius see Richter 2007, 93.
599 Platt 1908, 467. Not in García y García 1998. Cf. Brilli 1991, 24, 32.
600 Miltoun 1909, 216–217. He also informed his readers that artists stay at the Albergo Sole, while others stay at Diomede or Suisse. García y García 1998, no. 9263. His name is followed by O.N.I., which means, according to the *Oxford Dictionary of Abbreviations* (Oxford 1998), Office of Naval Intelligence. Miltoun was the *nom de plume* of Milburg Francisco Mansfield, journalist and travel writer from the United States.

By the time cars had become commonly used to travel across Italy, authors had stopped describing the technical aspects of their trips.[601] Illustrated books became increasingly popular, also thanks to portable photo cameras and improved printing techniques. Italy took a place of pride in the growing bulk of this new genre of travel book, which were often shorter and less profound in their descriptions, concentrating instead on seducing images of the *bel paese*. Some artists added comments to their images, like the French author Camille Mauclair and the painter Joseph-Félix Bouchor. In their series of illustrated Italian towns, Pompeii was a hit, since it was a gay town, well preserved under the ashes and did not appear a battered ruin like Paestum or Agrigentum.[602]

The Italian journalist Angelo Conti suggested that one should not go to Pompeii with an archaeologist, but with a beautiful silent woman, in order to fully appreciate the city. Pompeii was a creature that ought to be conquered.[603] Visits to the House of the Gilded Cupids and the House of the Vettii brought him into contact with the past, as if he transformed into one of the old inhabitants.[604]

---

601 In Léon Daudet's 1931 novel (see Chapter V, pp. 275–276) the party travels to Naples and, driving down through modern fascist Italy, they hail Mussolini's state for its accuracy and tidiness. The "picturesque" dirt of old has given way to cleanliness, whereas the good food has remained the same (Daudet 1931, 224): "Ils avaient traversé du haut en bas l'Italie fasciste, étonnante d'ordre et de civisme, pourvue d'autodromes, d'hôtels parfaits, ayant conservé une cuisine non internationale et même régionale [...] L'incurie ancienne, dite pittoresque, avait disparu, qui faisait ressembler certaines villes célèbres, et célébrées par les poètes, à des chambres pas faites, avec le pot de chambre sur la toilette, et les draps de lit bouchonnés à la fenêtre par une servante négligente." Also quoted in Clébert 1988, 416. Politically, Daudet was known as one of the most active members of the right-wing movement Action Française, founded in 1908. He quit this movement in 1940. However, the political allusions about the Italy of the Thirties are of no consequence for the remainder of the story.

602 Mauclair/Bouchor 1928, 126, 129, 130: "L'image n'est ni tragique, ni même triste. Le soleil la baigne. Le silence lui est doux. La catastrophe dont le souvenir a traversé les âges fut bien moins affreuse et convulsive que beaucoup d'atroces dévastations humaines. Asphyxiée par la pluie de cendres brûlantes, Pompéi fut ensevelie intacte dans sa grâce. Agrigente ou Paestum sont d'immenses motifs de mélancolie: Pompéi sourit encore. [...] Mais la pathétique du sort de Pompéi consiste précisément dans le contraste entre son ingénuité de cité modeste et gaie et l'effroyable déchaînement de cendre et de flamme qui s'acharna à l'anéantir avec Herculanum. Un si grand fléau pour un si frêle objet! [...] Il y a eu bien des disastres autrément grands: il n'y en a pas eu de plus touchants."

603 Conti 1907, 263–264: "A Pompei non si deve mai andare in compagnia di archeologi. Chi vuol godere l'incanto della città unica, deve andar solo; o al più insieme con una bella donna taciturna. La presenza d'una bella creatura che inceda e si muova con nobile ritmo e dolcemente sorrida, vale a farci perdere in quello spettacolo e a identificarci con quella vita lontana, assai più di molte pagine o di molte parole di arida e inutile dottrina." García y García 1998, no. 3219.

604 Conti 1907, 266: "Si entra, la porta ci si chiude alle spalle e si rimane soli. La nostra vita non

The philosopher Walter Benjamin from Berlin also tackled the cliché of meeting ancient inhabitants at Pompeii, which will be described in greater length in Chapter VI. During a visit to the catacombs of S. Gennaro at Naples, the guide represented Pompeii as the explanatory key of all antiquities. In contrast, the guide argued, modern Neapolitans did not visit the ruins, but the Cathedral of the Madonna in modern Pompei.[605]

For the psychiatrist Carl Gustav Jung, who worked on "subconsciousness" Pompeii only was capable of feeding his impression of ancient Italy. After a visit to the excavations in 1917, he decided never to go to Rome, where, after all, he would never come face to face with ancient Romans. In his opinion, Pompeii was a better alternative: here people encountered the daily life of the old Romans more intensively than in the capital of the Roman Empire.[606]

Between 1930 and 1932, the Italian journalist Nino Savarese wrote a series of sketches on Italian places and landscapes, collected in *Cose d'Italia*. In these texts, buildings and objects play the principal role. During a stroll through Pompeii in the late afternoon, the light was losing intensity and dark shadows were growing on the Via dell'Abbondanza.[607] Savarese felt as if he were walking in a real, living city – "una città vera, intendo una città viva" – in which he could have a drink in the bar of Sittius in front of the brothel, among living people or spirits of ancient Pompeians (fig. 6). If he had had to pass a night in the ruins, he would not have been alone, but rather among the spirits of the people whose eternal rest was disturbed by the excavations, who had missed the opportunity to turn into dust again, which, according to the Bible, man had to do.[608] Savarese warned against

---

è più del presente momento della storia; siamo divenuti antichi, siamo forse ritornati i cittadini del tempo passato. Respiriamo versi d'Orazio e di Virgilio."
605 Benjamin 1980, 308–309: "Einer der Alten führt und hält die Laterne dicht vor ein Bruchstück frühchristlicher Fresken. Nun läßt er das hundertjährige Zauberwort ertönen 'Pompeji'. Alles, was der Fremde begehrt, bewundert und bezählt, ist 'Pompeji'. 'Pompeji' macht die Gipsimitation der Tempelreste, die Kette aus Lavamasse und die lausige Person des Fremdenführers unwiderstehlich. Dieser Fetisch ist um so wundertätiger, als ihn die wenigsten von denen je gesehen haben, die er ernährt. Begreiflich, daß die wundertätige Madonna, die dort thront, eine nagelneue kostbare Wallfahrtskirche bekommt. In diesem Bau und nicht in dem der Vettier lebt Pompeji für die Neapolitaner. Und immer wieder kommen Gaunerei und Elend schließlich dort nach Hause." This sketch of daily life was published in 1925. This fragment is partly quoted in Zintzen 1998, 71. Not in García y García 1998. In his *Wanderjahren in Italien*, Gregoriovius (1953, 309) defined the catacombs of Naples as a Christian form of Pompeii: the cult of the dead was vigorous, with its *agapè* and the festoons.
606 In Jaffé 1971, 291–292. Quotation in Richter 2005, 25. Not in García y García 1998.
607 Savarese 1940, 121–128; 1991 129–135, quotations pp. 130 and 133, in VI. Pompei – Via dell'Abbondanza. García y García 1998, no. 11.970.
608 Savarese 1940, 133: "Nemmeno il conforto di scomparire, polvere nella polvere: siamo ancora qui, pietrificati, inchiodati all'atto di quel momento, e in mezzo alle nostre cose di un tempo."

Fig. 6: Bar of Fortunata along the "Consular Road", allegedly showing imprints of coffee cups or wine glasses (photo Stephan Mols). Remains like these inspired authors to write the numerous bar scenes in their novels and short stories.

disturbing the inhabitants during the night. The brief text is admirable for its ability to place the reader in a world of living and dead Pompeians at one time.

Simone de Beauvoir and Jean-Paul Sartre were on tour in Italy in 1936. Like most tourists, these French philosophers paid more attention to the cultural history of the country than to its Fascist regime. In *La force de l'âge*, De Beauvoir quotes a letter from Sartre, who was clearly disappointed by the banality of the paintings seen in the Naples museum. These paintings served to enlarge the small living rooms of the Pompeian idlers by inserting columns and perspective. Figural scenes presented mythology instead of real Roman life. Painting was a classicist art which did not communicate the reality of normal life at all. Pompeii offered an entirely different experience, where one could touch ancient inhabitants and see firsthand how they lived in the houses and among the other monuments. For sure, De Beauvoir concluded, Pompeii was a busy town, not unlike modern Naples.[609]

---

609 De Beauvoir 1960, 278–279. Quoted in German translation in Richter 2005, 136–139 apart from the following story of the brothel (see next note). Not in García y García 1998.

Sartre had a curious adventure in Naples. A drinking companion invited him to a brothel to see a *tableau vivant* of scenes inspired by the great frieze of the Villa of the Mysteries. Only Sartre was allowed to enter, and saw a girl performing in various positions similar to those on the frieze. Sartre declined the invitation to make use of other services, and later told De Beauvoir that in the brothel, he had experienced *dépaysement*, "disorientation," delivery to the unknown. This word became the title of a short story.[610]

The Hungarian author Sándor Márai and his wife Ilna Matzner, known as Lola, lived in Naples and Sorrento for a couple of years after their escape from Hungary in 1948. In an undated entry in his diary from 1948, he wrote about the colours of Pompeii, mainly red and blue, that mirrored the taste of the *nouveaux riches*. A painter in ancient times was like a modern photographer, simply doing what his client asked. Yet, Márai continues, the art of ancient Pompeii also illustrates the beauty of the human body in antiquity, contrasted with the bodies of modern people, which, according to him, gradually grew ugly after the Middle Ages. Ancient harmony and poetry, finally, found their expression in the bronze statues from the Villa dei Papiri ("Danzatrici"), and even in animal sculptures.[611]

The Italian poet Guido Piovene compared Pompeian landscape paintings with his own native region, the area of the Brenta river in the Veneto. He even felt the presence of the famous eighteenth-century playwright Carlo Goldoni within the walls of Herculaneum and Pompeii.[612] Pompeii was like a chatterbox, very

---

610 De Beauvoir 1960, 280. See Sartre 1981, 2123–2132, for the account of this short story.
611 Márai 2001, 103–104: "Die Grundtöne der Räume in Pompeji, das Blau und das Rot, zielten auf die Gunst der Parvenüs ab. Der neureiche Beamte und der Kaufmann ließen für ihre Wohnhäuser die Abbildungen ihres täglichen Lebens hübsch schnörkelig malen; der Expreßfotograf in Pompeji und Herculanum tauchte den Wein, das Brot, den Fisch, die Verwandten und die Hausgötter in dieses Blau und Rot, um seine Auftraggeber geschmacklich – in der ganzen Lichtfülle! – für sich einzunehmen. Lola macht mich darauf aufmerksam – was die griechischen Skulpturen, die makellosen Körper in Bronze und in Marmor, beweisen –, daß der menschliche Körper in der griechischen Zeit noch nicht 'degeneriert' war; in den Bildern des Mittelalters und der Renaissance allerdings ist er bereits häufig verfettet und deformiert. Aus den vier Tänzerinnen in Bronze sind Tanz und Vers der Antike exakt abliesbar. In diesen vier Körpern in Bronze ist das klassische Versmaß bewahrt, in dem das feierliche Lebensgefühl der lebendigen Kultur seinen Ausdruck gefunden hat. Doch auch in den Bronze-Tieren – im Wildschwein, in den Hunden, im Pferdekopf der Quadriga – ist dieser innere, versfußartige Rhythmus lebendig." I did not see the original *Napló 1945–1957*, Budapest 1994.
612 Piovene 1957, 360: "Si direbbero lacche venete, cineserie settecentesche e ci richiamano la riviera del Brenta. Un veneto come me, nel museo di Napoli, come del resto a Ercolano e a Pompei, sente alitare intorno il chiacchericcio di Goldoni." García y García 1998, no. 10.706

vivid and properly Neapolitan.⁶¹³ Therefore, when at Ostia, he made a comparison between its harbour and Pompeii. In his eyes, Ostia was an industrious town with broad functional streets, which were occupied by merchants and officials. Pompeii, in contrast, had small "promiscuous" streets, occupied by prostitutes and people wearing masks.⁶¹⁴

Around 1960, the Dutch poet Bertus Aafjes stayed in Albergo Sole for several months and visited both modern and ancient Pompeii. In nice miniatures, he brings to life the skeletons found in the House of Sacerdos Amandus as the family of this priest, as well as other victims in the surroundings. Matteo Della Corte, the 84 year old former director of the excavations (see p. 140), showed Aafjes graffiti and seemed to recognize Gina Lollobrigida and Sofia Loren in the girl Primigenia.⁶¹⁵ Aafjes likes the mythical and erotic images, which feature great nudity, and critizes local authorities as hypocrites for not showing such scenes in the brothel and the House of the Vettii to women. In this way, love making becomes "porn."⁶¹⁶ He would have got a positive reaction from the journalist Duncan Fallowell, if this English journalist had known his work. Fallowell drove from London to Noto, seen as a modern sort of Pompeii after the earthquake of 1693, in a blue Ford Capri. The graffiti at Pompeii reminded him of the same practice in Naples. Death and Eros intermingle:⁶¹⁷

> Pulses of eroticism ripple through the site without cease, not least because of the presence of Vesuvian death. One is reduced and switched on by the great pistons of History, Time, Death. But these erotic pulses come too from the natural and unafraid sexuality of the Pompeians themselves. This is the pre-Christian world. Human nature, in both its joyous and cruel aspects, has not yet been twisted into agonised shapes. Desire is no taboo here – but it is organised.

Nevertheless, the idea of a sex-driven city does not get out of people's mind easily. A mother traveling with her daughter to Italy in 2009 might still be shocked by

---

613 Piovene 1957, 362: "Tutta Pompei è parlante; Pompei e Napoli sono congeniali. L'archeologia napoletana ha il genio di vedere le cose antiche come se fossero d'oggi, e di ricostruire la vita d'allora come un quadro di genere o una commedia verista."
614 Piovene 1957, 634–635: "Ostia è piú riservata, meno espansiva. È silenziosa, quanto Pompei è loquace; le sue vie sono ampie, quanto sono fitte le vie nelle città morte della Campania; la fantasia le vede gremite di mercanti e di funzionari, mentre le vie promiscue e strette di Pompei ci appaiono affollate di comari, di etère, di personaggi coloriti, di maschere."
615 Aafjes 1960, 86–97. Another charming chapter is dedicated to Libero D'Orsi's discoveries in Stabiae (pp. 49–58). García y García 1998, nos 1 and 6502 ("Haafjes")
616 Aafjes 1960, 118–120, 133: "Naakt is de natuurlijke kleding op een pompejaans fresco" ("Nudity is the natural costume in a Pompeian fresco").
617 Fallowell 1989, 148 and 150. Not in García y García 1998. Noto had suffered great damage from an earthquake.

phallic souvenirs and conclude: "This is a very dirty place."⁶¹⁸ The motif of a dead and living city returns in an impressive way in a travelogue by the Canadian novelist Rachel Cusk, who made a long trip through Italy with her family. Visiting the museum in Naples, she experiences Pompeii as a living reality:⁶¹⁹

> It is disconcertingly alive, this vanished world of Pompeii. The silent museum seems filled with noise, with faces and glancing eyes and conversation, chattering pots and barking dogs and birdsong. It is as though the volcano did not extinguish the day, but took its cast exactly, its sound and smell and atmosphere, its structure, like the skeleton of a fern fossilized in a heap of rust.

Conclusion

After some early accounts of surprise, describing the existence of a subterranean town, travelogues concentrate on the remains themselves and their value for the knowledge of antiquity. These works of the second half of the eighteenth century show a deep respect for the material culture of the ancient Romans, but express a certain degree of disappointment as to the artistic value of paintings, sculptures and so on. The architectural remains are entirely neglected, even when the first open-air excavations at Pompeii reveal streets and houses.

Gradually, visitors lose interest in Herculaneum; the few remains visible under thick layers of volcanic material cannot match Pompeii's ruins. Nevertheless, even at Pompeii, visitors rarely have a good first impression of the city, since there is no logic to the excavations, which consist of small unconnected pits in seemingly random spots. The houses, standing erect under the bright Campanian sky, seem to have just been abandoned by their inhabitants, who are imagined to be shopping, working, relaxing, or just somewhere hidden inside. These impressions colored many accounts of the late eighteenth and the nineteenth century. Modern visitors were able to touch these ancients, speak with them, and learn about their lives and emotions. The combination of these sensations with the overwhelming nature of the Bay of Naples strengthens the notion of happy Italy. Like the *lazzaroni* in Naples, old Pompeians apparently were *fannulloni*, basking under the sun. Their small houses only provided shelter at night or during rainfall. At the same time, the ruinous state of the site and the lack of the original

---

618 Christmas 2009, 199. Despite this conservative outlook, this is a very witty travel book, with original views of Italy.
619 Cusk 2009, 176.

objects *in situ* evoke the disappointment of those who hope to see a town in its pristine splendor, but find it decayed in both antiquity and modern times.

During the nineteenth century, authors tried to become involved with the vicissitudes in the ancient town. It was a challenge to virtually penetrate into the past and to let personal feelings speak. The notion of destruction, therefore, became more important than before. Individual impressions dominate these texts; descriptions are less extensive and lack importance.

When the modern world, including mass tourism and mass transportation, arrived at Pompeii, tourists began looking upon the ruins as they did their own growing towns. The rapid urbanization of major population centers in Europe deprived townspeople of the simple, rural lives of former days. Thanks to its modest dimensions, Pompeii provided a model of an ideal ancient Roman town. This appreciation of the town's properties also evoked a greater interest in the scientific work carried out. Fiorelli's radical changes after the foundation of the Kingdom of Italy in 1860 came at a good time, coinciding with the modernization of Italian society and the appropriation of Pompeii by the new state as a national property rather than a Bourbon playground. The Pompeians became ancestors of the whole nation, and Fiorelli was the man to realize that by his great explorations.

Pompeii represents both the origin and the development of our society through the ages. The fact that it is not a gigantic town, with enormous temples and palaces, makes it sympathetic and of a human scale. Due to its human size, it did not frighten the average visitor to the extent Rome did, since it did not feature such immense monuments. The elitist visitors of the first hundred years, who themselves lived in large houses, villas, and palaces, were disappointed by the city's modest dimensions. But even they argued that Pompeii was luckier than Rome, because despite having suffered due to the excavations, it was always existent and living. Thanks to the sudden blow of A.D. 79, which froze this city in its place, it became the ideal manifestation of ancient life, which itself was open to interpretation. Everyone, therefore, was able to create his or her own ancient Pompeii, which is what was to dominate most fiction for the next two hundred years.

III Pagan Pompeii in Fiction

Novels about pagan Pompeii belong to the genre of the historical novel, which enjoys an incessant popularity among general readers, and aims to bring the past to our attention. Authors have different reasons and follow different strategies to evoke the past, but their fascination with history clearly forms the main reason for writing such books. Despite copious studies on historical novels, little attention has been paid to many of the works discussed and often resuscitated in this book.[620] This may be due to the literary weakness of some of these works or the fact that many authors and titles never enjoyed much fame. In his monograph on the historic novel in the nineteenth century, the literary historian Hannu Riikonen states that the historical novels playing out in Antiquity rarely reach the level of the best works by Sir Walter Scott and Victor Hugo.[621] In Riikonen's study, literary quality was less relevant than the author's choices in terms of how the ancient towns and their inhabitants were portrayed. Riikonen understood these works as products of what would become "cultural memory."[622] This notion sees monuments as expressions of the cultural identity of a nation, of a specific group of people and so on. "Pompeii" forms a sort of classical paradigm of ancient life in the eyes of many Europeans and Americans and serves as a mirror of people's modern lives. Nationality, in his case the Italian one, however, does not pay such a role prior to 1860 (see Chapter II, p. 101).

The historic novel really came to life during the eighteenth century in France and Britain. Around 1800, Sir Walter Scott created a new writing style, with novels based on a meticulous study of historical works and monuments. Scott's critics and subsequent authors alike, despite their high esteem for the author of *Waverley* and *Ivanhoe*, found that his lengthy descriptions of historical details obstructed the development and depth of the characters. In the second half of the nineteenth

---

620 For more on the historical novel, see Lukács 1965 (fundamental), on which all newer studies rely: Riikonen 1978, Sanders 1979 (Victorian Britain), Müllenbrock 1980 and 2003; Malinowski 1989 (late nineteenth century France); Wesseling 1991; Schaller 1992, 6–23 (America); Neumann 1993 (twentieth-century Britain); Orel 1995 (nineteenth century); Bernard 1996 (nineteenth-century France); Durrani/Preece 2001 (Germany); Gengembre 2006; Cichocka 2007 (mainly Latin America, but excellent theoretical approach, pp. 1–134); R. Maxwell in Maxwell/Trumpener 2008, 65–87 (nineteenth century). On archaeology and historical novels, see Zintzen 1998; Fitzon 2004; David-De Palacio 2005, 301–314; Zimmerman 2008; Blix 2009. Heinz-Joachim Müllenbrock, one of the great experts in this field, shares the historical novel among "den interessantesten Neuerungen der Literatur des 19. Jahrhunderts" (Müllenbrock 2003, 96; cf. p. 129).
621 Riikonen 1978, 9. Similar verdict in Leppmann 1966.
622 For the paradigm of "cultural memory" not yet fully applied to Pompeii, see a recent overview of approaches edited by Astrid Erll and Ansgar Nünning (2010); especially the contributions by Ann Rigney (pp. 345–353) and Astrid Erll (pp. 389–398).

Fig. 7: Pompeii: map of the monuments that play a role in the works of fiction discussed in this book (drawing René Reijnen, Radboud Universiteit). 1: Villa of the Mysteries, 2: Villa of Diomedes, 3: Tomb of Ampliatus, 4: Tomb of Umbricius Scaurus, 5: Villa of Cicero, 6: *Schola* of Mamia, 7: Tomb of Cerrinius Restitutus, 8: Herculanean Gate, 9: Bar of Nympherois, 10: House of the Vestals, 11: House of the Surgeon, 12: House of Sallustius, 13: Bar of Fortunata, 14: House of Pansa, 15: Temple of Apollo, 16: Porta Marina, 17: Antiquarium, 18: Temple of Venus, 19: Basilica, 20: Sarno Baths, 21: House of Queen Carolina, 22: Doric Temple, 23: Theaters, 24: Temple of Isis, 25: House of the Menander, 26: House of the Sarnus Lararium, 27: Nocera Gate, 28: Palaestra, 29: Amphitheater, 30: House II 5, 1, 31: *Praedia* of Julia Felix, 32: House of Cornelius Tages, 33: House of Sacerdos Amandus, 34: House of Paquius Proculus, 35: House of Ceii, 36: Fullery of Stephanus, 37: House of Cryptoporticus, 38: House of Cither Player, 39: House of Holconius Rufus, 40: Eumachia Building, 41: Forum, 42: Temple of Jupiter, 43: Macellum, 44: House VII 11, 11, 45: Lupanar, 46: Bar of Sittius or the Elephant, 47: House of Siricus, 48: Stabian Baths, 49: House of Centenary, 50: House IX 1, 26, 51: Bar of Asellina IX 11, 2, 52: House of the Chaste Lovers, 53: Nolan Gate, 54: House of Obellius Firmus, 55: House of Marcus Lucretius, 56: House of Marcus Lucretius Fronto, 57: House of the Restaurant, 58: House of the Skeletons, 59: House of the Baker, 60: House of Bacchus, 61: Bar VII 4, 15, 62: Temple of Genius Augusti, 63: Forum Baths, 64: House of the Tragic Poet, 65: Bar VI 10, 1, 66: House of the Faun, 67: House of Caecilius Iucundus, 68: House of the Silver Wedding, 69: House of the Gilded Cupids, 70: Castellum Aquae, 71: Vesuvian Gate, 72: House of the Vettii, 73: House of Meleager. ▶

century, many works either endorsed the contemporary social and political developments, or suggested escapes from a harsh daily reality. In the twentieth century, works began to mirror the biggest concerns of the period during which they were (and are being) written, like social inequity, abuse of natural resources, and moral issues.

Turning the attention to Herculaneum and Pompeii, I start with a statement by an author who never even wrote a historical novel about Pompeii or Herculaneum. Massimo Tapparelli d'Azeglio, who would become an important politician in nineteenth-century Italy, writes in his 1867 memoirs about how in his youth, like all young men of the Romantic era, he started writing poetry, and hoped to compose a short "romantic archaeological" epic about the end of Pompeii.[623] D'Azeglio had

---

[623] D'Azeglio 1867, 417 (Part II, chapter X): "Dopo le terzine mi passò pel capo di far un poemetto romantico-archeologico coll'azione a Pompei, ed il finale alla sua distruzione. In cupa notte l'angiolo sterminatore evocava il demone del Vesuvio, e gli segnava la città condannata all'esterminio: la ragione non me la ricordo, ma sarà stato al solito il secolo corrotto. Sorgeva lo spettro rovente dal cratere alla voce dell'angiolo, mostrandosi dalla cintola in su come Farinata e mentre colla forcina plutonica solleva le lave del vulcano, coll'altra mano sparge di ceneri la città condannata. Questa l'introduzione. L'interesse della favola si fondava sull'amore figliale. Un soldato classario vuole riscattare sua madre schiava. Nel Circo, a chi vincesse un gladiatore

III Pagan Pompeii in Fiction — **167**

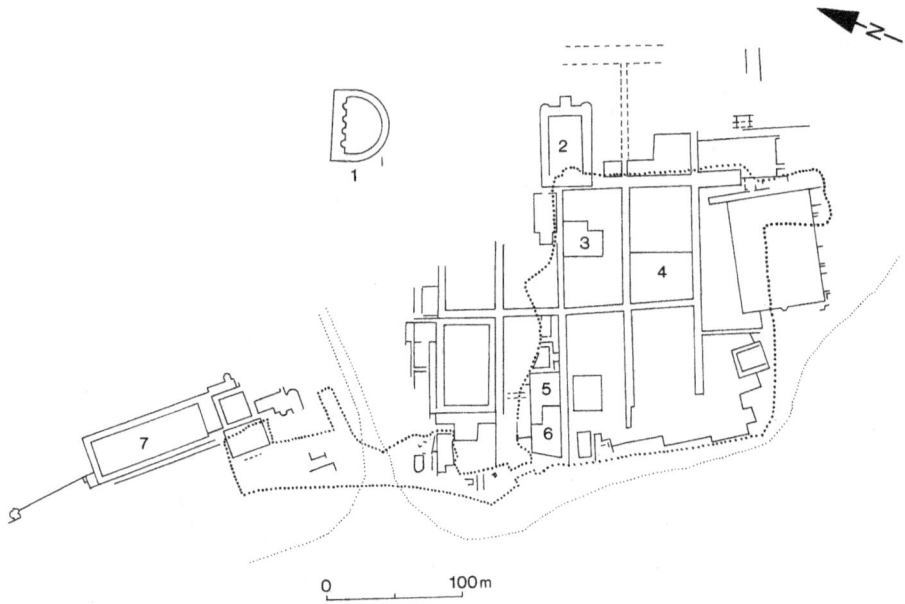

Fig. 8: Herculaneum: map of the monuments that play a role in the works of fiction discussed in this book (drawing René Reijnen, Radboud Universiteit). 1: Theater, 2: "Basilica", 3: House of the Skeleton, 4: Public Baths, 5: House of Aristides, 6: House of Argus, 7: Villa of the Papyri.

visited the excavations during two stays at Naples, in 1820 and 1827. His list of themes to be inserted into such a tale about ancient Pompeii includes many standard topics of fiction books, and his inventory might reflect his knowledge of similar novels. In his eyes, Pompeii met its end due to the moral corruption of its time.

famoso si prometteva una somma che bastava al riscatto. Il figlio lascia la sua coorte, si traveste, vince l'avversario, riceve il premio, libera la madre! ma è scoperto, il suo centurione lo mette ai ceppi, per poi giudicarlo. La madre gli è al fianco, lo conforta, lo abbraccia, gli annunzia libertà dopo breve castigo: intanto è notte, comincia lontano un sordo fragore, cresce, si mesce ad ululati e grida; la terra freme sotto i piedi, le mura si scuotono, una luce sanguigna illumina il cielo, scoppiano i tuoni, e vien giù tutto il *bataclan*, rompedo, abbattendo, sotterrando la città. La povera madre scongiurata, spinta dal figlio a fuggire, lo vorrebbe sciogliere, ma i ceppi sono grosse travi, ogni speranza è perduta, ecc., ecc. Come potrà facilmente immaginare con questa trama c'era da battere la gran cassa su tutti i tuoni. [...] Il poema rimane in progetto." Sogliano 1888, 12 and Leppmann 1966, 227 suggest that this epic poem had really been published, I think that he never wrote such a book on the basis of the clear-cut conclusion in his memoirs. See on these memoirs Audano 2009.

Had it been written, D' Azeglio's book would have become an example of a pagan novel, which is the first of several categories of written works, distinguished from the others on the basis of their contents. Next to (1) "pagan" novels, epics, and short stories, there are (2) "Christian" books, (3) "contemporary" works and (4) "time machine" fictitious publications.[624] The first category comprises books about pagan Pompeii and Herculaneum in antiquity, like *Pompeii* by Robert Harris. In the second category, Christians play some role in the society of the two towns, as in Bulwer-Lytton's *Last Days of Pompeii*, which is the predominant work. Category (3) focuses on the experiences of modern people in the excavations. Two examples are *Corinne* by Germaine de Staël and *Gradiva* by Wilhelm Jensen. The fourth category centers on modern people who encounter ancient inhabitants in dreams or paranormal experiences, as in Gautier's *Arria Marcella*. Of course, some works contain elements of more than one category.

This chapter deals with the first category, featuring books in which the plot highlights vicissitudes just before the eruption of Vesuvius of 79, or fiction that plays out (long) before. In the latter case, the plot is less predictable than in the 79 works. I will use the history of Pompeii as a guideline in the following discussion, but start with some early timeless remembrances (figs 7–8).

Medieval and Renaissance Predecessors

Herculaneum and Pompeii never fell into full oblivion after the great eruption. A few medieval works attest to a faint consciousness or, rather, to knowledge of ancient testimonies, although the most important source, the letters by Pliny the Younger, were not yet known. I recall Boccaccio's *Comedia delle Ninfe fiorentine* from 1341–1342 (see Chapter I, pp. 9–10).[625]

In 1358, Francesco Petrarca described Naples and its surroundings at length in a letter containing an itinerary for a trip to the Holy Land, which he wrote to his friend, the influential Milanese nobleman Giovanni Mandelli. This letter, written in Latin, became popular in Italian translations, and includes many learned details Petrarca had gleaned from ancient authors. Petrarca wrongly interprets Seneca's description of the A.D. 62 or 63 earthquake to be the cause of Pompeii's destruction and his "Pliny" is a mix of both the Elder and the Younger:[626]

---

624 Moormann 2007, 123. For (2) see Chapter IV, for (3) see Chapter V, for (4) see Chapter VI.
625 Boccaccio 1964, 761. García y García 1998, 61–62 gives some other early testimonies.
626 Petrarca 1990, 62, paragraph 40: "*Hinc tandem digresso, biceps adherit Vesevus (vulgo Summa monti nomen) et ipse flammas eructare solitus. Ad quod olim spectaculum visendum cum experiendi noscendique cupidine perrexisset Plinius Secundus, vir scientie multiplicis et eloquentie*

After parting finally from here [Naples], there will be Vesuvius with its double heads (vulgarly called Somma), which usually emits flames. To study this spectacle long ago, Pliny, a man of various knowledge and florid eloquence, came with eagerness to experience and learn it. He succumbed, because the wind moved up ashes and flames: a miserable end for such a great man! So Naples possesses the bones of both the Mantuanian [Virgil] and the Veronese. [...] A very beautiful stretch of land at the left hand side contained Pompeii and Herculaneum, once famous towns, now empty names, which were destroyed by earthquakes, as we have learned from Seneca, one witness among others.

Around 1500, the Neapolitan poet Iacopo Sannazaro wrote *Ecloga piscatoria* V. In it, he demonstrates his interest in the ancient towns hidden by Mount Vesuvius in 79. The poet introduces the *locus amoenus* of the fishermen Dorylas and Thelgon. When Thelgon invites the mythical sea creature Triton to sing about his love Galatea, their environment is described:[627]

Galatea was sitting with me under this rock. I was looking afar at both Capri and the countryside that keeps the names of the Sirens. In the other direction Vesuvius from his charred crest pinpointed the ancient ruins of Hercules.[628]

In *Arcadia*, a charming work of the pastoral genre published in 1504, Sannazaro describes how storyteller Sincero follows a nymph, hoping to find his (dead) lover and his fatherland near the Sebeto River. The unnamed girl shows him all the underworld places known from mythology and history:[629]

---

floride, vento cinerem ac faviliam excitante compressus est: miserabilis tanti viri exitus! Sic Neapolis, hinc Mantuani, inde Veronensis civis ossa custodit. [...] Pulcherrimus terrarum tractus ad levam Pompeios atque Herculaneum habuit, celebres olim urbes, nunc inania nomina, quas terremotibus eversas Seneca inter ceteros teste didicimus." García y García 1998, 61 gives another Petrarca reference. García y García also lists a testimony in Giovanni Pontano's *Hendecasyllabi*, which I could not find.

627 Sannazaro 1689, 60; Sannazaro 2009, 138–139: "*Rupe sub hac mecum sedit Galatea: videbam / Et Capreas, et quae Sirenum nomina servant / Rura procul; veteres alia de parte ruinas / Herculis ambusta signabat ab arce Vesevus.*"

628 In the *Ecloga Piscatoria* III, Chromis praises the surroundings of Naples for their rich population of fish, so in line 87: "*Herculaeae mullarum rupes*" (the cliffs of Herculaneum/Hercules for its mull). See Sannazaro 2009, 124–125.

629 Translation by Ralph Nash in Sannazaro 1966, 137–138. Sannazaro 1961, 115–116 (*Arcadia* XII, 28–34). Here quoted from Sannazaro 2004, 239–241: "Cosí ancora sotto il gran Vesevo ti farei sentire li spaventevoli muggiti del gigante Alcioneo; benché questi credo gli sentirai quando ne advicinaremo al tuo Sebeto. Tempo ben fu che con lor danno tutti i finitimi li sentirono, quando con tempestose fiamme e con cenere coperse i circonstanti paesi, sí come ancora i sassi liquefatti e arsi testificano chiaramente a chi gli vede. Sotto ai quali chi sarà mai che creda che e populi e ville e città nobilissime siano sepolte? Come veramente vi sono, non solo quelle che da le arse

So also under lofty Vesuvius I would make you hear the fearful groaning of the giant Alcyon; though these, I believe, you will hear when we draw nigh to your Sebeto. Time was indeed, that all the neighboring populace heard them, to their hurt, when he covered with tempestuous flames and with ashes the surrounding countryside, as the liquefied and blackened rocks you clearly testify to him who sees them: under which who will there ever be that can believe that peoples and villas and most noble cities are buried? As truly they are, not only those that were covered by pumice ash and by the mountain slide, but this that we see before us, which without any doubt (being at one time a famous city in your region, called Pompeii, and washed by the waves of the chill Sarno) by sudden quake was swallowed by the earth, the firmament whereon it was founded failing, I understand, from under men's feet. Surely, a strange and horrible kind of death, living people to see themselves stricken in a moment from the number of the living! Save that ultimately one always arrives at one destination, nor is there any travelling on from there except to death. –

And speaking these words, we already were next to the town she mentioned of which we could see the towers, houses, theaters, and temples almost complete. For our swift pace I wondered whether we could have arrived in so brief a lapse of time here from Arcadia, but one could clearly acknowledge that we were driven by a greater force than a human one.

Sannazaro was widely read, translated into various languages and had literary imitators in the sixteenth and seventeenth centuries.[630]

The Pompeians in the Novels

In Pompeian fiction, one observes certain stock figures. To give the people names, authors use those recorded in inscriptions and graffiti: Diomedes, Pansa, Sallustius (sometimes confused with the Roman historian from the first century B.C., Gaius Sallustius Crispus), and many more. In the twentieth century, the local

---

pomici e da la ruina del monte furon coperte, ma questa che dinanzi ne vedemo, la quale senza alcun dubbio celebre città un tempo nei tuoi paesi, chiamata Pompei, e irrigata da le onde del freddissimo Sarno, fu per súbito terremoto inghiottita da la terra, mancandoli credo sotto ai piedi il firmamento ove fundata era. Strana per certo e orrenda maniera di morte, le genti vive vedersi in un punto torre dal numero de' vivi! Se non che finalmente sempre si arriva a un termino, né piú in là che a la morte si puote andare. – E già in queste parole eramo ben presso a la città che lei dicea, de la quale e le torri e le case e i teatri e i templi si poteano quasi integri discernere. Maravigliaimi io del nostro veloce andare, che in sí breve spazio di tempo potessemo da Arcadia insino qui essere arrivati: ma si potea chiaramente conoscere che da potenzia maggiore che umana eravamo sospinti." Also quoted and examined by Cremante 2008, 113–114. Partly translated into English in Kidwell 1993, 65–66. Lefèvre 2006 is a very dense analysis of other examples of Sannazaro's interest for lost towns, but he omits Pompeii and Herculaneum (cf. Kidwell 1993, 48–50). García y García 1998, no. 11.918.

630 See Mauro in his edition, Sannazaro 1961, 427–430. Cf. Sogliano 1888, 14–15; Leppmann 1966, 59; García y García 1998, 61. Fernández Murga 1965, 7 mentions Spanish elaborations. For Maizony de Lauréal 1837 and Sannazaro, see chapter IX, p. 344.

archaeologist Matteo Della Corte enthusiastically invented people and their properties by completing and interpreting partially preserved texts rather uncritically.[631] In his footsteps, the Dutch journalist and poet Bertus Aafjes wrote biographies of victims found in houses on the Via dell'Abbondanza. The Italian author Sebastiano Patanè brings these Pompeians to life by means of portraits sketched by G. Eleno, a made-up historian, who with these images enlivens the town in its last days. The novelist Alex Butterworth and ancient historian and archaeologist Ray Laurence present a mix of scientific and fictional images of the inhabitants of Pompeii in their attractive monograph.[632] A number of their characters have namesakes in Petronius' *Satyrica* (or *Satyricon*): Gaius Pompeius Diomedes is a freedman like Trimalchio who possesses properties at Pompeii, who has made a great fortune of 800,000 sesterces and is a real showoff. Some others are Gaius Iulius Proculus, Norbanus, and Pansa.[633] Rare are historical persons known from ancient texts, like Cicero in evocations by Candido Augusto Vecchi from 1864 and Max Brod from 1955. Many protagonists belong to the upper levels of society or to the circles around them, including servants and slaves. The Vettii brothers – seen as *nouveaux riches* and rather banal people – get their place in fiction from the very moment of the excavation of their house at the end of the nineteenth century, in Jean Bertheroy's *La danseuse de Pompéi* from 1899 (fig. 9).

With Diomedes, we encounter one of the many Greek-named slaves and freedmen, as well as free and high-ranking Greek characters conceived without any concern for the severe social rules that governed Roman society, which would have prevented such people from actually existing. These characters transform Pompeii into a cradle of Greek civilization (cf. Chapter I, p. 71, and below, p. 176), where in reality, Greeks and their children decidedly did not belong to the upper class. Most of them would have been slaves or freedmen. Especially in "Christian" books, lower-class people also tend to stem from Palestine, Gaul, and Germany.

From D'Azeglio up to the most recent novels, there are recurrent topics, like descriptions of temples, public buildings like the amphitheater and the theater, the protagonists' houses, daily life, and family ceremonies. Descriptions of daily

---

[631] Della Corte 1926, 1965. The book is still for sale in Pompeian bookshops. Cf. Chapter II, p. 140 for criticism, and see García y García 1998, 384–385; Della Corte's enormous production is listed there under nos 3965–4151. Hunink 2014 provides a representative anthology of graffiti with English translations.
[632] Aafjes 1960; Patanè 2007; Butterworth/Laurence 2005, who state about these people and their portraits (p. 8): "The accounts of all their lives should be treated as firmly grounded conjecture, but conjecture nevertheless."
[633] Diomedes: *Satyrica* 38.10; Proculus: *Satyrica* 38.16; Norbanus: *Satyrica* 45.10; Pansa: *Satyrica* 47.12.

Fig. 9: Jean Bertheroy, *La danseuse de Pompéi*, cheap illustrated edition of the 1899 book, around 1900, front cover in art deco style. The girl – probably the protagonist Nonia – is represented as a dancing girl from Moulin Rouge or some other Paris cabaret.

life and ceremonies seem to follow a template that might stem from ancient textual sources rather than from knowledge of Pompeian objects or buildings, and include wedding ceremonies[634] (not simply protagonists' weddings, but even those of non-distinct citizens next door), funerals,[635] dinner parties,[636] visits to baths,[637] and theater[638] and amphitheater outings.[639] Meals in particular form one ingredient that either – positively – illustrates the notion of Pompeii as a city of great wealth and luck or – negatively – conveys the image of a rotten society. If we may believe ancient sources like Petronius' *Satyrica*, Martial's *Epigrams*, and Juvenal's *Satyrae*, rich Roman people came together to consume, in endless quantities, extremely expensive and absurd foodstuffs like exotic fish, peacock tongues, and singing birds hidden within large boars, and used costly vessels made from crystal, gold, or silver. Moreover, we read about the alleged custom of guests lying on luxurious beds and drinking *ad nauseam*, which contrasts with the modern – and more civilized – habits of dinner parties. Most of the authors of the books to be discussed here, however, did not understand the criticism hidden under the witty descriptions of these Latin sources that focused on the extreme luxury of the upper class and the *nouveaux riches* (that is, the freedmen who had gathered gigantic capital and displayed their wealth), and attacked this excess as an un-Roman weakness. In her narrative *Le ragazze di Pompei* (The Girls from Pompeii), the Italian author Carmen Covito recently presented a mock manuscript in the shape of Petronius' *Satyrica* and with the same orientation as novel.[640] But in real Roman life, most people never ate such meals and even the happy few could not go beyond the severe rules and etiquette of their peers when they organized a dinner party.[641]

---

634 E.g. Becker 1838 and 1849, Conforti 1888, Carozzari 1899, Rouland 1984, Vandenberg 1989, Lasky 2007.
635 E.g. Conforti 1888, Bertheroy 1899, Visser 1911, Rouland 1984, De la Rochefoucauld 2001.
636 E.g. Mazois 1819, Becker 1838, Gregorovius 1858 (1872), Bertheroy 1899, Behrend 1907, Visser 1911, Formont 1914, Saul 1966, Lerme-Walter 1968, De Corcelles 1982, Rouland 1984, Vandenberg 1989, Davis 1990, De la Rochefoucauld 2001, Lenk 2002, Harris 2003, Comastri Montanari 2005, Lasky 2007.
637 E.g. Mazois 1819, Carozzari 1899, Visser 1911, Formont 1914, Vandenberg 1998, Lenk 2002, Comastri Montanari 2005, Lasky 2007.
638 E.g. Gautier 1852; Vecchi 1864, Conforti 1888, Bertheroy 1899.
639 E.g. Vecchi 1864, Conforti 1888, Bertheroy 1899, Carozzari 1899, Saul 1966, Lerme-Walter 1968, De Corcelles 1982, Rouland 1984, De la Rochefoucauld 2001, Pagliara 2003, Lasky 2007, Russell 2008. A party from Baiae visits a gladiatorial show in Pompeii in a thriller from the SPQR series by John Maddox Roberts (2007, Chapter 3).
640 Covito 2012. In my opinion, it is less witty, less rough, and less explicit in describing sex scenes than Petronius. García y García 2012, no A1172b.
641 See on the Roman dinner party most recently, Schnurbusch 2011. He gives a long list of dishes on p. 116–117, note 371.

Especially in the nineteenth century, these novels repeat details either from these sources or popular handbooks[642] or even from older novels and short stories. The learned novels, which will be briefly presented shortly, inspired later authors. I shall leave out discussion of these stock themes, and only highlight peculiar variations worthy of being mentioned.

Of course, the ancient people featured in fiction generally speak the language of the author, but there is a striking amount of Latin to be found in this genre. This ranges from technical terms, names, and brief remarks, to quotations from graffiti and literary texts, to entire conversations invented by the author. This "word dropping" was intended to provide an authentic flavor to the stories, but often results in a forced and sometimes absurd form of authenticity. An extreme example is *Giallo Pompeiano* by Giuseppe Pagliara, whose characters not only speak Latin and Greek, but also the modern dialects of Rome and Naples, and whose descriptions abound in technical terminology.[643] Pagliara invents linguistic rules to make his Latin a vividly spoken language. For the poor readers who have not mastered these linguistic skills, there are hundreds of notes translating the terms into Italian. The result is macaroni Italian printed in a mix of italics and roman. To quote one example, in the following, spectators react to gladiatorial combat in the amphitheater:[644]

> E tutti a gridare, neanche si fosse già alla *sportula*, al *munus sine missione* in anfiteatro, col suo copioso spargimento di *vilis sanguis*, e non a un allenamento o, se si vuole, e per cosí dire, a una *lusio* o *prolusio*:
> '*Verbera, iugula, ure; habet, hoc habet; mitte; pollice verso; arma submitte; ferrum recipe!*'

---

642 Think of influential manuals like Ludwig Friedländer's *Darstellungen aus der Sittengeschichte Roms in der Zeit von August bis zum Ausgang der Antonine* (Leipzig 1862–1871; many reprints and translations) and Karl Joachim Marquardt's *Das Privatleben der Römer* (Gotha 1864, second edition edited by August Mau, Leipzig 1886, also re-issued and translated), written with Becker, present in this book with his *Sabina* (p. 190). On these studies, see Schnurbusch 2011, 34–35 (Marquardt), 38–40 (Friedländer).
643 Pagliara 2003. The book is a crime story in which "Petronius" is the detective. García y García 2012, no A3370. On the genre of crimes stories, see Cramme 2004 and 2009; Rocchi 2006–2007 and 2008.
644 Pagliara 2003, 80: "And everyone screams, although they had not yet arrived at the lunch (basket=*sportula*) and the merciless fight (*munus sine missione*) in the amphitheater, with its copious shed of vile blood (*vilis sanguis*), and not yet at a training or, if you want, and to say it in this way, a play (*lusio*) or prelude (*prolusio*): 'Flog, slay, burn, he misses, he hits, send, thumb low, lay down the arms, take the stroke of the sword.'" (*verbera* etc.)

"Greekness" in Fiction

Although he never visited the South, Friedrich Schiller was fascinated by the excavations in Pompeii and Herculaneum, thanks, perhaps, to the stories of his friend Johann Wolfgang Goethe. In his poem *Pompeji und Herculanum* (1797) Schiller describes buildings and objects familiar to him from Volkmann's travel guide. He begins his majestic poem by pondering the miracle of an ancient city being revealed by the ongoing excavations. When we ("wir": whether or not the poet is including his reader is unclear) asked for good water sources, the earth sent us life from under the earth. What had been living under the lava? Lost generations of Greeks and Romans, who were now returning to the world. He invites the reader to come with him and "see ancient Pompeii."[645]

Greek names of inhabitants known from inscriptions, like that of the freedmen Arrius Diomedes led to the creation of Greek protagonists in fiction. The villa opposite the tomb of Arrius and his wife Arria was labeled the Villa of Diomedes and would become a feature in many novels.[646] It was unclear to many authors whether the Pompeians spoke Latin or Greek, and in their fiction, they often created a great distance between a sophisticated upper class with Greek names and the *hoi polloi*, who were labeled Roman.

As explained above, in choosing Greek names for their characters, these authors demonstrate their unawareness of the low social status of freedmen and other non-Romans in the hierarchically rigid Roman town. The role of Roman citizens remains either underestimated or limited to public functions. Madame Bertheroy uses Greek names for Pompeians in *La danseuse de Pompéi* (fig. 9). The son of Aulus Vette (Vettius) is called Hyacinthus (an impossible name in Roman circles), and the priest of Apollo, who acts like a Christian clergyman, bears the name Chrestus. Bulwer-Lytton (as we will see in Chapter IV) portrays Pompeii and its inhabitants as full-blown Greeks, and his protagonists Glaucus and Ione even tell their story in Athens. These quasi-Greeks are upper class English landlords, living in leisure and looking down at hard-working Romans like the aedile Pansa and Diomedes, who in turn strongly contrast with the Egyptian priest Arbaces, a symbol of decadence.

---

[645] First lines: "Welches Wunder begiebt sich? Wir flehten um trinkbare Quellen, / Erde! dich an und was sendet dein Schoos uns herauf? / Lebt es im Abgrund auch? Wohnt unter der Lava verborgen / Noch ein neues Geschlecht? Kehrt das entflohne zurück? / Griechen! Römer! O kommet und seht, das alte Pompeji." Quoted from Schiller 1943, 276–277. A comment is to be found in Schiller 1991, 304–307. Leppmann 1966, 163: "mattes Gedicht"; Zintsen 1998, 92, 218–222.

[646] See also Zintzen 1998, 248–254; Moormann 20001, 12–15. On the villa V. Kockel in Guzzo/Tagliamonte/Lucchetti 2013, 58–63.

In Jensen's *Gradiva* (see Chapter V, pp. 265–268), Norbert's girl friend is called Zoe, Greek for "life." Moreover, the evocations of Greek poets and mythological figures lead to reflections on time and the characters' personal past. The Meleager of the House of Meleager, where Norbert meets Zoe, could either be named for the Hellenistic poet of that name or for the mythological hunter himself. The story is full of Greek references, and the author sees art in Pompeii and Herculaneum as a Roman remake of Greek art. Another Zoe features in Toudouze's *Cécube* (see Chapter V, p. 267; Chapter VI, pp. 321–323).

Entirely different is the Greekness in Daudet's *Les bacchantes* (see Chapter V, pp. 275–276). The reenactment of a Dionysian orgy in the Villa of the Mysteries stimulates Daudet to evoke a luxurious Greek atmosphere: among the most frequently used words are "débauche," "orphisme," "phallus," and "volupté."

Even in the entirely Italian, viz. Roman, world of Lowry's *Present Estate of Pompeii* (see Chapter V, pp. 301–304), Greek elements are hidden. The two protagonists, Tansey and Roderick Fairhaven, climb Vesuvius with a party of Greeks who were, as Tansy says, "visiting their old stamping ground."[647] Their guide, pointing at the bronze bust of a young Apollo in the Temple of Apollo, remarks that he has "'...a lady-face, because the Greeks made everything so sweet and gentle, but the Romans make everything like this:' – he drew down a growth of savage air from his chin – 'with beards.'"[648]

Greek works of art rarely feature as a topic in Pompeii fiction. Many novelists use descriptions of masterpieces as catalogued in Pliny's *Naturalis Historia*. Pliny knew the Vesuvian cities very well, and consequently could have described works of art in Herculaneum, Pompeii and Stabiae.[649] Madame Bertheroy, for instance, briefly introduces a shipbroker from Corinth, who lives on the "Acropolis" and possesses pictures by Zeuxis and other famous painters. Before her, Mazois evoked Greek art works in his *Le palais de Scaurus*. Erotic paintings by Parrhasius, in a sort of "Venereum" (see p. 191) in which the lord of the house receives geisha-like girls, embarrass the Gaulish prince Mérovir.

---

647 Lowry 1961, 186.
648 Lowry 1961, 198.
649 Pliny is recorded at length by Maizony 1837, Book VI–VII (death of Pliny). P. Levi (1984) dedicated the poem "Plinio" to the polyhistor.

Skeletons Get a Second Life

> "Nearby were the chained skeletons. 'The ones which were chained long ago,' Job said, 'don't suffer any longer and don't hear the voice of the executor any longer.'"[650]

In her 2008 description of ancient Pompeii, Mary Beard interprets the bones and plaster casts as the remains of human beings with real biographies, which in no way differs from the fiction authors who are the subject of my study.[651] To date, skeletal remains of some 1,100 victims have been found at Pompeii. If we assume a population in 79 of around 10,000, some 10 to 15 percent died during the eruption. Both numbers are not exact, though, as all estimations of Pompeii's population are results of certain guesswork, and the bones and cavities of victims missed over 250 years of excavating would substantially increase the number of dead.[652]

In Herculaneum, almost no victims came to light during over two hundred fifty years of investigations until in 1981, more than 200 people were discovered in the boat houses on the town's beach, delivering a horrid spectacle of human drama.[653] The first scholar to study these victims was the physical anthropologist Sara Bisel, who unfortunately died before she could work out her data. In a slim children's book, in which she appears in almost every photograph, she reports on her osteological research. To give the bones life, she presents a brief story about a slave girl named Petronia who has to do all sorts of jobs for her tyrannical mistress Flavia Theodora.[654] Among other thing, she serves as a second (and better) mother of Flavia's son Julius. When Vesuvius lets loose its fatal surges, Petronia, trying to save herself, sprints to the boat houses with Julius, but there meets her end, and is finally found by archaeologists in 1981.[655]

In the first hundred years of digging in Pompeii, excavators often found the bones of victims, as they correctly observed, on a higher level than the floors of the

---

[650] Chateaubriand 1968, 119; 1969, 1474, at the sight of the Barracks of the Gladiators behind the big theater in Pompeii [in 1803]: "Près de là étoient les squelettes enchaînés: 'Ceux qui étoient autrefois enchaînés ensemble, dit Job, ne souffrent plus, et ils n'entendent plus la voix de l'exacteur.'"
[651] Beard 2008. See also Butterworth/Laurence 2005, esp. 293–312.
[652] Reading *PAH*, the number of skeletal remains recorded is small. For more on these numbers, see De Carolis/Patricelli/Ciarallo 1998; Guzzo 2003b, 56–72; Lazer 2009, 73–76. Bonucci 1827, 151, gives the number of 170 skeletons at Pompeii in 1826, K. von Hase (1830, edited in 1891, 197) gives a number of over 100.
[653] Capasso 2001; Mühlenbrock/Richter 2005; Wallace-Hadrill 2011, 123–130; Lazer 2009, 28–32.
[654] Bisel 1990.
[655] Bisel 1990, 48–58 also 'identifies' other victims, like a sturdy soldier and the witch Portia, who foretold the tragic end without being heard.

houses. Sometimes, cavities in the volcanic debris were recognized as the traces of the dead. Apparently, the excavators did not breach the cavities caused by the bodies' decomposition, but as soon as they reached the edges, stopped and tried to extract the bones while leaving the shape intact. These remains and impressions of corpses in the *lapilli* evoked intense reactions.[656] One traveler observed skeletons of people who had been making love[657] and others collected bones as souvenirs;[658] guides even sold them to tourists for good money.[659] The plaster casts of victims as "invented" by Fiorelli in 1863 add an ever-lasting impression of a visit to Pompeii.[660] They function as veritable mediators between past and present, and come to life as protagonists in a wide array of texts (p. 314, fig. 13).[661]

---

[656] E.g. Hamilton 1777, 172–173: "In the street, just out of the gate of this Villa, I saw lately a skeleton dug out; and, by desiring the labourers to remove the scull and bones gently, I perceived distinctly the perfect mould of every feature of the face, and that the eyes had been shut. I also saw distinctly the impression of the large folds of the drapery of the toga, and some of the cloth itself sticking to the earth."

[657] Audot 1835, 147: "Se précipitant dans les bras l'un l'autre, les dernières convulsions d'une mort affreuse ne purent même les séparer! Qu'il devait être puissant ce sentiment qu'ils préféraient à la vie! Quand je les vis découvrir, il me semblait qu'autour d'eux s'émanait encore, après tant de siècles, quelque chose de cet amour si fort, si courageux, presque inconnu de nos jours." Also in Overbeck 1866, II, 30, here note 661.

[658] Latapie 1953, 223–248 (lecture of 1776); quotation at 240: "[...] certaines personnes veulent en emporter des morceaux s'il leur est possible, ce que je n'ai pas manqué de faire, afin de posséder dans mon petit muséum un os qui ait plus de 17 siècles." Also Denon, quoted in note 666.

[659] Bartels 1791, 128.

[660] See the fascinating study by Dwyer (2007). See also Zimmerman 2008, 115–118; Lazer 2009, 247–264; Stefani 2010.

[661] Overbeck 1866, II, 30, gives the most famous cases (key words underlined by me): "Ueber die Situation, in denen man die Gerippe fand, in denen also die alten Pompejaner gestorben wären, sind eine Masse romantischer aber unbewährter und zum Theil sicher falscher Erzählungen im Schwange. Ein paar Beispiele mögen hier Platz finden. Da will man in der ersten kleinen Grabnische links vor dem Herculaner Thor einen <u>Soldaten</u>, den Speer in der Rechten, die Linke vor dem Mund gehalten gefunden haben. Das soll nun die Schildwacht gewesen sein; die kleine Nische macht man trotz ihrer deutlichen Grabinschrift zum Schilderhaus und ergeht sich in sentimentalen Lobpreisungen des wackeren Mannes, der auf seinem Posten ausharrend, gestorben sei; als ob er gegen Eruptionen des Vesuv geschildert hätte! Vielleicht noch rührender ist die Geschichte <u>eines jungen liebenden Paares</u>, dessen Gerippe man in der innigsten Umarmung in der Strasse von den Theatern zum Forum gefunden haben will. In der überwölbten Halbkreisnische rechts an der Gräberstrasse soll eine <u>Mutter mit 3 Kindern</u> gefunden worden sein, die vielleicht einen Augenblick auf ihrer Flucht dort rastend, daselbst erstickt und begraben wäre; gleiches Schicksal hätte nicht weit davon mehrere <u>Männer</u> ereilt, welche einen kurz zuvor verstorbenen Freund oder Verwandten zu seiner letzten Ruhestatt geleitet und im triclinium funebre sein Leichenmahl, auch das ihrige, gefeiert haben sollen. Von einigen <u>Isispriestern</u> erzählt man, sie seien länger als rathsam in den Nebengebäuden des Tempels zurückgeblieben; den einen

A large group of victims was discovered in December 1771 in the Villa of Diomedes located amidst impressive tombs outside the city gate, along the road to Herculaneum. For many generations of visitors, the skeletons of a group of fleeing citizens who had sought shelter in an underground corridor were unforgettable. In the garden two more skeletons were found, one holding a purse of money, and the other a key,[662] both giving rise to speculations on their identities. The most exciting find was the impression of a woman's breast left in the hardened mass of volcanic material. The oldest description of these victims is by the excavator Francesco La Vega in his report of December 12, 1772.[663] The workmen came across eighteen adult skeletons, and one each of an adolescent and a young child. The enormous mass of bones urged them to work carefully in order to unearth the skeletal remains intact. In the ashes, they found hair, teeth, and skulls, as well as impressions of fine and thick clothing. La Vega observed that the fugitives had wrapped their garments around their heads, sometimes in several layers, and that the feet were clad with fabric socks; most of them wore shoes. One lady stood out, thanks to her particularly rich attire. Most of her bones stayed *in situ*, whereas her skull and the impression of her breast were taken out under La Vega's command and sent to Portici. Unfortunately these finds can no longer be found in the museum.[664] In his 1777 account, Hamilton mentions twenty-three skeletons and one more in the street. Saint-Non records twenty-seven skeletons, some of them still with jewelry.[665] According to Denon, some people

---

habe man unfern eines Tisches mit Speiseresten (Hünerknochen) gefunden und er scheine plötzlich erstickt zu sein, den anderen hätte die Verzweiflung der Todesangst zu einem gewaltsamen Rettungsversuch getrieben: mit einer Axt hätte er, da die Thür versperrt war, bereits zwei Wände durchhauen, um sich einen Ausweg zu bahnen, vor der dritten wäre er ebenfalls oder erschöpft erstickt zusammengesunken. Ein dritter hätte allerlei Tempelkostbarkeiten zusammengerafft und wäre mit ihnen geflohen, aber er hätte nur das *Forum triangulare* erreicht, wo man das Gerippe mit allerlei Gegenständen des Isiscultus fand." In his notes 4–5 on p. 339–340 he refers to *PAH* I: sentinel 13-8-1763; funeral triclinium 14 and 28-1-1775; niche 14-12-1811. The latter in Kockel 1983, 159–161, Nord 9; see below, p. 185.

662 These had been found previously, viz. May 25, 1771 (*PAH* I, 255), but other skeletons are reported on February 6, 13 and 20, 1773 (*PAH* I, 271–272). Similarly, two more persons in the corridor (*ibidem*, 272). See on the reactions Pucci 2012.

663 *PAH* I, 268–269.

664 Maiuri 1998, 39–42 observed the loss of the breast imprint already some decades ago (note from the 1950s).

665 Saint-Non 1782, 129: "C'est au bas de l'Escalier qui y [Cave K] conduit, que l'on a trouvé vingt-sept Squélettes de Femmes qui vraisemblablement, dans le trouble & l'effroi, s'étoient cachées dans cet endroit reculé. Elles s'étoient toutes refugiées, les unes auprès des autres, dans un des coins à côté de la Porte; & on a retrouvé avec leurs os, l'empreinte & la forme de leurs corps moulés & conservés dans les cendres, avec les détails de leurs habillemens. L'on fait voir même

counted twenty-six persons, but now there was one fewer, because Denon took away the skull of another lady.[666]

Not all authors reacted as succinctly and aptly as did Chateaubriand, quoted at the beginning of this chapter, who defined the making of the imprint as follows: "Like a sculptor, Death formed its victim."[667] The poet and playwright Auguste Creuzé de Lesser recognized the *pater familias* among the corpses.[668] Seeing the impression of the breast in the museum, Dupaty imagined the woman whose breast it had been as young, beautiful and tall.[669] The cast made a great impression on the zealous traveler Hester Lynch Piozzi:[670]

---

encore, au Musaeum de Portici, l'empreinte de la gorge de l'une d'elles, avec leurs anneaux, leurs bracelets, les chaînes qu'elles portoient au col, & leurs boucles d'oreilles." He quotes Hamilton's explanation in a lengthy and richly illustrated section on the villa (Saint-Non 1782, 125–132, pls. 78–80 "Maison de Campagne").

666 Denon 1997, 118: "Je ne sais si on continuera d'en montrer vingt-six, mais j'avoue qu'il ne peut plus y en avoir que vingt-cinq véritables, car je ne pus résister au désir d'avoir en bonne fortune la tête d'une dame romaine; et, ayant trouvé moyen de l'emporter à l'aide d'un très grand manteau que j'avais, je suis parvenu à la faire passer en France, où nos jolies Françaises pourront s'étonner de la dimension et des formes qui faisaient la beauté de ce temps."

667 Chateaubriand 1969, 1474: "… la mort, comme un statuaire, a moulé sa victime." He visited Pompeii in 1804. Cf. the short mention of the skeletons in De La Roche 1783, 65: "ossemens" found in a cellar. Other brief recordings in Andersen's diary (Barüske 1980, 200); Colet 1862, III, 120; Von Rochau 1852, II, 135.

668 Creuzé de Lesser 1806, 195: "Là, tous les sentiments humains furent brisés; là, au milieu d'une nuit profonde, et parmi les cris de l'angoisse, un vieillard, un chef de famille, fit entendre ses derniers adieux à son fils qui le cherchoit, à sa fille qui le soutenoit encore, à toute sa génération qui s'éteignoit avec lui."

669 Dupaty 1789, II, 131–132: "Je ne dois pas omettre un des monumens les plus curieux de ce cabinet célèbre; ce sont des fragmens d'enduit de cendres, qui lors d'une éruption du Vésuve, surprirent une femme, & l'enveloppèrent en entier. Ces cendres, pressées & durcies par le temps, autour de son corps, l'ont pris & moulé parfaitement. Plusieurs fragmens de cet enduit conservent l'empreinte des formes particulières qu'ils ont reçues. L'un possède la moitié du sein; il est d'une beauté parfaite; l'autre, une épaule; l'autre, une portion de la taille: ils nous révèlent, de concert, que cette femme étoit jeune, qu'elle étoit grande, qu'elle étoit bien faite, & même qu'elle fuyoit en chemise: car des morceaux de linge sont attachés à la cendre." During a second visit, the skeletons still horrify him (1789, II, 190): "Remontons, le coeur, ici, n'est pas à son aise." The villa is called "maison de campagne d'*Aufidius*" (1789, II, 191). For more on Dupaty, an eminent lawyer and civil servant, see Doyle 1985, esp. 77–79, 111–113; Mozzillo 1992, 55–78. Cf. Galiffe 1820, 88, 89; Valéry 1838, 445.

670 Piozzi 1789, II, 35–36. She recognizes the impression of a foot (p. 36) of a "sick female, known to be so from the *stole* she wore, a drapery peculiar to her sex; her bed, converted into a substance like plaster of Paris, still retains the form and covering of her who perished quietly upon it, without ever making even an effort to escape." Cf. De Gonzague 1797, 234: "Dans ce cabinet est aussi quelque chose de très-curieux; c'est l'empreinte de différentes parties du corps d'une femme, moulées dans des cendres massives. L'empreinte de la gorge surtout est parfaite; on y peut encore apercevoir les traits de la draperie fine et légère dont elle étoit couverte. On y

> How dreadful are the thoughts which such a sight suggests! how *very* horrible the certainty, that such a scene might be all acted over again to-morrow; and that, who to-day are spectators, may become spectacles to travellers of a succeeding century, who mistaking our bones for those of the Neapolitans, may carry some of them to their native country back again perhaps; as it came into my head that a French gentleman was doing, when I saw him put a human bone into his pocket this morning, and told him I hoped he had got the jaw of a Gaulish officer, instead of a Roman soldier, for future reflections to energize upon.

The German poet Elisa Von der Recke wrote romantically about the impression of the breast, beneath which the heart had stopped beating so abruptly. She felt a real connection with the people of Pompeii, and even heard one of their voices, speaking about their gifts to the gods.[671] A barrister from London and friend of Shelley, Thomas Jefferson Hogg, was less impressed by the remains he saw during his visit:[672]

> We saw the skull of a female, said to be the wife of Diomedes of Pompeii; the custode assured us, that her eyebrows might be seen; it was so dark that I did not see them: on the lava, or rather hardened mud, was the impression of her cheek and bosom: my companions instantly began to admire the form of her bosom from the impression which it had made; I could hardly distinguish it: in this instance, at least, I was insensible to the impression of a lovely bosom.

---

voit les anneaux, les bracelets, le collier, les pendans-d'oreilles et autres bijoux de tête, le tout en or, dont cette infortunée étoit parée pour être engloutie dans les entrailles de la terre." Similarly, Stolberg 1822, 95: "Eine Frau, deren Schädel verwahrt wird, fand man in Asche liegen. In die durch die Zeit consolidirte Asche hat sich ihre eine Brust deutlich abgedruckt. Sie war mit goldnen Armbändern geschmückt, und mit einem Halsbande."

671 Von der Recke 1815, III, 72: "Innig erschüttert erblickte ich hier in einem Stück zu Stein gewordner Krater-asche die eingedrückte Form einer weiblichen Brust, unter welcher einst das Herz so plötzlich aufgehört hatte zu schlagen. Ich fühlte mich über die vielen Jahrhunderte zurückgehoben, ganz in die Kreise der Menschen in den verschütteten Städten versetzt: es war als flüsterte mir eine Stimme die Geschichte manches zarten Weihgeschenkes zu; als sähe ich vor den kleinen Idolen die Andachts stehen, und hörte die frommen Gebete." She would become a learned scholar, see Müller 2012 (on her journal, esp. pp. 265–270). Another German reaction of 1813 was similar (Von Charpentier 1820, II, 199): "Auch sah ich hier einen mit Glas bedeckten achtzehnhundertjährigen, und dennoch schön geformten, – aber negativen Weiberbusen, nähmlich einen bloßen Abdruck davon. Eine gewiß schön gestaltete Pompejianerin flüchtete sich im Jahre 79 nach Christi Geburt bei dem fürchterlichen Ausbruch des Vesuvs in einen Keller, und wurde hier von dem hereinströmenden Aschenbrei erstickt, und ganz umflossen. Die dichte Asche umgab ihren ganzen Körper und erhärtete, und als man bei der Ausgrabung Pompeji's in jenen Keller kam, fand man die Gebeine und einigen schönen goldenen Schmuck (der jetzt in den Studien aufbewahrt wird). Der Abdruck der Brust der unglücklichen Frau in der erhärteten Masse wurde unverletzt aufbewahrt." García y García 1998, no. 2899.
672 Hogg 1827, 99. Similar: Von der Hagen 1818–1819, III, 93–94: "Wenig erfreulicher aber ein Stück fester Erde, worin sich der schöne Busen eines verschütteten Weibes abgedrückt hat, deren Schädel und Gebeine nur noch übrig sind."

Another less enthusiastic voice was that of the caustic Pompeii critic James Augustus Galiffe who wrote indignantly about the sentimental approach to the corpses.[673] The same is true for the Russian Count Orloff in his travel book dedicated to Tsar Alexander I. Orloff considered the imprint of the woman left in the *lapilli* an invention of the guides[674] Charles Swann combined his impressions of the *lazzaroni* in Naples with that of the stand-out lady:[675]

> Hark! she comes; I hear the rustling of her garments, and the Roman virgin will presently appear in all her classic dignity! Alas! such dreams would be dissipated by very different objects. The rags of some itinerant lazzaroni might occupy the image which the flowing folds of ancient costume had elicited; and a putrifying sore surrounded with coagulated filth, like Vesuvius amid its lava, would be presented for the fresh glowing countenance of a youthful maiden, just emancipated from the luxury of the bath.

Upon leaving the Villa of Diomedes during his first visit in 1817, military officer Paul Crombet encountered an old gentleman, and imagined him as an ancient Pompeian, familiar with the woman whose breast had become famously imprinted in the lapilli.[676] Louis Simond was struck by the remains of a mother and

---

673 Galiffe 1820, II, 119–120: "I am aware that this account of Pompeii is calculated to repress the romantick anticipations of many of my readers. But I shall not be sorry if it produces that effect. For I was myself so much disappointed, in consequence of having been seduced by the reports of others, into a belief that I should really see an habitable ancient city, which wanted people alone to restore it to its original state, – that I feel it a duty to guard others against a similar vexation. And I think it better even to fall short of the truth in such a description than to be beyond it."
674 Orloff 1819–1821, V, 428–429: "Avec un peu d'attention on distingue sans peine l'endroit de la cave où la lave s'arrêta: la cave ne fut point entièrement rempli, ainsi les malheureux qui s'y étaient retirés ne furent point engloutis, mais suffoqués, desséchés par la vapeur brûlante de la lave. [...] Elle est probablement l'invention des *ciceroni*."
675 Swan 1826, 47–49, quotation 48–49. The baths mentioned are those next to the Forum, just excavated in 1826.
676 Crombet 1941, 31: "Mais est-ce un rêve qui frappe mes sens? Serait-il possible que cette espèce de fantôme que je vois là, fixement arrêté devant moi, fût encore un ancien habitant de Pompeia? Il est vrai que ses cheveux blanchis par l'âge, que les rides profondes qui sillonnent son front annoncent la plus grande vieillesse. Il est vrai que la tristesse visible qui règne dans tous ses traits paraît annoncer que le temps n'a pu encore le consoler du désastre de sa ville. Cependant dix-huit siècles! ... Ah! oui, ce ne peut-être qu'un rêve qui s'est emparé de mon imagination. ... Mais quel trait de lumière! la certitude remplace enfin la doute ... Non, on ne m'avait pas induit en erreur... Ce vieillard était réellement un habitant de Pompeia; né il y a soixante-dix ans dans les ruines, dont il est un des gardiens, et l'affliction dans laquelle il était apparemment plongé n'était que le piège dont se servent ordinairement les mendicants pour exciter la sensibilité et la générosité lorsqu'ils se préparent à tendre une main suppliante."

child.[677] The painter Théodore Chassériau made a sketch of the room in which he represented the suggestion of the victims' shapes on the wall.[678] Joseph Santo-Domingo was indignant about the man with the purse found in the garden, who, he assumed, had never given alms, but who had merely spent money on himself.[679] The American Rev. John Mitchell suggested that the amphorae in the cellar still contained wine.[680] While many later travelers repeat these assertions, the American Joel Tyler Headley in March 1843 refuses to repeat the same old stories, and gives his personal impressions.[681]

These descriptions are testimony to the changes travel writing underwent in the late eighteenth and early nineteenth centuries. Whereas the first authors gave meticulous descriptions, with little space for personal feeling or observations, the late eighteenth century saw expressions of horror and emotion, combined with interpretations of the skeletons as specific people. This continued in the early nineteenth century, and ended several decades later, since authors evidently felt that the skeletons' stories had been told.

We observe a similar change of tenor in learned works and travel guides. Mazois, for example, associated the cast of the breast with a beautiful girl, still

---

[677] Simond 1828, 407: "Some of the skeletons were found standing against the wall: one of them, a woman holding a child by the hand, probably was the mistress of the house, as she wore valuable rings on her fingers, a gold chain, and other trinkets. Her whole form in its native plumpness, although since wasted to the bone, was found distinctly moulded into this hardened substance. We saw a part of that extraordinary mould, that is, the breast and drapery over. The head and the femur of the skeleton have also been preserved."

[678] Betzer 2010, 476–477, pl. 11; Pucci 2012, 73, fig. 1. Chassériau wrote a long comment on his sketch, which is quoted by Betzer and Pucci. John George Francis (1847, 137–138) recognizes traces of violence: "On a wall near its extremity the outlines of human figures are visible, an indelible stain made by fire and blood!"

[679] Santo-Domingo 1829, 222–223: "Ce vil harpagon ne dépensa jamais son or que par ostentation; combien de fois des infortunés réclamèrent-ils en vain son secours! Combien de fois refusa-t-il l'obole à l'indigence! Il entend tout à coup une voix sourde et tonnante; c'est le terrible Vésuve qui vient lui demander et la bourse et la vie." He counts 17 skeletons and, as to the imprint of the woman (for him probably the *domina*) in the ashes, he observes at p. 224: "J'ai considéré avec admiration les formes semi-sphériques de son sein, qui sont empreintes et moulées dans un morceau de cendre durcie sur lequel elle était appuyée en mourant; on y voit quelques parcelles de sa robe. On peut en conclure, sans être taxé d'inconséquence, que madame Diomède avait les chairs très-fermes et une belle gorge. Je doute que les dames parisiennes, surtout depuis la mode des corsets à busc, puissent laisser de pareils moules à la postérité."

[680] Mitchell 1845, II, 132. He wrote extensively about the negative aspects in continental society caused by the Catholic Church as seen on his tour through Europe in 1843–1844.

[681] Headley 1845, 71. Some other references: Skene 1937 [= 1802–1803], 214; Dwight 1824, 117; Le Riche 1825, 73; Lemercier de Longpré 1835, II, 208; Dumas 1846/2001, 407–408; Cross 1860, 158; Blessington 1839, 287 (= Clay 1979, 70).

pure and a virgin. Her dress was of the finest fabric. Seeing the cast, one could only reflect on the many centuries passed over the corpse of the Pompeian girl.[682] Dyer is among the last authors to spill ink on these types of emotions:[683]

> This [story] the reader will probably be inclined to think might do very well for the conclusion of a romance, but why invent such sentimental stories to figure in a grave historical account? It is a remarkable instance, perhaps the strongest which has yet occurred, of the peculiar interest which the discoveries at Pompeii possess, as introducing us to the homes, nay, to the very persons of a long-forgotten age, that every circumstance of this tale can be verified by evidence little less than conclusive.

The Sentinel of the Herculanean Gate

A frequently told tenacious, but surely fictitious story is about a Roman guard who remained on duty during the eruption. The way guides told it was that the excavators had found the guard's corpse in a small niche outside the city gate.[684] Today this niche on the west side of the street (p. 154, fig. 5) interests few visitors, and indeed, the excavation report from 1763, which wouldn't have been viewed by anyone but King Carlo's administration, simply described it as the tomb of Marcus Cerrinius Restitutus, a priest of the Roman Emperors cult, based on an inscription. Winckelmann published this information in 1764, relying on La Vega's personal account. As the excavation report itself was never published, Winckelmann

---

682 Mazois 1824, II, 90: "La fille, jeune et d'une beauté dont un hasard miraculeux ne saurait nous permettre de douter, vêtue, comme on l'a reconnu, d'étoffes précieuses, se retira dès les premières alarmes dans un souterrain de la maison, suivie de sa mère et de ses domestiques. " Mazois 1824, II, 91: [the cast] "prouve en faveur de l'infortunée qui périt âgée à peine de quelques lustres; jamais le beau idéal dans les ouvrages de l'art n'a offert de formes plus pures, plus virginales. On remarque sur le plâtre les traces d'une étoffe bien visible, mais dont la finesse rappelle ces gazes transparentes que Sénèque appelait du vent tissu. Lorsque l'on contemple ce fragment unique et miraculeux, on se sent ému d'un sentiment tout-à-fait douloureux; en vain se représente-t-on la fragilité de la vie, la nécessité de la mort, en vain compte-t-on les siècles écoulés que ne devait jamais voir l'intéressante victime de Pompéi, la jeunesse, la beauté et le malheur semblent être là d'hier pour exercer sur le cœur toute la puissance de la pitié." He refers to 17 corpses. Cf. Breton 1855, 244–245; 1869, 299–301. His compatriot Charles Hequet, who worked for three years (1859–1862) at Pompeii, did not deem the skeletons worth noting in his booklet about the villa (Hequet 1869 = García y García 1998, no. 6720).
683 Dyer 1868, 493–494.
684 For this story, see Moormann 2001, 11–13; Behlmann 2007; Lazer 2009, 40–41, with fig. 1.4 by Lancelot Seed (in an edition of Bulwer-Lytton's Last Days): "Amidst the crashing elements: he had not received the permission to desert his station." See also Overbeck 1866, II, 30 (quoted in note 661); St Clair/Bautz 2012 384, fig. 15.

remained the only printed source available for a long time.[685] Around 1800, Starke reinterpreted the niche as a sentry box.[686] Mazois argued that the niche was a street shrine devoted to a road-protecting divinity. He mentioned paintings representing this god as well as an altar.[687] Galanti mentioned the interpretation of the sentry box as an alternative, as did Donaldson, who recorded Mazois.[688] We may presume that Starke and Gell heard the sentry box story from a guide, and that thanks to these influential authors, it gained momentum. Lady Blessington heard it from Gell personally, when he brought her to Pompeii in September 1823:[689]

> On the right is an arched alcove, round which is a bench of marble. An altar, with a very beautiful bronze tripod,[690] stood in the centre, (and are now in the Museum,) and this gave rise to the supposition that the alcove was dedicated to some sylvan deity. To me it appeared rightly as a *reposoir*, erected for the convenience of persons to wait in until the gate was opened, as it stands very close to it. [...] A skeleton, with a spear still grasped in its hand, was found in the *reposoir*, and is supposed to have been that of a sentinel, who met death at his post, the spear held even in dead attesting his constancy to duty.

Some travelers thought that they saw the sentinel's helmet (with or without the skull of his head) in the museum. Young Rollo even saw the skull and the helmet

---

[685] Karl Weber in *PAH* I, 152–153, 13 August 1763. Inscription: *M. CERRINIVS /RESTITVTVS /AVG- VSTALIS /LOC. D. D. D* ("Marcus Cerrinius Restitutus, priest of Augustus. The *decuriones* gave the grounds [for the tomb]"). Winckelmann 1764, 20–21; 1997, 19 (comment p. 64); Martini 1779, 115 (tomb), 333–334 (inscriptions), *CIL* X 994. For the tomb, see Kockel 1983, 47–51.

[686] Starke 1802, II, 105 (observation from 1798): "The *City-Gate* is highly interesting; here is the sentry-box for the Guard ..." Cf. Starke 1828, 315: "*Sentry-Box*. This small Edifice, in the form of a niche, and close to the City-Gate, seems, judging from the lance, the crest of a helmet, and the skeleton found here, to have been the station of a soldier who died at his post." Johann Isaac Gerning (1802, II, 225–229), who was there in the same year 1818 (cf. Starke 1828, 305), did not mention any sentinel. Starke's book formed the basis for Murray's Italy of 1836 (cf. Chabaud 2000, 85–86, 87, here p. 129). This is the beginning of a successful story, to start with Joseph Sansom and Gell: Sansom 1805, II, 218: "Sentry-Box for the City Guard remains just within [sic] the Town Gate"; Gell/Gandy 1852, 63.

[687] Mazois 1827–1838, I, 27–28: "consacré sans doute à quelqu'une de ces divinités qui président aux chemins, et que les anciens appelaient *Viales dii*." A mix of shrine and skeleton in Clarke 1847, 71, 556 (no. 21 on his plan p. 536–537). Bonucci 1828, 74 (as the first: Kockel 1983, 49). So Vinci 1831, 53. Summary of these opinions in Von Agyagfalva 1825, 54 ("Kleines Gemach").

[688] Galanti 1832. II, 340; Donaldson 1828, 22–23. Similar interpretations in Ducos 1829, 321 and Power 1846, 15.

[689] Blessington 1839, 276; Clay 1979, 61. Cf. Power 1846, 156: "the one [tomb] attributed to Cerrinius, from its vicinity to the gate and its style and structure, was probably a sentry box."

[690] This is another alien element, viz. the famous tripod with the ithyphallic satyrs which stems from the *Praedia* of Julia Felix, see chapter II, p. 117. Hamilton 1777, 168 locates it here as the first of a long series of authors (.e.g. Clarke 1847, 71, 556).

together.[691] Bulwer-Lytton could not fail to insert the sentinel into his novel: when the protagonists are fleeing, they pass the city gate and its guardian.[692] As a military officer, Crombet was evidently struck by this example of courageous behaviour, and he referred to a number of soldiers.[693] Louise Colet wrote about the stoicism of Roman soldiers.[694] Classens de Jongste admonished youth in general by referring to the braveness of the soldier.[695] Mark Twain was rather cynical about the heroic nature of the sentinel:[696]

> But perhaps the most poetical thing Pompeii has yielded to modern research, was that grand figure of a Roman soldier, clad in complete armor; who, true to his duty, true to his proud name of a soldier of Rome, and full of the stern courage which had given to that name its glory, stood to his post by the city gate, erect and unflinching, till the hell that raged around him *burned out* the dauntless spirit it could not conquer.
>
> We never read of Pompeii but we think of that soldier; we can not write of Pompeii without the natural impulse to grant to him the mention he so well deserves. Let us remember that he was a soldier – not a policeman – and so, praise him. Being a soldier, he staid, – because the warrior instinct forbade him to fly. Had he been a policeman he would have staid, also – because he would have been asleep.

Overbeck supported the sentinel theory in his work, while his colleague Breton agreed with Mazois.[697] In his romanticized autobiography, Garibaldi referred to

---

691 Abbott 1858, 171: "His head, with the helmet still upon it, was carried to the museum at Naples, where it is now seen by all the world, and everyone who sees it utters some expression of praise for the courage and fidelity which the poor fellow displayed in fulfilling his trust." Cf. Cross 1860: 146: "There was the helmet of the soldier whose skeleton was found guarding the gate of Pompeii, where he had stood 1678 years – the helmet and nothing else!"
692 Bulwer-Lytton 1834, V, VI, and see note 685. In a note Bulwer-Lytton observes that more sentries of this kind were found. He probably refers to Bonucci 1828, 151, on guards next to the Temple of Jupiter: "Gli avanzi di due soldati che non vollero abbandonare il posto, ove forse erano di guardia, giaceano in questo sito: uno di essi era stato schiacciato d'una colonna. Una sola moneta di bronzo, ed una visiera si raccolsero presso di loro." Göbel 1993, 153: he even would have received the skulls of Arbaces and Calenus in 1859!
693 Crombet 1941, 28–29. Cf. the soldiers in the barracks mentioned, p. 46.
694 Colet 1862, III, 118: "[...] peut-être s'écria-t-il en riant: 'On ne passe pas!' car les soldats des légions romaines avaient de ces gaietés stoïques en face de la mort."
695 Classens de Jongste 1841, 30–32. Cf. Weed 1866, 530.
696 Twain 1869, 327–336; 1984, 264–265, chapter XXXI. The man would have died in a fire that started during the eruption, according to von Rochau 1852, II, 134–135.
697 Overbeck 1856, 291; Breton 1855, 98. Similarly brief are Micheletti 1846, 334; De Musset 1865, 411; Monnier 1865, 87.

the sentinel as an example of ancient Roman discipline displayed all-over the globe by the Roman legions.[698]

Finally, Fiorelli's publication of La Vega's excavation report urged most authors stop perpetuating this story.[699] Around 1880, Rudolph Karl Schramm, a minister from Bremen, wrote about a typical Roman sentinel who had looked for shelter in a tomb. In doing so, Schramm combined the two interpretations of the much-contested niche, and added a group of a mother and her children, probably known to him from Overbeck.[700] The German political philosopher Oswald Spengler used the sentinel motif as late as 1932, sketching a dark scenario of the "Untergang des Abendlandes" in which "coloured" people ("blacks" and "yellows") and the Russians (communists) would take over political and military power in the western world. Spengler believed in a brief life full of deeds and fame (rather than a long and empty one), and promoted living life like the Pompeian soldier in order to demonstrate the greatness and pureness of one's race.[701] A similar vein is present in Garro's *Juventus*, in which the young soldier Romano reveals both his Roman and Christian qualities in standing at his post until the bitter

---

698 Garibaldi 1874, 48: "Questi due fatti d'insuperabile disciplina, sono forse la chiave di quella severissima disciplina Romana, che condusse le Legioni su tutto l'orbe conosciuto e di cui si trovò un saggio sotto le ceneri di Pompei, d'un Legionario che, coll'arma al piede lasciossi coprire dalle ceneri senza muoversi." I thank Nathalie de Haan for the discovery of this interesting case.

699 Breton 1870, 114; Dyer 1868, 531: "Unfortunately, however, this story is a pure fable. The Journals of the Excavations know nothing of this soldier, although they always particularly record the discovery of skeletons, because in most cases some coins or other property were found near them." Murray 1873, 230: "The story of the skeleton of a soldier, fully armed, having been found here, led to its being considered at one time as a *sentry-box*; but as there is no authentic record of such a skeleton, the pleasing fable of the Roman soldier dying at his post must be abandoned (1763)."

700 Schramm 1890, 265–266, included the story and probably relied on an old edition of Overbeck's work (quotation here in note 661). In a similar way De Séranon 1877, 64–65; Lagrèze 1892, 65, 91; Blasco Ibáñez 1980 (travel book of 1896), 190–191 ("la más commoveda [tragedia] ... Se comprende que soldatos así conquistasen el mundo").

701 Spengler 1932, 88–89: "Lieber ein kurzes Leben voll Taten und Ruhm als ein langes ohne Inhalt. [...] Wir sind in diese Zeit geboren und müssen tapfer den Weg zu Ende gehen, der uns bestimmt ist. Es gibt keinen andern. Auf dem verlorenen Posten ausharren ohne Hoffnung, ohne Rettung, ist Pflicht. Ausharren wie jener römische Soldat, dessen Gebeine man vor einem Tor in Pompeji gefunden hat, der starb, weil man beim Ausbruch des Vesuv vergessen hatte, ihn abzulösen. Das ist Größe, das heißt Rasse haben. Dieses ehrliche Ende ist das einzige, das man dem Menschen nicht nehmen kann." I owe this quotation to Gemma Jansen and Robert Kragting. On Spengler's interest in archaeology, see Gere 2009, 147–149.

end (fig. 10).⁷⁰² In the German periodical *Der Spiegel*, Sándor Kopácsi, the chief of the Budapest police, was quoted, comparing the Pompeii sentinel to his own men during the revolt of 1956. His men had to maintain their position against the Russian tanks in the way the brave Pompeian soldier had done during the eruption.⁷⁰³ Most recently, the sentinel appeared in Rebecca East's novel of 2003.⁷⁰⁴

Antiquarian and Timeless Pompeii Novels

Various fiction books regard a "timeless" Pompeii, the town in its pre-eruption phase. Some of them try to recreate the classical world on the basis of antique texts and – more relevant to our case – archaeological remains of the ancient cities. These books, popular at the end of the eighteenth and in the first decades of the nineteenth century, excellently reflect the attitude towards antiquity during that time. Generally, they barely have plots and are unspecific as to time, and the authors focus on a young person learning about the (classical) world and about the way of life in ancient culture. An early example is the influential *Voyage du jeune Anacharsis en Grèce* by *abbé* Jean-Jacques Barthélemy from 1788 that describes the Pausanias-like tour the young title hero takes through Greece in the fourth century B.C., visiting historically important and sacred places like Delphi and Olympia and meeting great personalities. The *abbé* invented a lot of monuments, but made use of new discoveries in the South of Italy, like the Greek temples at Paestum and the Vesuvian cities. Barthélemy presents Anacharsis as a foreigner who wants to learn about Greek civilization; he is the grandson of

---

702 Garro 1942, 226–227, 228 (last lines): "Alla Porta Ercolanese appunto il legionario Romano regolava l'afflusso dei fuggiaschi con altri due soldati. I tre archi della porta offrivano un riparo abbastanza sicuro, ma in quell'ultima furia vulcanica quello di mezzo crollò, seppellendo i due militi. Gli archi laterali, nel nembo di pietre e di cenere, furon presto ricolmi, e i profughi, che ancora lì intorno si aggiravano, o caddero per non più alzarsi, o ricacciati indietro, trovarono morti più lungi. Lì, presso un pilastro – diritto, immobile, appoggiato alla sua lunga asta – rimase il solo legionario Romano. Quello era il suo posto; di lì – egli pensava – non doveva muoversi. [...] Quando, nella pioggia continua, se la sentì ammassata alla bocca, il legionario Romano volse in giro lo sguardo per vedere ancora lo spettacolo terribile che infuriava d'intorno, poi, – esempio sublime di fedeltà al dovere – chiuse gli occhi, abbandonandosi in Dio.
E la cenere – che tutta ormai copriva Pompei – ricoperse anche lui." For more on this book, see Chapter IV, p. 248.
703 *Der Spiegel* 1979, week 37, p. 156. Mentioned in Kockel 1983, 49, note 5.
704 East 2003, 29: "A fully armored soldier stood guard at the gate of Herculaneum and died standing on his post." For more on East's book, see Chapter VI, pp. 326–327.

the Scythian Anacharsis who belonged to the "Seven Sages."[705] He attends a theatrical performance in Athens. The description of the theater building matches that of the theater in Herculaneum by Cochin and Bellicard.[706] Barthélemy's presentation of Greek houses relies heavily on Vitruvius and the remains in Pompeii. Perhaps predictably, Barthélemy never visited Greece, but was in Naples in 1755 to buy coins and medallions in his role as the director of the Royal Coin Cabinet in Paris. In his vivacious letters, addressed to the Comte de Caylus, he only mentions the excavations by way of complaining about their slow progress.[707] The popularity of the *Anacharsis* made the publication of an accompanying volume of maps and illustrations an interesting enterprise.[708]

For all its bookishness, it does serve as a predecessor to Mazois' *Scaurus*, Dezobry's *Rome*, Becker's *Gallus*, and *Sabina oder Morgenszenen im Putzzimmer einer reichen Römerin* by the German archaeologist Carl August Böttiger.[709] Sabina, a lady of noble rank in the time of Domitian, starts her day by applying a complex array of makeup, the description of which leads to numerous digressions about the daily life of an elite Roman woman. This true example of nineteenth-century *Altertumswissenschaft* has lengthy footnotes that are full of quotations from ancient texts and descriptions of archaeological objects. Clearly, the author is no uncritical admirer of antiquity; instead, he hails modern social innovations. Böttiger concludes that the Romans lived in great luxury and that the Trimalchios of those days only sought to placate their gluttony.[710] In Böttiger's

---

705 Barthélemy 1788. In Herodotus' *Historiae* (4.76-78), the old Anacharsis is a symbol of non-Greeks who want to know Greek civilization. A text by Lucian of the second century A.D. has the same name. For more on Anacharsis and the equally famous Scythe Toxaris, see Visa-Ondarçuhu 2008 and Schubert 2010. On Barthélemy and antiquarianism, see Blix 2009, 36; on Barthélemy and Greece, see Güthenke 2008, 58-59. On Anacharsis' fortune, see Th. Schmitz, in A. von Möllendorff/ A. & L. Simonis (eds), *Historische Gestalten der Antike* (Der Neue Pauly Suppl. 8), Stuttgart/Weimar 2013, 69-76.
Barthélemy's predecessor is Fénelon's *Les aventures de Télémaque*, Paris 1699. In this novel, Telemachus, the son of Odysseus is in search of his father and gets an ideal Greek education. The book conferred a political criticism of the king, but was also an ode to Greek culture.
706 Barthélemy 1788, Chapter LXX. His Chapter III gives 30,000 spectators. Cf. Barthélemy's note on the "Théâtre & Bacchus" at the end of the book. Cf. Seznec 1949; Praz 1979, 39.
707 Sérieys 1801, 120 (letter XX, 7-4-1756). Cf. Chapter I, pp. 31, 38 for Caylus.
708 Du Bocage 1788, map 23 and Chapter LXX: "Théâtre grec." A (third) edition of 1790 contains explanations for a book binder of the Voyage in 4º and 8º, so that we may assume that the plates were inserted into the text volumes. The introduction (pp. i-xliii) is of little interest.
709 Mazois 1819, 1820, 1822; Dezobry 1846-1847; Becker 1849; Böttiger 1803 and 1806. See Riikonen 1978, 61. I leave out Dezobry 1846-1847 as it lacks Pompeian elements.
710 Böttiger 1806, IX-X: "Denn er [the author] ist fern davon, durch seine antiquarischen Schilderungen bloss reitzen oder gar kitzeln zu wollen. Eine solche Absicht würde sich weder mit dem

eyes, their atrocious treatment of slaves could not but evoke feelings of shame and disgust.⁷¹¹

While Böttiger concentrates on a lady, Wilhelm Adolph Becker's *Gallus* focuses on the daily activities of a gentleman, Gaius Cornelius Gallus, a successful politician, soldier and poet within Augustus' circles in Rome, who was disgraced because of his arrogance, and committed suicide.⁷¹² Despite Becker's attempt to create a vivid character, *Gallus* does not come to life.

François Mazois' *Le palais de Scaurus* forms a *summa* of his research in Pompeii. It is composed as a series of letters written in Rome by Mérovir, the son of Ariovistus, King of Gaul.⁷¹³ Chrysippe, a Greek philosopher, shows Mérovir around Rome, which is virtually reconstructed on the basis of his own research in Pompeii. Therefore, the description is accompanied by illustrations from *Les ruïnes de Pompéi*.⁷¹⁴ Mérovir lives in the house of Scaurus.⁷¹⁵ Mérovir's every move is linked to a footnote containing a quotation from a Greek or Roman author, used uncritically; Mazois uses neither distinction of time (Homer next to Juvenal), genre (poet next to historian), nor attention for the context of the source he is quoting. Mérovir is prudish and reacts with awe at seeing the *venereum* of the House of Sallustius,⁷¹⁶ in which the *dominus* would receive ladies (such was one early nineteenth century interpretation). Mérovir wants to leave this shameful room, but Chrysippe tries to calm him down by explaining that, like the lord of the house, the *matrona* had her own section, called *gynoeconitis*,

---

Ernste seines äussern Berufs, noch mit der Stimme in seinem Innern jemals in Einklang bringen lassen. Nein, er wünschte vielmehr dem grausam-wollüstigen Launenwechsel einer römischen Pandora die frevelhafte Genussgier eines römischen Trimalchio entgegen zu stellen und seine Leser da einzuführen, wo die raffinierteste Lust mit der gröbsten aller Sinnlichkeiten, der unersättlichen Essbegierde, im engsten Bund erscheint, zu einem Saturnalien-Schmauss des Sabinus." A long make-up scene is included in Menduni De' Rossi 2011.
711 Böttiger 1806, XXIII: "Willkommen sey also dem Verfasser und brüderlich gegrüst jeder Leser, jede Leserin dieser Szenen, deren Wange von Schaam und Unmuth erglühet, wenn sie die hier aufgestellten Schilderungen üppiger Grausamkeit und frecher Prunksucht lesen. Nichts ist hier übertrieben oder zu sehr ins Dunkle gemahlt."
712 Becker 1838. I saw Becker 1849, much expanded. I give some gleanings from its Preface by Wilhelm Rhein. Becker is mentioned by W. Stroh in his lemma on Gallus in *Der Neue Pauly* 3 (1997) 192–193. See on Becker, Schnurbusch 2011, 31–32.
713 Mazois 1819 [edited anonymously]; 1822. Already attributed to Mazois in the German translation (Mazois 1820, V–VI).
714 E.g. Mazois 1822, 46 (inscription Salve), 47 (zodiac), 50 (cave canem), 83, 86 (lararium).
715 Scaurus is the son of the man, also called Scaurus, who had built an extremely luxurious theatre in wood when he was *aedile* in 58 B.C. (Pliny, *Natural History* 28.15).
716 Mazois 1822, 99–107. See Chapter I, note 189. Gautier's Arria Marcella receives Octavien here (see Chapter VI, p. 313).

which was guarded by eunuchs. Clearly, Pompeii's fame as the town of carnal love, as developed in the eighteenth century, is fostered in scenes like these. The city's lavish bath culture does not please the Gaul either.[717] Mazois' *Scaurus* became widespread thanks to many editions and translations. Some thought that Mazois was describing the real house of Scaurus. In his famous *Cicerone*, Jacob Burckhardt praises Mazois for his splendid evocation of the house of Scaurus in his novel.[718]

Written forty years later, Candido Augusto Vecchi's *Pompei* goes through Pompeii's history from 81 B.C. to A.D. 72.[719] His eight short stories are dedicated to scholars, artists and politicians who made themselves invaluable in the Italian struggle for independence. To complete his work, Vecchi stayed five months at Pompeii, where he had frequent contact with Fiorelli. All the Pompeians portrayed are based on skeletons or inscriptions found by Fiorelli's team.[720] Vecchi included numerous vehement invectives against the Roman Church, as was fashionable in *Risorgimento* political circles around Mazzini and Garibaldi, and believed that paganism was one of the most attractive aspects of antiquity. But, he argued, ancient society had been in decline as it grew more decadent, and without explicitly saying so, he suggests that the disaster of 79 was a logical end to the debauchery of Roman life. Vecchi compares the past to the present and expresses his distaste for modern Neapolitan life, especially the mendicant priests roaming the streets of Naples and begging in the name of God.[721] This is despite his feeling

---

[717] Mazois 1822, 231–246. His reference to Tacitus, *Germania* 12 is mistaken. In this essay on the Germans, Tacitus says in par. 22.1 that they wash with hot water because of the cold temperature. The correct sources are Tacitus, *Agricola* 21–31 (the inhabitants of Britannia are becoming effeminate because of steam baths), and Dio Cassius 62.6.4 (queen Boudicca sees hot baths as a Roman form of effeminacy). On the impact of Tacitus' *Germania* in Mazois' era see Krebs 2011, 153–181

[718] Burckhardt 1869, I, 56: "Von dem Palast des Scaurus auf dem cölischen Berge hat bekanntlich Mazois in einem angenehmen Buche (das in allen Sprachen vorhanden ist) wirklich ein solches Gedankenbild aufgestellt; an Ort und Stelle ist indes kein Stein davon nachzuweisen. " According to ancient sources the house was not situated on the Caelius ('dem cölischen Berge') but at the foot of the Palatine near the Arch of Titus: E. Papi, *Lexicon Topographicum Urbis Romae* II (1995) 26; Tomei 1995 (remains found).

[719] Vecchi 1864; 1868. Mentioned by Sogliano 1888, 28; García y García 1998, nos 13.887–13.889. On Vecchi, see Ficcadenti 1981, 79–267. On Vecchi's book, see Ficcadenti 1981, 238–239. Vecchi lacks in Avvisati 2010 on Garibaldi and Pompeii.

[720] In letters to Vecchi, Fiorelli refers to these skeletons (see Ficcadenti 1981, 315–318). Cf. Curti 1872–1874, I, 173.

[721] Vecchi 1864, 102; 1868, 143: "I sacerdoti antichi dicevano – 'Spendete; e le Ombre amate godranno nei Campi-Elisi delle ricchezze che avrete profuso nel loro mortorio!' – E i sacerdoti moderni pur dicono – 'Spendete; e allor suoneremo campane, canteremo, borbotteremo in latino e tratteremo con Dio come fosse un giudice borbonico; e a furia di danari dati a noi, noi costrin-

that the people of Naples are, by nature, the most intelligent of all Italians, and as a result of these priests, are demoralized and start committing crimes.[722] He sees the cult of Isis as one of the most perfect religions in Pompeii because of its pure rituals and absence of falsity.[723]

Thanks to his profound knowledge of the ruins, Vecchi was able to insert accurate descriptions of monuments and objects, about which there had been an enormous growth in awareness since Mazois.[724] Vecchi was eager to incorporate new findings into his work, since he was proud of the fervent zeal for archaeology displayed in southern Italy thanks to the new Italian kingdom. This also holds for historical characters: among the persons portrayed in *Pompei* is Cicero, who, fed up with Roman politics, has retired to his Pompeianum and writes *De consolatione*. Vecchi makes Cicero and others spokesmen for his own political views, which he shares with Fiorelli (who, Vecchi insists, is a strong advocate of the modern Italian regime, which is no longer a series of "ministates" dominated by the Catholic Church). Like other authors, Vecchi does not succeed in conveying living history, despite his numerous dialogues; his style is swollen and the text abounds with unnecessary learnedness.

Cicero, one of Vecchi's favorites, is the protagonist of a novel by Max Brod, an author more famous for his work about Franz Kafka's literary heritage than as the novelist of *Armer Cicero*,[725] which portrays the orator-politician after the murder of his rival Caesar. The reader gets a good impression of Cicero by what his friends and personnel say about him. Brod represents Cicero as a man struggling against tyranny and bloodshed, which was especially pertinent in 1955,

---

geremo lui a riconoscere in un'anima ribalda una onesta.' –" As a matter of fact, time and again Vecchi curses the Italian clergy; see note 722.
722 Vecchi 1864, 61; 1868, 79: "Sono passati diciotto secoli e la tradizione rimane ancor verde. Vi ha tal gente in Napoli che lautamente vive di una siffatta speculazione ladra ed infame. Il cattolicesimo vi presta la sua mano sacrilega. – Sozzi frati colla bisaccia sul collo; sozzi preti con un bussolo che scuotono nelle botteghe nel nome santo di Dio; sozza bordaglia, coperta di un sacco, cinto da una corda sui lombi, chiede danaro e l'ottiene a pro di turpi speculatori e per cause non vere. – E quel buon popolo – il migliore d'Italia per pronta intelligenza, per docilità di carattere, per esuberanza di cuore – su ricchissimo suolo, vegeta sudicio, lacero ed infingardo. – Demoralizzato dai preti, commette opere inique e crudeli. – Abbuiato dalla paura, dimentica il domani della vita e sciupa il sopravanzo dei suoi guadagni nello inutile tentativo di spegnere il sacro incendio del purgatorio cattolico, apostolico, romano."
723 Vecchi 1864, 13; 1868, 20: "uno dei più completi e dei più ricchi [culti] che fossero in Pompei."
724 This might explain Carmine Modestino's reproach of Vecchi of a poor use of the classical sources (letter reproduced in Ficadenti 1981, 319–320).
725 Brod 1955. Not in García y García 1998.

during the aftermath of the Holocaust. *Armer Cicero* exemplifies the bad luck of one of the great men of Roman history, whom Brod clearly admired.[726] The attention Brod pays to mystery cults reflects his disdain for fanatical religious sects and secrecy. Among them features a group of Jewish Essenes, sketched as sweet people.[727] Brod claims that Pompeii did not offer Cicero what he had wanted: rest from the turmoil dominating political and social life in Rome. Despite its status as a smaller city of little importance, it was no peaceful place, but full of unrest and political stress.

Norbert Rouland's *Les lauriers de cendre* highlights Pompeii as a lucky retreat in the turmoil of the late Republic, in which the protagonists Lucius and Aurelia have to endure many sorrows.[728] The city is a mixture of Greeks, Samnites, Jews and Orientals, and displays a warm Greek hospitality.[729] For all the story's merits, the town remains a façade, for in the novel, the city has no characters apart from the happy couple. Rouland, a historian and lawyer, explains his ideas of the historical novel genre in an afterword.[730] A historical novel, he argues, is a good means of evoking antiquity, if written with reference to the sources, which give it a realistic image. The reader might wonder if it is for this reason that the book has so many explanations of details. Rouland represents Lucius as a traditional, incorruptible Roman. In contrast, his loving marriage to an equal partner seems more a construct of the 1980s than of Roman times.

For the most part, the authors of these "timeless" novels know Pompeii very thoroughly, so that they can transform it into a hot crime scene. Many tales portray the site as awesome and awful at the same time, focusing on the dangerous and crime-ridden society Pompeii the authors supposed it had been. This focus, of course, is a characteristic typical of thrillers, which are surprisingly abundant in Pompeii fiction of the last four decades.[731] The town's attractiveness lies in the possibility of rendering the stories believable by inserting archaeological and historical details, while the villains are often people known from authentic documents like raffiti.

---

726 Brod 1955, 279.
727 Brod 1955, 21.
728 Rouland 1984. On this book, see Moormann 2008, 387–389. Not in García y García 1998.
729 Rouland 1984, 237.
730 Rouland 1984, 419–425: "Pour un nouveau roman historique."
731 Cf. Cramme 2004. Rocchi 2006–2007 and 2008 discusses thrillers focusing on Pompeii. I have not the ambition to discuss all of them.

Murder and Crime

Les mystères de Pompéi by Cristina Rodríguez[732] is the story of Kaeso, the son of a German mother and a Roman father, who becomes head of the Pompeian militia under the reign of Tiberius.[733] Murder by poison and circulating false coinage are among the crimes he has to solve in an atmosphere of distrust of the emperor. Tiberius' successors Caligula and Claudius take part in the action, too, and become real protagonists.[734] Kaeso's pet leopard Io is a witty persona who evokes all sorts of reactions, including fear at times and laughter at others.

Rodríguez presents Pompeii in a cursory way, mentioning few Pompeian loci, persons and buildings, except for the Temple of Isis and its priest and priestesses.[735] Only in this novel is Pompeii depicted with explicitly dirty and poor neighborhoods next to luxurious ones, but given the archaeological records, it is quite certain that this is merely fiction. When, at the end of the novel, Kaeso leaves for Rome, he confesses that he is happy to have experienced living in the small provincial town that is Pompeii.

A novel by Stéphanie de la Rochefoucauld bears almost the same title: *Le mystère de Pompéi*.[736] In the year 64, the painter Labius discovers machinations that have caused several mysterious murders. His research continues until the eruption of 79, which he only narrowly escapes. The reader recognizes not only Pompeians known from inscriptions and graffiti, but several skeletons, too, which "come to life" in the novel. De la Rochefoucauld inserts data about the history and archaeology of Pompeii.[737] Other juicy elements are soft sex, politics, mysterious religions including occult sessions with flagellations, and slavery. One particular detail is the installation of vases to collect urine according to a rule decreed by Vespasian in Rome, who famously said: "Money doesn't smell."[738]

---

[732] Rodríguez 2008. The author has published other novels about the ancient Roman world, whereas she is also active as a numismatist (see frontispiece of her book). Not in García y García 2012.
[733] Kaeso is also featured in *Meurtres sur le Palatin : Une enquête de Kaeso le prétorien* (Paris 2009).
[734] A peculiar activity is Caligula's editing of Claudius' scientific treatises (Rodríguez 2008, 337).
[735] Rodríguez 2008, 101–103 (priestesses too much perfumed); 199–200 (priest not suitable to be a holy man because of gluttony).
[736] De la Rochefoucauld 2001. García y García 2012, no A2661–A2662. Cf. Moormann 2008, 389–390.
[737] There is a small bibliography. Some notes explain Latin words, situations and historical facts. Despite this touch of learnedness, the orthography of some names is incorrectly mixed, i.e. pure Latin ones (Nero for Néron) and Gallicized ones.
[738] Suetonius, *Vespasianus* 23: *pecunia non olet*; De la Rochefoucauld 2001, 243. This urine served for treatment of cloth. Some old houses are in use as fulleries (De la Rochefoucauld 2001, 54). They feature in many other novels and stories (see my index s.v. fullery).

In Danila Comastri Montanari's series of fourteen thrillers, we read about Publio Aurelio Stazio, a senator with a good relationship with Claudius. The Emperor asks him to carry out investigations, and like a real detective he resolves crimes in a Pompeii portrayed as a living mix of people from all over the world.[739] The description of oriental Sandelio is similar to that of Arbaces in Bulwer-Lytton's *Last Days of Pompeii*: black hair, sharp eyes, and aquiline nose, with a character difficult to unravel.[740] All male inhabitants seem oversexed, occupied with legitimate and illegitimate relationships. Phalli, present everywhere in Pompeii, the city of Venus, are visible symbols of this avidity.[741] Publio is a concoction of Epicurean stability and soberness, sexual interest and masculinity, and, finally, defense of moral order. The city's intellect is personified by Castore and Ipparco, both Greeks, and exoticism by people from Asia Minor. Despite this "hot" atmosphere, Pompeii is a provincial town, lacking the grandeur of Rome and displaying bad taste.[742]

Lindsey Davis wrote another series of thrillers, with Falco as a spy for the emperor Vespasian between 70 and 76. In *Shadows in Bronze*, the second of her eighteen popular Falco novels, the actions takes place in Pompeii and Herculaneum.[743] Society is seen through his eyes and those of Vespasian's mistress. I shall not give away the plot of this thriller, and concentrate on the image evoked of the Vesuvian towns. When Falco, his dear friend Petronius and their family members look for accommodation in the area, their impression is not very positive:[744]

> Pompeii was too brash, Herculaneum too prim, and the thermal spa at Stabiae chockablock with wheezing old gentlemen and their snotty wives.

---

[739] Comastri Montanari 2005, 104–105: Phrygians, Jews, Samnites, Etruscans, and Oscans; 196: Isis cult; 264: arcane Cilician rites of Attis. One character, Aulo Tiburnio Pio, expresses negative ideas about Eastern people (Comastri Montanari 2005, 105). García y García 2012, no A1097.

[740] E.g. Comastri Montanari 2005, 234: Sandelio was a "gran bell'uomo, con un fisico alto e asciutto e due occhi stranamente chiari che spiccavano come zaffiri in mezzo alla folta peluria nera. Il naso aquilino gli dava un'aria nobile e canagliesca insieme, e da tutta la sua persona emanava un atteggiamento pacatamente imperioso che doveva far girare la testa a più di una donna."

[741] E.g. Comastri Montanari 2005, 11, 270. Nevertheless, the text lacks descriptions of sexual intercourse.

[742] E.g. Comastri Montanari 2005, 78: interior of a house. In sum, it is a good example of golden average, *aurea mediocritas* (Comastri Montanari 2005, 183).

[743] Davis 1990. Davis holds a PhD in classics, but believes that fiction is more important in this genre of novels than fact. Therefore, she gives neither notes nor bibliography. Not in García y García 1998 and 2012.

[744] Davis 1990, 92. The spa of Baiae also features in Roberts 2007.

Pompeii is "'A place that intends to last!' One of my [Falco's] sharper remarks."⁷⁴⁵ As a result of the earthquake, the forum is still full of debris. The Temple of Isis is an "educational spot" for Petronius' son Larius. Phalli are signs of Venus, "a prostitute outside a genuine bordello." Herculaneum is a sleepy town, without stepping stones as at "dirty Pompeii."⁷⁴⁶

> [Herculaneum] had tasteful, well-scrubbed houses owned by people of little character who thought a lot of themselves. [...] Frankly, Herculaneum made me want to jump on a public fountain and shout a very rude word.

As if this is not enough, it is built upon "a pedantic Greek grid."⁷⁴⁷ Even though Davis creates a lowbrow image of Roman society as seen through the eyes of the utterly non-aristocratic Falco, she incorporates elements about antiquity which are familiar to historical novels. People are referred to (in both the first and second person) with the formal three names (*tria nomina*). Expensive and luxurious residences of the wealthy (like Oplontis), and the extreme poverty of the lower classes and slaves are efficiently sketched. Pompeii and Herculaneum are not specific in the narrative – Falco is traveling all over ancient Italy – but have the advantage of being particularly well-known towns of that era. Davis makes light of the disaster of 79 by having Falco refer to this date.⁷⁴⁸

Steven Saylor brings us a third crime serial by introducing "Gordianus the Finder" in well-written and thoroughly researched novels and short stories. Pompeii plays a subordinate role in a brief (and in my opinion not very salty) espionage story about a first-class fish sauce, the Pompeian *garum*, in 75 B.C.⁷⁴⁹ During a brief visit to Pompeii, which is not described or highlighted at all, Gordianus solves the crime of copying a specific precious Pompeian fish sauce and selling the imitation as the genuine one.

One may wonder whether Davis, Saylor or Comastri Montanari invented the idea of the serial Roman investigator. During the same twenty years, each worked arduously to establish an impressive corpus of similarly formatted crime novels. Thanks to their use of English, Davis and Saylor have a larger audience and are more popular.

---

745 Davis 1990, 98.
746 Davis 1990, 155.
747 Davis 1990, 157.
748 Davis 1990, 216: when Falco ascends Vesuvius, he remarks that the mountain will be lower in the future.
749 Saylor 2005, 71–79. The story dates from 2003 and was previously published in periodicals (García y García 2012, no A4085). The series started in 1991 and includes nine novels and two sets of stories (Saylor 2005, XI–XIII; for their chronology, see pp. 261–264).

Ronald Leslie Bassett's concern in *The Pompeians* is the lowest stratum of society, slaves in a Pompeii sinking into a moral morass.[750] The author concentrates on the harsh treatments and cruel punishments slaves have to suffer. Pompeii is rich, yes, but only for a very small elite of *nouveaux riches*, whereas the old Roman gentry can no longer afford a safe and luxurious life. Basset's Pompeians come from various parts of the globe, and symbolize the multifaceted Roman Empire, full of roughness and abrupt changes of fortune. Basset effectively intermingles real elements of Pompeii with his own fantasy, and does not burden his novel with the unnecessary information found in so many Pompeii stories.

Gordon Russell ventures a similarly hard-boiled image, in his modern thriller *La congiura di Pompei* ("The Conspiracy of Pompeii"), in which none of the protagonists survive the eruption.[751] Glauco, a Greek painter, is confronted with murder, adultery, bribery, and many other crimes. Pompeii, he feels, reeling from moral corruption and aggravated by earthquakes and sticky weather, is certain to end with total destruction, but his admonitions fall on deaf ears. He concludes:

> The town crumbles down, with the unlimited luxury of some houses, and the flocks of beggars crouching in the corners or with avid faces in front of the shops and around the Basilica that accommodated negotiations, with the corrupt and conceited *duoviri* who walked up and down the portico of the Forum in want of a breeze.[752]

Russell – behind whose English name hide the Italian writers Vanna de Angelis and Dario Battaglia[753] – attractively intermingles data from archaeological research and antiquarian knowledge.[754] Pompeii's monuments are essential in sketching the local atmosphere and the circumstances in which Russell's characters live. Graffiti are quoted to illustrate the license of the inhabitants.[755] Sex is not described, but

---

750 Bassett 1965, 171: "The Gods are destroying the rottenness that was Pompeii, and the vermin that might crawl from its ruins should be exterminated." Not in García y García 1998.
751 Russell 2008. García y García 2012, no A3972.
752 E.g. Russell 2008, 383: "La città gli [viz. to Glauco] sembrò allo sfacelo, con il lusso smodato di certe case, con i mendicanti a frotte accucciati negli angoli o con le facce avide davanti alle botteghe e intorno alla Basilica che accoglieva le contrattazioni, con i duoviri corrotti e tronfi che andavano avanti e indietro per il portico del Foro cercando un refolo d'aria."
753 Russell 2008, 427–428: brief *curricula vitarum* and titles of other novels playing out in ancient Rome.
754 Rather pedantically and inconsequently, Russell uses the Latin names of towns (hence always "Pompeii" instead of Italian "Pompei"), whereas all other names are Italianized. However, the title of the book, *La congiura di Pompei*, has "Pompei"! There is a bibliography and a list of technical terms at the end of this book.
755 E.g. Russell 2008, 224, reference to the prostitute Asellina (also in Lundgren 2001, here Chapter IV, p. 249).

is hidden behind every door.[756] Russell's paramount interest in gladiatorial games leads to lengthy descriptions of arms, costumes, and training sessions.[757] These and other digressions interrupt the narrative, yet the authors' fascination for Pompeii is clear on every page and is stressed by two remarks the young Pliny makes at his departure to Misenum: "Will we ever stop speaking and writing about Pompeii?" and "How can we not return to Pompeii?"[758] Russell's passion is the same as that of many other authors. Pompeii, Russel believes, is a means of bringing modern people in contact with the past, which differs little from our world in respect to beauty and ugliness or good and bad.

Like others before him, Philipp Vandenberg, a German crime author, found inspiration for the protagonist of his novel *The Pompeian* in the gypsum cast of a man now exposed in the Stabian Baths.[759] In his book, Pompeii essentially belongs to ancient Greek culture, unfortunately contaminated by rough Roman customs. Vandenberg's Rome – "diese stinkende, sterbende Stadt"[760] – exercises negative influences on Pompeii, like cruel slavery and prostitution. The citizens are known from inscriptions and graffiti, working people have jobs named in election inscriptions, and the author introduces strangers from Palestine – fugitives and convicts from after the Jewish revolts – and Carthage.

In Vandenberg's novel, which takes place during the years 62 to 79, a certain Aphrodisius meets St. Paul, who he believes has cured the lame Fabius Eupor, and who makes a great impression on him. Even an old Pompeian priest, Amandus, believes in Paul's living god and a Christian community is founded.[761] By inserting history and interweaving gossip and facts as told by Tacitus and Suetonius, he skillfully combines the different subplots into a juicy concoction – albeit one of the coldest and harshest views on Pompeii in fiction – of Roman history and Aphrodisius' experiences. As a result, Vandenberg is as ambitious as Bory (see Chapter VII, pp. 348–349), although digressions like his inclusion of sex scenes slow down the rhythm of the story, stripping the plot of its thrill and the reader of his or her interest.

Probably only surpassed by Bulwer-Lytton in popularity, Robert Harris has won fame and money with his 2003 novel *Pompeii*, which plays out between

---

[756] Brothels are everywhere (Russell 2008, 245). Pompeii is "licenziosa;" see the graffito *Sodom et Gomorrha* (Russell 2008, 28; here Chapter IV, p. 236).
[757] Dario Battaglia organizes reconstructions of games (Russell 2008, 428). See on his publications concerning gladiators M. Junkelmann, *Journal of Roman Archaeology* 23 (2010) 530–532.
[758] Russell 2008, 366, 368: "Si può mai finire di parlare e scrivere di Pompeii?" and "Come si fa a non tornare a Pompeii?"
[759] Vandenberg 1989, 326–327: Epilogue. García y García 1998, nos 13.834–13.835.
[760] Vandenberg 1989, 125.
[761] Vandenberg 1989, 42–43, 76.

August 22 and 25, 79, featuring the protagonist Marcus Attilius Primus, the new *aquarius* of Pompeii. Harris includes the town's famous brothel, and clearly believes that on account of its existence, Pompeii is a licentious place.[762] Sex, however, is only hinted at and not described. The ex-slave Numerius coins Pompeii "a hustler's town,"[763] rather rich, but with dark and dangerous sides and nasty smelling workshops.[764] Religion plays a secondary role in this book in the form of official celebrations for the gods, although many protagonists do not even believe in these gods, first and foremost Pliny and Attilius. Harris lets the pyroclastic surges do their lethal work as late as the morning of August 25, when Pompeii becomes a sepulcher for 2,000 inhabitants under the thick layer of pumice and ashes:[765]

> This ash hardened. More pumice fell. In their snug cavities the bodies rotted, and with them, as the centuries passed, the memory that there had even been a city on this spot. Pompeii became a town of perfectly shaped hollow citizens – huddled together or lonely, their clothes blown off or lifted over their heads, grasping hopelessly for their favourite possession or clutching nothing – vacuums suspended in mid-air at the level of their roofs.

One particular detail struck me: the blind slave boy Tyro (the counterpart to the blind Nydia in Bulwer-Lytton's *Last Days*), the guard of the *castellum aquae*, leads Attilius to the house of Popidius through the small streets of Pompeii.[766] This walk serves as Harris' excuse to describe the town in the same way other authors do.

Harris includes a bibliography as well as acknowledgements of consulted scholars. This endorses the suggestion that Harris has written a science-based novel, using relevant ancient sources and modern scholarship properly (most of his characters' names are known from official sources and inscriptions).[767] We encounter the former gladiator Brebrix in the retinue of Numerius, and the rich

---

[762] Harris 2003, 76. Three Jewish prostitutes are called Aegle, Maria, and Martha. These women were often considered Christians, like Zmyrina (p. 156). See Chapter IV, p. 235. García y García 2012, no A2331.
[763] Harris 2003, 99; 98: "It was imposing for a provincial town."
[764] E.g. Harris 2003, 107–110, 148. He mentions pots for the collection of urine to be used in the fulleries.
[765] Harris 2003, 335. People begin their day normally at 6 A.M., and surges arrive at ca. 8 A.M. (Harris 2003, 320–328, 334).
[766] Harris 2003, 106. The *castellum* would function according to Vitruvius' rules, which modern scholarship no longer believes.
[767] Harris 2003, 340–342. An interview conducted by Shelley Hales and Joanna Paul with Harris (in Hales/Paul 2011, 331–339) is very informative. Pesando (see note 768) somewhat impudently notes flaws and lacunae, especially the negligence of Italian publications. See also J.-A. Dickmann in Stein-Hölkeskamp/Hölkeskamp 2006, 494–495.

lady Julia Felix gets lost in the turmoil of the town's last hours. Fortunately for the modern reader, people do not speak Latin, although technical terminology is explained, but dirty words are frequently uttered by hot-tempered and uncivilized Pompeians. Harris makes sensible use of ancient sources, quoting Strabo, Seneca, and Pliny through the novel, while also referring to the giants on Vesuvius as described by Dio Cassius (quoted in Chapter IX, p. 344). The Elder Pliny dictates observations to a slave, which will end up, some thirty years later, in the famous letters of his cousin.

The archaeologist Patrizio Pesando aptly observed how Harris' work can be seen as a novel about violated nature.[768] Sulfur from the eruption infected the water, the water conduits were broken by the earth's shakes, the ground was covered by "dust," water no longer ran down, and the Sarno became arid. Even the *Piscina mirabilis* nearby Misenum was entirely drying up. The reason, Pesando claims, for this disorder of nature was people's abuse thereof for their own short-lived profit, without any thought to the future. In this way, Harris' novel fits well in with a stream of novels published in the last decades dedicated to the devastation of our planet by mankind, that express "ecocritical" concerns.[769]

While modern novels for adults generally (and logically) refuse to prettify Pompeii, some youth books do not hide the dark sides of ancient society either. Two good examples are German crime stories for children that revolve around technical themes. Fabian Lenk, in his *Anschlag auf Pompeji* (Assault on Pompeii), describes how the inspector of the water supply, the *curator aquarum* Aurelius Tulla Nigidius, is engaged in repairing the aqueduct outside Pompeii after the earthquake of 62 and has trouble with terrorist attacks by unknown Pompeians, which endangers his work. Aurelius' twin sons Marius and Caius discover the culprits and the well-told story has a happy end.[770] Despite the damage from the earthquake, Lenk's Pompeii functions as a rich and happy town. The author presents his young readers with descriptions of various customs, like a dinner party and a visit to the public baths, a Pompeian house, and some historical facts that fit into the story and lack pedantic overtones.

---

768 Review in *Rivista di Studi Pompeiani* 15 (2004) 242–245.
769 Called ecocriticism. I thank my Nijmegen colleague Marguérite Corporaal for her information on this topic. See Garrard 2004, esp. 85–107 ('apocalypse'). Rocchi 2008, 168 note 33, recalls the great interest in water management in this genre of novels. See here the next example, the novel by Lenk.
770 Lenk 2002. I read a third unchanged edition of 2007. The book belongs to a series "Tatort. Ratekrimis aus der Welt des Wissens," subdived into Tatort Geschichte [i.a. this book], Tatort Erde, and Tatort Forschung. García y García 2012, no A2700. On this and other detective stories for children see Rutenfranz 2004, 2009; Rocchi 2008, 166, 171.

In *Die verflixten Fälle aus Pompeji*, (Damned Cases from Pompeii) by Germund Mielke, protagonists Julia and Marcus discover a case of sabotage, when they assist their uncle, the *aedile* Antonius, to solve various irregularities in Neronian Pompeii.[771] The tale describes Pompeii as an agreeable town of 15,000 souls and is accompanied by informative drawings by the author. Yet Pompeii has its dark, criminal and violent sides, which also come to the fore very clearly in Harris' *Pompeii*, although Harris most likely did not get his inspiration from Lenk or Mielke, whose German books for children were out of his reach.

Marcelle Lerme-Walter wrote a terrifying story about slave children and their struggle for freedom in *Les enfants de Pompéi ou Le Jeu du roi*. This excellent novel was intended for twelve to fifteen year old girls, the age of its protagonists. Although these girls are not anachronistic "abolitionists" but believe that slaves are merely their buyer's property,[772] they advocate for the good treatment of that property, as was done by moderate Stoics like Seneca. However, the girls mourn for David, a poor Jewish slave boy who has been killed in his cell, and find the culprit of this crime. They also succeed in forcing the fuller Ululitemulus, called Ululi, to set free his badly treated slaves. Maybe because of the children for whom the book is written, the episodes that deal with animals and gladiators lack gory details, but are suggestive enough that any young reader would understand their cruelty. Thus, Sérapion, a young slave acrobat who plays Icarus falls down from heaven in the amphitheater. Although the end result of this well-known story would have left the slave dead, fortunately he does not die and he is able to escape from Pompeii.[773] Another theme is that of the witch, Orcanie, who makes a potion and magic tablets for Ululi. Lerme-Walter's Pompeii is a city inhabited by wealthy idlers who do not have any great sorrows and merely enjoy the climate and the city's beautiful surroundings. Freedmen like Ululi make up the lower classes, and strangers in the story, like the witch and her assistant, are given specific functions. As for archaeological data, the author mainly uses elements from the excavations around Via dell'Abbondanza, like the unsympathetic boy Successus, portrayed in a painting playing with a bird in house I 9, 3, and Sacerdos Amandus, Paquius Proquius, Loreius Tiburtinus, and Ululitremulus, who all are inhabitants of this quarter.

Lois Hamilton Fuller, in her boy-centric book *Fire in the Sky*, introduces the schoolboy Rufus, son of the fuller Stephanus. Rufus and his friends discover the culpable person behind aggressive attacks on candidates during a hard election

---

771 Mielke 1999. The book forms part of a series with similar stories in ancient Greece, Egypt, and Rome. García y García 2012, no A3040. See Rutenfranz 2004, 2009, 40–41.
772 Lerme-Walter 1968, 61, 162. Not in García y García 1998.
773 See Coleman 1990 on this sort of charade testified in ancient sources; cf. here Chapter IV, pp. 251–252.

campaign in June 79.⁷⁷⁴ The author paints a very realistic picture of the ancient town as the background of his captivating story. His characters' names and jobs are taken from archaeological monuments along the Via dell'Abbondanza, as in Lerme-Walter's novel. Rufus and his friends even find a treasure, which is the silver hoard from the House of the Menander, discovered by Amedeo Maiuri in 1930.

Eilís Dillon's *The Shadow of Vesuvius* is a youth book about the painter Scrofa ("Sow") and his slave apprentice Timon, also called Tullio or Tullis.⁷⁷⁵ Scrofa's previous apprentices died under mysterious circumstances, and as the story progresses, some of these mysteries are solved. Despite doing well for himself, Scrofa dislikes Pompeii, which is full of easygoing people who do not heed nature's warnings. Vesuvius' eruption is not fatal for the protagonists, who get away before it happens, but for the sake of history, the volcano has a prominent place in the narrative. Dillon inserts a few Pompeian features, of which the House of the Vettii is the only monument described in detail.

Clearly a pun on the title of Bulwer-Lytton's book, Kathryn Lasky wrote a novel for girls entitled *The Last Girls of Pompeii*.⁷⁷⁶ Lasky connects some of the protagonists with casts of victims found in Pompeii:⁷⁷⁷

> [T]he most arresting images were those casts of life trapped in that moment of dying [...] For a writer, visiting Pompeii was an almost intoxicating experience. Through this strange alchemy of ash and mud and rock, history had been frozen in time, an intimate history. It was the mingling of the macabre with ordinary domestic, of the beauty of life with the hideousness of violent death that I found so compelling.

Lasky succeeds in bringing together the two aspects she admires so much, the gypsum casts and the history frozen in time. She uses many clichéd elements to describe wealth in general, and the pleasure women get from their jewelry, make-up and apparel. Other standard motifs are visits of clients at Cornelius', the morning ceremony in front of the *lararium*, and the process of fulling fabric.

Like Davis and Comastri Montanari, the American classicist and archaeologist Caroline Lawrence wrote a series of thrillers, only for children.⁷⁷⁸ As far as I

---

774 Fuller 1965. Included are a short bibliography, a preface and acknowledgements. *Nomen est omen*: fullers are important in Fuller's book as in Lerme-Walter 1968 and Lundgren 2001. Also observed by Rocchi 2008, 168. Not in García y García 1998.
775 Dillon 1978. Not in García y García 1998.
776 Lasky 2007. Not in García y García 2012.
777 Lasky 2007, 180, 181.
778 Lawrence 2001. Part 2 of *The Roman Mysteries*, consisting of seventeen volumes. This and other works have been translated into various languages. On Lawrence, see Rutenfranz 2004, 2009, 38–40.

know, she is the only author to write about the fortunes of the people who survived the eruption.⁷⁷⁹ In *The Secrets of Vesuvius*, four kids solve Pliny the Elder's riddle about a young blacksmith with a clubfoot appropriately called Vulcan. In the sequel, *The Pirates of Pompeii*, which focuses on the same and other children from various social and ethnic groups, Lawrence describes an encampment of people brought together by fate near Stabiae, in which everyone from wealthy citizens to slaves try to find lost family members before heading elsewhere. In contrast with many other novels, Lawrence has characters from an array of social classes and ethnic backgrounds form friendships with each other. Children, naïve and pure by nature, play a positive role in creating this tolerance and equity (both of which form an educational element of the story) among the Pompeian refugees. Although not exactly angels, the children are not yet contaminated by Roman social laws, playing and having adventures together without any problems. In this book, they prevent an attack of pirates who want to hijack some rich people nearby, and succeed in having the pirates arrested and sentenced. Logically, Pompeii itself no longer plays an important role, but its traditional villa culture, with its opulent meals and costly interior decorations, resembles that of other Pompeii books. Lawrence skillfully enhances the *Pirates* story with historical information. One boy's father recounts the fall of Jerusalem, and emperor Titus visits the camp to give solace to his unfortunate citizens.

The novels briefly presented in this section are good examples of the shift that historians, archaeologists, and other students of ancient society have also made over the last decades. Pompeii, no longer thought of merely as an idyllic place for the rich and famous, is now shown housing both poor people and society's elite within the same city walls, as they meet with the problems of everyday life. In the children's books, the young people simultaneously act in their own right as children and play a reconciliatory role as they bring together people from strongly divergent backgrounds in catastrophic circumstances. These books, therefore, are important testimonies of a more realistic, less idealized image of ancient society.

Masterpieces of Art in Pompeii

Although Pompeii has not given us many real masterpieces of Greco-Roman art, some authors dedicate their stories to artists who had created superb artwork, some destroyed by Vesuvius, some not.⁷⁸⁰ This is the case with *Euphorion*, a

---

779 Lawrence 2002. Part 3 of *The Roman Mysteries*. García y García 2012, no A767, A2677–2678.
780 On this genre, see Fitzon 2002b, 309 note 26.

long poem by the German historian Ferdinand Gregorovius published in 1858. Mainly known for his scholarship on Rome in the Middle Ages, Gregorovius visited Pompeii many times from 1852 to 1874 in combination with doing research in Naples. In Pompeii, in a bewildering and hot summer atmosphere, the empty houses reminded him of tombs.[781] The poem, in the form of a classical epic in hexametres and subdivided into four canti of identical length, was initially called *Der bronzene Candelaber*, and was conceived at the beginning of 1854, probably after the author visited the museum in Naples and saw the large number of bronze candelabra there.[782] An artistic masterpiece is a candelabrum made by the titular hero that is more or less similar to a lampstand found at the Villa of Diomedes, where the story takes place.[783] The bronze object carries four lamps representing the figures after which the four *canti* are named.[784] Euphorion is the name of a Hellenistic poet, but a more likely namesake for Gregorovius' epic is the son of Faust and Helena in Goethe's *Faust II*, in which Euphorion emulates the great English poet Lord Byron (and even similarly dies too young). Goethe and other

---

781 Gregorovius 1991, 47, note from June 23, 1853: "Dies [Pompeii] ist ein Wesen, welches entzückt und abstößt. Die Häuser stehen wie leere Särge; Straßenreihen, Tempel, Theater, Forum – alles totenstill, vom Sommerzauber flimmernd. Nie fühlte ich solchen Wehmut. Nur Dichter können sie sagen." At Pompeii, he met Jacob Burckhardt and Friedrich Althaus (cf. Knight 1995, 92).
782 Gregorovius 1991, 53 (31-1-1854). The first edition of *Euphorion* is from 1858, the fifth one from 1883. Here the "Prachtausgabe" with illustrations of 1872 is used.
783 Cf. Gregorovius 1991, 182 (Augustus 15, 1864): "Ich ging lange in Pompeji umher, auch im Haus des Diomedes, und ich bedachte meinen eigenen Lebenslauf, zumal jene Zeit, wo ich das Gedicht 'Euphorion' schrieb. Auch dies ist schon mit Asche verschüttet; die Empfindungen, die mich damals belebten, sind verklungen; kaum vernahm ich davon einen leisen Nachklang im Haus des Diomedes, oder vor dem alten Kandelaber in den Studien." And on September 24 of the same year (Gregorovius 1991, 185): "Ich wanderte dort ungestört umher und ich saß lange auf der Terrasse des Hauses des Diomedes, wo mir Euphorion und Jone wieder erschienen, schon schattenhafte, aber freundliche Wesen aus jener Vergangenheit, als ich mich zum Licht des Ideals emporgerungen hatte." Meeting Fiorelli on September 24 of the same year, he wrote (1991, 185): "Dieser Mann von sehr sympatischem Äußern hat sich bereits unsterbliche Verdienste um Pompeji erworben." On May 28, 1874, Gregorovius (1991, 342) made a nocturnal visit: "Im Zauberlicht des Vollmonds sahen wir Pompeji."
784 Gregorovius 1872, 5–7. The candelabrum was illustrated in many books, i.a. *Museo Borbonico* V (1829) pl. 13; Clarke 1846, II, 296–29, with plate; Trollope 1854, 34–35, pl. XV.5; Overbeck 1866, II, 59, fig. 253; 1875, 387, fig. 232; Dyer 1867, 545–546; Roux/Barré 1870, VII, 3e série, 5–8, pl. 5; Overbeck/Mau 1884, 435, fig. 233; Mau 1908, 395, fig. 219. On the inspiration and start of the poem, see Motekat 1986, 219, and Osterkamp 1993, 197–201. The lamp found in the villa has oil containers in the shape of snails (*PAH* I, 265, found on June 13, 1772); picture in Roux/Barré 1870, VII, 3e série, 2, pl. 1. Mau 1908, 395, fig. 220, however, gives a tree-like lamp with five *lucernae* as found in the Villa of Diomedes.

poets in the nineteenth century greatly admired Byron, as Gregorovius admired both Byron and Goethe.[785]

Gregorovius did not view *Euphorion* as his masterpiece, and modern criticism tends to have similar negative judgments of its poetic qualities. Ernst Osterkamp has discussed the poem as a product of mid nineteenth-century German interest in classicism combined with the poetical form of a "Versepos," used by popular authors like Paul Heyse and Hermann Lingg.[786] The lovers are "blutleer" despite the romantic setting.[787] Art, the main theme does not enliven the work. Euphorion, a slave by "trade," is also a slave to his art and, therefore, he is not capable of producing any original artwork that shows artistic talent instead of mere craftsmanship. Despite its flaws, the poem had some success in its time, and suggested the notion of happiness as an impetus for artists' best work.

The German novelist Otto Behrend contended that Greek art was superior to Roman art in his 1907 *Der Bildhauer*, which focuses on the Greek sculptor Charmos from Aegina. Behrend's opinion was common in Germany from the time of Winckelmann onward.[788] Charmos, living in Pompeii in 79, falls in love with Agariste, one of his models for his statue of Psyche. When Vesuvius erupts, the couple escapes, carrying with them the statue, and when it breaks in their cart, they abandon the marble fragments. Their relationship, based on the love for a work of art, is modeled both after the Pygmalion motif about the artist falling in love with his own creation and Oscar Wilde's *Picture of Dorian Gray*, in which Dorian identifies with the portrait of himself made for him by his friend Basil Hallward, and dies when he see how ugly it has become due to his evil deeds. Pompeii provides an ideal background for the decadent atmosphere Behrend wants to sketch. Antiquarian details are mainly given in the first part, when the reader enters Charmos' world. The names of some Pompeians stem from local graffiti; the main characters bear Greek or Judeo-Christian names. A handful of "Nazarenes" plays a minor part.

In a book for teenagers by a productive Dutch author of children's books, P. Visser, with the same title as Behrend's, young Valerius, who enjoys a great career in Pompeii as a sculptor and jewel maker,[789] also loses his work to Vesuvius in 79. Visser presents Pompeii as Rome's littler sister, and describes its various social

---

[785] On the Greek poet, see Acosta-Hughes/Cusset 2012. Goethe, *Faust*, Zweiter Teil, 3. Akt, and *Paralipomenon* 196.
[786] Osterkamp 1993, 194–196; Zintzen 1998, 13–14. Cf. Motekat 1986, 215, 218, on the "poetic realism" of Heyse and others. For more on Lingg, see Chapter VIII, pp. 377–378.
[787] Osterkamp 1993, 197.
[788] Behrend 1907. García y García 1998, no 1486.
[789] Visser 1911. Not in García y García 1998.

layers and their protagonists who fill the streets and forum, including workmen and magistrates. The author compares Romans with amphibians due to their fondness for bathing.[790] Although he criticizes several Roman customs and the overly rich lives some people lead, Visser manages to avoid being moralistic.

As we have seen, artists form a small category of their own in Pompeii fiction, sometimes associated with works of art and other products found by the excavators, and sometimes merely placed in Pompeii to give them a good environment for their artistic expressions. Although the authors of these stories would have been able to use contemporary archaeological finds as the works of art being produced by their artist-protagonists, they instead largely preferred to invent fictional works of art. The lack of real masterpieces might be one reason for that choice.

Love, Wealth and Isis

Jean Bertheroy's *La danseuse de Pompéi* describes the religious and mental struggle of Hyacinthe, who, in A.D. 59, has to choose between his devotion for Apollo and his love for Nonia, the dancer from the title (p. 173, fig. 9).[791] Many elements of this book are identical to those present in the Christian novels. The cult of Venus (earth, love) sharply contrasts with that of Apollo (heaven, sun, spirit), who could almost be read as "Christ." In fact, the priest of Apollo is called Chrestus[792] and Orpheus is the Redeemer ("Rédempteur"). Despite this, *La danseuse* has no place for Christianity, and expresses a deep love for ancient paganism. The formula "sensuous pagan elegy," coined by Göran Blix for a poem of the same vision, aptly characterizes this novel.[793]

During a stroll in Herculaneum, Hyacinthe and Nonia, an amorous couple, compare it with Pompeii (which Bertheroy presents as a city full of refined luxury, art, and poetry) and Oplontis. Pompeii is noisy and vivid, Oplontis has

---

[790] Visser 1911, 142.
[791] Bertheroy 1899 (see Riikonen 1977, 210); Aziza 1992. The writer's real name is Berthe Jeanne Corinne Le Barillier. Aziza 1992, 996. I have used the reprint in Aziza 1992. On this book, see Moormann 2008, 380–382; here p. 272, note 1052. García y García 1998, nos 1578–1580.
[792] Yet, that was a rather common name. Baudy 1991, 28 gives an example in Suetonius, *Life of Claudius* 25.4. Tacitus, *Annals* 15.44 speaks about *chrestiani* as followers of Christ. Another Chrestus features in Lundgren 2001 (see pp. 249–250).
[793] Blix 2009, 74. For an opera inspired by this novel, see Chapter VIII, p. 371. The illustration of fig. 9 belongs to a cheap undated edition of the 1899 edition, with many nudes in an art déco style.

an embalmed sweetness, and Herculaneum is nothing but rich.⁷⁹⁴ In her narrative, Bertheroy frequently uses terms like "débauche," "volupté", "voluptueux," "séduction," "race dégénerée," and "nu." Bertheroy assumes that naked women fought in the amphitheater. Although this adds another element of Roman debauchery to her catalog, historically speaking, women did not fight in the arena at all, except for the Christian victims of persecution described in early Christian literature (see Chapter IV, pp. 251–252). Finally, rich women dress delicately so that their beautiful bodies are visible under the fabric. Bertheroy incorporates new information about the excavation; the recently excavated and restored House of the Vettii is the topographical focus of his book.

Two decades after Berthéroy, Maxime Formont dedicated *Visions antiques* to Psyché, another dancing girl. As a variation on novels about Rome, Formont's novel takes place in Baiae and Pompeii in the time of Vespasian and Titus; the text, he writes, will convey antique elements more or less reliably, but flaws do not matter, since not everything about ancient society is known.⁷⁹⁵ In Pompeii, a blithe town, the protagonists enjoy life at all costs, so that when Vesuvius begins its devastating work, they do not try to escape, despite the warnings by one of the protagonists, a soldier named Elius, and die in happiness. The author presents the Bay of Naples as an earthly paradise, unfortunately contaminated by the foolish temperaments of the people living there.⁷⁹⁶ Despite this, Pompeii is an ideal retreat for those who refuse to partake in the social and political life of Rome and no longer wish to show off, as is necessary in the Roman capital. Moreover, Pompeii displays its eternity in the form of its citizens' tombs. There are no serious archaeological flaws in the descriptions, and the writer inserts recently excavated monuments like the House of the Vettii. Formont's couple is not attracted to public life, and therefore, the reader does not meet other inhabitants of Pompeii. Perhaps the political situation in the year of publication, 1914, was one reason the author chose to include details like the couple seeking shelter in a time of menacing disaster, much as Europeans would have been doing during the early days of the Great War.

---

794 Bertheroy 1992, 674: "C'était vrai ; et c'était précisément cela, ce bruit, ces couleurs, toutes ces outrances, qui faisaient de la petite cité osque une ville unique au monde, c'était cela que Nonia aimait par-dessus tout, et qui la rendait indifférente à la douceur embaumée d'Oplonte, à la paix déserte de Retina, à l'incomparable richesse d'Herculanum." Bertheroy distingues Retina from Herculaneum.
795 Formont 1914, I–III, "Avertissement." For more on this book, see Moormann 2008, 384–385. Not in García y García 1998.
796 Cf. David 2001, 283.

Gustav Adolf Müller's novella *Im Lupanar* plays out in the time of Claudius, focusing on the nobleman Cnejus Valerius and what he calls his "novel of the heart" about a beautiful Helvetian slave girl.[797] Although the two are a social mismatch, Pompeii, a modern, rich and lucky town, where people live merrily and without limitations, serves as the happy stage for this romance. Cnejus' retirement from Roman politics illustrates his longing for a continuous *otium*, and he even leaves his Alban villa to more fully enjoy the Pompeian lifestyle. This motif is similar to Vecchi's and Brod's stories about Cicero, and Rouland's *Cendrier*.

The 63–64 liaison of Emperor Nero and his wife Poppaea, who stems from a Pompeian family, forms the basis of Covito's *Le ragazze di Pompei* about independent women in Pompeii who benefit from the elite's luxurious way of life. Dinner parties, extravagant houses like the House of the Faun, bathing, make-up, gossip and politics are what occupy these people's lives. Pompeii does not become a living element, although Covito tacitly inserts modern scholarship when she alludes to a deluxe hotel with a painted representation of Nero as Apollo amidst his Muses.[798]

Fiction works often include Egyptian personages, given the relationship between all things Egyptian and the portrayal of a luxurious town.[799] The discovery of the Temple of Isis at Pompeii in 1764 tickled the fantasy of the visitors about the Egyptian cult and its gatherings. Serapion in Gregorovius' *Euphorion* helps survivors go to Egypt. Böttiger and Nerval also demonstrate a fascination with Isis.[800] A decidedly sympathetic Egyptian is Memnonès in *La prêtresse d'Isis*:

---

[797] Müller 1900, 54: "Herzensroman [...] dessen Gegenstand eine wunderschöne helvetische Sklavin." Later on, she comes from Tomi, which is in modern Romania. This 78 page booklet also includes stories about Catilina, and Titus in Jerusalem, and belongs to the series "Eckstein's 50 Pfennig-Bibliothek" (no. 30). Not in García y García 1998. Müller's novel *Das sterbende Pompeji* (Müller 1910) is discussed in Chapter IV, pp. 244–246.

[798] Covito 2012, 111–112. Painted by Fabullus, known as the artist who decorated Nero's Golden House in Rome. The paintings of Nero and the Muses would be those found in Murecine (o Moregine) in 1959 and 1999 and interpreted in this way by Marisa Mastroroberto in A. D'Ambrosio et al. (eds), *Storie da un'eruzione. Pompei Ercolano Oplontis*, Naples 2003, 479–523.

[799] In this chapter: Böttiger 1837–1838, Vecchi 1864, Lerme-Walter 1968, Rouland 1984, Davis 1990, Rodriguez 2008.

[800] Böttiger 1837–1838, II, 210–230; with plate IV: "Die Isis-Vesper: nach einem Herculanischen Gemälde." Quotation at p. 211: "Ihre genaue Kentniss mag einen hellen Lichtstrahl auf Entstehung und Fortpflanzung neuer Liturgieen [sic] und Kirchenbräuche werfen und schon in sofern den Alterthumsforscher vor dem Vorwurf sichern, daß er, wie dort Foote in einer bekannten Farce auf die Alterthümler spottet, frische Milch von alten Böcken melke und zum Eichelschmauss einlade, wo lockeres Weizenbrot winkt." The two fragments are Museo Nazionale inv. 8919 (night scene) and 8924 (priests in front of temple). Along with many more fragments, they come from a house found in the earliest excavations of Herculaneum and can be dated to the first half of the first century A.D. (Moormann 1988, 122–123). See here p. 361.

Légende de Pompeï by Édouard Schuré.⁸⁰¹ His favorable presentation of Isis and her worshippers should not surprise readers, because Schuré was one of the main instigators of oriental studies in France, and simultaneously subscribed to Madame Blavatski's esoteric ideas of theosophy. His books, re-edited many times, had a lot of avid readers.⁸⁰² This novel is an interesting attempt to determine the benefit of this cult, which offered ideas about redemption and afterlife and formed an attractive and morally less burdensome alternative to Christianity. Pompeii stands for moral and political decline, debauchery, idleness, and lust. The fine and pure Isis followers – Memnonès, his adopted daughter Alcyone and the couple Helvidius and Helvidia – are in sharp contrast with those who believe in the old Roman gods and lead an immoral way of life. Among them are the wealthy Hedonia (name derived from Greek *hedone*, lust) and the Roman ambitious officer Ombricius.

Hints at soft sex, arcane Egyptians, lustful masters of beautiful young female slaves, Titus becoming an emperor and his military companion Marcius: all these heterogeneous elements come together in an overloaded novel by Martin Saul. The author clearly hints at Bulwer-Lytton's book in the title of his book, *The Last Nights of Pompeii*.⁸⁰³ A baby found on the steps of the Great Temple of Jerusalem in 69 later becomes a full-grown beauty. She comes from Parthia, and lives in the wealthy house of her stoic and chaste master Marcius. The Jewish officer and historian Flavius Josephus has a small role among the Jewish captives, and has contact with Pliny the Elder.⁸⁰⁴ Pompeii is a nice town, rich thanks to the fervid restorations after 62. Saul does not even try to describe Pompeii on the basis of archaeological data; any other Roman town could just as easily have served as the backdrop for the story. Pompeii is merely a familiar name, an easy location. Saul introduces Jews and Christians, seen by the Romans as filthy people, as well as African Isis worshippers. We read lengthy descriptions of cruel amphitheater

---

801 Schuré 1907. On this book, see Mercier 1980, 606–607; Moormann 2008, 382–384. García y García 1998, nos 12.287–12.289 (including translations). The author visited Pompeii in 1904 and found there a "latinité encore baignée d'hellénisme" (Mercier 1980, 556).
802 Schuré was one of the most influential authors of esotericism and theosophy of his time and his *Les grands initiés*, Paris 1889, has been published and translated many times over. In this work Pythagoras, one of the great examples for Memnonès and his friends, features as one of the 'initiated' and visionary spiritual leaders. See J.-P. Laurant in W.J. Hanegraaff (ed.), *Dictionary of Gnosis & Western Esotericism*, Leiden/Boston 2005, II, 1045; Zander 2007, 1019–1026.
803 Saul 1966. Not in García y García 1998. I could not find any information about the author. See for a good review http://glorioustrash.blogspot.nl/2010/06/last-nights-of-pompeii-by-martin-saul.html (visited June 24, 2012).
804 Saul 1966, 76, 98: he is called Josephus ben Mattathias of Jotapata.

games attended by Titus, dinner parties in Pompeii and on Capri, and strange rituals in the Temple of Isis.

Louis de Corcelles published a "letter found in a bottle" containing the adventures of a woman from Pompeii in the time of Piso's conspiracy against Nero in 65.[805] Fleeing to the far West, she and her friends live until their death on an uninhabited island. De Corcelles skillfully describes archaeological data without showing off. The author is likely making an "ecocritical" plea to "return to nature," since he spends so much time describing the woman's difficult time surviving on the island. If so, it would imply a touch of ecocriticism we have seen in Harris' *Pompeii*.

The amphitheater of Pompeii is the oldest permanent building of its kind in the ancient Roman world, and has always been the object of much fascination, especially in Christian novels (see Chapter IV, pp. 251–253). The Ferrarese-born author Raphaelis Carrozzari contributes to this theme a short epic in Latin, entitled *Leo gladiator seu Pompeii Vesuvii montis conflagratione obruti*.[806] The *epyllion* of 331 lines tells about the gladiator Leo and his love for Vettia.[807] Carrozzari's victims are those who have been "reconstructed" by the guides and archaeologists over the last hundred years. Vettia's father Vettius is a newcomer, a man connected with the House of the Vettii, which had recently been excavated when Carrozzari wrote the book. The drama is all a bit unlikely: a gladiator and an upper-class girl would have barely been an acceptable couple in Roman society, and Vesuvius' eruption by night is evidently a more dramatic backdrop for the story than the actual historic daytime eruption.

Another gladiator is featured in Luigi Conforti's *Pompei*, an epic of some 4,200 lines.[808] The love between Cestilia, a Greek slave girl, and Marcello, the son of a succesful Roman officer in the Judean War, is unacceptable in Pompeian society.[809] Pompeii is luxurious, and possesses precious stones, glittering gold and perfumes are used in abundance. In the chapter "Diluculum – Ganea" a rhetor

---

805 De Corcelles 1982. Not in García y García 1998.
806 Carrozzari 1899. García y García 1998, no. 2659. It was submitted to the *Certamen Poeticum Hoefftianum* in Amsterdam, a well-known contest for modern Latin poetry for the 1899 edition. Although he did not win a medal, his text was "magna lauda [sic!] ornatum" and edited by the organizing committee. Carrozzari also participated in the *Certamen Hoefftianum* of the years 1894, 1895, 1900, 1912, and 1913, but never won a prize.
807 The name Leo, of course, means lion: the man is a lion fighting against other lions.
808 Conforti 1888. The work is subdivided into a prologue and six chapters bearing Latin names which correspond to different times of day, and are dedicated to friends and colleagues like Fiorelli, Sogliano, Edmondo De Amicis and Woldemar Kaden. García y García 1998, nos. 3179–3199 includes this and other works.
809 Conforti 1888, 50–51.

visits the bar of Portio in Pompeii, where he eats lavishly. The clientele includes gladiators, merchants, slaves, and actors.[810] The forum is full of Athenenian courtesans and blond young men.[811] At one point, Marcello makes sure not to miss a visit to the baths, because he wants to be there at a time when women are present too.[812] Renzo Cremante has made clear that Conforti adopts the style and verse forms of the great Italian poet Giosuè Carducci, at that time a standard for many poets.[813]

Conclusions

Although numerous, pagan novels do not display a very variegated vision of Pompeii. Despite the town's small size compared to Rome, authors do not present great differences in the quality of life, but merely see the potential for creating stories, and possibilities to offer ancient society in all its facets to astonished readers. For the most part, the authors are eager to describe relevant details, and not only what is necessary for the plot, but to show their familiarity with the excavations. Other Greek and Roman excavations never excited the fantasy to such a degree that all classes of society as well as public, religious and private buildings, could be similarly portrayed. The absence of comparable vestiges of antiquity in other towns apparently would have demanded too high a degree of imagination for authors to have situated their novels elsewhere in the ancient world. At the same time, the tradition of fiction about Pompeii itself could have formed a compelling source of inspiration for subsequent works of fiction. Another attraction of Pompeii was the presence of authentic-seeming inhabitants who are featured as protagonists, since they were discovered both in the shape of the victims' gypsum casts and names recorded in inscriptions and graffiti. As a consequence of this epigraphical wealth, the inhabitants of fictitious Pompeii bear names known from these texts rather than names merely known from other classical sources. Nevertheless, the traditionally fostered classical literary sources are of paramount importance as well to construct a fictitious Pompeian society. Characters' lives need to be filled with activities and juicy details about the maintenance of slaves, lavish dinner parties, weddings and burials. In using these sources, the modern writers Davis, Russell, and Harris differ little from nineteenth-century

---

810 Conforti 1888, 29.
811 Conforti 1888, 60.
812 Conforti 1888, 84. It is like the famous tepidarium painting by Théodore Chassériau from 1853 show in Musée d'Orsay, Paris (on which see Betzer 2010).
813 Cremante 2008, 116–134, with information about Conforti's life.

authors like Bulwer-Lytton, Vecchi, and Bertheroy. Children's books include the same narrative themes, which are essential stone cubes in the mosaic of Roman society for all categories of readers. In pagan Pompeii novels, Vesuvius' eruption is an unavoidable intervention of nature that leads to the city's destruction. This is in contrast with the Christian determinism to explore the specific reasons for the city's demise, as will be discussed in the next chapter. The escape of a happy few has little to do with particular characteristic qualities, but is the result of dumb luck or the survival of the fittest.

In the run of about 200 years, fictitious portraits of Pompeii have become more and more detailed, enriched by each successive discovery. Around 1900, the House of the Vettii "replaced" old mansions like the Houses of Sallustius, the Tragic Poet, and the Faun, just as the Houses of Sacerdos Amandus, Paquius Proculus, and the Menander known from Spinazzola's and Maiuri's excavations along Via dell'Abbondanza would do some decades later. An old love, the brothel not far from the Stabian Baths, remained ever present in these books next to the Forum Baths.

While older books concentrate on upper class Greco-Roman people, modern works include protagonists from a variety of classes and ethnics. Nowadays slaves often serve as examples that illustrate how cruel Roman society was, and are portrayed as increasingly independent thinking creatures, not unlike the emancipated lower classes in modern western society. As a consequence, many recent works present Pompeii as a more multifaceted and harsher society, complete with usurpation of power and lawlessness, infrastructure problems, and urban development. Contrasts of wealth and poverty are drawn with a stronger emphasis, conveying what is a more or less realistic view of ancient society.

For many authors and readers, Pompeii still has great value as a representative example of ancient society. The increasing number of Pompeii novels over the last twenty years corresponds with the growing interest in the devastated and resurrected town, as becomes clear by the exploding numbers of visitors to both the excavations themselves and exhibitions all over the world that propagate captivating images. Documentaries, films, internet sites, and games also stimulate people to read about Pompeii. Sold as the best preserved specimen of Roman culture, in both a positive and a negative sense, Pompeii makes a great impact on this vast audience, which will recognize features found in these novels. In modern fiction, the victims found in the excavations undoubtedly have become satisfactory intermediates between the past and the present, while also becoming the sacrifices for our antiquarian wisdom.

Fig. 10: Emilio Garro, Pompeiana Juventus, Turin 1942. Cover by Luigi Melandro.

IV Jews and Christians in Pompeii Novels

While the historical "pagan" Pompeii novel became popular the middle of the nineteenth century (and still enjoys this popularity today), fiction concentrating on the rise of Christianity and its struggle in the Roman Empire was a mainly nineteenth-century topic.[814] This is especially true for works situated in Pompeii and Herculaneum. Edward Bulwer-Lytton[815] set a trend shortly after 1830 when he introduced Christians among the inhabitants of Pompeii. Following Chateaubriand's 1809 *Les Martyrs* and preceding, among others, Cardinal Wiseman's 1854 *Fabiola*, Lew Wallace's 1880 *Ben Hur: A Tale of the Christ*, and Henryk Sienkiewicz's 1896 *Quo Vadis?*, Bulwer-Lytton and others portray Christians as a persecuted but strong small sect that survives the eruption of Vesuvius. In our context, *Les Martyrs* has a certain relevance. Although this story plays out in the time of Emperor Diocletian and focuses on his persecutions of Christians, Rome and the Bay of Naples "act" in the same way as they do in novels focusing on Pompeii and Herculaneum.[816]

Three aspects may have enhanced the choice of Pompeii and Herculaneum as stages of Christian novels. Many authors assumed that the first – and purest – communities of Christians after the death of Christ would have been found in Italy. Believers from the Holy Land would have followed St. Peter and, especially, St. Paul to Italy. In 59 or 60, after a famous voyage by sea, which is described in the *Acts of the Apostles*, Paul landed in Puteoli (modern Pozzuoli, north-west of Naples), the main Roman harbor of the Italian peninsula at that time.[817] In many authors' collective assumption, Pompeii, situated a short distance from Puteoli, was a likely residence for a new Christian community. The first two doctors of the Church may have died in 64 under the reign of Emperor Nero.[818] A second event

---

[814] This chapter relies on Moormann 2006 and 2011a.
[815] Lytton was added to his family name Bulwer when he inherited the estate of his deceased mother in 1843. *The Last Days of Pompeii* was published anonymously "By the author of Pelham", referring to Bulwer-Lytton's first, successful novel of 1828.
[816] Chateaubriand 1969, 11–678, esp. 173–193, Livre V. Pliny and Herculaneum are mentioned, and there is a hermit on the slopes of Vesuvius, now a Christian (p. 82: "Je suis le Solitaire chrétien du Vésuve"). On historical novels on early Christianity, see Goldhill 2011, 193–244.
[817] *Acts of the Apostles* 28.13–30. See about St. Paul also Schnabel 2002, 882–1424; Nippel 2003.
[818] Tacitus, *Annals* 15.3–8 tells how Nero had Christian people crucified and burnt in the Gardens of Gaius (now the Vatican complex), when they had been accused of causing the great fire of A.D. 64. St. Peter and St. Paul, however, would not have been executed there, as is reported for the first time under Domitian by Clement of Rome (*ad Epistulam ad Corinthios* 1.1). Sallustius (*Nero* 16.3) estimated this persecution as one of the few good deeds of the emperor. For the earliest phase of the Church in Italy see Lepelley 2000, 227–266; Schnabel 2002, 778–796; Lampe 2003.

that recurs throughout these novels is the destruction of the Temple in Jerusalem and the abduction of Jews to Italy in 70. In various stories, Pompeians have dealings with these unfortunate people or their children. A third common theme in these books is that the eruption of Vesuvius serves as punishment for those who do not follow the way of the Righteous: God rescues only his own flock – in other words, those who converted to Christianity. The characters in these tales are not radically different from those in pagan novels. Stock elements include – to repeat the list from Chapter III – wedding ceremonies,[819] funerals,[820] dinner parties,[821] visits to baths,[822] the theater,[823] and the amphitheater.[824] In this context, Roman features speak to the rottenness of society and demonstrate the decay that has come to its apocalyptic end. These tropes become either negative examples of society or illustrate the old customs now happily replaced by new ones, as is explained in *The Vestal*:[825]

> I [Lucius] have been thus minute in describing the two rites of sepulture and marriage, not only from the deep impression they then made on my mind, but because as I now transcribe my history for my children, should I be so fortunate as to become a father, it may not be uninteresting to them as Christians or as men to be informed of the nature of the rites practiced by their fathers, which are already hastening to be done away and forgotten, in the increasing light and simplicity of Christianity. At the same time they will rejoice that I spare them any account of the nature of the feelings that agitated and occupied my own mind during the day, from the presence of the Vestal.

Along with the question of whether Christians and/or Jews indeed lived in Pompeii, these (and other) works of Christian fiction are the topic of this chapter. The first authors, including Bulwer-Lytton, did not question their historical presence or absence and freely invented their stories. Later generations of writers included either real or imagined evidence from the excavations in the form of quotations and references. I start with a few predecessors of Bulwer-Lytton that were of no consequence in later texts and had the misfortune of being entirely forgotten.

---

[819] E.g. *Vestal* 1830, Holt 1886.
[820] E.g. *Vestal* 1830, Kaden 1892, Garro 1942.
[821] E.g. Nicolai 1818, *Vestal* 1830, Bulwer-Lytton 1834, Méry 1834 and 1837, Alberti 1872, De Graaff 1874, Holt 1886, Bassanville n.y., Müller 1910, Garro 1942, Rosoni 1970, Lundgren 2001.
[822] E.g. Bulwer-Lytton 1834, Alberti 1872, Holt 1886, Rosoni 1970.
[823] E.g. Nicolai 1818, *Vestal* 1830, Bulwer-Lytton 1834, Müller 1910, Lundgren 2001.
[824] E.g. *Vestal* 1830, Fairfield 1832, Bulwer-Lytton 1834, Alberti 1872, Bassanville n.y., Kaden 1892, Müller 1910, Garro 1942.
[825] *Vestal* 1830, 56.

Christians in Pompeii before Bulwer-Lytton

The oldest work, from 1818, in which Christianity plays a (modest) role is *Das Grab am Vesuv*, a brief novel by Carl Nicolai. It was presented as a bundle of letters, a popular style in eighteenth-century fiction, and represents a mock manuscript (a genre that we will address in greater detail in Chapter VII). Nicolai's protagonist Marcus Praetorio met Christians in Jerusalem in 69–70, and learned that their God would conquer the world.[826] Back in Italy years later, he sometimes remembers this friendly sect as he goes through a difficult patch in 79, the last year of Vespasian's government. Titus, Vespasian's son and successor, seems a monstrous and immoral suitor of women and power, but Marcus and his lover Julia subsequently better understand Titus' deeds so that his image comes across positively in the end. Although allusions to Christianity are few, Julia's moral conduct and Titus' pardon seem inspired by Christian ideas. Pompeii and Herculaneum, icons of luxury, are not described in detail, and their destruction is necessary to bring the story to its sad end.

An anonymous author from Boston portrays Pompeii in much greater detail in his *The Vestal or A Tale of Pompeii* published in 1830.[827] A visit to the site and references to modern literature serve as the author's evidence of his precision in his attempt to bring back to life the dead city:[828]

> Pompeii as she now is, has sat for the portrait of what she once was. [...] But in the following tale I have not only entered the houses of the Pompeians, I have even occupied their very bones. The character of the priest of Isis is built upon the manner in which his bones were found; and they may seem to afford but a narrow basis for the superstructure reared upon them. He might himself smile perhaps, could he look over the pages of this veracious history, and compare himself as delineated here, with what he actually was.

Despite this, he takes some questionable liberties. For example, he describes a shrine to Vesta administered by a group of Vestal maidens living in the House of the Vestals, introduces catacombs, and postpones Vesuvius' eruption to 95, as – so he ventures – the chronology is still rather uncertain.[829] Like Nicolai's book,

---

[826] Nicolai 1818, 35: "... in kurzer Zeit wurde die gantze lebende Welt von ihm entflammt!" Not in García y García 1998, but see Fitzon 2002a, 491.
[827] Here quoted as *Vestal* 1830.
[828] *Vestal* 1830, iii (preface). Bonucci 1828 is quoted at length in endnotes next to some other works.
[829] *Vestal* 1830, iii-iv. The "House of the Vestals" was found in 1769, and belonged to the frequently visited monuments. Its imaginary name probably derives from the *lararium* found in it. For Domitian see Lepelley 2000 and here note 818. For Vestals in nineteenth-century fiction, see Goldhill 2011, 225–226 (omitting *The Vestal*).

it is a mock manuscript. As Lucius, the protagonist, is new in town, Pompeii is described in detail. The streets are narrow and the gate is guarded by a sentinel (cf. Chapter III, pp. 185–189). As to places where the city had not yet been unearthed (the road from the forum to the theaters, the temple of Isis, and the amphitheater, to name some), no details are given at all – and hence they do not exist; the protagonists "skip" from one place to the next. A luxurious meal in the novel includes turbot and lamprey.[830] Some protagonists are modeled after skeletons of victims discovered in 1811, and Bonucci must have been "ignorant of the veracious story contained in these pages."[831] The Egyptian priest is an amiable gourmand who likes to offer food and drinks to his friends and helps them in their difficulties.[832] Due to their vow of celibacy, the Vestal maidens acting as early Christians suggest an association with Catholic nuns. Moreover, Vestals were pious women by nature, highly esteemed by the Romans, and their conversion to Christianity provoked a thrilling effect. The chronological shift to the reign of Domitian – who personally attends gladiatorial games with Christians as victims – is likely a literary trick to aggravate Domitian's negative reputation Concerning the conversion to the new religion, Lucius vehemently defends his decision of becoming a Christian to his father and sister, and although he is met with their incomprehension, he is not expelled from the traditional Roman circles. Vetellius, the leader of the Christian community sees the eruption of Vesuvius as "the vengeance of the Almighty."[833]

The work probably had some dissemination in the United States, but remained unknown in Europe. As stated, the front page does not bear the name of the author. The catalog of the Library of Congress in Washington D.C. lists Thomas Gray as the author, while that of the British Library lists the book as anonymous.[834] The best evidence for the attribution to Gray is a note in Fairfield's *Last Night of Pompeii*, discussed below, referring to "Dr. Gray from Boston."[835] One tiny detail betrays the American provenance of the writer, viz. the story about an American elm.[836] Curtis Dahl sees this anonymous American novel as "too much of an archaeolog-

---

[830] Expensive fish are a constant element at a luxurious Roman meal; there is a gigantic turbot in Juvenal, *Satire* 4.37–52.
[831] *Vestal* 1830, 183.
[832] He is frequently called "good-natured" (e.g. *Vestal* 1830, 95 and 109), likes wine (*Vestal* 1830, 97–98) and brings food and wine to prison (*Vestal* 1830, 135). In note 20 on p. 202, it is stated that these priests were supposed to remain chaste, but in real life licentiousness was the rule.
[833] *Vestal* 1830, 176.
[834] Dahl 1956, 188 and García y García 1998, no. 6285 also report Gray. Of course, this Gray is not the well-known poet who had been in Herculaneum in 1740 with Horace Walpole (here chapter II, pp. 103–104).
[835] Fairfield 1832, 309.
[836] *Vestal* 1830, 75, with a footnote.

ical treatise and moral homily to be a good novel."[837] In my opinion, however, the story is told well, at a good pace and with the right amount of tension, with the archaeological digressions being neither too burdensome nor too long. The notes, on the other hand, are superfluous to a good understanding of the story. The Christian aspect is characterized by a great degree of desire to convert the reader, something a more gripping story could indeed have done without.

The legibility of this novel strongly contrasts with the tedious style of the 191 page verse novel by Sumner Lincoln Fairfield, written two years later.[838] Three *canti* in iambic pentameter tell the story of the Jewish girl Mariamne and her lover Pansa, both converted Christians, who are for that reason destined to be rescued from the decadence and decline of the Romans. The eruption of Vesuvius is seen as a sign from God. Like Nicolai's Marcus, Pansa has served as a soldier in the Jewish Wars, and witnessed St. Paul's crucifixion (in fact, he was killed with a sword) in Rome. Like that town, Pompeii abounds with sin and decadence; the *praetor* Diomede epitomizes its degenerate civilization. The Iseum surpasses all limits of luxury, with marble, precious stones and gold everywhere. For the pagans, the Christians are a nuisance: Pansa, once an excellent decurion, now is

> [...] the plague
> of the new Heresy and Love, at once,
> infected.[839]

As a reaction, Pansa foretells the future fall of Rome, including assaults by Vandals and the plague of the Roman pope.[840] In this way he ends up as the prey of a lion in the amphitheater.

Fairfield includes almost no antiquarian descriptions, and the evocation of luxury and debauchery is of a purely literary character. As we know from Fairfield's biography by his wife, he never visited Italy. The ancient town of Pompeii did not

---

837 Dahl 1956, 188–189. See also Zimmerman 2008, 110–111.
838 Fairfield 1832. With an average number of 25 verses per page, it is some 4,500 lines in length. Dahl 1956, 187; Reinhold 1984, 271; Lacerenza 2004, 252–253. García y García 1998, no. 5102 also gives the name Fairfax and mentions an unpublished translation into German (his no. 1558).
839 Fairfield 1832, 124.
840 Fairfield 1832, 134: "I see a hoary head o'ercrowned / By three diadems of earth, hell, heaven," which is explained on p. 307, note 38: "The Pope – whose tiara was the very meteor of ruin." That Fairfield was an antipapist comes again to the fore on p. 179 where Pansa says: "And from the palace of the Sacred Hill / The thrice crown'd pontiff shall to earth dispense / The awful edict of his mighty will" etc. In note 39 on p. 308 the Jews are called "that strange people." However, Jane Fairfield (1847, 59) states: "Though bred a Protestant, he doubted the genuineness of all creeds except the Catholic. *This church he believed to be the church of Christ, founded by him and his apostles*." This contrasts sharply with his remark about the Pope!

interest him, except to show how mankind brings destruction upon itself when its fails to follow the path of Christ. When Vesuvius starts to erupt, Pansa therefore concludes:[841]

> Ye hear no thunder – but Destruction's howl!
> Ye see no lightning – but the lava glare
> Of desolation sweeping o'er your pride!
> Death is beneath, around, above, within
> All who exult to inflict it on my heart,
> And ye must meet it, fly when, where ye will,
> For in the madness of your cruelties
> Ye have delayed till every hope is dead.

Notwithstanding these dire words, the poem ends in happiness and peace, with the Christians safe and alive:[842]

> Dayspring and dewbeam, thus, year after year,
> Dawned and departed, and the seasons had
> Their own peculiar joys in Pansa's home.
> And there – the Roman Convert's testament –
> The storm-nursed heritors of Faith, blasphemed,
> Throned Liberty on Alpine pinnacles,
> And bade her temple be the Switzer hills.
> There in love worshipped, there with hoar hairs died
> The Christians, but the deathless spirit Rome
> Gave to her son, and Mariamne's heart,
> Bequeathed – in Freedom and God's holy Law,
> With tyrant Wrong warred through Guilt's thousand years.

The book is of little literary quality and seems overburdened with admonitions, at least in the eyes of modern readers.

Joseph Méry's 1834 poem, edited in the same year as Bulwer-Lytton, should be briefly mentioned.[843] Méry would later gain fame as the author of the textbook for Verdi's opera *Don Carlos* (1867). His libretti include *Herculanum*, with music by Félicien David (see Chapter VIII, pp. 364–365), which presents a small Christian community as well as some Jews in Herculaneum in 79. Although the poet does little to evoke Herculaneum, a mere synonym for an agreeable lifestyle, both it and Pompeii are portrayed as lovely towns enjoying their wealth in a fertile area, and

---

841 Fairfield 1832, 158.
842 Fairfield 1832, 200.
843 Méry 1834; 1837 [in *Scènes de la vie italienne*], 147–163. García y García 1998, no. 9154.

comparable to Sybaris.⁸⁴⁴ Despite the admonitions of a Jew, their towns' inhabitants feast until the very end, when Vesuvius erupts. So, Méry concludes, everything vanishes under the ashes apart from the "living Jew" seen by a seaman from Misenum.⁸⁴⁵ These last lines introduce Ahasverus, the Wandering Jew, a famous motif in many nineteenth-century literary works, and also in tales by De Graaff and Müller (see pp. 247, 253).⁸⁴⁶ At first glance, Méry seems to hesitate between the inherent rightness of the Jewish religion and the appeal of the free Roman way of life. Should we die in happiness or take the difficult road to eternity? He concludes that we may well prefer to vanish rapidly under the lava than to stay alive in misery.

Intermezzo: Briullov's Pompeii

Although I leave out art works inspired by the Vesuvian towns in this book, I must briefly describe *The Last Day of Pompeii*, a 456.5 × 651 cm painting by the Russian artist Karl Pavlovitsj Briullov. The enormous canvas, which Briullov made between 1830 and 1833, had a great impact on novelists of his time (fig. 10). It was on show in Briullov's Roman studio, traveled to Milan, and would reach its final destination in the Russian Museum in St. Petersburg in 1834.⁸⁴⁷ The painter had been to Pompeii as early as 1827 and would come back several times.⁸⁴⁸ The painting

---

844 Méry 1837, 153: "Pour ces villes d'amour l'azur fut prodigué, / Tout, jusqu'à leurs tombeaux, était riant et gai, / Comme dans Sybaris, autre ville odorante / Qui dort au bruit des flots du golfe de Tarente."
845 Méry 1837, 163 (final lines): "Tout disparut... Après l'épouvantable scène, / Un nautonier craintif venu du cap Misène, / Laissant flotter sa voile abandonnée au vent, / Sur Herculanum mort vit un Hébreu vivant!"
846 See Goldhill 2011, 236–237 on the "foundational tale" of this topic, and George Croly's 1828 *Salathiel*.
847 Lo Gatto 1971, 140–143; Leontyev 1996, 24–31; Glücklich 2008, 65–68; Gardner Coates/Lapatin/Seydl 2012, 140–142, with bibliography; Rowland 2014, 129–136; references in the following notes. Briullov lived and worked in Italy from 1823 to 1835. The painting was commissioned by M.G. Razumovski and A.N. Demidov as a gift to Tsar Nicolas I. Men like Pushkin, Glinka, and Gogol saw the image as a typical expression of catastrophe in their age (see below notes 849–850). Blix 2009, 155, figs 10–11, suggestively presents a painting by Frédéric Henri Schopin from ca. 1850 as a canvas inspired by Briullov's work (see also Gardner Coates/Lapatin/Seydl 2012, 142–143). Robert-Boissier 2011, 212–213 suggests that the girl with the black hair and one bare breast lying in the centre might be inspired by the famous woman's cast from the Villa of Diomedes (see p. 180), which I think is very likely, as are most associations mentioned in my brief description.
848 Lo Gatto 1971, 142, quotes, in Italian, a May 1842 letter from Briullov's brother Aleksandr, also a painter, to their parents. Cesare di Castelbarco dedicated a poem to this painting (Lo Gatto 1971, 141–142).

evoked various reactions among Briullov's compatriots. Gogol ventured that it was an achievement satisfying the demands of the times, when he saw the work in August 1834.[849] It lacked both the harshness of Michelangelo and the soft touch of Raphael, and was realistic, transparent, a "Sea of brilliance."[850]

Set against a dark night full of fire and with crumbling tombs and a turreted city wall, groups of people are shown struggling to escape from Pompeii. On the left goes a bearded old man carrying a torch and what seem to be a golden trinket and a silver incense burner. Next to him a kneeling woman, clasping two children, recalls the three skeletons described in this way in the hemicycle next to the Herculanean Gate. Behind them, a group of young people, some of them carrying their possessions on their heads, moves in front of the tombs. The man with the crate full of painting utensils might be a self-portrait of Briullov. A girl with a bronze or golden bowl on her head gazes in the direction of the viewer. Towards the centre, a half nude man runs to the left with his wife, who clutches an infant and young nude child, almost treading on a supine woman with beautiful black hair, whose jewelry box has spilled out onto the ground near her head, and whose baby grasps her. Behind the two running parents, a man clad in white and with a headband looks like Homer; he is likely a pagan priest trying to rescue his earthly possessions, which are gathered in a bundle under his arm. The center of the painting's foreground is almost empty, but beneath the fiery sky, the background is full of chaos. Together, this creates a certain depth in the composition. A man lying on his back has fallen from a dark horse. In front of him a helmeted man and a boy carry a bald old man in a green garment. This group recalls Aeneas, Anchises and Ascanius fleeing from the burning town of Troy, but also is suggestive of a "Taking from the Cross" by one seventeenth-century painter or another. Next to them a young man tries to give solace to a kneeling woman with black hair (seen as Pliny the Younger and his mother). Behind, an almost nude rider tries to master his panicking horse. At the far right, a young girl holds a still younger, probably suffocated girl with a flower garland on her head.

---

849 Gogol 1982, 205: "The underlying thought corresponds exactly to the style of our century, which, generally speaking, seems aware of its own terrible process of disintegration and is striving to unite all genres into general groups and is selecting violent crises experienced by the vast mass of the population." Quotation from "The Last Day of Pompeii" (pp. 203–210). Gogol was in Naples in the winter of 1846–1847, but did not refer to Pompeii in his work, as far as I could deduce from the English translations in Proffer 1967, 166–175. On Gogol in Italy, see Lo Gatto 1971, 124–140.
850 Gogol 1982, 208. Aleksandr Pushkin wrote some sketches of a poem on this work. Lo Gatto 1971, 140 points out that according to the poet the painting expressed "il sopragiungere dell'elemento distruttore nell'uomo."

Fig. 11: Karl Pavlovitsj Briullov, *The Last Day of Pompeii* (1830-1833), canvas, 456.5 × 651, St. Petersburg, Russian Museum.

A detail, mostly not observed, makes Briullov's work relevant in my discourse: the bearded old man, described first, wears a chain with the small cross around his neck, so that he must be a Christian.[851]

Bulwer-Lytton's *Last Days of Pompeii*

Bulwer-Lytton had already published some novels and volumes of poetry when he toured Italy in 1833–1834, accompanied by his wife Rosina Wheeler, with whom he had a very difficult relationship.[852] They left their little son Edward Robert behind in England.[853] Bulwer-Lytton had been elected MP in 1831 and stood at the beginning of an impressive political career. He was currently working on *Rienzi*, a novel about the fourteenth-century Roman politician Cola di Rienzo, and hoped to enjoy a pleasant stay with his wife under the Mediterranean sun. In Milan, he was struck by Briullov's canvas, and immediately wanted to start a novel about the same dramatic topic.[854] It is not unreasonable to suggest that Bulwer-Lytton took Briullov's innovative element of the Christian cross into account when he wrote *The Last Days of Pompeii*. The party continued their voyage southwards and in Naples they met Sir Walter Scott as well as Gell. *Rienzi* disappeared into a drawer and the first sentences of the new book were written under a pergola at Naples: "Italy, Italy, while I write, your skies are over me."[855] The result was

---

[851] Also mentioned in Harris 2007, 163–165.

[852] The trip to the South ought to ameliorate the bond, but the couple separated and Rosina had an especially unlucky life until her death (Mitchell 2003, 31–41 and *passim*; Bulwer-Lytton 20008, I, XIII–XXVIII; Goldhill 2011, 193–194). André Maurois wrote a brief novel *Les derniers jours de Pompéi* in which he sketched this unhappy marriage (Maurois 1928).

[853] See Andrew Brown, *Oxford Dictionary of National Biography* 34 (2004) 979–987 for a brief overview with bibliography. Some biographies will be cited in the following. Christensen 2004 contains the proceedings of a congress on the occasion of the second centennial of his birthday in 1803, in which the following contribution is relevant for the topic at hand: A. Easson, *ibidem*, 100–115. See also Lacerenza 2004, 249–252; Harris 2007, 165–172, 192–194; Zimmerman 2008, 114, 123–124; Goldhill 2011, 193–202; Stephen Harrison in Hales/Paul 2011, 75–89; Meilee D. Bridges, *ibidem*, 90–104; W. St Clair & A. Bautz in Gardner Coates/Lapatin/Seydl 2012, 92–95; St Clair/Bautz 2012; H. Schlange-Schöniger in Reinsberg/Meynersen 2012, 98–106; Reimers 2012, 180–187. On Bulwer-Lytton and Italy, see Mitchell 2003, 157–159.

[854] Leppmann 1966, 111 suggested that Bulwer-Lytton got his inspiration when he met Carlo Bonucci at the excavations after having separated from his friends, planning to return to the hotel for lack of interest.

[855] Bulwer-Lytton 1834, II, IV. As there are countless editions and translations (see García y García 1998, nos 2306–2310), I give Bulwer-Lytton's own subdivisions in books and chapters. In the * note to the preface Bulwer-Lytton states: "Nearly the whole of this work was written in

published in London in September 1834 and became by far the most popular work of this prolific author, both in and after his lifetime. *Rienzi* came out in 1835 and, although politics were increasingly occupying him, Bulwer-Lytton remained active in literature.

The Last Days of Pompeii relates the love-story of Glaucus and Ione, two young Greeks whose love is obstructed by Arbaces, a lustful priest of the Isis cult and the symbol of utter sin. The subplot concerns a group of Christians, connected to the protagonists by Ione's brother Apaecides, who is initially Arbaces' assistant, but, doubting the rightness of his religious choice, converts to Christianity. After various adventures in Pompeii, ending with Glaucus' condemnation "to the beasts" in the amphitheater, and a narrow escape from the eruption of Vesuvius, Glaucus and Ione travel to Greece and become Christians, too. In an epilogue, Bulwer-Lytton recounts that the twenty skeletons found in the Villa of Diomedes are the mortal remains of some of the protagonists.[856] Impressive characters are Arbaces, the symbol of absolute evil, and the blind slave girl Nydia, important as a mediator between the lovers, an obstruction to the realization of Arbaces' plans, and a (secret) lover of Glaucus. She refuses to follow him to Greece, and at the end, commits suicide.

Both Scott and Bulwer-Lytton spoke about Pompeii as the "City of the Dead."[857] They contended that for authors and readers of historical novels alike, Antiquity was more difficult to grasp than the Middle Ages, because the people of the latter era, at least, were Christians. The chosen period, nevertheless, was "the most civilized period of Rome" and, therefore, the most tangible of ancient society.[858]

Omniscient narrators who make digressions into other times and places than those of the plot was a common technique in historical novels of the nineteenth century. At the beginning of the last Book, the narrator foretells that the

---

Naples last winter (1832–3)." In the footnote of the first edition (Bulwer-Lytton 1834, V–VI), he writes: "Nearly the whole work was written the winter before last at Naples. On my return to England I was, indeed, too much occupied with political matters to have a great deal of superfluous leisure for works, purely literary, except in those, not unwelcome, intervals when the parliament going to sleep, allows the objects of life to awake; – dismissing its wearied legislators, some to hunt, some to shoot – some to fatten oxen, and some to cultivate literature."

856 Bulwer-Lytton 1834, V, XI. I had omitted this important case in previous publications; see G. Pucci in *Alma Tadema* 2007, 121 note 13. See Chapter III, pp. 180–185 on the human remains in the Villa of Diomedes.

857 Characterization attributed to Scott by Gell. See Scott 1890, II, 464 (with reference to Gell in a footnote): he went to Pompeii with Gell ("the coryphaeus of our party") on February 10, 1832. On this and similar characterizations, see Zimmerman 2008, 111–112. On Scott in Italy see Gell 1957; Scott died after his return to Britain in the same year, 1832.

858 Bulwer-Lytton 1834, Preface. This point is discussed by Blix 2009, 48–49.

day described therein is the last in Pompeii's history.⁸⁵⁹ Bulwer-Lytton also wants to demonstrate his command of the sources. In this case, he thrusts upon us a comparison of the two famous and frequently-cited letters of Pliny the Younger. Despite the use of authentic literary and archaeological sources, the book is a "historical costume romance." "Romance and sensationalism, rather than historical analysis, give the book its shape and power."⁸⁶⁰ The characters are not fully developed and remain more or less one-dimensional. The historical and antiquarian elements, namely the descriptions of objects and old customs occupy much of the novel. As noted, in his scrupulous attempt at accuracy, Bulwer-Lytton repeatedly interrupts the story to explain differences between the past and the present. Footnotes with references substantiate this accuracy, although readers of fiction probably do not expect such depth of information. The many references in Bulwer-Lytton's novel to petty facts also told in travel books make *The Last Days* a sort of new travelogue, an approach to the traditional theme that no other book apart from De Staël's *Corinne* (see Chapter V, pp. 258–260) had made. This means that even if readers forget the story, they will keep the impression of Pompeii's importance as a document of Roman society.

Bulwer-Lytton does not define the layout of Pompeii in detail, but offers a sketchy presentation that contrasts with his detailed description of the houses and the Temple of Isis. Apparently, he did not want to risk errors in topography and preferred not to use his imagination (cf. pp. 318–319, fig. 14). It is, therefore, an excellent ploy to make Nydia blind:⁸⁶¹ "Every street, every turning in the more frequented parts was familiar to her."

The buildings used for the locations of the various episodes – the Houses of Sallustius and of the Tragic Poet as well as the Villa of Diomedes and the Temple of Isis – became hallmarks for tourists. Bulwer-Lytton got an extensive tour of Pompeii by Gell and used the latter's publications as one of his main sources, which he duly acknowledges in a footnote.⁸⁶² Some rooms in the Villa of Diome-

---

859 Bulwer-Lytton 1834, V, I. A similar remark pertains to Ione's jewelry that she will never wear: "They were never fated to grace the fair form of Ione; they may be seen among the disinterred treasures of Pompeii, in the chambers of the studio at Naples" (Bulwer-Lytton 1834, III, IV).
860 Campbell 1986, 73. About the novel, pp. 72–76.
861 Bulwer-Lytton 1834, II, VII. In his Preface, Bulwer-Lytton refers to an anonymous Englishman in Naples for this motif: "Speaking of the utter darkness which accompanied the first recorded eruption of Vesuvius, and the additional obstacle it presented to the escape of the inhabitants, he observed that the blind would be the most favored in such a moment, and find the easiest. In this remark originated the creation of Nydia." Cf. the person of Tyro in Harris 2003 (here Chapter III, p. 200).
862 Bulwer-Lytton 1834, I, VIII. The first edition has a dedication to Gell, dated September 21, 1834, omitted in all later editions. Bulwer-Lytton hopes that the book will please him, who succeeds in stimulating the study of antiquity after bad times. For Gell's reaction see Clay 1976, 155.

des are skillfully sketched, e.g. that of Iulia, a rich Pompeian matron who does her hair like a lady of the Flavian period, according to "the latest fashion in Rome."[863] Glaucus lives in a dwelling that resembles an apartment for a wealthy bachelor like those in London's Mayfair.[864] Like these dwellings, Vesuvius is one of the characters: its presence is always perceptible, and it harbors the suspense that gives the book its tension.

One feature of *The Last Days* that would certainly have been attractive to the contemporary English reader was the equation of certain "good" and "bad" aspects of Pompeian society with then present-day Britain and the Continent. Bulwer-Lytton contended that most of the bad could still be seen in Italy, primarily around Naples, while most of the good still existed in English society. These comparisons enhance my conviction that the book resonates with the atmosphere of upper class English society, which is seen as a successor to the Roman upper class. Bulwer-Lytton – and his readers from the same class – would have looked down upon the primitive society of southern Italy, which in their opinion had not developed substantially since Antiquity. The ancient community described in the book barely differs from Bulwer-Lytton's own contemporary milieu. There are distinct differences between social groups, and the protagonists pass their time with appropriate "leisure" pursuits and some business on the forum, but stay far away from daily politics. They show distaste for the super-zealous *aedile* Pansa, but also loudly evoke their opinion that public and religious functions should be entirely controlled by the upper class. Bulwer-Lytton seems to imply that in his ideal world, modern Catholic priests should not earn money, but should be independently wealthy.[865] Members of both the ancient and modern upper class have visiting cards and wallets, although "with this difference – the ancients' wallets were usually better furnished."[866] Bulwer-Lytton notes that ancient schoolboys would have received floggings much like contemporary ones (as represented in one of the forum scenes), and he warns "young readers" about the consequences of bad behavior.[867]

The forum of Pompeii resembled the streets of modern Paris from the point of view of the busy traffic, but also London's Inns of Court – complete with its

---

863 Bulwer-Lytton 1834, III, VII. For the make-up scene, see Böttiger's *Sabina* (1803, 1806; here Chapter III, pp. 190–191).
864 The House of the Tragic Poet. Bulwer-Lytton 1834, I, III. Bulwer-Lytton lived in a luxurious apartment on Mayfair, separated from his wife, and was seen as a dandy (Mitchell 2003, 87–91).
865 Bulwer-Lytton 1834, II, II. Cf. Vecchi 1864, here Chapter III, pp. 192–193. See on this matter also St Clair/Bautz 2012, 366–367.
866 Bulwer-Lytton 1834, I, VII and II, II.
867 Bulwer-Lytton 1834, III, I.

lawyers.[868] A visit to the theater or amphitheater required the purchase of a ticket, "not much unlike our modern Opera ones."[869] Other similarities include the Roman and English love of gardening and topiary (clipping of trees and shrubs into modeled forms, Latin *nemora tonsilia*), as performed by a "retired [...] Hackney at Paddington."[870] Sport, too, forms a principal aspect of life and is widely discussed in pubs by the lower classes, in both ancient and contemporary society. In Bulwer-Lytton's novel, the "professionals" themselves, the gladiators, meet in a *caupona*.[871] At home, rich people ate off "bone china,"[872] but they did not display their wealth in the conspicuous way of the nouveau riche Diomede, when he showed off his villa to his stupefied visitors in the way Trimalchio had done in Petronius' *Satyrica*. Bulwer-Lytton even contrasts this behavior with "[his] refined English notions which place good breeding in indifference."[873] In the meantime, the *hoi polloi* demonstrated a "lively vehemence of their Campanian blood." Nydia is a better flower seller than modern girls;[874] Pompeii has a storyteller like modern Naples; horse and cart has not changed and a sacrifice in a temple resembles a Catholic mass.[875]

Some elements in the book belong to the Gothic Novel.[876] This genre had developed in the mid-eighteenth century, in the wake of an interest in the Middle-Ages at the expense of Antiquity and the Renaissance. Walpole's *Castle of Otranto* (1764) and Beckford's *Vathek* (1780) heralded this trend. They were followed at the beginning of the nineteenth century by Mary Wollstonecraft Shelley's *Frankenstein* (1818). The weather in these books is often suffocating; there are storms and black skies.[877] In an unforgettable description, Bulwer-Lytton's

---

868 Bulwer-Lytton 1834, III, I refers to paintings showing the forum excised from the walls of the atrium of the *Praedia* of Julia Felix. See *PPM* III, 247–257.
869 Bulwer-Lytton 1834, V, II; see Gell 1832, I, 92 and II, 50 vignette. These bone tokens frequently feature in travel books and are referred to as expressions of civilization.
870 Bulwer-Lytton 1834, III, III.
871 Bulwer-Lytton 1834, II, I.
872 Bulwer-Lytton 1834, I, VIII.
873 Bulwer-Lytton 1834, IV, III.
874 Bulwer-Lytton 1834, I, II. Another Pompeian flower seller features in *A la joie morte*, a poem by Hugues Rebell (1894, 25–26) of which I quote the opening lines: "La petite âme qui chantait, / La fleurette toujours épanouie et souriante, / Qui à tous les hommes offrait son calice parfumé, / Pour que chacun s'en embaumât, / La petite âme qui chantait, / S'est envolée avec l'oiseau, avec le pétale, avec le brin d'herbe; / Elle est mêlée à l'air subtil, / Et en le respirant, nous respirons son souvenir." For more on this poet (pseudonym of George-Joseph Grassal) see David 2001, 155. Not in García y García 1998.
875 Bulwer-Lytton 1834, III, IX and I, II respectively.
876 Cf. Riikonen 1978, 79 ("Elemente des Schauerromanes"). On *The Last Days*, pp. 81–89.
877 E.g. Bulwer-Lytton 1834, III, IX.

reader encounters a witch on the slopes of Vesuvius. The Doric temple on the Triangular Forum is "timeworn and half in ruin." These and other aspects serve to "prove" that Pompeii was a symbol of moral decay.[878]

The Pompeians of the novel think that strangers cannot be trusted. Apparently the Greeks and Christians form an exception, which Bulwer-Lytton partly explains in his Preface with the claim that Pompeii was a Greek colony founded by Heracles (cf. Chapter I, p. 63, note 245). Arbaces is the example of an extremely bad foreign character, the caricature of Lucullian and sexual lust, not living for spiritual feelings despite his function. For Bulwer-Lytton, decadence is not the Greek or Hellenistic spread of luxury, but Oriental debauchery.[879]

Both Fairfield and Bulwer-Lytton[880] represented the Christians in Pompeii as examples of "pure" Christians who are an example for modern times. Both may well have taken into account the – rare – early travelogues in which the eruption is explained as a punishment by God similar to the destruction of Sodom and Gomorrah. In 1831 Selina Martin, for instance, wrote about the heathen Pompeians:[881]

> In vain they did call on their gods to deliver them. They were made of metal and stone, they could not hear. At the omnipotent command of the Most High, from the mountain issued forth coals of fire.

In his Preface, Bulwer-Lytton observes how the early persecutions of Christians inspired him, and emphasizes the purity and moral richness of the early Christians, who he contrasts with those living in Britain.[882] This opinion might reflect Bulwer-Lytton's adherence to the then still very young Oxford Movement. In 1833 a number of theologians of the University of Oxford rebelled against the reigning opinions of the Church of England, which according to them, was too greatly influenced by liberalism and too much tied to the state. The ancient communities of Christians were to serve as examples of a spiritual revival in which the Eucharist and the presence of Christ were the principal aims. People were looking for a

---

[878] Bulwer-Lytton 1834, V, IX (quotation), II, I.
[879] Bulwer-Lytton 1834, I, VII (Arbaces). He even inserts a discussion on the dependence of the Etruscans on the Egyptians as advocated by Arbaces (Bulwer-Lytton 1834, III, X, note). Malamud 2009, 132–133 illustrates how in America Arbaces was seen as a symbol of Islam and the Ottoman Empire.
[880] In Moormann 2007, I address how Bulwer-Lytton was accused of plagiarism by Fairfield (see Fairfield 1835). Here, I leave out the quarrelsome relationship between these two defenders of Christianity in Pompeii.
[881] Martin 1831, 68. García y García 1998, no. 8782.
[882] Bulwer-Lytton 1834, IV, I. Christians make their first appearance in Bulwer-Lytton 1834, III, III. See Campbell 1986, 74–75 and Goldhill 2011, 198–202 on Christianity

more intimate and personal belief and the intense commitment to Christ formulated by the first Christians inspired them.[883]

While Nicolai, *The Vestal* and Fairfield fell into oblivion, Bulwer-Lytton's novel elicited great acclaim despite his own repulsion, and would generate many "offspring" in the shape of novels, operas, poems, stage works, and ultimately, movies.

Bulwer-Lytton's Fortune

From its publication in 1834 up to the twentieth century, *The Last Days of Pompeii* has remained the most influential Christian Pompeii novel. Many other literary works and stage adaptations (see Chapter VIII, pp. 367–370, 372–377) rely on this work. In the following, I briefly sketch its reception immediately after its publication.

In Britain, Bulwer-Lytton's political associate Benjamin Disraeli and Lady Blessington (see Chapter II, p. 125) immediately praised his work after its publication. On October 23, 1834, Bulwer-Lytton wrote to Blessington that it was not among his favorites.[884] While visiting Pompeii for the second time some years later, Mary Shelly took the occasion to reflect on the novel:[885]

> Bulwer [...] has peopled its silence. I have been reading his book, and I have felt on visiting the place much as if *really* it had once been full of stirring life, now that he has attributed names and possessors to its houses, passengers to its streets. Such is the power of imagination. It can not only give 'a local habitation and a name' to the airy creations of the fancy, and the abstract ideas of the mind, but it can put a soul into stones, and hang the vivid interest of our passion and our hope upon objects otherwise vacant of name and sympathy. Not indeed that Pompeii could be such, but the account of its 'Last Days' has cast over it a more familiar garb, and peopled its desert streets with associations that greatly add to their interest.

---

883 G. Biemer, Oxfordbewegung, *Lexikon für Theologie und Kirche* 7 (1998) 1239, with extensive bibliography; Gadille 1995, 230–236. Other private reasons which might have inspired Bulwer-Lytton are evaluated in King/Engel 1981. They sketch Bulwer-Lytton's personal development, in which his becoming an MP in 1831 plays an important role. He becomes aware of his political responsibility and his heroes become more "social" than "romantic." On the contrary, Mitchell 2003, 138–139 sees Bulwer-Lytton as a non-religious person.
884 Lytton 1913, 443–444 [letter Disraeli], 446–447. Quotation on p. 460. On these relationships Mitchell 2003, 94–96 (Blessington, with illustration on p. 86 of her salon with Bulwer-Lytton, Disraeli, and Dickens), 99–102 (Disraeli), 119–120 (Dickens).
885 Quotation taken from Dahl 1956, 191. Mary had been there with her husband Percy Bysshe Shelly in 1818. Then he wrote his 'Ode to Naples' in which fine lines on Pompeii can be read (cf. Chapter I, p. 71–72).

A non-literary reason for Bulwer-Lytton's immediate success might have been the eruption of Vesuvius in August 1834. Just one week before his novel came off the presses, the news about the enormous disaster had arrived in London, and the September edition of *The Athenaeum* suggested that the book came out in time.[886]

There are translations of Bulwer-Lytton's work into numerous languages.[887] Like the works of Scott and other historical novels, it was also revised for children until far into the twentieth century.[888] Adrien Lemercier's 1841 children's version was very popular in France.[889] This writer followed Bulwer-Lytton precisely, in contrast with his compatriot Eugène Meuris in *Glaucus et Arbaces ou le dernier jour de Pompeïa*.[890] In Meuris' version, the dialogues are shortened or entirely omitted, whereas the contrast between Glaucus and Arbaces is sharpened and the Egyptian priest plays a larger role.

The Last Days of Pompeii became a hit in the United States thanks to the presence of the early Christians.[891] One expression of Nydia's popularity in America – she would be as popular as the little matchstick girl in Andersen's fairy tale – is William Randolph Rogers' statue "Nydia, the Blind Girl of Pompeii." In 1850, the marble creation was first exhibited in the Pennsylvania Academy of Fine Arts at Philadelphia. The Metropolitan Museum acquired a copy in 1859 and many American museums followed. A large exhibition in Philadelphia in 1876 had no less than six versions on show.[892]

---

886 Quoted in Simmons 1969, 104–105. See now also St Clair/Bautz 2012, 368.
887 See García y García 1998, nos 2307–2310 (translation into German, French, Italian, and Spanish). Dutch: *De laatste dagen van Pompeji*, Amsterdam 1835; Swedish: *Pompeii' sista dagar*, Stockholm 1835. Cf. Ernst 1992, 82–90; Zintzen 1998, 205, 3–208. On Germany Fitzon 2002b, 306, 314–315 note 45.
888 E.g. Bunce 1960. Many examples in nineteenth-century Germany, e.g. Körber 1849, Nieritz 1850, Höcker 1889 and Moritz 1892.
889 Lemercier 1841. I also saw an anonymous version: *Les derniers jours de Pompeï. Imité de Bulwer*, seventeenth edition, Tours 1868 (volume in Bibliothèque de la jeunesse chrétienne approuvée par Mgr l'archevêque de Tours). García y García 1998, no. 7898 has the thirtieth edition. The copy I read contains some steel engravings with images in the vogue of the Middle Ages (dress, figures, attributes).
890 Meuris 1868. García y García 1998, no. 9163. Bulwer-Lytton is not mentioned at all.
891 Margaret Malamud (in Hales/Paul 2011, 199–214) has pointed out how the rapid social changes in the 1840s evoked feelings of anxiety about the instability of the world. This led to an increasing interest in religion, especially that of the early Christians. Bulwer-Lytton's book formed a stimulating lecture for these seeking Christians. See chapter VIII, pp. 367–370, 372–377 for the impact of drama after Bulwer-Lytton.
892 See Jon Seydl in Hales/Paul 2011, 215–231, about this "1876 Philadelphia Centennial Exposition."

Nydia has even been highlighted in poetry. For instance, Nannie Montfort, in her preface to *Nydia and other poems*, ventures that the verses are meant to divert the reader from their daily sorrows and bring comfort. There is no reference to Bulwer-Lytton, but the "Nydia" of the main poem is without a doubt Bulwer-Lytton's flower girl. After a short description of Pompeii she is introduced:[893]

> Love gave to Nydia his rare, effulgent beams,
> Almost beyond her lost and fondest dreams,
> Revealed through dull, emotionless, night band eyes
> That kept concealed all outward mysteries
> Which voice the inward language more
> Than all dear utterances in the ample lore
> Of lovers, and keep mere speech in least most
> Restraining when most distracting silence cost
> High vantage ground.

Because Glaucus loves Ione, Nydia must seek comfort with God. The main part of the long poem concentrates upon Nydia's devotion. It finishes – like the other poetry of the book – extremely piously.[894]

Bulwer-Lytton's *Last Days* also received less favorable criticism. I single out a statement by the Dutch critic Conrad Busken Huet, who once observed that the "destruction of Pompeii" was not a very good theme for a historical novel. In an attack on Bulwer-Lytton's novel, he argued that it "featured all of the genre's flaws and some additional weaknesses, due to the circumstance thatit is a novel playing out in antiquity. Who can remain, from the beginning to the end, a poet, when he is obliged a coupe of times to give class on Greek or Roman antiquities?" The author insists on pausing the narrative to explain Greek or Roman antiquities.[895] Besides his distaste for the genre, Busken Huet clearly disliked the numer-

---

[893] Montfort 1917, 13–25; quotation at p. 16.
[894] Montfort 1917, 25: "Biogenesis and logic or Soul is God inert / And God apparent, designated by power to divert / Unclarified Energy into varied currents / Of immature, specific attributes, making deterrents / Of counter laws, or degenerative system which / Prepare ways for rehabilitation or law-ditch / Between manifest life and transcendent existence / Called wall which closes all avenues or assistance / To eternal law or earth procreation or mortal, / Insulating crust – body – and less the stark portal / To electrifying, individualized Ego, / Learning the I Am to manifest in spheres so / Remote from Dust insignia that all preconceived dear hopes / Are miraged, but ardent near facts lying along the slopes / Of Eternal Progression, which leads to Almighty God – / Ladder reaching down from Him and resting on the rod."
[895] Busken Huet 1877, 43, chapter VI: "Dit boek vereenigt in zich al de gebreken die van het genre van den historischen roman onafscheidelijk kunnen geacht worden, en nog eenige andere gebreken erboven, voortvloeiend uit de omstandigheid dat het een roman is die in de oudheid

ous explanations of antiquarian details, which distracted the reader from the story itself.[896] A second problem Busken Huet had with Bulwer-Lytton and others is that their plots are too precisely defined by the historical theme of the eruption of Vesuvius: the reader knows beforehand the end of the story, viz. the destruction of an entire city and that a possible escape is not at hand.[897] This argument is less convincing than the first, since many successful literary works renarrate well-known themes. Greek tragedies are a prime example of this. In the case of Pompeii novels, however, after a study of a large series of novels, novellas and stories, I often felt that I had seen and read this tale several times before; for that reason I was positively struck by Busken Huet's opinion.

Among modern literary scholars, Leppmann believes that the spell of Bulwer-Lytton's novel is convincing and that the antiquarian setting vanishes, whereas Riikonen sees the author as the best example of the antiquarian tradition.[898] Bulwer-Lytton's biographer Campbell notes that his novel, despite its broad diffusion, was not his best or most important work. This is unfortunate in a certain way, because Bulwer-Lytton was not a mediocre writer. He had a rich fantasy and knew how to invent fine and subtle plots, but his style was rather ineloquent.[899] Zintzen stresses the strong realism and the antiquarian trustworthiness of the work, whereas, in describing Pompeii, Bulwer-Lytton used many visual metaphors to create a vivid atmosphere of the ancient town.[900] The philologist Timm Reimers also stresses the reliability of the archaeological evidence.[901]

The importance of Bulwer-Lyttons' novel cannot be underestimated, even if the author himself found it a lesser work than other publications. Many readers – and followers – were captivated by the plot and the intriguing interplay between the characters and the Pompeian setting, which apparently enhanced the book's dramatic tension. As we will see in the remainder of this chapter and in the fol-

---

speelt. Wie kan van het begin tot het einde dichter blijven, wanneer hij bij tussenpoozen genoodzaakt wordt kollege te geven in de Grieksche of Romeinsche antiquiteiten."
896 This sort of problems is a flaw of the genre and, as we have seen, also pertains to the historical novels discussed in Chapter III (cf. p. 174). Cf. Göbel 1993, 149–161, who refers to various scholars and critics on that point. Cf. also Riikonen 1978.
897 Busken Huet 1877, 44.
898 Leppmann 1966, 171–181; 8, 64–67 observes (p. 65) "einen gelehrten Anstrich." Riikonen 1978, 64. On the technique of inserting antiquarian details into the story, *ibidem* 64–68.
899 Campbell 1986, 129. Another biographer does not pay much attention to the work, but recalls its success of 32 editions until 1914 (Mitchell 2003, XVI). Göbel 1993 meticulously analyses various novels and offers an excellent panorama of Bulwer-Lytton's capacities. On the – doubted – literary qualities of the novel, see Goldhill 2011, 193–194.
900 Zintzen 1998, 203–208, 228–233.
901 Reimers 2012, 181.

lowing chapters, Bulwer-Lytton is never far from any intimation of the disaster of Pompeii, both in literature and art and drama.

Before pursuing my survey of Christian fiction, it is relevant to assess whether there really were Jews and Christians in Pompeii and Herculaneum.

Jews and Christians in Pompeii before 79?

> I think that if such air, such climate, and such nature existed everywhere, there would be many fewer saints and sages and many more happy and carefree sinners. From the religious point of view, people cannot be allowed to live on this sensual shore; and, who knows – could the ardent prayers of the first Christians have influenced the eruption of Vesuvius, which destroyed Pompeii and Herculaneum?[902]

Although the debate about the presence of Jews and Christians in the Vesuvian cities has nowadays somewhat abated, it is relevant in our context to cast a glance at the archaeological evidence. What is known about their presence, and if any, were these believers part of Jewish and Christian communities, or were they simply individuals? Did they have houses of worship? Then there is the question of whether the modern authors made use of such data, or whether they entirely invented their historical narrative themes. Believers searching for Christian roots and hoping to find them in Campania are convinced that Jews and Christians lived and worked in Pompeii. Some scholars have tackled the problem and the following synopsis is based on their works.[903] Giancarlo Lacerenza, a Neapolitan scholar of Hebrew Studies, has found out that Raffaele Garrucci, an important mid-nineteenth century scholar of early Christian art, was the first to believe in

---

[902] Aleksandr Herzen (1995, 97), letter from February 25, 1848, in translation by Judith E. Zimmerman. See Lo Gatto 1971, 180–192, 216–220.

[903] E.g. Baldi 1964; Giordani/Kahn 1965, 1974, 2001 (see the critical review by L.V. Rutgers, *Bibliotheca Orientalis* 60 (2003) 188–189); Castrén 1975, 36; Maulucci Vivolo 1990; Vitale 2000, 127–161; Lacerenza 2001 and 2004; Schnabel 2002, 794–796; Lampe 2003, 7–10; Glücklich 2008, 41–44. Varone (1979) states that he wrote his book for interested lay people of Catholic inclination, but his work is relevant both scientifically and religiously for other readers as well, due to Varone's balanced opinions. He discusses pros and cons and is mostly skeptical concerning the Christian character of doubtful cases. Among the most zealous defenders of the presence of Jews and Christians at Pompeii were Pio Ciprotti (1975) and Della Corte. Della Corte 1965 has numerous suggestive allusions to the "Nuova Fede" (p. 312). See also note 911.

the presence of Christians, which would be two decades after the publication of the novels discussed.[904]

The sources adduced mainly consist of graffiti on Pompeii's walls in which names occur that are or are supposed to be Jewish or Christian. There are also graffito texts that have been interpreted as referring to the message of Jesus. Another category of sources consists of artistic objects and figural representations in decorations of houses.[905] No remains of cult rooms have been found (or seen as such) in either houses or public buildings, so that the existence of synagogues or churches – the latter would only come into being in the second century in Rome – is excluded. This does not constitute a problem, however, as it is known that worshippers often met in private homes to celebrate their communions. Jews might have been the more visible, judging from references in ancient literature and the existence of a synagogue in late Antiquity at Ostia.

A few graffiti contain names that imply a provenance of the mentioned persons from Palestine: the names Jesus, Maria and Martha occur a few times. One citation of Martha, written in the toilet of the House of the Centenary, is not very flattering:

Marthae hoc trichilinium / est nam in trichilinio / cacat
"This dining room is Martha's, for Martha shits in the dining room."

Apparently a servant of Palestinian birth had been taken on by some relative or acquaintance.[906] One of the three Marias found on Pompeian walls worked with Aegle and Zmyrina in *thermopolium* IX 11, 2.[907] Aegle is a Greek name meaning light of the Sun or the Moon, and Zmyrina is named after Smyrna, modern Izmir in Turkey. Probably all of them were slaves or at most free women of low status, and their services probably extended beyond delivering drinks. Consequently, Hebraic names may well represent people from Israel. As we have seen, many inhabitants of that region were forced to go to Italy as captives after the Jewish

---

904 Garrucci 1853, 69, although by that time no "evidence" had yet been found. See Lacerenza 2004, 254–255. On Garrucci, see C. Ferone, *Dizionario Biografico degli Italiani* 52 (1999) 388–390.
905 E.g. the Pygmies acting in a scene like Salomon's Judgment from House VIII 5, 24 (House of the Doctor), now National Museum Naples inv. 113.197 (*PPM* VIII, 604–606), seen as a proof of the presence of Jews and Christians by De Feis 1906 and Müller 1910 (see below p. 246). The theologist John W. Burgon, Fellow of Oriel College at Oxford (1862, 288) recognized Christian tokens in depictions of branches, pigeons, anchors and in words like *elpis*.
906 *CIL* IV 5244, found in 1879. A Marthe [sic] is recorded in *CIL* IV 3763.
907 Maria: *CIL* IV 7866; Aegle: *CIL* IV 7862; Zmyrina: *CIL* IV 7863–7864. The girls also feature in novels: Lundgren 2001 and Harris 2003.

Revolt of 69–70 (see p. 252, note 974). The existence of these poor slave people, however, does not necessarily imply the existence of communities that worshipped Yahweh or Christ in the towns of Vesuvius.

One of the most studied graffiti is that containing the word *christianos* as part of a longer text which faded shortly after its discovery in 1862 on the south-western wall of the atrium of house VII 11, 11 in the Vicolo del Balcone pensile, not far from the brothel. The story of the find and its documentation by the classicist Karl Zangemeister and others contains so many questionable assertions so as to make it rather suspect.[908] The two transcriptions of the text show great differences, including the spelling of the word itself, for which reason it has been suggested that the graffito was actually a fake. Fiorelli, who produced a third copy of the text, interpreted *christianos* as the name of a wine. Margherita Guarducci, an epigraphist renowned within and beyond Catholic circles alike for her scientific research on the tomb of St. Peter (underneath the papal altar in St. Peter's Basilica in Rome), reconstructed the sentence as follows, although without explaining its reasoning:[909]

> *Bovios audi(t) christianos / s(a)evos o[s]ores*
> "Bovius listens to the Christians, those cruel haters."

In 1995 the theologian Paul Berry argued that the portico of the house had served as a house church for a small community, despite the *lararium* with a painted image of a genius and Heracles.[910] Berry includes the *Sodoma* and *Rotas* inscriptions (see below, p. 237) as additional evidence. He sees the text *Rex es* ("you are the king"), recorded in House II 5, 1 in 1957, as a citation from the Bible.[911] According to Berry, it becomes clear from these texts that the members of the community spoke Latin, not Aramaic or Greek.

The graffito *Sodom[a]/Gomor(r)a*, found in house IX 1, 26, offers a clear reference to the episode about these two sinful cities in the Bible, for which reason the writer may have been Jewish or Christian.[912] Speculations have been made about

---

[908] *CIL* IV 679. Apparently written with charcoal; seen by Alfred Kiessling. Cf. Della Corte 1965, 204–205; *PPM* VII, 464; Schnabel 2002, 796; Lacerenza 2004, 256–257.
[909] Guarducci 1965 and 1967.
[910] Berry 1995. Pellegrino 2004, 319–341 interprets this portico in the same way.
[911] *CIL* IV 10.193. Della Corte (editor of this *CIL* volume) and Ciprotti (see supra note 903) published it in the Vatican paper *Osservatore Romano della Domenica* of December 1, 1957. Elsewhere the authors presumed that the contents were not necessarily Christian. Nowadays, there are good reasons to assume the presence of a brothel in this house: Guzzo/Scarano Ussani 2011, 63, note 3.
[912] *CIL* IV 4976. Cf. *Genesis* 13.13 and 19.24. Ultimately, H. Solin, *Gymnasium* 121 (2014) 103–104: written by a Jew at some time before A.D. 79.

why and when this remark was scratched on the wall: did a Christian foresee the absolute decline of the Roman culture; did the text refer to the earthquake of 62 or the eruption of Vesuvius in 79? Or should we presume a visit from a Christian or Jew – even as a robber – to the ruins after the 79 cataclysm, who left this line as his explanation of the disaster? Or does it simply refer to Pompeii's luxury and debauchery? There is no definite answer possible, the graffito being lost nowadays.

Not less famous in this debate is the following palindrome text that can be read in all directions:

SATOR ROTAS
AREPO OPERA
TENET TENET
OPERA AREPO
ROTAS SATOR

This inscription's "backbone" is *tenet* ("he/she takes/holds") in cross form. One can recognize other words like *sator* ("sower"), *opera* ("works") and *rotas* ("wheels"). The term *arepo* is enigmatic and no meaningful sentence can be constructed on the basis of these words. The text is also known from other contexts in the ancient world; it was used in the Christian world of late Antiquity in Egypt and even occurs in the Middle Ages.[913] The Egyptian papyri in which the formula occurs are of a magical character, containing spells. The origin of the saying, however, is not necessarily Christian. The term has the same force as "abracadabra" or other incantations and appears to have accidentally entered the Christian context.

The examples found at Pompeii were seen in 1925 in the House of Paquius Proculus and in 1936 in the Great Palaestra.[914] In 1925, the text was not considered proof of Christian habitation by Della Corte, its discoverer, while the 1936 graffito was presented by the same scholar as a sound proof for the existence of Christians thanks to two words next to it, *Sautran / Val*.[915] The French archaeologist Jérôme Carcopino stuck to a late dating of other *sator* inscriptions and, therefore, argued that the Pompeian text had been written decades later by a person who had descended in search of his own possessions or someone else's, a hypothesis which cannot be proven and only makes the discussion more difficult. This constituted an insult to Della Corte, as it insinuated that (1) he had not observed that

---

[913] Lampe 2003, 8–9: not before ca. 500 in a Christian context. See the extensive overview in Sheldon 2003.
[914] *CIL* IV 8123 and *CIL* IV 8623. Garro 1942, 168: the Christian soldier Romano writes this text in the palaestra.
[915] *CIL* IV 8622a-b.

ashes and *lapilli* would have been disturbed by such an intervention; (2) he had not observed that the script was more recent; or (3) that he, himself, must have been a forger! Guarducci gave short shrift to these insinuations. In the first place, she argued, the text was authentic, and in the second place, although without concrete contents, it was magical and hence mysterious and impenetrable.[916]

The *sator* inscription has become the topic of many monographs in which various interpretations are given to solve the enigma. In some, it is claimed that it refers to the foundation of Rome, or forms a very succinct message of Jesus Christ himself, or another form of reference to Christianity.[917] The French classicist Alain Le Ninèze presents a rather dry collection of alternative readings, one more unlikely than the next in his novel *Sator*, composed of letters by Lucius Albinus, procurator of Judaea in 62–67 and his uncle Publius Balbus Pison, which is preserved in a (mock) manuscript in the Vatican library.[918]

The *sator* text has an essential but puzzling role in Osman Lins' 1973 Brazilian novel *Avalovara*.[919] Around 200 B.C., Publius Ubonius and his slave Loreius are fascinated by the text's associations with magic, astronomy, and Pythagoras.[920] The master proposes setting his slave free if he can find the solution. Loreius knows the solution, but wants to manipulate Publius. Yet, during a visit to the prostitute Tyche – Destiny – he betrays the solution and commits suicide.[921] Later in the book, in modern times the narrator comes across a Greek version in a manuscript in the Biblioteca Marciana in Venice, but there is no connection made between these imaginary sources and the plot. The quadrate is combined with a spiral on top of it in Lins' book. The composition forms the basis of eight stories, each connected with one of the text's letters and playing out between 1908 and 1966, which are all intertwined with each other. It is not clear why Pompeii plays no substantial part in this section of Lins' book. He may simply have known of the *sator* texts in Pompeii and recalled them as predecessors to his learned, some-

---

[916] Della Corte 1965, 311, 406; Carcopino 1953, 47–72; Guarducci 1965 and 1967. Not Christian according to Gigante 1979, 78–79 (with bibl.). Lacerenza 2004, 252, 262–265 sees it as a fake.

[917] I mention very few recent proposals: Cammilleri 1999 (evidence of Christians in Pompeii); Vitale 2000, 127–141 (announcement of the arrival of the Savior); Pascolini 2006 (Jesus Christ); Iannelli 2009 (Romulus and Remus; no Christians in Pompeii). Overview in Sheldon 2003, esp. 248–252, 265–266.

[918] Le Ninèze 2008.

[919] I read an English translation (Lins 1980). The Pompeii scenes are in "Spiral/Square" nos 5, 6, and 7. The only archaeological connection I could find is the profession of Anneliese Roos' husband, who is a nautical archaeologist (Lins 1980, 181).

[920] Lins 1980, 12, in a Pompeii "then at the height of its splendor."

[921] The two readings are (Lins 1980, 53): "The farmer carefully maintains his plow in the furrows" or "The plowman carefully sustains the world in its orbit."

times witty and intriguing story.⁹²² In a booklet full of word plays, the famous semiologist and novel writer Umberto Eco presents mock riddles inspired by the *sator* inscription, gathered from various sources or composed by himself.⁹²³ Like Lins' his view of the text is devoid of Christian symbolism.

Another puzzle was provided by alleged images of the Holy Cross discovered in Pompeii and Herculaneum. The first case was a stucco relief in the bakery in the luxurious House of Pansa, seen by Mazois as an "espèce de croix." Only Mazois ever recorded this lost piece of possible evidence, which in his (and my) view might have been something else anyway, like a tool used in the bakery.⁹²⁴ Still visible today is the cross-shaped cutting in the wall plaster of a room on the upper story of the House of the Bicentenary at Herculaneum. This find elicited a fiery debate, only quieted in the last decades. Skeptics seem to have won the argument: the incision simply served for the insertion of two interconnected wooden laths to support a small plank.⁹²⁵ This notion, however, has not met approval with the Swiss Catholic priest Paul Georg Bruin, who focuses on that "sign of the holy cross" in a historical essay.⁹²⁶ His booklet turns into a short story about the rich corn merchant Diomedes and his (Christian) slave Petronius, who has a wooden cross in his room in Herculaneum. Without explicitly saying it, Bruin sees the ruins of Herculaneum as the remains of a town where our forerunners in belief walked and worked. Some utterly unlikable features of the Vesuvian cities are linked to passages from the New Testament, such as the mosaic of the watch dog in the House of the Tragic Poet in Pompeii: *cave canem* is also a dictum in St. Paul's letter to the citizens of Philippi.⁹²⁷

---

922 There are a certain amount of studies about this Borges- and Calvino-like author. See Simas 1993; Dalcastagnè 2000 (i.a. chronology and line of story); C.D. Damasceno Ferreira, I. Ribeira Gomes, and J. Paganini in De Faria/Ferreira 2009, 51–59 (structure of novel), 129–141 (poetics), 143–156 (playing motif).
923 Eco 2006, 66–75, in the tradition of the group of literary authors united in OULIPO (e.g. Italo Calvino, Raimond Queneau, George Perec) like Lins.
924 Mazois 1824, II, 88.
925 See Falanga 1981; Mols 1999a, 58, figs. 162–163; Lampe 2003, 9. For a vivid description of the find see Maiuri 1998, 241–248 (chapter "Inventio crucis," dated March 1939). Nevertheless, see Pellegrino 2004, 321–323: here a rich family (p. 322) "practiced a polytheist version of Christianity known as Gnosticism." The cupboard is called an oratory and the food found within it should be seen "evidently as part of a religious rite."
926 Bruin 1979. García y García 1998, 2210.
927 *Letter to the Philippians* 3.2. Bruin 1979, 13. He suggests that the excavations at Pompeii only started in 1861. The mistakes concerning the chronology of Nero illustrate the author's lack of knowledge. As the cover says, the book is recommended as a gift for Catholic children's ceremonies like Confirmation.

Berry takes Tertullian's A.D. 197 *Apologeticus*, one of the few ancient records of the destruction of Pompeii, as further proof of the presence of Christians in Pompeii. Tertullian, an intellectual from northern Africa who converted to Christianity, wrote a vehement defense act for the Christians, arguing that they could not be blamed for the disasters that had befallen the Roman world. They were no sinners against the State; rather it was the heathens who were responsible for everything. The orator demonstrated this through, amongst other things, references to other great disasters from the past. In the *Apologeticus* we read:[928]

> But neither Tuscia nor Campania lamented about the Christians when fire from heaven covered the inhabitants of Vulci, and fire from her mountain covered Pompeii. Hitherto no one in Rome worshipped the real God, when Hannibal mowed down in a bushel the Roman ancestors near Cannae in his slaughter. All your gods were venerated by all, when the Gauls occupied the Capitol itself.

Tertullian argues that because – or if – people are non-believers, such disasters will befall them, but at least since the rise of Christianity, there have been fewer catastrophes of this kind.[929] The author simply suggests that Pompeii was the victim of Vesuvius, and that there were no Christians there at all. The fall of the city is perceived as similar to that of Vulci and Rome's Capitol Hill, destroyed before the birth of Christ.[930]

Upon examining when the discoveries of these possible (or imagined) proofs of the presence of Jews and Christians in Pompeii were made, we can conclude that none of them were known when the hitherto discussed authors wrote their respective works. As noted previously, the texts used by our authors do not refer to Christians, which is also true for later publications like Fiorelli's. The writers of the books discussed must have therefore invented the theme themselves. Their written work accommodated the tastes of their times: historical situations in which the righteous man and woman sought a path to heaven.

---

928 *Apologeticus* 40.8: *Sed nec Tuscia iam atque Campania de Christianis querebantur, cum Vulsinios de caelo, Pompeios de suo monte perfudit ignis. Nemo adhuc Romae Deum verum adorabat, cum Hannibal apud Cannas Romanos anulos caede sua modio metiebatur. Omnes dei vostri ab omnibus celebrantur, cum ipsum Capitolium Senones occuparunt.* Cf. Berry 1995. Pesando/Guidobaldi 2006, 14 give references to Tertullian (here above) and *Apocalypse* 8.8–9 (translation St. James Bible): "And the second Angel sounded the trumpet: and as it were a great mountain, burning with fire, was cast into the sea, and the third part of the sea became blood; and the third part of the creatures which were in the sea, and had life, died; and the third part of the ships were destroyed."
929 *Apologeticus* 40.9.13–15.
930 In a similar vein Lampe 2003, 7; Lacerenza 2004, 249–252.

Jews and Christians at Pompeii after Bulwer-Lytton

> Ici le Germain et le Gaulois, nos ancêtres, se sont entr'égorgés pour le plaisir des esclaves de Rome; ici encore, les premiers confesseurs de nos saintes croyances ont été déchirés sous les yeux des prêtres des idoles. Telles sont les réflexions du voyageur, et quelques amères qu'elles soient en elles-mêmes, elles font pourtant diversion à d'autres regrets.[931]

Despite little (or nonexistent) evidence of Christians or Jews living in Pompeii, authors of the second half of the nineteenth century started to use material like the names of the graffiti mentioned above. There are various children's books among these evocations, meant to edify the young souls for a sane and pure life. A good example is Eduard Alberti's *Marcus Charinus, der junge Christ in Pompeji*.[932] During a dinner party, Pompeian elite debate whether the Nazarenes are hypocrites ("Heuchler") or not. They do not arrive at a definite conclusion.[933] In Alberti's novel, the Christians' strong confidence in God provides them a narrow escape from Pompeii in 79, and gives them strength to follow His example.[934] The differences between this narrative and stories for adults are not great, apart from the concentration on young people of around 14–15 years as protagonists. Some adventures demonstrate their faith and courage. Pompeii suffers from vices like slavery and corruption, while opulent eating and bathing prove the town's weakness. Alberti uses Pompeii as a location for a debauched Roman "Sittengeschichte" and does not insert specific Pompeian details.

---

[931] Mazois 1838, 86, after a lengthy description of the amphitheater of Pompeii (pp. 77–86): "Here, the German and the Gaul, our ancestors, slaughtered each other for the pleasure of the slaves of Rome; here also, the first confessors of our holy beliefs were torn apart under the eyes of the priests of idols. Such are the thoughts of the traveler, and, how bitter they are as such, nevertheless they let us forget other regrets."
[932] Alberti 1872. Not in García y García 1998.
[933] Alberti 1872, 26.
[934] Alberti 1872, 111–112: "In dem Schwall des Verderbens, unter den Betäubten, Suchenden, Jammernden waren Wenige so gefaßt und besonnen wie die Glieder jenes Zuges, der, von Fackeln vorangeleuchtet, seinen Weg durch die Stadt in der Richtung nach der Küste und nach Stabiä sich bahnte. Charinus war es mit Marcus und seinen Sklaven, die in der Noth und dem Elend ihren Herren nicht verließen, wie es so viele thaten. Warum schritten sie so sicher, so unerschrocken dahin? Hielt die Voraussicht dieses Schreckentages ihren Muth noch aufrecht, nun er erschien? Stärkte sie der Gedanke, daß sie die Mutter, die Herrin des Hauses, drüben in Surrentum in Sicherheit wußten? Beides mochte der Fall sein, aber mehr hob sie der gläubige Aufblick zu Dem, in dessen Hände sie ihr Leben empfohlen, mehr ermannte sie der freundliche Trost, daß kein Unglück groß genug sei, um sie Schaden nehmen zu lassen an ihrer unsterblichen Seele."

Emily Sarah Holt's *The Slave Girl of Pompeii* from 1886 focuses on girls. The Christian slave girl Sophronia ('Modesty'), child of a Greek father and a Jewish mother from Palestine, convinces their pagan masters to convert. During the eruption panic assails all but the Christians. Sophronia's mistress Camilla, who has the same age as the slave girl, wonders why:[935]

> "Is this the difference between us and Christians?" said Camilla to her own heart. "Then I would I were one of them! It would be worth the cost of life, if one could feel thus when death stands at the door!"

Holt uses antiquarian knowledge about Pompeii to enliven her story, and includes digressions on house interiors, sacrificial ceremonies, a wedding that includes the bride's bath, and the Jewish history as told by Flavius Josephus. In this sense, Holt is more of an antiquarian than Alberti. Christian rectitude is a dominating factor and the impeccability of the characters becomes too cloying an element throughout the story. Nevertheless, thanks to the vivid atmosphere, the good dialogues and the realistic protagonists it is not the worst book on the topic.

The Christian theme was met with acclaim in Italy as well. In the Reverend Antonio Bresciani Borsa SJ's 1850 *L'Ebreo di Verona*, a group of young people roaming Pompeii experience the somber, silent and desolate atmosphere which comes from the loss of the city's inhabitants.[936] The party sees debauchery as the main reason of the inhabitants' destruction, for they had not known God, and for their nonbelief had had their town destroyed.[937] Bresciani feels obligated to warn the young readers of his work about the dangers thereof. An excellent *memento mori* is the street of tombs, built for the forefathers of those who had died under the ashes of Vesuvius.[938] 1846–1849, the years indicated in the subtitle,

---

[935] Holt 1886, 57–58. García y García 1998, no. 6879A. Camilla's name might refer to the Volscan queen in Virgil's *Aeneid* 7.803–817, who gradually got the reputation of a profetess (see G. Arrigoni, *Enciclopedia Virgiliana* 1 (1984) 628–631), but also to the word *camilla*, a female servant in religious matters.

[936] Bresciani 1872, 59–60 (Part II, ch. LII, "La battaglia di Santa Lucia"): "Tutta la città offre alla vista dell'osservatore un aspetto funesto di solitudine, di silenzio e di desolazione a veder tutte le case senza tetti, le lunghe strade vuote d'abitatori, i fondachi derelitti, le officine spoglie d'operai." García y García 1998, nos. 2092–2095.

[937] Bresciani 1872, 60: "Il viaggiatore che la contempla, vede tanta agiatezza, sì gran copia di piaceri, di delizie, di conforti e di voluttà, che già da gran tempo teneano aggravate e sepolte nell'obblio di lor nobile dignità le anime immortali di quelle misere genti che, convolte fra il lezzo d'ogni turpitudine e vizio di natura, aveano fornicato da Dio; il quale nell'eterna giustizia del suo braccio volle profonder la città e sotterrarla eziando ne' corpi, e nelle mura, e nelle piazze, e ne' pubblici e privati monumenti."

[938] Bresciani 1872, 62: "[I] sepolcri de' Pompeiani, edificati alla memoria dei cari estinti da que'

were a difficult period for Pope Pius IX and his Papal State: he fled to Gaeta (and visited Pompeii), where Bresciani, head of the *De propaganda fide* ('Propagation of Faith') College in Rome, visited him, while Mazzini was in power in Rome. Bresciani's work, therefore, also warned against the rise of non- or rather anti-catholic political movements in his country. The book would stay in print until after the foundation of the Italian Kingdom, and the admonitions within continued to gain momentum with the majority Catholic population in Italy.[939]

Religious Sunrise at Pompeii

The German author Woldemar Kaden lived for many years in the south and published fiction and travel memories on his beloved Italy. Jews and Christians are protagonists in his 1892 *In der Morgenröthe*.[940] To my knowledge, it is the only Christian novel to play out between 59 and 62. A central figure is St. Paul, who arrived in Puteoli in 59, the year of the street fights in Pompeii between Pompeians and inhabitants of Nuceria, which are described in the novel by the character Chrysogene. As major players in his story, Kaden also included Seneca (who committed suicide in 65), and Nero, allegedly the worst emperor of the first century. This timeframe freed Kaden from the stereotypical final chord other novelists always played. The main characters bear a mix of Greek and Latin names, not names known from Pompeian inscriptions. Explicit elements inspired by the New Testament are the fight for Agathemeros' clothes, a clear hint at what happened at Golgotha with the clothes of Christ,[941] and, as examples of the Seven Works of Mercy, the cure for the sick and cure for the dead, performed by Christians during epidemics regardless of the fact that the victims are pagans. The Isis people are untrustworthy easterners like Bulwer-Lytton's Arbaces.

Kaden presents a Pompeii in decay: although the Republican times of Cicero had been pure, during the ascent of Christianity, the city's richness and idleness

---

cittadini, a cui, poco appresso, tutta la città dovea tornare in sepolcro, che gli avrebbe vivi vivi assorbiti e sotto le roventi ceneri del Vesuvio affogati e compresi."
939 For the Pope's visit to Pompeii; see *Pio IX* (1987). On Bresciani, see A. Coviello Leuzzi, *Dizionario Biografico degli Italiani* 14 (1972) 179–184.
940 Kaden 1892, 1–228. The author calls it a novella, but it is a substantial novel. García y García 1998, no. 7261. On Kaden see the introduction by C. von Thaler in Kaden 1892. For another of Kaden's novellas see Chapter V, pp. 270–271.
941 Kaden 1892, 196. Cf. Matthew 27.35; Marcus 15.24; Lucas 23.34; John 19.23–24 (most extensive version).

drags it down.⁹⁴² Christians are not yet capable of stopping this negative development. Peppered with laurel bushes and cypresses and with the backdrop of green Vesuvius, vineyards, the forum, temples, theaters and other buildings, Pompeii is "like a pearl in the bosom of the pearl shell on the bottom of the sea," a treasure hidden within its ugly case.⁹⁴³

Gustav Adolf Müller was another German addict of the South who studied archaeology. He was in Italy several times and participated in excavations in Rome. As one of his many works dealing with the world of both the Old and New Testaments, *Das sterbende Pompeji. Ein Roman aus Pompejis letzten Tagen* focuses on Christians surviving the hell unleashed by Vesuvius.⁹⁴⁴

Müller's book dramatizes a clash between two religions. Some Romans, among whom is the rich Vettius, have heard about new religious ideas stemming from Palestine, and come across Jews and newcomers like Ahasver living in Pompeii. There are also other religious people, like Isis priests Tutmose and Cerrinius and their follower Pansa. Isis' temple is among the most venerated shrines in Pompeian society.

In the last chapter, "Wie Pompeji starb," Vettius and his friends embrace Christianity, and are happy to participate in several rituals: addressing the lamb standing on the throne, they ask to be washed with His blood, and say "O Lord, have mercy on me."⁹⁴⁵ Clearly, according to these feverish believers, a pagan Pompeii has no future and must perish. It is not said in clear words whether, according to them, God single-handedly causes the eruption or not, but implicitly, this seems to be the case. At any rate, Fate is merciless for Pompeii, Herculaneum, and Stabiae, and nature takes her own life while creating a deep tomb for thousands of unsus-

---

942 Kaden 1892, 102, 103: "Die Philosophie, die man in Pompeji findet, ist eine Philosophie, die ihren Mann im Allen schadlos hält, ihn wie ein verwöhntes krankes Kind in die Arme nimmt, ihn einzulullen nach den Schmerzen der Welt zu einem großen Traum des Glückes."
943 Kaden 1892, 99: "Dort liegt es, wie eine Perle im Schoße der Muschel, im Grunde des Meerbusens, in welchen die neugierigen Augen Bajaes, Puteolis und Neapolis nicht dringen können. Nah hinter der Stadt steigt die Kuppelbauruine des Vesuvs auf, dicht umrankt, wie altes Gemäuer von Epheu, von Weinreben, über welche hinaus der Fruchtbaum wächst; auch das stille Thal zu seinen Füßen ist von lieblichem Grün erfüllt. Und jetzt schon kann man sie deutlich erkennen, die graziösen Formen der glänzend heitern Tempel, das säulenragende Forum, die schöngerundeten Theater und Marmorhallen, die im reichen Statuenschmuck in breiten Treppen zu der blauen Welle niedersteigenden Landhäuser, umgrünt von Pinien, Lorbeerbüschen und Cypressen."
944 García y García 1998, no. 9671. Müller was in Pompeii in 1888, 1893, 1897, and 1909.
945 Müller 1910, 384: "Schon öffneten unsichtbare Hände diese Pforte dem geliebten Mann [Vettius]. Sie [Myrtis] spürte bereits das Nahen der heiligen Stunde, wo er, Hand in Hand, mit ihr eintreten, und zum Lamme, das auf dem Throne steht, sagen durfte: 'Wasche mich mit deinem Blute. Herr Jesus, erbarme dich meiner.'"

pecting people.⁹⁴⁶ The group of survivors picks the fruits of true belief and gradually begins to understand God's mystery. While the pagan temples crumble, the light of the holy cross becomes a rejuvenating sun. "Dying Pompeii was for them a great parable. [...] *Christus regnat in aeternum!*"⁹⁴⁷

In contrast with most other novelists, Müller starts his book with a long mission statement, worthy of being summarized here. In his preface, he argues that Pompeii unfortunately fell prey to decadence and was devastated for its lustful life. However, the sun cast its rays on Pompeii's pure beauty and real love reigned among the inhabitants who were not afflicted by filth.⁹⁴⁸ During one of his visits to Pompeii, Müller had a vision of the wonder of love in Pompeii and the great death ("das große Sterben") in that town. While sitting on the Foro Triangolare (see Chapter I, p. 28–29), he asked whether these inhabitants really ignored pure beauty, which was shrouded in a mantle of purity.⁹⁴⁹ In contrast with Bulwer-Lytton in his outstanding work, Müller adds, the modern author can rely on new

---

946 Müller 1910, 419: "Erbarmungslos war die Natur, eine Mörderin ihres eigenen Lebens. Ein gleich jähes Verderben, ein jähes Grab hatte sie Tausenden ahnungsloser Menschen, hatte sie Guten und Bösen bereitet! Sie aber, die alles erlebt hatten, sie fuhren in der Finsternis dahin, um rettendes Land zu gewinnen."
947 Müller 1910, 425: "Niemals sahen die Geretteten das versunkene Pompeji wieder. Was Großes sie an die Vergangenheit band, das war und blieb in ihnen lebendig und trug Früchte des Segens. Immer klarer ward ihnen das dunkle Geheimnis göttlicher Führung. Sie sahen, wie die Tempel des Götterwahns veröedeten, und wie das strahlende Licht des Kreuzes zur alles verjüngenden Weltensonne wuchs. Das sterbende Pompeji ward ihnen zum großen Gleichnis. [...] *Christus regnat in aeternum!*"
948 Müller 1910, VIII: "So nennen viele Pompeji, die Stadt der Venus, nur eine Stätte der Greuel. Gleich Sodom und Gomorrah fluchen sie ihm und meinen, der Aschenregen vom Vesuv habe, da er Pompeji verschüttete, nur die niedrigste Sünde, nur wahnsinnstolle Lust erstickt. Wirklich?
Leuchtete über Pompeji nicht auch jene Sonne, in der sieghaft das reine Bild der Schönheit erstrahlt? Kannte es die Liebe nicht, deren Haupt die Sterne berühren, deren Gewandsaum nicht vom Kot der Straße bespritzt wird? Lebten keine Menschen, deren Augen so hell und begeistert sahen, daß sie die echte Schönheit unter tausend unechten Geschwistern erkannten?"
949 Müller 1910, IX: "Damals – jäh, wie eine Vision, erschaute ich das Liebeswunder und das große Sterben von Pompeji. Auf der Erhebung des *Forum triangulare* saß ich und sah gen Himmel und auf den Vesuv und lauschte in die von wachsendem Donner erschütterte Stille. Der letzten Tage von Pompeji gedachte ich, und die Frage kam wieder: Ihr, die euch unter Donner, Blitz und Erdbeben die höllische Asche verschlang, kanntet ihr jene Schönheit nicht, die im schneeigen Gewand der Reinheit über das Menschenland schreitet? Kanntet ihr die Liebe nicht, die wie ein Edelhirsch den Trunk aus der Pfütze verschmäht und nach den irisfarbenen Sturzbächen der Berge lechzt?" The "sitting on the triangular forum" is probably modeled after Edward Gibbon's 1764 "I sat musing amidst the ruins of the Capitol," where he gets the idea for his *Decline and Fall of the Roman Empire*.

archaeological information, no longer needs to use Naples as an explanation of the ancient way of life, and must refrain from a Bulwer-Lytton-like bookishness.

Müller attempts to deliver a realistic image of ancient life. "His" Pompeians neither speak too learnedly nor use modern colloquialisms.[950] Like Busken Huet, Müller is well aware of the problem of the predictable finale of the book, for which reason he hopes to concentrate on the narrative as a whole rather than immediately hinting at the catastrophe. He claims the presence of Jews in the local community, taking as proof the allegedly converted Pompeian Umbricius Scaurus, the painting of Salomon's judgment, and the names of Martha and Maria in graffiti.[951] The same would be true for Christians, but the author remains reluctant in this respect and limits himself to the introduction of the symbolic "Wandering Jew" called Ahasver. So, Müller concludes, Pompeii will become a symbol of the old, dying world that, like Jesus, was sentenced to death in Golgotha.[952]

Müller's is a passionate book, full of love for the ancient world and, above all, the young Christian community. He has a sound grasp of the *pompeiana* and classical *faits divers* and uses these data to intersperse the story with descriptions of ancient customs and religious rituals. Vettius' home is a collage of various Pompeian dwellings: the vestibule has the *cave canem* mosaic from the House of the Tragic Poet, and many halls are lavishly ornamented with images from the House of the Vettii. Pompeii is essential within the story and does not simply function as a backdrop of an antique episode as it does in other works. It is no great wonder that, contrasting directly with Kaden's work, the novel's characters bear names from graffiti, inscriptions and other evidence.

Another Ahasverus appears in a Dutch short story from 1874 about the "Destruction of Pompeii" by a nowadays entirely forgotten author of political and

---

950 Explaining his literary play, Müller (1910, XIII–XIV) argues: "Aus fast jedem Beiwort meiner Sätze soll ihm [Leser] eine Spur jeder Kulturtage entgegenleuchten. Dabei aber will ich mich hüten, dem Leser ein Bild des Lebens und des Verkehrs zu zeichnen, das für Pompeji nicht passen *kann*; ich darf ihm nicht mehr, wie dies noch Bulwer wagte, nur von einem durchaus 'glänzendem' Straßenleben, gar von vielen schönen und geschmackvollen 'Equipagen' reden, die in prunkvollem Korso durch Pompejis Gassen fuhren, denn wir wissen heute, welche Grenze dem Wagenverkehr in Pompeji gesetzt war; auch wird es rätlicher sein, gewisse allzu kühne Szenen mit 'magischem Effekt' – wie sie sich leicht in 'historische' Romane stehlen – zu vermeiden; und keineswegs wollen wir das Mißbehagen daran wecken, daß etwa die Personen einen in Übertreibungen sich ergehenden, bald allzu naiven, bald allzu gelehrten Dialog betätigen; andererseits darf der Erzähler nicht die eigenartige Sprache jener Zeit und ihrer Menschen überhören und diese – allzu 'modern' sprechen lassen."
951 Müller 1910, XV–XVI. On the Salomon's Judgment see note 905.
952 Müller 1910, XVI: "Das sterbende Pompeji wird uns zum Symbol der sterbenden alten Welt, über die seit dem Tage von Golgotha das Todesurteil gesprochen war."

literary texts, Martinus Hendrik de Graaff.[953] De Graaff portrays Ahasverus as a man of around forty years old, who did not help Jesus when He made His way of the cross and was damned by Him to become the Wandering Jew. De Graaff's Pompeii is a "Roman town full of beauty and luxury, instructed by Greek civilization and graced by Roman vanity," where a "laughing and pagan death" reigns,[954] enriched in the story by the usual accoutrements of ancient debauchery: shrines, villas, skeletons of fugitives carrying treasuries, and the cult of Isis.

As we will see in Chapter VI, the notion of trespassing borders of time and the possibility of contacting dead people were very popular in the nineteenth century. Two examples pertain to the theme of Christians in Pompeii. A spiritualistic, anonymously published work from 1888 mixes Christian ideas with mesmerism. Some protagonists pass from the present to the past.[955] During a séance, Caïus "becomes" the seventeenth-century poet Rochester evoked by Vera Kryzhanovskaya in a "réunion extra-terrestre." The story contains a mix of experiences the same people have in both past and present while time traveling, and expressions of Jewish and Christian religious sentiments in ancient Pompeii. Pompeii is only the medium through which people pass from one era to the other and does not get a face of its own.

In the Countess of Bassanville's "La maison maudite," published around 1880,[956] the guide Dom [sic] Francesco takes a gentleman to Pompeii to the Villa of Diomedes, and shows him the skeletons we have seen in Chapter III. They are the victims of God's vengeance, which is a good thing according to the guide.[957] Francesco tells the story of some antique Pompeians, and the visitor gradually begins to realize that, in a former life, Francesco was Glaucus, a slave of Diomedes and member of a Christian community. He and his beloved mother Nysida did not escape and died like the pagans. The names and some episodes coincide strikingly with those in Bulwer-Lytton's book, but there are considerable differences as well. The most important aspect is the *metempsychosis* or reincarnation of Dom Francesco as ancient Glaucus. This high degree of intimation with people from

---

[953] De Graaff 1874. Not in García y García 1998. My Nijmegen colleague Rob van de Schoor who has a thorough knowledge of nineteenth-century Dutch literature pointed it out to me.
[954] De Graaff 1874, 9, 12.
[955] Rochester 1888, 266–267. This part is signed by ROCHESTER. I was unable to find more information about this work and its author.
[956] Bassanville n.y., 248–334. Not in García y García 1998 (he mentions another book about Naples under no. 1340, which I did not see). The fact that Herculaneum has been discovered some 160 years earlier (p. 249) gives a rough indication to date the book around 1880.
[957] Bassanville n.y., 252: "Dieu est juste, me dit dom Francesco; il punit les crimes que les hommes ne savent pas atteindre, et, si vous connaissiriez l'histoire des derniers habitants de cette maison, vous les plaindriez bien moins, je vous assure."

the past is the force behind this merging of two characters. Another guide will experience the same, but without any reference to Christianity, in De Lamothe's *Le fou du Vésuve*.[958]

Twentieth Century Fiction on Christians

The genre of Christian novels waned after World War I. In film, Christianity as a rising power within Roman society remained a constant source of inspiration until recently. When twentieth century fiction of any sort concentrates on Pompeii, Bulwer-Lytton's "Urfassung" is clearly never far away from the author's consciousness.

Emilio Garro's 1942 *Pompeiana juventus* revolves around a Pompeian branch of Roman *juventus*, a youth organization we know little about (fig. 10). Its members provide a warm welcome to the emperor Vespasian when he visits the town in 79. One of them, Aurelio, has contact with converted Jews and becomes a Christian. The protagonists' connections go back to the Jewish Revolt of 69 and its aftermath, whereas the arrival of St. Peter and St. Paul in Italy form departing points for subplots. Rome and Pompeii serve as the ideal stages for these events. Many of Garro's characters bear names from Pompeian sources. The archaeological features are painstakingly precise and must have been checked before publication.[959] The accent on youth, the Augustan *juventus*, made the work a politically correct book for children in their teens. The ancient institution of *juventus* was a prototype of corporate fascist associations for young Italians like Balilla. In 1924, Della Corte had published a study on a – supposed – *juventus* in Pompeii, which relied on extremely meager evidence, but remained influential for many decades.[960] Garro's book betrays a strong preference for the simple, not yet corrupted Christian community. The mix of *juventus* and Christian elements tallies with the fascist policy of being friends with the Catholic Church, enforced by the 1929 Treaty of the Lateran. Jews have no good repute unless they are baptized

---

[958] De Lamothe 1881, here, see Chapter VI, pp. 300–301.
[959] Garro 1942. García y García 1998, no. 5746. Maybe Garro got professional assistance: Maiuri and Della Corte recommend the work on the inner side of the cover. All Latin and Greek terms are explained.
[960] Della Corte 1924: his main argument is the epithet *juvenis* used in election inscriptions. Complexes connected with the supposed *juventus pompeiana* are the Samnite palaestra next to the Temple of Isis and the Caserma dei Gladiatori (collapsed in 2011). Castrén 1975, 33, 1112, 115, denies the existence of a *juventus*. Bracco 1983, 32 sees this book as an upbeat to the development of Balilla, but Della Corte's book does not refer to modern times. On Balilla, see Schleimer 2004.

and become Christians.⁹⁶¹ In this aspect Garro probably supported the anti-Jewish laws in fascist Italy, in vigor from 1938 onwards.⁹⁶²

Jews, Stoics and Christians all stroll around Pompeii in *Amore e morte a Pompei*, a 1970 novel by the Italian medical doctor Oscar Rosoni. As it was for Bulwer-Lytton, Rosoni argues in a preface, Pompeii's fate is the starting point. First, he sketches a matter-of-fact image of the town. Rosoni's dryness harms descriptions of daily life, gambling, and games. Considering his profession, it is no wonder that medical matters dominate the story.⁹⁶³ The representation of Pompeian society in this book had not evolved beyond Bulwer-Lytton's, and the city is extinguished on account of its lust and depravation. The protagonist Marco is a weak person, easily influenced by young friends, falls in love with his patients, does not trust his pal Lucilio,⁹⁶⁴ and converts to Christianity after having lost all of his friends. A Jewess, Abra, is portrayed as a sensual infidel who at the end is cruel, too, who "boasts" of the great qualities of her faith, but does not live according to it. These negative characteristics are highlighted in a way that makes Rosoni's book a rather anti-Semitic novel.

A vivid sketch of Pompeii in the last two years of its existence by Marja Lundgren gives the stage to lower-class people known from graffiti or houses in the ancient town. Two core groups are highlighted in *Pompeji*:⁹⁶⁵ a small comedy troupe, and three prostitutes in the brothel of Asellina and the *caupona* of Sittius, the Elephant.⁹⁶⁶ Maria, one of the prostitutes, belongs to a sect of Christians, together with a gladiator and other lower-class people, who read letters from St. Paul which arrive posthumously and encourage the group to be brave and chaste. The messages announce Pompeii's sudden end due to its debauchery. Lundgren's Pompeii offers a mixture of good and bad, ugly and beautiful, rich and poor. Venus is the patron of the town, and Pompeii is sluttish, which becomes clear in the wording of many dialogues. Many sentences are quotations from graffiti

---

961 Various examples of conversion: Matthaios Ben-Barraba (Garro 1942, 101), Valeria exorcized and baptized by Pope Linus in Rome (Garro 1942, 105–111), etc.
962 Garro 1942, 5 (Jews building the Colosseum), 47–48 (Jews cursing Vespasian and clad in old rags), 58 (Christians are no Jews!), 142–143 (converted Jews, writing the graffiti we have seen before).
963 Rosoni 1970. The novel is published in the series "Collana di medici narratori e saggisti." Rosoni does not explicitly claim to be a physician, but there are several detailed descriptions of deceases and accidents. García y García 1998, no. 11.658.
964 He might be the Lucilius known as the addressee of Seneca's letters.
965 Lundgren, won several Swedish prizes for her 2001 novel. Translations into French and Dutch (both 2002), of which I read the latter.
966 VII 1, 44–45, excavated in 1862. *PPM* VI (1996) 462–464. The name of Sittius is known from a lost text (*CIL* IV 806). Thanks to the image of an elephant, the *caupona* was also known under that name and features in various works (e.g. Garro 1942; see here also Chapter VIII, p. 376).

or composed of sexual terms and allusions. Maria writes *Sodoma et Gomorrha* on a wall as a reflection upon St. Paul's warnings. The storyteller is omniscient: she makes comparisons with things in Pompeii's aftermath, "time traveling," as it were, by referring to unexcavated parts of Pompeii or by mentioning skeletons of victims of the eruption.[967] Thanks to its loose composition, the book reads like reportage rather than a tightly composed novel.

Most recently, the pharmacist S. Menduni de' Rossi published a bizarre novel about the find of the remains of a female follower of Isis, *Il prodigio del sistro*.[968] The victim is recognized thanks to the *sistrum*, the ritual music instrument found next to her. The victim's spirit begs the excavator to take her to the excavator's home. The invisible girl recounts her story: shortly before Vesuvius' eruption, she had wanted to convert to Christianity, a wish she still hopes to fulfill in the Cathedral of St. Mary in modern Pompeii. The motif of the religious errand of the lost Pompeian priestess dominates the story. After a series of implausible adventures, the book ends with an epiphany of this old Pompeian inhabitant, who converts in the Cathedral and ascends to Heaven, all with the consent of the pious excavator. Although the book has an archaeological dig in Pompeii as its point of departure, the old town does not play a role in the narration. The reader encounters some of the excavator's colleagues and learns about the strict rules concerning the procedures in an archaeological excavation, passages which unnecessarily interrupt the story and do nothing to improve its narrative quality.

The only novel about Herculaneum as a town with a Christian population is Richard Llewellyn's 1955 *The Flame of Hercules*.[969] Garvan from Gaul gets involved in a religious struggle between followers of Diana ("Dianists") and Christians ("Anointed"), who are led by a wealthy lady-merchant, Lydia of Samaria. Some of them have met St. Paul and St. Peter in Italy. Diana's worshippers kneel in front of her effigy and want Garvan to do the same.[970] Making sacrifices to the gods is good for yourself[971] and no love for other gods is needed. This selfish principle causes the death of all wicked Romans.

---

967 Two comparisons involve Swedish places. The rich part of Pompeii is like the quarter of Österholm in Stockholm; without Venus, Pompeii would be like the small town of Skövde.
968 Menduni de' Rossi 2011. García y García 2012, no A 3023a.
969 Llewellyn 1955. García y García 1998, no 8086 has a different title. Carmen Covito's 2013 novella *Il processo di Giusta* has one Christian character, but this is a detail within the story of the girl Giusta, playing out in higher circles in Herculaneum.
970 Llewellyn 1955, 157. This is a Christian anachronism.
971 Llewellyn 1955, 183. In fact, a principle of Roman attitudes towards the gods with whom they make virtual contracts: *do ut des*.

Llewellyn's Herculaneum is merely a name, not a town that rises from its ashes in a virtual reconstruction. Its topography is pure fantasy, displaying some grand houses, temples, and public buildings, like a law court and a prison. This is odd, since the author would have been able to profit from Maiuri discoveries made since 1927. The protagonists drive chariots or are carried in palanquins. Thanks to Garvan, we get glimpses into the rough world of slaves, poor workers and pubs. The disaster of Vesuvius is described in few words. Llewellyn evidently sought to contrast the apocalypse of a decadent society with the rescue of the noble Christians. For Llewellyn, the non-Roman background of the protagonist is a strong positive quality, – as is his Christian belief – and distinguishes him positively from the decadent Romans, as he is not yet contaminated by Roman debauchery.

The moral message of a deserved punishment, finally, makes the topic not less than applicable in literary sermons. In *Le chanoine Brousillard à Herculanum* by Jacques Debout the preaching priest Brousillard addresses an "antivolcanic brotherhood" the Confréry Antivolcanique. His sermons have the objective to pray against the eruptions of Vesuvius as well as the more frequent and possibly less feared lusts of Debout's times.[972] Although the text does not convey any feeling for Herculaneum, it is interesting as an example of the idea of Vesuvius as avenger of sin.

Christiani ad bestias

"Christians to the beast" or "to the lions" is a cry often heard in Christian novels, plays, and operas (see Chapter VIII). The punishment of being sent *ad bestias* officially existed and is referred to in martyrs' acts.[973] From the Counter Reformation onwards, the Colosseum was seen as the classical locus of Christian martyrdom and became the home of martyr chapels. This does not mean, however, that there is any proof of Christians being slaughtered there; the sources contradict each

---

972 Debout 1930, 7–8: "L'objet de cette œuvre pieuse est non seulement, comme son titre le laisse prévoir de combattre par des prières spéciales les éruptions du Vésuve, mais encore celles de la concupiscence, plus fréquente et peut-être moins redoutées." Debout is the nom de plume of the priest René Roblot, who was active in the emancipation of the Catholic lower classes and published both theological and literary works. His "chanoine Brousillard" is also the master of other collections of sermons by the same author.
973 See Coleman 1990. The amphitheater is also popular in pagan novels; see p. 174, note 639.

other.⁹⁷⁴ Another source of inspiration was the execution of Christians in Rome by Nero in 64 after the great fire that devastated large parts of the town, known from Tacitus' *Annals* 15.44. The Colosseum construct inspired Chateaubriand and other travelers to meditate upon destiny. Although the Colosseum was not yet completed in 79, Garro enthusiastically used it as the symbol of Christian martyrs.

The fact that Pompeii possessed an amphitheater similar to the Colosseum stimulated our Christian authors to include the martyrs' punishment as a thrilling happening before the great finale of Vesuvius' eruption. The descriptions of these scenes may rely on martyr acts, like the *Passion of Perpetua and Felicitas*, in which the gruesome deaths of Christians in Carthage in 203 are described at length.⁹⁷⁵ The rumor that a lion's skeleton had been found next to the entrance of the amphitheater at Pompeii completed the story.⁹⁷⁶

In one of the oldest works herein discussed, *The Vestal*, an old Christian who calls for his daughter Marcia is trampled by an elephant. A ferocious lion does not attack Vetullius, but addresses him kindly, apparently because they "know" each other. This meek animal is based on the story of "Androclus and the lion" described by Aulus Gellius in the second century A.D., and often read by children in their first Latin lessons.⁹⁷⁷ Fairfield, the author of *The Last Night of Pompeii*, adapted the motif, while he was clearly inspired by *The Vestal*:⁹⁷⁸

> But while I am happy to acknowledge both the pleasure and benefit I have derived from that elegant story, I must be allowed to say that the causes of the lion's submission are unlikely. He cowers at the feet of the aged Christian in that work, because he sees an old master; here [in Fairfield], he is made to submit on the well-known principle familiar to naturalists, that during any great convulsion of nature, the most savage animals forget their common animosities, and that the lion will not attack a man who steadily fixes his eyes upon him.

---

974 The construction of the Colosseum was financed by the booty from the sack of Jerusalem, as we know from a palimpsest inscription *CIL* VI 40454a: Alföldi 1995. M.C. Cartocci, Amphitheatrum, *Lexicon Topographicum Urbis Romae* I, Rome 1993, 35, gives inconsistent late-antique sources referring to persecutions under Decius and Diocletian. Clement of Rome (see p. 215, note 818) mentions hundred women slaughtered in the guise of the Danaids or Dirce. See for the dearth of indications for Christian martyrs and the Christianization of the Colosseum U. Sinn in Stein-Hölkeskamp/Hölkeskamp 2006, 435–437; Wegerhoff 2012, 67–107. See for the enactments of mythical themes in the amphitheater Coleman 1990, esp. 65–66.
975 *Passio Perpetuae et Felicitatis* 18–21. Coleman 1990, 53, 55 gives other examples of people thrown *ad bestias*.
976 Starke 1802, II, 97–105; Bonucci 1827, 196. *Vestal* 1830, 215 refers to Starke.
977 Gellius, *Noctes Atticae* 5.14. A meek lion also in Reece 1872 (see Chapter VIII, pp. 375–376).
978 Fairfield 1832, 309. Motif in *Vestal* 1830, 68.

Indeed, Fairfield's fierce lion does not pounce on the Christians, here in the person of the – almost standard – old wise man:[979]

> Next, bent and trembling, blind and dumb with fear,
> A Christian came (from noisome catacombs
> Dragged forth to prove his feebleness of faith,)

Bulwer-Lytton's lion is also inert. Müllers's *Das sterbende Pompeji* tells a story of a lioness that refuses to attack some Jews, who are despised by gladiators. The moment this happens, Vesuvius erupts, and as the Pompeians see the Vesuvian night fall over them, they cry: "Great dying has arrived! Our gods are dead!"[980] In Bassanville's novella, neither the lion nor the tiger attacks Glaucus, but the author adds a new element: Glaucus' mother Nysida weeps when her son appears in the arena, totally naked apart from a belt and a dagger. The beauty of the young man deeply impresses the spectators. He simultaneously feels like a hero and a god, and feels disdain for the audience members who gaze at his splendid body.[981] The physical description of the young gladiator has something of the erotic evocation of a movie star and might have been inspired by popular paintings like Jean-Léon Gerôme's *Pollice Verso* of 1872 (now Phoenix Art Museum, Phoenix Arizona). Strikingly, the beauty of the denuded victims is a topic we encounter in martyr acts as well.[982]

---

[979] Fairfield 1832, 153.
[980] Müller 1910, 409: " Da – ein dumpfes Getöse, gewaltig wie das Zusammenbrechen großer Felsmassen und aus der Tiefe der Erde kommend, schlägt an das Ohr der Pompejaner. 'Die ewige Nacht kommt!' 'Das große Sterben ist da!' 'Unsere Götter sind tot!'
Arme fuchteln hoch. Ein wildes Schreien bricht wieder und wieder los."
[981] Bassanville n.y., 328: "Quand le jeune Grec vit tous les yeux des spectateurs fixés sur lui, une vive rougeur couvrit ses traits, un sourire de mépris glissa sur ses lèvres et, oubliant un instant les préceptes d'humilité de la religion à laquelle il sacrifiait volontairement sa vie, il se redressa de toute la hauteur de sa taille bien prise. Alors l'élasticité de ses membres, la grâce de sa personne et la sérénité de son front firent courir un frisson, sinon de remords, du moins d'émotion, chez tous les spectateurs de la lutte terrible qu'il allait avoir à soutenir contre son féroce adversaire. Il semblait à la fois un héros et un dieu."
[982] *Passio Perpetuae et Felicitatis* 20.2: the girl's body, exposed to the male gaze. See Marco Formigano in *Passio* 2008, 55–57. For visualizations and evocations of Christian martyrs, see Vance 1989, I, 48–54, who gives examples of artistic evocations like Gérôme's *The Christian Martyrs' Last Prayer* painted on demand of William T. Walters between 1863 and 1883, and – indeed – now in the Walters Art Museum in Baltimore. On Christians in the amphitheater as presented in Christian novels, see also Goldhill 2011, 228–229, and H. Silbermorgen, Leidenslust und Leidenschaft. Katakombenromantik und Katakombenpropaganda, in *Imperium der Götter*, exhibition catalogue Karlsruhe 2013, Stuttgart 2013, 439–450.

Conclusion

Literary works which highlight Christians and Jews in Pompeii and Herculaneum use these towns as stages on which to depict these early communities in an overtly hostile Roman society. Jews had suffered much during the Jewish Revolt in 69–70, and some of them had experienced the edifying effects of the new faith. Pompeii, I think, was an ideal backdrop for these stories, because its destruction could function as a parallel for the devastation of Jerusalem, although this is never explicitly written in these stories. In Christian fiction, Pompeii's end became the result of a perceived decline in Roman ethics and the inclination of the pagan Romans towards immorality. The presence of an Egyptian shrine in the city – a fairy tale nicety also used in so many other Pompeii evocations – "proved" the lack of consistency in Roman religion at the same time as it argued for the "trueness" of the Christian religion. How, these books smugly ask, could the Romans tolerate the presence of an outlandish Oriental faith within the walls of their city? These arguments implicitly circle around a very closed view of society, with only one true ideological system: Christianity. Of course, not tackled in these novels are the variations of Christianity, which would likely have diminished the strength of any given author's message.[983]

Christian authors adopt quotations from graffiti as well as manuals and guides at hand. The representations of Pompeii include descriptions of varying lengths of the monuments excavated by the time a given work was published, sometimes with a tinge of admiration, always with criticism of Pompeii's extreme wealth. The authors who visited the site must have benefited from their reconnaissance. The earliest authors were not able to benefit from the graffiti and other materials, which were found among Pompeii's ruins in later decades and were sometimes considered marks of the presence of Jews and Christians.

As a rule, the Jews and Christians in fiction operate in small groups, often guided by a wise person who has lived long enough to know the public life of Jesus, thanks to personal encounters or from firsthand testimony. He – never she – has often lost a child or parent, and meets this lost relative in Rome or Pompeii. The congregations gather outside of town in crypts of pagan tombs, like those outside the Herculanean Gate, or in catacombs, fearing discovery by the Romans. They work in the households of prominent Pompeian citizens and encounter the rich and their immoral way of life. Intimate contact between family members and slaves creates opportunities for exchanges about the Christian belief, so that pagans gradually are convinced of the "truth." Members of the two non-pagan

---

[983] I owe this observation to Aaron Ostrow.

religions rarely deal with each other together, and for the most part, Jews convert to Christianity. Believers usually bear Hebrew or Greek names, which underline their low social status as slaves or freedmen.

Hidden reunions, persecutions, death sentences in the amphitheater and salvation of Christians, the main themes of non-Pagan Pompeii fiction, would also be introduced in fiction that plays out in later eras of the Roman Empire. The formulas used by the Christians in awkward situations are similar to prayers and apologetic phrases of early-Christian acts of martyrdom. Strikingly, descriptions of corporal punishment or torture are not in the repertoire of the authors at hand. The eruption of Vesuvius is the "final solution," bringing liberation for the Christians and death to the pagans. In this framework, Pompeii represents a rotten society, polluted by bad customs and weak character. Its pagan inhabitants are the prey of luxury, lust, corruption, and selfishness, and do not understand the power of the pure belief of the Christian God. Therefore, they will be punished like the citizens of Sodom and Gomorrah. Authors greedily insert descriptions of luxurious celebrations similar to those in the pagan novels described in Chapter III. The way in which Pompeii is presented in other Christian novels does not change considerably with respect to Bulwer-Lytton's portrait of the city. What is more, Bulwer-Lytton's novel exerted a stronger influence on many fiction authors than the excavations themselves.

Therefore and without hesitation, we may credit Bulwer-Lytton for proffering a very prolific theme for historical fiction. He paved the way for novels featuring Jews and Christians in Pompeii. One might even ask whether the immense popularity of *Last Days* dictated the agenda of later generations of Pompeii excavations and research.[984] Jews already lived in Italy long before the destruction of Pompeii. As far as I know, no fiction author ever dedicated an entire work to them as inhabitants of Pompeii.[985] Pompeii was a convenient vehicle of addressing the topic of Jewish and Christian monotheism, given the events of the 50s through the 70s A.D. Featured in these stories are appealing historical figures like St. Paul, Nero, Vespasian, and Titus, all of whom lived during these decades. Often at the fore in various tales of Christian fiction are historical figures like Caligula, Seneca (and his fictitious correspondence with St. Paul), and Domitian. Pompeii offered an appealing home for the people who acted in these books, and visitors to the excavations could almost experience that lost world while roaming the old

---

984 I owe this suggestion to Stephan T.A.M. Mols.
985 Apart from a recent Hebrew novel I cannot read by the archaeologist Natalie Messika: *Adamah Shehora* [Black Earth], Rosh Pina 2008. See http://www.nataliemessika.co.il/black%20earth.htm (consulted on April 16, 2012). For Jews in nineteenth-century fiction on Roman antiquity, see Goldhill 2011, 234–242, who concludes that Jews were mostly sketched in a negative light.

streets and peeping into the houses. Although there were no (or very few) proofs of the presence of Jews and Christians within Pompeii's walls, the people known from skeletal remains, graffiti and artistic products all-too-easily functioned as the protagonists of these books. From the old man with the cross fleeing from the scene in Briullovs' painting, to the spirit of the excavated Isis priestess, the Christians in Pompeii fiction get a safe home, whether it's outside Pompeii after a narrow escape, or whether it's alongside the victims of the eruption, in Heaven. Thus, these almost certainly purely fictional Christians become emblems of pure and righteous life, ancient models for the wide readership of these novels in the Christian western world of the nineteenth and twentieth century.

V Modern and Contemporary Visits to Pompeii in Fiction: A Perilous Affair

> "Nature, like the catastrophe at Pompeii, or the metamorphosis of a nymph, freezes us into an accustomed cast of countenance. In the same way, the intonation of our voices expresses our philosophy of life, what one says to oneself at each moment about things."[986]

The excavations of Pompeii not only stimulated authors to write about Pompeii in ancient times, as we have seen in the previous chapters, but also about contemporary adventures or even time travel (see Chapter VI). Franc Schuerewegen once put forth the – fundamental – question: What happened – and happens – after the eruption?[987] The volcanic material destroyed Pompeii's status as a living Roman town, but also formed – and forms – the optimal way of preserving its remains. Seeing these vestiges evokes a range of reactions and often changes the visitor's experience of Pompeii to an utterly memorably once in a lifetime encounter.

Imaginary and real encounters with the archaeological site of Pompeii have been the topic of literary works and parts of memoirs and travel books since the first decades after Pompeii's discovery up until the present. Authors describe their own adventures or those of historical figures or imagined characters. In various cases these people seem to experience the presence of the lost inhabitants as living creatures. Such encounters apparently exert a great influence on the psyche of the protagonists of such texts. Thanks to these characters' encounters with the past – in the form of ruins and (suggestions of) inhabitants – these books suggest a radical change in the mindset of authors and/or fictional characters about their view of the past in general and Pompeii in particular.[988]

---

[986] Proust, 1954, I, 909; 1988, II, 262: "La nature, comme la catastrophe de Pompéi, comme une métamorphose de nymphe, nous a immobilisés dans le mouvement accoutumé. De même, nos intonations contiennent notre philosophie de la vie, ce que la personne se dit à tout moment sur les choses." In *A l'ombre des jeunes filles en fleurs* II. *Noms de pays: le pays*; translation J. Grieve, *In Search of Lost Time* 2, London 2002, 486. M.J. Versluys drew my attention to this text. Not in García y García 1998. On Proust see below p. 284–286.
[987] Schuerewegen 1991, 326.
[988] See Fitzon 2002b.

How Ruins Can Change Your Mind

Especially among early nineteenth-century writers, Pompeii was a melancholic symbol of the unavoidable end of life. Once so beautiful and rich, and situated in the loveliest country in the world, Pompeii was wiped away in a single day. For that reason, old authors warned all travelers to the south to beware of Pompeii's vanity.

In 1797, when French troops arrived in Naples, the King of Naples fled to Palermo with his friend, the British ambassador William Hamilton. This dramatic period inspired several French and Italian authors to write good novels. Pompeii gets a small role in Henri de Latouche's *Fragoletta. Naples et Paris en 1799*. Marius d'Hauteville encounters Camille, an extraordinary boyish girl, called Fragoletta ("little strawberry"), and Eleonora Pimentel Fonseca, the well-known revolutionary noblewoman of the Parthenopean Republic.[989] Marius considers Fragoletta's gender ambiguity a defect. For that reason, she is not a complete person in his view, but it nevertheless fascinates him and brings him closer to her. He feels the same fascination for the Pompeian antiquities, which are also defective: Fragoletta and ancient ruins satisfy his imagination more than complete or perfect people or works of art.[990] The archaeological finds can be admired for their purity, and for not having been damaged by modern restorations, which prevent us from having an unbiased opinion.[991]

Germaine de Staël's *Corinne* is a novel about the love between Corinne, an Italian author of British origin, and her travel companion Oswald Nelvil, a Scottish gentleman. At the same time it is what Elisabeth Chevallier calls an "itinéraire romancé"[992] De Staël got the idea for this novel after her father's death in 1804,

---

[989] De Latouche 1829. *Il resto di niente* by Enzo Striano from 1986 is a fascinating novel about Pimentel Fonseca.

[990] Cf. Smith 1996 on androgyny. See also Costa 1996, 89–94. Algernon Charles Swinburne dedicated a poem to this androgynous Fragoletta, opening pointedly: "O love! What shall be said of thee / The sun of grief begot by joy? / Being sightless, wilt thou see? / Being sexless, wilt thou be / Maiden or Boy?" (Swinburne 1905, I, *Poems and Ballads*, 83–85).

[991] De Latouche 1829, 82 (chapter IV): "Si, par quelques accidens du désastre, une ou deux de ces statues nous ont été rendues un peu mutilées, nous voyons du moins que leurs fragmens sont restés fidèles; tandis que tout ce qui a passé par la main des hommes, de génération en génération et sans interruption d'héritage, a été dénaturé. Ainsi, tout est confondu dans nos prétendues restaurations."

[992] Chevallier 1980, XL. In the following I quote from De Staël 1841, but will indicate the books and chapters. Cf. Martinet 1996, 120–121, 157–158; Costa 1996, 76–83; Barbara Witucki in Hales/Paul 2011, 62–74. Especially in the last decade many studies have been dedicated to her and Italy: Casillo 2006; Alfonsetti/Bellucci 2010; Szmurlo 2011. On Staël studies, see M. Gutwirth and K. Szmurlo in Szmurlo 2011, IX–XIX and 1–20. García y García 1998, nos. 13.183–13.193; he dates the

when she visited Naples in 1805 to get inspiration.⁹⁹³ Many of the experiences of Corinne and Oswald find their origins in De Staël's *carnets de voyage*. The love story plays out during a grand tour through Italy, in the first half of which Corinne is the authority who introduces the neophyte Oswald into Italian society. The section about Naples, Pompeii, and Vesuvius forms the middle of the book, and the encounter with Campania is presented very dramatically. Corinne and Oswald are impressed by the overwhelming forces of Campania's nature and history. Just as they fear becoming objects of destruction (in their case, the destruction of the bond of their intimacy), Vesuvius and Pompeii as a "couple" symbolize the destroyer (of fortune) and the object of destruction. In the first half of the novel, the love between the two young people is growing, while in the second half, disaster strikes rapidly and without warning, and their relationship is disrupted by the emotional volcano.

In their admiration and bewilderment, Corinne and Oswald differ little from many travelers before and after them. For Corinne, Pompeii is "la ruine la plus curieuse de l'antiquité," where one gets the best picture of the Roman past. She compares Rome's impressive ruins of public buildings, its politics and grandees, to Pompeii's narrow streets and glimpses into private lives.⁹⁹⁴ Corinne wants to "pénétrer dans le passé" and experience the eternity of life, as she has seen in Pompeii, with its dead victims who nevertheless continue to live.⁹⁹⁵ She reaches the conclusion that these ruins teach more than any classical text can, and for our lovers, ancient Pompeii becomes a model of harmony and luck. The debris, however, is a general warning about death and a reminder of the possibility of dying in the same way as Pompeii's ancient inhabitants died. After all, Pompeii is a "Ville des morts."

De Staël herself experienced Vesuvius as grand and threatening, "as a starting empire of hell, an appearance of the night, a silent march of sparkling lava, an abyss of fire, a noise like that of wind and water."⁹⁹⁶ She visited Vesuvius on Feb-

---

episode to 1794–1795 (p. 1140). De Staël 1930 shows that she did not record Pompeii visits in her letters to Vincenzo Monti, her only correspondent in that period.
993 S. Balayé in De Staël 1971, 94. She made this trip from February 21 to March 9. She paid a second visit to Italy in 1816, although that time, to the North (De Staël 1971, 407–432).
994 De Staël 1841, II, 27 (book XI, chapter 4): "A Rome, l'on ne trouve guère que les débris des monumens publics, et ces monumens ne retracent que l'histoire politique des siècles éroulés, mais à Pompéia c'est la vie privée des anciens qui s'offre à vous telle qu'elle étoit." Also quoted in Aziza 1992, 33–38; Jacobelli 2008, 67–68.
995 De Staël 1841, II, 32 (book XI, chapter 4). Ibidem, p. 29: "Qu'il y a long-temps que l'homme existe! qu'il ya a long-temps qu'il vit, qu'il souffre et qu'il périt!"
996 De Staël 1971, 120: "Empire de l'enfer qui commence, apparition de la nuit, marche silencieuse de la lave scintillante, un gouffre de feu, un bruit semblable à celui du vent et de l'eau." She also mentions the hermit on Vesuvius known from many other accounts (p. 127).

ruary 26, and Pompeii on February 27, 1805, but reversed the order in her novel to increase the dramatic effect.[997] Corinne and Oswald feel the power of nature on Vesuvius, and Corinne expresses her need to escape from this "desert," insisting on returning to Naples. Not an amenable part of nature, the volcano is a mysterious power that shuts the door on the possibility for a more peaceful existence.[998] One of the consequences of Vesuvius' destructive powers is infertility instead of fertility, which affects Corinne and Oswald's liaison.[999]

Corinne was very popular in the nineteenth century, especially among women.[1000] Pompeii archaeologist Antonio Sogliano noticed in it a "soave melancolia" towards the dead.[1001] According to the literary historian Wolfgang Leppmann, the novel is a dull example of the classic romantic narrative, in which the fashion of the times accounts for the choice of Pompeii as the location of the crisis in Oswald and Corinne's relationship. Pompeii is a "landscape of the soul" in which Corinne and Oswald "dig" into their own personalities, as excavators do in the ruins.[1002] Even if Leppmann is right about his observation on romantic literary fashion, De Staël's image has its own value: Pompeii's decay fits in with the crisis in the author's own life.[1003]

Alphonse de Lamartine was another French author who traveled extensively to the South in 1811–1812, and fell in love with Pompeii.[1004] His charming 1851 novel *Graziella* was inspired by his love for Antonella, a girl in Resina. Italy is the country where real love is possible, although its climate precludes a stable life.[1005] Pompeii represents life and decay, love and terror, extremities like those in *Corinne*: it was beautiful and rich, but was mercilessly destroyed by nature.

---

997 De Staël 1841, II, 83–87 (book XIII, chapter 1).
998 See Schuerewegen 1991, 319–322.
999 De Staël 1841, 87 (book XIII, chapter 1). In their haste, they forget to visit Herculaneum. This town is less macabre, for one encounters no victims, and it may be for that reason that it plays no part in *Corinne*. See De Staël 1971, 137: "Herculanum. Ce théâtre sous terre. Moins d'effet que Pompéia. C'est trop près de la mort minée. La mort fait surtout effet avec l'apparence de la vie, la danse des morts fait plus d'effet que les tombeaux ; quand vous exigez de terreur, elle vient moins."
1000 Chapman/Stabler 2003, 1–4. Cf. Jameson 1826, 115–116. The name of Corinne is that of the Greek poetess Corinna, friend of Pindar. Our protagonist was also a literary author of fame.
1001 Sogliano 1888, 20–21.
1002 Leppmann 1966, 121–142, esp. 126 ("Landschaft der Seele"), 131 and 134. See Jacobelli 2008, 59–72 on the Pompeii section in comparison with (other) travelogues.
1003 See good discussions in Jaton 1988, 25–35 and Rothemann 1996, 74, 76–77.
1004 He would return in 1820, 1825 and 1844.
1005 De Lamartine 1867. Cf. Jaton 1988, 32–33. For the French historians Ernest Renan and Hippolyte Taine, the country had a negative connotation due to the lack of working and moral discipline among the inhabitants, and it was believed that the climate influenced the human soul and body and in the case of Campania, created lust and laziness rather than industry and progress.

A German book that conveys the author's personal experiences and touches on the theme of Pompeii is the hyper-romantic *Titan* by the Bavarian romantic writer Jean Paul, who never visited Italy and assembled the necessary topographical details from travel books.[1006] In *Titan* two friends, Albano and Dian, are wandering through Italy. On top of Vesuvius, Dian writes to his lover Linda, in Capri, about the gruesome and idyllic characteristics of this volcanic area. His letter mixes notions of Greek horror and friendly people in touch with nature. People dance amidst ancient columns, and friars and fishermen stroll around. Vivid Portici contrasts with Herculaneum, hidden under Portici's houses.[1007] Albano and Dian see Herculaneum as a cemetery next to Vesuvius; Vesuvius is the cemetery's marker as the Pyramid of Cestius in Rome is the marker at the edge of the non-Catholic cemetery, which forms a striking comparison. Studying the town to learn about ancient life, they reflect that the victims would be altogether dead even without the eruption of 79. They wonder if the victims would have liked modern Germany. The sight of a terracotta head, marker of a tomb, makes them shudder, because in it they see their own future.[1008]

1006 Written between 1792 and 1802 and published in parts between 1800 and 1803. Here cited after Jean Paul 1961. Vgl. Jean Paul 1933, 9, 280–281. Not in García y García 1998. In 1816, August von Platen praised Jean Paul's descriptions of Italian nature without having visited the South (Platen 1896, I, 408). On the travel books cf. Jean Paul 1961, 1060; Leppmann 1966, 163, and works cited in the following.
1007 He writes his letter in the hut of the hermit on the slope of Vesuvius. Jean Paul 1961, 645 ("114. Zykel" in the "29. Jobelperiode"): "Immer dieselbe große, durch dieß erhabene Land ziehende epische griechische Verschmelzung des Ungeheuern mit dem Heitern, der Natur mit den Menschen, der Ewigkeit mit der Minute. – Landhäuser und eine lachende Ebene gegenüber der ewigen Todesfackel – zwischen alten heiligen Tempelsäulen geht ein lustiger Tanz, der gemeine Mönch und der Fischer – die Gluth-Blöcke des Bergs thürmen sich als Schutzwehr um Weingärten, und unter dem lebendigen Portici wohnt das hohle todte Herkulanum – im Meer sind Lavaklippen gewachsen, und in die Blumen schwarze Sturmbalcken geworfen." Jean Paul 1961, 648: "Hat mich der erhabene Säulenstuhl des Donnergottes neben mir so sehr erschüttert, oder denk' ich zu lebhaft an das hole todte Herkulanum unter mir, wo Eine Stadt Ein Sarg ist: weinend und beklommen seh' ich über das Meer an die stille Insel, worauf du [i.e. Linda] wohnst."
1008 Jean Paul 1961, 652–653: "Er besuchte nun die unterirdische Stadt in ihrem Gottesacker, gleichsam neben der Cestius-Pyramide des Vulkans. Dian ging mit ihm das Herkulanum als ein antiquarisches Lexikon durch, um ihm die ganze Haushaltung der Alten bis zum Mahlen hinauf aufzublättern; aber Albano war bewegter als sein Freund von dieser mitten in der Gegenwart wohnenden Vergangenheit, von den stillen Häusern und nächtlichen Gassen und von den häufigen Spuren der fliehenden Verzweiflung. 'Wären denn nicht diese Leute alle jetzt doch todt ohne den Vesuv?' fragt' ihn Dian heiter im heitern Lande. 'Ich frag' Euch lieber (fuhr er fort), ob ein Baumeister, wenn er aus dieser Kunstkammer oder Kunststadt gekommen, in Eurem Deutschland noch viel Lust haben kann, nach der größten Ruin der Erde die erbärmlichen winzigen für Eure Fürstengärten anzugeben.' – Sie sahen in einem dunkeln Vorhaus eben eine irdene Maske an, die

For Jean Paul, De Staël, and Lamartine, Vesuvius is the unaccessible power of nature in the background of blissful Campania, symbolizing how people's destiny can change all of a sudden. The excavations of Pompeii and Herculaneum are a strong demonstration of this. The victims of the eruption still seem to warn visitors, and change the visitors' very vision on the world.

Grasping the Past?

Some people are said to live in the past: they have internalized the history of persons they are fascinated by or are spellbound by old places. I start with Gérard de Nerval, who visited Pompeii in 1834 and 1843, and used memories of these visits in two short stories.[1009] In *Octavie* a French tourist guides his English lover through Pompeii.[1010] When they are in the Temple of Isis, the girl seems to experience the ancient cult as an active member or as if she were an old witch.[1011] The two tourists do not develop a serious relationship and lose contact. Ten years later, when they meet again at the same spot, she is the wife of a crippled gentleman. Apparently, they were not obliged to take a local guide, and could walk around freely. A second story by Nerval, *Isis*, shares the Isis theme with *Octavie*. *Isis* describes a masked ball held in the excavations of Pompeii.[1012] The cult,

---

man in Gräber stellte, mit Lampen wie Augen dahinter. Da blickte ihn Albano starr an und sagte: 'Sind wir nicht blitzende Larven aus Erde am Grab?' – 'Pfui, die häßliche Idee!' sagte Dian." As to "Mahlen," Jean Paul 1933, 287–288 has "malen." Both commentaries give each alternative. The old one means "to paint," the new "to mill" (in the context of "Haushaltung"). In the old German orthography, the words are homonyms and both solutions are acceptable (Jean Paul 1961, 1104).
1009 For his visits, see letters to his father published in Nerval 1989, 1408. As to Nerval and his Naples novellas, see Jaton 1988, 147–163.
1010 Nerval 1993, 605–611. Alo published in Aziza 1992, 483–492. The sketch was edited together with "Isis" in *Les filles du feu*, Paris 1854, dedicated to Alexandre Dumas. García y García 1998, no. 9808–9811. Jaton 1988, 151 suggests that the name of Octavie derives from the village Ottaviano, but I wonder whether such an insignificant place would really have inspired the author. "Octavie" is the French version of the Latin name Octavia, among others both a full and a half sister of Augustus.
1011 Nerval 1993, 611: "Elle voulait jouer elle-même le personnage de la Déesse, et je me vis chargé du rôle d'Osiris dont j'expliquai les divins mystères."
1012 Nerval 1993, 612–623. According to the Pléiade commentary (Nerval 1993, 1248) and Aubaude (1997, 29) Nerval was inspired by Böttiger (Böttiger 1838, 210–230, pl. IV; see here Chapter III, pp. 190–191) and *The Golden Ass* by Apuleius. According to Böttiger, Judaism can be a good religion for people looking for comfort and afterlife, whereas he personally prefers the cult of Isis with the same elements and imagery (p. 212): "Die Sinnlichkeit forderte bestimmtere, tastbarere Formen der Anschauung und Anbetung." On Nerval and Egypt Aubaude 1997 and Versluys 2002, 389–390, with bibliography. See also Olmos Romera 1993b.

which worshipped Isis for her goodness,[1013] is depicted as including ablutions, abstinence from food, and punishment of the flesh, and is judged to be a predecessor of Christianity, a likely reason for Nerval's fascination for Egypt. Like his friend Gautier, Nerval loved pagan cults much more than modern Christianity. Pompeii represented the ideal place of worship and, consequently, of luck. Modern people, Nerval believed, might attain the felicity that existed in Roman Pompeii by opening their minds to these old religions. Pompeii serves as a stage for the final part of Gautier's novel *Jettatura* from 1856, when a duel takes place in the Forum Baths.[1014] No explanation is given for this macabre setting, since there is no thematic connection between the duel and Pompeii.

Two Italian writers of the nineteenth century, Giacinto Bianco and Diego Vitrioli, have the reputation of an intimate bond with the Roman era, since their works suggest that they thought and felt like the ancient Romans and seemed even to live in the Roman past. The storyteller of Bianco's *Una notte sulle rovine di Pompei* believes that thousands of spirits of deceased Pompeians were floating around him during a nighttime visit to Pompeii. In a melancholic mood, he thinks about entering the past again and speaking with the dead.[1015] As Virgil was Dante's guide in Hell, Pliny the Elder is Bianco's. In five nighttime meetings ("colloquii") during which the narrator hopes to see visions of his own, he and Pliny discuss Pompeii's fate, and, hence, the fortune of mankind.[1016] Some historical figures associated with the area drop by during these sessions. We encounter Cicero defining the Pompeians as corrupted by the erring spirit of Rome,[1017] and the leader of the slave revolt Spartacus as a dead spirit (*larva*), as well as the

---

[1013] Nerval 1993, 615: "Les idées superstitieuses attachées à de certains jours, les ablutions, les jeûnes, les expiations, les macérations et les mortifications de la chair étaient le prélude de la consécration à la plus sainte des déesses de mille qualités et vertus, auxquelles hommes et femmes après maintes épreuves et mille sacrifices, s'élevaient par trois dégrées."
[1014] Gautier 2002, 399–482. First edition, Paris 1856. Also in Aziza 1992, 529–534 (this fragment); García y García 1998, no. 5807. The Italian translation by Alberto Consiglio (Naples 1991) has a good introduction. The passage about the duel in the baths is on p. 113–118. Gautier also wrote a poem "Jettatura" (Gautier 1970, 309–312), without anything about Pompeii or Naples. We will see in Chapter VI, pp. 313–317 how Gautier erected a monument for Pompeii with *Arria Marcella*.
[1015] Bianco 1833, 8. García y García 1998, no. 1646.
[1016] Bianco 1833, 12: "Scelsi la notte come la più adatta alle alte contemplazioni del dolore meco portando la speranza di potere diventare nuovo spettatore di notturne visioni, come in altro tempo fu dato a *Genio Insubro*." Pliny asserts that his partner evokes in him mortal wishes and carnal changes (Bianco 1833, 25): "Uomo tu fai rinascere nel mio petto mortali desiderii; e quantunque sostanza intelligibile sento ridestarsi degli effetti, che sono modificazioni della carne."
[1017] Bianco 1833, 42: "popolo di Pompei, lingua mendace turbò poc'anzi questi silenzii di morte, e libero spirito dolendosi di Roma osò ben anche mettere pe'l fango il nome mio: ma l'oratore Arpinate M. Tullio è qui per giustificare se medesimo alla presenza di tutti."

mythical founder of Pompeii, Hercules – unnamed but recognizable by his club and lion's skin.[1018]

Although the approach is charming, Bianco, who came from a class of Neapolitan intellectuals that felt the need to enhance the region's prestige, comes across as a pompous, bookish, and chauvinistic southern Italy. The rivalry he writes about between Pompeii and Rome equates to that between Naples and Rome in modern times, with the proud feeling of supremacy of the vibrant local Neapolitan culture.

Diego Vitrioli was a later colleague of Bianco from Reggio di Calabria who had great prestige as the author of excellent Latin verse. In his prose sketches *Veglie Pompejane*, he paints the beauty of ancient Pompeii against the background of a dire modern Italy.[1019] As in antique pastoral dialogues, the storyteller visits Pompeii on a hot day with his friends Teagene, Cerinto, and Cariclea.[1020] They define Pompeii's importance by the fact that it features both Greek and Roman elements, and has better preserved ruins than, say, Agrigentum or Selinus. Here, we see a still tangible, genuine life without decadence.[1021] Ancient art is presented as the mother of modern (Italian) art. By night, the friends meet old Pompeians, including Pliny the Elder. At the end the book, they see the tombs near the Herculanean Gate which make them aware not only of the present, but also of the inevitability of their own eventual deaths and burials in tombs, albeit most likely not due to disaster, but at home.

Both in its title and contents, there are parallels with *Noctes Atticae* by the second-century Latin writer Aulus Gellius: the title of each work refers to evening

---

1018 Bianco 1833, 78: "Tremò di rabbia l'ombra del Fondatore, e battendo colla picca il suolo disse: perfida Roma, iniqui Romani troppo tardi noti a questo braccio! Quale scelleraggine appellar col nome di benificenza l'opprimere il manomettere, e dopo aver spogliato un popolo, chiamarlo in tuo linguaggio pace! Ma non sorse fra voi, nobile sangue, un qualche generoso, che vendicò cotanta offesa?"
1019 Vitrioli 1930, II, 59–159. It was dedicated to his father and dated April 30, 1858. García y García 1998, no. 13.977. On Vitrioli, who was only in Pompeii in 1845, see the hagiographic sketch by Aliquò-Lenzi (1933, esp. 41–44) and Moormann 2013.
1020 In these names we recognize the Greek names Theagenes, Kerinthos, and Charikleia. The first is a frequently found name of authors and philosophers, whereas Kerinthos is a Gnostic Judeo-Christian preacher of the late first century A.D. Charikleia, finally, features in the late antique novel *Aethiopica* of Heliodorus. The story's characters do not correspond to any of these classical persons.
1021 Vitrioli 1930, II, 69: "Ma che dissi? Pare che i Pompejani fruiscano tuttora il dolce lume della vita: vieni, ti fieno schiusi gli usci; e tu, rimosse le seriche cortine, vederai le madri ninnare soavissimamente i bambini; le giovanette volgere a lo speglio i lumi; le ancelle intente al fuso ed al pennecchio. Forse ne udrai gli occulti parlare, e fino il pestìo de' piedi. Quì niente è mutato, nè si mosse un'unghia."

meetings in ancient towns (Pompeii and Athens), and each contain debates on various topics by learned people. Vitrioli uses a highbrow language similar to that of Renaissance Arcadia. The comparisons between antiquity and modern times do not flatter the modern Italian side of the coin. Therefore, from his nostalgic historical point of view, Vitrioli finds Pompeii attractive as a source of glimpses into a more desirable ancient life.

A nice medley of fact and fiction that once again plays out at night is Vittorio Imbriani's 1863 novella *Pompei notturna*.[1022] Imbriani, a Neapolitan scholar and republican politician, had been in exile for political reasons before becoming professor of Aesthetics in his maternal city. In the story, the author (who is also the protagonist) hopes to meet an ancient Pompeian, and feels that in case he encounters Cicero, he should know some Latin phrases, so he starts studying his old schoolbooks.[1023] The night, he thinks, offers the greatest chance of such an encounter happening, since then the spirits of the deceased Pompeians come to life again, and the dim light makes the city look merely damaged, not destroyed and deserted.[1024] On this night of his attempt, a statue of a sleeping Ariadne comes to life upon contact with the fresh air. At sunrise, much to Imbriani's dismay, she will be brought to a museum to become a mere inventory number and a dead object once again. Imbriani's plea for a local "musealization" of the finds was one of the main reasons he wrote this charming work.[1025]

The play between past and present works out excellently in Wilhelm Jensen's *Gradiva. Ein pompejanisches Phantasiestück* from 1903.[1026] In Jensen's story, Norbert

---

1022 Imbriani 1992, 3–21. Garcia y Garcia 1998, no. 6959 mentions other editions.
1023 Imbriani 1992, 5: "Dicono che gli spettri amano le rovine come il capelvenere: ed io pensai di passare una nottata a Pompei, nella dolce speranza d'imbattermi con l'anima di qualche infelice abitatore insepolto; e fors'anche con Marco Tullio Cicerone, che tornasse al suo caro Pompeianum. Ripresi grammatica e dizionario, mi mandai a mente una dozzina di buoni latinetti, e qualche frase degli *Ufficii*, tanto per non iscomparire."
1024 Imbriani 1992, 7: "Pompei sembra una città danneggiata, non una città distrutta e deserta: forse tal si mostrava dopo il tremuoto che precedette di pochi anni l'ultima rovina. A mano a mano che la veglia si protrae, quando gli uccelletti cominciano a cantare, ed i carri a gemere in lontananza, e le tenebre ad esser dissipate dall'alba, tu t'aspetti a veder la vita rinascere per quelle vie, come rinasce il fil d'erba che tu strappi dalle fenditure delle muraglie."
1025 Imbriani 1992, 15: "Ma quando un Monumento è chiuso in uno degli infecondi chiostri che si addimandano Musei, egli è morto, e nulla può surrogarlo. I tesori estetici accumulati ne' musei sono tolti alla circolazione, sfigurano!" The motif of sleep is important, since the figure is a "Sleeping Beauty" who, however, can no longer be brought to active life again. Think of the impact the famous "Sleeping Ariadne" in the Vatican Museums makes on Dorothea in George Eliot's *Middlemarch* of 1871. For some more references to the idea of musealization of finds *in situ*, see Chapters I and II.
1026 I use Urban/Cremerius 1973 for both texts. See i.a. Rohrwasser 1996, and works quoted in the following notes. García y García 1998, nos 5509–5512.

Hanold, a young archaeologist, is seeking true love by way of a Roman relief on which is depicted a young woman in profile walking to the left, with one foot on the ground and the other tiptoeing, called Gradiva by Norbert.[1027] He meets Gradiva in the person of a neighboring girl from his hometown, Zoe, in Pompeii, and the story has a happy ending.

Nowadays, the novella suffers from a burden of psychoanalytic reading, which was prompted by Sigmund Freud's famous 1907 analysis. Freud, who visited Pompeii in 1902, was spellbound by the analogy of Pompeii's history and the apparitions of spirits. Pompeii was repressed by Vesuvius' eruption, and revealed, as in an analysis, by the excavations.[1028] According to Freud, Jensen's novella contains an example of a dream as an unfulfilled wish.[1029] Apparently, a living girl named Zoe – despite the fact that her very name means "Life" – interests Norbert less than a dead girl named Gradiva on an ancient relief.

Jensen found Freud's analysis convincing, but denied having conceived of such an explanation beforehand.[1030] This analysis was pathbreaking, as it was one of the earliest adaptations of psychoanalysis. In Leppmann's eyes, it showed both its possibilities and its limitations, and was, in fact, better-written than the story it analyzed.[1031] The literary scholar Ika Willis suggests that the book portrays a specific method of telecommunication, much like the first telephone contact between Bell and Watson. According to Willis' attractive suggestion, Gradiva's way of walking matches the use of Pompeii's stepping stones by both ancient and modern people roaming the ancient town. The archaeologist in Norbert is satisfied by finding the girl as if she were an archaeological object connected with, among other things, these stepping stones.[1032]

1027 He has a plaster cast of the relief representing Winter, now in the Vatican Museums (Museo Chiaramonti no. 1284 = Leppmann 1966, pl. 17; Urban/Cremerius 1973, fig. on p. 22; Andreae 1995, II, 433; III, 41*, bibliography). Freud also possessed a copy of it. There is even a periodical named after the heroine, *Gradiva: revue européenne d'anthropologie littéraire*.
1028 Freud 1989, 12. García y García 1998, nos 7196–7197. Cf. Freud 2002, 164: "Wir waren heute in Pompeji, wo es extra heiß war." Sorrento made Freud think of Goethe (p. 159), and he thought that the Naples museum was fantastic (p. 162). On Freud's fascination for archaeology, cf. Armstrong 2005, 12–25 (Jensen); Williams 2008, 48–50; Gere 2009, 153–160; Daniel Orrells in Hales/Paul 2011, 185–198 on "Freudian archaeology." Cf. Pint 2010 for psychological and philosophical readings like Freud, Lacan, Lotringer (see index p. 289); idem in Lothane 2010.
1029 "Traum als unerfüllter Wünsch." Cf. Urban/Cremerius 1973, 140.
1030 Urban/Cremerius 1973, 12.
1031 Leppmann 1966, 192–206.
1032 Willis 2007, 227. In a similar vein are studies by Jacques Derrida (1980 and 1995, 129–155: "Thèses" and "Post-Scriptum"). On Derrida's Gradiva, see Orrells 2010. For another psychoanalytic reading of the novella, see Bellemin-Noël 1983. The photographer Victor Burgin (2006, 88–93,

One may ask whether Jensen knew Gustave Toudouze's *Cécube*.[1033] As in Jensen's novella, in Toudouze's short story, there is a girl by the name of Zoe. The girl's name symbolizes the living bond between the present and the past. Another element in common is the omnipresent Italian wall lizard, animal of the sun and eternity, stronger than death. Yet, *Gradiva*'s Zoe does not trespass time or belong to ancient Pompeii. This fact explains why she is considered an alien object within the archaeological environment, for she is a northerner and is not representative of (the cliché of) a Mediterranean sensual beauty.[1034]

The German literary historian Christiane Zintzen observes another important similarity in her comparison of *Gradiva* and *Arria Marcella*. In both works, the protagonist seeks a living person based on the ideal of an archaeological object, which at the same time doubles as a search for the protagonists' self.[1035] Imbriani and Douglas in *Nerinda* (see Chapter VI, pp. 317–320), we may add, use the same motif – that of inspiration by a statue or a cast. Casts provide one more similarity between *Gradiva* and Gautier's *Arria Marcella*: while Octavien falls in love with the impression of a breast, Norbert is fascinated by the impressions of Zoe's feet in the dust.[1036] Pompeii hides life in sepulchres or in impressions in the volcanic material that covers the town. In my view, as an archaeologist, Norbert has to unpeel the past and question the material in order to find himself and the lost girl. The excavation of his own persona is similar to the excavation of Pompeii, where eventually, he will find Zoe and his own identity.

I also see a thematic correspondence with Thomas Mann's 1912 *Der Tod in Venedig*. The protagonists – Norbert in Jensen and Aschenbach in Mann – depart suddenly from their homes, not yet knowing where they are going or what they are looking for. Their love for their lovers – Zoe and Tadzio respectively – is not

---

94–95) made work inspired by the novella. Burgin argues in a similar psychoanalytic vein: "Like a photographic plate, the surface of the city has received the imprint of an event that has irreversibly transformed it. In a neologism, Pompeii is a *catastrographic image* (one which, unlike Dresden and Hiroshima, remains so in its entirety and in perpetuity), any photograph of Pompeii is therefore the impression of an impression, the index of an index."

1033 Toudouze 1877 (see on this story Chapter VI, pp. 321–322). Urban and Cremerius (1995, 40–41) give other possible sources of inspiration.
1034 Interesting observations in Rothemann 1996, 74–75, 79–81.
1035 Zintzen 1998, 77–81. Other references on pp. 14, 44–45, 124–125, 221 and 327–328. Martinet 1996, 175–179 points out that the whole story is based on an object.
1036 Impressions of a dog's feet in Voltaire's *Zadig* also lead to a reconstruction of events. See Gere 2009, 7–8. In Freud's psychoanalysis, the foot plays a major role as a sexual symbol. See also Gautier's *Le pied de momie* (here p. 313, note 1191).

returned. In contrast with *Der Tod in Venedig*, *Gradiva* has a happy ending, which also contrasts with Kaden's and Gautier's evocations of a Pompeian lover.[1037]

Two film versions were made of Jensen's story, both heavily relying on the psycho-analytic interpretation: Giorgio Albertazzi's very literal 1970 *Gradiva*, and Alain Robbe-Grillet's 2006 *C'est Gradiva qui vous appelle*. In the latter movie, John Locke is looking for traces of the French romantic painter Eugène Delacroix in Morocco. Meeting a mysterious girl provokes various sexual dreams and experiences.[1038]

In *Eine Halbtagsstelle in Pompeji* ("A half-day job at Pompeii"), Jürg Federspiel moves between past and present and uses archaeological data as a means of contact.[1039] Wolfgang Vonderach, the protagonist, is killed by a stroke after a walk with his family outside Basel, and awakens at Pompeii, where he meets Kurt, a skeleton-like being ("Wesen"), who becomes his guide and describes Pompeii as a concentration camp where cruelty and lack of essential materials are propagated by culturally well-bred people. It is an awful town whose poor people are badly treated by local SS troops ("Untersklaven," "low slaves") who themselves are under the command of "high slaves." And, as if this were not repulsive enough, rich ladies "screw" gladiators.[1040] Film, another virtual world, dominates the dialogues between Wolfgang and Kurt, who also has a "modern" identity and (German) name next to his ancient ego.

Federspiel describes Pompeii as a sinister City of Death that contains a mixture of the corpses of the rich, who lived in opulent houses and were buried in precious tombs, and those of the poor, who left no trace. Kurt probably belonged to the latter category. As a guide, Kurt keeps Wolfgang in an iron grip, making him dependent like the "Untersklaven." The tourists, seen as dead people by Kurt, are perhaps ideal mediators between Pompeii's ancient past and Wolfgang's family in Basel in the present. At the end of the story, Wolfgang inexplicably dies again, and returns as if nothing has happened, to the scene of his walk outside Basel at the beginning of the story. I fail to understand this authorial choice, because Pompeii seems entirely alien to Wolfgang's family life. The literary scholar Sabine Rothemann recognizes in this short story the eternal succession of phases

---

1037 Cf. Fitzon 2002b, 325–330.
1038 See the script publication in Robbe-Grillet 2002.
1039 Federspiel 1993, 117–153. Not in García y García 1998.
1040 Federspiel 1993, 144: "Pompeji war eine grausame Stadt. [...] Die Reichen prunkten auf, schämten sich nicht. In den Straßen schleppten sich die Gerippe der Häftlinge des Konzentrationslagers Pompeji dahin, getreten und erniedrigt von den lokalen SS-Truppen, den Untersklaven, die selber von den verdummten Obersklaven erniedrigt wurden. [...] und die reichen Damen verbrachten lange Stunden unter den Leibern der Athleten, heiße Stunden [...]."

of destruction, resurrection and fall, in which the deaths of Kurt and Wolfgang are necessary elements.[1041] If this attractive suggestion is true, we may conclude that Pompeii represents both destruction and fall, while Wolfgang's family life in Basel signifies the era of resurrection. Kurt's equation of Pompeii with Nazi terror has no parallel in any other literary evocations I know of.

A psychologically dense interpretation of Pompeii plays a role in *Blauwbaard* ("Bluebeard"), a Dutch novel from 2000 by Pauline Slot. Edu, an archaeologist, and Maria, a psychiatrist, live together as a couple in an atrium-like house in Leiden built many decades earlier by an architect who has written a book on Pompeian architecture.[1042] For Edu, Pompeii is a living town, the impression of which is enhanced by the fact that he had fallen in love here with his first lover, Rianne, and with his wife, Maria.[1043] Tourists enliven Pompeii like the ancient inhabitants did. It gradually becomes clear that Edu and Maria have complicated histories, with unknown family bonds, various lovers, and adventures not common for "normal" people like them. The Bluebeard theme is evidenced by Edu's five-room house in Leiden. Although Edu serves as a modern Bluebeard, Maria does not become one of his victims. Pompeii is the cradle of all of Edu and the girls' relationships, and in some crucial moments, the action takes place in the excavations. A room in the House of Marcus Lucretius Fronto[1044] is the locus where Edu had made love with both Rianne and Maria; despite leaving no concrete traces, the virtual ones they leave there make it a sort of Bluebeard's Castle. Edu digs here as an archaeologist, while the other protagonists dig, especially the psychiatrist Maria, like Freud, inside their psyches to find their roots.

Art Works of the Past and the Present

J. Paul Getty's fame relies, among other things, on the museum he founded in Malibu. The building is modeled after the Villa of the Papyri at Herculaneum and contains a wealth of antiquities. He wrote down his memories about some of the more peculiar acquisitions. In one of his short stories, Getty invents a pedigree of

---

1041 Rothemann 1996, 83–84. See also Richter 2005a, 119–126.
1042 Slot 2000. Leiden is not mentioned by name, but Edu works in a museum of antiquity described as the Rijksmuseum van Oudheden (see Slot 2000, 61–62, 256–257) and lives within biking distance. I do not know of any translation of this excellent novel.
1043 The name Rianne has the same roots as Maria, being an abbreviated form of Marianne, which may imply that the women are actually one and the same.
1044 This house was the subject of Dutch research in the 1970s (see Peters 1993). The author may have chosen to feature it for that reason.

the Heracles Lansdowne. He liked the statue because it had been found in Hadrian's Villa near Tivoli; it was subsequently sold to the Marquess of Lansdowne in 1792, and now belongs to Getty's collection. In his story, the Heracles was brought from Corinth to Italy by Daphne and Glaucus, a couple in love, and later, was the proud possession of Calpurnius Piso and exhibited in the Villa of the Papyri at Herculaneum.[1045] Whereas the first part of the story slowly gains momentum due to lengthy descriptions of the couple's sea travel from Corinth to Campania and seamen's stories told on board, the second part is livelier and passes more quickly. It finishes with a nice synopsis of the collector's history:[1046]

> Then, like many other choice works of art, the young Herakles from Corinth, silent witness to the courtship of Daphne and Glaucus, to worlds long since gone, and to man's age-old struggles, followed the sun westward to the New World.

It is not exactly known from where Getty got his inspiration to use the Villa of the Papyri as the model for his museum in Malibu, which opened in 1974 (see note 1045). He was, however, in Campania often, and saw the finds in the Naples museum (some bronzes there are mentioned in his story). In Getty's eyes, Pompeii was a prosperous town of some 20,000 inhabitants who made a living selling fish sauce. The image he sketches presents the imperial-period town of the first century A.D., set back to the middle of the second century B.C for the sake of the story.

In Kaden's 1892 *Des Ikarus Flügel*, Isidor Carus (Icarus), a German artist, tries to outdo the superior artistic level of antique art in the Bay of Naples, where he begins a love affair with the marchioness Felicetta De Bajo. Failing at both endeavors, he suddenly dies.[1047] Like Gregorovius' Euphorion, Isidor hopes for the freedom to practice his art as he pleases, but is not wholly accepted by society.[1048]

1045 Getty 1955. Not in García y García 1998. On Getty and the Campanian cities, see K. Lapatin in Zarmakoupi 2010, 129–138 and in Hales/Paul 2011, 270–285. On the villa, see Comparetti/De Petra 1883; Mattusch 2005; Sider 2005; Zarmakoupi 2010. I thank Kenneth Latapin from the J. Paul Getty Museum in Malibu for some extra information.
1046 Getty 1955, 329 (last sentence). In this story, Hadrian is the wisest, culturally most doted emperor of the Roman world. There was peace in the empire and he personally displayed a good taste for ancient art (Getty 1955, 327–329).
1047 Kaden 1892, 272. Carus is buried in Boscoreale on a cemetery for strangers in this area (cf. Richter 2005b, 229–234). While sitting next to the corpse, the storyteller cites the Icarus passage from Goethe's *Faust* (Kaden 1892, 349). Kaden was a teacher in the German school in Naples (Richter 2005b, 220). On this novella, see Fitzon 2002b, 319–321. Another novella is presented in Chapter IV, pp. 243–244. Kaden (1892, 287) inserts "Die Lampe der Venus" from Vecchi's 1864 *Pompei*, a tale about the passion for art causing death (cf. Chapter III, pp. 192–193).
1048 Cf. Fitzon 2002b, 319. On *Euphorion*, see Chapter III, pp. 204–206.

Another clash, which concerns matters of belief as well as cultural differences, is between the Lutheran northerner and the Catholic priest Don Giacinto.[1049] In his tale, Kaden describes the mental abyss between North and South, and between Protestants and Catholics. These poles will never meet despite the Eden-like atmosphere in the Bay of Naples.

In Otto Eichhorn's *Maddalena* from the 1930s, another artist, the German painter Peter Trenk, meets the particularly lustful Maddalena, and falls in love with her. She is similar to Fragoletta, Graziella, and Felicetta in the novels by De Latouche, De Lamartine, and Kaden.[1050] In 1936, Trenk returns to the South and meets Maddalena's daughter, who shares her mother's name. Eichhorn plays with the idea of a combination dead and living city and a dead and a living Maddalena. Trenk, who lives in modern Pompeii visits the church and speaks with the locals during one part of the day, but spends the other part drawing and studying in ancient Pompeii. In Trenk's eyes, the South of Italy implies warmth, sun, luxury, love, and liberty, but also decay and danger. All these aspects come together in the two manifestations of Pompeii (old and new), and in the stories of the older and younger Maddalenas. The young man meets the girl; he proposes making a portrait of her in order to get to know her better, which leads Trenk to doubt his love for Maddalena, despite his lust. The adventures with each Maddalena both end with an unexplained death. The older Maddalena dies first, Peter dies second, and they are reunited again in heaven. Despite the Catholic elements, the novella displays no strong religious feelings and depicts the couple merely as a sample of the local population.

1049 Kaden 1892, 322–323: " Don Giacinto hatte zwar nichts Absonderliches an sich; in seiner Erscheinung war nur der katholische Priester scharf ausgeprägt mit einem Stich in den Fanatismus, das zeigten die harten kalten Augen, die zusammengezogenen Augenbrauen mit der tiefgegrabenen Längsfalte dazwischen und das energische Kinn in einem langen hagern fast olivenfarbenen Gesichte. [...] Seine düsteren Blicke auf mich – den er entfernt schon kannte – und auf meinen jungen Landsmann bewiesen mir zur Genüge, daß er die Glaubensgegensätze in uns, den Protestantismus, das Lutherthum schon herausgewittert, schon gerichtet habe, daraus ergab sich von selbst, daß er auch den Marchese verurtheilen, zum wenigsten beklagen mußte, solche Gesellen in sein Haus eingeführt zu haben."
1050 Eichhorn n.y. García y García 1998, no. 4885 mentions the year 1934, but since he returns after twenty two years and the House of the Menander, excavated in 1936, gets special attention, it must be 1936 or later. On pp. 10–11, he describes Maddalena: "Klug waren die schwarzen Augen, die eine seltsame Mischung von Schwermut und verhaltenem Feuer ausstrahlten. Es mußte ein Geschöpf sein, für das es keine Probleme gibt, das sich auf seine Instinkte verläßt, wie ein intelligentes Tier." Maddelena's daughter will have the same eyes and sensuality (Eichhorn n.y., 41): "Augen [...] blickten teils kindlich-lieb, teils wildkatzenartig-schlau. Die Lippen etwas wulstig, vermitteln neben gesunder Sinnlichkeit auch ein trotziges Selbstbewußtsein."

The North-South contrast also fascinated Pierre Gusman, an artist and art historian who published a lavishly illustrated book on Pompeii in 1899.[1051] He also embellished Bertheroy's *La danseuse de Pompéi*.[1052] Four decades later, Gusman took up the theme of Pompeii with *Elskée. Au jardin de Vénus*, illustrating it himself, as he had done with his previous publications (fig. 12).[1053] *Elskée* is presented as a memory Gusman has from around 1900, and recounts the love story of Elskée, a Danish girl whose name comes from the Danish verb *elske* ("to love"), and Aurelio, a local guide at Pompeii. After a rather happy period together, they separate and Elskée returns to her native Denmark, but feels nostalgia for Pompeii and returns once more to the South. During a trip to Capri with some Danes, she visits the Grotta Azzurra and drowns. Despite the long descriptive passages of Elskée, her character remains rather flacid. Aurelio is a simple Latin lover, good for a one-night stand and a "philosophical" talk.

This rather sad love story contains a lot of polar opposites, including perceived conflicts between the sun and the clouds, warm and cold, north and south, and men and women, who each have their particular desires. Pompeii and Denmark are each clichéd metaphors of these antagonisms. Elskée witnesses the merging of past and present in ancient Pompeii, and experiences the charm of Isis and the double mystery of life and death. Aurelio believes in a mix of the Venus of ancient Pompeii and the Madonna of modern Pompeii both seen as protrectresses of the city and embodying, respectvively, the ancient and modern vitality of the two Pompeiis.[1054] For Elskée and Aurelia alike, therefore, ancient Pompeii is no mere mass of stones, but a vital and essential part of their lives. However, Pompeii does evidently exert a negative influence on them both, as it is a dead and mournful place where the decadence of the past serves as a poor example for the living.

Pompeii is a vehicle of death in the fictitious diary of the fictional writer Albert Einhart, included in a novel by Friedrich Theodor Vischer.[1055] As the story goes, in 1865, "A.E." had rescued the unnamed storyteller in the Alps, and became

---

[1051] Gusman 1899 and 1900 (American edition, translated from the French). García y García 1998, nos. 6487–6489. Cf. David 2001, 134, 414–417, who gives examples of Gusman's approach of the study of the ruins and, especially, inscriptions.
[1052] David 2001, 145; on the book (Bertheroy 1899) see Chapter III, pp. 207–208.
[1053] Gusman 1936. Private press edition in few copies. García y García 1998, no. 6492.
[1054] Gusman 1936, 23–24: "La religion du *soprastante* était également faite d'un christianisme païen, logique d'un paganisme mystique, et qu'unissaient en naturelle communauté les croyances antiques et les dogmes modernes. Dans la Madone, patronne de Valle di Pompéi, Aurelio voyait une belle image, l'image de la femme idéale, la femme éternelle, conciliable avec Vénus céleste, épouse au nimbe d'or, à la robe étoilée, telle qui est présentée l'antique protectrice de Pompéi."
[1055] Vischer 1918; first edition 1878. García y García 1998, no. 13.973 mentions his *Briefe aus Italien*, Munich 1907, with pp. 128–132 for our matter, but does not include this novel.

Fig. 12: Pierre Gusman, *Elskée. Au jardin de Vénus* (1936), figure on p. 66, next to the start of part 4, "La maison jaune," the yellow house. Gusman depicts the amphitheater from the southern side looking north toward Vesuvius. The book is a rare gem, with only 362 copies having ever been produced.

"Auch einer," more or less "one more" or "a man like him." A.E. sends his *Eine Pfahldorfgeschichte* ("Story of a Pile Village") from Venice to the storyteller, who some years later finds personal belongings of Albert Einhart, including a passport, dated 1869. When the storyteller visits Einhart's house, he learns of Einhart's death shortly after the Battle of Sedan in 1870. The diaries, which were also found among the personal items, tell A.E's – or Einhart's – biography, including a voyage to Italy, where a visit to Pompeii in 1866 evoked expectations of death.[1056] In his diaries, Einhart refers to the gypsum casts of victims, which are described as modern artists' models, and relays his hope not to be resurrected in a similar way, although a rapid and cruel death doesn't sound bad at all.[1057]

The Pompeii theme applies well to mankind in general. Einhart (or "Auch einer") is the traditional "Every Man" who is seeking both past and future, in his case by contemplating the victims of the eruption, but at the same time, he functions as Vischer's *Alter Ego*. As a matter of fact, A.E. exhibits many of the characteristics of Vischer himself, who had become an important philosopher in his time. In his view, Italy – represented in A.E's diaries by Pompeii – is a paradise, since it lacks bonds with regular society and enables people to live off what is given to them by nature.[1058]

1056 Vischer 1918, 286: "Todesahnung." The storyteller "edits" the diary (Vischer 1918, 350–562; end).
1057 Vischer 1918, 535: "Pompeji. Die Gipsformen der Toten – genau in dem Moment, wie sie vor fast zweitausend Jahren im Todeskampf zuckten. Sonderbar – das tut sonst der Bildhauer aus Kunstzweck: er fesselt einen Zeitmoment im Raume. Hier hat die Natur dasselbe getan: die Sterbenden erstickend umhüllt, die Umhüllung verhärtet und nach achtzehnhundert Jahren einem scharfsinnigen *direttore degli scavi* so die Gußform dargeboten, die er nur ausgießen durfte. / * / Ich möchte gerade nicht in einer solchen Todeszuckung nach Jahrtausenden als Gipsfigur wieder aufstehen, übrigens rasch und gewaltsam sterben ist doch auch so übel nicht." Cf. Chateaubriand's remark, quoted at p. 181, note 667 and the simile in Gamper 1915, 162: "In Gebärden und Bewegung zeigen sie [the gypsum casts] Rodins heiße Kraft." I owe this reference to Nathalie de Haan.
1058 Many interesting data on Vischer and this book in Pottharst/Red 2011, e.g. Th. Althaus, pp. 169–190 on the *Pfahldorfgeschichte*, which was meant to be a critical assessment of the enthusiastic excavations of prehistoric remains in and near the Lake of Zurich at the same time Vischer was professor in that town (1855–1866). The time table (pp. 335–338) lists Vischer's many travels to Italy, but only the first, in 1839–1840, included a visit to Naples. See also Berger-Fix 1988, 84, 88–89: reproductions of Pompeian objects in Vischer's study.

Amoral or Immoral Behavior in the Villa of the Mysteries

One of the very rare more or less explicitly erotic novels situated in Pompeii is Léon Daudet's 1931 *Les bacchantes, roman contemporain*. Like his father Alphonse, Daudet was a prolific author of novels, political essays and memoirs. *Les bacchantes* is not presented as a burlesque; it has a very serious tenor. Romain Ségétan, a highly esteemed French scholar, wants to gather with his friends to re-enact the orgies depicted on the painted frieze in the Villa of the Mysteries at Pompeii, which, according to him, date to the fifth century B.C.[1059] Since Ségétan and his friends see the representations as a large erotic depiction of Bacchus and his followers, the activities they plan includes a mix of "volupté réelle et la catastrophe simulée" – that is to say: sex, eating, drinking, and if necessary, murdering those who cannot or choose not to become initiates into the cult of Bacchus[1060] In the last chapter, Ségétan and his friends kill various people they suspect might report their suspicious – not to mention forbidden and obscene – activities to the archaeological authorities or to the police. The novel unfolds amidst rumors of an impending war, referred to at the beginning of the story, when the party is preparing the expedition in a rural French community. The motif of the impending war no longer plays any role once the story shifts its focus to ancient Pompeii, where the participants are fully engaged in their re-enactment of the mystical orgies.

Some technical devices used in the novel betray Daudet's interest in both technology and politics (especially in terms of national defense), in addition to spiritualism and telepathy, aspects in which Daudet was also strongly interested.[1061] This fascination was common among Italian and French futurists of the 1920s, many of whom shared fascist and right wing views as well. The Bacchic women of the work's title are simultaneously the figures painted on the ancient frieze and the ladies in Ségétan's Dionysian orgiastic re-enactment party. Ségétan tries to make a sensible connection between these two worlds – ancient Pompeii and its Dionysian enthusiasm, and the contemporary free spirit of his friends. The work includes thoughts on the interpretation of the iconography of the paintings, which was up until this time alien to works of fiction. Some vigorously debated principal theories on ancient religion come to the fore, and Daudet might have

---

[1059] Daudet 1931. García y García 1998, no. 3641. On Daudet, see p. 158, note 601.
[1060] Daudet 1931, 266.
[1061] Vatré 1987, 250–252, 253. E.g. Daudet's novel *Un jour d'orage*, Paris 1925, with a magician. Cf. Willis' reading of *Gradiva* (supra note 1032) with similar telephone metaphors (Willis 2007, 235–237).

read scholarly interpretations of the frieze, which were already considerable in number at the time.[1062]

Ségétan is a composite of Daudet and Jean-Martin Charcot, the famous twentieth-century doctor whose clients belonged to high society Parisian circles, like the Proust and Daudet families.[1063] Antiquity and Italy were not primary focus points among Daudet's topics,[1064] but his curiosity about the meaning of the painted friezes in the Villa of the Mysteries fed his fascination for spiritualism and mystery. Passion and love – or better, eroticism – characterized Daudet and his works.[1065] Interestingly, *Les bacchantes* was banned by the Catholic Holy *Officium* and placed on the *Index* of prohibited books. Be that important or not, after reading this book, I remain puzzled by the absence of any condemnation of the sexual and culinary debaucheries – let alone the murders – which are never repented by the amoral protagonists.

Since their discovery, the Villa of the Mysteries paintings have become the most "quoted" Pompeian decorations in books and films, typically conveying a touch of the arcane. Over the last century, the images have been the subject of the wildest allusions; Daudet's is not even the most radical, and some interpretations go beyond strict iconographic or iconological rules. The psychotherapist (Eleanor) Nor Hall sees the room of the Villa of the Mysteries as the ideal realm of women, and follows Jung's archetypal methods along with ideas about hidden female practices formulated by ancient historian Jane Harrison, Jung's pupil Linda Fierz-David and poet Hilda Doolittle.[1066] Hall recognizes herself in the characters painted on the walls as women willing to be initiated into this matriarchal cult.[1067] Erminio Paoletta enthusiastically identifies the painted women as Nero's wife Poppaea and her friends, despite the chronological distance of some one

---

1062 E.g. Vittorio Macchioro, *Zagreus. Studi sull'orfismo* (Bari 1920). See the chronological list of publications in Sauron 1998, 157. Sauron also reads the frieze as the representation of the initiation of a girl.
1063 Vatré 1987, 270; Clébert 1988, 415–416. Charcot appears several times in other works as well (cf. Vatré 1987, index, and Clébert 1988, 46), e.g., Proust's *À la recherche du temps perdu* (see index in Proust 1954, III and 1989, IV).
1064 Daudet wrote a historical novel on Sulla (*Sylla et son destin*, Paris 1922). Cf. Vatré 1987, 283 (visits to Venice with his father Alphonse).
1065 Vatré 1987, 269–270 sees *Les Bacchantes* as an expression of "cette passion sexuelle dévorable."
1066 Hall 1988; Fierz-David 1989 (but from 1957). Other feminist views in Gazda 2000. A homosexual view based on Fierz-David might be David Cannon Dashiell's "Queer Mysteries," a set of 28 paintings in the Museum of Modern Art in San Francisco from 1993 (see Syme 2004, esp. 88 note 27).
1067 See Gere 2009, *passim*.

hundred thirty years. In this room, Paoletta claims, Poppaea would have been initiated into esoteric circles.[1068]

Politics, Crime and Murder in Pompeii

Pompeii is featured as a locale for crime stories in many novels. Next to those playing out in Antiquity (Chapter III), various works feature Pompeii as a modern city of crime or place it in a political thriller or historical novel. Several other novels evoke the dramatic Neapolitan vicissitudes of the late eighteenth and early nineteenth centuries.

In her 1992 *The Volcano Lover*, Susan Sontag portrayed Sir William Hamilton and his wives, Catherine and Emma. The excavations of Herculaneum and Pompeii do not play a paramount role, except as curiosities visited by famous travelers like Sade, Beckford, and Goethe.[1069] Hamilton's desire to purchase objects from the excavations is not satisfied until later on, when his relations with the court enable him to collect certain items.[1070] Hamilton's feelings are the principal topic of this romanticized biography, a true psychological masterpiece. One strange historical mistake pertains to Catherine and Beckford's visit to the Villa of the Mysteries, which would actually only have been possible after 1910.[1071]

Gustave-Georges Toudouze's 1908 *La sorcière du Vésuve (1808)* pays homage to the French occupation of Naples in the Napoleonic era.[1072] In the ruins of Pompeii, Roger de Viornes meets the witch ("sorcière") Orsola Rocco, the mother of the head of the bandits De Viornes and his French soldiers are supposed to catch. After complicated vicissitudes, the brigands surrender to De Viornes, who becomes a supervisor at Pompeii and produces plans and descriptions of the site like the (excellent,

---

[1068] Paoletta 1989. The paintings date to 70–60 B.C. Even though I do not agree with Gilles Sauron and Elaine K. Gazda, and rather believe in a purely mythical interpretation as scenes from the life of Dionysus, I refer, once more, to Sauron 1998 and Gazda 2000 for overviews of the many interpretations. See on the villa D. Esposito and P. Rispoli in Guzzo/Tagliamonte/Lucchetti 2013, 69–79.
[1069] Sontag 1992, 65, 94–95, 156.
[1070] Sontag 1992, 7, 123. Recall the *Pompeiana* Goethe saw in Hamilton's residence (here Chapter II, p. 150).
[1071] Sontag 1992, 94–95.
[1072] Toudouze 1908. García y García 1908, no. 13.611. Toudouze was a son of the novelist Gustave Toudouze (see here p. 267) and, among others, a member of the French Schools in Athens and Rome. He also showed his interest for the Vesuvian region, as he wrote about the auction of paintings from the Villa of Boscoreale at Paris (García y García 1998, nos. 13.609–13.610).

of course) work done there by the French. De Viornes is especially spellbound by the Temple of Isis, where Orsola finds material for her "magic."

Guido Milanesi's *Sancta Maria* is a sort of Cold-War novel *ante litteram*.[1073] In this novel, two Russian sisters, separated during the Revolution of 1917, meet again in Naples. Ninel (an anagram of Lenin), works for the Soviet propaganda machine, while Elena has fled to the west, converted to Catholicism, and married a Neapolitan nobleman. Ninel is impressed by the remains of ancient Pompeii and grapples with the bright side of materialism, examples of which she observes in Pompeii, where people understood the vanity of mankind, while still enjoying being vain. Gradually she turns down her old communist ideology and embraces the western world. The novel has an evident political obsession in the form of an intense hatred of communism. Milanesi neither hints at the fascist regime, nor compares West and East, but focuses on atheism, which rules communism, and Christianity, which warrants liberty.[1074]

In David Rice's 2007 thriller *The Pompeii Syndrome*, Pompeii serves as a locale for terrorist attacks. An Arab terrorist plot against Ireland and Britain aims at the destruction of a nuclear plant in Freshpark, which could cause a disaster much worse than Chernobyl. A Dominican priest, Father Frank Kane, is making a film about the destruction of Pompeii "briefly before 2013," and refers to such disasters as "Pompeii syndromes." In Kane's eyes, these "syndromes" are like Cassandra's foretelling. Just as no Trojan believed Cassandra's warnings during the Trojan War, no one believes the danger of the syndromes until it is too late.[1075] The captivating book is a thriller rather than a science fiction fantasy thanks to investigator Jack Stokes, who tracks down the terrorist leader from Saudi-Arabia, sheik Kemal Aboud, who owns a park near Galway, Ireland, which serves as a cover-up for the plot against the nuclear installation. The book contains few Pompeian elements, notwithstanding various references to the documentary film. Victims of other catastrophes are described similarly to those sketched by Pliny. There is also a far-fetched reference to Pompeii in a rather poorly conceived equation between a mythical tree and the fume of Vesuvius' eruption:[1076]

1073 Milanesi 1936; I read the twelfth edition of 1944. García y García 1998, no. 9240 lists eight editions. See on this former naval officer http://www.treccani.it/enciclopedia/guido-milanesi (accessed November 18, 2014).
1074 There are many quotations of graffiti. Milanesi might have followed Della Corte's interpretations. E.g. the House of Loreius Tiburtinus, now known as House of D. Octavius Quartio. It was excavated in 1916, 1918, 1921, and again in 1933–1935. For Loreius Tiburtinus as a fantasy name see Della Corte 1965, 370–375 and the criticism in Castrén 1975, 184. See also p. 140, note 531.
1075 Rice 2007, 148. He mentions April 3, 79 as the date of Pompeii's destruction.
1076 Rice 2007, 207. The Yggdrasill is the Tree of Life in the old-Nordic mythology as described in the *Edda*.

Nordics had their great Tree of Life – Yggdrasill I think they called it – the World Ash Tree [...] But on the other hand the people of Pompeii had a Tree of Death / Pliny´s pine tree that rose into the sky above Vesuvius and brought extinction to them all.

In a postscript, the author recalls how he got his inspiration for this novel, standing in the Forum of Pompeii in 2002.

In 1974 William Melton eternalized the stirring adventures of Larry Wheeler in *Nine Lives to Pompeii*. Wheeler is a charming crook based on Felix Krull from Thomas Mann's famous novel, who narrowly escapes nine attacks on his life in the run of the novel. He wants to put an end to a plague of destructive plants in Pompeii with "weedex," his own invention, and meets local hostility.[1077] Melton's is a book with much action, witty dialogues and charming portraits of the main characters. The approach to Pompeii is original and touches on a real problem – the injuries caused by exuberant vegetation, which sincerely worries the players in the story.[1078]

In one of his short stories, the Dutch archaeologist and writer Frédéric Louis Bastet portrays a nameless archaeologist who studies water management at Pompeii.[1079] The protagonist's visits to Pompeii have two goals: to do his professional research and to escape the presence of his wife, an intolerable chatterbox. When she comes to the excavations, the archaeologist, in a moment of despair, pushes her into a deep old cistern, hoping to regain rest for his tormented soul. He writes down his story in jail. Bastet has a great sense of humor, but also exhibits a (maybe exaggerated) high degree of misogyny. Making use of his own experiences as a researcher, he describes the protagonist's research clearly and without using too many technical terms. He recalls the (bad) Albergo Sole with its slavish servants, the struggle to get the permissions to enter locked houses and the quiet hours when the tourists had finally streamed out of the gates. Every scholar who has

---

[1077] Melton 1974. An "Author's Note" (p. 278) informs that the director of the excavations, Donelli, is not based on Maiuri, but is his own invention. To me, Donelli is a look-alike of Alfonso de Franciscis, Maiuri's successor. García y García 1998, no. 9107.
[1078] An early awareness of ecocriticism? Cf. the analysis of Harris' *Pompeii* in Chapter III, pp. 199–201.
[1079] Bastet 1986b, 29–40: *Resten van een dagboek* ("Remains of a Diary"). Not in García y García 1998. The topic studied surely is not a Bastetian research theme, being too technical. In the same volume (p. 91–99) the story *Een echtpaar* ("A Couple") tells about an unfortunate ascent up Vesuvius. As an archaeologist who worked extensively on Pompeian painting, Bastet was well-known, but he also published several novels, short stories, memoirs, and poetry, as well as books on the Dutch author Louis Couperus and on the relationship of Chopin and George Sand. Obituary by P.G.P. Meyboom, *BABESCH* 85 (2010) VIII–XI.

ever worked at Pompeii is able to narrate similar practices – save, let us hope, for savage spousal murder.[1080]

Jacqueline La Tourette's *The Pompeii Scroll* focuses on an American and an Italian colleague of the unfortunate (and nameless) Dutch archaeologist in Bastet's story.[1081] Joyce Lacey and Antonio Casale, search an ancient papyrus scroll. Although she is an archaeologist,[1082] Joyce does not know Pompeii. Apart from a visit to the brothel and her discussions with Antonio, the Pompeii theme is limited to the lost manuscript, surely a fictional creation, as no Pompeian papyri are known (see Chapter VII). Like Gusman and others, La Tourette notes the emotional differences – standard as claimed by so many authors – between Europeans ("Northerners") and Italians ("Southerners"). While the former are cool and keep their emotions in check, even under the strange circumstances of the story, with mysterious murders occurring in Pompeii and other adventures, the latter frequently have emotional breakdowns.

In *Was im Dunkeln bleibt. Ein Neapel-Krimi*, Barbara Krohn provides her readers with a clichéd image of Pompeii, situating a modern murder in the brothel of ancient Pompeii. The action of her thriller plays out between Naples and the excavation, with chief inspector Gennaro Gentilini and his German lover Sonja Zorn as the lively protagonists. Ancient Pompeii is portrayed as an open-air brothel, giving occasion to stealthy meetings, as it would have done in antiquity. For that reason, the choice of the *lupanar* is emblematic. Sonja's first visit does not move her very much at first,[1083] but this changes when she sees the gypsum casts of the victims. Later on, the story seems dominated by Priapus' phalli, symbols of uncontrolled sex of which the Gabinetto segreto in the museum holds many examples.

1080 Antiquity is not the only theme Bastet tackles in fiction, but the setting in the Mediterranean is predominant. One novel is situated in Crete, another on Capri (the title *Lava* suggests a connection with Vesuvius).
1081 La Tourette 1975. A French translation, *Le papyrus de Pompéi*, appeared in a monthly series "Modes de Paris" written by "un des auteurs favoris du public féminin. " García y García 1998, no. 7751.
1082 She tries to take away a piece of volcanic stone from a Pompeian house and is deservedly admonished by Antonio – not proper behavior for a real archaeologist!
1083 Krohn 2007, 36: "Sie konnte diese Häuser, diese Straßen, diese Plätze an den Brunnen einfach nicht mit Leben füllen." She only sees tourists (p. 37). I know of this book thanks to Agnes Allroggen-Bedel.

Children as Archaeologists in Herculaneum and Pompeii

Some children's books about Pompeii belong to the category of thrillers or adventure novels. They are also interesting for adults, for they illustrate ways to bring young readers into contact with the ancient world. Pompeii offers authors the occasion to describe children's adventures, and some children "actively" participate in excavations and discoveries. This Indiana Jones feeling appeals to the general public's notion that archaeology means excavating treasures.

Although written during the era of the French government in Naples, Mary Edgeworth's moralistic children's book about two poor boys, "cunning" Piedro and "honest" Francisco has no references to the French, but evokes Herculaneum.[1084] Francisco escapes poverty, earns his own money and develops into a nice young man. Through English residents of Naples, he meets a modest artist with whom he sees the Roman paintings in the museum and starts drawing. He also descends into the excavations to make sketches of both the old tunnels and the open-air digs.[1085] In this didactic novel, Francisco's spiritual development stands in the foreground. Edgeworth includes several Italian sentences, translated in notes, and references to studies by Hamilton and others.

A short story by Henry Howard Clark from 1883 tells the adventure of an American midshipman named Tom Morgan who is in Naples shortly after the eruption of Vesuvius in 1872.[1086] During a visit to ancient Pompeii, Morgan mentions a house "which was being excavated in honor of General Grant's visit, which had been made to the city a short time previous."[1087] Not a "cultural" person, Morgan is driven by curiosity. When he finds some ancient objects in an illegal excavation, he is fair enough not to conceal the finds from the official authorities. As compensation, director Fiorelli gives Morgan some trinkets, which is meant to convey a happy ending to the story. Clark's thoughtful tale was meant to introduce the excavations to American children in their teens. The book demonstrates the bravery and honesty of American citizens abroad, even as ancient European treasures tempt them. The young people who read the book would have been stimulated to visit the old world, much like Morgan and General Grant had done.

[1084] Edgeworth 1808. I also saw later editions from 1811 and 1819. Not in García y García 1989. Curiously, Piedro and Francisco are Spanish rather than Italian names.
[1085] Edgeworth 1808, 445 (with a long note about the excavations), 453.
[1086] Clark 1883; 23 unnumbered pages. Clark's name is followed by "U.S.N.," viz. United States Navy, which might explain the choice of his topic. On the 1872 eruption see Scarth 2009, 253–259. The story is the first of a series of short stories by various authors. Not in García y García 1998.
[1087] Indeed, the former president Ulysses Grant visited Pompeii on December 19, 1877. See Young 2002 (=1879), 77–81, with an illustration of the event on p. 80.

Edouard Maynial's French novel from the 1920s tells the story of three poor children who seek refuge in a Pompeian villa in an abandoned part of the site, and struggle to survive, like Robinson Crusoe on his deserted island.[1088] One of the children, François thinks that he is an orphan of French-Italian background, while the other two, Mario and Lina, are orphans from Calabria who refuse to emigrate to America with their rude uncle Giuseppe. Maynial is well informed about the excavations and succeeds in letting the kids discover treasures with their own eyes in this well-written story. They learn to look at paintings; the portrait of a couple similar to that of Paquius Proculus and his wife, and friezes with *amorini* like those in the House of the Vettii, are singled out. The author does not separate real and imaginary elements, and appropriately mixes his account with antiquarian information. There are clear allusions to the effects of World War I on both adults and children, especially at the surprising end, which I shall not betray here.

Some passages show Maynial's (and his protagonists') strong sensitivity to antiquity. Because of the way it deals with the theme of death, I single out an episode that describes the tomb where the children reluctantly live. François explains to Mario and Lina that death was not something the Romans were afraid of, and that the tombs reflect the happy and luxurious life in town (cf. p. 134, Taine). The Pompeians were very pious, he argues, and showed a great deal of respect for their deceased family members. He also points out that ancient Pompeii was separated from us by the eruption of Vesuvius,[1089] and by doing so, displays a good understanding of the two categories of deceased people in Pompeii: those respectfully entombed by family members, and those buried suddenly by the violent 79 eruption.

Carla degli scavi is a novel by Renée Reggiani dedicated to Libero d'Orsi, a schoolteacher who rediscovered Stabiae in the 1950s.[1090] The story is told from

---

1088 Maynial 1922, with illustrations by André Cahard. Not in García y García 1998.

1089 Maynial 1922, 94–95: "Tout d'abord, Lina et Mario avaient montré quelque répugnance à élire domicile dans un tombeau. Mais François leur avait expliqué que les tombes romaines n'avaient point ce caractère funèbre et désolé qu'éveille la vue d'un cimetière moderne. C'étaient des véritables monuments disposés le long des routes, dans la campagne, exactement la dernière demeure des vivants, qui conservaient l'aspect souriant, les commodités et souvent le luxe des habitations proprement dites. Les morts étaient brûlés, les cendres enfermées dans des urnes, les urnes disposées dans des cases le long d'un mur. Et seul le souvenir des morts habitait la grande maison silencieuse, où la piété des vivants, assis sur les grands bancs de marbre qui précédaient le tombeau, se plaisait à rêver, dans les belles soirées d'été. Mais c'était si loin, ce souvenir des vieux Pompéiens ensevelis avec leur ville dans la formidable éruption du Vésuve, que nulle profanation n'était possible." See also p. 154, fig. 5.

1090 Reggiani 1969. In an introduction, Carla Poerio presents the book as a novel for children. It

the perspectives of Carla Clerici, D'Orsi's niece from Milan, and D'Orsi himself. In a flashback while at Pompeii, Carla experiences the eruption as a girl from two thousand years ago. The book is a straight eulogy of D'Orsi, an amateur archaeologist who, thanks to his perseverance, made important discoveries, but was not respected by the official authorities. In fact, he was officially banned, but despite this, D'Orsi pushed on with his work at various sites, and made important finds. In the book, these discoveries are made in the company of Carla, who, in admiration for her uncle, argues that they would not have been made if he had given in to the opposition from officials. Reggiani hints at contrasts between Italians from the North and from the South, with the former often disdaining the latter on account of their alleged laziness and sloppiness. Carla, from Milan, is a positive messenger of the notion that even in the South, people do their best and achieve thrilling results.

Pompeii as Symbol of War and Destruction

Authors often compare towns destroyed by nature (here, Vesuvius) and towns destroyed by man during wars. The main purpose of these similes is the reason for and the method of destruction. Many recent examples concern damage caused by wars and therefore are defined as manmade, whereas Pompeii was hit by the unpredictable eruption of a volcano. The eruption itself is commonly thought of either as some form of punishment, the consequences of God's wrath (as we have seen in some Christian novels in Chapter IV) for the decadent lifestyle of the ancient Pompeians, or as one of those unstoppable natural disasters that take place all over the world. Pompeii, unique because of the unprecendented state of its preservation, allows authors to flesh out their stories with images of an intact world that has suddenly faded away, like the cities destroyed by men in later times.

In 1826, the Austrian playwright Franz Grillparzer composed a letter, written by the imaginary Tomes Dikson to his father and dated "vor der Donau im Jahre 2826." In the letter (which remained unpublished during Grillparzer's life), Dikson

---

does contain explanations of difficult words. There are digressions on cars which include technical qualities explained in detail, apparently a hobby of the author, who published other children books as well. García y García 1998, no. 11.230. On the old and new excavations, see Barbet/Miniero 1999. The diaries of D'Orsi have been edited in D'Orsi 1996. Reggiani includes a dialogue between the eighteenth century excavators Alcubierre and Weber on their first discoveries at Stabiae (see on them Chapter I, pp. 19–21). D'Orsi also appears in De Meuse 1967 (translated by D'Orsi himself from the first 1961 French edition).

recalls a volcanic eruption in 1826 that destroyed Vienna, which bears its ancient Roman name, Vindobona. The only surviving inhabitant – a sinner – can only find eternal peace if somebody frees him from his sins.[1091] Dikson tells his father that he would like to find the remains of the old site under the debris, as archaeologists did so many years earlier at Herculaneum and Pompeii.[1092] So he begins to excavate, and here the letter finishes abruptly. According to a comment on the letter, this piece is satirical, and is meant as a protest against the Emperor's censorship in 1826, which entailed a morally and intellectually devastated Vienna.[1093] Although Grillparzer knew Pompeii (he had been in Naples in 1819 during a trip through Italy), the ancient city in itself is not really relevant in Dikson's letter.[1094]

The Polish poet Władysław Kulczycki claimed in his long poem *Pompeii* that the destruction of Pompeii was comparable to Poland's misfortune in the nineteenth century.[1095] Although the Polish people would have to work hard to reach independence, he sees glimpses of hope for his fatherland, since it was not the victim of Vesuvius.[1096] Unfortunately, Kulczycki would die before Poland was set free, which only happened after World War I.

This catastrophic war evoked very different reactions from Marcel Proust, whose Pompeian reminiscence is quoted at the beginning of this chapter. Baron

---

1091 "Schreiben des jungen *Tomes Dikson* an seinen Vater in Philadelphia." See Grillparzer 1930, 105–106: "Sie [the father] müssen nämlich wissen, daß der letzte Bewohner dieser Mühle, ein ungerechter Mann, in der Blüte seiner Sünden von den Trümmern der einstürzenden Vindobona erschlagen, so lange als Geist zu wandeln verurteilt ist in diesen Mauern, bis jemand sich findet, der ihn erlöst, indem er so viele gute Gedanken hat, als jener schlechte." The letter was probably written April 8 or 9, 1826. Not in García y García 1998.
1092 Grillparzer 1930, 106: "Nur konnte ich den Gedanken nicht los werden, nach dem Vorbild von Herkulanum und Pompeji, unter der Lava Wiens nach Spuren und Überbleibseln entschwundener Zeiten zu forschen."
1093 Grillparzer 1930, 362–364.
1094 Grillparzer n.y. The diary of his stay in Italy reports a visit to Vesuvius on the late afternoon of May 14, 1819. There is nothing on Pompeii. On Grillparzer and Italy, see Leroy du Lardonnoy 2012.
1095 Kulczycki 1897, 9–17. The book has an introduction by Kulczycki's son, and was translated by Alinda Bonacci Brunamoti. The poem is dated August 1, 1884. García y García 1998, nos 7600–7601.
1096 Kulczycki 1897, 15, 16: "Nel tempio augusto del celeste azzurro / Incenso e luce la montagna innalza, / Come un'ara selvaggia, ove perenne / È l'olocausto. / O mia dolce Polonia! / O novella Pompei! Te pur ricopre, / Cimitero di prodi, la squallente / Cenere della morte. Innanzi a questo / Reboante Vesuvio, oscuro e muto / Sembra il tuo sacrifizio. / [...] / Oggi il vacuo sei tu, lo spettro, il nulla / D'un cimitero. Indarno io cerco l'ara, / Cerco indarno la fiamma. Oh Patria mia, / Fuma e risplendi! I popoli diranno / Di te, siccome di Pompei: mirate; / Ella è un tempio in rovina, ma il Vesuvio / Su lei rosseggia di presaghi lampi."

de Charlus, one of the protagonists of Proust's *À la recherche du temps perdu*, describes Paris threatened by German attacks in 1916, and compares it with Pompeii. The dangerous gases from the volcano are like the atrocious chemical waepons used in the trenches on the battlefield:[1097]

> Social amusements fill what may prove, if the Germans continue to advance, to be the last days of our Pompeii. And if the city is indeed doomed, that in itself will save it from frivolity. The lava of some German Vesuvius – and their naval guns are no less terrible than a volcano – has only to surprise these good people at their toilet and to eternise their gestures by interrrupting them, and in days to come it will be part of a child's education to look at pictures in his school-books of Mme Molé about to put on a last layer of powder before going out to dine with a sister-in-law, or Sosthène de Guermantes adding the final touches to her false eyebrows; these things will be the subject of lectures by the Brichots of the future, for the frivolity of an age, when ten centuries have passed over it, is matter for the gravest erudition, particularly if it has been embalmed by a volcanic eruption or by the substances akin to lava which a bombardment projects. What documents for the future historian if asphyxiating gases, like the fumes of Vesuvius, and the collapse of a whole city, like the catastrophe which buried Pompeii, should preserve intact all the imprudent dowagers who have not yet sent off their paintings and their statues in safity to Bayonne! And indeed, for the last year, have we not already seen fragments of Pompeii every evening: people burying themselves in their cellars, not in order to emerge with some old bottle of Mouton Rothschild or Saint-Emilion, but to conceal along with themselves their most treasured belongings, like the priests of Herculaneum whom death surprised in the act of carrying away the sacred vessels? Attachment to an object always brings death to its possessor. True, Paris was not, like Herculaneum, founded by Hercules. But how many points of resemblace leap to the eye! And this lucid vision that is given to us is not unique to ourselves, it has been granted to every age. If I reflect that to-morrow we may suffer the fate of the cities of Vesuvius, these in their turn sensed that they were threatened with the doom of the accursed cities of the Bible. On the wall of a house in Pompeii has been found the revealing inscription: *Sodom et Gomorrah*.

Shortly after in the narrative, sirens announce a bombardment, and there are fires. Marcel, the narrator and Charlus' friend, runs into a brothel "by accident" and sees Pompeian paintings on its walls. The "Pompeian" association pertains both to the color – Pompeian and brothel red – and to the images, which depict sexual intercourse. Later, he reflects about his narrow escape from this brothel with Charlus. He recalls the prophetical text "Sodom" applied by Charlus on one of the brothel's walls, which told the same story as the famous ancient Pompeian

---

1097 Translation C.K. Scott Moncrieff et al., *Remembering of Things Past* III, New York 1981, 834–835 = Proust 1954, III, 806–807 (Le temps retrouvé); 1989, IV, 385–386. To my knowledge, the only scholar who paid attention to Proust and Pompeii is Francesca Spiegel (in Hales/Paul 2011, 232–245). The "priests of Herculaneum" might be the famous Isis priests' skeletons found in and near the Temple of Isis at Pompeii (see Chapter II, p. 141).

inscription (see Chapter IV, p. 236).[1098] He compares the brothel's clients with the ancient Pompeian victims. The former steal into the Paris metro – which is as dark as the catacombs – to continue their sexual intercourse, much like the latter, whose skeletons have been covered by the Vesuvian ashes.[1099]

"Sodom and Gomorrah" refers to the Pompeian inscription, but also to the homosexual inclination of Charlus and the other clientele coming to this brothel.[1100] By its nature, and like ancient Pompeii, the brothel is destroyed for being filled with sinners, like the Biblical town of Sodom. Now, as a ruin, it becomes a new type of brothel, much like Pompeii became a new type of city. Consequently, Paris is like a new Pompeii. Although the Pompeii theme comes up very briefly in Proust's novels, it has great importance for the definition of Paris during the war as a perpetual place of sin.[1101]

A similar connection between Paris and Pompeii – this time written during World War II – was made by Felix Hartlaub in 1941. *Kriegaufzeichnungen von Paris* describes his work in German offices in Paris. These war records form a mix of merry and sad impressions of a city that has not yet fully lost its grandeur and *joie de vivre*, but already shows a patina of depression and destruction caused by military force and a sliding standard of living. The once grand Ministry of Foreign Affairs suffers from German misuse. Calendars show the date the Germans entered Paris; time is frozen. The sudden retreat of the French, who left everything they

---

1098 Proust 1954, III, 833–834; 1989, IV, 412. In the translation of C.K. Scott Moncrieff (see note 1097), p. 863: "But my thoughts had turned to another subject. I was thinking of Jupien's house, perhaps by now reduced to ashes, for a bomb had just fallen very near me just after I had left it – that house upon which M. de Charlus might prophetically have written *Sodoma*, as the unknown inhabitant of Pompeii had done, with no less prescience or perhaps when the volcano had already started to erupt and the catastrophe had begun. But what mattered sirens and Gothas to the men who had come to seek their pleasure?" Briefly discussed in Syme 2004, 82–83.
1099 Proust 1954, III, 834; 1989, IV, 413. In the translation of C.K. Scott Moncrieff (see note 1097), p. 864: "Some of these, like the Pompeians upon whom the fire from heaven was already raining, descended into the passages of the Métro, black as catacombs."
1100 The previous volume of the cyclus also bears the title *Sodom et Gomorrhe*.
1101 The equation of modern sexual license and ancient Pompeian brothels briefly returns, in a similar Proustian way, in *La rambla paralela* by the Columbian author Fernando Vallejo (2002, 79): "De la lista del carriel me quedaron faltando sus paranoias y animadversiones, que pasaban de mil, y un raro sentido de pérdida de lo no vivido. Que añorara a Antioquia y su niñez, vaya, ¿pero el burdel de Pompeya? ¡Cómo es que no había entrado, aunque fuera a ver! Ese burdel no frecuentado de hacía dos mil años que le cubrió el Vesubio le quitaba el sueño. Y el Versalles de Luis XIV con sus salones de espejos y sus arañas de mil luces bailando rigodón… Al rato cambiaba de parecer y la tachaba de 'corte empelucada de roñosos sifilíticos.'" I owe this addition to my Nijmegen colleague Brigitte Adriaans, who sees Vallejo as one of the most exciting modern Latin-American authors.

were working on as it was, provokes a comparison with Pompeii's last day. The invaders have broken open hundreds of doors and damaged countless pompous writing desks, whose drawers are open, documents spilling out onto the floors. The dust covering everything creates "Pompeian effects."[1102] Hartlaub does not restrict his comparison with Pompeii to the stoppage of time and the destruction; in his eyes, personal effects like novels, umbrellas or top hats suggest that the old inhabitants of the offices will return shortly.

Hartlaub studied archaeology in Naples in 1933 and in letters to his parents he tells them about his experiences, although he barely mentions Pompeii.[1103] He certainly had an interest for Antiquity, but it scarcely permeates his literary work.[1104] After studying history in Berlin, he was required to join the German army under the nascent Nazi regime. The fact that he was occupied with military functions until his never-resolved disappearance in April, 1945 made it difficult, at first, to view him as a "good" German. However, since the first publications of his work in the 1950s, it became immediately clear that Hartlaub would have become one of the major German authors of the twentieth century, and nowadays, biographers and essayists see many reasons to interpret his work as a way of "inward emigration," or even a stealthy opposition against a world he was unable to quit.[1105] As we see, Pompeii forms a tiny fascinating tassel in Hartlaub's oeuvre. Hartlaub's evocation of Pompeii exhibits a clear affinity with the desolate one Proust had created after World War I, and leads me to come to the conclusion that most likely, Hartlaub had read Proust.

There are other comparisons beteen Pompeii's destruction and the cataclism of World War II. In Lowry's *Present Estate of Pompeii* (discussed on p. 301–304),

---

1102 Hartlaub 1955, 88; Hartlaub 2002, 119: "Die Zimmer zu Hunderten an den langen Gängen. Jede Tür aufgebrochen, jeder Schrank, jeder Schreibtisch geknackt. Kläglich hängen die Schubladen aus den pompösen 'Bureaux d'acajou.' Ströme von Briefen haben sich zur Erde ergossen, der Zug blättert in Photoalben, Staub liegt schon einen halben Finger dick. Pompejanische Effekte: Die Kalender zeigen alle den 14. 6. 40. Die von der Sonne ausgezehrten Zeitungen: des formations blindées ennemies ont réussi à s'infiltrer […]." On this fragment, see Rothemann 1996, 81–82. See also Leppmann 1966, 234–235; Rothemann 1996, 75, 81–82; G.L. Ewenz in Hartlaub 2002, II, 1–40; Marose 2005. Not in García y García 1998.
1103 Hartlaub 1955, 451 (letter to his parents from March 11, 1934): "Heute vor einem Jahr mag ich ungefähr das erste Mal nach Pompeji hinausgefahren sein, kurios. "
1104 G.L. Ewenz in Hartlaub 2002, II, 20; Marose 2005. Partly unpublished pieces with classical themes: *Dädalus gründet Cumae* (Hartlaub 1955, 361–363), *Der Tyrann*, and *Sodoma-Gomorra* (see Marose 2005, 45). He also wrote a novella about the French occupation of Naples in 1799: *Parthenope oder das Abenteuer in Neapel* in which no mention of Pompeii is made (Hartlaub 1955, 294–352; see G.L. Ewenz in Hartlaub 2002, II, 23–24; Marose 2005, 97–98).
1105 The so-called "innere Emigration." Cf. G.L. Ewenz in Hartlaub 2002, II, 22–25; Marose 2005.

Roderick Fairhaven looks at Pompeii as if it were Coventry or Rotterdam. A similar case is Primo Levi's poem *La fanciulla di Pompei*. It starts with the contemplation of the gypsum cast of a Pompeian girl, and then turns to the catastrophy of World War II. Anne Frank has left a record of her existence in the form of her diary, while an anonymous Japanese girls risks being forgotten:[1106]

> The Girl-Child of Pompeii
>
> Since everyone's anguish is our own,
> We live yours over again, thin child,
> Clutching your mother convulsively
> As though, when the noon sky turned black,
> You wanted to re-enter her.
> To no avail, because the air, turned poison,
> Filtered to find you through the closed windows
> Of your quiet thick-walled house,
> Once happy with your song, your timid laugh.
> Centuries have passed, the ash has petrified
> To imprison those delicate limbs for ever.
> In this way you stay with us, a twisted plaster cast,
> Agony without end, terrible witness to how much
> Our proud seed matters to the gods.
> Nothing is left of your far-removed sister,
> The Dutch girl imprisoned by four walls
> Who wrote of her youth without tomorrows.
> Her silent ash was scattered by the wind,
> Her brief life shut into a crumpled notebook.
> Nothing remains of the Hiroshima schoolgirl,

1106 Translation by Ruth Feldman and Brian Swann (Primo Levi, *Collected Poems*, London/Boston 1988, 34). Levi 1984, 42–43. "Poichè l'angoscia di ciascuno è la nostra / Ancora riviviamo la tua, fanciulla scarna / Che ti sei stretta convulsamente a tua madre / Quasi volessi ripenetrare in lei / Quando al meriggio il cielo si è fatto nero. / Invano, perchè l'aria volta in veleno / È filtrata a cercarti per le finestre serrate / Della tua casa tranquilla dalle robuste pareti / Lieta già del tuo canto e del tuo timido riso. / Sono passati i secoli, la cenere si è pietrificata / A incarcerare per sempre codeste membra gentili. / Così tu rimani tra noi, contorto calco di gesso, / Agonia senza fine, terribile testimonianza / Di quanto importi agli dei l'orgoglioso nostro seme. / Ma nulla rimane fra noi della tua lontana sorella, / Della fanciulla d'Olanda murata fra quattro mura / Che pure scrisse la sua giovinezza senza domani: / La sua cenere muta è stata dispersa dal vento, / La sua breve vita rinchiusa in un quaderno sgualcito. / Nulla rimane della scolara di Hiroshima, / Ombra confitta nel muro dalla luce di mille soli, / Vittima sacrificata sull'altare della paura. / Potenti della terra padroni di nuovi veleni, / Tristi custodi segreti del tuono definitivo, / Ci bastano d'assai le afflizioni donate dal cielo. / Prima di premere il dito, fermatevi e considerate. / 20 novembre 1978." Alessandra Corda drew my attention to this poetic gem, which I cited in Moormann 2001. A German translation is in Richter 2005a, 144. Not in García y García 1998.

> A shadow printed on a wall by the light of a thousand suns,
> Victim sacrificed on the altar of fear.
> Powerful of the earth, masters of new poisons,
> Sad secret guardians of final thunder,
> The torments heaven sends us are enough.
> Before your finger presses down, stop and consider.
>   20 November 1978

Apart from Anne Frank's notepad, the references to victims are rather vague. Nevertheless, there appear to have been concrete sources for Levi. The archaeologist Giuseppe Pucci has suggested that the gypsum cast Levi refers to is that of a victim found in the House of the Cryptoporticus in 1914.[1107] As for the Hiroshima girl, I think that Levi is referring to a shadowy imprint of a victim incinerated by the bomb's 3000 degree Celsius blast. This token of the disaster was visible on a stair of a financial bank in the center of town, until it was removed to the Hiroshima Peace Memorial Museum in 1971.[1108]

Over the last decade, Roberto Saviano has shocked the world with his revelations of Naples as strangled by the Camorra. The town is at war and the many victims cannot be dismissed as the results of conflicts between gangs and families only. When seeing one of these corpses, he writes:[1109]

> It looks like one of the figures that emerge from the ashes of Vesuvius when the archaeologists pour plaster into the void left by the body.

The comparison of Pompeii's "fall" and the attack on the Twin Towers in New York on "9/11" (2001) is nowadays rather frequent, and I refrain from an exhaustive list of references. In Rice's novel, which we have seen earlier, a certain Doctor Postlethwaite thinks of 9/11 and of New York's Twin Towers.[1110] In *Ghosts of Vesuvius*, Charles Pellegrino pays a lot of attention to manmade and natural disasters. He dubs the chapter on the 2001 attack "Vesuvius in New York"[1111] and claims that Pompeii's destruction might even have been caused by God's wrath.[1112]

[1107] Pucci 2012, 82. He also cites some more poems that make associations between and are dedicated to victims of Auschwitz and Pompeii.
[1108] Burgin 2009, 31, note 37. Cf. on his Hiroshima simile note 1032.
[1109] Saviano 2007, 82 (in the chapter "The Secondigliano War").
[1110] Rice 2007, 153.
[1111] Pellegrino 2004, 382–455. A specific comparison is formulated on pp. 418–420.
[1112] Pellegrino 2004, 19–29. He refers to Dio Cassius' Giants (quoted in Chapter IX, p. 344) and to the rise of men, as told in the *Apocalyps* 8.2.

What would happen if Vesuvius became active again, and consequently wiped out Pompeii for the second time? This is the theme of a fable-like novel by Helmut Krausser, who studied archaeology for a couple of years. In *Die wilden Hunde von Pompeii* (*"The Wild Dogs of Pompeii"*), the protagonists are Kaffeekanne[1113] ("Coffee Pot"), a small but tough (and funny) Pompeian stray dog, and his fellow strays.[1114] The names of the animals reflect their rudeness (Ferox, Nero, Saxo), wisdom (Plinius/Plin), sweetness (Clio, Chloe, Agrippina/Grippi, Kaffeekanne's lover), and others.[1115] Dogs outside Pompeii's walls belong to modern society, in contrast with the protagonists themselves, who live somewhere between past and present. In his most important adventure, Kaffeekanne prevents an impending Vesuvian eruption by going down into the crater and closing one of the volcano's openings. The story ends with the various groups of dogs coming together and ending their feuds. Thanks to the dogs' positive influence, ancient *and* modern Pompeii can continue to attract visitors from all over the world, who in turn, will cherish the dogs for their "service." The choice of dogs as protagonists in a novel is original and witty, but also relevant, since the excavations have always been full of dogs, both wild and tame.

As any good fable does, this novel has a clear set of morals. Man is a bad keeper of his own world. He causes his world to suffer from crime and ecological misuse (here, Krausser inserts a touch of ecocriticism, which we encountered briefly in Chapter III, p. 201). The dogs are like men (or alternatively, men are nothing but dogs). We can only rescue Pompeii when we take into account its precious state and not concern ourselves solely with commercial profits. We should respect both the history and the modern, living environment, and try to find harmony between these two distinct sides.

Guiding and Being Guided in Pompeii

> I've read little about the malaise of travellers, even the sense of tragedy that must come over them sometimes at their lack of relation to their environment.[1116]

1113 His dead half explains this name – a "respelling" of *Cave Canem*, or "beware of the dog" – and refers to the mosaic in the House of the Tragic Poet: Krausser 2004, 121–122.
1114 Krausser 2004. There are suggestive illustrations by his wife Beatrice Renauer.
1115 A group with suggestive names is that of dog gladiators who tackle Saxo (Krausser 2004, 180–181): Kingkong, Stalin's Last Wish, Eviscerator, etc. These are fighting dogs in the human world, killing each other for money like gladiators in antiquity (Krausser 2004, 188–189, 191–192).
1116 Lowry 1961, 177. This section is a reworking of Moormann 2003a.

As we have seen in Chapter II, guides working in the excavations of Pompeii and Herculaneum, in the museums of Portici and Naples, and on Vesuvius itself, evoke all kinds of reactions. However briefly their role as leaders endure within a given tour, guides and "their" tourists become intimate partners who need to develop a certain level of mutual trust during the brief time they are together in order the guide-tourist relationship to function smoothly. Especially in the first decades of tourism, travelers needed the assistance of local people because there were no adequate descriptions available and many practicalities needed to be organized. As an alternative to hiring a guide, in 1811, Domenico Romanelli, a learned Italian priest and librarian, presented his *Viaggio a Pompei, a Pesto e di ritorno ad Ercolano*.[1117] The *abate* held the guides in low esteem, as exemplified by a man he met working in Pompeii who used to tell the visitors to the House of the Vestals that Pompeii was originally only inhabited by Vestals, the Roman priests who had to regard their chastity and kept burning the holy fire of Vesta.[1118]

Paul Crombet, a Belgian navy officer, formulated a sort of definition of a guide in the early nineteenth century.[1119] A *cicerone* is a lower class man who has followed in footsteps of his father and grandfather, and become a guide. He does not possess a thorough knowledge and is not inclined to answer questions, let alone react to his clients' remarks. His only advantage is that he is not aware at all of mistakes he makes, since he is (and his mistakes are) genuine. Crombet does not highly esteem the human dignity of these guides. Presumably most upper class travelers dealt with the guides in the same manner.

1117 Romanelli 1811, 2: "perchè niuno si è occupato a fare un itinerario esatto di tutti i luoghi restituiti al giorno, e molto meno a dare un dettaglio di tutte le antichità, che vi sono state raccolte." It was dedicated to Queen Caroline, the wife of King Joaquin Murat.

1118 Romanelli 1811, 62: "Un *Cicerone*, ch'è solito di guidare i forestieri per Pompei, ci assicurò con aria di fermezza d'esser questa l'abitazione delle *Vestali*, e ci raccontò finanche il loro dovere di serbare e la castità, ed il fuoco sacro, e la pena a chi trasgrediva. Noi lo lasciammo in possesso della sua erudizione, e passammo avanti." Vestals occur in various novels, e.g. *Vestal* 1830 and Lasky 2007 (see pp. 203, 217).

1119 Crombet 1941, 52–53 (note of October 1817): "Un *cicerone* est un homme du bas peuple dont le principal métier est de conduire les voyageurs et qui, possédant par une tradition, qui lui est parvenue de père en fils, une connaissance superficielle et souvant fausse des antiquités de son pays, débite à chaqu'un ce qu'il en sait, sans jamais varier d'un seul mot, sans pouvoir jamais répondre à la moindre objection, absolument comme ces hommes qui montrent dans les foires des animaux étrangers et rares, dont il font, sans s'arrêter, l'histoire en termes ampoulés, mentant horriblement et donnant quelquefois par un long cervier, et cela je l'ai vu, un chien d'aspect un peu sauvage. Sans un certain rapport cependant l'avantage reste du côté des *cicerones*, parce qu'au moins ils sont de bonne foi, et s'ils vous trompent, s'ils vous induisent en erreur, ce n'est pas leur faute."

Travelers could hire a guide, either in Naples or at the entrance to the excavations. Like today, complete day tours were on offer, and included a guide, a coach with horses, a picnic and anything else, as needed. Until the railway opened in 1844, a trip from Naples to Pompeii took an entire day. An excursion to Herculaneum was commonly combined with an ascent up Vesuvius and a visit to the museum in Portici, in a one-day trip. Some voyagers went to Pompeii first, and "did" Herculaneum and Portici on the way back to Naples. Torches were necessary at Herculaneum, and were better purchased in Naples for a fair price instead of being gouged at Resina.[1120] Mariana Starke provides practical information, including her recommendation of purchasing food for the whole day, since there was no café yet in the excavations.[1121] As to the unavoidable tips, Starke lists the various persons involved: for the two coachmen, the boy assistant, and "the Man who throws water on the paintings, one or two *carlini*," while the guide gets a *ducato*.[1122] Bribery was necessary to get access to the newest excavations. Denon, working for Saint-Non's *Voyage pittoresque*, had to tip his guide, rather a greedy workman, who impeded his research.[1123]

A serious handicap was that of communication and mutual understanding. Many travelers spoke some Italian, but the local dialect was – and is – another matter. Hogg noted that his visit to Vesuvius was "a well-organized bore" because his guide spoke

> the asinine dialect of the Neapolitan tongue; which is, perhaps, a dialect of the Italian, which is a dialect of the Latin, which is a dialect of the Aeolic, which is a dialect of the Greek, which, with a slight admixture of Pelasgic, is doubtless a dialect of the Sanscrit [sic]...[1124]

The *Encyclopédie* is probably the only major reference work that eternized one specific museum guide. The author of the lemma "guide," Louis de Jaucourt, critically informs his readers that in Portici there is a certain Filippo Cartoni, a barely instructed young man.[1125] Another complaint concerns the hurry with which one

---

1120 See De la Roche 1783, 43–51.
1121 Starke 1802, II, 97, 109, quoted in Chapter II, p. 130.
1122 Starke 1802, II, 108, 109.
1123 Denon 1997, 118. Cf. Saint-Non 1782: "Nous corrompîmes, comme nous nous l'étions promis; mais comme notre coquin de ce jour-là n'était qu'un coquin subalterne, qu'un ouvrier qui avait envie de garder notre argent sans cesser de faire son métier de sentinelle, il nous tourmentait pendant notre travail, et nous ne pûmes que lever une très petite partie du plan qu'il nous faillait, et que nous eûmes à force de soins, de tentatives, de travail et d'argent."
1124 Hogg 1827, II, 112 and 113 (he visited the area in December 1825).
1125 C., Herculanum in *Encyclopédie* Supplément 3, 1777, 349–358, quotation on p. 352: "un jeune homme très peu instruit." There is a similar passage in Volkmann 1777–1778, 310: "Der jetzige Auf-

had to visit the museum.[1126] This haste became still more irritating in combination with the prohibition against taking notes or sketching objects, which provoked the same reactions modern tourists – and scholars – have to plaques at museum and site entrances that say "no photographs."[1127] Hogg's long description of his visits to the museum in Naples in 1825 is very instructive as to the practice of those days.[1128] On December 7, Hogg received a personal welcome from Andrea De Jorio, keeper of the *Galleria dei Vasi* in the museum and scholar of a wide array of archaeological topics, who obtrusively tried to hawk his own books. De Jorio would become famous thanks to his study on gesture, his 1832 *La mimica degli antichi investigata nel gestire napoletano*.[1129] The guards were pushy as well. In theory, every room was open, but one had to tip the guards, albeit very moderately, which prevented a concentrated and tranquil study of the objects.[1130] We have very few testimonies dedicated to guards and guides in the museum from more recent times. Some travelers observed that too many idlers – *fannulloni* – were milling about at the entrance, while many exhibition rooms were (and/or are) closed. This situation has not changed much in modern times.

Until 1860, the archaeological sites themselves were guarded by veterans, called *invalidi*, who had sometimes, indeed, been disabled in battle or work, and

---

seher Filippo Cartoni, welcher es den Fremden zeigt, versteht wenig von den Alterthümern, und ist daher selten im Stande neubegierigen Reisenden von den Sachen, die er zeigt, Rechenschaft zu geben." and in De Lalande 1786, VII, 425: "jeune homme très-peu instruit [...] on ne recevoit de lui aucune lumière."

1126 E.g. Hog 1824, 202: "[people] are conducted on by a cicerone in the king's livery, with rather too much rapidity for such an exhibition." García y García 1998, no. 6872.

1127 See an interesting example of scholarly irritation formulated in Hannestad 1999.

1128 Cf. Galignani 1819, 453–455, who warns for tipping: "a silver key is of no use." García y García 1998, no. 5665; G. Guilcher in Chabaud 2000, 81–93.

1129 Translated into English and commented by Adam Kendon (2000). Hogg 1827, II, 57: "[He] has published a great many useful guides; but is a little too anxious to sell them. To an English traveller, it is peculiarly distressing to find a gentleman puffing his own works, as it is so totally different from our habits; and with all the strangers, it must have a tendency to impede the end proposed, the sale of books; for the often reiterated recommendations must lead them to suspect, that they do not possess the merit which they really have." Also quoted in the biographical sketch of De Jorio (Kendon 2000, xlix, note 41). On De Jorio's publications, see García y García 1998, nos 3915–1925; Kendon 2000, xxxviii-li. See also p. 127, note 473.

1130 Hogg 1827, 59: "The galleries are open every day, but not so open as they ought to be; there is much locking and unlocking, and feeing servants; not that the sums expected are great, because I was taught by a Prussian, who had long resided in Naples, that copper does as well as silver on all occasions; so that you give, it matters not how much, or how little; but to make these frequent and trifling donations is an interruption of the perfect freedom essential to study." The same in Crombet 1941, 180: the museum entrance was free, but the guards' services were not.

lacked instruction about the site they were meant to look after. Some actually lived in ancient houses, or in cabins built nearby inside the site. In 1802, in the area south of the big theater, Benkovich, a German traveler, observed a garden maintained by the guards containing lettuce, broccoli, and other vegetables.[1131] Benkovich describes these guard-gardeners in such a way as to suggest that they only barely "make the cut" as *homo sapiens*, a descriptive style all too typical during this period. The British author Anna Jameson found Pompeii dull at first sight, but her enthusiasm grew rapidly thanks to an active "lazzarone boy" guide when she witnesses a sham performance in which the anonymous boy excavates an object in front of an admiring crowd of visitors. Despite her enthusiasm, she characterizes him as little more than a monkey:[1132]

> I followed him to a spot where a quantity of dust and ashes was piled against a wall. He began to scratch away this heap of dirt with hands and nails, much after the manner of an ape, every now and then looking up in my face and grinning. The impediment being cleared away, there appeared on the wall behind a most beautiful aërial figure with floating drapery, representing either Fame or Victory: but before I had time to examine it, the little rogue flung the earth up again so as to conceal it completely, then pointed significantly at the other workmen, he nodded, shrugged, gesticulated, and held out both his paws for a recompense, which I gave him willingly; at the same time laughing and shaking my head to show I understood his knavery. I rewarded him apparently beyond his hopes, for he followed me down the street, bowing, grinning, and cutting capers like a young savage.

The English traveler Anna Miller bothered little about the rules and the guardians of those rules. She wanted various inscriptions, like that of the *theatrum tectum*, copied by a member of her party.[1133] Miller also would have liked to make drawings in a house, but was not allowed to do so by the guardians. At lunch, everyone relaxed, including the local personnel, and "M-" was able to copy down an inscription. In the afternoon the greatest attention was paid to the Temple of Isis:

> I amused our guide, by walking towards some paintings, that appeared at a little distance, while M- took down this inscription in the temple. Whilst he was copying this inscription, I came to the painting in view. [...] I took a pencil out of my pocket, and began to make a rude sketch from this stag, and intended, if possible, to do the like from the perspective view;

1131 Benkowitz 1806, 34. He also notes another garden: "Er brachte jedem von uns einen Blumenstrauß, und zwar aus dem Impluvio des Hauses, wo er einen kleinen Garten angelegt hatte. Dies Verschenken der Blumen und das dafür gelöste Trinkgeld scheint sein Erwerbszweig zu seyn." See also the drawings of the Villa of Diomedes in Hamilton 1777, here p. 43, note 161.
1132 Jameson 1826, 244 and 245–246.
1133 Miller 1776, 296: "By a stratagem, M-, unseen by our guides, copied it exactly as follows: C. Ovinctius [etc.]." Following quotations in Miller 1776, 302–303, 304, 305.

but my guide, in the most pressing manner imaginable, begged me to desist: he assured me he saw some soldiers on an eminence not very distant; that should I be perceived, he must suffer for his inattention, and even I should be sharply reprimanded by government. [...] I continued my work during this harangue. [...] But to return to our poor Cicerone, he really was in the right as to the soldiers.

Apparently, these soldiers were standing on a not-yet-excavated edge of the site, not far from the temple. The text "M-" must have copied is the inscription recording the restoration of the Iseum on the expenses of Popidius Celsinus (see Chapter II, p. 143).

The British painter Jane Waldie was clearly glad about being able to walk "in perfect liberty." She argued that members of her party did not break any serious rules by picking up small pieces from the excavations to take home, or making notes and sketches.[1134] In 1842, Penry Williams, an English painter who lived in Italy for many decades, claimed that, with all the disrespect for the site of Pompeii and the local people, any attention paid by the guards to this disrespect was a necessary good for its preservation and longevity.[1135]

The French traveler L. de Sivry met one of the *invalidi*, a veteran of the Napoleonic period, which was an experience that he, as a French patriot, very much appreciated. This *invalido* had seen Murat and Napoleon "with his own eyes," and repeatedly exclaimed these venerated names. Telling De Sivry the things he knew about the Villa of Diomedes, the veteran could not refrain from recounting Murat's death.[1136] De Sivry's compatriot Gautier records in *Arria Marcella* how a

---

1134 Waldie 1820, III, 120: "To do us justice, however, with the exception of a few broken bits of marble, of little value, which we pilfered as remembrances of the place, we made no other bad use of the opportunities thus afforded, than that of breaking through a royal edict. Without an express permission from the king, no one was allowed to sketch at Pompeii; but I found my usual dispatchful style of drawing enable me to evade the regulation, and to secure such views of the place as I wished, quite as effectually as if all the crowned heads in Europe had been graciously pleased to approve of my doing so."
1135 Williams 1847, 138: "The custodes who accompany the visitors have eyes like lynxes. This is not a matter for surprise, as out of the hundreds of parties who explore these ruins, there are very few individuals indeed who do not consider frescoes, statues and mosaic pavements fair objects for plunder and spoliation. To such an extent has this been carried, that no sooner is any object of curiosity brought to light, that it is immediately placed under lock and key, and sent on the first opportunity to the museum at Naples."
1136 De Sivry 1843, 320: "invalide [...] qui, pendant tout le temps que j'employai à parcourir ces ruines vénérables, ne me parla pas d'autre chose que de Murat et de Napoléon, *qu'il avait vus de ses propres yeux* [...] Voici la maison d'Arrius Diomède, l'atrium, l'impluvium: Napoléon, Murat, Marengo! [...] Ceci est la chambre à coucher. Le lit était placé sur une estrade, au fond d'une alcove fermée par des rideaux, et le cabinet de toilette où l'on retrouva encore des fioles, des

guide forced the three friends to hire him.[1137] The New York politician Thurlow Weed was satisfied with the guides,[1138] as was the Bremen minister R. Schramm, whose guide opened every sentence with "Would you be so kind" ("Haben Sie die Gewogenheit"). This guide "even" refused a tip after the tour – presumably following the rules Fiorelli had established. Schramm's positive judgment depended on the fact that his guide came from Piedmont and not Campania, and was for that reason alone reliable and zealous. Schramm clearly used the ineradicable prejudice of the low esteem northerners had of southerners, the same opinion contradicted by Carla in *Carla degli scavi* (see above, p. 283).[1139]

A writer by the name of Lewis Engelbach had a peculiar guide in Michele, who led him around the excavations in 1802. Everything they visited, Michele claimed, was fake:[1140]

---

pafums, des essences, des flacons de toute espèce… Ils l'ont fait fusiller! Mais les braves soldats, commmandés pour faire feu, sans se donner le mot, tirèrent tous en l'air." De Sivry's real guide was Giacomo (p. 315). Thanks to all these words, De Sivry was treated satisfactorily (p. 324): "Je quittai Pompéi, l'esprit tout rempli de souvenirs romains auxquels venaient se joindre agréablement des fragments précieux de l'histoire contemporaine racontés par un témoin oculaire, à qui la nature, toujours secourable aux malheureux, avait accordé en éloquence, pour la plus grande gloire du roi Joachim Murat, et de l'empereur des Français, Napoléon le Grand, tout ce que le pauvre homme avait laissé de jambes et de bras sur les champs de bataille."
1137 Gautier 2002, 289: "[ils] prirent un guide à l'osteria bâtie en dehors des anciens remparts, ou, pour parler plus correctement, un guide les prit. Calamité qu'il est difficile de conjurer en Italie." Cf. Lowry 1961, 184: "And as a matter of fact he [Roderick] half remembered Tansy saying that you couldn't escape these clutches, you were legally bound to take a guide."
1138 Weed 1866, 531: "The King keeps intelligent guides at Pompeii for the twofold purpose of showing Visitors through the City and protecting its treasures." Weed was also allowed to excavate (Weed 1866, 529): "We were allowed to use the Pick, but not to take away any of the Spoils, though like other Visitors, we did obtain a few specimens, among which were fragments of stucco and Etruscan ware." The "Etruscan ware" would have consisted of some pottery shards.
1139 Schramm 1890, 277–278: "Er war kein Neapolitaner, sondern ein Piemontese, und diese hier im Süden recht häufige Anstellung der Norditaliener durch die Regierung erweist sich als eine vorzügliche Maßregel, einmal um tüchtige und brauchbare Beamte zu bekommen, mitten unter einer sonst ziemlich unzuverlässigen Bevölkerung, sodann aber auch zu dem andern Zweck, die verschiedenen italienischen Stämme durch einander zu würfeln und miteinander bekannt zu machen. Einstweilen ist freilich die Eifersucht und Mißgunst, der Neid und Argwohn der neuen Provinzen gegen diese piemontesischen Eidringlinge noch groß genug; wo immer man sie findet, hört man Klagen über sie, die zum Theil berechtigt sein mögen, im Ganzen aber doch meistens nur darauf hinauslaufen, daß die stramme piemontesische Art und Zucht den schlafferen Süditalienern unbequem ist."
1140 Engelbach 1815, 60. He makes a comparison with Torre del Greco, devastated various times – even recently – by Vesuvius, in contrast with Pompeii, which was struck only once. At Herculaneum the guide was unintelligible (p. 147).

The cold replies which I received to some of my expressions of admiration at the objects around us, convinced me presently that he participated but little in my gratification; but I was far from suspecting the monstrous hypothesis of which his brains were breeding all the while, and the birth of which was only retarded by the too close presence of our guide. [Michele argues:]

What I wonder at, is that a man of your sense, who has learned and seen so much, should suffer himself to be imposed upon in such a barefaced way by this artificial rubbish, reared on purpose to deceive those that in their blind antiquarian zeal can swallow the dose so artfully prepared for them. Pompeji indeed! Believe me, dear sir, none of these structures, columns, painted walls, and other antiquarian nonsense, are even of so old a date as our houses on the Infrescata, the building of which I perfectly remember. All you here behold has been fabricated (at an immense expense to be sure) by our Neapolitan government, partly out of foolish pride, but chiefly to attract travelers from all parts of Europe, and to make them spend money in the kingdom.

That was probably also true for Ventisei ("Twenty-six"), the man who, in the mid–1860s, made the American author and critic William Dean Howells conclude that Pompeii was like a book of fiction.[1141]

In the late eighteenth century, guides began enthusiastically describing stains on the marble counter of an ancient bar. There was not yet much to be shown, so the guides felt they had to entertain the travelers, and exhausted them with futilities. Round marks of wine glasses or coffee cups would have been visible on the marble counter of a bar found in the earliest excavations along the Via Consolare (p. 160, fig. 6). Such stains would prove the irreversibility of the catastrophe. It would be nice to know how and when the story came to be known by travelers and first appeared in their accounts.[1142] As in the case of the sentinel (see Chapter III, pp. 185–189), Starke was instrumental in the divulgation of the explanation of these stains:[1143]

1141 Howells 1988, 59: "Pompeii is so full of marvel and surprise, in fact, that it would be unreasonable to express disappointment with Pompeii in fiction. And yet I cannot help it. An exuberant carelessness of phrase in most writers and talkers who describe it had led me to expect much more than it was possible to find there." Cf. p. 58: "He was Roman, spoke Italian that Beatrice might have addressed to Dante, and was numbered Twenty-six." Mr. 26 is a sympathetic veteran who pops up various times in the run of this chapter.
1142 It was the *Caupona* of Perennius Nympherois or Nympheros VI 1, 2, excavated in 1770 (*PPM* IV, 1993, 1–2). The oldest mention known to me is that in Watkins 1792, 418, in a letter dated January 20, 1788: "[...] on the sill of a window stains of some such liquor as chocolate or coffee, made by the bottoms of the cups." Another mention a short time later is Anna Amalia in 1789 (Hollmer 1999, 67). He also features in Le Riche 1820, 63–64 (see note 1145).
1143 Starke 1828, 316. Italics are Starke's. Cf. Starke 1802, 105 "One of the shops (in appearance a soap-boiler's) had soap found in it – another shop evidently was a coffee house and the marks of the cups still remain upon the marble dresser." Other recordings by both English and Germans: Dwight 1824, 115; Swan 1826, 45; Friedländer 1819, II, 236; Kephalides 1822, 161 ("die eingeätzten Ringen"); Dickens 1998, 169.

> *Building on the left, commonly called a Coffee-house*; but more probably a *Thermopolium*, or *Shop, for hot medicated potions*. Here we find a Stove; and likewise a marble Dresser, with marks upon it, evidently made either by cups or glasses; and consequently the contents of these cups, or glasses, must have been (as medicated liquids frequently are) *corrosive*.

The Danish ambassador to Naples, Edmond de Bourke, saw rings of "souscoupes" in 1795 in the *thermopolium* of Perennius Nympherois, where he surely would have stopped to drink. Unfortunately, the bartender was dead and De Bourke traveled in the country of shadows.[1144] The French artist J.M. Le Riche regarded the stains as the result of a drink enriched with honey.[1145] For the poet Samuel Rogers, these stains provoked strong reactions of emotions about the living and the dead.[1146]

One of the wittiest and most hilarious accounts of guides is that in Alexandre Dumas' literary portrait of Naples, *Le corricolo* from 1841–1843.[1147] Dumas spent three weeks there in November 1835 and fostered warm feelings for the town, despite his political problems with the local government and the clandestinity of his sojourn. The essential point Dumas stresses is the flexibility of the Neapolitans, and their capability of "arranging" anything, whatever it was, and regardless of whether or not it was forbidden. According to Dumas, foreigners tended to protest immediately against the local rules, proclaiming their nordic democratic freedom. In contrast, the Neapolitan *lazzaroni* had a fine talent for securing everything tourists wanted. This meant that the lazzaroni needed to do

---

1144 De Bourke 1823, 209: "J'aurais volontiers demandé quelques refraîchements au maître de la maison; mais je voyageais, pour ainsi dire, dans le pays des ombres, où il n'y avait plus que des souvenirs." De Bourke wrote this book in 1795, but it was published postumously by his widow. He was an ambassador for Denmark in Naples (1792–1797) and later in France, and stemmed from an old Irish family. Audot (1835, 129) saw the same peculiarity in the *taberna* of Fortunata: "tasses, dont la liqueur a corrodé le marbre, ce qui ferait supposer qu'on la composait avec du miel." Caupona VI 3, 18–20, excavated in 1806 (p. 160, fig. 6). Morgan (1821, III, 108) refers to a rumor: "A modern traveller has added that the marks of the coffee cups were visible; a remark also made by our guide from whom perhaps he copied the observation."

1145 Le Riche 1820, 63–64: "[...] l'empreinte des tasses dont la liqueur, que l'on suppose faite avec du miel, a corrodé le marbre. Sur le même comptoir sont situés les petits gradins destinés à poser les tasses."

1146 Rogers in Hale 1956, 259: "[...] stain of the liquor glasses. As we looked down into the vintner's-Shop & on the jars enclosed in the counter cased with various bits of Marble, I thought I saw the man serving his customers – and as the shadows of the evening came on, & standing alone, I looked up the street of tombs toward the city-gate, the strange silence & deserted air of the place almost overcame me." Rogers was at Pompeii on March 1, 1815 and repeats the observation during visits on March 3 and 15 (pp. 260 and 267). As to his feelings, on March 6 (p. 264), he felt here "a melancholy to be found nowhere else."

1147 Dumas 2001, 101–106. For more on Dumas, see Chapter I, p. 74.

things on the behalf of tourists that were severely prohibited, such as gossiping about the King, copying paintings, or stealing statues. Money was important, but nothing compared to the help of the local *lazzaroni*.[1148] Dumas obviously exaggerates the stupidity of both the local people and the tourists – English only! – as well as the severity of the rules. He presents examples of a typical British tourist's improper behavior and failure to understand, and the equally typical witty reactions and practical solutions to problems offered by a Neapolitan guide.

Because they feared punishment by the local authorities, local guides were unable to give in to the often-ludicrous demands of tourists, but this didn't stop them from suggesting that (especially British tourists) take guides who were unable to take responsibility due to specific handicaps. Dumas' own experience with the police might have been the starting point for the series of suggestions which he might have heard from various Neapolitan ciceroni. A Brit whose goal it was to curse against the King of Naples and his entourage, was told to be prudent and remain silent, or take a deaf guide who cannot betray him to the secret police. The English visitor who wanted to make sketches in the excavations was advised to take a blind *invalido*. And since no one was able to buy genuine finds as souvenirs from the excavations, it was recommended that visitors simply steal something, and take an invalid guardian ("un invalide boiteux") who was unable to run after the fleeing thief. In the end, it comes out in the story that the ideal guide was both deaf and blind. To increase the chapter's humorous effect, Dumas "copies" the dialogues between the British tourists and Neapolitan guides in a curious French-gibberish mix.

As described in Chapter I, in the 1860s, Fiorelli implemented new rules for guides, which were met with approval from visitors. Jan Willem Staats Evers, a Dutch lawyer and politician who had visited Pompeii in 1840, and again after these new regulations on guards and guides, compared the new situation with the old one, and concludes:[1149]

> The city now is both surrounded and guarded by an excellent corps of gendarmes who, as it were, are on the heels of every stranger so that damaging or stealing treasures now has become impossible. Thirty two well disciplined guides are at the disposition of the traveler. Near Pompei itself a museum and a library have been erected and hundreds of workmen

---

1148 Dumas 2001, 102: "L'Anglais avait fait les trois choses les plus expressément défendues à Naples: il avait dit du mal du roi, il avait copié des fresques, il avait volé une statue, et tout cela, non pas grâce à son argent, son argent ne lui servi de rien pour ces trois choses, mais grâce à l'imaginative d'un lazzarone."
1149 Staats Evers 1872, 105–106.

are usually working in the excavations during the winter.[1150] These digs are now finished for approximately a third of Pompeii's area, but there is reason to suppose that the most important zone of the town, with the forum, temples, amphitheaters, theaters and many public offices, have now been unearthed.

Guides in Literary Fiction

Some of the examples of guides and guards discussed in the previous paragraphs were surely fictitious personages who were created to enliven the memoirs of the travelers. Straight fiction also includes examples of the fascination writers had for these persons.

In *Le fou du Vésuve* by Alexandre de Lamothe, the unnamed storyteller's wish to visit Pompeii is answered by his host with the recommendation of signor Carlo, who, the host says, will be a better guide than Fiorelli himself would have been.[1151] One topic of their lively conversation is ancient window glass. Carlo refers to a past client of his, a learned German who, so he told, had written a thick book on the non-existence of windowpanes in Pompeii, and who reacted, upon seeing an ancient windowpane, by exclaiming: "Das ist eine Einrede" ("that's a contradictory proof").[1152] In the "morgue of Pompeii," a room with skeletal remains, Carlo explains that two particular victims of interest were found near the Villa of Diomedes. This leads Carlo to begin to tell his story, which continues during a long stroll through the ruins. Carlo claims that he used to be called Minucius Félix, and was a friend of the Villa of Diomedes victims, some of whom were Christian slaves. These slaves stimulated him to study their ideas, but he never shared their beliefs because of their miserably low status as slaves.[1153] Although the storyteller pays attention to Carlo's (Minucius') words during their long walk, Carlo finishes his story rather abruptly by stating that he does not belong to this world any longer, and wants to return "home" to ancient Pompeii. Finally, the storyteller notes that he never saw him again during the remainder of his stay at and around

---

1150 Cf. Fiorelli 1873, 9 (here Chapter I, pp. 74–81).
1151 De Lamothe 1881. This is the first and longest (138 pp.) of a series of novellas and short stories in a volume bearing this title. García y García 1998, no. 7685.
1152 De Lamothe 1881, 20. The presence of glass was discussed from the first years onwards. See examples of window panes from Pompeii in many exhibition catalogs, e.g. Meller/Dickmann 2011.
1153 De Lamothe 1881, 127: "J'avoue qu'à partir de ce moment la religion du Nazaréen commença à me paraître digne de respect, et peut-être aurais-je songé à l'étudier si l'idée de devenir le frère de misérables esclaves ne m'eût pas retenu."

Pompeii, but assures the reader that he will never forget Carlo.[1154] That Carlo was said to be a better guide than Fiorelli might be explained by the fact that he is a genuine ancient Pompeian inhabitant. Yet, Fiorelli remained the most important and ideal guide.

Modern people meeting ancient inhabitants in their dreams or during a walk is a common occurrence in Pompeii fiction, but the guide – Carlo – who tells his own history is one of a kind, as far as I know. Carlo misses his past life in lucky and prosperous Pompeii, including his talks with the Christians. As in most nineteenth-century novels, ancient Pompeians, with the exception of Christian slaves, belong to the highest social levels of society. In his role as a guide in the modern Pompeians ruins, Carlo yearns for the socio-cultural status that Minucius, his previous self, enjoyed in ancient Pompeii. Therefore, Carlo is a tragic figure who is comfortable neither in the past nor in the present and who feels like he has failed by not adhering to Christianity in his former life. The novella demonstrates De Lamothe's good knowledge of the monuments, and he aptly adopts tropes used in fiction, such as the Diomedes family, graffiti, and Christians in the amphitheater, who are "saved" at the very end by the eruption of Vesuvius. The name Minucius Félix, corresponds with that of an early Christian author, who in the second or third century A.D. wrote the dialogue *Octavius*, in which a pagan and a Christian Roman discuss Christianity. De Lamothe's book is a sort of new version of this *Octavius*, and uses Pompeii as an ideal backdrop for the creation of a Roman atmosphere.

Malcolm Lowry, the author of the famous *Under the Volcano*, wrote a relatively unknown short story called *Present Estate of Pompeii*, which plays out at Pompeii some years after World War II.[1155] He created it in 1948 after a trip through Italy with his wife. It describes the touristic stroll of Roderick McGregor Fairhaven and his wife Tansy, a Canadian couple from Eridanus, British Columbia

---

1154 De Lamothe 1881, 138: "– Partons, dit-il brusquement: ma place n'est plus ici, le bonheur n'y habite plus pour moi; rentrons dans notre prison.
Un instant après, installés dans la voiture qui par son ordre était venue nous attendre en cet endroit, nous roulions de nouveau sur la route poudreuse de Naples.
Dans le trajet, il ne m'adressa pas trois paroles et me quitta sans vouloir écouter mes remerciements.
Je ne l'ai pas revu depuis, mais je ne l'oublierai jamais." The remark about the absence of luck alludes to the inscription found in the House of Pansa: *Hic habitat felicitas*. Cf. Chapter II, p. 127.
1155 Lowry 1961, 175–200. There are few discussions about this short story: Leppmann 1966, 207, 235–238; Rothemann 1996, 74–75, 82–83; Bowker 1995, 509–511. Maybe it is not superfluous to say that Lowry's masterpiece *Under the Volcano* does *not* deal with Pompeii, but is situated in Mexico, since it is listed in García y García 1998, no. 8175; Lowry 1961 is no. 8176. I cannot but offer my recommendation to read this dense and beautiful text, rather than many other texts herein discussed.

with their guide, Signor Salacci. The couple has lunch in a small restaurant called "Vesuvius" near the Circumvesuviana railway station. Consulting her guide book, Tansy concludes that they only have time for a short tour.[1156] The visit prompts Roderick to reflect on ruins and the decay of humanity, and he compares Pompeii to the ruins of Liverpool. Salacci equates Pompeii with St. Malo, Rotterdam, and Naples, all also destroyed during the war, and mentions the bombs dropped on Pompeii itself. The great difference, Roderick thinks, is that society preserves the ruins of Pompeii, but throws away the debris of the other cities.[1157] Salacci twice asserts that he is a Pompeian.[1158] The city was purportedly destroyed by God "for its wickedness."[1159] Because Salacci dresses like an old-fashioned businessman, he reminds Roderick of his older brother.[1160]

> And there was no doubt about it, Roderick thought again, this town, that both was and was not there, was obviously very real and complete to the excellent Signor Salacci: he saw it all.

In the House of the Vettii, Salacci begins concentrating his explanations to the couple on the topic of love in Pompeii, albeit – in nearly all cases – paid "love," without which, he says, life decays rapidly. The painted Priapus in the *vestibulum* is invisible behind shutters, and erotic paintings in the room next to the kitchen are locked behind a door, but Salacci has a key and shows the paintings to his clients. The Priapus is "a Cyrano engaged in weighing, it seemed at first sight, upon a sort of Safeway scale, his nose, which emitted curious carmine sparkles."[1161] According to the guide, the brothel represents real life.[1162] Roderick begins to

---

[1156] Lowry 1961, 183 might quote an existing guide: "The ruins are open to visitors daily, free of charge, from nine to seventeen o'clock. At the entrance, and even at the station, Italian, French, German and English-speaking guides (tariff!) press their services on the tourists. [...] The time required for a conducted tour is from one and a half to two hours, but to view the place properly, four or five hours are necessary. Visitors are not allowed to take food in with them."
[1157] Lowry 1961, 187, 188, 193, 199. On those bombs, see García y García 2006 and Chapter I, p. 88. Lowry had been impressed by the ruins seen at Rotterdam (Bowker 1995, 432). The comparison between Naples and Pompeii is also used by Curzio Malaparte in *La pelle* from 1949. Roblès 1986, 61 describes a visit shortly after the bombardment of a couple in love; the atmosphere at Pompei is described as depressing.
[1158] Lowry 1961, 185, 200.
[1159] Lowry 1961, 185.
[1160] Lowry 1961, 187.
[1161] Lowry 1961, 190. The pun hits on the *phallus* similar to or identical with Cyrano de Bergerac's enormous nose. Apparently Lowry sees a similar figure in the painted Priapus. "Safeway" is a grocery chain in the United States and Canada.
[1162] Lowry 1961, 191: "There are, unless you happened to be Toulouse-Lautrec, few things in life less profitable than going to a brothel, unless, Roderick reflected, it was going to a ruined brothel."

feel a budding hatred for Pompeii, for all the wrong things have been preserved! And even more so, since Salacci merely shows his clients what he enjoys (and what he wrongly assumes will lead to bigger tips) – out-of-use brothels, shops, and bakeries. Roderick gets obsessed with the notion of "decay" and remembers a night walk in which he reflected upon the ideas of Volney and Toynbee about the matter. Hence his thought:[1163]

> Well, St Malo was wiped out, Naples defaced, but a cock in the street outside an antique Pompeian brothel still survived. Well, why not?

Finally Roderick understands his own irritation: he is "the visitor from Ultima Thule," and gets "a feeling that there was not going to be time" to really understand the ruins of Pompeii. In contrast to those made during World War II, Pompeii was not a "man-made ruin."[1164] He thinks that he has come to Pompeii too late, but, despite his hatred for Salacci's absurd knack for dwelling on such banalities, feels that this visit is important to him.

Eridanus, which returns in other short stories in Lowry's book, may be associated with the underworld river mentioned by Virgil in *Aeneid* 6.659: *plurimus Eridani per silvam voluitur amnis* ("the stream of Eridanus is twisting through the wood in all his strength").[1165] Since Lowry's prose is always learned and full of open and hidden references to great literary works from antiquity onwards, this correspondence is not without meaning.[1166] Eridanus forms part of the Hades visited by Aeneas during his descent to hell, his *katabasis*. Lowry's insertion of a modern and an ancient Eridanus also serves as a reference to modern and ancient Pompeii, another omnipresent duality. What transforms the Fairhavens' tour into a descent to hell is their fear of the ruins and their guide's behavior. Salacci, with his swindler's traits, represents a sort of Hermes-Mercury character who is only concerned with money. The great difference, of course, between that and the

---

1163 Lowry 1961, 194 and 195 (quotation). He partly cites the title of Volney 1791: *Les Ruines ou Méditations sur les révolutions des empires*, written during the bloodthirsty days of French Revolution (briefly also mentioned in Rothemann 1996, 83). He also refers to Arnold Toynbee (1948). From both books quotations are inserted, dealing with the destruction of the wrong things.
1164 Lowry 1961, 199. Levi (1984) makes the same distinction in "La fanciulla di Pompei"; see above p. 288.
1165 See M. Scarsi, Eridano, *Enciclopedia Virgiliana* II (1985) 365; A. Setaioli, Inferi, loci, *ibidem*, 953–963, esp. p. 955. Eridanus – otherwise known as the name of the Rhône and the Po – is a frequent topic in Lowry's work. It is even applied (as a name) to his house on the west coast of Canada in a short story also with this title (see Bowker 1997, 305–306, 417, *passim*). Fairhaven is a really telling name in combination with the Eridanus references.
1166 Moreover, Virgil is mentioned writing the *Aeneid* (Lowry 1961, 188).

manmade hell in World War II is that Pompeii's hell was a creation of natural forces. Manmade ruins can be swept away, but Pompeii cannot. Consequently, Salacci becomes a *Hermes psychopompos*. All his observations on life relate to deceased Pompeians. He explains the labyrinth-like structure of the town, especially the curved street where the brothel is located, which tempts an image of the Underworld.[1167] Finally, one may ask whether "present estate" in the title – actual property – refers to Salacci and his appropriation of Pompeii. Lowry's story is a most impressive evocation of Pompeii as the city of the dead. His protagonists truly feel as if they are being drawn into hell and becoming part of the city of the dead. Lowry makes fine use of mythical symbols from classical sources, and mixes banal notions with learned ones, but this learnedness does not burden the story; rather, it refines it. Archaeology is only relevant in that the author singles out monuments that underline his ideal about the hell and the past. The Fairhavens' visit is both ordinary and peculiar at the same time. Tansy and Roderick are impressed with what they see at Pompeii, but they are irritated by the way Salacci introduces them to it. Although their experience is on one level exactly like the hundreds of thousands of visitors who feel obliged to follow their guides blindly, but feel like plunging into the past more thoroughly.

Roger Peyrefitte visited southern Italy around the same time as Lowry, and published an anthology of impressions in *Du Vésuve à l'Etna*. The sketch "Le gardien de Pompéi"[1168] contains quite a humorous monologue in which a guide voices his distaste for visitors who want more than a short and stereotypical tour of Pompeii. Peyrefitte listens to this grumbling guide, and reluctantly acknowledges that indeed, he, other writers, scientists and journalists do often ask for more than the average hour. Some thoughts – surely those of the author himself – but also of certain intelligent guides, are worth mentioning here. The anonymous guide is proud of his profession; unlike museum guides watching over lifeless objects displayed behind glass, he brings to life living rooms, barber shops, bars, soap makers, and brothels.[1169] He claims that shop keepers and citizens – and not only

---

1167 Lowry 1961, 195. The guide makes a pun with curva, curved street and – according to him – "lost woman" (p. 198). I could find no evidence for this pun. The late Marcello Gigante from Naples and Camillo Neri from Bologna confirmed my doubt orally during a stay at Vandoeuvres, Fondation Hardt (June 2001). Neri said that in Serban curva has this meaning. Did Lowry know that and confuse the two words? For the topography of the underworld cf. the lemma by Setaioli cited in note 1165.
1168 Peyrefitte 1976, 158–168 (chapter XII). Briefly mentioned by Leppmann 1966, 143, 233 as an example of "gehobene Belletristik".
1169 Peyrefitte 1976, 160: "Ce qui nous distingue des simples gardiens de musée, c'est justement que nous gardons autre chose que des objets d'art. Nous ne sommes pas voués à contempler éternellement des salons; nous pouvons nous délasser chez le barbier, chez le cabaretier, chez le

wealthy families – had nice paintings on their walls. Art and pleasure were accessible to every inhabitant.[1170] The American bombardments of 1943 brought ruin to ruins. Fortunately, the guide says, we now see a town resurrected for the second time.[1171] According to him, Pompeii is a place where politics do not apply, arguing that he has received soldiers from many nations – including Nazis, fascists and Allies, and not to mention Hindus and drunk Americans – who were all equally interested in seeing the miracles of Pompeii.[1172] Since touring the brothel on Vicolo del Lupanare brings tips to guides, Peyrefitte's guide includes it on his tour of the ruins. Still, Peyrefitte writes, the modern town has received the Madonna di Pompei as a moral compensation for the sins of its ancient forerunner.[1173]

Conclusion

Many works of fiction and travelogues use Pompeii as a locale for stories about foreigners vising the ancient monuments. Local people are rarely represented in these works, unless they are guides or guards, and Italians from other parts of the country appear only in books written by Italians. Among these visitors are tourists, artists, and archaeologists, who all experience an event from their unique perspective. Most of these stories play out in summer, when the sun and lizards create a lazy and dreamy atmosphere. A striking element featuring in various stories presented in this chapter is the nighttime encounter of modern visitors with ancient Pompeians or people who suggest that they had ancestors in the

---

savetier, et il y a toujours, au coin d'une rue, le symbole revigorant que nous indique le chemin du lupanar. Tout cela nous attache à ces pierres et nous les fait aimer."
1170 Peyrefitte 1976, 166: "Ce qui fait aimer Pompéi, c'est que ce luxe et ce goût n'y aient pas été le privilège des riches. Vous avez vu, dans de simples boutiques, des peintures aussi exquises que celles des plus grandes demeures. Voilà, je crois, ce qui caractérisait la vie antique: l'art y était à la portée de tous, comme le plaisir."
1171 Peyrefitte 1976, 161–162: "Au cours de la guerre, des renseignements erronés avaient fait croire que les Allemands truffaient de munitions des ruines de Pompéi. Elles furent, pendant trois jours, le point de mire de l'aviation américaine: cent soixante-deux bombes ajoutèrent des ruines aux ruines, sans faire toutefois des dégâts irréparables aux édifices principaux. Mais c'est miracle que vous puissiez encore visiter Pompéi! [...] Bref, Pompéi a ressuscité, une fois de plus. Elle a survécu à la pluie de feu, comme elle avait survécu à la pluie des cendres."
1172 Peyrefitte 1976, 163–164: "Nous sommes en dehors de la politique et des régimes: nous avons vu avec indifférence les soldats allemands venir saluer les croix gammées des mosaïques, et les miliciens fascistes venir saluer le temple du génie d'Auguste. Nous avons conduit au lupanar des bataillons de nègres, apaisé les rixes entre Anglais et Hindous, fait arrêter des Américains ivres qui volaient des squelettes."
1173 Peyrefitte 1976, 167.

ancient city. Tourists made nocturnal visits to Pompeii in the nineteenth century, hoping to catch some of the spell that had this town in its grip. As in fairy tales, the night seemed to turn dreams into reality, and at night, ancient and modern people apparently were interchangeable (and did in fact switch places), did unusual things, and took greater risks.

In contrast, stories tend to be more realistic when they take place by daylight. A science fiction novel or a thriller, for instance, has no need for the night, but the past is still important, since Pompeii forms a historical backdrop.

The eruption of A.D. 79 often serves as a comparison for a great disaster like the twentieth-century World Wars, and invites people to reflect on the possibility of improving their own situation (or not), using the debris of Pompeii as the negative extreme with which to compare. The ruins become a construct of a living atmosphere of ancient people devastated by nature rather than by human forces. At the same time, ancient Pompeii is often considered a peaceful society modern people would have loved to see.

Contrasts between South and North also come to the fore in various works. Hyperborean visitors penetrate the allegedly simple and happy realm of the Mediterranean world, but also experience the corruption and rottenness clearly visible in the ruins of the once decadent ancient towns. The spells that Pompeii and Herculaneum cast on Northern visitors, therefore, can be dangerous, and infect them with the Mediterranean culture's vices.

For many guests, the play with the past is Freudian in nature. With or without psychoanalysis, thanks to coming into contact with ancient Pompeii and its inhabitants, these visitors discover hidden feelings in themselves. Pompeii, consequently, is no innocent locus; long after its destruction it still exerts a spell on modern man. Corinne, Zoe, and Elskée redefine their relationships of love, and children encounter people who exert both positive and negative influences on them. In the shape of a fable, dogs appear in the mirror when men gaze into it. When we read all of these works, we might as well conclude as Primo Levi did: "stop and consider."

The guides highlighted in the last section convey either general knowledge, clichéd information, or their own creative ideas concerning the ancient town. Some have internalized the history they tell their clients so strongly that they actually become ancient Pompeians, or bring the visitors directly into ancient city life, and even, at least in Salacci's case, as a *Hermes psychopompos*. The power of the guides, some authors would argue, ought not to be underrated. Guides can not only brainwash their clients, but transport them to truly dangerous places.

VI Time Traveling to Ancient Pompeii

To get from the present to a time or place in the future or the past, one needs to use a time machine. Pompeii, with its appeal as a once-living city slumbering under the ashes, is an attractive destination for such an exercise. Indeed, literary attempts to reach Pompeii's ancient inhabitants are plentiful and encompass over one hundred fifty years of writing. Pompeii prompts writers to create such imaginative and seemingly impossible travel, because time traveling enables the travelers to meet the city's ancient inhabitants, who are still present in the ruins either by virtue of their corporeal remains or their names scribbled on walls. Stories of this kind testify to the profound desire – not only of the authors, but of scholars who work with the archaeological evidence – to know the ancient Pompeian people better. Although we have already seen some examples of time traveling in Chapter III, I have collected most of these cases in this separate chapter in order to give them a place of their own.

In *A World Full of Gods*, Keith Hopkins' book on the rise of Christianity that was published briefly before his untimely death, Hopkins, an economic historian, discusses various hypotheses of why Christianity became so successful in as time passed. The approach is both scientific and fantastic, both serious and funny – a mixture of which not every scholar approves.[1174] At the beginning of his book, the storyteller (Hopkins?) publishes an announcement asking people to go to ancient Pompeii to look for possible Christian evidence. Martha and James, a typical lower class British couple, are sent down as volunteers to visit Pompeii, Ephesus, and Egypt.[1175] By means of an implant they can communicate with ancient people easily. In Pompeii, they observe a strong presence of phalli and other sexual devices, but find no Christians.

Although Hopkins is not the only twentieth-century author to jump into the past, this genre is most prevalent in nineteenth century writing. In some travelogues we observe suggestions of close contact with ancient inhabitants of Pompeii in the form of brief dream-like descriptions. James Skene, a Scottish traveler, antiquarian, and friend of Sir Walter Scott, wrote in 1803 that he had a vision of standing face to face with the dead citizens.[1176] This feeling incited authors to

---

[1174] Hopkins 1999. In his review, Glenn W. Bowersock (*Journal of Roman Archaeology* 13, 2000, 763–766) offers his very negative opinion. On p. 765 he tackles the notes, which he calls "seriously apotropaic" – which may be true for many of my footnotes as well.

[1175] Martha is also the name of alleged Christian girls in Pompeii, see Chapter IV, p. 235.

[1176] Skene 1937, 214: "I feel now as if I had been conversing all day long *tête-à-tête* with an ancient Roman on the particulars of their domestic economy, for Pompeii is so much uncovered that the rubbish is perfectly cleared away from the pavement of the streets, the houses are swept,

personalize victims. William Stamer, for example, presented "well-known" Pompeians like the aedile Pansa, Sallustius, M. Holconius Priscus – the builder of the theater – and also met the participants of a Roman funeral in the Street of Tombs. Stamer knew, of course, that these people were dead, yet he beckoned them to come to the present:[1177]

> Augustals of Pompeii! – my lords spiritual and temporal. Decurions! – the honorable members of our Lower House. In the manner of your election, in the supernal wisdom of your debates, in the cleverness you display in finding out how not to do it, you are birds of a feather.
> [...] Priest of the different temples! – the clergy of the Holy Catholic Church, who, in default of sacrificial meats, sell indulgences and anything and everything for which a purchaser can be found.

As demonstrated in the previous chapters, the fictitious Pompeians, like Stamer's, often are recreations of people known from local evidence. These data – especially bones and gypsum casts (p. 314, fig. 13) – play a paramount role in the works discussed in the following. As in other instances, Stamer used Pompeii as a screen on which situations and projections of the Present could be projected.

Chatting on Mamia's Bench

Cyprian Norwid lived most of his life in exile, having left Poland in 1842. In Italy he took residence in Florence to study sculpture and made trips to all the important Italian towns. He wrote *Pompeja*, his 175 line poem, in 1849 after a visit to the site in 1848.[1178] The interrupting punctuation and lacunae suggest that the poem is a mock papyrus (cf. Chapter VII). A visitor sits outside the Herculanean Gate on the *schola*, a semicircular bench made in honor of the priestess Mamia (p. 154, fig. 5). He reflects on the tombs nearby and notices the presence of an agreable old gentle-

---

the walls still painted, in short, one can walk about as in a deserted town." García y García 1998, no. 12.497. Although he was British, Skene was able to travel to Italy during this time thanks to the Peace of Amiens.
1177 Stamer 1878, 179, 205.
1178 It would be published in 1863 at Leipzig. Text in Norwid 1968, 17–25; commentary on pp. 408–410; with French translation in Norwid 1974, 29–41. I got the latter version with the friendly help of Esselien 't Hart. This English translation is by Paul Hulsenboom MPhil, a former student of mine. Norwid's motto is from the Old Testament, *Ecclesiastes* 1.13 (English Standard Version): "And I applied my heart to seek and to search out by wisdom all that is done under heaven." García y García 1998, no. 9915 also gives other editions. See on Norwid (esp. in Florence) Woś 2006, 68–70, fig. 19; Kalinowka 2011, 547–562.

man next to him: Balbus, consul of Pompeii "in long-distant times". He presents himself as a man suffering from the sad history of his fatherland:[1179]

> I was curious – I carefully observed the old man,
> Comparing his profile to the well-known busts of famous men,
> I was thinking of asking him, but as I wanted to do so I shivered;
> – There is a shiver however, which arouses boldness,
> So, as I was plucking my leaf, I said: "My lord, I
> Would be pleased to know with whom I have the
> pleasure of exchanging words and of sitting here."
> To which he replied: "People called me the consul of the city,
> Their master; if you will, a king, so to speak,
> For I do not know how that position is nowadays called;
> But my name is Balbus – now, my guest, be so kind
> As to return the favor..." So I answered: "Shadow,
> It will suffice for me to tell you that I am of a people
> Not unacquainted with the lives of shades... which
> slumbers... which is nameless – and that I have
> therefore since my youth accustomed myself to a
> Way of living which will not bother you...
> Besides, what more should I tell about myself,
> now that you know this?!"

The two chat until the arrival of a young Greek poet crowned with a laurel wreath. He lives in a house now visited by travelers – based on the circumstantial evidence of its description, that of the Tragic Poet – and tells them about the town from the perspective of a relative outsider, being Greek. Balbus describes his job and about strolls through Pompeii accompanied by lictors, the official guards of magistrates. The reader gets a portrait of the Greek (cultural) and Roman (practical) sides of Pompeian life.[1180] This illusive encounter is interrupted by the arrival of the storyteller's guide, who suggests that they continue the visit of the excavations. Norwid

---

1179 Lines 57–71: "Ciekawy byłem – dobrze starca uważałem, / Mierząc profil z znanymi biusty wielkich ludzi, / Myśliłem spytać, ale spytać chcąc zadrżałem; / – Że jest jednakże drżenie, co odwagę budzi, / Więc, skubiąc liść mój: 'Panie – rzekłem – rad bym wiedzieć, / Z kim szczęście mam zamieniać słowo i tu siedzieć?' / A on mi na to: 'Zwano mię miasta konsulem, / Przełożonym; jeżeli chcesz, to niby królem, / Bo nie wiem, jak się godność ta dzisiaj tłumaczy; / Imię zaś moje Balbus – również gość niech raczy / Zamienić to zwierzenie...' Więc ja rzekłem: 'Cieniu, / Dosyć będzie, gdy-ć powiem, że jestem z narodu, / Któremu żywot cieniów... w pół-śnie... w bez-imieniu / Nieobcym jest – że przeto nawykłem od młodu / Sposobu-bycia, który nie zaciąży tobie... / To zaś wiedząc, cóż mówić zresztą o osobie?!'" Translation Paul Hulsenboom.
1180 Norwid evidently subscribes to the rather standard notion that Greece stands for "culture" and Rome for all things "practical." Pompeii exhibits aspects of both sides. See Chapter II, pp. 71–74 for the discussion of Pompeii as a "Greek" city.

creates a highly melancholic atmosphere, with gentle people from a timeless past who reappear in the present as "spectres." The poet may have read Bulwer-Lytton's *Last Days of Pompeii*, since he singles out the residence of Glaucus. It is not entirely clear whether the "I" of the poem himself trespasses time or not; if not, Balbus and his friend have come alive in a new reality in some version of the present.

I do not know whether Norwid knew Friederike Brun's poem *Pompeji*, which contains an invitation to meet the people entombed along the Street of Tombs. Sitting in the same *schola*, the poetess feels as if the priestess personally calls her to join the peace of the deceased. The *schola* actually addresses the visitors as a speaking person in the second part, and in the last lines the dead Pompeians, the "voice of the shade," entombed in the funerary monuments, warns them that they too might suffer from a lethal disaster. *Pompeji* evokes the impression of houses still inhabited.[1181]

A similar poetic incantation is *The House of the Tragic Poet*, a short story in the shape of eleven poems by the Czech poet Vladimír Janovic, in which Aeschylus, the fifth century Greek tragic poet, rises from death in Pompeii as the Tragic Poet of the famous Pompeian mosaic.[1182] In ancient Pompeii, the *chorodidascalus* rehearses Sophocles' satyr play *Ichneutai* ("Trackers") with six untalented actors. When the storyteller visits the House of the Tragic Poet with his guide Atanasio, he does not know who the last Pompeian owner was, whereas Aeschylus' younger colleague Sophocles is still famous thanks to his tragedies:[1183]

1181 *Der Neue Teutsche Merkur* 2 (July 1810) 149–151: "Flüstern Schatten um mich? Wer trat die Spuren im Steine? / Wo die Wägen, die tief höhlten das sinkende Gleis? / Wo die Pfleger des Heerds, des heiligen Heerds der Penaten? / Freundliches Salve wo ist, der dich dem Fremdling entbot? / Seht das Triclinium hier, es ladet zum gastlichen Schmause, / Hat erst das kühlende Bad schmachtende Glieder erfrischt. / Näher säuselt's mich an, wie schwirrender Flug der Cikaden / Weht's um die Wangen mir her, klagend mit zirpendem Laut: >Unstet schweben wir hier um halbgesprengete Grüfte / >Doppelt verlieh sie Natur, Neugier verschonte sie nicht. / >Sängerin wölb' uns ein Grab an der Ostsee grünenden Küsten; / >Friedlich schlummern wir dort, Schatten begehren nur Ruh.< / *** / Das Grab der Priesterin Mammia mit der Exedra vor dem Thore von Pompejo. / Müde Fremdling', o Mammia, ladest du freundlich zur Ruhe, / So wie du selber auch ruhst dort in gewölbeter Gruft. / Durch Jahrtausende dringt die sanfte Stimme der Wehmuth; / Dankend weilen wir hier, opfernd den lauteren Trank. / Stimme des Schattens. / >Frevelnde Händ' entheben der Mammia heilige Urne, / >Ach, dieß doppelte Grab schütze die Schlummernde nicht! / >Unser Gebein ist verstreut, Unheilige schaut den Titanen! / >Wißt, der in Asch' uns begrub, heget noch Gluthen für Euch!<" See Fitzon 2002a, 495 notes 5–6, who also quotes other texts, and Fitzon 2012, 137–141. Not in García y García 1998. I thank Thorsten Fitzon for a copy of the poem. Its form clearly imitates Schiller's famous *Pompeji und Heculaneum*, and will return in Gregorovius' *Euphorion* (here pp. 176, 205–207). On Brun and Italy, see Müller 2012, 258–263.
1182 Janovic 1988 (translation from the Czech by Ewald Osers). Not in García y García 1998.
1183 Janovic 1988, 16.

The last owner of the house was a merchant
More of a practical poet. Why tragic indeed?
(To both sides of the door are shops)
He loved pictures – frescoes and mosaics
That's all we know of him
And it isn't important
Salve lucrum!
The tragic poet on the other hand
is immortal

The storyteller calls Aeschylus back to life and Aeschylus asks:[1184]

Tell me, why do you bring me back to life? –
The question hits its mark
– If I knew the answer
I wouldn't be writing a poem
But I tell you this much:
Ever since I was a child
monsters the shape of mushrooms have been rising
from our seas
Compared with them the friendly polychrome
of your smoking Vesuvius
(I know it from the brightly-coloured postcards
of Vincenzo Carcavalla)
is a harmless trifle
In similar volcanoes
we now build our thermal pools
hotels casinos bars –
The tragic poet was alarmed:
– You are blaspheming like that priest in Greece
who scoffed at the
Eulysian mysteries –[1185]
I flared up then: – What about you?
You blaspheme even in your choice of word
when to a mixing bowl for wine and water
a vessel used in banqueting
you have given the name of *crater*
Is that not asking for catastrophe?

1184 Janovic 1988, 28.
1185 Apparently "Eleusinian," i.e. from the Demeter mysteries at Eleusis near Athens (modern day Elefsina), is meant.

In a later encounter they discuss eternity. Aeschylus warns of the forces of Vesuvius and finds the narrator too light-hearted.[1186] After some digressions[1187] the poet returns to Aeschylus: his actors nowadays are youngsters with *motorini* in the streets of modern Pompeii, no longer interested in ancient drama:[1188]

> – My dear old poet
> who was so confident that humans
> could overcome their raving fury
> don't you understand people any more?
> I'm coming from a floodlit Pompeii
> where your Valenses race motorbikes
> and your Licinuses hang about juke boxes in bars
> Believe me Aeschylus each of them would rather
> go to a wild party at Paquius's house
> than to rehearsal with you
> Will you condemn them for this?

Nevertheless, poetry will remain while other things fall to pieces. After leaving, the narrator asks himself: is it possible that the old tourist guide Atanasio he met before in the excavation is a reincarnation of Aeschylus?

Thanks to sufficient archaeological details, this poem betrays Janovic's fine familiarity with the site. Janovic is sorry to see Pompeii's destruction, but, as we see in the quoted passage on the eruption and the photographic illustrations, he maintains a positive outlook concerning the attractiveness and importance of the archaeological site for future generations.

1186 Janovic 1988, 42: "Aeschylus angrily broke out / a pebble from a ruined wall: / – Just look ... *opus incertum* / and yet it holds for centuries / Everything here's uncertain / When you must call for help / you'll cry even in an empty forest / Surely you too are longing for a poem / in which innocent victims would /give real pain to the living –"
1187 Janovic 1988, 43–62, nos VII and VIII. In no. VII, Janovic introduces Numerius Popidius Celsinus, the restorer of the Temple of Isis (see Chapter II, p. 143), now a man of 23 years. Others are Gaius Cuspius Pansa, the aedile who inspects the quality of the water in the baths, Vedius Siricus, Epidius Rufus (brick seller), and Marcus Holconius Priscus. All are devoted to Venus (p. 50), as Paquius says, making a gross pun to the Christian eucharisty: "Brothers let this spread table / be an altar for us / and this dinner a dinner for Our Lady / No splinter from the cross of Golgotha / courses in *our* blood / Food is food and wine is wine / We receive the body in the body." In poem VIII Marcus Spurius Mesor is visited by the usurer Lucius Caecilius Iucundus, wittily described after the bronze portrait in his house with "the raders of the old man's bat-like ears" and "the cone-shaped pimple/on the banker's left cheek" (pp. 60, 62).
1188 Janovic 1988, 65.

Love for Deceased Girls

In 1852, Théophile Gautier set a trend of prose stories about time traveling to Pompeii with his delicious novella *Arria Marcella*.[1189] Gautier visited Naples in 1850, and was expelled by police on November 8 on charges of being a socialist writer.[1190] That experience did not impair his appreciation for Pompeii, which was, in his eyes, an exemplary pagan society free of Christian moralism. The excavation offered an excellent *mise-en-scène* for reflections on the contact between modern man and the past in the form of reincarnation or *metempsychosis*, a theme that returns in other works by Gautier and contemporary authors (fig. 13).[1191]

In *Arria Marcella*, the young French traveler Octavien[1192] is spellbound by the shape of a female breast exposed in the museum in Naples. Covered by fine fabric impressed in volcanic material, it is a symbol of disaster and the veil of lost beauty; the breast, Octavien concludes, must have belonged to a charming young woman.[1193] As we have seen in Chapter III, Octavien is not the only literary traveler who has stood still in the Villa of Diomedes and fantasized about a woman whose remains are captive in the Vesuvian waste. Octavien's contemplation becomes a sort of fetishism like that of the man who is obsessed by the foot of a mummy in Gautier's *Le pied de momie* (see note 1191). According to Gautier, Pompeii displays its paganism with every column, is not distant from modern life and Christianity, and exudes a strange atmosphere.[1194] Octavien meets Rufus Holconius and Tyché

1189 Gautier 1852, 2002. Also in Aziza 1992, 501–527. García y García 1998, no. 5807. On this novella, see Schuerewegen 1991; Olmos Romera 1993c; Martinet 1996, 173–175; Costa 1996, 125–131; David 2001, *passim* (as a work of reference for later authors); Blix 2009, *passim*; Genevieve Liveley in Hales/Paul 2011, 105–117; Pucci 2012, 73–76. Also see works quoted in the following notes.
1190 See M.-H. Girard in Gautier 1997, Introduction. The book does not contain impressions of Naples and its surroundings. David (2001, 130) refers to Gautier's recollection of Pompeii in 1850, in an article in *La Presse* from June 24, 1853, about Chassériau's painting "Le tépidarium."
1191 Similar aspects in *Le pied de momie, Avatar, Le roman de la momie* and *Spirite*. Claudine Lacoste-Veysseyre sketches this trend in the nineteenth century (in Gautier 2002, 1311). See also the very rich "Notice" by Pierre Laubriet, in Gautier 2002, 1286–1298. On *Le pied* Malinowski 1989, 256–274. On *Momie* Blix 2009, 98–105. Cf. Shelley Hales in Hales/Paul 2011, 153–170.
1192 Octavien would be a portrait of Gautier's friend Gérard de Nerval (Jaton 1988, 125; see here Chapter V, p. 262). His name, in that case, is a recording of Nerval's *Octavie* (contra Jaton 1988, 152).
1193 Cf. Schuerewegen 1991, 326–327 on this paradox.
1194 Gautier 2002, 289: "L'aspect de Pompeï est des plus surprenantes; ce brusque saut de dix-neuf siècles en arrière étonne même les natures les plus prosaïques et le moins compréhensives; deux pas vous mènent de la ville antique à la vie moderne, et du christianisme au paganisme; aussi lorsque les trois amis virent ces rues où les formes d'une existence évanouie sont conservées intactes, éprouvèrent-ils, quelque préparés qu'ils y fussent par les livres et les dessins, une impression aussi étrange que profonde."

Fig. 13: Late nineteenth-century photo of the gypsum cast of a victim of the eruption of A.D. 79 in the Antiquarium of Pompeii.

Novoleja[1195] at night, who bring him into contact with Arria Marcella. Arria makes herself known as the girl of the breast impression in the museum.[1196] Her father, Arrius, warns his daughter that Octavien does not belong to her era, but she begs her father to leave her alone with Octavien and to keep his gloomy ("morose") reli-

---

1195 This name must be a variation of Naevoleia Tyche, known from a tomb outside the Herculanean Gate (Kockel 1983, tomb south 22). A person with this name returns in Toudouze's *Cécube* (see below pp. 321–322).
1196 Gautier 2002, 309: "'Oh! lorsque tu t'es arrêté aux Studj à contempler le morceau de boue durcie qui conserve ma forme', dit Arria Marcella en tournant son long regard humide vers Octavien, 'et que ta pensée s'est élancée ardemment vers moi, mon âme l'a senti dans ce monde où je flotte invisible par des yeux grossiers; la croyance fait le dieu, et l'amour fait la femme. On n'est véritablement morte que quand on n'est plus aimée; ton désir m'a rendu la vie, la puissante évocation de ton coeur a supprimé les distances qui nous séparaient.'" As Octavien says, he was attracted by a sort of magnetism (Gautier 2002, 310). He likens her to the Aphrodite from the east pediment of the Parthenon, who wears body-sticking clothes.

gious beliefs to himself.[1197] Her father, who has converted to Christianity, hopes that Arria will follow in his footsteps before her death. When she refuses, he curses her and she once again becomes a heap of bones and ashes. Arrius succeeds in destroying the bond between ancient and modern lover, because as he believes, with or without the aid of Christian belief, such a relationship cannot exist. In my view, this means that Arrius knows what happened to the two lovers on that terrible eruption day. Arrius is the stereotype of the average Christian (grey, old, probably wise) in Christian novels (see Chapter IV). Octavien reacts to the interruption by Arria's father like a modern person, in that he does not concern himself with any religion, be it Roman pagan or Christianity.[1198] He envisions himself as Faust resurrected, which explains the story: like Goethe's fascinating character, Octavien lives in the present, past and future, and his love for Arria spans all three as well.[1199] Unfortunately, this comparison between Octavien and Faust is also true for Arria's unhappy ending: Arrius functions in a similar way to Goethe's Mephisto in the destruction of the bond between two lovers.[1200]

Arria might have inspired the female protagonist in Leopold von Sacher-Masoch's *Venus im Pels*, in which Severin von Kusiemski tells the story of his love affair with Princess Wanda von Dunajew. In the course of their relationship, he role-plays as her slave and is often whipped. Since she likes to wear fur mantles, he gives her the nickname "Venus in Fur." In the South, she experiences paganism, warmth, and sensations of love. Pompeii, villas, baths, and temples were constructed in and for the pagan mind, not for thinkers from the north.[1201] Both

---

1197 Gautier 2002, 311–312: "'Arria, Arria,' dit le personnage austère d'un ton de reproche, 'le temps de ta vie n'a-t-il pas suffi à tes déportements, et faut-il que tes infâmes amours empiètent sur les siècles qui ne t'appartiennent pas? Ne peux-tu laisser les vivants dans leur sphère, ta cendre n'est donc pas encore refroidie depuis le jour où tu mourus sans repentir sous la pluie de feu du volcan? Deux milles ans de mort ne t'ont donc pas calmée, et tes bras voraces attirent sur ta poitrine de marbre, vide de cœur, les pauvres insensés enivrés par tes philtres.' – 'Arrius, grâce, mon père, ne m'accablez pas au nom de cette religion morose qui ne fut jamais la mienne; moi, je crois à nos anciens dieux qui aimaient la vie, la jeunesse, la beauté, le plaisir; ne me replongez pas dans le pâle néant. Laissez-moi jouir de cette existence que l'amour m'a rendue.'"
1198 Gautier 2002, 310: "des élans insensés vers un idéal retrospectif".
1199 Like Faust's relationship with Helena in Faust II. The couple would get Euphorion as a child, probably the same as Gregorovius' artist Euphorion (here Chapter III, p. 205). Octavien's later marriage to the English girl Ellen is a repetition of the theme: one foreigner with a name very similar to Helena conquers another stranger.
1200 Some interesting observations in Rothemann 1996, 74–75, 78–79.
1201 Von Sacher-Masoch 2003, 8–9: "'Und doch diese ewig rege, ewig ungesättigte Sehnsucht nach dem nackten Heidentum, ' fiel Madame ein, 'aber jene Liebe, welche die höchste Freude, die göttliche Heiterkeit selbst ist, taugt nicht für euch Modernen, euch Kinder der Reflexion. Sie bringt euch Unheil. *Sobald ihr natürlich sein wollt, werdet ihr gemein.* Euch erscheint die Natur

Wanda and Arria are attractive to their respective lovers primarily due to how mentally different they are from them – with Arria in the past and Wanda in the South. They are also attractive due to their genuine (in Arria's case) or attempted (in Wanda's) warm southern nature. Both women are mysterious, remote, and in fact, unreachable, and neither Octavien nor Severin really understands his lover, which in part, at least, adds to the attraction.

Gautier's fascination was based on the impression that Rome was not yet a victim of primness; indeed, he advocated the human nude as the purest theme in his many articles on art. Apart from eroticism, which was often seen as something typical of Naples by people from the North,[1202] and reincarnation, *Arria Marcella* possesses other elements familiar from Romanticism, and elements of the Gothic novel, like the ghost-ridden gray ruins that evoke Medieval buildings, and shudder-inducing night walks.

Antonio Sogliano, one of the nineteenth-century excavators of Pompeii, underscored Gautier's construction of the girl – bleak, brown, noble shape and so on, defining the novella as a learned capriccio,[1203] while the French author Marc Monnier considered *Arria Marcella* to be Gautier's best story.[1204] The literary historian Wolfgang Leppmann[1205] defines it as a sequel to Bulwer-Lytton, because it starts with the cast of the girl which appears at the end of *The Last Days*. In Octavien's dreams and hallucinations, Leppmann sees similarities with Poe, Hugo, and Flaubert. He correctly notices the Pygmalion motif in that Octavian first loves a lifeless cast of the female breast in the museum. The red color, as Leppmann

---

als etwas feindseliges, ihr habt aus uns lachenden Göttern Griechenlands Dämonen, aus mir eine Teufelin gemacht. Ihr könnt mich nur bannen und verfluchen oder euch selbst in bacchantischem Wahnsinn vor meinem Altar als Opfer schlachten, und hat einmal einer von euch den Muth gehabt, meinen rothen Mund zu küssen, so pilgert er dafür barfuß im Büßerhemd nach Rom und erwartet Blüthen von dem dürren Stock, während unter meinem Fuße zu jeder Stunde Rosen, Veilchen und Myrthen emporschießen, aber euch bekommt ihr Duft nicht; bleibt nur in eurem nordischen Nebel und christlichem Weihrauch; laßt uns Heiden unter dem Schutt, unter der Lava ruhen, grabt uns nicht aus, für euch wurde Pompeji, für euch wurden unsere Villen, unsere Bäder, unsere Tempel nicht gebaut. Ihr braucht keine Götter! Uns friert euer Welt!'" The pilgrim with the rod must be Tannhäuser, the protagonist of Wagner's opera, who makes a pilgrimage to Rome.

1202 See Jaton 1988, 73–86.

1203 Sogliano 1888, 29–30: "Questo cachet de beauté, trovato nella casa di Diomede, porge al Gautier il destro di evocare nella sua fantasia la fanciulla pallida e bruna, dalle linee fidiache, della quale una nobile forma, caduta in polvere da duemila anni, grazie al capriccio della eruzione, è pervenuta sino a noi."

1204 Monnier 1865, 91: "son chef-d'oeuvre peut-être, et, en tout cas, un chef-d'oeuvre." He connects this observation with Gautier's fine description of the Villa of Diomedes.

1205 Leppmann 1966, 181–192.

observes, is a playful detail symbolizing the erotic atmosphere of *Arria Marcella*.[1206] The Spanish archaeologist Ricardo Olmos Romera also recognizes the Pygmalion theme and stresses the importance of the name of Tyche ("Destiny"), who introduces Octavien to Arria.[1207] Zintzen observes that even modern guide writers tend to personalize this cast, in a process of "Sinnstiftung," the desire to enliven the dead past.[1208] Indeed, Gautier did this in a radical form and managed to attract a number of followers. An interesting suggestion about a possible source of inspiration is Giuseppe Pucci's reference to a statue of a "woman bitten by a serpent" by Auguste Clésinger from 1847, which evoked Gautier's enthusiasm.[1209]

Norman Douglas's novella *Nerinda*, composed for the most part in the form of a diary, is almost identical to *Arria Marcella* in its fascination for the remains of a Pompeian girl (fig. 15). During a visit to Pompeii with his sister Bertha, Donald, the protagonist, falls in love with a gypsum cast exposed in the Antiquarium:[1210]

> There was one of a young woman, with eyes half closed as though in pain. It seemed to fascinate Bertha by its life-like grace and beauty.
> 'Poor girl!' she said at last, after standing entranced before it. 'Chained up in that narrow case! Who can she have been? Perhaps the daughter of some patrician, hurrying away to escape the awful vengeance of her gods. It is revolting,' she added, 'to expose even her ashes to the gaze of the whole world.' A truly womanly afterthought.
> I said I thought she looked more like a nymph.

Donald returns several times to see her alone, each time doing his best to avoid interacting with the old museum guard. In a dream, she reveals to him that her name is Nerinda, and defines her status as the daughter of an ocean king. Still in his dream, he prays in front of her and achieves his goal of bringing her back to

---

1206 Leppmann 1966, 189; Zintzen 1998, 118–119, 123 (on red; cf. the power of red in the fragment quoted from *Venus im Pelz* and Proust's red, here Chapter V, p. 285).
1207 Olmos Romera 1993c, 52 and 56. He judges Arria's reply (see note 1197) to her father as splendid, "hermosísima."
1208 Zintzen 1998, 248–254. Cf. Maiuri 1958, 39–42; La Rocca/De Vos 1976, 340.
1209 Pucci 2012, 75, fig. 3. The statue is in the Musée du Petit Palais, Paris.
1210 Douglas 1929, 26. This novella, written in 1899 and printed for the first time in 1901 (Author's Note p. 69–79), was Douglas' only piece of fiction. Douglas reveals in this note that the alleged storyteller suffered considerably from his experience with Donald and had to be admitted to a psychiatric clinic. He had a sort of "dislocation" (p. 73), being a "paramorphic insanity," as formulated by a certain Henry Maudly. Not in García y García 1998. See i.a Fussell 1980, 119–130; Pucci 2012, 78–80.

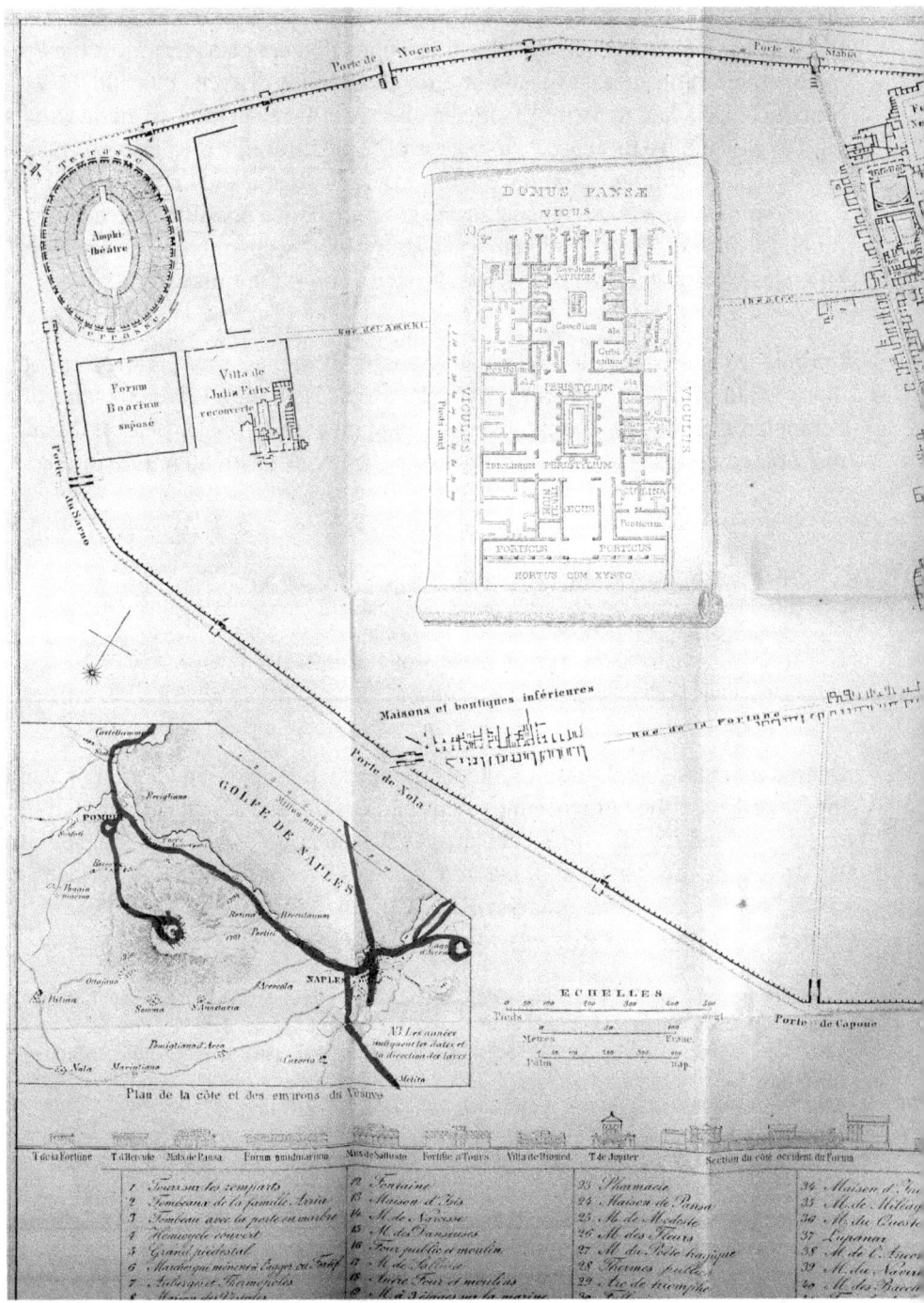

Fig. 14: Stanislas d'Aloë, *Les ruines de Pompéi jusqu'en 1858*, plan of Pompeii dated 1859. The railway station and the Hotel of Diomedes are visible at the right hand top corner. In the empty space between Amphitheatre and Theatres, a plan of the House of Pansa is inserted, whereas

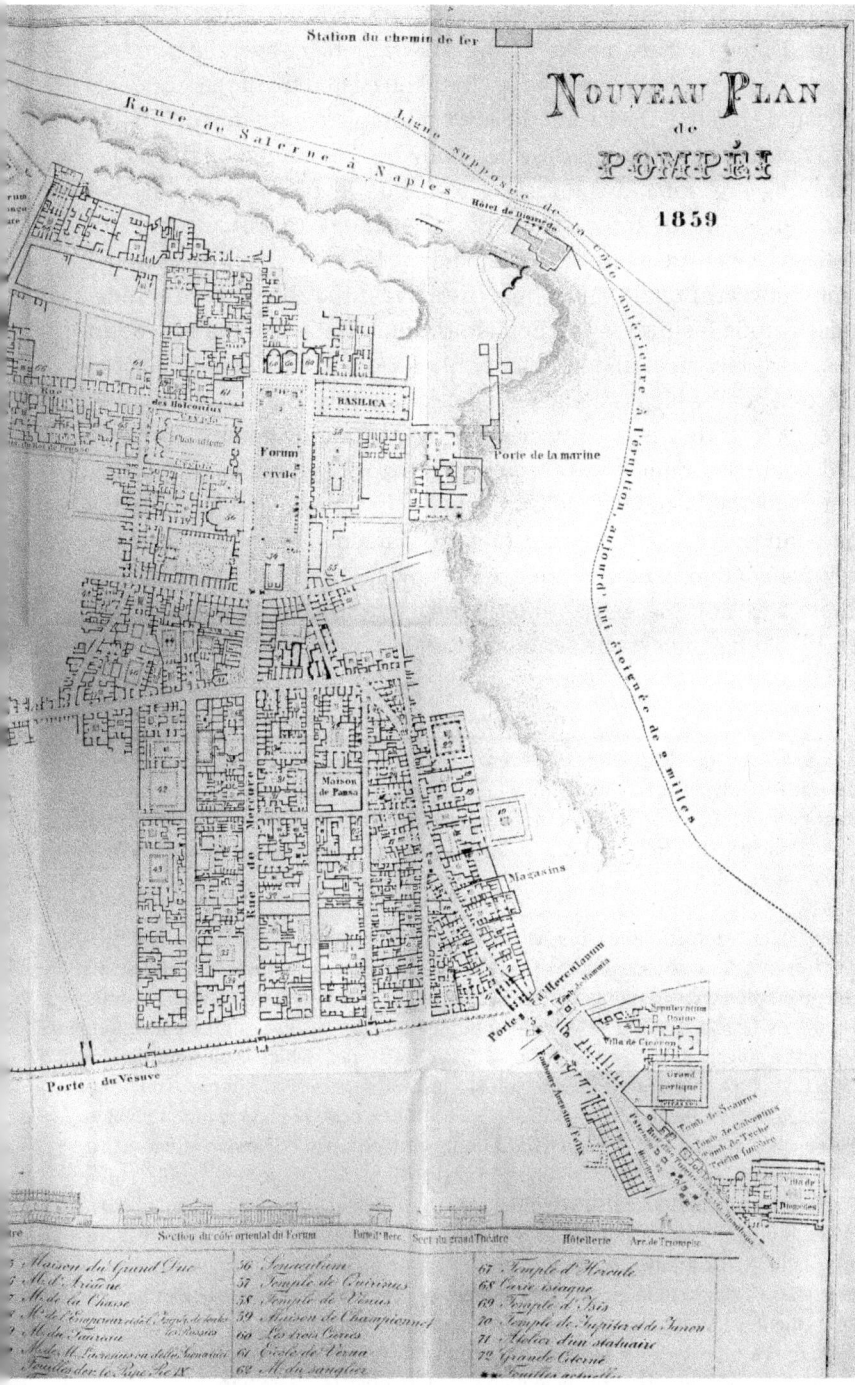

the reinterred *Praedia* of Julia Felix is rather correctly drawn next to the Amphitheater. This plan served authors like Gautier and Nerval, as well as Gautier's protagonist Octavien.

life.¹²¹¹ Later on, he imagines seeing her near the shore and thinks about the girl constantly. Here, Donald's diary breaks off and a narrator takes over the storytelling. A local paper reports that robbers have killed the custodian of the Antiquarium in the museum, and that the cast of the girl "is completely shattered."¹²¹² The storyteller also reveals that Donald's drowned body has been found in the port.

Old and young are notable contrasting elements in the novella. The old museum custodian is directly contrasted with the (very old) cast of a young girl, which symbolizes premature death. The custodian acts as a *Hermes psychopompos*, mediating between Donald and (the gypsum cast that becomes) Nerinda. The cast arouses erotic feelings in the English traveler. But since she is dead in reality, the two will only meet in death, and only if Donald sacrifices himself to achieve his second goal, which is being with her for eternity.

Undeservedly forgotten is a witty novella by Alexandre Pothey. *Un vieux lapin* ("An Old Rabbit") contains the account of a trip of a young man, Camille, to Castellammare di Stabia and Pompeii.¹²¹³ Camille thinks a lot about Aphrodite. Although the goddess' reputation – and that of Pompeii – is not solely noble, upon an attentive contemplation of the ancient town, Camille cannot but conclude that there was nothing extraordinarily negative in comparison with the modern town.¹²¹⁴ Pothey mocks the seriousness of other authors and archaeolo-

---

1211 Douglas 1929, 47–48: "And lo! It happened even as I expected. Her cheeks coloured and her curved lips quivered slightly, ever so slightly, like an anemone flower trembling in the breeze. Life, for one short moment, flowered through those delicate veins. As for her eyes – I gazed, and methought I looked into another world." It is possible that the name Nerinda stems from Nereus and his daughters, the Nereids.
1212 Douglas 1929, 63.
1213 Pothey 1883, 103: "Pompéi! Cette ruine vivante, avec ses temples, ses maisons, ses rues bordées de hauts trottoirs, les traces des chars profondément gravées sur ses larges dalles volcaniques, vous ramène en pleine vie romaine, malgré la silence lugubre qui vous enveloppe et vous glace." Not in García y García 1998. In 1870, Pothey published *La Muette*, a similar collection, and therefore uses the adjective "nouveaux" for his 1883 set of stories, which is also entitled *La Muette*. The "Muette" is a circle of friends who tell stories, impressions, and report vivid dialogues. On *Un vieux lapin*, see David 2001, 125, 128–129, 163–164. A novella playing out in Stabiae only is Jean de Meuse's *Flaviana*. The unnamed narrator meets a group of Pompeian refugees in a grotto and is rescued from death by Flaviana, daughter of the Highpriest of the Sun, Lucius Vetius (De Meuse 1967; García y García 1998, no 9165; I did not see the original French edition from 1961).
1214 Pothey 1883, 106; 107: "Pompéi était sous l'invocation de Vénus Physica. […] Les fresques sont obscènes, sans l'être. La preuve, la voici: l'on m'a raconté qu'une grande dame, une princesse russe, mise en goût par la défense pour les femmes d'y pénétrer, finit par tromper la vigilance du gardien. Une fois là, elle dit, avec une sorte de déception et de dépit, au guide qui l'accompagnait et qui me l'a rapporté: 'Ce n'est que ça?... Qu'y a-t-il d'extraordinaire?'" David 2001, 163–164 also highlights the comparison of ancient and modern objects and situations.

gists, to whom the tiny bones found in an ancient dining room become important and serve as proof of Epicuran philosophy. Pothey reduces them to gluttony. In one of the numerous ancient "cafés" – some of which even house billiard tables like modern cafés in Paris – Camille sees the bones of a rabbit laid out on a small table. This skeleton, it turns out, is what remains of an ordinary meal enjoyed by the café's clientele.[1215] Again, nothing has changed! Pothey's vision of Pompeii is full of irony. The absence of (skeletal remains of) the Pompeian diners makes the situation still more absurd: the small animal has "survived" the disaster, but the people have vanished.[1216] The author might also blame the ancient inhabitants for fearing death rather than enjoying life like Epicureans.

A more dangerous trip is that of the architect Louis B*** in Gustave Toudouze's *Le Cécube de l'an 79*. As he is looking at a small lizard in a glass captured the same afternoon during a stroll in the excavations, Louis asks the host at his Pompeian hotel for a good wine. He receives an old bottle bearing the text *M. Spurio Cons. / LXXIX Ann / Caecubum*.[1217] *Caecubum* hints at the name of the famous ancient wine that gives its name to the novella, full bottles of which would have been found during the French excavations of the early nineteenth century in the cellars of the House of Pansa. As Louis sips it almost 2,000 years after its production, it still has its intended effect.[1218] As if on cue, the architect breaks his glass and with it the glass cage which holds the lizard. It gets dark and Louis hears someone say "ΖΩΗ" – zoë or life – and sees a beautiful girl who introduces herself as Naevoleia Tyche and whose tomb Louis recalls having seen during his visit to Pompeii. Toudouze's use of a couple of well-chosen aspects – the tomb of Naevoleia and ancient wine, to name two – creates a fine short story about impos-

---

1215 Pothey 1883, 111–112: "Le pauvre lapin! Il reste encore la tête et les os blanchis de quelques membres. Quand tu viendras à Pompéi, tu verras le tout au musée. Les maîtres du lieu, épicuriens sans doute, avaient probablement voulu mourir avec grâce. Et, Dieu me pardonne, ils festoyaient gaiement. Ils s'étaient, ma foi, couronnés de roses, car voici encore quelques feuilles conservées sous la lave. Je t'en envoie une. Mais ils ont apparemment eu peur et se sont sauvés lâchement, à l'approche de la catastrophe, car il ne restait pas le moindre trace du corps de ces capons. Je t'avoue que je leur en ai voulu." The mentioning of the museum might refer to a pastry form of a hare, found in Pompeii.
1216 See also David 2001, 128–129. David points at the "balthazar," an enormous bottle of wine, that underlines the opulence of the dinner party.
1217 "Under consul Marcus Spurius, the year 79. Caecubum." "A.D. 79" is of course the modern chronological indication, so that the inscription sounds odd. See David 2001, 422–423 on this and other mock inscriptions.
1218 Toudouze 1877, 15: "A peine est-il approché la liqueur de ses lèvres qu'une chaleur extraordinaire courut dans ses veines, se répandant par tout son corps; quelque chose de subtil, d'indéfinissable, lui monta au cerveau." García y García 1998, no. 13.613.

sible love.¹²¹⁹ Naevoleia reproaches Louis for disturbing her peaceful second life as a lizard in her family's tomb and promptly vanishes, advising him to drink the wine. The wine serves as a means to bring the protagonist into a state of bliss in a town that is a symbol of lucky and untroubled life. The girl is like another Arria Marcella, the heroine in Gautier's novella, who, for just one night, has a happy encounter with a modern man.

La Coupe d'Hercule, another of Toudouze's stories, is a complex story written as if it were an ancient papyrus that was allegedly buried in the year 863 *ab urbe condita* – that is A.D. 110 – where Pompeii was once located, that is later revealed to be a hoax.¹²²⁰ In this story, visitors to Pompeii also come across the ancients via their tombs, and encounter Zoè, another girl of the same name, as well as wine and lizards. In the ruins of Pompeii, Jacobus Androscapanès, an old professor from Paris with a German father and a Greek mother,¹²²¹ meets Antonius Severus Marcus Caïus Cornelius Lentulus, a Roman who has left Rome thirty years earlier. The two speak Latin. The Roman claims to be a linear descendant of the Lentulus family from the time of Cicero. He does not recognize Pompeii in its contemporary "dead" form, no longer a living and merry city, and blames Androscapanès for trying to deceive him into believing that they are, in fact, in Pompeii.¹²²² They realize that they are meeting on August 23, a terrible day, the day before the eruption, of a non defined year in the 1870s! Lentulus is shocked by the ruins, prompting Androscapanès to ask whether Lentulus knows nothing about the eruption of 79. Strolling under a burning sun, they see thousands of lizards, but no people.¹²²³ The new friends meet a potpourri of ancient Pompeians, and Lentulus falls under the spell of Julia, who is being carried on a luxurious chair with bearers, followed by the priest of Isis. In the excavation's museum, they see these people's skeletal

---

1219 The small booklet probably forms part of a larger collection, given the suggestion of García y García 1998, no. 13.613, which mentions the collection "Visions antiques." On Toudouze and the tomb of Naevoleia Tyche see David 2001, 133, 135–136.
1220 More on mock papyri in Chapter VII.
1221 His name Androscapanès means "ax man." Toudouze 1878, 167: "l'homme pioche, Ἀνὴρ σκαπάνη."
1222 Toudouze 1878, 21–22: "autour de nous tout est mort, tout respire la désolation, la solitude. Non, ce n'est pas là Pompéi. Pompéi vit, Pompéi chante, Pompéi va de fête en fête, et les jeux du cirque n'y chôment jamais. Ah! tu [Androscapanès] n'es qu'un vil imposteur!" Later, he does recognize Pompeii (Toudouze 1878, 51): "Pour le Romain, c'était une intense souffrance, la cruelle douleur d'un homme amené au milieu des décombres et des ruines qui viennent d'engloutir tout ce qu'il a de plus cher, de plus précieux et de plus sacré. Le désespoir l'envahissant peu à peu, il ne pouvait voir une ruine nouvelle sans ressentir aussi une torture nouvelle." García y García 1998, no. 13.613.
1223 Toudouze 1878, 45: "myriades de petits lézards gris."

remains, which show their agony. The two men are pained to realize the torture the Pompeians faced as they died, suffocated by the ashes and killed by poisonous gases.[1224]

Toudouze displays a good knowledge of the monuments and the inhabitants of Pompeii as known from inscriptions, and may have used Breton's *Pompéia*. His fascination for crossing the border between life and death is evinced on every page. Since a character named Lentulus figures in a novel by Paul Bory from 1890 (see Chapter VII, pp. 348–349 and fig. 14), one may ask whether there is some relationship between the two texts, which are both presented as mock manuscripts. But the men cannot be the same, since the Lentulus in Toudouze's story dies in 79, at which point Bory's Lentulus had already been dead for eight years. But it is not implausible that Bory knew of Toudouze's Lentulus. The same might be true for a connection with Jensen's *Gradiva*, in which we also find the recurring theme of lizards, a girl named Zoè, and an ancient person transforming into a modern character, or vice versa. But any influence on Jensen by Toudouze isn't very likely due to the obscurity of Toudouze's text.

Another echo of the fascination for Isis forms the gist of Cesare Peri's 1996 *Avventura a Pompei*.[1225] An American archaeological team digs in a house near the Temple of Isis and finds the remains of a priest of Isis, the priest's daughter Cecilia, and Egle, their Greek slave girl. Peri stresses the symbolic value of digging: it reveals not only the past, but one's own spirit as well.[1226] Isis is the alternative to the Christian god and her mysteries strongly inspire modern people. In that way, Peri adroitly mixes clichéd images of the treasure-hunting archaeologist, psychology, and wild speculations about skeletons, which come together to yield a rather farfetched story, which might have inspired the following work.

1224 Toudouze 1878, 97: "Ce sont d'atroces agonies, des crispations à donner le frisson. Le coeur se serre, l'émotion devient irrésistible lorsque, en face de ces tristes reliques, on analyse les tortures de ces Pompéiens étouffés, de ces Pompéiennes luttant d'une manière désespérée contre le lent et implacable ensevelissement de la cendre fine tombant sans arrêter, contre une atmosphère embrassée, contre les exhalaisons méphitiques des gaz, contre les empoisonnements sulfureux que les crevasses ouvertes partout et les mille fissures du sol lançaient contre les survivants."
1225 Peri 1996. There are footnotes explaining both technical terms and difficult Italian words. Every chapter has a short questionnaire. Therefore, the book seems to be a textbook at the level of the first years of high school. Peri is the author of many Latin courses. García y García 1998, no. 10.471A.
1226 Peri 1996, 174: "Hai capito che scavare, smuovere terra, pietre e lapilli, ha il fascino di un gesto simbolico, come per l'alpinista scalare la vetta e per il pilota lanciarsi nell'azzurro. Scavare non è altro che cercare la verità, attraverso i vari strati della storia dell'uomo e di noi stessi…" Freud's metaphor comes to life again; cf. p. 266.

In her recent novel *Il prodigio del sistro dalla Pompei sepolta*, Stefania Menduni de' Rossi, a pharmacist and amateur novelist from the Pompeii area, portrays Eva Berchet, an Italo-American archaeologist who discovers a sistrum next to the cavity of a victim during the excavation of a villa on the north side of Pompeii. This Egyptian musical instrument belongs to Elpidia Sabina, an Isis priestess who appears as a spirit and urges Eva to keep her stay hidden from the other archaeologists. Elpidia reveals that she was on the brink of converting to Christianity when the eruption took place. Now, she belongs neither to the world of the living nor to that of the dead, and neither to Isis nor to Christianity.[1227] De' Rossi makes the time machine motif work; Elpidia seeks contact with modern people and visits the Catholic cathedral in modern Pompeii, where she becomes obsessed with the Virgin Mary, clearly a new identity of ancient Isis. During a baptism, she disappears and is apparently brought to Christian heaven. At the end, Eva finds Christian tokens in the excavations and thanks St. Mary for her help saving Elpidia. More than anything else, this novel is an extremely pious Catholic story in which archaeology is but an instrument to rescue ancient Pompeians from their pagan world. The description of the excavation, which is full of secrets and contains little detail about the remains, is rather unrealistic and only serves as a backdrop for the portraits of Eva and Elpidia. Clearly, the neighborhood of both the pagan excavations and the Catholic cathedral nearby stimulated the author to compile her novel.

A Siren or an Opera Singer?

Gilbert Augustin-Thierry's *Leucosia* has a complicated plot.[1228] The title derives from a wall painting in Pompeii that shows a nymph whose name is inscribed next to her head.[1229] There are two protagonists: Esther Mosselman, an opera singer, and Marcel Lautrem, a composer who is hopelessly in love with her. Armand Blondel, a painter, tells Lautrem's story, in which Esther plays the role of Leucosia as a Siren living in the Blue Grotto on Capri in the time of Tiberius, who converts

---

1227 Menduni de' Rossi 2011, 20: "Non appartengo più al mondo dei vivi e neppure a quello dei morti."

1228 Augustin-Thierry 1912. He was a prolific author of novels and opera libretti like César Franck's never-completed 1888–1889 opera "Giselle." Not in García y García 1998. The first story in *Leucosia* is of pagan character and concentrates on the irresistible forces of passion; the second is about Christian love. According to the author (Introduction, p. II) the short stories' plots may differ, but their general theme is "déterminisme."

1229 See David 2001, 423 on this mock inscription. Cf. above note 1217.

to Christianity and practices her seductive forces on Christians. Both Blondel and Lautrem are fascinated by Pompeii, which they see as the "town of death."[1230] Lautrem interprets the *Leucosia* painting as the image of a prostitute, because the image is located in an obscene atrium adorned with Priapi.[1231] Lautrem hears the Siren's voice calling him "Marcellus." She then comes to life, and turns out to be an oriental-Greek-Jewish prostitute living in this house, which is devoted to the oriental sister of Aphrodite, the love goddess Astarte. Lautrem becomes spellbound by Leucosia's strong character and is unable to escape from her supernatural forces.[1232] Apparently Lautrem loses consciousness in the excavations, and is brought back to life by a workman. Various adventures follow, and the story ends in a way I shall not betray here.

As Jensen does in *Gradiva*, Augustin-Thierry plays with time by using an ancient painting as the primary means for Lautrem's self-identification as a lover. Pompeii stands for free love and debauchery, decadence and loss of morality. The modern characters are prey to their passions and clearly fit into the mainstream of fin-de-siècle decadent literature and symbolism.[1233] Augustin-Thierry's authorial choice to include a Siren works out well: with her voice, Esther seduces men who are destroyed by their lack of self-consciousness.[1234] Throughout the novel, the author flirts with vaguely oriental and ambiguous connotations of the Siren and Aphrodite, equivalent to the Pompeian Venus, as well as Jewish symbols. In this way, he follows the late nineteenth-century current of orientalism, mixed with (quasi) mystical ideas Schuré had explored in *La prêtresse d'Isis* (see Chapter III, pp. 209–210).

1230 Augustin-Thierry 1912, 38: "cette ville de la mort."
1231 Augustin-Thierry 1912, 43: "l'atrium n'était qu'une écœurante obscénité. De lubriques emblèmes, d'ordurières priapées en décoraient le pourtour, et sur les marches du *tablinum* on avait érigé un autel, à triple figure de bouc. Ce postibule était une sorte de temple clandestin où d'immondes initiés avaient adoré jadis quelque divinité d'infamie, la Pandêmos, la Vénus Athor, ou la Mylitta…"
1232 Augustin-Thierry 1912, 47: "Salut! Tu veux m'ignorer, mais tu me connaîtras. Nous nous retrouverons, car en dépit du Golgotha, la Bête régnera toujours sur le monde. Tu apprendras alors que, par moi vivifiée, toute chose vivante obéit à la fatalité de ma loi. Ton âme s'efforcera de me fuir; mais passée en ta chair, je te dévorerai tout entier. Tu aimeras; tu aimeras; tu aimeras, – subissant la douleur, te débattant contre l'opprobre, accomplissant le sacrilège, commettant le crime, disparaissant dans la démence… oui, toi dont le dédain m'outrage, tu n'auras plus désormais d'autre Dieu que moi…"
1233 Augustin-Thierry 1912, 89: In a paper, Lautrem is called "le prince du symbolisme." Cf. David 2001, 142–143
1234 Augustin-Thierry 1912, 209: "Pareille à la Circé du mythe hellénique, l'Astaroth l'avait transformé en bête, et cette bête quémandait encore de l'amour… Hélas! qui de nous, en sa chair ou dans son coeur, ne recèle aussi une Astaroth?"

As for the twentieth century, the romantic idea of mesmerism no longer played a part, but there are various other means of transporting people through history, to the past or to the future.

An American Student Turns into a Pompeian Slave Girl

Rebecca East's 2003 novel *A.D. 62: Pompeii* portrays Miranda, a PhD student of Classics in her final stage at Harvard. Miranda is both the omniscient storyteller and the main character, which gives East control over the development of the plot as far as Miranda is concerned, but is also limiting in that East isn't easily able to widen the horizon beyond the girl's experiences.[1235] A silver chip has been planted in Miranda's arm, which along with a time machine allows for her transposition to antiquity and for her to return at any time. The situation is similar to that of the couple Hopkins sends to Pompeii, discussed at the beginning of this chapter. Miranda becomes a slave to a wealthy Pompeian, Marcus Tullius. She gradually makes progress within the *familia* and becomes an intimate of Marcus' daughter Tullia. Marcus even falls in love with her and takes her as a *hetaera*, despite his wife Holconia's hatred for her (and for Marcus himself). Miranda is set free and adopted by Julia Felix, and later still, marries her former master. She wins the townspeople's hearts by telling stories about King Arthur, Romeo and Juliet, and Scheherazade, and she bewilders Roman ears by playing folk songs, Medieval tunes, and Mozart on her recorder. All these vicissitudes are intermingled with scenes of daily life, feasts, ceremonies, and stories that Pompeians tell her, since Miranda is a stranger from an unknown country.

As Miranda looks at Pompeii with her modern science-trained eyes, she simultaneously experiences the rough life of an ancient Roman slave. She wonders how Marcus Tullius will behave towards other women in the future and whether or not she will return to her former life as a Harvard PhD student. Slavery is the main theme of the book; as a slave, she suffers mentally and physically, contemplates the pros and cons of a life in the difficult Pompeian society as a person without family or a relationship, and contrasts it with the modern American life of a free, independent woman.[1236] Her appreciation for Pompeii, therefore, is a mix of aston-

---

[1235] East 2003, 289–292 reveals her sources of inspiration and knowledge and refers to her website www.rebecca-east.com. She presents herself as an archaeologist with knowledge of ancient society and, especially, Pompeii, which is clear from her lengthy descriptions of and comments on Pompeii and its inhabitants in the years 61–62.

[1236] E.g. East 2003, 137: "I didn't want to become comfortable with the idea of being a slave. But under the circumstances, a Stoic resignation to the situation seemed about the best I could hope for."

ishment, admiration, and disgust, whereas her love for Marcus Tullius is intermingled with doubts about status. In the course of her realizations, she suffers from conflicted internal monologues and attempts to weigh the positive and negative aspects of the ancient society she had willingly become a part of:

> I was falling in love with a slave owner, although I despised the idea and practice of slavery. I wanted him to love me, and I wanted to feel some sense of belonging in this time. And yet I realized that as a slave I could never be loved or respected equal, or have any sort of freedom in my relations with him.[1237]

In East's novel, the characters of the ancient protagonists often seem to be based on fictional personages in other Pompeii novels or people known from graffiti and inscriptions, especially rich people like Julia Felix. Despite Miranda's status as a slave, her slave "colleagues" are not described. Instead, we are introduced only to wealthy slave owners and other "elite" members of Pompeian society. Marcus Tullius bases his authority on his status of *pater familias*, whereas Holconia is a schemer who relies on the power and wealth of her family. Miranda, with her interest in magic, fairy tales and astrology, seems to be an odd mixture of "flower power" girl and inquisitive-minded Harvard scholar in-the-making.

Miranda's decision to remain in Roman Pompeii and not return to her former life in the modern world make East's novel original. This construction serves as an excuse for East to make long comparisons between antiquity and modern times, but by no means does she portray all things modern as better. She especially wants her readers to consider modern "illegal" workers who have no rights. These poor people, although "free" in today's world, are often less sure about what tomorrow will bring than were ancient slaves. As a fugitive from a far-away land beyond the Pillars of Hercules, Miranda's inquisitive nature is satisfied by the endless opportunities to learn about Pompeian culture by asking the locals about their lives. As a result, the book is highly informative about Pompeii in the time of Nero in general, and specifically about the upper class way of life there.

Back to the Future

Surprisingly, there are some Pompeii stories that take place in the future, probably because in the minds of the authors, readers likely wouldn't have expected such a twist. *Pompeii in Massachusetts*, a short story by Louis Golding from 1934, tells the hilarious story of the rivalry between two rich industrialists in the

---

[1237] East 2003, 159.

2060s.[1238] Jabez Q. Pappenheim, a sausage maker, and Silas F. Birnbaum, a gumboots producer, each boast about their plans to erect cultural monuments for the people of Massachusetts. Birnbaum is proud of having transported "waters of the more illustrious European lakes, in great suboceanic pipes, to his native land" of Massachusetts. Meanwhile, as a reaction to Birnbaum's enormous ongoing enterprise, Pappenheim constructs a replica not only of Pompeii, but of a "real" live Vesuvius, and obviously not according to his plans, is killed when it accidentally erupts. Golding, a Ukranian Jew, blames the two *nouveaux riches* Jewish nabobs for their stupid expenditures of money in public. This was a timely theme, since at the time of writing the entire world was in the throes of the Great Depression. The author's use of Massachusetts and Pompeii can be explained by the reputation of each for wealth. Pompeii itself is described with little detail, but its historical fatal end serves as a fitting parallel to the sudden finale to Pappenheim's adventure. Golding seems to consider the disappearance of Pappenheim's mock Pompeii as significant as the destruction and disappearance of the real archaeological site.

Amélie Nothomb's *Péplum* is a puzzling novel. The title might refer to the Greek *peplos* or – more likely – to the genre of historical movies.[1239] The storyteller – A.N. – is in a hospital on May 8, 1995 and awakens in the twenty-sixth century in an unspecified place. On May 27, 2580, she meets Celsius and becomes engaged in a long dialogue, a narrative style common in many of Nothomb's works. Celsius dresses A.N. in a "péplum," whereas he wears a "hologramme." He claims that the eruption of Vesuvius took place only the year before, i.e. 2500 years *after* the date generally believed. He views the eruption as one of the most beautiful gifts ever given to archaeologists,[1240] and rather oddly, believes that future scientists, whose goal it will be to preserve the ideal ancient city under the ashes and who are capable of visiting the past, are somehow responsible for the eruption.[1241] Celsius, in his self-proclaimed role as "démiurge," asserts that he had created the ruins of Pompeii just before his meeting with A.N., and insists that there had been nothing there before. A.N. objects to his explanation, arguing that many evocations of Pompeii are known from before 1995, like Bulwer-Lytton's *Last Days* and

---

1238 Golding 1934, 242–251. Not in García y García 1998. Following quotation at p. 242.
1239 The interpretation of *Péplum* in this way is mine.
1240 Nothomb 1996, 8: "les scientifiques du futur, qui auront les moyens de voyager dans le passé, sont les responsables de l'éruption du Vésuve en 79 après Jésus-Christ. Mobile du crime: préserver, sous les cendres et les laves, le plus bel example de cité antique – mieux: le joyau historique de l'art de vivre! Qu'est-ce que vous en pensez?" Not in García y García 1998. See P.G. Guzzo, *Rivista di Studi Pompeiani* 8 (1997) 191–192 for a rather skeptical review of this novel.
1241 A similar explanation is given by Blix 2009, 171, in his chapter on the motif of lost and hidden towns (pp. 155–199).

peplum films. Celsius does not know them and even ignores Pliny's letters about the eruption.

Although both Celsius and A.N. speak French, they do not understand each other, so that the greater part of the dialogue consists of quibbling, misunderstandings and denials. The reader learns that Celsius is one of four oligarchs under a Tyrant modeled on the Athenian Peisistratus of the sixth century B.C. The world is no longer divided into North and South, the latter having been devastated in the twenty-second century, but into "Levant" and "Ponant," East and West. Love no longer exists and people are divided into classes on the basis of their IQ. The past is still venerated and can be seen in museums, but Pompeii is more than a museum, "la vie même."[1242] Celsius had unearthed the city with a "vulcanovore" in four minutes and descended into the ruins as if he were Orpheus incarnate. Celsius recounts his emotions upon seeing the city to A.N., which are similar to those we know from "traditional" accounts. He admires the buildings, which were not monumental but gracious, and proclaims that the most beautiful things in Pompeii were the paintings. At the conclusion of their long conversation, A.N. wakes up from a dream, and finds herself back in her country in 1995, writing a book about this strange encounter in another time.

The novel is a genuine science fiction story thanks to details of futuristic technological innovations like the "vulcanovore" and the societal order with a "demiurge," and the like. The main differences with respect to the readers' (and author's) historical period are the organization of the state and the population's class system. Except for its eternal beauty and as a clichéd image of a lost city, there is no real justification for the use of Pompeii.[1243] The ancient town seems to become a newly clichéd version of Atlantis, the unknown prehistoric town that was destroyed. Nothomb seems to be seeking an alternative for known histories, and uses iconic Pompeii as a starting point to combine Celsius' imaginatie future with twentieth-century disasters like the World Wars and nuclear explosions. The book takes places in a hypothetical time period called Uchronia,[1244] in which historical elements and science come together in fiction. In that sense, *Péplum* is a fascinating experiment.[1245]

[1242] Nothomb 1996, 78.
[1243] The author lived for several years in Italy as the daughter of the Belgian ambassador in Rome, and surely knew the excavations from personal visits.
[1244] Wesseling 1991, 100–105 explains the term and discusses some examples.
[1245] Elements of this Uchronian style of writing can also be found in Golding's critique on his own society, expressed in a detour in time. Since Golding defines himself as a critical Jew, his characterisation of the two protagonists is a sort of self-image. Cf. Wesseling 1991, 110–114.

Frederick Pohl's final novel, *All the Lives He Led*,[1246] was published when he was 92 years of age. It takes place in 2079, the bimillenary of the eruption of Vesuvius. Pompeii is a touristic highlight enhanced by the use of "virts," virtual reconstructions of monuments that no longer exist, or exist only in incomplete form, plus mock Pompeians re-enacting ancient life with visitors. Bradley Sheridan, who works there, is trying to forget the disasters and subsequent impoverishment he experienced in the United States, where in 2062 Yellowstone exploded,[1247] covering the greater part of his fatherland with volcanic ashes and devestating its economy and political power. The world in 2079 suffers from terrorist attacks, inexplicable natural disasters, and an epidemic disease called "Pompeian flue" that has killed thousands of people.[1248] As told by Brad, Pompeii is limited to gladiatorial shows (virtual and live-action) in the amphitheater, fulleries (which, happily, do not smell, since they are virtual), brothels (real and virtual), and wine bars that sell bad (real) wine, one of which is on the Via dell'Abbondanza, with Brad as its manager. Pohl's Pompeii is more or less the clichéd image already depicted in many other Pompeii books. For this reason, there seems to be no real justification for the story to take place there, as opposed to anywhere else, unless the authors felt the need to use the trope of the destruction of civilisation as symbolized by the obliteration of Pompeii.

Conclusion

Time machines provide authors with opportunities to experience not only time and space, but also the emotions of modern and ancient people suddenly meeting somewhere therein.[1249] Pompeii, a well-known metaphor for a culture suddenly lost – while at the same time a living, modern town – is an excellent setting in which to experience this. I have only to recall the observations made by the travelers in Chapter II and my own experiences showing people around the excavations. Many get the impression that the inhabitants are out and about, doing errands, strolling, or drinking coffee at a bar.

1246 Pohl 211; its title seems to refer to Melton 1974 (see Chapter V, p. 279): *Nine Lives to Pompeii. A Novel of Suspense.*
1247 That year commemorates the Pompeian earthquake of A.D. 62, but there is no mention of it.
1248 Pohl 2011, 155 mentions 80,000 people killed in one week, "dying in excruciating pain and horrid disfigurement." He might be comparing them to the Pompeian victims without explicitly saying so.
1249 Blix 2009, 106–115 discusses various examples of literary evocations of people "resurrecting" from the past by diverse methods like time machines and mesmerism.

Surely, the earliest authors would have had more intense reactions of this sort, but later writers also experienced this feeling personally. Gautier was fascinated by the idea of time and culture shocks, an interest he concretized in other works as well (see note 1191). In *Arria Marcella* the jump into the past is the consequence of an encounter with the negative remains of a victim. Especially since Fiorelli began filling the cavities with plaster to make casts, the drama of what had been the suffering of these poor people became almost tangible. Decadent authors of the late nineteenth century responded to their encounters with the drama of the victims in various ways, either enthusiastically giving in to a form of hopeless love, or trying to avoid it, as they realized that natural forces were working too strongly to remain entirely free from these citizens' spells.[1250] Modern writers all have their own agendas, but still depend on the archaeological remains, whether they were found in the past or have yet to be explored (at least in fiction) in the future.

1250 Cf. David 2001, 113–122.

Les salons que lui ont prêtés ses amis, etc.

Fig. 15: Paul Bory, Mémoires d'un Romain. Vie privée de l'ancienne Rome, Tours 1890, 43: "Les salons quelui ont prêtés ses amis, etc.," the drawing rooms lent to him by his friends, etc. In this mock papyrus book, Lentulus and his friends sit in the atrium of the House of the Tragic Poet, next to the garden. The room has a flat roof as in most reconstructions of the nineteenth century. Artist unknown.

VII Real and Fictional Manuscripts from Pompeii and Herculaneum

> *Defles adsidue combustos igne papyros?*
> *Pone metrum: lacrymas terge, Mnesylle, precor.*
> *Nam procul hinc efflat sulphur, flammaque Vesevus;*
> *Nec patulos libros ustulat ille tuos.*
> *Qui et mercator munita condidit arca:*
> *Cum sale porcinae carnis eruit.*[1251]

In 1752, 1,800 scrolls of papyri were discovered in a villa being excavated since 1750 on the northwest side of Herculaneum, appropriately called the Villa of the Papyri.[1252] Surprisingly, this discovery was not immediately regarded as a step forward in the study of ancient literature.[1253] Only once the first scraps were deciphered did these scrolls become a paramount branch of literary studies in Naples, with the *Academia Herculanensis* taking over the task of deciphering and publishing the ancient texts.[1254] In order to accomplish this work, in 1753, father Antonio Piaggio was asked to come to Portici to unroll the scrolls, a task he would continue to work on until his death in 1796. Piaggio had previously worked in the Vatican Library as a Latin scribe and *custos* of miniatures, and did not yet know Greek.[1255] Although he was criticized for working too slowly, his invention of a device that unrolled the papyri in a relatively harmless way brought him the

---

[1251] Vitrioli 1930, 134; 1998, 122: *Elegia* LXXVIII: "I papiri ercolanesi" ("Do you constantly weep about the fire-burnt papyri? Don't exaggerate: please, dry your tears, Mnesyllus. For far from here Vesuvius emits sulphur with a flame; and he does not char your broad books. The vendor who hides them in a strongbox, takes them out with salty pork meat.").

[1252] This chapter takes up elements from Moormann 2010 and 2012.

[1253] The number of scrolls varies from description to description, probably due to the varying number of destroyed or partially preserved pieces in different accounts. Capasso (1983, 126–129) lists 800 unrolled scrolls, 800 scrolls not yet unrolled, Delattre (2006, 22–23) only lists 650–700 scrolls. For the history of the excavation and the afterlife of the Villa of the Papyri see Mattusch 2005, 40–54, on the papyri 49–51, 57, figs. 2.13 and 2.22; Sider 2005; Delattre 2006. New excavations were carried out between 1996 and 1998, not on behalf of the Superintendency, but of a consortium especially established for that goal (cf. *Ercolano* 2008, introduction, and Zarmakoupi 2010).

[1254] Nowadays, the *Cronache Ercolanesi*, started in 1971 by Marcello Gigante, is the most important publication of the *Officina*, apart from monographs.

[1255] According to Winckelmann 1762, 90; 1997a, 127. See i.a. Longo Auricchio 2000 and Longo Auricchio/Capasso 1980 and M. Capasso, *ibidem*, 61–69; cf. the following notes.

praise of scholars and travelers alike.[1256] In 1754, the first text to be deciphered was *Peri mousikes* ("On music") by Philodemus, and sixteen more scrolls would follow in the subsequent forty-two years.

This slow progression and the seemingly lazy Neapolitan scholars did not meet with approval from the learned public and travelers. Yet authors pointed to the importance of the scrolls and hoped that the corpus of texts would be enriched. Athanasius Grün, to single out just one of these authors, was very enthusiastic about the scrolls' potential. Grün praised the charcoal-like forms that hide treasures that are like pearls in their ugly shells.[1257] He did not bother to speculate about their contents, mainly treatises of Stoic and Epicurean writers of the Hellenistic and late-Republican era, while many other observers expected to read lost masterworks from ancient literature. The English surgeon Samuel Sharp had little hope of finding jewels.[1258] Consequently, the desire for literary or historical texts inspired creative authors to write their own.[1259] In these works, the circumstances for finding the mock manuscripts are more or less identical: a visitor meets an excavator, a merchant or one of the editors of the Herculanean papyri

---

[1256] There is a huge bulk of recent literature on the library, the history of decipherment, and the texts themselves. Of special note are studies which began in Naples in 1969, stimulated by the late Marcello Gigante, Secretary of the Centro Internazionale per lo Studio dei Papiri Ercolanesi upon his death; i.a. *Contributi* 1980; Gigante 1986. For a good introduction, see Sider 2005. Nice images are in Capasso 1983. Piaggio's machine was illustrated in several books, i.a. Bartels 1791, 107; cf. Capasso 1983, 116–121; here p. 41, fig. 2. See also Sarnelli Cerqua 1993. There were written guides for visitors: De Jorio 1825; Castrucci 1858. There are models of Piaggio's machine on display in the National Museum in Naples in a room next to the main finds of the Villa of the Papyri, and in the *Officina dei Papiri Ercolanesi* in the National Library in Naples. Some letters regarding Piaggio's nomination as "unroller of the papyri" and containing some of his own memories are also known. See Gigante 1981, 9–14. Micheletti (1846, 325) names father Antonio Baschi as the inventor of another unrolling method. On Spanish visitors see López Martínez/Sabater Beltrá 2011; Romero Recio 2012, 23–44.

[1257] Grün 1849, canto II, couplet 11: "Gruß, Musen, euch! Dort die Papyrusrolle, / Verkohlt und morsch, wahrt noch im Eingeweide, / Gleichwie der Muschel Schrein, der perlenvolle, / Wohl manche Perl' aus eurem Festgeschmeide." For Leopardi see here pp. 53–54, 136; other examples in Moormann 2010.

[1258] Sharp 1766, 150: "The learned have, probably, a great loss in this disappointment; they flattered themselves that the remaining books of *Livy*, and other valuable writings, might have been found in this collection; now it is to be feared that, though they should be there, we shall not avail ourselves of the possession."

[1259] See David 2001, 397–403 on some French examples, esp. Bory 1890 (see below pp. 348–349); Blix 2009, 54–55. For fictitious manuscripts related to Sappho see Reynolds 2000, 170–174. On old and later mock manuscripts, see Herman/Hallyn 2009. On forgeries of antique texts in general, see Martinez 2011.

working in the *Officina,* and hears about a mysterious text which has not yet been edited. The visitor buys or lends it, makes a transcription and/or a translation, and returns the original, which subsequently disappears. As a result, the only surviving "edition" of the antique manuscript is this transcribed or translated version. The "editor" eagerly presents it to the public, while asking for patience and mercy for any mistakes.

The oldest fictitious manuscript purportedly found in Herculaneum that I know is by an anonymous author and bears the long title *Some Account of the Roman History of Fabius Pictor; From a Manuscript lately discover'd in Herculaneum; the Underground City near Naples.*[1260] In a preface, dated "November 17/6, 1748" – despite the oddity of the date's format, four years before the discovery of the scrolls in the Villa of the Papyri – the "editor" apologizes for not having sent notices to his friends about recent finds from the buried cities. He hopes to compensate for this lack of news with a manuscript, discovered in a room next to the theatre of Herculaneum, which proves, according to the editor, that the citizens of Herculaneum were literate. A cavity under a mosaic floor housed a cedar box containing five book scrolls:[1261]

> Not to hold you any longer in suspense; it was but about ten days ago, that some of the workmen, in penetrating about forty yards to the east of the theater (which I described to you in a former letter) met with two fine marble pilasters of the Doric order, and a sort of marble door-case; which seemed to lead to a handsome apartment. [...] As the workmen were clearing away the earth from the middlemost of these three lower squares [of mosaic], they found (by the sound of their instruments upon it) that it was hollow; and suspecting that there might be some treasure hid within, they repeated their blows with such violence, and so much impetuosity, that they broke it into twenty pieces (which they soon found, they need not have done; for it was made to move, in a groove, downwards.) As soon as they had thus opened it, they discovered, by the light of their torches, that there was a cedar-box in it. This was locked too; but they burst it open: and were greatly disappointed at only finding some large scrolls of old paper, tied up in five bundles, in the inside of it.

The editor makes clear that the text on two of the scrolls is written in Carthaginian language; three of them bear the title CAII. FABII. PICTORIS. HISTORIA. ROMANA ("Roman History of Gaius Fabius Pictor"):[1262]

[1260] *Some Account* 1749. Not in García y García 1998.
[1261] *Some Account* 1749, 3–5.
[1262] *Some Account* 1749, 6, 7. The dates indicated in the passage are the Seven Kings (753–510), the actions of the *decemuiri legibus scribundis* of 451/450, that is the commission that wrote the "Laws of the Twelve Tables", and the invasion of the Gauls in 387, when Marcus Furius Camillus was appointed dictator.

All the inside is written in capitals too; on a sort of paper, made of the bark of trees. [...] The first volume contains the reign of the seven kings; the second concludes with the fall of the Decemvirate; and the third reaches to the destruction of Rome by the Gauls, and the restoration under Camillus. You see how fairly they are written; and how little the worse they are, for all the centuries they have lain there. He is an admirable writer! And gives us a thousand lights, that we before wanted.

Luckily, the guard of the museum, Ottavio Antonio Bayardi (see Chapter I) permits the editor to read and translate a fragment of the manuscript, which concerns a debate that took place during the consulate of Marcus Valerius and Postumius Tubertus about the treachery of priests who contacted and venerated the "Tyrant, and his two sons," viz. Tarquinius Superbus.[1263] *Some Account*, which is presented as a mock papyrus, alludes to the Senate of Rome, but in reality is a political pamphlet in which the Senate stands for the English Parliament. The opposition of the sacral ministers in the scroll's ancient Rome is a metaphor for Parliament's opposition, which supported the still-popular Jacobites after the 1745 rebellion in Scotland. "Bonnie Prince Charlie" – Prince Charles Edward Stuart, grandson of James II – had gathered enemies of the now reigning Hanoverians and gone to war against England. The author of the pamphlet evidently presented it as an old manuscript in order to placate the hostility against the Catholics in Britain. A cry made by one of the Senators about the temple being in danger would have been familiar to contemporary readers, as they would have known clergyman and politician Henry Sacheverell's 1709 sermon "The Church is in Danger."[1264]

Another cryptically-presented political pamphlet has the same provenance as *Some Account* – that is, ancient Herculaneum: *A Fragment of the Chronicles of Nathan Ben Saddi; A Rabbi of the Jews Lately Discovered in the Ruins of Herculaneum*.[1265] Allegedly from "Constantinople: printed in the year of the Vulgar Era

---

1263 It is not among the fragments attributed to Fabius Pictor. See Beck/Walter 2001, 55–136. His work was written in Greek and entitled Ῥωμαϊκά ("Roman matters"), also known as *Annales* ("Yearbooks"). For the history, see F. Münzer, *RE* XXII.1 (1953) 948–949 s.v. Postumius no. 64. There is no exact reference, but one might consult Livy (2.16) and Dionysius of Halicarnassus (5.44–5.47) on this period. In 2.15, however, Livy describes a debate on liberty without the kings, in which the main figures are the consuls Publius Lucretius and Publicola (who is Publius Valerius, consul in 503, who died shortly after). This scene might have inspired our anonymous author.
1264 *Some Account* 1749, 21: "the temple, the temple, is in danger!" This temple was the Temple of Jupiter on the Capitol, commisioned by Tarquinius Superbus. I am much indebted to my Nijmegen colleague Frans Korsten, who pointed to Sacheverell's words. The pamphlet was edited by the Catholic printer Mary Cooper.
1265 *Fragment* 1758. Not in García y García 1998. The comment in the catalog entry of the work in the library of the University of Michigan at Ann Arbor, where I found it, says: "A mock-Bibli-

5707," the book was published in Philadelphia in 1758 by James Chattin. "Nathan Ben Saddi" was a well-known mock-author in the 18th century.[1266] *A Fragment* is a libel edited by William Smith from Aberdeen, who was a fervid worker in the educational and religious sectors of public life in Philadelphia.[1267] Amidst fervent discussions about taking a firm position on the question of the British occupation during the growing conflict that would eventually lead to American Independence, Smith apparently published pamphlets that paint him as not exactly the strongest supporter of the British. Nowadays it is difficult to understand fully what Smith was pushing for in this mock manuscript. No reference whatsoever to the Vesuvian cities is made in *A Fragment* and the provenance of Herculaneum given on the title page only suggests that the reader holds a genuinely old book in his hands.

Fictional Manuscripts from Antiquity

The literary trick of inventing a manuscript dates to antiquity. As early as the fifth century B.C., stories were written about unearthed bronze plaques containing texts and manuscripts. Pompeii specialist Pietro Giovanni Guzzo's fascinating 2004 essay claims that these ancient imaginary works are testimony to an early form of archaeology and the Romans' acute awareness of a material past.[1268] The Roman historian Livy and other classical authors describe two such imaginary manuscripts. Like *Some Account* and *A Fragment*, there is confusion about the context of their discovery and their contents. In Livy's version, two peasants discover the tomb of King Numa Pompilius at the foot of the Janiculum in Rome in 181 B.C. Apart from skeletal remains, the grave contains fourteen books – seven in Greek and seven in Latin. The Latin books deal with the laws of the priests, those in Greek treat the learning of wisdom. The public magistrates do not know what to do with these apparently embarrassing texts and decide to burn the manuscripts.[1269]

---

cal account of the arrest of William Smith for allowing a translation of an article for Benjamin Franklin's Pennsylvania Gazette to be published in the German newspaper under his control."
1266 E.g. *The Chronicle of the Kings of England: Written in the manner of the ancient Jewish Historians*, written by Lord Chesterfield and edited by Robert Dodley in his *Trifles* (London 1740).
1267 R.M. Calhoon, Smith William, *American National Biography* 20, New York/Oxford 1999, 305–306.
1268 Guzzo 2004, 27–55, where the example singled out is discussed on pp. 30–31 no. 6 and 47–53 Appendix 2. For another point of view, see Martinez 2011.
1269 Livy 40.29.2–14.

Another Latin author, Valerius Maximus, tells the same story,[1270] and Pliny the Elder has a slightly different version, in which he refers to a lost account by Varro, a Roman scholar of the first century B.C. Saint Augustine, the fourth-century Church Father, also mentions Varro, citing his *Liber de cultu deorum*.[1271] In all these versions of the story, details differ. For example, the grave's location is either at the top or at the foot of the Janiculum, and the exact number of books within varies, as does the contents themselves of the Latin books. The Greek texts are *praecepta* of philosophy, that is, "instructions" or "rules." The Greek philosopher Pythagoras is said to be the author, or at least the leader of the school from which the books originated, and Livy even makes his relationship with King Numa explicit. In all of these versions of the story, the Roman public magistrates burn the books without making the contents public.

Also reflected in Livy are the Roman authorities' panicked reactions to unknown philosophical texts. A few years before the discovery of the books, in 186 B.C., Rome had suffered greatly from the scandal of the *Bacchanalia*, a Dionysian festival of Greek origin that had broken many public order laws, so the authorities' fear of provoking new riots by publishing the philosophical books was understandable.

Modern authors of fictitious manuscripts never betray their sources of inspiration. The King Numa story, nevertheless, might be one ancient source of inspiration for the tradition of creating these fictitious manuscripts. The Phrygian author Dares' eyewitness account of the fall of Troy is another likely source. Cornelius Nepos, a biographer who lived in the first century B.C., claims to have found Dares' old autobiographical Geek manuscript in a letter written to his colleague Sallustius. With the intent of making it known to the Romans, Nepos then presents the reader with a Latin translation of the Greek *Daretis Phrygii de excidio Trojae historia* ("Dares the Phrygian's History of the Destruction of Troy"), a didactic novel that was very influential in the Middle Ages.[1272] Nepos claims it is a much more trustworthy source than Homer, who had never written about the destruction of Troy, since his *Iliad* finishes some weeks before its final destruction. Whoever actually penned this fictional letter and account – some unknown author most likely from the fifth of sixth century A.D. – must have decided that

---

1270 *Factorum et dictorum memorabilium* 1.1.12.
1271 Pliny, *Naturalis Historia* 13.84–88 (section on the history of the use of paper); Augustine, *De ciuitate Dei* 7.34. Augustine dealt with Numa Pompilius as instigator of various religious rules in various works, see Bruggiss 2009.
1272 For the text of Dares' *History*, see Beschorner 1992, 12. Cf. Beschorner 1992, 64–76 (commentary). Beschorner 1992, 67–68 gives other examples of ancient mock texts.

attaching it to the names of Nepos and Sallust would attract the reader's interest and enhance the text's importance.

A counterpart to Dares' work is Dictys' *Ephemeridos Belli Troiani libri sex* ("Six Books Containing the Journal of the Troian War"), a Greek text known only from a Latin translation.[1273] A preface and a prologue introduce Dictys, a Cretan, as a companion of Diomedes, the Trojan War hero. In antiquity, Cretans were set down as liars, which might be another reason for naming Dictys' origin. Sometime during the thirteen years of Nero's reign, in A.D. 66/67, peasants had supposedly found the text in Dictys' tomb and brought it to the Emperor, who recognized it as an old Greek scripture that required transcription. However, while Dictys' original Greek text was allegedly written – at the earliest – in 66 (but probably around 200), the Latin version we have, which was allegedly translated by a certain Lucius Septimius, dates to the fourth century. Septimius would have given it to his friend Quintus Aradius Rufinus.

Novels from Greece

One of the most popular novels of the late eighteenth century "stemming from Herculaneum" is Etienne-François Lantier's *Voyages d'Anténor en Grèce et en Asie*, the translation of a Greek manuscript allegedly found at Herculaneum.[1274] It is not an adventure story; it is a description of the costumes and libidinousness of the Greek way of life, relying heavily on Barthélemy's *Anacharsis* (see Chapter III, pp. 189–190). The Preface begins with a description of the author's visit to Herculaneum (a "habitation des gnomes") and Portici, where people are at work deciphering the scrolls. One of them, Abbé Spalatini, is dismayed about the nature of the texts that have been unrolled, which keep turning out to be philosophical treatises and not, as he hopes, great works by historians or tragic authors. When the author inquires about a very thick Greek scroll to the side, Spalatini dismisses it indignantly, thinking it to be a worthless work of an unknown author.[1275] As his Greek is too feeble to read the text on the spot, the author receives permission to

---

1273 What follows relies on Merkle 1989, 73–80 (discovery; comparison with the Numa episode), 243–286 (chronology Greek and Roman versions).
1274 Lantier 1795, 1798. García y García 1998, no. 7718. Translated into various languages (García y García 1998, nos. 7719–7721). Cf. Blix 2009, 54–55, who mentions another fictitious manuscript I have not seen: [anon.,] *Le sacre du Numa, ou Égerie* of 1775, also allegedly found at Herculaneum.
1275 Lantier 1795, 1798, Avant-Propos: "un rouleau très volumineux, dans l'idiôme grec, dont le titre étoit: *Voyage d'Anténor en Grèce et en Asie*. Je demandai à l'abbé s'il connoissoit cet ouvrage. – 'Non; je n'ai pas le loisir de lire un si grand fatras, qui d'ailleurs est d'un auteur très-inconnu.'"

take the book to Paris, where he hopes to find curious scholars and laymen who are interested in ancient costumes. Still in the Preface, and almost as a last resort to advertise the manuscript to women as well, the author claims that within this work, ladies will find romantic adventure stories as a remedy against boredom and sweet food for their more sensitive side.[1276] Finally, the author of the Preface reveals that the author of the ancient scroll is Anténor from Ephesus, the son of Euphrosyne, a priestess of Diana. Anténor would have written the work when he was 108 years old.[1277] Little in this work betrays connections with the excavations in Herculaneum.

In 1836 Father George Croly published *The Young Enchanter – From a Papyrus of Herculaneum*.[1278] It is supposedly a papyrus that was found in Herculaneum in the same year as its publication, and includes a miniature drawing of a painting of Mount Olympus. Croly's storyteller claims that a similar painting had been unearthed in 1815 in the "House of Alcmaeon" upon the happy occasion of King Ferdinand's return to Naples.[1279] *The Young Enchanter* is presented by the storyteller as a translation, which is kept in the *Officina* under the auspices of "Chevalier Collini." There are many lacunae in the manuscript, and as the story starts *mediis in rebus*, Croly finishes his prologue by saying:[1280]

> One of the most formidable of these mutilations occurs in the commencement, and still defies all the ingenuity of Italian scholarship to fill up the chasm.

Croly's tale, which begins in a villa on the Bay of Naples, describes a complicated love affair between Sempronius, a Roman officer, and Euphrosyne, a girl portrayed in a painting. After many vicissitudes, Sempronius finds his Euphrosyne and the couple can marry happily. Their companion, the philosopher Callias, finishes with a humorous observation in the style of *Much Ado About Nothing*:

1276 Lantier 1795, 1798, Avant-Propos: "Heureux si les savans me lisent par curiosité, les gens du monde par désœuvrement, pour acquérir sans peine quelques notions sur les moeurs et les usages antiques! Les femmes pourront trouver dans les aventures amoureuses un remède contre l'ennui et les vapeurs, et un doux aliment pour leur sensibilité."
1277 Antenor's name either refers to a wise man from Troy known from Homer's *Iliad*, or – less plausibly – to the maker of the statuary group of Harmodius and Aristogeiton on the Athenian Agora after 510 B.C. On both Antenors see the brief entries in *Der Neue Pauly* 1 (1996) 727–728.
1278 Croly 1836. See on him Goldhill 2011, 237–239.
1279 This is the House of Sallustius, also called House of Actaeon in Pompeii. Famous as the living quarters of one of the protagonists of Bulwer-Lytton's *Last Days* (here chapter IV, p. 226) and highlighted for its *venereum* by Mazois 1819 (chapter III, p. 191).
1280 Croly 1836, 10.

"but, in the name of Cupid and Venus, again I ask, why take all the trouble?"[1281] What we read is an adventure story similar to Greek novels of the Roman era like Achilles Tatius' *Leucippe and Clitophon*, full of misunderstandings, recognitions of lost persons, and shipwrecks. The Greek world is depicted as full of luxury and richness, with Asia and Greece lands of uncontrolled emotions and cruelty, while Campania, and especially Pompeii, denote rest. A non-Greek priest in the story is a barbarous and untrustworthy person, similar to Arbaces in Bulwer-Lytton's *Last Days*. Interestingly, Euphrosyne is none other than Anténor's mother in Lantier's *Voyages d'Anténor en Grèce et en Asie*.

For sure, the story would have sunk into complete oblivion if not for Charles Baudelaire, who published a French translation in 1846 as a piece of his own called *Le jeune enchanteur. Histoire tirée d'un palimpseste d'Herculanum*. In his complete works published in 1869, "Herculanum" becomes "Pompeia," among other changes. In 1950 the literary historian W.T. Baudy discovered that Croly was, in fact, the source of Baudelaire's story,[1282] and painstakingly demonstrated Baudelaire's lack of mastery of the English language by comparing the two versions. Baudelaire frequently ran into the trap of false friends: "actual" becomes "actuel" instead of "réel" "lovely" is rendered "amoureux" rather than "joli," "charge with" becomes "charger de" and not "accuser," and so on. Baudy cannot explain why Baudelaire committed this act of plagiarism under the pretence of a translation, but rightly defines it as such.[1283] Baudy's suggestion that Croly might have even seen Baudelaire's version remains speculative, as there is no evidence of that ever happening.

Less a novel than a philosophical treatise wrapped in a thin story line (albeit one that achieved great popularity and was often reprinted and translated) is *A few days in Athens, being the translation of a Greek manuscript discovered in Herculaneum* by Frances Wright d'Arusmont, who addresses her readers with a *captatio benevolentiae* in the preface:[1284]

> That I may not obtain credit for more learning than I possess, I beg to acknowledge the assistance I have received in my version of the curious relict of antiquity now offered to the public from the beautiful Italian MSS, of the erudite Professor of Greek in the university of *****.

1281 Croly 1836, 38.
1282 Baudy 1950. This discovery got no general knowledge (García y García 1998, no. 1400 has Baudelaire only). For Blix 2009, 36 and 244 note 37 Baudelaire's is an original story, with an English "keepsake" as source. Cf. Leppmann 1966, 89, 191. See Baudelaire 1975, 1405–1407 (comment by Claude Pichois). Because of the false attribution it is logically lacking in Baudelaire 1980 (mentioned on p. XIX). First publication on February 20–22, 1846, in the daily paper *L'esprit public*, then half a year later in the monthly *Le magasin littéraire*.
1283 Baudy 1950, 238: "Ainsi donc un plagiat sous les espèces d'une traduction."
1284 Wright 1822, I. Not in García y García 1998.

This "I" received a torn manuscript in Naples in 1817, and completed the lacunae in order to publish a reconstructed version of the Greek text in Italian. Wright, for her part, now presents an English translation. However:[1285]

> I have only to add, that the present volume comprises little more than a third of the original MS.; it will be sufficient, however, to enable the public to form an estimate of the probable value of the whole.

As the story goes, Theon, a young man from Corinth, has arrived in Athens to study with Zeno, the famous Stoic, but instead meets Epicurus, who invites him to come to his garden. Most of the twelve chapters are situated in Epicurus' garden and contain a series of dialogues – some between the two philosophical rivals and others with Cleanthes, another philosopher, explain the beauty of Epicurean thinking, so that Theon finally joins that opposing school. Wright does not present her mock manuscript with the artificial lacunae so often found in other works of this genre; hers is a complete work. Wright, a Scottish feminist *avant la lettre* who traveled through the United States in 1818–1820 and worked there as an abolitionist from 1824 until her return to Europe in 1839, believed in equal rights for all people. The contents of her book, written in Scotland in 1818, illustrate this clearly. One of Epicurus' pupils, the girl Leontium, seems like a self-portrait of the author when she suggests a lively involvement in Epicurus' doctrine of tolerance.[1286] Herculaneum is used only as a vehicle to "publish" an antique-like Epicurean text that conveys Wright's political ideas.

Giants Destroy Herculaneum

The only mythical poem about the destruction of Pompeii and Herculaneum is Joseph-François-Stanislas Maizony de Lauréal's French epic, *L'Héracléade ou Herculanum enseveli sous la lave du Vésuve, poëme de L. A. Florus*.[1287] Although Ingres, the famous French painter, sketched Maizony's portrait in Rome around 1813, I was unable to find much information about him.[1288] Thanks to his work

---

1285 Wright 1822, VIII. She adds that Italian scholars have no monopoly any longer to study old classical texts, especially when they are not of religious nature and pertain the classical era. This refers to the arrival of people like Hayter and Sickler (see Chapter II, pp. 128, Chapter IX, p. 401).
1286 Morris 1992, 16–17. More on this work in Morris 1992, 66–67 and 134–135; E.M. Moormann in Mattusch 2013, 195–199.
1287 Maizony de Lauréal 1837. García y García 1998, no. 3949.
1288 Drawing in Musée Bonnat at Bayonne, reproduced in Mattusch 2013, 190. The internet catalogue entry http://www.museebonnat.bayonne.fr/index.php?rub=recherche&fiche=95CE17291

for the Napoleonic government in Rome, Maizony must have known Italy well. As indicated on the frontispiece of *L'Héracléade*, he was a member of the *Academia Pontiana* at Naples. Here, he presents a translation of a mock ancient manuscript allegedly found in Naples in 1812–1813 and later stolen by a Neapolitan ruffian. In contrast with other purloined manuscripts from Naples, this work allegedly dates to a later time, since it is dedicated to Pliny the Younger and the "author" – not indicated, except in the title of the publication – is assumed to be Florus, a historian who lived at the beginning of the second century (see p. 345). Publishing a poetic translation based on the original prose of the manuscript, the "editor" mixes various elements of the "lost manuscript" genre and supplies voluminous commentary. The resulting poetic elaboration consists of ten *Chants* ("Songs") in alexandrines with the rhyme scheme AA-BB-CC.

The epic tells of the struggle of the eastern goddess Cybele and a mythical underground people, the Giants, against the Olympian gods, and focuses on the destruction of Herculaneum. The Giants are irritated by the fact that Herculaneum sits on the flanks of Vesuvius, which they consider their property. The Giants try to kindle the fire under Vesuvius by means of a tunnel full of fire that connects Vesuvius to Mount Etna, its sister volcano. As a result, the eruption is worse than war, and devastates the area such that the landscape resembles the moon and looks as if it has been afflicted by a deluge.[1289] Hercules, whose "playground" in the form of Herculaneum has been lost, complains bitterly, and Father Jupiter intervenes, explaining to him that the oracular prophecy will come true: something new will come and the old city will never suffer from future wars. With this consolation, the poem – in which new archaeological splendor is announced – comes to an end.[1290] The theme of this epic is the Giants' revenge for their defeat

---

&typ=2&type=3&fiche=95CE7364 (accessed December 22, 2011) states: "Monsieur de Lauréal, qui vécut à Rome de 1811 à 1814, était greffier à la Cour impériale dans cette ville. Son épouse et lui tenaient un salon que fréquentaient les artistes français, dont Ingres. Il rencontra ainsi Madeleine Chapelle, future première épouse de l'artiste." Brief mentions in Maizony 1837, XI, note 1. Everist 2002, 108 recalls him as the libretto writer of *Louis XII ou La Route de Reims* by Alphonse Vergne of 1825, on which work see his pp. 158–167, 169. See also J.M. Quérard/F. Bourquelot/C. Louandre, *La littérature française contemporaine. XIXsiècle*, Paris 1854, 241.

1289 Maizony de Lauréal 1837, 237: "Partout la cendre morte, et presse de son faix / Les murs, les toits rompus des hameaux, des palais; [...]"

1290 Maizony de Lauréal 1837, 255: "Dévoilée à l'éclat de leur flambeau magique / Ta ville secouera sa cendre léthargique, / Et reverra le jour, mon fils, et son tombeau / De ses murs rajeunis deviendra le berceau. / Pompéia, qui subit le destin d'Héraclée, / Comme elle à la lumière en ces temps rappelée, / Vivante sortira de son sépulcre épais; / Et de toute insolence affranchis désormais, / Nos temples radieux, peuplés de leurs images. / Du monde émerveillé recevront les hommages, / Et les peuples divers et leurs pasteurs pieux / De Rome triomphant adoreront les dieux." He gives a reference to the 1828 excavations in the commentary on p. 433.

in the mythical war against the Olympian gods, known as the Gigantomachy, which the gods only won thanks to the help of (mortal!) Hercules; this new Gigantomachy is unique in fiction about Pompeii and Herculaneum. The presence of the Giants relies on a rumor recorded by Dio Cassius and repeatedly referred to in novels and travel accounts:[1291]

> Numbers of huge men quite surpassing any human stature – such creatures, in fact, as the Giants are pictured to have been – appeared now on the mountain. Now in the surrounding country, and again in the cities, wandering over the earth day and night and also flitting through the air.

The Giants were extremely popular in Roman poetry and Maizony might have taken bits and pieces from various sources.[1292] He did his best to write a poem that fitted into the Latin and Greek tradition of learned epic poetry. His main source of inspiration was the anonymous poem *Aetna*, ascribed to the poets Virgil, Claudius Claudianus, and to Lucilius, the addressee of Seneca's letters. Seneca's *Letter* 79 researches the natural phenomenon of vulcanology in which mythological figures like the Giants (and their revenge) and Winds play major roles. Both the form and contents of the passage on Virgil's voyage through Hell in Dante's *Divina Commedia* might have been another of Maizony's literary inspirations. Finally, Maizony quotes Sannazaro's *Arcadia* in his commentary and may have been influenced by him directly.[1293]

Maizony's epic was called out as a hoax as early as 1854 in an anonymous American essay about French literature:[1294]

> So late as 1837, Maizony de Lauréal presented to the public a French translation of a poem by the Roman Florus, upon the destruction of Herculaneum; but, unfortunately, he has hitherto omitted to produce the Latin original, and consequently the general opinion is that the whole affair is a hoax.

1291 Dio Cassius, *Roman History* 66.22.2, translation Foster 1955, 305.
1292 Maizony de Lauréal's commentary contains a dense collection of quotations from ancient and modern texts that demonstrates a good command of the relevant literature. For a good overview of Roman evocations see F. Vian, Gigantes, in *LIMC* III (1988) 193–196; Johnston 2005; Smolenaars 2005.
1293 Maizony de Lauréal 1837, 311–312, 415.
1294 Anon., Literary Impostures, *The North American Review* 78 (1854) 305–345, quotation p. 314. I credit this reference to Thomas Willette, who also remembered the insertion of the *Héracléade* in Furchheim 1891, XXIII, 23 as a scholarly publication.

The attribution of the manuscript to Florus is rather unconvincing.[1295] Maizony would have been better off attributing it to another writer of this era of Silver Latin, like Statius, a poet from Naples, who became very popular for his epic poems in the last decade of the first century. Or would Tacitus have been a better candidate? Apparently, Maizony had wanted to link his work to Pliny the Younger, who had described the eruption so forcefully in his letters to this historian. One error Maizony commits is making Pliny the Younger the son of the Elder, which can be explained as the result of Maizony's desire to strengthen their affectionate bond and to enhance the family drama. An allusion to Herculaneum's peace under the earth reflects the decay of ancient monuments in towns like Rome, which are always visible under the sky, always suffering from the devastating forces of nature and of man. It is worth noticing that Leopardi offers a similar solace in his *Paralipomeni* (see Chapter I, pp. 53–54).

Maizony's interest in Vesuvius upholds a strong tradition. I recall Mme De Staël's interest in this mountain in *Corinne* and in her *Carnets de voyage*. Mankind is not able to control the hidden forces of this mountain, which so suddenly caused the disaster in 79.[1296] The emotions evoked by the volcano even stimulated a group of politically driven women in 1848 to name themselves Vésuviennes.[1297]

As to the composition, Maizony's work is entirely French in style and character. After looking in vain for similarities with seventeenth-century classics, I turned to Voltaire's 1728 *Henriade*, to which Maizony had actually written an addition.[1298] It is not difficult to find a series of similarities between the writing style, language usage, and composition of dialogues, language and style. Other exam-

---

1295 As for who Florus is, we know a poet (Annius Florus), an orator (P. Annius Florus), and a historian (L. Annaeus Florus or Julius Florus), who might all be the same person! See Von Albrecht 1997, II, 1411–1420, esp. 1411 note 1. Maizony de Lauréal 1837, vii has Annaeus Florus. The historian Florus' remarks on the Vesuvian cities are in his *Epitome* of Livy 1.11.3–6 and 2.8.45, but they do not pertain to the eruption.
1296 Schuerewegen 1991; here Chapter VI, p. 259. Cf. P. Larousse, *Grand dictionnaire universel du XIXe siècle*, Paris, X, 1873, 267–268 s.v. Lave; XV, 1876, 963–964 s.v. Vésuve, 964 s.v. Vésuvien, -ienne, 1169–1170 s.v. Volcan. Here many references to the 79 eruption are made.
1297 *Les Vésuviennes ou la constitution politique des femmes, par une Société de Françaises*, Paris 1848. Women ask for freedom and civil rights and explain the name as follows (p. 14): "C'est le premier nom de dérision qui a servi à nous désigner au ridicule, et nous mettons notre amour-propre à le réhabiliter.
Puis il peint merveilleusement notre position et plus qu'aucun autre il exprime notre pensée; seulement, la *lave* si longtemps contenue, qui doit enfin se répandre autour de nous, n'est nullement incendiaire, elle est toute régénératrice." See i.a. Schwegman 2008, 16.
1298 *La petite Henriade ou l'enfance d'Henri IV, poème en trois chants avec des notes historiques et littéraires; présenté à S.A.R. Mgr le Duc de Bordeaux*, Paris 1824.

ples of congruence are the use of pagan gods, and personifications of natural phenomena and the force of nature (these personifications are more logical in Maizony's *L'Héracléade* than in Voltaire's *Henriade*, which is a historical account of King Henri le Grand of France),[1299] the presence of ten songs in alexandrines, each with a synopsis ("Argument"), and the learned commentary at the end. Both Voltaire and Maizony insert long stories as foundations of their respective narratives. The most striking use of a type of allegory is the image of Discord flying to Rome, seeking help against Henri, in Chant IV of Voltaire.[1300] In *Héracléade*, Cybele acts as a parallel to Voltaire's Discord.[1301] While Saint Louis XII encourages Henri in a dream (Chant VII, similar to the visits to Hades by Odysseus and Aeneas), in the *Héracleade*, Jupiter comforts Hercules, his son. The hell in Voltaire's Chant VII also likely showed Maizony how to evoke the horrid underworld, whereas Chant IX sings about the beautiful land of Love, which would match Maizony's description of Campania.[1302]

1299 See the extensive introduction and comments in Voltaire 1970 and see Besterman 1976, 97–105. There were some 50 to 60 editions during Voltaire's life only and many imitations (Besterman 1976, 101; *Héracléade* not mentioned).
1300 She arrives at the battlefield when D'Aumale has just been wounded, Chant IV, vs. 96–98 (Voltaire 1970, 445): "La Discorde le vit, et trembla pour d'Aumale: / La barbare qu'elle est a besoin de ses jours: / Elle s'éleve en l'air, et vole à son secours." See for Discordia also Virgil, *Aeneid* 8.702.
1301 Cf. Maizony de Lauréal 1837, 31: "Comme un homme courbé, qui, la houe à la main, / A travers le coteau, la plaine, le jardin, / Écartant chaque obstacle, ouvre une route sure / Au ruisseau qu'il conduit loin de sa source obscure, / Et qui, par une pente en sa course emporté, / Roule devant son guide un flot précipité; / L'ingénieux Vulcain, délaissant son enclume, / D'île en île construit des canaux de bitume, / Et jusqu'au bord d'Hercule amène sous les eaux / Des feux éoliens les immenses ruisseaux; / Travail digne d'un dieu!" with Voltaire's Chant IV, vs. 157–166 (Voltaire 1970, 447–448) about Discorde's devastating work: "La Discorde aussitôt, plus prompte qu'un éclair, / Fend d'un vol assuré les campagnes de l'air. / Partout chez les Français le trouble et les alarmes / Présentent à ses yeux des objets pleins de charmes : / Son haleine en cent lieux répand l'aridité ; / Le fruit meurt en naissant, dans son germe infecté : / Les épis renversés sur la terre languissent ; / Le ciel s'en obscurcit, les astres en pâlissent ; / Et la foudre en éclats, qui gronde sous ses pieds, / Semble annoncer la mort aux peuples effrayés."
1302 E.g. Chant VII, vs. 127–140 (Voltaire 1970, 517–518): "Henri dans ce moment, d'un vol précipité / Est par un tourbillon dans l'espace emporté / Vers un séjour informe, aride, affreux, sauvage, / De l'antique chaos abominable image, / Impénétrable aux traits de ces soleils brillants, / Chefs-d'œuvre du Très-Haut, comme lui bienfaisants. / Sur cette terre horrible, et des anges haïe, / Dieu n'a point répandu le germe de la vie, / La Mort, l'affreuse Mort, et la Confusion, / Y semblent établir leur domination. / 'Quelles clameurs, ô Dieu! quels cris épouvantables! / Quels torrents de fumée! et quels feux effroyables! / Quels monstres, dit Bouron, volent dans ces climats! / Quels gouffres enflammés s'entr'ouvrent sous mes pas!'"

Herculanean Manuscripts and the Third Life of the Villa of the Papyri

When we return to the time of the discovery of the papyri in Herculaneum, the first fictitious work connected with them is *Lettres de Julie à Ovide*. There are various versions known of Charlotte-Antoinette de Bressay's epistolary novel,[1303] a genre that was popular in the eighteenth century. In Julie's fictional letters, she writes to the poet Ovid about his *Ars amatoria*. Ovid had been banished to Tomis (modern day Constanța, in Romania) in A.D. 8. Although De Bressay wrongly thinks that her "Julie" is based on Julia, the daughter of Augustus, the first Roman emperor, it is more likely that her story is based on Augustus' granddaughter, Vipsania Julia. After the death of her second husband (and Vipsania Julia's father), Marcus Agrippa, Augustus had forced Julia into an unhappy marriage to Tiberius on the demand of Tiberius' mother Livia. This reputedly led her to adulterous liaisons with various noblemen, and she was sent into exile on the island of Pandataria in 6 B.C. Vipsania Julia was born in 19 or 18 B.C., and like her mother, was accused of living an adulterous lifestyle and was exiled to Trimerus, a small island on the Apulian coast, in the same year that Ovid was exiled to Tomis. She would live on Trimerus until her death in A.D. 28. The connection of Vipsania Julia with Ovid is doubtful, and hypotheses about her being the Corinna in Ovid's *Amores* lack a sound foundation.[1304] As to De Bressay's mock manuscript, there is no preface or introduction to the letters recording their discovery at Herculaneum. This prov-

---

1303 De Bressay 1753, 1756. Claude-Joseph Dorat is also mentioned as the author. Not in García y García 1998. According to *Grand Dictionnaire des femmes de l'ancienne France* it was the marquis's son who made De Bressay's name public. There are also German and Italian editions of this work, and a similar work entitled *Lettre de Julie, fille d'Auguste, à Ovide*, Paris 1766, containing a 20-page letter written in iambic hexameter, with a rhyming scheme of AA-BB-CC. According to the "Avis de l'éditeur" it had been printed in 1760 in two editions and has now been re-edited and greatly altered, because the author "n'a pas conservé trente vers de l'ancienne façon; & il a cru le sujet assez piquant pour lui donner tous ses soins." Julie, the protagonist, asks Ovid if he is on a shipwreck or an uninhabited island. She is imprisoned by her father (12) "ou plûtot mon tyran & mon persécuteur," exposed to (p. 14) "Méprisables Romains, Romains infortunés / Assassins aujourd'hui, demain assassins." *Lettre de Julie* belongs to an anthology of love letters in verse, *Lettres en vers, ou épitres héroïques et amoureuses*, Paris 1766.

1304 Cf. Ovid, *Tristia* 2.103 and 3.5, 49. On Julia's adultery, which began after a conspiracy involving one of her husbands, L. Aemilius Paulus, see Suetonius, *Augustus* 65; Tacitus, *Annals* 4.71; *Scholia in Iuvenalem* 6.158. see on the fortune of both Julia's A. Simonis, in A. von Möllendorff, A./ A. & L. Simonis (eds), *Historische Gestalten der Antike* (Der Neue Pauly Suppl. 8), Stuttgart/Weimar 2013, 535–540, esp. 536 [Julia] and 721–734, esp. 726 [Ovid].

enance only appears in the subtitle of the anonymous English translation of the French original.[1305]

The French author Paul Bory wrote a mock manuscript, *Mémoires d'un Romain. Vie privée de l'ancienne Rome*, which was allegedly found in the "Maison du philosophe," probably the Villa of the Papyri (fig. 14). Four scrolls contain the diary of Decius Cornelius Lentulus Ocella, who passed away in 827 *ab urbe condita*, i.e. A.D. 71. Lentulus, a man of noble birth and a member of the Roman *Cornelii* family, penned his own diary, which covers the years 47 to 71, in a frank and highly informative manner.[1306] The "editor" of the mock manuscript states that although the text is already encumbered by many lacunae, he has left out additional parts deemed indecent. Lentulus, the editor continues, tried to follow the traditional Roman *mores*, and avoided Greek influences that led to debauchery – examples of which come to the fore in the run of the text. In 62, Lentulus finally withdrew from public life, having decided to live a peasant life in the countryside in "Cratère,", the Bay of Naples, leaving behind the turmoil of urban society.[1307]

In his mock memoir, Bory includes some elements commonly found in historical novels, including the marriage of an old man to a thirteen-year-old girl. In Alexandria, Lentulus attends a funeral, and witnesses the corpse's embalming, following Egyptian tradition. Christians feature a couple of times. In 54 Lentulus refers to "rites effrayantes" of the "Nazaréens."[1308] After this diary entry, Lentulus does not mention Christians in the narrative until he notices that Stipontus, his slave, is a Christian. Lentulus is typical member of the Roman upper class. Although he is always aware of his high social status, he admits that when danger is afoot, like during the earthquake of A.D. 62, class distinctions lose all meaning.[1309]

1305 *Letters from Julia, the daughter of Augustus, to Ovid. A manuscript discovered at Herculaneum. Translated from a copy of the original*, London 1753, Preface, p. VIII states the find in the ruins.
1306 Bory 1890, 20: "C'est une sorte d'autobiographie dont le personnage était incontestablement de bonne naissance." Not in García y García 1998. The protagonist is a fictitious member of the family of the *Cornelii Lentuli*. See *RE* 4 (1900) 1355, s.v. Cornelius nos. 172–241, and in some of the supplements (see *Register*, Munich 1980, 89 nos. 177–238). See also *Der Neue Pauly* 3 (1997) 173–176. This branch of the family had died out by the end of the first century A.D. Another Lentulus features in Toudouze 1878 (see Chapter VI, pp. 322–323). On this book, see Moormann 2008, 378–380.
1307 Bory 1890, 158: "où les moeurs plus rudes me garantissaient le succès, un domaine de mon goût, de l'espace, des champs et des paysans."
1308 Bory 1890, 88–89.
1309 Bory 1890, 173: "Dans ce premier moment de confusion il n'y avait plus de distinction de classes, le plus orgueilleux comme le plus humble étant également misérables; on peut même dire que les plus riches étaient les plus dépourvus."

Bory's main sources are Suetonius' *Lives of the Twelve Caesars*, and Tacitus' *Annals* and *Historiae*. Bory tries to exemplify the Romans' decadence, as incarnated by the debauchery of their emperors. Pompeii stands in the middle of this decadence. The fall of Pompeii – and of the Roman Empire later on – is determined by the way these Romans live. Greece, with its own rambunctious debauchery, is the origin of Rome's suffering.[1310]

The book belongs to the typically French *illustrés* of the late nineteenth century, novels lavishly illustrated thanks to the modern technique of steel engravings. Several illustrations look familiar to those in contemporary Pompeii textbooks.[1311] The character of these images ranges from picturesque plates in the style of nineteenth-century painters like Gérôme and Alma-Tadema, to modern photographs and simple line drawings known since the time of John Flaxman, the British neoclassical artist. Some illustrations demonstrate incorrect concepts of reconstructions that were in style during Bory's time, like flat-roofed atriums, despite the reconstructions in several manuals which already showed the inclining roofs of the *compluvium* (fig. 14).

In the 1990s, excavations of the Villa of the Papyri were meant to uncover new manuscripts and to re-explore the remains excavated in the 1750s. After a long period of rest, with truly new archaeological research being carried out again, these excavations also inspired two authors to write thrillers.[1312]

Michela Ascione's 2007 *La Villa dei Papiri*, is about a group of destructive treasure hunters excavating in the Villa of the Papyri, in which official research is being carried out simultaneously.[1313] Its dry title (and the fact that Ascione is an archaeologist from Naples) does not immediately betray that her book is, in fact, fiction. Ascione's protagonist, Francesca Gargiulo, is a young archaeologist who discovers clandestine excavations in one of the Bourbon galleries in which charred papyri have been discovered as well as rooms belonging to the complex. At the same time, she discovers that Giovanni Corcione, her old professor in Naples who had been planning a scientific project to carry out investigations in the Bourbon galleries, has vanished. Although she fails to reach him, she gradually discovers that he is one of the unsanctioned treasure hunters. At this point,

---

1310 See also David 2001, 62 (with a long quotation from Bory 1890, 35–36 about Greece), 158 (determinism), 250 (emperors). See also, as mentioned at p. 64, note 249, Livy's Preface to his *Ab urbe condita*.
1311 E.g. Bory 1890, 379 = Lagrèze 1887, 105; Bory 1890, 331/351 shop = Overbeck 1856 and 1866, fig. 202.
1312 On the Villa of the Papyri, see publications mentioned in note 1253.
1313 Ascione 2007. Not included in the essay by Stefano Rocchi (2006–2007) on thrillers and detectives.

Margherita, the story's narrator, interrupts with the news that she has just heard from a friend that Francesca's adventure, which she has written as fiction, is not, in fact, the fictional story she had believed it to be but a real event: illegal excavators are now being arrested by the police thanks to her novel. This sudden change from one fictitious situation to another (that is, from the thriller about Francesca and her professor to the discovery of clandestine excavations thanks to Margherita's book) is a literary technique also known from Italo Calvino's *Se una notte d'inverno un viaggiatore*.[1314] Ascione's profession justifies her insertion into the narrative of precise, scholarly details about the Villa of the Papyri and the excavations of Herculaneum, whereas the fact that she was born in Naples enhances the reader's impression of her strong empathy for the city and its environs.

Carol Goodman's 2008 *The Night Villa* features a more elaborate plot that circles around an American excavation project that is more an Indiana Jones story than a scientific enterprise.[1315] Sophie Chase, a professor of classics at the University of Texas at Austin, participates in an expedition to Herculaneum set up by the Greco-American "software millionaire" John Lyros. The team's adventures intermingle with a story read on a papyrus found during these excavations, so that gradually, the modern archaeological team becomes a part of the ancient story. Their quest for two scrolls – one by Pythagoras entitled *Golden Verses*[1316] and one that contains the diary of Iusta, a slave girl – leads to horrifying adventures in old tunnels. I shall not betray the outcomes of either story. Almost no Italians feature in the novel, apart from insignificant personnel and an archaeologist named Maria Prezziotti, and the American excavators work autonomously without contacting local archaeologists or the local authorities responsible for the site.[1317] Superstition, sacred and secret organizations, great wealth, and American university culture abound in Goodman's book. The Villa and Herculaneum both get little detailed attention. According to Phineas, the author of the ancient papyrus,

---

1314 Turin 1979. Translated by William Weaver as *If on a winter's night a traveler* (New York 1981).
1315 Goodman 2008, 147. Tunnels are roughly drilled through antique floors to reach the supposed hiding place of Phineas' scrolls. Members of the team hide information from each other and (want to) steal objects for private reasons. Remains other than the scrolls and the figural mural decorations get no attention.
1316 Goodman 2008, 325: this cryptic text would contain an announcement of the birth of Christ.
1317 The official excavation authorities of Herculaneum never obtain the results or discussions of our team. The only archaeologist referred to is Wilhelmina Feemster Jashemski, who researched gardens in the area of Vesuvius in the 1950s–1980s (Goodman 2008, 171, 192–193). Several names are misspelled. The waitress Giulia is called Guilia or Guila. Her twin sister is Theresa instead of Teresa. Maria is from the Pontificia Instituto Archeologia Sacra (p. 131), which must either be the Pontificio Istituto di Archeologia Cristiana or the Pontificia Commissione di Archeologia Sacra.

Herculaneum lives in "pleasure of the flesh."[1318] Walking through the town, he sees obscene graffiti.[1319] Iusta belongs to a community of Christians who live in a poor quarter of the town.[1320]

Sophie and other team members successfully translate the Latin scroll *a prima vista* into fluent English. When she finds another manuscript in a terracotta statuette, its letters vanish as soon as they are exposed to the light, but she is able to "transcribe" a translation. Lacunae in the scrolls are rare and do not hamper the understanding of the story. The "Latin" parts, which chiefly focus on ambition, love and hatred, do not differ stylistically from the "American" ones, and display the unorthodox behavior of the Roman protagonists, who are as selfish as the team members discovering them. Goodman skillfully explains some ancient habits and rituals. *The Night Villa* is a thrilling dual story in which the characters of the protagonists – both ancient and modern – change back and forth several times. Yet, as a whole, the book has less to do with ancient Herculaneum than with the obsession of sects and occult beliefs.

In *Le ragazze di Pompei*, Carmen Covito (see Chapter III, p. 209) presents a translation of a fictitious Latin manuscript without a provenance, unless we are meant to believe that it derives from *Codex Herculanensis Novissimus A1*, a Latin manuscript about the life of three Pompeian girls. *Codex* constitutes a female pendant of Petronius' *Satyrica*, with all sorts of debauchery and transgressions of civilized Roman ways of life.[1321] The narrative is interrupted by the editor's comments and notes, which refer to (made up) modern scholarship and contain quotations from and allusions to unknown texts of ancient authors like Hippocrates, Nossis and Ovid, as well as ancient culinary recipes.[1322] Instead of the male point of view advocated by Petronius, the unnamed author of Covito's mock manuscript represents an – anachronistic – female view of antiquity, with women as independent and free citizens.

1318 Goodman 2008, 79. This seems one of the reasons for Lyros to work here (Goodman 2008, 226–227).
1319 Goodman 2008, 174. She describes the terrace of Nonius Balbus and the Suburban Baths.
1320 Goodman 2008, 299. Again a trope of fiction: Christians are depicted as lower-class people or slaves. Cf. Chapter IV.
1321 Covito 2012, 39.
1322 Covito 2012, 39–41, 63–65, 98–99, 119.

Manuscripts from Pompeii

Pompeii, thus far, has offered up no texts other than inscriptions, graffiti, wax tablets, and dipinti. The thrill of the prospect of finding a manuscript in some ancient mansion has nevertheless inspired authors to create their own. Some of these are La Tourette's *The Pompeii Scroll* (see Chapter V, p. 280), Mazois' *Scaurus* (see Chapter III, pp. 191–192), and *The Vestal* (see Chapter IV, pp. 217–218).[1323] *The Vestal* starts with two friends traveling through Italy. At Nettuno, they receive an old manuscript from a priest, who is not mentioned by name. The remainder of the book presents the translation of the priest's manuscript, which ends with some sentences uttered by a certain Piso.[1324]

A subtle comparison between old and new manuscripts and their loss forms part of a fascinating thriller from 1874–1875. In Wilkie Collins' *The Law and the Lady*, Eustace Macallan is accused of having murdered his first wife, Sara. Upon this accusation, out of shame and remorse, he separates from Valeria, his current wife, who incessantly searches for the truth, believing that her husband is innocent. In the style of Agatha Christie's Miss Marple, she resolves the murder mystery. The search for evidence of Eustace's innocence is described as if it were an archaeological expedition at Pompeii.[1325] The town plays a role in the story, when documents have to be excavated in a garbage heap next to the house in which Sara's body was found under suspicious circumstances. Whereas Playmore, the attorney, doubts that any papers will be found that are crucial to her case, Valeria is hopeful, and refers to Pompeii, where fragile objects were found undisturbed:[1326]

> By way of encouraging Mr Playmore, I now reminded him that the eruption which had overwhelmed the town had preserved, for more than sixteen hundred years, such perishable things as the straw in which pottery had been packed; the paintings on house walls; the dresses worn by the inhabitants; and (most noticeable of all, in our case) a piece of ancient

---

[1323] La Tourette 1975; *Vestal* 1830. A mock correspondence on the *sator* riddle is that "edited" in Le Ninèze 2008, presented here in Chapter IV, p. 238.
[1324] *Vestal* 1830, 162. Piso is also the surname of the supposed owner of the ancient Villa of the Papyri, Lucius Calpurnius Piso Caesonius (see M. Capasso in Zarmakoupi 2010, 89–113 on various proposals).
[1325] Collins 1998, 285 (chapter XXIV); Zintzen 1998, 33–34, gives another interesting passage from Collin's detective novel.
[1326] Collins 1998, 340, chapter XLIII. The excavation almost gets scientific dimensions, thanks to the use of sciences and the employment of a chemist (pp. 351–352). Cf. Zimmerman 2008, on Victorians and new methods of excavating. On dust heaps and excavations, see Zimmerman 2008, 162–168 (there is no mention of Collins). Valeria visited Pompeii with her father (Collins 1998, 265).

paper, still attached to the volcanic ashes which had fallen over it. If these discoveries had been made after a lapse of sixteen centuries, under a layer of dust and ashes on a large scale, surely we might hope to meet with similar cases of preservation, after a lapse of three or four years only, under a layer of dust and ashes on a small scale?

Valerio Massimiano Manfredi's *La torre della solitudine* is a novel full of oddities in the vein of Dan Brown's *The Da Vinci Code*. It revolves around Desmond Garrett, an independent scholar, whose self-proclaimed purpose in life was to unravel the mysteries of seven ancient tombs in the Near East and northern Africa. During one of his research trips, he went missing, and his son Philip is now seeking his lost father. Thanks to hints hidden in a book by his father, he meets strange Vatican librarians and descends under a convent in or near Naples, where he finds a Roman house containing the remains of a victim of Vesuvius holding a Greek manuscript on parchment. Philip is unable to grasp the manuscript, but manages to take a photograph, and eventually succeeds in deciphering the text, which contains more clues leading to his father.[1327] Manfredi's use of Pompeii is logical for the sake of the story, but, much like his concise evocations of Aleppo, Palmyra, and Petra, he does not convey a specific impression of the ancient town.

Modern Mock Manuscripts in the Guise of Ancient Papyri

Mock papyri need not be ancient, as we have seen with the texts of Fabius Pictor and Nathan Ben Saddi at the beginning of this chapter. Modern fiction that pretends to be ancient is often merely assigned an ancient date, and hides allusions to anything modern. But this is not the case with a collection of texts by the fictitious Mr. Price of Cardiganshire, presented in the authorless *Democritus: Or the Laughing Philosopher*. In the introduction, the anonymous "editor" of *Democritus* tells of how he met Mr. Price in Naples:[1328]

> I knew him well at *Naples*. About a week before he left this city, he was led by curiosity to venture himself among the ruins of *Herculaneum*, where the manuscript of the following book was either dropt by him out of his pocket or stolen from him. It was brought to me by one of the *Miners* in that *subterranean* city, after Mr. *Price* was gone to *Rome*. About a month after his arrival there he died of fever. To prevent the loss of so valuable a treasure to the public, I have now printed it, as soon as I could after my arrival in *England*.

1327 Manfredi 1996 (2006), chapter VI. The transcription mentions an Etruscan text by Avle Vipinas, a man we encounter in the prologue of the book during an expedition in the desert.
1328 *Democritus* 1771, V–VI, Preface. Not in García y García 1998.

What follows is a series of satirical discussions about English politics, rhymes and riddles, not one of which has anything to do with Pompeii or Herculaneum.

Another rather bewildering work is a bundle of American nursery rhymes attributed to one Thomas Appleton, which is proudly announced as a manuscript found at Herculaneum. The texts contain no hint of this source. Nor do they describe ancient themes; all are simply pleasant verses for young children accompanied by simple illustrations.[1329]

Yet another puzzling work is *Homardiana*, an anonymous poem written in iambic hexameters with the rhyme scheme AA-BB-CC.[1330] That it is in the form of an ancient papyrus is suggested by the lacunae in the text, indicated with dotted lines and incomplete words. The poet recounts the tale of a dinner party where a lobster is served at midnight. While the orchestra is playing a sad march, another lobster marches in seeking the cooked lobster, his wife. The host asks a medical doctor to bring the she-lobster to life. Despite the doctor's modesty – he is no veterinarian – she is resurrected, and everyone there dances into the night. A touch of antiquity is betrayed in the first line, which sounds like the beginning of a classical epic: "I sing about these lobsters, ancient crustaceans, giant fish saved from the flood and served upon Mr. D's table to brighten a gloomy ball."[1331] The illusion of this being an ancient manuscript is shattered, however, by a reference to contemporary French upper-class society, in which a certain gentleman is libeled. This enigmatic yet playful poem is still a mystery to me; unfortunately, I still cannot determine to what or to whom it is referring.

1329 Appleton 1872. There is a brief poem by him called "Pompeii," published in *Faded Leaves*, Boston 1872, 169: "The silence there was what most haunted me. / Long, speechless streets, whose stepping-stones invite / Feet which shall never come; to left and right / Gay colonnades and courts, – beyond, the glee, / Heartless, of that forgetful Pagan sea. / On roofless homes and waiting streets, the light / Lies with a pathos sorrow fuller than night. / Fancy forbids this doom of Life with Death / Wedded, and with her wand restores the Life. / The jostling throngs swarm, animate, beneath / The open shops, and all the tragic strife / Of voices, Roman, Greek, Barbarian, mix. / The wreath / Indolent hangs on far Vesuvius' crest; / And over all, the glowing town and guiltless sea, sweet rest." Not in García y García 1998.
1330 *Homardiana* 1861. Not in García y García 1998. For the text, see Moormann 2010, 244–245.
1331 *Homardiana* 1861, start: "Je chante ces Homards, antiques crustacés, / Gigantesques poissons du déluge sauvés, / Et qui, pour égayer un bal inégayable, / Furent chez Monsieur D*** servis dessus la table." The lobster dance also reminds the lobster-quadrille in Lewis Carroll's 1865 Alice in Wonderland, Chapter 10 (suggestion made to me by Prof. Wessel Krul, University of Groningen).

Manuscripts not Found at All?

In poetry, there are means of suggesting varying degrees of preservation of manuscripts by leaving unfinished verses, inserting empty lines or adding dotted half sentences. In David Citino's collection of poems, *The News and other poems*, aspects of both ancient and modern daily life and politics are integrated.[1332] Italy is highlighted, complete with its historical treasures and modern problems. The fragmentary state of the poem makes it look like a papyrus or a crumbled piece of paper thrown into the garbage, a form that well corresponds with the poem's words, which concern the millions of unruly tourists who damage the ruins by stealing archaeological objects and scribbling on the walls (and it can be implied, leave their garbage behind). The poem bemoans the serious decay of paintings and mosaics, despite the limited access to the Roman houses that contain them. We recognize some classical elements, like graffiti, Pompeian red paintings, old houses and Vesuvius, which silently presides over the landscape. The corpses preserved as plaster casts are the most impressive remains of death. The "doll houses" remind the reader of Goethe's "Puppenschränke" (see Chapter II, p. 149).

> Pompeii in Danger
>
> – Reuters
>
> Tourists, pretty thieves,
> graffiti
>   diddlers,
> the weather
>   of southern Italy –
> the current peril, not
> moody, fuming Vesuvius.
> In 1956
> 64 Roman houses
>   open to the public.
> Today, but 14.
> Last year,
>   two million sweating visitors.
> They pry up
> mosaics.
>   Fondle
>   frescoes. *Pompeii Red*
> dulls to flat pink.

1332 Citino 2002, 28–29.

>   Where art
>   is concerned
> (not to mention
> reality)
>   people are
> the problem.
>   Cemetery doll houses.
> Grave petting zoo.
> Romans
>   writhe,
> contort in plaster.
>   Living couples
> come to touch,
>   to screw,
> imagining tours
>
> of art
>   falling
>   on their backs
> like snow, muffled moans,
>   the night
>   a mountain
> coming down.

Conclusion

We have seen various styles of manuscripts found in the Vesuvian cities: (epic) poems, historical works, libels, and novels. Bory's novel and the Greek short story of Croly and Baudelaire are actually presented as physically incomplete manuscripts full of lacunae, most of which do not thwart at least a basic understanding of the running text. Bory meticulously describes his manuscript, as does the author of the Fabius Pictor text. The fact that the pamphlets "by" Rabbi Nathan and Fabius Pictor were so libelous explains why the authors' identities are unknown. The pamphlets' age is a handy argument for their provenance from the Vesuvius area, although their antiquity is not specifically stressed. Conversely, Julia's mock letters to Ovid do actually "play out" in antiquity, so a Bay of Naples provenance is even easier to argue. Anténor's novel also has its ancient topic as a pretext for being from Herculaneum. Mazois' *Scaurus* is presented as a Roman pendant in the style of the nineteenth-century *histoire des moeurs*, which offer literary descriptions of life-style and manners. The manuscript character, however, is not very recognizable in Mazois' novel. The *Vestal of Pompeii* also takes place in a historical setting and the text would have been written after 95. Authors may have chosen to use the manuscript form to impart a higher degree of authenticity in their historical tales. This is also true for "mixed" stories like Goodman's *Night Villa*, about modern scholars working with ancient papyri.

Apart from their titles, there is nothing in the anonymous 1771 English *Democritus* or the 1861 French *Homardiade* that suggests that they are truly ancient manuscripts. Instead, each merely contains contemporary stories. As in the early texts of Fabius Pictor and Rabbi Nathan, mystification plays its part; the absurdity of these texts comes from the improbable combination of modern with ancient. Maizony's mistake was truly strange, in that his manuscript "found" at Herculaneum deals with the destruction of that very town.

Clearly, the ancient scrolls discovered in the Villa of the Papyri inspired modern authors to invent their own papyri and pull them from the ruins at Herculaneum and Pompeii. The very existence of this genre demonstrates an immense fascination with the excavations and the potentiality of hidden treasures. And, as we have seen with *Democritus* and Citino's poem, the genre has also given way to a form of satire in which modern manuscripts lost at Herculaneum are found by the explorers. With the examples discussed in this chapter, the possibilities are not yet exhausted: other cases make appearances in various chapters throughout this book.

Fig. 16: George Herbert Bonaparte Rodwell, Buy My Flowers, first page of score for Soprano and Piano, New York, c. 1835-1838. Song sung by blind Nydia in Bulwer-Lytton's The Last Days of Pompeii (Chapter I, II).

VIII Pompeii on Stage and Screen

The disaster caused by Vesuvius has inspired playwrights, composers, and filmmakers in different ways, but they all share the fascination for the drama of a town's final moments and destruction. As we will see, most of them end up with a reworked version of Bulwer-Lytton, but there are other responses to the eruption as well. Pompeii operas are testimony to Pompeii's popularity as well as the constant need for new operas in Italy, France, and Germany, where, especially during the nineteenth century, the demand for municipal opera houses was enormous. Few productions enjoyed a reprise in later seasons or in other theaters. One may therefore ask what dictated the perpetual choice to use Pompeii as a subject. Was it the artists' or the public's genuine interest in the ruins and ancient town, or was it merely the result of a demand from the opera houses and drama theaters, and – later – from film producers? Drama needs a public, is expensive, and can only achieve a moderate amount of financial success or a good artistic reputation if it is produced well. The motif of the destruction of Pompeii became rather popular in nineteenth-century opera, because scriptwriters and composers could easily shape stories according to the reigning template of the genre. *Belcanto* opera in Italy, *grand opéra* in France and Italy, which usually included ballets, *grosse* or *romantische Oper* in Germany, all included complicated love stories, and a mix of different styles of scenes: some with large masses of soloists and choruses, and other more intimate scenes of one or two protagonists expressing their love, hatred, anxiety and relief.

From the time of Pacini to that of Nouguès – that is, for almost the entire nineteenth century – many composers endeavored to create their own Pompeii opera, of which we still know many titles, a dozen libretti and only a handful of music scores and recordings. Bulwer-Lytton's *Last Days* inspired composers to write musical elaborations in the same way Schiller and Shakespeare's plays and Scott's novels inspired playwrights and composers to adopt their plots. The Pompeii theme came at a good moment: the demand for historical plays that included ordinary people playing major roles was enormous, while tragedies and operas about ancient history and mythology which focused on gods, kings and emperors became obsolete.[1333]

In accordance with the conventions of the tragic opera, two male opponents strive for one beautiful and innocent girl. All Bulwer-Lytton operas focus on the lovers Glaucus (tenor) and Ione (soprano), who are frustrated by the villain Arbaces (baritone or bass). Nydia (soprano) – not always blind – is in love with

---

1333 Kimbell 1991, 407–408, 501.

Glaucus, as is Julia (mezzo-soprano or alto) who functions as Arbaces' accomplice. Nydia is often a very important character who unites the various subplots.[1334] The same can be said for prose drama. Bulwer-Lytton forms the principal starting point, but dramatists later chose their own themes and stage forms that vary considerably, including television and radio plays.

A great problem that arises when conducting a study of operas is the lack of sound: apart from Pacini's *Ultimi giorni*, Petrella's *Ione*, and David's *Herculanum*, to my knowledge no Pompeii opera has been staged in the past decades, let alone recorded on LP, CD or DVD. We must therefore rely on libretti, full scores, or (incomplete) piano excerpts. The existence of the latter illustrates the popularity of these operas, at least in the private sphere. Yet, even these sources are difficult to find.[1335]

Operatic Stirrings in The Bay of Naples

The theme of Pompeii first pops up briefly in Mozart's last two operas, *Die Zauberflöte* and *La clemenza di Tito*, both from 1791. Mozart and his father visited Herculaneum and Pompeii during their stay in Naples in June 1770, but Leopold's letters from the Bay of Naples to his wife are almost completely mute about their experiences there. There is a concrete reference to Pompeii in *La clemenza*, in which the Roman Emperor Titus is introduced as a good sovereign. This is in accordance with the occasion for which the work was written, namely, the coronation of

---

1334 An extra "feature" of this character is that she sings original songs from the novel like "Buy my flowers" (Bulwer-Lytton 1834, I, II), e.g. in Von Montowt 1903, act I ("Tra la la! Kauft nur ab diese Sträuße!") and Fox 1892, act I. Here Rodwell c. 1835, fig. 16.
1335 For Pompeii in music, see the list in Reischert 2001, 1, 788–790 s.v. Pompeji: 35 compositions written between 1825 and 1994. Some musical works have titles that offer no clues as to their contents: Johan Magnus Rosén 1855 (symphonic piece); Castellano 1893 (ballet); Edouard Mathé 1908 (ballet); Herbert Aberlkin Godfrey 1910 (stage music); Jean Paul Ertel 1912 (symphonic poem); Karl Alexander Raida 1923 (stage music); Walter Niemann 1953 (piano); Jiří Válek 1970 (symphony); Gustav Kneip 1992 (opera); Alexander Sojnikow 1994 (opera). I also found Walter Niemann's undated *Pompeji. Kleine Suite für 2 Flöten und Streichorchester* opus 48. I could not find any concrete proof of the existence of the 1924 opera *La rosa di Pompei* by Francesco Cilea (text by Ettore Moschino), although it is mentioned in *Enciclopedia dello spettacolo* 3 (1956) 759 s.v. Cilea, Francesco, and on http://en.wikipedia.org/wiki/Francesco_Cilea (accessed January 18, 2014). However, the opera is not mentioned in other *important* sources, to begin with Cilea's memoirs (M. Grande, *Francesco Cilea. Documenti e immagini*, Reggio di Calabria 2001) and in standard encyclopedias: W. Ashbrook, *The New Grove* 4 (1980) 391–397; R. Meloncelli, *Dizionario Biografico degli Italiani* 25 (1981) 503–509; J. Budden, *The New Grove of Opera* 1 (1992) 865–866; J. Streicher, *Die Musik In Geschichte und Gegenwart. Personenteil* 4 (2000) 1115–1116.

Emperor Leopold II of Austria, as King of Bohemia in Prague. Titus' benevolence is evidenced by his plan to help the devastated Campanian cities.[1336] Since this theme of humanitarian aid does not ever materialize, it is secondary to the plot of the opera, which was not Mozart's invention. The text, by Caterino Mazzolà, is an adaptation of a frequently-used 1734 libretto by Metastasio.[1337]

The Magic Flute contains Egyptian elements which became very famous and inspired many artists to represent Egyptian and other similar motifs. The Dutch archaeologist Frédéric Louis Bastet once suggested that Mozart got his inspiration for *The Magic Flute*, written in 1791 on a textbook by Wolfgang Schikaneder, albeit late, from the Temple of Isis in Pompeii. Bastet argues that two paintings from Herculaneum, which show Egyptian ceremonies being performed in front of a temple, might be an iconographical source for the beginning of *The Magic Flute's* second act, when Sarastro stands in front of the temple.[1338] These images had been published in the second volume of the *Antichità* of 1760; the original and its pendant were on show at Portici.[1339] The Neapolitan letters of father and son to mother and sister at home, however, only announce visits to the ruins and no specific objects or monuments, so that Bastet's idea seems too far-fetched.[1340] We

---

1336 Act 1, scene 4. "Romani, unico oggetto / è de' voti di Tito il vostro amore [...] / Udite: oltre l'usato / terribile il Vesevo / ardenti fiumi / dalle fauci eruttò; scosse le rupi; / riempié di ruine / i campi intorno e le città vicine. / Le desolate genti / fuggendo van; ma la miseria opprime / quei che al foco avanzar. Serve quell'oro / di tanti afflitti a riparar lo scempio. / Questo, o Romani, è fabbricarmi il tempio." With *La clemenza* Mozart returns to the *opera seria*, with recitatives and arias, probably having been forced to do so by the ceremonial occasion. On Titus' assistance to the victims of Vesuvius' explosion, see Suetonius, *Life of Titus* 8.3–4.
1337 See Lühning 1983 on Titus operas. For a long list of Titus operas, see Reischert 2001, 1, 948–951.
1338 Bastet 1986a. Old images in *Antichità di Ercolano* II (1760); Saint-Non 1782, 26, no. 104 (= Lamers 1995, 316 no. 341). See also Assmann 2005, 93; U. Pappalardo in *Egittomania. Iside e il mistero*, Naples 2006, 220–229; Rowland 2014, 91–119. Letters on their stay in Naples in Mozart 1962, 292–412. Cf. Basso 2006, 75–77, 199–209, 432. See also p. 209, note 800. For more on the Temple of Isis, see Chapters I–III.
1339 Another well-known reproduction was the illustration by Pâris in Saint-Non 1782, 26, no. 104 (reproduced in Lamers 1995, 316 no. 341).
1340 In a letter of 16 June to his wife, Leopold announces a visit to the area (Mozart 1962, 361): "Montag und Erchtag etc: werden wird den Vesuvius etwas näher betrachten, Pompea und das Herculaneum die Stätte wo man ausgrabt und die bereits gefundenen Seltenheiten bewundern, Caserta etc: und Capo di Monte besehen etc: welches alles Geld kosten wird." According to a postscript, they went down into the excavations of Herculaneum: "Man muß alle seltenheiten zu sehen allezeit eine flambo mit haben, indem vieles unter der Erde ist. Ich und der Wolfg: waren mit unserm bedienten ganz allein, wir hatten 6 Schifleute und den Cicerone, die alle ihre Verwunderung nicht bergen konnten den Wolfg: zu sehen, indem die 2 alten graubarteten schifleute sich erklärten niemals einen so jungen knaben dieser Orts gesehen zu haben, welcher diese Alterthümer zu sehen an diese Orte gekommen wäre." For Leopold's complaints about costs, see Basso 2006, 24.

should also take into account the amount of time that passed between Mozart's visit to Pompeii and the creation of *The Magic Flute* as well as the fact that the text was written by Schikaneder. The exotic Egyptian features are instead stock elements of the massonic language used by Schikaneder.[1341]

Another early musical evocation was the 1803 *Il trionfo di Vitellio Massimino e la Distruzione di Pompejano*, a large narrative ballet composed by Luigi Belloli and based on a text by Luigi Romanelli, an opera librettist. It is unclear what might have served as the inspiration for this ballet.[1342] All of the characters are portrayed as guilty sinners and seem to accept that the gods are punishing them with the eruption of Vesuvius.[1343] Stage directions mention fitting locations in Pompeii, but its choice as the locus of the drama mainly depends on Vesuvius' eruption.

Whether incited by Belloli or not, Giovanni Pacini would soon add a jewel to this genre with *L'ultimo giorno di Pompei* ("The last day of Pompeii"), staged in Naples on November 19, 1825 to celebrate the name day of Queen Maria Isabella.[1344] Pacini, the successor to Gioacchino Rossini as the principal composer at the San Carlo Theater, achieved an enormous amount of esteem with *L'ultimo giorno*, which was based on a libretto by Andrea Leone Tottola. Appio, a suitor who also loves Ottavia, disturbs her happy married life with Sallustio. When Ottavia rejects his advances, Appio accuses her of adultery and Ottavia is sentenced to death following a trial presided over by her husband. The end of the opera describes the horrible chaos caused by Vesuvius' eruption. People trying to escape alone or in groups run in all directions. Rain pours down, punctuated by thunder and

---

1341 See Assmann 2005 (p. 93: very brief reference to Pompeii).
1342 Romanelli 1803: "The triumph of Vitellius Maximinus and the Destruction of Pompei[anum]." Four years later, the work was combined with an opera, for which it probably served as an intermezzo: *Castore e Polluce* with music by Vincenzo Federici and ballet by Pietro Angiolini (Romanelli 1807, 19–34). All have brief entries in *New Grove* and *The New Grove Dictionary of Opera*.
1343 Romanelli 1803: "Occulti tradimenti ordì Flacco Vellejo per vendicare l'estinto suo Padre, e chiamò a parte delle sue trame Simplicio, irritato già per vedere impedite le nozze di sua sorella con Vitellio, sicchè tutti si resero colpevoli di gravi delitti espiati dal Cielo colla distruzione di Pompejano lor Patria, che restò sepolta sotto l'eruzioni [sic] del fulminante Vesuvio." Similar phrasing in Romanelli 1807, 24.
1344 Main source: a CD recording from 1997, under the baton of Giuliano Carella (Dynamic CDS 178/1–2), the result of performances in Martina Franca and Catania, Pacini's birthplace, in 1996; with an analysis by G.C. Ballola in the liner notes. See M. Rose, *New Grove* 14 (1980) 66–70; Black 1988; S. Henze-Döhring, *Pipers Enzyklopädie des Musiktheaters. Oper. Operette. Musical. Ballett* 4 (1991) 607–609; S.L. Bathazar/M. Rose, *The New Grove Dictionary of Opera* 3 (1992) 808–812; Loubinoux 1998; R. Kleinertz in Reinsberg/Meynersen 2012, 147–149. García y García 1998, nos. 10.037–10.041, 13.608 (also later performances). He refers to A. Scherillo, Il Vesuvio e Pompei nel melodramma italiano dell'800, *Atti dell'Accademia Pontiana* 33 (1984) 331–338, which I could not find.

lightning.[1345] As Pacini confesses in *Le mie memorie artistiche*, he got his inspiration for the story from Antonio Niccolini, a stage engineer.[1346] Thanks to Niccolini, the set depicted Pompeii rather authentically. The House of Sallustius, the forum, the Street of Tombs next to the Herculanean Gate, the Villa of Diomedes, and Vesuvius were all represented quite faithfully.[1347] Tottola adapted the story for the stage, creating a spectacle full of special effects, mass scenes and intimate moments that focus on one or two protagonists. *L'ultimo giorno* is indeed a brilliant *belcanto* opera, entirely in line with Rossini's work, in which Pacini has dared to give Ottavia and Appio – and as counterpart, Ottavia and Sallustio – the freedom to sing "tormented" arias and duets, outbursts of intense sadness due to supposedly broken hearts.[1348] Ottavia and Sallustio's duet in which they pray next to her tomb is one of the genre's very first melodramatic conjugal duets, a motif that became popular thereafter. Gérard Loubinoux, a French drama and music scholar, demonstrated the underlying motivation of the story: the volcano erupts to punish the volcanic ardor of Appio, with the eruption itself a successful metaphor of the passion of love.[1349]

The success of the November evening performance was enormous, and Pacini got a ludicrous contract from Domenico Barbaia, the mighty local impresario who forced many a composer and singer to strive for perfection when working for his productions. In his memoirs, Pacini never recalls visits to Pompeii, but boasts that the Pompeii opera was the most successful of his early days.[1350] *L'ultimo giorno*

1345 "Gli abitanti sbalorditi e sparsi in vari gruppi procurano salvarsi colla fuga. Le madri spaventate seco trasportano i ragazzi, ed i bambini; altre co' loro prezioni arredi. Le Vestali fuggono colla gran Sacerdotessa. Tutto è confusione, e presenta il quadro della desolazione. La pioggia cresce, mista ai lampi, ed a' tuoni. Si cala il sipario."
1346 Pacini 1865, 51. Like that of Romanelli, Pacini's piece was most likely not based on an existing narrative.
1347 Loubinoux 1998 gives some examples of the stage directions, which are not included in the CD's liner notes. As for the forum, the libretto gives the following description: "Foro di Pompei festivamente adorno. In prospetto il tempio di Giove e lateralmente ad esso i due archi trionfali, da' quali vaggonsi le contrade, che introducono al Foro, e di lontano i vari edifici della Città. A sinistra una tribuna, ornata di ghirlande." Kimbell 1991, 410–411 discusses similar descriptions of Pompeii monuments, substantiating Loubinoux' remarks. On the stage decorations Jacobelli 2009.
1348 See G.C. Ballola's analysis in the CD liner notes (see note 1344). Cf. Kimbell 1991, 467–470 (*L'Ultimo giorno* not discussed).
1349 Loubinoux 1998, 507. He makes an interesting comparison with Auber's 1827 *La muette de Portici*, where the 1631 revolution in Naples also ends with an eruption of Vesuvius.
1350 Pacini 1865, 49: "[...] *L'ultimo giorno di Pompei* fu il maggior trionfo della mia prima epoca artistica. Porrò ogni modestia da parte per essere semplicemente espositore della verità." There is a witty portrait of Barbaia and Rossini in Dumas 2001, chapter V. On Barbaia and Rossini, see Kimbell 1991, 448–466.

was performed in many other theaters until the 1850s, when it went out of fashion and singers who were able to master its extremely difficult score stopped materializing.[1351] Paul Crombet (see Chapter III, pp. 183, 187) wrote an early and partly enthusiastic review of a performance he saw in 1826 in the San Carlo Theater. The stage showed a realistic Pompeii, including its edifices, and the eruption revealed itself as a shower of real ashes. The music was brilliant, but too artificial to keep his attention for the entire duration.[1352]

There is only one opera that was inspired by Herculaneum. In 1859, the Paris Opéra staged Félicien César David's *Herculanum*, which most likely would have been a spectacular production.[1353] The eruption of Vesuvius functions as a Last Judgment, with God punishing the pagans through his "vengeur," the volcano. Interestingly, according to the libretto, this happens a year after the destruction of Jerusalem.[1354] The preface to the program booklet argues that Vesuvius was thought to have avenged pagan cruelties practiced in Jerusalem as well as persecutions of Christians all over the Roman Empire.[1355] The story begins with a

---

1351 See Loubinoux 1998, 498; Ballola (as note 1344).

1352 Crombet 1941, 175–176: "On peut aller contempler, à quelques lieues de la ville, les temples, les places et les portiques que vous ont fidèlement offerts de magnifiques décorations. Tout est exactement imité, même la fatale éruption du Vésuve qui termine la pièce. On dirait que c'est une pluie réelle des cendres et de feu qui tombe sur le théâtre et va tout en fuite. La musique de Pacini est aussi brillante, mais il y a trop peu de naturel pour inspirer de l'intérêt." Similar reactions in Valéry 1838, II, 445; Risi 2004, 353, 364–367.

1353 Méry/Hadot 1859, libretto by T. Hadot, on the basis of Méry 1834 and 1837 (see Chapter IV, pp. 220–221). García y García 1998, nos 3643–3648 (numerous editions). I also found *Ercolano. Opera in quattro atti*, Italian translation by Marcellino Marcello, Milan 1858. Not in Reischert 2001. See Leppmann 1966, 176 (no title given); A. Gerhard in *Pipers Enzyklopädie des Musiktheaters. Oper. Operette. Musical. Ballett* 1 (1986) 683–685; Pitou 1990, 651–653; P. Schleuning in Mühlenbrock/Richter 2005, 213–217; Blix 2009, 77; Brango/Giroud 2008, 11. Loewenberg 1978, 938–939 mentions 74 performances from opening night on March 4, 1858 up to 1868, and mentions a reward bestowed upon him by Emperor (and amateur archeologist) Napoleon III for this excellent representation of ancient Herculaneum. *The New Grove's* 7 (2001) 47 indicates that it was reworked by Joseph Méry with the title *Le dernier amour*; the text I saw belongs to this reworked version. The work was also staged in the Opéra Royal de Versailles on March 8, 2014. The fragments of the music I heard in a radio transmission (Radio France, April 2014) betray a mix of Berlioz, Spontini, young Verdi, and other contemporary composers of good quality. I thank the music experts Jan Zekveld and Mauricio Fernandez for their comments upon the music (mail J. Zekveld of April 30, 2014). In the same program, a "Souvenir d'Herculanum" by the German composer Sebastian Lee was broadcasted.

1354 Jerusalem was destroyed in A.D. 70. But see Méry/Hadot 1859: "L'action se passe en 79, sous le règne de Titus, un an après la prise et la dévastation de Jérusalem."

1355 Méry/Hadot 1859, 5: "[...] aux impiétés païennes commises dans Jérusalem, et aux persécutions recommencés contre les chrétiens en Orient, dans la presqu'île de Corinthe et dans

despotic easterner, Olympia, who hopes to conquer and orientalize the Roman Empire. Jews in Jerusalem, she claims, have lost their leading role in history and a new faith will rule the world, despite the heathen struggles to continue Roman civilization. She loves the young Christian Hélios and drugs him with a poison so that he leaves his lover Lilia. Of course, the story ends with the eruption of Vesuvius; Hélios and Lilia escape, while Olympia remains in her orgiastic atmosphere and dies. Although the Eastern world dominates the story, it portrays Herculaneum as a small, yet very rich and sex-driven town, which serves as a backdrop for a clash between the pagan East and the Christian West. The "Etruscan" interior in the last act symbolizes decadent richness. The dinner party and ballet of the bacchants are instrumental in enhancing this almost perverse realm.[1356]

Musicologist Peter Schleuning sees David's work as an expression of the composer's political persuasion.[1357] David was a fervid member of a group of *Saint-Simonistes* who preached a simple and noble society like that of the early Christians. According to Schleuning, *Herculanum* demonstrates the struggle between a decadent society and a fine sect of early "social" worshippers, and therefore implies David's opposition to the bourgeois world. This does not, however, prevent him from using that same world's greatest form of artistic expression, the *grand opéra*. The music and stage would have indulged the audience with spectacular mass scenes and the intimate encounters of lovers and rivals, which were sometimes interrupted by Satan himself. It would have made for an ideal mix, perfectly matching the format of the *grand opéra* genre and meeting the public's expectations.

Political allusions are also important in *Le roi carotte*, an 1872 French operetta that partially plays out in Pompeii.[1358] A humorous masterpiece by Jacques

---

la Grande Grèce, surtout à Naples et en Sicile. [...] Le Vésuve fut regardé comme un vengeur." Conclusion (p. 7): "L'œuvre lyrique d'*Herculanum* a donc été composée avec ces légendes, ces traditions, ces faits historiques, ces documents, qui, par leur date, s'associent à la plus grande catastrophe de l'ère chrétienne, à la destruction de trois villes englouties sous un déluge de feu, dans le plus beau pays du monde."

1356 David 2001, 165–167 gives two splendid reactions to the opera and its distorted vision of Antiquity, viz. an ocular testimony in the novel *Les Vertiges* by Camille Gros (Paris 1876) and a critique by Villiers de l'Isle-Adam from 1859 (both quoted). The latter text is also in Villiers de l'Isle-Adam 1986, II, 766–770, who argues that this opera offers a complete and intimate image of Herculaneum. See also David-de Palacio 2005, 336.
1357 P. Schleuning in Mühlenbrock/Richter 2005, 213–217.
1358 Sardou/Offenbach 1872. *Le roi carotte* is a piano score with full texts for the singers, but without the spoken texts, stage directions and necessary explanations of the plot. The genre was called "opéra-bouffe-féerie." Faris 1980, 165–167; A. Lamb, *New Grove* 13 (1980) 509–513 [Offenbach]; C.N. Smith, *ibidem* 16 (1980) 497–498 [Sardou]; J. Heinzelmann, *Pipers Enzyklopädie des*

Offenbach, one of the wittiest composers of the nineteenth century containing a Pompeian scene, it is unfortunately performed very rarely. Composed on a text by the famous playwright Victorien Sardou, it would have been a gigantic spectacle, with a great number of protagonists. *Le roi carotte* is about Fridolin, a weak and bankrupt prince who has been deposed by the pompous and ridiculous King Carrot, the ruler of the vegetables and insects under the earth. When Fridolin tries to regain his power, Quiribibi, a magician, advises him to time travel to ancient Pompeii, where he will find a magical ring that once belonged to the biblical King Salomon and which has been brought to Italy by a Roman soldier. When Fridolin, accompanied by friends, travels back in time, they expect to find "le peuple effacé [...] fantômes du passé" (people faded away, phantoms of the past), but in a scene called "Pompéï restaurée," they meet practitioners of some 25 professions, including artisans and merchants, on the forum.[1359] Fridolin and his friends enjoy the blithe attitude of these Pompeians, who view them with great astonishment on account of their non-Roman clothing, pipe smoking, and songs about modern trains. Fridolin procures the ring just before Vesuvius erupts, and his party manages to escape. After other vicissitudes, the story ends with Fridolin in power once again, having married a nice girl.

The aspect of time travel in Gautier's *Arria Marcella* (see p. 313), and the motif of a subterranean kingdom in Leopardi's *Paralipomeni* (see p. 53) might have been sources of inspiration for Sardou. King Carrot calls himself a "gnome," for which reason we can compare him with the spirits of the deceased Pompeians resting underneath the earth, who were often called gnomes in other works as well. Sardou wrote a first draft in 1869 as a funny but critical portrait of Napoleon III. It most likely would have been staged only after the Emperor's fall in 1870, and with Offenbach, Sardou reworked it into the 1872 operetta. Either Fridolin or King Carrot might be said to represent Napoleon; for both there have been arguments put forward.[1360] As for the theme of Pompeii, I note that the pubic admired the lavish ancient costumes and the image of the ancient town on stage. Because

---

Musiktheaters. Oper. Operette. Musical. Ballett 4 (1991) 557–560; Yon 2000, 435–446; M. Jährmärker, *Die Musik In Geschichte und Gegenwart. Personenteil* 12 (2004) 1317–1334 [Offenbach]; A. Gier, *ibidem* 14 (2005) 965–967 [Sardou]. See also http://fr.wikipedia.org/wiki/Le_Roi_Carotte (accessed, December 28, 2013), in which Pompeii is mentioned because of Sardou's wish to include it in his comedy. Josef Heinzelmann gives the number of 149 performances in Paris, followed by English versions in London (1872) and German ones in Vienna (1867).

1359 Sardou/Offenbach 1872, 177. These Pompeians have both Greek and Latin names like Gurgès, Harpax, and Numérius.

1360 Clear explanation of both possibilities in Heinzelmann (see note 1358). Faris 1980, 165–167, Yon 2000, 442: both see Fridolin as an alter ego of Napoleon.

Napoleon had a "maison pompéienne" in Paris, this link might well have been visualized in the scenery as well.[1361]

Operas Inspired by Bulwer-Lytton's *Last Days*

Pacini's continuous success might have held back other Italian composers from attempting to write their own Pompeii operas until 1858, when Errico Petrella did just that in Milan. It was with Petrella that the elaborations of Bulwer-Lytton's 1834 novel (discussed in Chapter IV) first materialized. Several operas actually bear the same title as Bulwer-Lytton's novel.[1362] The Christians, a motif singled out in novels following Bulwer-Lytton, generally play a subordinate or nonexistent role, which can be explained by the tendency of operas to accent love stories and the little potency Christianity had to dramatize a plot.

After first being performed with modest acclaim in 1858 in the Scala in Milan, Petrella's *Jone o l'ultimo giorno di Pompei*[1363] held the stage until the beginning of the twentieth century. Petrella follows Bulwer-Lytton's plot, leaves out Christians, and makes Nidia a powerful person who refuses to give in to the lust of the Egyptian priest Arbaces. Listening to the music, it is difficult to imagine her as the young slave girl of the novel. As equally dramatic sopranos, Nidia and Jone are musical rivals, and occupy the stage much more than the male characters. Petrella did ignite the theme of the funerary march accompanying Glauco's entrance in the amphitheater, which has remained popular. The music historian M. Rose considers *Jone* "the best known of Petrella's serious operas," but without being able to assess performances of his other operas, I consider this work a middle-of-the-

---

1361 Faris 1980, 167; Yon 2000, 441. On the Maison pompéienne, built between 1856 and 1858 and destroyed in 1891, see A. Milanese in Guzzo/Tagliamonte/Lucchetti 2013, 39–40 (with bibl.) and S. Hales, Living with Arria Marcella: Novel Interiors in La Maison Pompéienne, in Leander Touati forthcoming.
1362 However, it is not clear whether all of them were inspired by it. See Reischert 2001, 1, 788–790. As in my discussions of other works in this and other chapters, I cite the names of characters as used in scores, libretti, and tragedies and comedies, so that Glaucus becomes Glauco, Nydia Nidia etc. Werr 1999, 89–90 mentions a ballet by Girolamo Albini after the novel, staged in Milan in 1837: *Jone e Glauco ossia Gli ultimi giorni di Pompei*.
1363 Petrella 1858. Libretto by Giovanni Peruzzini. García y García 1998, nos. 10.505–10.515, 10.571–10.573 for the numerous versions; Loewenberg 1978, 930–931; Reischert 2001, 1, 789. There is an LP of a performance in Caracas in 1981 (anniversary of the Teatro Municipale, that had opened in 1881 with the same work) under the direction of Eduardo Muller (Bongiovanni, Bologna 1982). The liner notes include a long list of previous performances.

road, deservedly-forgotten opera, which is also Sebastian Werre's conclusion in the only modern study about Petrella.[1364]

In 1869 the Parisian public enjoyed Victorin Joncières' *Le dernier jour de Pompéi* in the Théâtre Lyrique.[1365] Some protagonists bear names other than those of Bulwer-Lytton's characters, but the plot is exactly the same. Joncières stresses Arbaces' perversity, next to an extravagant luxury and horrific atmosphere. Burbo's inn, the Temple of Isis, and the amphitheater are all appropriate locations for subsequent scenes.

Few German Pompeii operas have survived, and those that have only survive in the form of mute text. Some are known only by name, like *Die Nazarener in Pompeji* by Joseph Muck.[1366] In August Pabst's *Die letzten Tage von Pompeji*, Arbaces tries to persuade Apäcides to remain a follower of Isis by showing him dreamlike visions of night and day and paradise.[1367] Like a Wagnerian Tannhäuser in the Mountain of Venus, Apäcides falls in love with these images. The opera ends with a chorus of Christians, somewhere near the harbor of Pompeii. Pabst effectively uses the witch on Vesuvius from Bulwer-Lytton's novel as an instrument to realize a happy ending. Apart from the witch's words about Christianity and the final chorus, there are no hints of Christianity. Ione's relationship with Arbaces is closer than it is in the novel, with the two of them living together under one roof, he acting as her foster father. Arbaces' gloomy character contrasts with the others, who largely come off as frivolous and happy young people. Yourij von Arnold's *Die Nazarener in Pompeji*[1368] has a much simpler plot and includes fewer of Bulwer-Lytton's protagonists, who have been partly changed. The three-act opera

---

1364 M. Rose, *New Grove* 14 (1980) 586–588, cit. p. 587; idem, *The New Grove Dictionary of Opera* 3 (1992) 984–985; N. Miller in *Pipers Enzyklopädie des Musiktheaters. Oper. Operette. Musical. Ballett* 4 (1991) 745–749; Werre 1999, 87–103.
1365 Joncières 1869. Dahl 1956, 191; Reischert 2001, 1, 789. The libretto is by Charles Nuitter and Alexandre Beaumont. I saw a piano score by Ed. Mangin, Paris (no year).
1366 Darmstadt 1887. Libretto by C. Gollmick and L. Bauer. García y García 1998, no. 9665; Reischert 2001, 1, 789; not in *New Grove*. I saw a ballet score: *Ballett aus der Oper: Die Nazarener von J. Muck. Arrangement für Türkische Musik*, Offenbach am Main, n.d. Reischert 2001, 1, 788–789 gives other German operas by Franz Lachner (1839), Peter Müller (1853), mentioning Bulwer-Lytton in the title, as well as those with the same title by Julius Urban (1879), Ernst Schwaiger (1888), Josef Forster (1917) and Franz Kessel (1931). None of these works in Loewenberg 1978, García y García 1998, and the *Grove* encyclopedias.
1367 Pabst 1851. García y García 1998, no. 10.272; Reischert 2001, 1, 788. Libretto by Julius Pabst, possibly a relative of the composer.
1368 Von Arnold 1863. The Russian composer, who also wrote the libretto, worked from 1863 to 1870 in Leipzig. García y García 1998, no. 916; Reischert 2001, 1, 789. *New Grove* 1 (1980) 620 gives the Russian title *Posledniy den Pompei* (no date) among works "of academic interest only." Not in Loewenberg 1978.

circles around the Nydia, a Christian girl, and her lover, Sextus. Von Arnold clearly highlights the Christians. The gruesome Arbaces opposes the praetor and his son, and other noble Romans. Their religious and moral conflicts are worked out in the protagonists' duets and arias. Archaeological details are scarcely described in the libretto. Reinhold von Montowt had some success with his *Die letzten Tage von Pompeji*, executed in Lübeck and Magdeburg, and possibly in other places as well, which features many more singers than Pabst's opera, one of whom is the Egyptian goddess Isis.[1369] In Von Montowt's version, Glaukus and Ione rise to heaven in a Christian apotheosis. "Old things die, time changes and new life blooms out of the ruins."[1370] Nydia is rather unimportant and probably not blind either. Pompeii is but a cardboard backdrop and plays no important role.

Marziano Perosi's *La cieca di Pompei* ("The blind girl from Pompeii") is an Italian opera inspired by Bulwer-Lytton, which enjoyed some success in Austria and Germany. It might be for that reason that I found only one German libretto, written for performances in Vienna in 1912, with texts by Karl Schreder and Robert Maria Prosl.[1371] Perosi's connections with Pompeii would become concrete with his appointment as the chorus master and organist in the modern city's cathedral from 1918 to 1921. As a Christian meeting place, in *La cieca* Perosi invents a "Garden of Cybele." When Vesuvius starts its devastating eruption, Perosi describes the dramatic changes of the environment in a Wagnerian way as if the end of the work were the finale of *Götterdämmerung*. The violence of the music conveys the destruction of Pompeii, after which there is rest, with soft and moving tones that paint a picture of the sea. The scene changes to an attractive landscape along the Bay of Naples, with pine trees, shrubs, and blooming roses. At a distance, dark clouds cover Vesuvius, and scattered pale fires rise from its crater. It is dawn, and a small boat lies on the shore.[1372] The title suggests that the blind girl,

---

1369 Von Montowt 1903. I saw an undated (but with an indicated 1903 copyright) program book including a synopsis (pp. 1–8) and full text, edited at Magdeburg. Reischert 2001, 1, 789 gives the premiere at Lübeck in 1900. Not in Loewenberg 1978 or García y García 1998.
1370 Von Montowt 1903: "Aus der Asche Pompejis steigen in der Apotheose Glaukus und Ione, die Vertreter des Christentums, zum Himmel empor. / Das Alte stirbt, es ändert sich die Zeit, / Und neues Leben blüht aus den Ruinen."
1371 Perosi 1912. García y García 1998, no. 10.492; Reischert 2001, 1, 789; *Die Musik in Gegenwart und Geschichte* 10 (1962) 1078; *Dizionario enciclopedico universale della musica e dei musicisti. Le biografie* 5 (1988) 648. Not in *New Grove* (1980).
1372 Perosi 1912, 75: "Die Musik schildert den Untergang Pompejis. Nach erreichtem Hohepunkt des musikalischen Ausdruckes vermindert sich die Gewalt der Töne und allmählig tritt Ruhe ein, um endlich in weiche, wogende Klänge überzugehen, welche die leichtbewegte Meeresluft schildern. Die Schleier werden langsam durchsichtig. Bald zeigt sich eine reizende Landschaft am Gestade von Neapel. Pinien umsäumen das Gefilde. Links unter blühenden Sträuchern ein Rosenhügel. Das Meer bespült den Strand. In der Ferne sieht man den Vesuv von dunklen Wol-

Nydia, has a special part, but she does the same things she does in the novel and in other operas. During the finale she kisses the sleeping couple Glaukus and Jone and drowns herself with the last words of the libretto: "Remember me!"[1373]

There is only one British opera based on Bulwer-Lytton: George Fox's *Nydia, the blind girl of Pompeii*.[1374] One protagonist is Olinthus, an old Christian who begins the opera with his announcement of the end of Pompeii ("Beware! Listen to the dread command!"). Nydia is indeed the musical protagonist, singing many of Bulwer-Lytton's original lyrics, including "Buy my flowers." There are few stage directions in the score, and the local Pompeian atmosphere is not specifically evoked. The music becomes turbulent and loud in certain passages. Another British contribution, Benoit Hollander's 1907 *Pompeii*, is a semi-staged lyrical work for voice and orchestra.[1375] As in most operas, there is no specific interest for Pompeii as an archaeological monument and the plot of Bulwer-Lytton's novel is the focus of this work.

Nydia's song "Buy my flowers" was also set to music by George Rodwell (fig. 16) and A.F. Winnemore, and arranged by I.C. Viereck.[1376] Henrietta G. Gubbins' score from around 1860 is a musical rendition of "The wind and the beam lov'd the rose."[1377] The same poem was also put to music by John Blockley.[1378] John Philip Sousa wrote a suite for wind instruments and without words called *The Last Days of Pompeii* in 1893. There are three parts: "In the House of Burbo and Stratonice," "Nydia," and "The Destruction of Pompeii and Nydia's Death." As indicated by Sousa himself by means of quotations from the novel inserted next to the headings, we can locate these episodes in Bulwer-Lytton's novel.[1379]

---

ken bedeckt. Ab und zu dringt ein schwacher Feuerschein aus seinem Krater. Morgendämmerung. Eine Barke liegt am Ufer."

1373 Perosi 1912, 76: "Gedenket mein!" Similar to the last words of Dido in Purcell's *Dido and Aeneas* ("Remember me").

1374 Fox 1892. García y García 1998, no. 5435. Reischert 2001, 1, 789 gives 1891 as year of staging and mentions Justin Huntly McCarthy as the librettist. Not in Loewenberg 1978 or *New Grove*.

1375 Hollander 1907. Reischert 2001, 1, 789. Not in Loewenberg 1978, García y García 1998, or *New Grove*.

1376 Bulwer-Lytton 1834, I, II. A.F. Winnemore, *The Blind Flower Girl. A Ballad, The Poetry from the Romance of The Last Days of Pompeii*, Philadelphia: G. Willig [1840s?]. Not in García y García 1998 or Reischert 2001.

1377 Bulwer-Lytton 1834, III, II. H.G. Gubbins, *Nydia's Song from the Last Days of Pompeii*, ca. 1860 [seen in the University of Michigan Library]. Not in García y García 1998 or Reischert 2001.

1378 J. Blockley, *The wind and the beam lov'd the rose: Nydia's song in Bulwer's "Last days of Pompeii."*, Philadelphia: A. Fiot [184?]. The score's notes announce that the English soprano Madame Collins had sung it. Not in García y García 1998 or Reischert 2001.

1379 There is a 2003 CD on the Naxos label (8.559092) by the Royal Artillery Band under the baton of Keith Brion. See on this work Brion's CD liner notes, in which he says that it was one of Sousa's preferred pieces of music. Not in García y García 1998 or Reischert 2001.

Ancient and Modern Pompeii Join Forces

In 1827, Louis Alexandre Piccini, the grandson of the famous composer Niccolò Piccini, wrote the music to René-Charles Guilbert de Pixerécourt's *La tête de mort*, an opera that plays out at Pompeii in Napoleonic times, but has little to do with the ruins themselves.[1380] Instead, it is about the occupation of Naples during the Napoleonic era, with French troops fighting against southern brigands around Pompeii. The ancient city serves both as a meeting place and as a tomb, which adds an element of horror to the plot, something that was fashionable in de Pixerécourt's era. With its inclusion of Napoleonic interventions in the south of Italy, the opera precedes French novels like De Latouche's *Fragoletta*, De Lamartine's *Graziella*, and Toudouze's *La sorcière du Vésuve* (see Chapter V, pp. 258, 260, 277–278).

Bertheroy's *La Danseuse de Pompéi* (see Chapter III, pp. 207–208) inspired Henry Ferrare and Henri Cain to write the libretto of *La Danseuse* for the composer Jean Nouguès,[1381] which includes quotations from Bertheroy's dialogues. The dancing girl, the ardent love story, jealous guys, and the dramatic end of the novel are excellent ingredients in a *grand opéra* that includes ballets, spectacular scenes, and romantic intimate moments. *La danseuse* precisely follows the novel, and includes a dinner party scene and others that were stock themes in Pompeii novels. Pompeii, the setting of the opera, is described in detail, which I assume must have been realized on stage.

The humorous and highly original 1921 *Giove a Pompei* is the only known major Italian operatic work about Pompeii from the twentieth century.[1382] It was composed by Umberto Giordano and Alberto Franchetti, with text by Luigi Illica and Ettore Romagnoli, two successful libretto writers. The four artists merge ancient and contemporary personages and inventions, like airplanes, telephones,

---

1380 De Pixerécourt 1827. Staged in Paris in the Théâtre de la Gaîté on December 8, 1827. See *New Grove* 19 (2001) 713–714. The booklet I have found, however, is not a libretto, but prose. Not in García y García 1998.
1381 Nouguès 1912. There is an Italian translation of the novel: *La danzatrice di Pompei*, Rome 1921. Blix 2009, 74, figs 3–4, gives examples of artworks inspired by the novel. On Nouguès and his very successful *Quo vadis* (text by Henri Cain) after Sienkiewicz from 1909, see R. Suchowiejko in Brango/Giroud 2008, 295–309, plate VII. Nouguès studied in Rome and Pompeii to gain a better understanding of the atmosphere of each before writing this and other works (ibidem p. 301).
1382 Illica 1921. Not to be confused with Franchetti's *Glauco*, written on the basis of a novel by Ercole Luigi Morelli, mentioned by García y García 1998, no. 5442 (Franchetti) and 9632 (Morselli), which is about the mythical Glaukos rather than Bulwer-Lytton's Glaucus and is not relevant for the Pompeii theme. Of this "Commedia musicale in tre atti" I found only a piano score, with music for voice as well. It is probably an extract of the original work, as there are only arias and ensemble songs, and the plot is undeveloped.

and post offices, as well as music styles. We simultaneously meet Parvolo Patacca, the director of the excavations, Aricia, the ancient city's High Priest, and a veteran from the Italian wars in Libya. Although his role is slightly ambiguous, Marcus Pipa, the Fire Chief, is most likely another modern personage. Giove and Ganimede are gods. "Little Patacca" is reminiscent of the popular folklore character Meo Patacca in Roman Trastevere. Clearly, the opera is a hilarious joke that mixes ancient mythology and history, and traditional ideas and modern notions and techniques. A motorcycle stands in for a Roman chariot, and Jupiter's eagle acts as an airplane. Modern people excavate and African *reduci* represent Italy's recent conquest of Libya, while the ancients and their gods stroll around simultaneously. This mix corresponds with the artistic current of Futurism, in which writers, musicians and artists expressed their interest in the advancement and supremacy of Italian technology in their works. Every operatic cliché is played with – from misunderstandings, to passion, and pathos. Pompeii is an ideal backdrop, since it is simultaneously a place of history, research, and tourism. The eruption of Vesuvius must have been a pyrotechnical spectacle. The role of the music, a pastiche of Mozart, Donizetti and Verdi, was to bring all this chaos to life, but it seems that the audience on the 1921 opening night in Rome admired the set and the second act ballet more than the music.[1383]

In January 2012, the Dallas Opera House announced plans to stage a "forgotten belcanto opera" entitled *Rosa Dolorosa, figlia di Pompei*, with music by Jake Heggie and the libretto written by Terrence McNally for the 2015–2016 season. According to a brief description, it will contain "two mad scenes, an erupting volcano."[1384]

Glaucus, Ione, and Nydia on Stage

The first American theatrical adaptations of Bulwer-Lytton's *Last Days* date to the 1830s. The English playwright Louisa H. Medina, who was popular in New York,

---

1383 C. Parmentola, *Dizionario enciclopedico universale della musica e dei musicisti. Le biografie* 3 (1986) 209 s.v. Giordano, Umberto: "[...] l'eruzione del Vesuvio vi assume il carattere di spettacolo pirotecnico: uno spettacolo che oggi si definirebbe 'dissacrante'." *New Grove* 9 (2001) 170 and 888: Giordano wrote a part of the opera "20 years earlier," which remained unpublished until 1921. Cf. M. Mattarozzi/M. Porzio, *Dizionario dell'opera*, Bologna 2005, s.v. Giove a Pompei.
1384 Adrian Stähli drew my attention to the announcement, which I consulted on February 26, 2012 (http://blog.dallasopera.org/2012/01/17/the-dallas-opera-proudly-announces-a-major-new-commission/). However, Mr. Heggie has kindly informed me in an email from March 19, 2012 that a work entitled Great Scott would contain nothing Pompeian. Rosa Dolorosa will be a (mock) opera that would (or would not) be staged within Great Scott.

had her Bulwer-Lytton piece successfully performed in the Bowery Theater as early as 1835, one year after *Last Days* was published. This and subsequent performances were instrumental both to the novel's success and to Pompeii's reception in popular culture in the United States.[1385] Medina closely follows the original plot, except for the presence of Christians in Bulwer-Lyttons' novel, and stresses the social tension between the wealthy elite and the poor. Glaucus symbolizes the "honor and pride of the oppressed artisan-craftsmen."[1386] Vesuvius' eruption puts a harsh end to the excesses of capitalism, as expressed by luxury and debauchery in the novel. Elements of suspense, like caves, hidden rooms, and Vesuvius itself, play an important role, whereas no monument in Pompeii except for the amphitheater is specifically recalled. In later plays, American audiences were spellbound by the motif of "Christians as survivors" in a catastrophe that punished wicked and debauched Romans. The American historian Margaret Malamud aptly characterizes this genre of drama as a "morality play,"[1387] a characterization that also pertains to a short play by the Reverend Lewis Griffa.[1388] Griffa inserts dialogues directly from the novel, evidently believing them to be vivid enough, and suggests in his preface that professionals as well as "Lady Amateurs" were more than capable of performing the work.

In 1885, Georg Henry Boker wrote his last two plays, both of which were based on Bulwer-Lytton's novel. Neither *Nydia* nor *Glaucus* were ever published – or, it is likely, performed – during his lifetime.[1389] Boker got acquainted with antiquity thanks to his diplomatic service in Istanbul from 1871–1875, where he was involved in Frank Calvert and Heinrich Schliemann's excavations at Troy.[1390] Boker's *Nydia* mirrors elements in Medina's, like the absence of Christians and Arbaces' scripted death under the architrave of an honorary arch on the forum.[1391]

1385 Medina 1857. Performances in 1836, 1840, 1843, 1844, 1849, and 1857 are remembered opposite the frontispiece. Not in García y García 1998. Cf. Yablon 2007, 192–193 and Malamud 2009, 34, 43–44, 123, 179. On stage productions, see also St Clair/Bautz 2012, 371–375.
1386 Malamud 2009, 44
1387 Malamud 2009, 190, in a discussion of Cecil B. DeMille's *The Sign of the Cross*. During the nineteenth century, Pompeii became a metaphor for decadence in American political debates (Malamud 2009, 111, 146, like Lew Wallace's *Ben-Hur* of 1880). On Bulwer-Lytton's impact on American culture, see Malamud 2009, 122–133 and Margaret Malamud in Hales/Paul 2011, 199–214 (cf. Chapter IV, p. 229, note 879).
1388 Griffa 1876. Not in García y García 1998.
1389 Written in 1885, but edited in Boker 1929 and 1940. Cf. Yablon 2007, 192.
1390 Allen 1999, 152, 159.
1391 Boker 1929, 98: "The death of Arbaces should be neatly managed. I have indicated a safe way of killing him, by a fall of a part of the arch. This seeming stone should be made, say of a square bag of inflated India rubber, guided to the floor by a wire, so that there may be no ridic-

Arbaces uses a *sistrum* to call his slaves as if it were a table bell.[1392] The characters are, for the most part, clichéd versions of their counterparts in the novel. Arbaces organizes "orgies," which Nydia sees. Glaucus is a smart, rich Greek hero and looks like Alcibiades, the proverbially beautiful Athenian politician. Ione, similarly, is smart and rich, and Nydia is intelligent, noble, and sees without seeing. The only clear guiding motif of each of these pure souls is their hatred against the cult of Isis, as explained by Glaucus to Arbaces:[1393]

> The filthy gods you worship, that your crime
> Failed of fulfillment; or their eyes had seen
> Your carcass swimming in your guilty blood,
> Here at her outraged feet! [...]
> There are no deities,
> Worthy the name, that are not ever found
> Upon the side of right. O, hide your head,
> Let your gods see you, and avenge themselves
> On your defiance of their majesty.

Edward S. Bradley, the editor of *Nydia*, thought that Boker's *Glaucus* was of low quality.[1394] Nydia's less significant role, Bradley writes in his introduction to the text, was due to the fact that Lawrence Barrett, the envisaged producer of *Glaucus*, was not a fan of the Nydia character in Bulwer-Lytton's the novel, which he had read, and wanted to produce a play that minimized her role. Boker, evidently, had taken this into account.

Marguerite W. Morton's 1896 *Scene from "The Last Days of Pompeii"* is a brief play in which the fatal last episode of Bulwer-Lytton's novel is visualized, with Olinthus and Glaucus rescued from cruel death in the arena, which collapses as people try to get away. The text is accompanied by extensive notes on how to perform the play and the diction of the protagonists.[1395]

---

ulous bouncing when it strikes. The stone should also be covered with debris that would fly off when it strikes Arbaces; and it should be managed by a carpenter concealed behind the top of the arch. If there should be any hitch in the death of Arbaces, the whole scene will be made ridiculous. The thing should be made as much like reality as possible."

1392 Boker 1929, 59: "The sistrum was an instrument peculiar to Egypt, and was used in place of a bell. It should be made of brass, so as to make a loud sound. [...] It was grasped by the handle and shaken like a child's rattle. This instrument you will have to get made." As a matter of fact, the *sistrum* was a sacred music instrument used in the Isis rituals (see p. 41, fig. 2).

1393 Boker 1929, 65.

1394 Boker 1929, XI. But see Boker 1940, 119–228.

1395 Morton 1896. Not in García y García 1998.

An English rather literal follow-up to Boker's plays is William L. Mansell's *Ione*, which retells Bulwer-Lytton's novel and accordingly finishes with Ione, Glaucus, Lydon and Nydia on their small boat. They do not speak, but perform a sort of tableau vivant that seems to suggest a happy ending.[1396] Robert Reece's *The Very Last Days of Pompeii* also closely follows Bulwer-Lytton, but is a comedy that contains puns on modern expressions and situations of the day. The first performance of the play, with music by A. Nicholson, took place on February 13, 1872. The text concentrates on Glaucus and Ione and has no Christian elements. There is a mix of dialogues and songs and the (numbered) rhyming lines run smoothly. Glaucus, Sallustius and Diomedes were all played by women. Glaucus introduces himself:[1397]

> Happily born beneath a Grecian sky,
> Trained in the soft refinements of my nation,
> Hail anything that promises sensation.
> I've seen all sports since I was ten, or greener,
> From classic skittles to the grand arena;
> Languid myself, *my* rule's in act diversion
> To patronize vicarious exertion.

Arbaces thinks Glaucus and the Romans are nothing but softies.[1398] Greek and Roman – which is to say, in Reece's eyes, English – education is superior to any foreign cult:[1399]

> Arbaces: 'Twas Egypt first sold pine-apples in slices. [...]
> Apaecides: I've heard 't was Egypt that invented *Isis*. [...]
> Glaucus: All high art 's derived from the *Attics*.

Anachronisms are part of the joke, as in the song "Perhaps she's on the railway":[1400]

> Perhaps it is the rale way, or you cut a shine,
> To plunder all your fellow-men and try the swindle line ...

1396 Mansell 1871. Not in García y García 1998.
1397 Reece 1872, lines 49–55. Not in García y García 1998 or Reischert 2001. The only modern reference I know is in St Clair/Bautz 2012, 376, who stress the play's popularity.
1398 Reece 1872, lines 93–100: "The Latin mind is weaker than I wish, / It's overcome by tricks with bowls of fish. / I never *can* from this conviction turn 'em, / Thus when I borrow handkerchiefs I burn 'em. / That real watches, rings and hats are smashed, / That *'tis* a pigeon in the paper squashed! / From such I turn half smilingly, half sadly, / Merely observing that I *don't do badly!*"
1399 Reece 1872, lines 149, 150, 163.
1400 Reece 1872, lines 147–148. "Rale" is a pun on rail. According to the Oxford Dictionary, the word means "abnormal sound additional to that of respiration," a sort of cough, now superimposed onto the sound of the train.

There is a happy ending; Vesuvius does not erupt. The comedy does not even try to evoke a serious image of the ancient town. The highlighted monuments are the usual suspects: a bar, a house, the amphitheater, and Reece also inserts clichés of Pompeian luxury, Roman civilization, death in the amphitheater, and love affairs.

More of a parody can be found in an undated play of the late nineteenth century. *The Last Daze of Pompeii: An Antiquarian Muddle* by J.W. Hogo-Hunt and J.F. Sunavill is a very witty and sometimes-tasteless comedy about some members of "The Erculean Helephant," a Pompeian gentleman's club formatted after a typically elite British club.[1401] The authors are the comic writers James Frank Sullivan and John William Houghton, but I do not know if the play includes allusions to an actual club and/or historical people.

In *The Last Daze*, Pompeii itself is but a vague background notion belonging to the original book, and the characters are stand-ins for Bulwer-Lytton's Calenus, Arbaces, and Glaucus, Ione's lover. The many songs almost make it a musical. Arbaces instills fear in all who approach him,[1402] and does not portray himself in the most flattering way:

> In me, I may inform you, you descry
> A villain of the very deepest dye,
> In fact, when old enough to use discretion,
> I took up villainy as a profession;
> And, being an unusually hardy 'un,
> I speedily became a Poor Law Guardian.
> But cash from that I found I couldn't pump any,
> So took to managing a joint stock company,
> And, as receipts were rapidly diminishing,
> Became a medium by way of finishing –
> For folks are gulled (who do not understand tricks)
> By *sleight of hand* and such like *slight off-hand* tricks!
> From these confessions you will gather I'm
> *Au fait* at each unpunishable crime.
> Yet I've so well pursued that little game
> That men have learnt to tremble at my name.

Remarkably, the story ends without Vesuvius' eruption, but with a call for a shower of flowers to fall upon Ione and Glaucus from the audience:

[1401] "Helephant" might refer to the Bar of Sittius or the Elephant in Pompeii, which frequently appears in Pompeii fiction.

[1402] Hogo-Hunt/Sunavill [1870]. Mentioned by M.D. Bridges in Hales/Paul 2011, 91. On Sullivan, see *Oxford Dictionary of National Biography* 53 (2004) 309–310. "During the piece, when it is possible, all the characters except Glaucus, display a crouching terror in approaching Arbaces."

> Ione: But where's Vesuvius – the Lava, dear?
> Glaucus: We must defer that incident, I fear.
> Yet, stay – There needs no trouble on that head
> (to audience) *You* overwhelm us with applause instead.
> For cinders substitute – well, say bouquets.
> Bewilder us with cheers – Prolong our *daze*.

Bulwer-Lytton's success in Spain was due to many Spanish translations of his novel and a popular adaptation by Juan Espantaleón, whose play starts with the scene *El perjurio* ("false oath"), situated in front of the Temple of Isis and some tombs. While Arbaces hopes to win over Yone, his former priest Apaecides joins the Nazarenes, an event that Arbaces and Caleno try to prevent. After a big argument with Arbaces about religion, Olinto, the leader of the Christians, is sent to the amphitheater. Espantaleón stresses the importance of the Christian theme that returns in later scenes of the play, which is otherwise true to Bulwer-Lytton's novel.[1403] Albert Boadella uses Bulwer's title as a pun in his *Ubú president, o, Los últimos días de Pompeya*, about the Catalan politician Jordi Pujol i Soley, which was staged in 1995. The use of Pompeii in the title represents decadence, something for which Pujol was notorious.[1404]

Pompeii in the Background

As with opera, theater turned away from Bulwer-Lytton at the end of the nineteenth century. Playwrights and authors tried to find their own way with the Pompeii theme.

Hermann Lingg's one-act love story *Clytia* premièred in 1883 at the Hoftheater in Munich.[1405] Lingg wrote many pieces in which history plays an important role, but antiquity was not his special period of interest. Apart from some tiny hints

---

[1403] Espantaleón 1892. R. Olmos Romera (1993a) studied the fortune of Bulwer-Lytton in Spain. The most successful translation is *Ione* by Celestino Barallat y Felguera (1888); frontispiece illustrated on p. 55. See García y García 1998, no. 2310 for other Spanish remakes. On Espantaleón, see Romero Recio 2012, 66.
[1404] I saw the text in Boadella 2006, 84–228. At p. 85: "En la obra de Boadella, la referencia es claramente irónica y alude a los últimos momentos del mandato de Pujol." Good introduction on pp. 11–83 by Milagros Sánchez Arnosi.
[1405] Munich 1883. García y García 1998, no. 8036 (incorrectly called "poema narrativo"). A 32 page booklet (Lingg 1883) advertises that a piano-score of *Clytia* is available. There are very few remarks on stage direction.

of the ancient town in *Clytia's* meager plot, specific reasons for using Pompeii as the setting are absent. The play is about a "normal" confusion of relationships between members of high society set in the ancient past. The name Clytia refers to a daughter of the sea god Oceanus, but also to a jellyfish and a butterfly.

It is not clear if (and if so, when and where) J. Cellarius' *Die Isispriester in den letzten Tagen von Pompeji* was ever performed. The complicated plot intermingles two themes: love and Christianity, which plays an ambiguous role.[1406] Although the characters bear different names, Bulwer-Lytton is never far away. We recognize depraved Egyptian priests, the Villa of Diomedes, and its owner, Diomedes himself. Cellarius's use of Pompeii is limited to the written script, for the onstage layout as described in the text shows no affinity with the site. Cellarius' aim is to demonstrate a sharp contrast between Sethos, the wicked, unreliable Isis high priest, and Timon, a wise Greek citizen. Diomedes and the small group of friends and relatives vacillate between the two religions, but finally decide to join Timon's sect.

A play that shines a positive light on Christianity is Ödön von Horváth's 1937 literary masterpiece *Pompeji. Komödie eines Erdbebens in sechs Bildern*.[1407] Von Horváth was the Austro-Hungarian author of twenty theater plays and three novels, who worked mainly in Germany and Austria, but fled in 1938 to the west to escape national-socialist terror. In Paris, he was accidentally killed by a falling tree in the same year. *Pompeji* was among his last works, and was only finally performed in 1959. It demonstrates a popular wish in the 1930s, namely, abolishing dictatorship in favor of freedom, real love, and solidarity, and in connection with that, the switch from paganism to Christianity. Actors wear "Pompeian" masks, apparently modeled after images from wall paintings, and act in a way that corresponds with how a twentieth-century audience would have expected them to, based on common associations contemporary people would have made with certain ancient professions, like traders, slaves, and seers, all of whom appear in the play. In the course of the play, however, each character gradually removes his ancient disguise, to reveal a "modern" character in modern times, which is the opposite of what the audience had come to expect, as it directly contradicts the function each plays in the plot. For instance, K. R. Thago, a wealthy Punic trader, changes radically from an extortionist plutocrat to a charitable man caring for the

---

1406 Cellarius n.y. Not in García y García 1998. I could not find any data about Cellarius in the *Neue Deutsche Biographie* or elsewhere. The dates of publication and, if any, performances are unknown, but looks as second half of nineteenth century because of spelling and style.
1407 Von Horváth 1972, 591–646. There was also a never-staged forerunner, *Ein Sklavenball. Mit Gesang und Tanz in drei Akten* (Von Horváth 1972, 539–590). See Von Horváth 1972, *9; Bartsch 2000, 119–120, 146–153; Ropers 2012, 154–180. García y García 1998, no. 6906.

poor and sick,[1408] leaving the other characters perplexed. The composition and several phrases reflect Plautus' comedies, to which Thago's slave Toxilus refers at the beginning.[1409]

Von Horváth's sense of humor is sometimes absurd, starting with K.R. Thago's name. Thago's adventure at sea resembles the vicissitudes of protagonists in ancient Greek novels, including shipwrecks, getting lost and other such plights. Indeed, Thago was shipwrecked and floated on a piece of wood, since walking on water was an ability given to one man only.[1410] Thago's slaves vainly hope for freedom after their master's alleged death. Christianity serves to turn the world's sinners into do-gooders.[1411] "Der Herr," who appears in the run of the piece, is none other than St. Paul. Toxilus the slave is said to have been thrown into a deep pit, from which being rescued was impossible, which serves as another biblical reference to the well into which Joseph is flung by his brothers. Apart from Dordalus' shop, which includes *dipinti* on its walls, Pompeii is not defined very precisely, but serves as the backdrop to a changing world in which everyone takes off their masks and the world becomes a peaceful and healthy place reigned by Christian love.[1412]

John Blauer and Rod McManigal's 1989 *Pompeii* was a play written for the (all male) members of the San Francisco Bohemian Club. Twenty nine protagonists along with a chorus, dancers, supporting actors and an orchestra present a play in the outdoor "Bohemian Grove" which mixes some elements from Bulwer-Lytton and the storyline of Merian Cooper's 1935 Hollywood movie *The Last Days of Pompeii* (see p. 383). Marcus, a former blacksmith, becomes rich as a gladiator. He earns a lot of gold fighting against Pontius Pilatus' enemies in Judea, where a "Man of Healing" heals his young son Flavius. Marcus and Flavius witness Jesus' crucifixion, and Flavius becomes a Christian. Many years later in Pompeii,

---

1408 Baumann 2003, 427–429 makes a comparison between Thago's transformation and Saulus' radical change into Paulus, that is, from an enemy of Christianity into a zealous missionary. This part of Horváth's piece is aptly called "Verwandlung." Ropers (2012, 161–162) stresses that Thago has no face any longer.
1409 For Plautus, see Ropers 2012, 156–157, 159–160 (i.a. names taken from Plautus' comedies). Bartsch 2000, 146–153, sees elements taken from Bulwer-Lytton's *Last Days*, but if so, these seem restricted to the Christian theme.
1410 Von Horváth 1972, 640. This detail implies that Thago has become a Christian. It obviously refers to Jesus walking on the Lake of Galilea (Gospel of St Matthew 14.22–31).
1411 Baumann 2003, 421–451 on theological allusions in the play. Ropers 2012, 170–171 gives examples of quotations from the New Testament.
1412 Zintzen 1998, 341: she also refers to Grillparzer 1930 and Grün 1849, see here chapters V, pp. 283–284 and VII, p. 334. Von Horváth's piece was elaborated into an opera by Horst Ebenhöh in 1971; see the composer's website: http://www.ebnet.at/werke/werke_fs.htm (visited January 7, 2012).

Marcus has become the manager of Pompeii's amphitheatre and welcomes his former comrade Pontius Pilatus to the games in the amphitheater, which have been organized in honor of Pilatus' visit. Flavius is condemned to death by the Romans on account of his Christian faith, and along with his friends is to die in the arena in front of his father and Pilatus. Marcus tries to rescue his son and other Christians just as Vesuvius begins to erupt, and ends up sacrificing himself under Christ's benignant eye.[1413] The work consists of prose dialogs, and songs and interludes composed by David Bowman, and the authors have fun with Bulwer-Lytton, changing Nydia's "Buy my flowers" to the blind fortune-teller Fortunata's "Buy my visions." The town of Pompeii is presented as the typical idealized backdrop, with scenes on the forum, a banquet at Marcus' and the amphitheater. When Vesuvius does its violent work, the only way out of danger is Christianity. The Olympian god Jupiter, the only pagan persona in the play, is shown looking down upon the actors from Olympus shaking his head, as he realizes that he is in the process of losing control over the world, which is transforming from a pagan society into a Christian heaven on earth.

Pompeii in Mass Media

Opera and theater plays, two more or less elite forms of public performances, led to popular counterparts, too. In the twentieth century, of course, came cinema, but before that, in the nineteenth century, came panoramas and pyrodrams. Both words are neologisms, concocted with Greek words, and mean, respectively, "view of everything / of all sides" and "drama with fire." The first panoramas, invented around 1800 in Britain, presented towns or landscapes in closed round rooms, which visitors could walk around. In subsequent decades, they became larger and were installed in special temporary buildings or tents. In painted or (later) photographic form, the large images conveyed a feeling of being plunged right into Pompeii itself, and were sometimes enhanced by lighting effects or moving elements.

The earliest Pompeii panorama that I know of was installed by Robert Burford in Leicester Square and Strand in London in 1825.[1414] A twelve-page descriptive booklet of Pompeii provided the visitor with necessary information. At the back of the booklet is a folded plate with an overview of the two parts of the frieze

---

[1413] Blauer/McManigal 1989.
[1414] However, in Dutch papers of 1807 a panorama of Naples, including the destruction of Pompeii, was presented by the French Opera in Amsterdam (see journals on the Dutch Royal Library website; hits under "Pompeji" + "panorama" – http://kb.kranten.nl/).

visible in the panorama, with added numbers referring to the written explanation of the image.[1415] The upper frieze displays the forum with the temples of Jupiter and "Venus or Bacchus" (= Apollo), the latter still surrounded by *lapilli*. The lower frieze depicts dancing peasants and a part of the city near the Herculanean Gate. After 1828, the German artist Carl Georg Enslen divulgated the panorama throughout Germany, and there was a large Franco-Belgian production in later decades.[1416] In 1886, a panorama was produced by the "Panorama-maatschappij Amsterdam" at the Plantage Middenlaan. A huge painting that was based on a design by Bobin, a "French architect," showed "Pompeii at the moment the eruption starts and terrified people fleeing from all sides to the coast."[1417] An accompanying pamphlet tells the story of Pompeii and cites Pliny's letters, and questions Dio Cassius' claim that the theater was full of people when disaster struck (discussed in Chapter IX, p. 393), since this pertained to Herculaneum. The pamphlet does not, however, question Cassius' claim that people were in the amphitheater in Pompeii when Vesuvius erupted. Also according to the pamphlet, a group of Christians was happy to get out in time. In the second section of the pamphlet, the panorama itself is described, with some houses, temples and the two theaters singled out.

Unlike panoramas, which were shown in special installments in various towns and villages, and visited over long periods of time by increasing numbers of people as their popularity grew, pyrodrams were singular onstage representations in huge spaces that took the form of *tableaux vivants*, with hundreds of actors accompanied by music and enlivened by fireworks. Considering the cost of putting on one of these spectacles, event organizers would attempt to gather thou-

---

1415 R. Burford, *Description of a View of the Ruins of the City of Pompeii, Representing the Forum with the Adjoining Edifices, and Surrounding Country, now exhibiting in the Panorama, Strand; painted from drawings taken on the spot*, London 1825 (1823 = Garcia y Garcia no. 2324). Donaldson, who wrote a lavishly illustrated book on Pompeii (Donaldson 1827), is acknowledged. The panorama was conceived immediately after the eruption of 1822. Hogg (1827, 80) recalls two panoramas in 1827: "faithful and exact." On other panoramas, see *Sehsucht* 1993; Kockel 2006; Leroy 2009, 14–82 (Burfort i.a. p. 57); Thomas 2010; V. Kockel in Cain/Haug/Asisi 2011, 23–48, esp. 29–30 (Pompeii); Oleksijczuk 2011 (panoramas until 1820).
1416 Kockel 2006 (Enslen); Leroy 2009 (France, Belgium).
1417 B., *Panorama van de verwoesting van Pompeii door de uitbarsting van den Vesuvius*, Amsterdam 1886, 11. It includes a plan of the excavation with all names in French and in the beginning Breton (1855, 1869) is quoted. "B" might be Bobin. See, however, *Sehsucht* 1993, 182 cat. II.124: paintings by Charles-Jules Castellani, brought from Copenhagen. On Castellani *Sehsucht* 1993, 54–55, 74–76 and Leroy 2009. The location was next to the zoo "Artis," so that there was a steady flow of people in this area until the zoo's closure in 1889. See also the Dutch journal site (see note 1414) for advertisements.

sands of spectators in advance of a scheduled performance. The oldest recorded Pompeii pyrodram took place around 1850 in Manchester. In the second half of the nineteenth century, the British entrepreneur James Pain was, perhaps, the most accomplished producer of Pompeii pyrodrams.[1418] Spectators were accommodated on wooden rows of seats. An 1879 show in Manchester was attended by 25,000 spectators, and later that same year, it was staged a couple of times in New York, each time attracting some ten thousand visitors. By 1914, Pain had organized dozens of successful spectacles on nearby Coney Island, with 1,300 "meticulously costumed actors" playing the inhabitants of Pompeii. Accompanying music by the popular composer and conductor Patrick S. Gilmore was "performed by a full military band."[1419] In this drama, Pompeians, being noble characters, perish due to a natural disaster, not because of their decadence. In his study on the theater of Fort Worth, Jan L. Jones aptly claims that "the plot had little to do with history, but guaranteed box-office appeal."[1420] Pain's productions also toured Australia and New Zealand and got enthusiastic reactions from the public.[1421]

Pompeii on Screen

Due to the introduction of film as a serious form of entertainment at the beginning of the twentieth century, the attraction of these spectacles waned. As with open-air pyrodrams, Bulwer-Lytton was the principle source of inspiration for early cinema.[1422] There was a flood of silent films on Roman Pompeii in the first several decades of the twentieth century. All entitled *Gli ultimi giorni di Pompei*, they were released in 1908, 1909, 1913 (two in one year!) and 1926.[1423] In those early times, films based on ancient themes were costly productions and enhanced the reputation of the young (and prestige-hungry) Italian Kingdom, as a shining follow-up to the Roman Empire. While the plots repeated the storyline of Bulwer-Lytton's *Last Days*,

---

1418 Yablon 2007; Malamud 2009, 177–179.
1419 Mayer 1994, 93, 100. The synopsis of this show is reproduced in Mayer 1994, 100–103. Jones 2006, 82–85 describes how in Forth Worth (Texas), Pain attracted 100,000 visitors over fifteen performances in October 1890. A second production in 1902 was a smaller success. See also Malamud 2009, 123, 150–151
1420 Jones 2006, 83.
1421 Colligan 2002, 130, 132, 145–147, 148–149 (1887 and 1888).
1422 Wyke 1997, 147–182; Mayer 1994, 90–103; Martin 2002; P. Pesando in Guzzo 2003b, 34–45; Harris 2007, 206–210; Glücklich 2008, 72–85, 96–99; Aziza 2009, esp. 77–78; Malamud 2009, 187; I. Lottini in Bayman 2011, 32–53; C. Catrein in Reinsberg/Meynersen 2012, 150–153. For antiquity in film also see Solomon 1978 and Fitzon 2002a.
1423 Kinnard/Davis 1992, 55; Yablon 2007, 190; Glücklich 2008, 73–74.

at least in the cases of the 1913 and 1926 films,[1424] the spectator "descends" from modern Pompeii into 79 Pompeii and gets involved in the ancient story. The Egyptian priest Arbaces is generally depicted with a distorted body, twisted eyes, a dark complexion, and fancy clothing. These serve as evidence of his extremely negative character, and as a political representative metaphor for Ethiopia and Libya, which had been conquered as a consequence of the imperialistic tendencies of the young Italian state. After World War II, imperialistic themes vanished from this genre of film, but politics would still dictate the choice of the historical theme. A 1950 Italian film of the same name, but which was also known as *Sins of Pompeii*, is a political statement of post-war Italy that claims that the Christian element should strengthen the political power of the new Catholic party, the Democrazia Cristiana.[1425]

Politics played no role in the world of Hollywood, unless one believes that no message is a message. Hollywood producers wanted nice love stories in a historical setting, and the narrative permitted the introduction of mass scenes and spectacular effects, elements familiar to audiences from *grand opéra*, which was still fresh in the public's memory. Still, the edifying forces of Christianity were attractive, and would dominate various "peplum films."[1426] A good example of such a film is Ernest B. Schoedsack and Merian C. Cooper's 1935 *The Last Days of Pompeii*. Its plot is almost identical to Blauer and McManigal's play written for the Bohemian Club (see above p. 379–380).[1427] Pompeii's amphitheater is represented in the film by the amphitheater in Verona.

Mario Bonnard's 1959 film *Last Days* features several characters that bear names from Bulwer-Lytton's novel, but the story is about gangsters terrorizing Pompeii who accuse the members of a small Christian community of performing illegal activities.[1428] A long climactic scene displays Pompeii's destruction and the death of most of the gangsters, but some Christians, including the protagonist Glauco, escape in small boats.

1424 On the 1926 movie (directed by Carmine Gallone and Amleto Palermi), see Redi 1994, who includes lavish illustrations.
1425 Made in 1948 and 1949, released in 1950. Directed by Marcel L'Herbier and Paolo Moffa.
1426 Malamud 2009, 186–207 and Bondanella 2009, 159–179, discuss peplum films in the context of American and Italian society respectively. Although the Pompeii theme is not singled out, many of their observations are relevant. A striking detail is the fight of beasts against Christians in the amphitheater, as in Cecil B. DeMille's 1932 *The Sign of the Cross* (see Malamud 2009, 187–193, fig. 7.2; cf. note 1387).
1427 I did not see this film and rely on Kinnard/Davis 1992, 52–56 and Glücklich 2008, 74–76. There is a 1960 Italian remake without Jesus. Kinnard and Davis provide photographs suggesting a depiction of a high degree of luxury in the amphitheater and other Pompeian buildings.
1428 Glücklich 2008, 76–77; Bondanella 2009, 163; F. Burke in Bayman 2011, 193–194. Martin 2002, 116 sees parallels with the anti-Jewish terror of the Nazis.

The British comic actor Frankie Howerd had a lot of success in 1970 with his "Up Pompeii" series on BBC television.[1429] He was the first to bring the Pompeii theme into the private homes of English spectators. His and other productions use Pompeii as a realistic locus for historical dramas playing out in antiquity and eternizing ordinary people, sometimes next to emperors and princes.[1430]

The Fires of Pompeii, written by James Moran, is a 2008 episode of the BBC television series *Doctor Who*. The title character is portrayed as an inventor in the 1960s, whose primary interests are now rescuing the world and destroying evil alien forces. Doctor Who and his friend Donna travel in their spacecraft TARDIS from modern London to Pompeii on August 23, 79. When Vesuvius begins to erupt, they realize that it is "Volcano Day," and Doctor Who discovers that aliens called "Pyroviles" are planning to destroy the world using Vesuvius' powers. Another destructive power is that of the arcane "Sibylline Sisterhood," members of which kidnap Donna. Among the Pompeian inhabitants depicted are Lucius Caecilius Secundus and his family. Caecilius is a sculptor who has made a futuristic work of art that converts energy into destructive powers for Lucius Petrus Dextrus, a priest and magistrate who envisages the destruction of society with the Pyroviles' help. After many adventures involving the Doctor, Donna, and the Caecilii, Donna persuades the Doctor to rescue the Caecilii from Pompeii as it is destroyed by the eruption of Vesuvius, and at the end of the episode, the four family members are depicted as successful businessmen in ancient Rome, where they venerate small portraits of the Doctor and Donna as their household gods. This ending is similar to the ending in Bulwer-Lytton's *Last Days*, in which the protagonists Glaucus and Ione look back from their house in Athens on all the adventures they have had in Pompeii. Thanks to a mix of special effects and ancient narrative elements, the episode is also similar to some of the novels that were discussed in Chapter VI, in which people jump into the past or into a futuristic Pompeii.[1431] The conversations in the episode are often very witty, and contain English wordplay mixed with Latin and science fiction jargon. The Caecilii bear the same names as the protagonists of the "Cambridge Latin Course" used in Britain since the 1970s. Caecilius is also the name of an ancient banker from Pompeii, whose banking records

---

1429 See for instance http://search.babylon.com/?q=Frankie+Howerd+&s=web&as=0&babsrc=HP_ss (visited January 7, 2012).

1430 I do not discuss more recent films, mostly produced for television and often consisting of various parts, like Peter Hunt's 1984 *The Last Days of Pompeii* and Peter Nichelson's 2003 *Pompeii, the Last Day*. See Pucci 2012, 81–82.

1431 E.g. Nothomb 1996, Hopkins 1999, East 2003; Pohl 2011. Hobden 2009 analyzes *The Fires of Pompeii* extensively. Easily accessible synopsis and further information is available on websites like Wikipedia.

were discovered in the nineteenth century in the House of Caecilius Jucundus and who features in various novels (see p. 312, note 1187).

The latest addition to Pompeii cinema is Paul Anderson's 2014 *Pompeii*. It uses 3D effects to create a spacious Pompeian panorama, and compellingly presents the consequences of Vesuvius' 79 A.D. eruption and the simultaneous tsunami. The story does not differ from many of the earlier fictional intimations. Milo, a Nordic Celtic man, has been captured as a slave, becomes a gladiator and is brought to Pompeii for a spectacular show in the amphitheater. Upon arriving in Pompeii, he rescues a young woman, Cassia, from a carriage accident by killing a horse that has gone crazy, which is just the first of several incidents involving horses. We come to realize that Milo is a natural horseman, as in later scenes, he is seen taming horses and riding them spectacularly.

Milo and Cassia are drawn to each other, but she is forced to marry Corvus, a Roman senator and former military officer. Interestingly, and although it never becomes quite clear why, Cassia and her family, as Pompeians, feel superior to the Romans, who are mainly represented in *Pompeii* by Corvus and his assistant Proculus. At the beginning of the film, Milo, portrayed as a child, witnesses these two men murdering his family in his home country. Against all odds, Cassia and Milo find each other as Vesuvius erupts, and die together under one of the deadly pyroclastic clouds. At both the beginning and the end of *Pompeii*, we see plaster casts of their bodies, which remind us of the long tradition in fiction of drawing inspiration from the remains of the victims, who become men and women of flesh and blood.

The movie includes many lengthy scenes of crude fighting and bloodshed, and pays little attention to character development. Gladiators are portrayed as the heroes who slay better-armed Roman legionaries. The film's depiction of the Roman world in general is highly inaccurate. Men's fashion and grooming are particularly implausible, including the extravagant leather or metal wristbands men are frequently seen wearing, their mostly curly hairdos, which only became fashionable in the second or early third century A.D., and their Caracalla-like beards during a time when the elite were normally clean-shaven. Corvus is clad in a cuirass rather than a toga, and roams Pompeii's streets with his entourage of legionary soldiers bullying the citizens, a kind of havoc inside a Roman city's walls that would have been unheard of during times of peace.

The film's use of Pompeii itself centers only on its tragic end, and not Milo's dramatic experiences as an orphan and subsequent life of forced slavery as a gladiator.[1432] One last historical inaccuracy to note: had a figure like Milo proven

---

1432 In this sense, Milo's life is similar to that of Maximus Decimus Meridius in Ridley Scott's *Gladiator* of 2000. See the hilarious analysis of *Pompeii* and another 2014 Pompeii film (*Apocalypse Pompeii*) by Giuseppe Pucci (2014a).

himself such a great fighter, show organizers would most likely have deemed him worthy of fighting in Rome, and not kept him in a provincial city like Pompeii.

Seen from the archaeological and antiquarian side, these films are peculiar concoctions that mix ancient reality and fantasy. They never show exact replicas of Pompeian houses or other buildings, but instead display diverting imitations, while copies of objects and mural paintings in the Naples museum enhance the atmosphere.[1433] In Nydia's house in the 1926 film, the *tablinum* contains the archaistic marble statuette of Diana from the House of Holconius Rufus, and the bronze boar being attacked by two dogs from the House of the Cither Player stands in the peristyle next to a copy of the Satyr by Praxiteles (which, as far as I know, was not actually found at Pompeii).[1434] A niche behind a fountain looks like the *lararium* in the House of the Sarno River. A portrait herm might be the likeness of the head of the banker Caecilius Iucundus. The plants in the garden are reminiscent of the peristyle gardens in the Houses of the Vettii or of the Gilded Cupids, both excavated and reconstructed shortly before 1900. The paintings in the houses are reproductions of drawings and watercolors made in the nineteenth century rather than copies of actual murals in the excavated houses. In Bonnard's 1959 archaeologically flawed film, what should be the cult statue of Isis in her temple is actually a pharaoh, the Colosseum-like amphitheater is adorned with the late archaic Athena statue from the Temple of Aphaea on Aegina (now in Munich), and the painted frieze of the Villa of the Mysteries embellishes the aedile Ascanio's office. The antiquarian details in the *Doctor Who* episode on Pompeii, such as the set of Pompeii, the house of Caecilius and the costumes, are very old-fashioned and look like they are from older movies, a feeling that is enhanced further by the use of the famous Cinecittà studios in Rome for the outdoor scenes of Pompeii. A tenacious anachronistic mistake made in this and almost all other Pompeii (and Roman) movies is many male protagonists' use of broad leather or metal wristbands, I already mentioned in relation to the 2014 *Pompeii* movie, which were not worn at all in antiquity.

Pompeian elements feature in other films, too, like Fellini's 1969 *Satyricon* and 1972 *Roma*. In *Satyricon*, Eumolpus possesses *objets d'art*, like the painted stellarium from the Villa of Ariadne at Stabiae. In *Roma*, frescoes found during the construction of the metro fade away; some details resemble the Villa of the Mysteries frieze, which also decorates a room in *Satyricon*. The first scene of Pastrone's 1916 *Cabiria* plays out during an eruption of Etna. The destruction of Catania and its

---

1433 Like the paintings by Alma Tadema (see *Alma Tadema* 2007). However, some 1950s decors resemble the street facades as reconstructed in Spinazzola 1953.
1434 Wyke 1997, fig. 6.5.

wealthy houses would have been a fitting scene at the end of a Pompeii movie. Carmine Gallone's 1937 *Scipione l'Africano* uses houses in Pompeii and Herculaneum as places of action.[1435] Rossellini's enigmatic 1954 masterpiece *Viaggio in Italia* is about Alexander and Katherine Joyce, an English couple masterfully played by George Sanders and Ingrid Bergman, settling a legal matter in Naples, where their troublesome relationship is put to the test. At Pompeii, by accident, they witness some archaeologists' discovery of two corpses, interpreted as a pair of lovers in their final embrace. Maiuri is seen for a fleeting moment as one of the excavators. In the National Museum, dimly lit bronze utensils haunt Katherine through gloomy still apparitions, which she understands as an announcement of her impending death.[1436]

Tourists Roam Pompeii on Radio

As far as I know, there are not many evocations of Pompeii written for radio. Henry Reed's *The Streets of Pompeii* is an intriguing exception, a radio play broadcasted by BBC London in 1952, 1955 and 1977.[1437] Reed sketches vivid portraits of various classes of tourists, especially British ones who barely come into contact with modern Italians. Attilio and Francesca, a young Italian couple who are roaming the streets of the excavation, are the instruments by which Reed brings the listener from one group of British visitors to another. Intermezzi of Sibylle and the Traveler bring the listener into contact with the past and work like the reflective choruses of Greek tragedies. To stress the differences between the various protagonists, each gets his own specific idiom and accent. Every character carries the burden of a historically loaded Pompeii from which there is no escape, and the script is full of words like "empty," "silent," "silence," "closes," "dead," and "oblivion," which to a modern listener symbolized solitude and being forgotten. Sibylle always speaks in verse; Traveler sometimes does so, while all other players use prose. There are musical interludes composed by Anthony Smith-Masters. In the context of our study, Sibylle and Traveler evoke the most striking impressions of Pompeii through their discussions of the notion of antiquity that the play wants to convey. Concerning the resurrection of the ancient town, Sibylle says:[1438]

1435 On this film, see Wyke 1997, 21–22, 51; Pucci 2014b, 302–306.
1436 See Hirsh 2007. See also Bondanella 2009 and Bayman 2011; Pucci 2012, 80–81. Pucci 2012 discusses other films in which gypsum casts play a role.
1437 Reed 1971, 125–172. García y García 1998, no. 11.224 has 1970.
1438 Reed 1971, 131.

> Here to the light of heaven returns
> From underground the skeleton
> Of dead Pompeii, disinterred
> By avarice or piety
> From underneath oblivion.
> Here in the Forum's emptiness,
> Erect the pilgrim stands between
> The fallen colonnades and sees
> Within a long look the smokeless hill,
> The cloven summit threatening still
> The shattered fragments of this place.

Traveler describes the history of the place and its discovery, and asks:[1439]

> Antiquity. Is it thus that the Land of the Dead will look at our first glimpse of it? At the moment of release into that long vacation, it is thus we shall see that country? [...] Set out in empty streets, the fractured grey boxes of strangers' houses living then, into eternity? Each containing something we cannot see, even though all seems shamelessly and horribly broken open to the still, new air, the new still air of the morning, the vagueness and the lightness of morning, of a holiday morning in a strange land.

All visitors to Pompeii feel the spell of death, even if they do not feel a special attraction to the monument or its history. Tourism is not seen as a negative activity: people can learn from it.

Modern Classics: Pink Floyd and Other Pop Songs

October 4–7, 1971, Pink Floyd recorded a concert with no audience in the amphitheater at Pompeii that was released as a movie in 1972. We mainly see the band standing in the arena with their backs to the main entrance. The film crew, led by Adrian Maben, is visible in front of them. Maben wanted the band to concentrate on their music in a cultural environment, without the cheering public they were accustomed to at festivals and concerts.

The cavea of the amphitheater is overgrown with weeds and in the arena heaps of grey ashes and lapilli are lying against the protective wall, suggesting that it has been unearthed recently. We see the band playing seven pieces[1440] and

---

[1439] Reed 1971, 137. Traveler is very similar to the Wanderer in Wagner's *Siegfried*.
[1440] I Echoes, Part I – II Careful with Axe, Eugene – III A Saucerful of secrets – IV One of These Days – V Set the Controls for the Heart of the Sun – VI Mademoiselle Nobs – VII Echoes, Part II.

sometimes roaming the slopes of Vesuvius or the smoldering *caldara* of the Solfatara. There are shots of ancient Pompeian monuments – e.g. the theaters, basilica, forum, and houses – that never show a living soul. At other moments, ancient wall paintings pop up behind the musicians, including the frightened woman and other figures from the Villa of the Mysteries frieze, images of Silenus, and the famous painted portrait of a couple found in the House of the Baker. Heavy clouds obscure the scene, alternated by sunny or starry skies. Even if Pompeii is not a subject of the songs, the town is a gloomy player in the drama.

One may ask whether this seminal recording inspired other pop artists to make songs or entire albums dedicated to Pompeii. It is a theme nowadays easily retraceable on the Internet. In the few examples I heard the disaster dominates the lyrics.[1441]

Conclusion

Most of the nineteenth century operas and theater plays discussed herein play out in the last days of Pompeii's existence, and Vesuvius punishes the town's inhabitants for being corrupt or fanatic pagans, or people perish due to their own foolishness. The playwrights almost always followed Bulwer-Lytton's novel (with the notable exception of Ferrare, Cain and Nouguès, who were inspired by Bertheroy's novel), but sometimes invented their own plots. Bulwer-Lytton's novel also provided the lion's share of material for *grand opéras*, with opulent ballets, complicated relationships and wicked characters struggling with noble ones. Bertheroy's 1899 *Danseuse* and Nouguès' remake marked the end of an era, just before World War I, when Bulwer-Lytton's novel also lost popularity, although cinema makers continued to adopt his work for their movies until the 1960s. Works for stage not

---

[1441] I shall not discuss the various pop songs in which Pompeii is about the subject. It is easy to find them on YouTube and via Google. I shall, however, mention some album titles: On New Triumvirat's 1997 Pompeii, Pompeii meets its end already in 62 ("The Earthquake 62 a.d.", text Jürgen Fritz); Nova Mob, released *Pompeii* in 1991; Anthrax released *American Pompeii* in 1995. Anne Hills sings "Last Days of Pompeii" on her 1992 album *Don't Panic*, while Michael Smith has a song with the same title on his 1991 album *Love Stories*. On The Flaming Lips' 2006 album *At War with the Mystics*, appears the German song "Pompeji am Götterdämmerung." The American band Bastille released "Pompeii" in 2013 as a free download. A rather popular German rock song is Herbert Grönemeyer's "Pompeji" on his 1979 debut album *Grönemeyer*, which has been performed frequently, even recently. A genre yet to be explored are video games, of which I shall only mention the 2008 *Escape from Pompeii*, in which Alabama Smith searches for an amulet, and her friend Anastasia rescues Alabama from an eruption of Vesuvius.

inspired by Bulwer-Lytton are rare and were mostly written after the war. Lingg's *Clytia* seems to have no relationship with antiquity, except for the plot's location and date. Fully original plays like De Pixerécourt and Von Horváth, and operas like Giordano and Franchetti's *Giove a Pompei* are rare birds in the cage of drama. The same is true for Reed, who uniquely brought to stage the reactions of modern tourists upon seeing Pompeii's ruins. Von Horváth and Reed tackle modern behavior in an antique setting by confronting the users of the ancient site with the devastating effects their behavior may be having on it.

Archaeological accuracy gets little attention in operatic, tragic, and cinematographic works, although stage directions and descriptions of settings sometimes betray an interest in historically accurate visualizations. Composers and stage producers tried incessantly to simulate the eruption of Vesuvius by means of grandiose musical outbursts or spectacular visual special effects, but this was not the only incentive to write works about the end of Pompeii. All of these intimations of Pompeii and Herculaneum betray a fascination for antiquity and the wish to visualize historically documented drama in orchestral or pop music and on stage, film, radio and television – and even in video games, which promises to give Pompeii new life yet. In this newest branch of virtual art, the sky is the limit in terms of purposefully-crafted stories based on ancient life in Pompeii or Herculaneum.

IX Herculaneum Under Vesuvius

This chapter focuses on poetry about Vesuvius and Herculaneum, which, except for Maizony de Lauréal's epic *L'Héracléade* in Chapter VII, is a topic that has not yet been herein discussed. A handful of poems betray a fascination for the volcano and its effects on ancient Herculaneum and Pompeii.[1442]

The Fiery Mountain of Vesuvius

The 1631 eruption led to a renewed interest in Europe and inspired poets to write about that great disaster. Seventeenth century Vesuvius poems by the German poets Martin Optiz and Jacob Bidermann stand out for their dramatic and effective evocations of the cities that vanished in 79.[1443] Opitz was read widely during his lifetime and thereafter, both in Germany and abroad, and is commonly regarded as a superb poet. In his 1633 *Vesuvius*, he attempts to explain the phenomenon of volcanism. Without describing the 1631 disaster, he explores the principles of volcanology and questions the possible role of God in the disaster.[1444] The poem

---

[1442] The earliest example is an epigram by M. Valerius Martialis, *Epigrammaton libri* 4.44: *Hic est pampineis viridis modo Vesbius umbris, /Presserat hic madidos nobilis uva lacus, /Haec iuga quam Nisae colles plus Bacchus amavit, /Hoc nuper Satyri monte dedere choros, /Haec Veneris sedes Lacedaemone gratior illi, /Hic locus Herculeo nomine clarus erat. /Cuncta iacent flammis et tristi mersa favilla, /Nec superi vellent hoc licuisse sibi.* Prose translation by D.R. Shackleton Baily, Martial (Loeb Classical Library), Cambridge Mass./London 1993, I, 313: "This is Vesuvius, but lately green with shade of vines. Here the noble grape loaded the vats to overflowing. These slopes were more dear to Bacchus than Nysa's hills, on this mountain not long ago Satyrs held their dances. This was Venus' dwelling, more pleasing to her than Lacedaemon, this spot the name of Hercules made famous. All lies sunken in flames and drear ashes. The High Ones themselves would rather this had not been in their power." Cf. Th. Mommsen, *Corpus Inscriptionum Latinarum* X, Berlin 1883, 90: "Epitaphium urbibus scripsit Martialis (ep. 4, 44) non invenustum" (Martial wrote a rather nice epitaph for the towns).
[1443] On this eruption and its aftermath, see Richter 2007, 51–70; Von der Thüsen 2008, 20–40; M.B. Bremen in Meller/Dickmann 2011, 104–111; Cocco 2013, 52–78 (mainly scientific responses), and works quoted in the following. This chapter contains parts of a paper published in Mattusch 2013, 189–204.
[1444] Opitz 1644, 43–84. About this posthumous edition, that was nevertheless prepared by Opitz, see E. Trunz in the facsimile edition of Opitz 1644 (Tübingen, 1967), 3*–9*. The first edition of this poem, dedicated to Duke Johann Christian von Brieg, is from 1633 (ibidem, p. 18*, 27*). Not in García y García 1998, Von der Thüsen 2008 or Williams 2008. See Richter 2007, 68–70, 127–128. As for the quotations in the following notes, Optiz used forward slashes ("/") as commas, which I have left intact. Therefore, I use pairs of square brackets ("[]") to denote line breaks.

is sprinkled with prose digressions in which Opitz demonstrates an impressive understanding of what the ancient sources say about volcanoes. Along with Bidermann (see below), Opitz was the first poet to describe the eruption and cataclysm of 79 from the perspective of Herculaneum; Pompeii is not mentioned. Opitz' powerful work starts with a description of the sudden disaster, which occurred despite the volcano's apparent serenity.[1445] People react without a plan, driven by fear and panic. Families try to flee together and some people die on account of their greed for money.[1446]

In a brief, but informative paper, the literary historian Michael Dronia discusses an interesting Latin poem by the German Jesuit philologist Bidermann, *Campanum seu Vesuvius flagrans*.[1447] Both Pompeii and Herculaneum are briefly described in stanza 28. Although no concrete ruins are detailed, the author lists features of the ancient towns probably known from ancient sources that suggest a certain knowledge of the sites:[1448]

1445 Opitz 1644, 56, 57: "Die Welt liegt unbesorgt mit sanffter Ruh ummgeben, [] Als alles Landt umbher beginnet zu erheben [] Sich selbst und was es trägt; es giebt der grossen Last [] Mit Furcht und zittern nach; das arme Volck verblast / [] Der Häusser Rücken bebt / die See wird auch erreget / [] Biß daß Aurora kompt noch bleicher als sie pfleget / [] Und ihren weissen Zug fast hinter sich läst gehen / [] Dieweil sie umb den Berg sieht eine Wolcken stehn / [] Dardurch ich heller Glantz mit allen seinen Strahlen [] Zu dringen nicht vermag / noch weiters weiß zu mahlen [] Das gantz betrübte Feldt. [...]" Description of the disaster pp. 56–61.

1446 Opitz 1644, 57: "[...] das alte Herculan / [] Das lustige Castell genandt Octavian / [] Viel Flecken voller Frucht und Dörffer stehn im Brande / [] Die Wässer fürchten sich und fliehen von dem Lande / [] Das Volck so nicht erstickt und gar wird fortgerafft / [] Kompt Athemloß daher / beraubet aller Krafft / [] Lahm / nackend und halb todt / und füllt mit Wehe und Zagen [] Den gantzen Himmel an / der gleichsam mit ihm klagen [] Und auch sich kümmern muß. Wie etwan ein Soldat / [] Wann daß er Feind und Todt vor seinen Fäusten hat / [] Und ihm der blinde Staub gleich under Augen stehet / [] Erhitzet Fewer giebt / und da er meynt er gehet [] In dessen auß Gefahr / so rennt er mehr hinein: [] Nicht anders lauffen sie auch ober Stock und Stein / [] Von Angst und Asche blind: der giebet seinen Wänden [] So brennen gute Nacht; der reißt mit beiden Händen [] Den armen Vatter fort / der nunmehr alt und schwach [] Gar kaum zu folgen weiß / und zeucht den Stab hernach; [] Der kan sein trewes Weib und Kinder nicht verlassen / [] Und jeglicher bemüht mit sich etwas zu fassen [] Das ihm für allen lieb: doch folgt der Raub nicht gar / [] und mancher kompt durch Geitz in Jammer und Gefahr / [] Bleibt selber wo sein Geld."

1447 Bidermann 1637 [first edition Lucerne 1635, third edition Venice 1668]. It consists of 47 stanzas of ten lines in hendecasyllabic verse. See Dronia 2006, from whose paper stem the two quotations. Not in García y García 1998.

1448 Bidermann 1637, stanza 28: *Heu, qualem dedit abstulitque vestrum /Vulcani rabies utrique formam! /Pompeios ibi nuper et superbi /Circumstantia videram Herculani /Templa et compita et atria et plateas /Et fastigia turrium et sacella. /Nunc vestigia nulla, nulla amoeni /Cerno signa loci, sed hinc superstes /Solum est nomen et inde campus, in quo /Pompeii steterunt et Herculanum.* These and other lines also in Maizony de Lauréal (1837, 415–416).

O, which beauty of yours was both given and taken away by the rage of Vulcanus! I shortly saw[1449] there Pompeii and temples, squares, atriums, streets, tops of towers and shrines here and there at Herculaneum. Now I do not see any vestiges nor signs of the beautiful spot, but from here remains only the name, from there only the field where Pompeii and Herculaneum were once standing.

The eruption and the catastrophe of 79 are the subjects of stanzas 33 and 34, in which Dronia recognizes information taken from Pliny, but the stanzas also seem to include information from Dio Cassius:[1450]

> While hostile chariots alternate with hard gladiatorial fights in the panting theatre, people start crying and the poor souls reach heaven with their lamentations: some of them stretch their hands to the burning stars, others sigh oppressed; ashes cover many people, as do falling stones. Some hope to escape and lose the opportunity at the last minute. Others meet their death while hesiating too long in their patriarchal house.
> Voices sound in great confusion: while one brother wants to help his brother, here grandchildren weep over their grandfather, there a sister weeps over her sister and elsewhere a host grieves for his guest, a husband for his wife, and a friend calls his mate; a hindered mother carries her child away and sons-in-law do the same with their very old fathers-in-law. Others in danger clutch those who are near to them or simply do not know what to do or whether Podalirius' final assistance will help them.[1451]

Almost hundred years later, *The Excursion* by the English poet David Mallet ventures a strong fascination for volcanoes. Nature and man-made towns disappear during an eruption of liquid death, which boils and moves under the earth:[1452]

1449 Dronia 2006, 33 translates *videram* with "hatte man dort ehemals sehen können", since one could have seen the remains in antiquity only. The *cerno* in line 8 might suggest autopsy of the author, similar to Holstenius' remarks (see chapter I, p. 11).
1450 Bidermann 1637, stanzas 33 and 34: *Tam severos inimica dum theatro /Alternant iuga lacrimante ludos, /It clamor populi suisque caelum /Obtundunt miserabiles querelis: /Pars ambusta manus ad astra tendunt, /Pars oppressa gemunt; favilla multos, /Multos saxa tegunt relapsa. Temptant /Hi sperare fugam fugamque in ipsa /Amisere fuga. Hi, moram in paterno /Dum nectunt lare, repperere mortem. //Vox confusa sonat, iuvare fratrem /Dum frater cupit, hic suum nepotes /Lamentantur avum, hic soror sororem, /Hic hospes dolet hospitem, maritus /Uxorem, socius vocat sodalem; /Infantem trahit impedita mater /Et grandem soceri gener senectam /Haerentque alter in altero et laborant /Ignari, quid agant opemque cuius /Supremam Podalirii fatigent.*
1451 Dronia 2006, 35 explains the mythical figure of Podalirius, a Greek doctor in the Trojan War (Ovid, *Ars Amatoria* 2.735) and a companion of Aeneas (*Aeneid* 12.304).
1452 Mallet 1728, here quoted from Mallet 1759, 6–110, reprinted in Gäumann 1977. García y García 1998, no. 8675. Not in Richter 2007, Von der Thüsen 2008 and Williams 2008.

> ... the *fluid lake* that works below,
> Bitumen, sulphur, salt, and iron scum,
> Heaves up it's [sic] boiling tide. The lab'ring mount
> Is torn with agonizing throes. At once,
> Forth from its side disparted, blazing pours
> A mighty river; burning in prone waves,
> That glimmer thro the night, to yonder plain.
> [...]
> Ruin ensues: towers, temples, palaces,
> Flung from their deep foundations, roof on roof
> Crush'd horrible, and pile on pile o'erturn'd,
> Fall total – In that universal groan,
> Sounding to heaven, expir'd a thousand lives,
> O'erwhelm'd at once, one undistinguish'd wreck!

Mallet's work, which is composed in blank verse, demonstrates the transience of mankind in a thrilling and dramatic way. The appearance of the volcano is deceptive:

> Yon neighbouring Mountain rising blank and bare,
> It's double top in steril ashes hid,
> But green around it's base with oil and wine,
> Gives sign of storm and desolation near:
> Store-house of fate! from whose infernal womb,
> With firey minerals and metallic ore
> Pernicious fraught, ascends eternal smoke [.]

Here and in the remainder of the poem, Mallet does not focus on victims or the emotional reaction of fleeing citizens. His interest lies with volcanology and with the impact eruptions have on the natural environment.

Atanasio Cavalli, a Carmelite father and an active geology and physics researcher who invented the first machine to register earthquakes, proffered similar ideas in his 1785 *Lettere meteorologiche romane*, which contain observations on volcanic activities.[1453] A large part of Cavalli's *Il Vesuvio* praises King Charles' politics concerning the development of the young Kingdom of Naples and the excavations of the buried towns.[1454] His style is rather pompous, at least in comparison with Bettinelli's fine poem from the same period (see p. 399).[1455] Cavalli describes

---

1453 U. Baldini, *Dizionario Biografico degli Italiani* 22 (1979) 716–718 s.v. Cavalli, A.

1454 Cavalli 1769, III–XLIX. The "poemetto" in hendecasyllabic verse – rather long despite its name – is subdivided into a great number of *canti*. The booklet in which it appears contains extensive commentary by the author himself. García y García 1998, no. 2786.

1455 Baldini (see note 1453) has a different opinion about Cavalli's "modesta, ma assidua attività poetica", focusing on his *Vesuvio*: "una certa spontaneità e inventiva fantastica che stentano

all twenty of Vesuvius' known eruptions by 1769; the mountain was, by that time, split into two peaks. Cavalli writes that the world should be grateful that Pompeii and Herculaneum are in the King's realm, because with his blessing we will once again see the rise of Herculaneum, in which the theater and a temple of Hercules have been excavated recently. We (the readers of his poem) are very much like the successors to Pliny the Elder, who had been able to see Herculaneum from his villa at Misenum.[1456]

Vincenzo Monti, a neo-classicist poet and a friend of Germaine de Staël, published *La Musogonia* in 1798, the same year Schiller published *Pompeji und Herculaneum*.[1457] The title, which means "The birth of the Muses," is an allusion to Hesiod's *Theogony* and like his ancient colleague, Monti hopes to bring the Muses back to life, as he states in his preface. In strophes 60–61 he addresses Vesuvius and remembers its victims Pompeii and Herculaneum:

> Do you, Vesuvius, refuse to put an end to this sort of plagues, if you still vomit your ashes and let suffer Naples and the Siren in its Gulf?

Monti implores the volcano to "Give solace to Naples." Pompeii and Herculaneum, he says, have endured cruel disasters that have caused people to suffer. While the archaeological aspect plays no role in the poem, Monti does allude to the unstable political situation in the Kingdom of Naples, with the King exiled to Palermo and French troops occupying Naples. Monti is highly critical of the King's administration and unlike other poets, does not praise the King for his excavations.[1458]

---

però a calarsi in una forma limpida e priva di durezza."
1456 Cavalli 1769, XX–XXI: "Che se dallo spuntare in sul mattino / Di rilucente Sol, può dir qual forza / Il di lui raggio avrà, nel pien meriggio / L'osservatore d'occhio acuto, e sano: / Ecco gli avvanzi d'un superbo tempio / A Alcide sacro, e le patère, e gl'altri / Sacerdotal' stromenti, e d'un Teatro / Magnifico, regal piccola parte." There is a whole genre of contemporary Vesuvius poems, e.g. Michelangelo Ciccone, *Il Vesuvio. Canti anacreontici tra Fileno, e Fillide ... dopo l'eruzione degli VIII Agosto del 1779*, Naples 1779. Ciccone's work is dedicated to Hamilton, and claims that nature is terrible and rude, but also creates beauty.
1457 Monti 1797; 1998, 237–264. The verse form is the *ottava rima*. García y García 1998, no. 9563. On Monti, see L. Frassineti in Monti 1998.
1458 Monti 1797; 1998, 259: "E tu pur dèsti agli empi sepoltura, / o Vesevo fatal, tu che la piena / versi iracondo di tua spuma impura / vicino, ahi troppo, alla regal Sirena. / Deh! Sul giardin d'Italia e di natura / i tuoi torrenti incenditori affrena, / e questa d'Acheloo leggiadra figlia / non far che per te meste abbia le ciglia. // Poco è forse alla misera il tiranno / Giogo che il collo già le curva e doma, / e incatenata il piè, carca d'affanno, / indarno sospirar sotto la soma, / se fecondo tu pur di strazio e danno, / il manto non le bruci e l'aurea chioma? / Deh! Non crescer ferite al suo bel volto: / Pompea ti basti ed Ercolan sepolto."

A decade later, Cesare della Valle wrote a poem about Vesuvius in which Pliny is his guide, as Virgil was for Dante.[1459] After describing the area and sketching out Vesuvius' history and eruptions, Della Valle travels into the volcano's interior and discusses theories on volcanism. Pliny tells him about the modern theories and explains the eruption of 79. Vesuvius is "the tomb of Herculaneum and the cradle of Resina."[1460] According to the poet, the disaster is the result of a Gigantomachy in which the Giants put an end to all beauty during their conflict with the gods. This gigantomachy might be a symbol of the conflict between the civilized and the barbarian. Pliny says that the Giants live inside Vesuvius. After the death of Seneca and Pliny, Della Valle suggests, the world became ignorant, Wisdom fled to Heaven, and society became devoid of law.[1461] But Della Valle is optimistic about the historical developments of the day. New intellectual studies in Italy and abroad are blooming, which feed culture – namely, arts, literature, and science. In the last *canto*, the 79 tragedy is compared to the fall of Troy.[1462] In the last lines, the poet personally ("io") rescues a mother and her child from the ashes and delivers them to the husband-father.[1463] Della Valle is not interested in the archaeological remains and provides an imaginative account of the panic that ensues during and after the eruption.

In Sade's *Histoire de Juliette* (see Chapter II, p. 119), the volcano plays a peculiar role. During Juliette's second visit to Naples, described in the Sixième Partie,

---

1459 Della Valle 1810. García y García 1998, no 4173. There are five *canti*, each with 31 or 32 strophes.
1460 Della Valle 1810, 6, *Canto* 1, 4: "Fu tomba ad Ercolan, culla a Resina."
1461 Della Valle 1810, 59, *Canto* 3, 23: "Al suo morir si spense il chiaro giorno / Di Roma e insiem del mondo. Età funesta / D'ignoranza e di sangue a noi ritorno / Di poi faceva; e dalla ria tempesta / Fuggì Sofia nel suo divin soggiorno. / Delle favole allor la schiena in festa / Rinacque in novo aspetto; e di natura / Tornò, qual pria, la legge ignota e oscura." The Giants also form the topic of Maizony's mock manuscript *L'Héracléade* (discussed in Chapter VII, pp. 342–343).
1462 For an example of a description of desperate people, see Della Valle 1810, 120, *Canto* 5, 27: "Parte ciascun di vario pondo onusto. / Quegli il picciol tesoro al seno stringe: / Questi l'uni le spoglie; e con robusto / Braccio amoroso ad arrestar s'accinge / Colui sul dorso il genitor vetusto. / L'altro il gregge d'innanzi a se sospinge: / Porta il padre per man la sua fanciulla: / Porta la madre il suo bambino in culla."
1463 Della Valle 1810, 123, *Canto* 5, 31–32 (end): "Illeso io giungo. Al palpitante seno / Mi stringe allor la disperata madre / E se perir degg'io, (diceami,) almeno / Mi salva il figlio e lo ridona al padre. / E poi sciogliendo a maggior pianto il freno, / Poneam' in sen colle sue man leggiadre / Quel caro pegno, a cui fra mille baci / Singhiozzando diceva: ah parti, ... e taci. // Tosti mi segue, o donna; io grido; è morte / Ogn'indugio per noi; mi segui e spera. / E fra dirupi e le crollanti porte, / E per nube di fumo e densa e nera, / Sulle mura dal foco infrante e assorte, / Col sen facendo al fanciullin visiera, / Con man sostengo alla tremante madre, / Salvi li rendo ed al consorte ed al padre."

Vesuvius plays a central role.[1464] Juliette and Clairwil are impressed by the tranquil mountain, and see the crater as its anal zone, due to its production of lava.[1465] This "anal" quality makes the girls crave some form of entertainment, so they throw their friend Olympe Borghèse into the crater, allegedly as a gift to nature and its sexual fulfillment, but in reality, we learn, it is because she has become too boring. Before performing this gruesome act, they undress Olympe and molest her, but do not kill her. Her screaming is heard for "more than six minutes" after her fall, and the girls throw her dress into the crater as well. The two murderers are conscious of the possibility of Vesuvius seeking revenge, but since this does not happen, they feel free to further pursue their lust – not only for death, but for each other. As a finishing touch, and in an attempt to forget their crimes, they both empty their bowels into the crater and make "tribadic" love on its edge. Relieved, they discuss theories on volcanism.[1466] Juliette and Clairwil define the volcano as a magic machine that, thanks to its hidden volcanic forces and its exterior shape helps them to realize their perverse actions.[1467]

Poetic Evocations of Herculaneum

In terms of research, touristic attention, and literary evocations, to name a few – Herculaneum is the disregarded younger sister of Pompeii, like Cinderella. In her introduction to *Pompei. La costruzione di un mito*, Luciana Jacobelli, an archaeologist from Naples, explains the enormous difference between *postpompeiana* and *postherculanensia* by the museum-like character of the excavations of Herculaneum in comparison to those of Pompeii.[1468] Herculaneum sits in a deep crater and can be visited only after a steep descent from the modern town above (fig. 17). In contrast, Pompeii is visible at ground level and sits immediately adjacent to the modern town which bears its name. Despite this, Herculaneum did inspire a solid collection of literary evocations, as evidenced by a handful of poems that testify to a fascination for Herculaneum. Before discussing some poetic evocations, I present here an extraordinary prose curio.

[1464] Early on in his travel book, Sade claims that he will describe Vesuvius, but, unfortunately, never does (Sade 2008, 236, 267). On Vesuvius as Juliette and Clairwil's "partner in crime," see Costa 1996, 57–61.
[1465] Johann Caspar Goethe used the image of intestines to describe the crater (here p. 146).
[1466] Sade 1998, 1100–1104. See M. Delon in Sade 1998, 1370–1371; Von der Thüsen 2008, 128–139, esp. 137–139 fig. 57. Note, interestingly, that Juliette will later murder Clairwil as well!
[1467] M. Delon in Sade 1998, 1570 aptly speaks about Vesuvius' "violence tellurique."
[1468] Jacobelli 2008, 7–8. See also the comparison made by Eugene Dwyer in Mattusch 2013, 245–263.

Fig. 17: Ernest Breton, *Pompéia décrite et dessinée* (second edition, 1855), pl. IX: "Maison d'Argus à Herculanum," Herculaneum, peristyle of the House of Argus. The guide in white jacket explains the site to the gentleman with a top hat.

Jacques Cazotte's *Le diable amoureux* (The Devil in Love) begins with a description of Herculaneum as a gloomy ruin haunted by wandering ghosts and spirits.[1469] This underworld forms an excellent starting point for a novel that little has to do with ancient Herculaneum. The Spanish officer Don Alvare de Maravilla bets his colleagues that he will personally meet the devil. One evening, they go to the ruins of Portici, once solemn monuments that are now in decay.[1470] The devil appears in the form of a camel's head, asking "Che vuoi?" (What do you want?) and later reappears, on Don Alvare's demand, as a spaniel, to change afterwards yet again into Biondetta, a pretty housemaid who falls in love with Don Alvare.

1469 Cazotte 1772. It is one of the first French "gothic" novels. García y García 1998, nos. 2815–2818 lists many editions and translations. Leppmann 1966, 191 mentions it as an example of fiction in which the dark side of Italy is evoked.
1470 Cazotte 1772, introduction: "Ces restes des monuments les plus augustes, écroulés, brisés, épars, couverts de ronces, portent à mon imagination des idées qui ne m'étaient pas ordinaires." Figure 2 of the first edition shows Don Alvare and the camel in a round room constructed in *opus reticulatum* and with a vault covered with stucco, which looks like a small bath room in Baiae.

Cazotte may have read some of the first accounts of the site of Herculaneum, in order to create an appropriate and realistic ambience for Don Alvare's first meeting with the devil. "Portici," which is to say, in Cazotte's novel, the underground excavations of Herculaneum, serves only as a locale in which to meet ghosts and spirits, one of which is the devil.

When we pass to poetry in the eighteenth century, we encounter a lot of praise for the King of Naples and enthusiasm about the papyri from the Villa of the Papyri. In the nineteenth and twentieth centuries, poetic expressions became more personal and convey the poets' fascination for the ancient town. Some early poems allude to the (im)permeability of the more than 20 meters of volcanic material that closed off ancient Herculaneum from the modern world.

One example of eighteenth-century praise for the King can be found in *Al Signor Abate Benaglio*, by Saverio Bettinelli, a well-known Jesuit scholar and teacher of rhetoric who traveled from Rome to Naples in 1754, accompanied by his colleague Francesco Benaglio[1471] and a party of tourists, among whom were the Van Limburg Stirum brothers, two young Dutch counts. The *epyllion* describes the Bay of Naples literally illuminated by Vesuvius in full eruption.[1472] Innocent Herculaneum had been destroyed, and now rises from her ashes in antique splendor, thanks to the explorations by King Charles, the new Titus ("Tito novello"). The number of monuments described is much higher than what would have actually been visible in the early exploratory tunnels.[1473] Unanimously, Italy stimulates this endeavor to unveil the treasures of the past, and to study and write about them.

1471 C. Muscetta, *Dizionario Biografico degli Italiani* 9 (1967) 738–744 s.v. Bettinelli, S.; C. Mulini, *ibidem*, 161–164 s.v. Benaglio, F.
1472 Bettinelli 1755; 1969, 625–626, vs. 259–279. The 340-line work is mentioned by Sogliano 1888, 26; not in García y García 1998.
1473 Bettinelli 1755; 1969, 626–627, vs. 297–332: "Infelice Ercolan, nido ed albergo / de l'arti greche, amica sede un tempo / del buon sangue roman, poi lutto acerbo / de' tuoi vicini, e preda iniqua al foco / non pur, ma al tempo e a l'obblio forse eterno. / Se non che omai fuor de le tue ruine, / benché lacera, ancor levi la fronte / a riveder dopo tant'anni il giorno. / Sì vedi e senti, che la man regale / vincitrice del tempo e de l'obblio / stende a sgombrar da lo squallor vetusto / tua perdita beltà Tito novello; / e già nove per lui sorgon di terra / eccelse moli a te, sorgon già novi / a te marmorei atri superbi e logge, / ove tu possa al rivedere in pompa / più vaga posti i simulacri vivi, / i tuoi quadri spiranti, ed ogni culto / de' sacri templi tuoi, de' tuoi teatri, / dimenticar tutti i passati danni. / Che se a le mense usate ancor ti piaccia / forse seder tra l'urne note e i cibi, / se veder ami l'ornamento antico / de' fini intagli in bronzo sculti o in marmo, / e i sacri vasi, e gli stromenti, e quanti / pesi o misure, e quante pietre o gemme / in feste, in giochi ed in altri usi mille / de l'umane vicende util ti furo; / t'allegra pur, che a' tuoi desir converse / corron l'arti novelle, e al regio cenno / s'affatica ogni man, studia ogn'ingegno, / e scritti ed opre Italia tutta aduna, / perché più bella al prisco onor renduta / tu cresca a lei l'avita fama, e a noi / per te ritorni in questa età cadente / un nuovo a rifiorire ordin di tempi."

The first British contribution is by Thomas Gisborne, a country parson and poet educated at St. John's College, Cambridge. *Herculaneum*, his Latin ode to the ancient town, was recited in 1777 in the Cambridge Senate House. I have only seen an 1833 translation or re-elaboration of Gisborne's text in English by Nicholas Lee Torre.[1474] Kings Charles and Ferdinand are once again acknowledged for the discoveries made during their reigns, and the poet states that Earth must accept the fact that people are always going to enter into her interior to reveal precious ancient objects. At the end of his poem, Gisborne suggests that the modern visitors can admire wall paintings which are equal to the lost works of Zeuxis and Parrhasius, ancient Greek painters. Gisbourne then expresses the hope that the papyrus scrolls will deliver texts by famous poets from Antiquity – preferably in Latin only, as he evokes some writers of the Golden Latin era:

> Nor yet hath envious age defac'd
> The breathing forms that Zeuxis trac'd;
> Surviving still Time's awful doom,
> The colours of Parrhasius bloom.
> Sketch'd on the wall with skilful care,
> The pencill'd figure still is there;
> Preserving still its glowing hue,
> Each faultless limb attracts the view;
> Still deck'd in smiles each feature seems,
> Still darts the eye its sparkling beams.
>   And ye, amidst the wreck secur'd,
> Too long in darkest night immur'd,
> That kindlier fates to light restore,
> Hail! sacred mines of classic lore,
> Hail, rescued volumes! though the strain
> Of Horace lives not here again,
> Though vainly may the Muse desire
> The thunders of a Virgil's lyre;
> Yet may perchance new Bards arise,
> Where Herculaneum buried lies;
> Some new Catullus prove his heart
> The prey of Love's envenom'd dart:
> There may some new Propertius tell
> The wily God's o'erpowering spell,
> And in sweet plaintive measures mourn
> The beauteous Nymph's unbending scorn.

1474 Gisborne 1833. Not in García y García 1998. Thomas Willette provided me with the translation. On the author, see R. Hole, *Oxford Dictionary of National Biography* 22 (2004) 356–357. As far as I know, Gisborne never traveled to the South.

Another poetic voice from Britain is that of John Hayter, King George IV's librarian and an eminent classicist who sojourned in Campania on research two times. A few years before 1800, he was there to study the volcanic phenomena of Vesuvius, and was back in 1802, thanks to a grant of the King, to test a new method of unrolling the papyri, for which he hired "unfolders." In an appendix to the travel reports, Hayter published a poem that is similar to one of his poems for which he had won a prize from Oxford in 1809.[1475] Strongly patriotic epic hexameters praise his Maecenas (King George), who has invited him to liberate Herculaneum for a second time, this time from the occupying French troops in Naples. Thanks to George's victory over France, the poet is able to travel to the South like a Greek colonist and to shed light on Herculaneum's finds:[1476]

> On your order, I personally crossed the waters of the long sea to settle finally on the face of the Euboian coast, together with the Saracen and Greek colonists in the Phlaegrean fields, and to go through the Argive remains in the area burnt by Vesuvius. Here I have to bring to light the monuments of the city of HERCULES, held in a grave of pumice, and the learned ashes from the deepest darkness and the giant Typhon.

John Hughes is the author of two poems on Herculaneum, one of which, *Herculaneum*, he wrote in Latin in 1811 as a student at Oriel College, Oxford.[1477] It uses convoluted Latin, but is generally of a good quality, and begins with the announcement that treasures have been discovered at Herculaneum which have been slumbering there for many centuries:[1478]

1475 Hayter 1811. García y García 1998, no. 6611 with brief remarks on his trips. M.J. Mercer, *Oxford Dictionary of National Biography* 26 (2004) 74–75. Cf. specifically Indelli 1980.
1476 Hayter 1811, 111: *"Ipse Tuo emensus longi maris aequora jussu /Euboici demum consedi ad littoris oram /Sarrasten, Graiosque Phlegraea in sede colonos, /Ut peragrem Argolicas loca per combusta Vesevi /Relliquias: ut pumiceo conclusa sepulcro /HERCULEAE monumenta urbis, doctasque favillas /Imis eripiam tenebris, molique Typhaeae."* Hayter is a learned poet who plays with his own knowledge and that of the public. With *"Euboici"* (from Euboia), Cumae is meant, the oldest Greek colony in southern Italy, not far from Naples.
1477 Hughes 1811. García y García 1998, 6926. The copy I saw in the Bodleian Library at Oxford contains some autographical remarks as well as a dedication by the author to Earl Temple, the father of the identically-named author of the 1857 *Tom Brown's School Days*. When relevant, I reproduce the notes by the author and, signed with "MS," some of his hand-written corrections.
1478 Hughes 1811: *"Per terram antiquâ Ditis caligine mersam / Tendere, et umbrarum sedes penetrare sepultas / Fert animus. Quinam mihi dux Cyllenius altum / Pandat iter? quaeve inferiae comitentur euntem, / Exsanguesque pio flectant libamine Manes?"* "Cyllenian leader" means Hermes, who was venerated on Cyllene, a mountain in Arcadia.

> My soul wants to penetrate the land covered by Hades' enduring darkness, and the houses buried in the shadows. Which Cyllenian leader will open the long road for me? And which dead gods of the Underworld will accompany me during my trip for a pious libation?

After the obligatory praise for the King, Hughes evokes works of art like statues on the forum (by which he must mean the so-called Basilica), temples and houses. Inside these buildings are utensils, larariums and other personal belongings still in their original places, and Hughes describes paintings at length. Nevertheless, we are aware of the tragedy hidden beneath the debris. We see bones and the shapes of bodies impressed into volcanic mud, which Hughes must have seen in Pompeii rather than in Herculaneum:[1479]

> Where am I being taken, out of my mind? Will these lighter songs be suitable for the sad ghosts? Their relatives did not bury them in their paternal earth and they did not speak any last words, and their souls were not calmed by weeping or by any ritual, but by a horrible heap which presses upon their limbs. For, here and there, my eyes meet sad remains in the streets and houses, and bones that maintain the shape of people pressed into the ashes who stiffened immediately after their death.

Hughes concludes that the disaster left nothing of the peaceful idyll Campania had been before. In the last lines he paraphrases Martial's Vesuvius poem (see note 1442). Now Herculaneum is emerging anew in a splendid way that Athens and Rome cannot match:[1480]

> But a friendly era covered and protected you, seat of Hercules, lucky by a stronger omen, while old age was shackling the fortress of the Capitol and the powers of the children of Romulus, and War was shackling the standing columns. But now finally, this new era

---

1479 Hughes 1811: *"Quo rapior demens? Num moestos carmina Manes / Haec leviora decent? quos nec tellure paternâ / Composuere sui, et dixere novissima verba, / Nec fletu mulceri animas, nec ritibus ullis / Contigit; at foedo tumulus premit aggere membra! / Quippe oculis passim occurrunt per strata domosque / Tristes relliquiae, servantiaque ossa figuram / Impressam cineri, quales jam morte sub ipsâ / Diriguere homines."* Cf. the visit of Casanova's lover Lucia described in Japin 2003 (p. 19, note 52).
1480 Hughes 1811: *"Vos autem, Herculeae sedes, potiore beatas / Omine, dum Capitoli arcem, fascesque vetustas / Romulidum, stantemque ruat Bellona columnam, / Pressit amica aetas, donec grandaeva sepulchro / Eriperet Latii spolia, et melioribus annis / Integros Sophiae tandem non invida flores / Panderet, antiquis retegens nova regna* [text has *tegna*, which does not make sense] *Camoenis. / Jamque, velut verno tepefactus sole resurgit / Arvorum redivivus honos, quem provida tellus / Obruerat, tutum hybernis sub flatibus Euri, / Sic vos, barbarici intactos sub turbine Martis, / Rumpere claustra dedit; lucisque oblita renasci / Jussit, avita fovens rediturae semina famae."*

takes the venerable spoils from the tomb in Latium[1481] and reveals them as fresh flowers of Wisdom for better years, while revealing new realms to the ancient Muses. And just like the honorable fields, which are warmed by a vernal sun, Herculaneum is reborn and blooms again after having been kept safe by fostering earth from the winter storms of Eurus. In such a way this friendly era has given you [citizens from Herculaneum], who have remained untouched by the turmoil of barbarian Mars, the possibility of breaking your fetters, and has forced things which had forgotten light to be born again, fostering the ancient seeds of fame, which is now bound to return.

Unlike Hughes, whose pompous texts betray his concern for British politics more than a genuine love of Herculaneum, the illustrious William Wordsworth, in 1819, at the age of 49, released *Poems of Sentiment and Reflection*, which tried to summarize his life.[1482] In the autumn of his life, the poet sees how many things – like health and love – are going less well, although there are still opportunities for aging poets. In *September, 1819* Wordsworth writes that these older poets no longer have any need to sing about their passions so their verses can remain fresh. He sees the Greek poets Alcaeus and Sappho from Lesbos as stimulating examples from Antiquity of everlasting reputation. In the last two stanzas of the poem is an allusion to possible treasures hidden in the library of the Villa of the Papyri. Addressing the excavators ("ye"), Wordsworth expresses his wish that they find examples of lost poems from Greek and Roman literature, exemplified by the sixth-century poet Simonides and the first-century poets Virgil [Maro] and Horace:

[...]
O ye, who patiently explore
The wreck of Herculanean lore,
What rapture! could ye seize
Some Theban fragment, or unroll
One precious, tender-hearted, scroll
Of pure Simonides.

1481 The author mistakenly situates Herculaneum in Latium (the modern day region of Lazio) rather than in Campania.
1482 Wordsworth 1908, 361–362, from *Poems of Sentiment and Reflection*, no. XXVIII; Wordsworth 1977, 401–402. Briefly referenced in Dahl 1956, 186 and Leppmann 1966, 129, 148. Leppmann stresses Wordsworth's love for northern Italy. Wordsworth visited Italy in 1822 (see his *Memoirs of a Tour on the Continent* from 1822) and 1842, but never went south of Rome (see Kneale 2010). We must not confound him with his later namesake, a fellow of Balliol College, Oxford. After working in India for some decades in education, this second Wordsworth retired in 1890 and went to Capri, where he lived until his death. He published two Pompeii poems in *Gleanings of Verse* (London, 1899), 38–39. García y García 1998, no. 14.453 ascribes these poems to the older Wordsworth.

> That were, indeed, a genuine birth
> Of poesy; a bursting forth
> Of genius from the dust!
> What Horace gloried to behold,
> What Maro loved, shall we enfold?
> Can haughty Time be just?

Two years later, Edwin Atherstone developed the theme of decay into a lengthy work,[1483] although he apparently did not know Herculaneum, and mistook it for Pompeii. According to Atherstone, Vesuvius was no longer reputed to be a volcano by the ancient inhabitants of Herculaneum, but when, on the day of the eruption, the atmosphere turned sticky and vapors rose from Vesuvius, they understood that they were in great danger:[1484]

> Terror was over all men: – what to fear
> They scarcely knew: – yet to the stoutest heart
> The panic shudderings crept; and in the brain
> Of wisest man work'd dire imaginings
> And shapeless horrors.
> [...]
> Each where he stood remain'd: – the mother hugg'd
> Her infant to her breast: – The father grasp'd
> The trembling hand of his beloved child: –
> Fast in the lover's arm the shrinking maid
> Was folded.

Some people stayed behind to pray, but were struck by lightning and turned to ash. No inhabitant can rest since "The dead sleep in the city."[1485] The gods do not respond to the prayers of the inhabitants, and a steamy hot, unhealthy rain falls like a "deluge, followed by more storms at night."[1486] Atherstone continues with an evocation of Herculaneum's luxury and of the final moments of the victims found during the excavations, like the prisoners under the temple of Jupiter, including a soldier and his small son:[1487]

1483 Atherstone 1821. The Herculaneum poem – his first publication – is 88 pages long. A translation of Pliny's two letters precede the poem. García y García 1998, no. 979. On Atherstone: A. Atherstone, *Oxford Dictionary of National Biography* 2 (2004) 808.
1484 Atherstone 1821, 4–5, 7.
1485 Atherstone 1821, 12.
1486 Atherstone 1821, 24, 30, 31.
1487 Atherstone 1821, 39, 41, 42, 44–45. In fact it is Pompeii's Temple of Jupiter. See p. 187, note 692.

> But miserable above all were they
> The dungeon captives, by their ponderous chains
> Chain'd to the ground: – helpless and hopeless: far
> From aid of man, or kindly sympathy,
> Cheering though vain:
> [... soldier]
> While yet
> The beard was new and tender on his chin,
> A stolen embrace had given a young one claim
> To call him father: – 'twas a rosy boy,
> A faithful copy of his sire
> In face and gesture. In her pangs she died
> [...]
> That gave him birth; and ever since the imp
> Had been his father's solace and his care.
> [...]
> The iron door was closed, – for them
> Nor to open more!

At the end of the terrible day of the eruption, there is nothing left but arable lands for the plowmen:[1488]

> 'Tis gone! where late
> The mighty city stood no trace is left; –
> Its costly palaces – its splendid streets –
> Its awful temples – all are gone. Remains
> A dark-hued plain alone, whose rugged face
> The lessening lightnings plough; – o'er which the flood
> Of lava slowly settles in a lake. –
> Years – ages – centuries – shall pass away
> And none shall tell where once that city stood.

In 1828, the Neapolitan poet and navy officer Michele D'Urso published *I nuovi scavi d'Ercolano* in Naples on the occasion of the beginning of open-air excavations at Herculaneum, which would yield the House of Argus (fig. 17).[1489] The tercets are dedicated to "Argia" – "girl from Argos." This name might refer to the excavation of this specific house, although "Argus" refers to the mythical custodian of Io, but also to Herculaneum, the city founded by Heracles, who was born in Argos, and therefore might also refer to his daughter. As Pompeii rises from the ashes, D'Urso

---

[1488] Atherstone 1821, 84, 88 (end).
[1489] D'Urso 1828, 3–4: preface. García y García 1828, no. 4816. García no. 4815 mentions *Ercolano. Versi*, Naples 1827, which might be the same. I could not find any other bibliographical data than what is indicated here.

observes how happy the excavation is. In contrast, Herculaneum, which bears the name of the mightiest ancient hero, is so unlucky to have been buried under layers of bitumen.[1490] Nevertheless, D'Urso continues, we must keep in mind that like Herculaneum, Tyrus, Carthage, and Troy, our civilization will one day vanish as well. Even Rossini's beautiful music will one day make way for "funerary wailings of the hoopoes, owls, and frogs."[1491]

Somewhere between a lyrical and an epic poem is Charles Room's 1828 *Herculaneum and other poems*, which contains a story about Helen, a beautiful young girl from Herculaneum, and her father.[1492] Helen is described as a Bacchic dancer; nowadays one would call her a disco girl. She and her friends are not concerned with the dangers of nature:[1493]

> Saw ye not, fondling o'er the infant germ
> Of innocence, the father's om'nous tear?
> A foolish dread – yet, still his soul could worm,
> Tho' undefin'd, some mystic cause of fear;
> [...]

Death attacks Herculaneum and even the Elder Pliny does not survive.[1494]

Canto 2 describes the natural beauty and fertility of Italy, which, however, is constantly threatened by Nature.[1495] In *canto* 3, Room tells the story of how some

---

1490 D'Urso 1828, 5–6: "Opportuno ver noi nuovi da lunghi, / Mentre del venir tuo quasi gioisse / Si gemina Pompei or che tu giunsi. // Oggi rivive perchè mal rivisse / Quella Città che si nomò dal Forte / Che il tricorporeo Gerion trafisse; // E più infelice della sua consorte, / Da cener no, ma da bitumi ardenti, / S'ebbe meschina una più cruda morte: // Quindi dal duro invoglio emerge a stento, / E par che rimembrando i danni suoi / Di nuovo al giorno ritornar paventi."
1491 D'Urso 1828, 9–10: "La tua rovescerà cruda alterezza, / Igneo Vesevo alterator di gente, / La folgore di Dio che i monti spezza: // Quello che verserai rubro torrente / Dello squallor della vallea Cumana / Queste contrade vestirà repente, // E di Rossini l'armonia sovrana / Li cangerà nel funebre ululate / Dell'upupa, del gufo e della rana." In 1824, Rossini left Naples for Paris, leaving Pacini as his successor (see Chapter VIII, p. 362).
1492 Room 1828, 13–63. Three *canti*, each subdivided in nine lines counting stanzas (*canto* I: 18 stanzas and some songs; *canto* II: 37 stanzas; *canto* III: 15 stanzas). Not in García y García 1998. I could not find any information about this author.
1493 Room 1828, 15 (I.IV).
1494 Room 1828, 22 (I.XVIII).
1495 The last stanza, no XXXVII (Room 1828, 45), summarizes this idea: "From joy to grief, life's changeful current flows, / Whose restless waves such quick transition bring, / From fortune's heights anon to heading woes, / They sweep earth's mightiest son, though sceptered-king, / Say what is happiness! – the bird of spring / That speeds its course to cheer youth's halcyon-day; / Stoops earthward, on its bright ethereal wing, / Deigns but one glance, but one celestial lay, / Descends, – bears heav'n to mortals, – sings, – and flies away."

people escaped from the disaster. Helen's father is one of the lucky escapees, but having lost his beloved daughter there can be no gratitude or joy:[1496]

> But, where the few rejoice, the many weep.
> Though wretches smil'd, and call'd destruction friend,
> There were, who mourn'd, in lamentation deep,
> Their much-lov'd city, and bewail'd her end.
> For some, in that sad night, had lost or friend,
> Sire, wife, or child: dear names which ne'er depart,
> But, in the soul, with tenderest feelings blend;
> Names, from whose thrilling sympathies to part,
> 'Tis death, 'tis worse than death – the shipwreck of the heart!
> [...]
>   Thus, thus, unbless'd,
> His sun went down, with none, he lov'd, to mark
> His dying wish, record that wish, confess'd;
> Thus sunk his weary age, eternally to rest.

Room's Herculaneum is a seductive trap: it is beautiful, has a luxurious nature, and the inhabitants are happy. Yet they get careless and forget their duties, which practically guarantees that punishment will come; beautiful Helen is a prime example of a victim. Archaeological notions are almost completely absent from the poem, with Room merely relying on images from texts to shape his own world.

Jacques Delille's 1800 didactic epic *L'homme des Champs, ou les Géorgiques françoises* sings about the benefits of country living and is based on Virgil's *Georgica*.[1497] Delille describes Vesuvius and recalls the ruins at its foot, about which the local hermit still tells stories. The poet recalls how the volcano erupted after air and water infiltrated the mountain's inner cavities.[1498] Vesuvius is terrible, and one day local people will discover the monuments hidden beneath it, and

---

1496 Room 1828, 51, stanza IV; 58, final stanza XIII.
1497 Delille 1800. There are many editions (the Bibliothèque Nationale at Paris has editions from 1801–1805, 1824, 1832, 1850, 1873). I know of a Dutch translation by the poet Willem Bilderdijk from 1803. Not in García y García 1998.
1498 Delille 1800, 102: "Mais j'aperçois d'ici les débris d'un village: / D'un désastre fameuse tout annonce l'image. / Quels malheurs l'ont produit? avançons, consultons / Les lieux et les vieillards de ces tristes cantons. / Dans les concavités de ces roches profondes, / Où des fleuves futurs l'air déposoit les ondes, / L'eau, parmi les rochers se filtrant lentement, / De ces grandes réservoirs mina le fondement. / Les voûtes, tout-à-coup à grand bruit écroulées, / Remplirent ces bassins, et les eaux refoulées, / Se soulevant en masse et brisant leurs remparts, / Avec les bois, les rocs et leurs debris épars, / Des hameaux, des cités traînèrent les ruines. / Leur cours se lit encore au creux de ces ravines, / Et l'hermite du lieu, sur un décombre assis, / Aux voyageurs encore en fait de longs récits."

the remains of the people who died trying tried to escape with their loved ones or their personal treasures.[1499]

The Irish poet Margareth Keogh's published a small collection of verse which is dominated by two poems about the Vesuvian cities.[1500] In the poem *Herculaneum*, Herculaneum's remains give the impression that people's happy lives were interrupted first by the eruption, and now, as it were, by the ongoing excavations. For ages, the town was hidden in history:

> [...]
> For ages, like Pompeii, sunk in night,
> Lo! Herculaneum struggles to have light;
> Entombed in lava, almost lost her name,
> She, too, revives with melancholy fame;
> Majestic, ev'n in ruins, behold her rise,
> Striving once more to look into the skies –
> Once more to feel the sun's benignant rays,
> And bask beneath them in the noontide blaze –
> Once more to breathe the balmy air of Heaven,
> And all the sweets to living cities given.
> [...]

Keogh thanks the excavators for having revealed the ancient town, whose fate can be experienced during a visit or by reading about its discoveries. The poet makes the same comparison D'Urso does, observing that great empires vanished, but that Herculaneum's resurrection from under the volcanic layers has brought it eternal fame. When the visitor goes down into the subterranean galleries, he or she experiences the eruption:

1499 Delille 1800, 105–106: "Un jour, peut-être, un jour les peuples de ces lieux / Que l'horrible volcan inonda de ses feux, / Heurtant avec le roc des restes de murailles, / Découvriront ce gouffre, en creusant ses entrailles, / Contempleront au loin avec étonnement / Des hommes et des arts ce profond monument; / Cet aspect si nouveau des demeures antiques; / Ces cirques, ces palais, ces temples, ces portiques; / Ces gymnases du sage autrefois fréquentés, / D'hommes qui semblent vivre encor tout habités: / Simulacres légers, prêts à tomber en poudre, / Tous gardant l'attitude où les surprit la foudre; / L'un enlevant son fils, l'autre emportant son or, / Cet autre ses écrits, son plus riche trésor; / Celui-ci dans ses mains tient son dieu tutélaire; / L'autre, non moins pieux, s'est chargé de son père; / L'autre, paré de fleurs et la coupe à la main, / A vu sa dernière heure et son dernier festin." The first six lines of this quotation are cited by Santo-Domingo (1829, 105) at the beginning of his chapter on Herculaneum.
1500 Keogh 1842, 5–9. Not in García y García 1998. I could not find any biographical data on Keogh. Other songs hail Victoria's accession to the throne and the birth of the poet's son. Thanks to my Nijmegen colleague Marguerite Corporaal, who brought Keogh's poem to my attention.

> What painful feelings rush upon the soul
> As o'er our heads we hear the chariots roll;[1501]
> Their sound recalls the dread volcanic shock,
> When Mount Vesuvius cast forth liquid rock
> And burning ashes, which in torrents came,
> Destroying all with unrelenting flame.

Of course, the visitor will also recognize the gruesome nature of the death of the victims, who were abruptly transported from their blissful lives to hell. While sitting in the theater, the ancient citizens of Herculaneum were listening to songs inspired by the Muses, which were interrupted by the noises of the erupting volcano. Nowadays, these poor citizens enter into our memories:

> Think, though in ruins now, there was a day
> Ere devastation here had held such sway;
> But if beneath the deep Lethean wave
> Your sufferings and your wrongs to death you gave,
> Let sweet oblivion ever there conceal
> What wounds the finer feelings to reveal.

Keogh muddles knowledge about and impressions of Pompeii and Herculaneum, leading the reader through Herculaneum by daylight, as if it were Pompeii, and introducing the reader to the victims of 79, who just happen to be away from their houses. In contrast to Pompeii, which had been mostly exposed already for a hundred years only a small section of Herculaneum had been excavated in Keogh's time.

In contrast to all of these poets, who give a rather uncritical image of the discoveries, Giacomo Leopardi, in his posthumously published *Paralipomeni alla Batracomiomachia*, questions the alleged splendor of the Neapolitans' discoveries in the ancient towns. According to Leopardi, the Neapolitans have neglected underground Herculaneum, and have failed to thoroughly study it or the finds, especially the papyri, which he views as potentially the most important novelty, thanks to their contents – that is, unknown ancient Greek and Latin texts (see also Chapters I and VII). As in his poem *La ginestra*, Leopardi tackles the scholars' vanity, and accuses them of working out of a sense of vanity and not public duty and of lacking a willingness to present the discoveries to the entire learned world.[1502]

1501 Various travelers hear the traffic in the streets of modern Resina-Ercolano.
1502 On Leopardi's poem, here p. 136; also see Moormann 2001 and Rothemann 1996, 74, 77–78.

Twentieth century poems

I know of only two lyrics from the twentieth century, both of which are of superb quality. The Dutch poet Gerrit Achterberg is not known as a particularly great admirer of antiquity. In his poems, Achterberg often uses terms and images borrowed from biology and other science-based knowledge. He plays with time and with the notion of an unreachable lover, sometimes because she is already dead, like Orpheus' wife Eurydice. *Herculaneum*, from Achterberg's 1941 anthology *Osmose* (Osmosis) is a clear example of his poetic style.[1503] In the second stanza of the poem, he writes about the "shell of time," which neither life nor death can penetrate. The screen of light (verse 1) denotes the distance from the reader to that of Herculaneum's extinguished life, whereas at the end of the poem there seems to be a glimmer of hope for being able to reach the dead. Achterberg never saw Herculaneum in person, so the simile of this difficult poem is not strictly archaeological. Instead, it is the thick layer of volcanic material that man can barely penetrate and which covers a hidden life, so that osmosis – the title of the collection – is impossible.

> Herculaneum
>
> A yellow screen of light
> in green morning, after years.
> The calyxes of your face
> blossom to death under the heavy
> shell of time, in stone leaves,
> the season stands outside the wall.
> No death can retrieve this,
> no life gives the fire.
>
> Am I in balance with you?
> Or will you, with the last strength
> of an indomitable backlight,
> pierce these shafts?

1503 Achterberg 1980, 196: "Een gele achterstand van licht / in groene morgen, sedert jaren. / De kelken van uw aangezicht / bloeien zich dood onder de zware / schil van den tijd, in stenen blaren / staat het seizoen buiten de muur. / Geen sterven kan dit achterhalen, / geen leven geeft het vuur. // Ben ik met u in evenwicht? / Of zult gij met de laatste krachten / van een ontembaar tegenlicht / doorboren deze schachten?" Winfred van de Put told me about this poem and suggested various interpretations for it. Not in García y García 1998. I could not find any reference to Achterberg's use of Herculaneum in a study on Achterberg and the classics (Kassies 1989, 25). The translation is mine.

The Austrian poet and novelist Ingeborg Bachmann lived in Italy for many years and dedicated a fine poem to the encounter of "hard" history in the excavations after reading "soft" literature in books. Only upon seeing the hitherto hidden corpses of the victims, can one know true love.[1504] The poet roams around the ruins of Herculaneum and touches the invisible remains with her fingers, as if she were blind. Lava, the nearby Vesuvius and darkness are singled out as specific images:

> Lessons in love
>
> Lessons in love
> from ten thousand books.
> taught in the sharing
> of barely variable gestures
> and foolish oats –
>
> initiated into love
> but first knowing it there –
> when the lava spilled over
> and its breath reached us
> at the foot of the mountain,
> when finally the spent crater
> surrendered the key
> to these locked bodies –
>
> We entered enchanted rooms
> and illuminated the dark
> with our fingertips.

Conclusion

Although Vesuvius has erupted many times since its infamous A.D. 79 eruption, the 1631 eruption rapidly became known throughout Europe as one of the great natural catastrophes of the modern era, and inspired poets who were fascinated

---

1504 Bachmann 1978, 141: "Unterrichtet in der Liebe // Unterrichtet in der Liebe / durch zehntausend Bücher, / belehrt durch die Weitergabe / wenig veränderbarer Gesten / und törichter Schwüre – // eingeweiht in die Liebe / aber erst hier – / als die Lava herabfuhr / und ihr Hauch uns traf / am Fuß des Berges, / als zuletzt der erschöpfte Krater / den Schlüssel preisgab / für diese verschlossenen Körper – // Wir traten ein in verwunschene Räume / und leuchteten das Dunkel aus / mit den Fingerspitzen." From *Anrufung des Großen Bären*, section "Lieder auf der Flucht" no. VI (1956). Also in Richter 2005a, 114. Translation: I. Bachmann, *Songs in Flight. The Complete Poems of Ingeborg Bachmann*, translation by P. Filkins, New York 1994, 228–229. Thomas Willette has been so kind as to give me a copy of this translation. Not in García y García 1998.

by the cataclysm itself and by its possible causes to compare it with the destruction of Herculaneum many centuries earlier. In these baroque poems, the poets evoke the towns' disappearance from the earth with images that are similar to those used in descriptions of modern eruptions, and rarely do the poets attempt to reconstruct a historically-sound Roman past. The genre did not change radically after the start of the excavations in Herculaneum in 1738, which were largely lauded as the result of King Charles' cultural policy. A growing interest in volcanology and the eruptions' causes led to some of the poems exhibiting an appreciation for a scientific approach. Simultaneously, epic stories about Giants living under the volcano were written for the first time. Volcano poems did not usually convey an impression of the poets' emotional reactions upon seeing the excavations. From the early nineteenth century onward, Vesuvius no longer received much poetic attention. The development of the study of volcanism apparently made poetic approaches obsolete, and lessened the mountain's romantic drama. Vesuvius had become a monster, following a nice characterization by Rachel Cusk: "It is corpulent where the town is abstracted. It has devoured it, and left the bones. [...] The volcano is a mere beast."[1505]

The literary evocations of Herculaneum clearly demonstrate the interest the ruins awakened from the start of the excavations in poets and other authors. The expressions gyrate between wonder and bewilderment and are intermingled with emotional reactions to decay and death. Poets express great praise for the daylight excavations in the nineteenth century, and another focal point is the Villa of the Papyri library, with its charred scrolls that contain unknown Greek and Latin texts. A few poems bemoan the absence of texts by the great classical authors among those unrolled.

Herculaneum in these poems is more a symbol of drama than an archaeological object from which we can glean knowledge about ancient society. The buildings and objects rarely play a concrete role in the evocation of this small Mediterranean town, which had been swallowed by Vesuvius in 79. Unlike the more or less concrete characters we have encountered as the inhabitants of Pompeii in numerous novels and short stories, Herculaneum's inhabitants have not been personalized to the same degree, but similarly serve as symbols of the gruesome fate nature or superhuman divine powers can bestow. The archaeological explorations have created touristic sites that anyone can freely visit. In contrast to the citizens of other great ancient empires which were destroyed in one way or another in the course of history, who left no trace behind, the citizens of Herculaneum have been recorded far more concretely. This "fame" is the only solace for these victims.

1505 Cusk 2009, 178.

X Intimations of Pompeii: By Way of Envoy

> "'Shall we never, never get rid of this Past!' cried he, keeping up the earnest tone of his conversation. – 'It lies upon the Present like a giant's dead body! [...]"[1506]

What Does This Book Tell Us?

In the following I recapitulate the main topics of this book's nine chapters, and focus on the malleability of Pompeii and Herculaneum and the notion of ancient urban constructs.

The excavations outlined in Chapter I began in the second quarter of the eighteenth century. During these early excavations, and up until the early nineteenth century, excavators rarely reflected on the reasons they were excavating. If they were there to hunt for treasure, they were soon deluded by the paucity of high-level works of art; if they were there to resurrect ancient towns, they were slow to learn and implement proper archaeological procedures, and due to their careless processes, lost a great deal of unique evidence, like certain buildings' structural and decorative elements. It took a long time before the cities could be appreciated on their own as unique monuments – monuments that have lavished the world with a tremendous amount of data, which is yet to be fully assessed. Their relevance to and importance for the research of antiquity was only slowly realized. A wide array of topics addressed in Pompeian graffiti opened scholars' eyes to aspects of the Roman world that they did not know from literary sources. The vulnerability of these ruins, which seem sturdy, but are in reality quite frail, was overlooked for so long that both treasure-minded and archaeological excavations have so sufficiently damaged them that they might now be considered man-made ruins, and not only Vesuvius-made. Indeed, the annals of the excavation history – the longest continually running archaeological project in the world – do not only record successes. We must conclude that, despite the advancements made in the field of conservation and restoration, these monumental sites provide archaeologists and local administrators with a growing list of concerns, not only due to the precarious state of the remaining edifices, but also due to the dearth of money for restoration and maintenance, and the political circumstances which create unstable working situations and are all-too-susceptible to corruption.

[1506] N. Hawthorne, *The House with the Seven Gables*, chapter XII (after N. Hawthorne, *Collected Novels* (The Library of America), New York 1983, 509).

Chapter II brings us images of Herculaneum and Pompeii as the product of some 250 years of site visits. Although the earliest travelers did not fully understand what they had seen at underground Herculaneum (but did admire the first finds in the Royal Palace in Portici) or in the few buildings unearthed at Pompeii, subsequent generations of visitors were increasingly aware of the unique monument that especially Pompeii was, since its streets and houses were (and are) unmatched in the known world. After several generations of travelers who made observations about Pompeii's uniqueness, still newer generations began to reflect on how modern visitors behaved toward it and toward Herculaneum, as more and more of that city was uncovered. Even today, visitors are astonished by the immediacy of the two cities, and how the victims from each seem to bring them to life.

Central to the experience of visiting or intimating Pompeii and Herculaneum have always been the skeletons and, later, the plaster casts of the victims. Without almost no exceptions, scholars and amateurs alike see these corpses as the remains of once living people, whose personalities and likenesses can be reconstructed. The narrative style that includes victims' portraits can be subdivided into several categories, which are the bases for Chapters III–IX. During the first hundred years after their discovery, Herculaneum and Pompeii were considered "Greek," in that they displayed evidence of Greek culture, which was so admired in the era of their discovery and the earliest excavations. Gradually, and especially in the past 150 years, the principal character of the towns began to take on more of a "Romanness."

The greatest number of fictional evocations focuses on or finishes with the last days of Pompeii or Herculaneum in A.D. 79. Few authors have bothered to write about the towns' earlier history, and when they do, they focus on the (very few) famous Pompeian men, like Cicero. Historical fiction in the form of novels, novellas, and short stories can be subdivided into two predominant categories: pagan and Christian.

The pagan novels discussed in Chapter III portray Pompeii as a classical Greco-Roman world in which the pantheon of gods rule from afar. Authors create an ancient microcosm and enliven it with people who bear names known from local texts and who live in the excavated houses. With varying degrees of precision, the authors build a Pompeii – or rarely, a Herculaneum – which readers might recognize in the way they recognize Rome, London, or New York as the central location in other books. In the lives of the ancient inhabitants, a number of events or themes recur as standard motifs: dinners, weddings, funerals, political intrigue, plays in the theater or amphitheater, motifs known from ancient sources as well, and uniquely evidenced by *in situ* material remains and numerous objects in the Naples museum. Pompeii's destiny, the abrupt end of the story, stimulates some authors to come up with original *finales* in which certain characters are rescued or save themselves, in ways that, realistically speaking, appear to be rather far-fetched. The reason for the eruption itself is explained in various ways, depending on the political, religious or scientific views of each author.

Christian novels, treated in Chapter IV, follow the theological motif of Pompeii and Herculaneum being punished by God. According to the authors of some Christian novels, the decadence of the Roman Empire did not begin in the late second century, but during the first century. In these novels, Christians – and sometimes Jews – live relatively poor lives in Pompeii in tiny groups, worshipping their respective god in secret, and are almost never represented as free-born citizens. The authors of these novels are usually Christians themselves, and paint sober and pious lives against a backdrop of sinful luxury and polytheism, practiced by the dominating pagan upper classes. Slightly disturbing for scholars is the complete absence of Jews and Christians in the archaeological record. The theme is evidently not as enticing to authors nowadays, either because of the lack of factual evidence or the changing position of Christianity in the modern world.

Logically, the same opulent scenes that are found in the pagan novels frequently pop up in Christian novels as well, so that both categories have much in common. Christians feature as amphitheater victims long before this would have actually occurred in the Roman world, but as a consequence of the eruption of Vesuvius, which puts a sudden end to the torture that these fictional Christians undergo, these early victims are not yet hailed as martyrs. In contrast, some that find their way out of the volcanic hell testify to the strength of the young religion. In this scenario, these early Christians are seen as worthy of being saved, whereas the pagans, who are not rescued by their gods, die in the eruption.

A third category, the topic of Chapter V, is that of modern people visiting the excavations and having extraordinary adventures. Some of these visitors are like the historical travelers seen in Chapter II, who are simply there to take in an ancient wonder, while others feel a change in their spiritual habitudes when they stand face to face with the old ruins. The concept of rebirthing – meeting a person from the past in the present – perpetuates the idea that the dead towns house the living dead. That these meetings often occur at night connects these books with works about modern people who trespass the borders of time, the subject of Chapter VI. In most cases, the protagonist goes back in time and encounters ancient citizens, with whom he (or rarely, she) shares an experience. This concretizes a common fantasy brought about by seeing a living human being through the façade of the remains or cast of a victim. These novels were especially popular and mostly written during the nineteenth century, and typically feature time-travelers who are in a semi-hypnotized state. A handful of fiction works brings readers to Pompeii in the future, during which it is still seen as a strong topic, though these books tend to view Pompeii from a more contemporary social viewpoint with regards to the abuse of political power, the devastation of natural resources and the mistreatment of men and women as slaves.

Chapter VII, which is devoted to mock manuscripts, also deals with jumping into the past. The discovery of papyri in Herculaneum led authors to invent their own purportedly just-discovered, previously unknown "classical" texts. While Pompeii and Herculaneum are often suggested to be the places these "ancient" texts were found, they are rarely the subject of – or indeed, even mentioned in – them. Many of these mock manuscripts imitate ancient novels, discuss historical events, or paraphrase ancient philosophical thoughts. Some of them do play out in the Vesuvian cities themselves. These are said to have been written by the actual inhabitants of the ancient towns, and typically consist of letters, diaries, and memoirs compiled by locals that reflect ancient daily life. It is important to note that without the papyri discovered at Herculaneum around 1750, authors would probably never have been prompted to write such mock texts. The dead towns are still the paramount source of inspiration for works that have to do with (lost and/or found) ancient knowledge.

In Chapter VIII the topics of Chapters III–VII come together in an anthology of works that require stage performances to come to life in full – operas, dramas, movies, and other stage productions, few of which offer images of the lost cities that differ from those described in novels. Numerous adaptations of Bulwer-Lytton's *Last Days* prove the popularity of this work in the age of Bulwer-Lytton and long after. Before the era of film, the enormous panoramas and spectacles with artificial fire and other special effects were very appealing to nineteenth-century spectators. After World War I, new subjects, including politics, the economy and societal disturbances, outgrew Bulwer-Lytton's popularity. Pompeii's fate is the baseline for later works that incorporate discussions about man's existence and which are dominated by modern society falling to pieces and mass tourism. This has endured in pop songs and computer games, so that even for young people who do not necessarily have a historical notion of Pompeii, the town becomes a reality, albeit a virtual one.

Vesuvius' eruptions from 1631 onwards have inspired authors to reflect endlessly on the destiny of the area around the mountain. Chapter IX focuses on works whose protagonist is Vesuvius, the culprit and primary source of destruction in all of these works, which despite this is largely absent – in terms of references to the physical mountain itself – from the majority of Pompeian and Herculanean recreations. New here in the spectrum of Pompeian themes is myth, since the Giants, the bewitched creatures who kindle the fire under the crater, and who were briefly evoked by Dio Cassius, became more popular in Vesuvius poems. These evocations frequently pertain more specifically to Herculaneum, since unlike Pompeii, it lies directly at the foot of the volcano. While Herculaneum novels and stories have a place in previous chapters as well, the section devoted to that town in Chapter IX records lyrical poetic recreations that are mostly devoid of narrative.

Some Numbers

If we add up all of the works discussed in this book – novels, novellas, short stories, poems, stage works, movies and TV shows – we come to a total of 255 works (see Appendix, pp. 425–428). It is no surprise that prose dominates. As for the poetry included here, most of it is lengthy, of the "epic" variety that tells stories, as well as lyric poetry about Herculaneum. This distorts the overall image, for I have chosen not to take into account the bulk of Pompeii poems, which are mostly lyrical and personal impressions of poets, who use their poems to meditate on their experiences during visits or on images grasped from reading other texts. As for dramatic works, I counted only the films, operas and other stage works for which I have seen at least a synopsis or libretto, and not the dozens of works I know only by title and mention in the notes. This brings us to the following distribution:

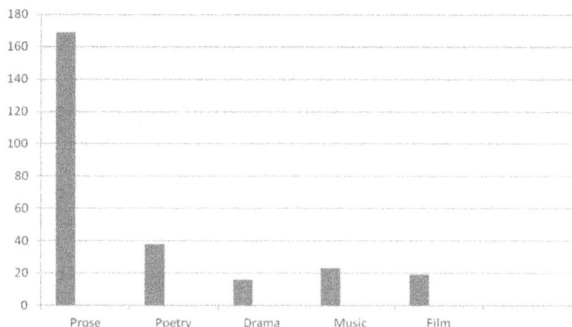

The publication or performance dates of these works show a rather regular distribution from the early 1800s onwards, and if we take into account that we are only a quarter of the way through the fifty-year period from 2000–2049, a recent increase in numbers is evident:

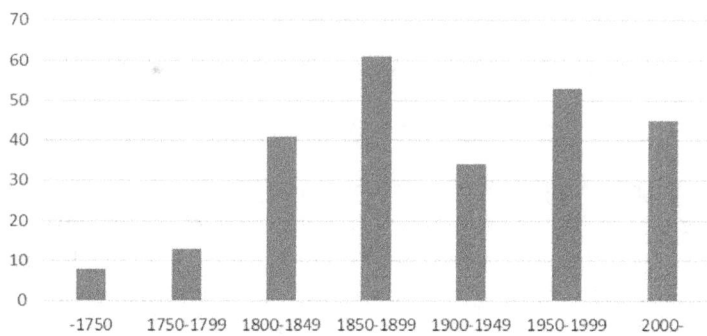

Pompeii's popularity in the second half of the nineteenth century can mainly be explained by the production of works inspired by Bulwer-Lytton, especially drama. The number of truly original works might therefore be smaller during these decades. We can conclude that there has been a constant production of some thirty to thirty five works every fifty years, or one every year and a half.

Finally, some words about the languages (and indeed, the countries) in which these works have been published. The category "Other" contains works in Dutch, Latin, Swedish, Spanish, Czech and Polish. There might be many more from countries and in languages that I have no access to, due to my lack of knowledge of these languages and my unfamiliarity with these countries' cultures. English – including American – and French works dominate, while Italian and German works make up a smaller, though still considerable number. The persistent interest in Roman history in the relevant countries, as well as intensive tourism to Italy must have contributed to the great attention paid to Pompeii: over time, readers gradually became increasingly aware of Pompeii and Herculaneum as a "product," which spurred authors to produce their intimations. The success of various works in the era in which they were published – and their translations, which this book does not take into account – should not be underestimated, even if they may have fallen into oblivion since their initial publication.

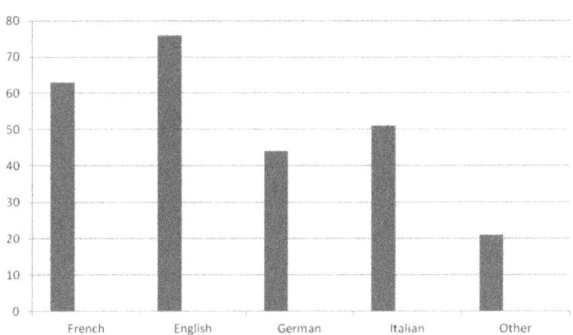

Customizing Pompeii and Herculaneum

The small Roman towns destroyed by the 79 eruption of Vesuvius have always provoked awe, fascination, and bewilderment among people all around the world. Herculaneum and Pompeii, which have continuously been explored since their discovery in the middle of the eighteenth century, have stimulated writers to create personally-colored reconstructions of the past, especially due to the number and condition of the remains that have been found. The re-creation of antiquity continues to fascinate us today, and produces many variations on the same theme: ancient Pompeii and Herculaneum as they might have been and as they are today. But why have authors so relentlessly chosen to highlight these towns as opposed to, say, Rome or Athens? The most likely reason is simply that the human drama of the 79 cataclysm continues to exert a spell stronger even than that exerted by the two majestic ancient capitals.

The casts of corpses and the skeletal remains, impressions, and voids left in the volcanic material covering the ruins constitute an indispensable extra compared with archaeological monuments like Rome or Athens, or even ancient burial sites at other excavations. The act of laying bare these victims in their original environment, rather than simply finding skeletons in tombs, conveys the sense of being able to experience these people's lives firsthand. Archaeology sometimes plays a decisive role in these reconstructions, largely because Pompeii and Herculaneum are the results of archaeological activities, and have yielded a unique case of material culture. For the authors interested in archaeology, the notion of the unhappy extinction is more appealing than the ruins themselves, and we find in their works a concoction of general ideas and clichés about antiquity mixed with some more specific *pompeiana*. At the same time, many re-creators ignored the material data and constructed their own historical realm instead.

Many Pompeii novels find their origins in countless eighteenth-century travel accounts, which detailed Northerners' trips to southern Italy. During these years, one experienced Pompeii and Herculaneum by contemplating artifacts in the royal collections at Portici rather than confronting the physical structures in the towns. Several decades would pass before the towns themselves became the main attraction of Vesuvian tourism. Since at first, the local authorities were blind to the value of the sites as attractions, tourists played an important role encouraging the authorities to change the purpose of the excavations from a mad grab for treasures into a program of clearing detritus from the ruins and leaving houses, courtyards, and public buildings on view.

As a consequence of these developments, the earliest Herculaneum or Pompeii fiction that adopted the archaeological remains in the story's plot came relatively late, in the 1830s. The appearance of these works corresponds generally with the growing popularity of historical novels, and particularly with the publication of detailed descriptions of the excavations. Most historical novels of the time concentrated on reconstructing life rather than evoking mighty sovereigns and mythical heroes. The low social and cultural profiles Pompeii had gradually obtained, as modern excavations and studies have increased in number, have made it an ideal object for authors of historical fiction, since it allowed them to focus on the daily lives of ordinary people.

Textual sources enrich the archaeological image of the past, although they rarely refer directly to Herculaneum or Pompeii. Bulwer-Lytton and his followers were – and still are – happy to insert negative aspects of ancient life, such as those conveyed by Petronius in *Satyrica*, Suetonius in *Lives of the Twelve Caesars*, and Martial and Juvenal in their satires. Few archaeological objects found in the excavations confirm the unparalleled degrees of gluttony, sexual depravation, and corrupt political behavior discussed so passionately in these texts. As citizens of the Roman Empire, Pompeians must have been similarly gluttonous and corrupt, albeit on a smaller scale.

Judging by modern historical and archaeological writing, the well-defined social classes known to have existed in Roman society rarely function as they should in historical novels and other fictitious representations. Love affairs often trespass social boundaries, mostly without awkward consequences. A freeborn citizen might indiscriminately get engaged to a non-citizen, freedman, or slave, and even marry such a person, despite his or her highly unequal status in traditional Roman eyes. Women act freely, unburdened by their husbands' or fathers' authority. Bafflingly, we encounter a greater number of fictional independent women in Pompeian novels than would have been living even in the societies in which many of these books were published and read, let alone in ancient Pompeii itself. Non-citizens have as much of a say in public affairs as their citizen counterparts. Foreigners, especially Greeks and Egyptians, enliven Pompeii and Herculaneum in large numbers, have jobs in town, and speak as equals with upper-class locals. Gladiators are sometimes seen as heroes and admired by citizens to a degree beyond what would have been appropriate in Roman society. The interactions between male and female characters are similar to what would have been (and is) acceptable in whatever period these novels were (and are being) written. Elite women have free access to things usually considered male matters, like running businesses, discussing politics, and going out in public without their husbands. Innumerable drinking scenes take place in Pompeian bars like "The Elephant," where all sorts of people pass the time, and embody a supposedly class-free society. The same literary evocations suggest that men from all social classes frequent the *lupanar* and other places where carnal diversions were offered, whereas in reality, only lower-class males frequented brothels on a regular basis.

The oldest archaeological publications presented only the finds and left out the context, so early visitors limited themselves to the study of utensils, paintings, and sculptures; the towns' urban layout was not yet a point of interest. The potential of Pompeii and Herculaneum as vehicles of ancient life would increase substantially thanks to the favorable reception of Bulwer-Lytton's 1834 *The Last Days of Pompeii*, which paved the way for that new thrill of actively involving Pompeians as protagonists rather than as mere names or anonymous users of artifacts found in the excavations. The adoption of specific houses as these protagonists' residences enabled Bulwer-Lytton to enliven the old ruins still more vividly. If they were lucky enough to visit the site itself, Bulwer-Lytton's readers could actually visit the houses of Glaucus, Ione, and Sallustius, the novel's protagonists, and reconstruct their lives in the context of these archaeological realities.

The professionalization of archaeology in the late nineteenth century contributed relatively little to a deeper understanding about the towns on the part of amateurs. Until architects began reconstructing ancient houses in order to convey to the visitors a more tangible idea of ancient residences than mere ruined walls, the results of new excavations – namely, more houses – were seen as being the same as the results of older ones. Only in the course of the nineteenth century did the professional study of the ancient remains turn toward the idea of the town as a whole, but publications available for the greater public were slow to publish new insights. Two things would have the greatest impact on the general public: the creation of plaster casts of the human victims by Fiorelli in 1863, and the discovery in the early 1980s of hundreds of corpses on the beach of Herculaneum. The recent reconstruction of the successive stages of the eruption by volcanologists has refined Pliny's iconic description and clarified how people died in Vesuvius' fatal cataclysm, and has made modern authors more sensitive to the motif of destruction than ever before. Another issue met with much interest by modern novelists has been the reopening of the Villa of the Papyri's excavations in Herculaneum in the 1990s and the hope of finding more ancient texts. In contrast, studies on Pompeii's previous historical periods have not yet been incorporated into many fictitious intimations.

The unending fascination for the Vesuvian towns is not generated from a passion for treasure hunting *à la* Indiana Jones, or a quest to unravel mysteries such as Atlantis, or a desire to decode previously untranslated languages, or to answer vexing questions about ancient cultures such as the Egyptians or the Etruscans. For such pursuits Pompeii and Herculaneum are too humble in their historical context. Still, mystery abounds in Vesuvian fiction, wherein religion and personal belief are important motivators for many protagonists. Scientists cannot easily reconstruct mystery cults and religious attitudes, for almost no primary written sources are known. The presence of non-Roman cults – principally that of the Egyptian goddess Isis – and the paintings in the Villa of the Mysteries stimulate authors not only to connect them with arcane non-Roman cults, but also to explore attitudes towards religious freedom and to suggest an early presence of Judaism and Christianity.

The ancient world is unreachable except by means of the collective imaginations of innumerable authors, whose common theme of psychological time travel in novels, novellas, and poems, illustrate their strong desires to experience this world firsthand. The ideal that many nineteenth-century authors tried to portray in Pompeii and Herculaneum was the absence of depressing moral rules, especially those dictated by Christianity and the Roman civil order. That we often read about freedom of religion and liberal interactions between characters from different classes and opposite sexes, leads to a more tangible version of Pompeii's past that we do not encounter in other works of fiction about antiquity.

People's attraction to Pompeii and Herculaneum, first and foremost, lies in their high degree of tangibility and in their easily understandable nature: one does not need to be an expert to comprehend Pompeian houses as the realms of extinct generations of Romans. Every visitor can imagine more or less how the ancient Romans would have moved through the streets and buildings in much the same way as these visitors move through the streets and buildings in their own contemporary cities and towns of origin. Common modern reactions to the ruins, like "did Pompeians know this?" or "could they already make that?" imply that in the eyes of these beholders, Pompeians were "ordinary" (that is, relatively modern) men and women. In this respect, the scale of the urban environment is a relevant point of consideration. In contrast with Rome, with its Colosseum, huge baths and other monumental complexes, and Greek cities with their grand temples, Pompeii and Herculaneum were humble, and apart from the amphitheater and the two theaters, did not feature such prestigious buildings.

The earliest visitors – typically high-ranking officials and aristocratic Northerners – were actually let down by the "small" dimensions of the houses, the narrow streets and the "provincial" character of the finds, which did not stimulate them to experience the sublime and which did not seem to be endowed with "simple greatness," which Winckelmann had written about in various influential publications as a special quality of Greek and – to a lesser degree – Roman civilization. Pompeii's provincial nature might have disappointed these early visitors while satisfying later tourists of more modest circumstances, but it didn't prevent them from writing down a great deal of direct and spontaneous reflection on the disaster and its victims.

Luckily, as time passed, most of the negative judgments about its small-town nature faded away in both travel books and fictional intimations, and these formerly unfavorable aspects became advantages: in Pompeii and Herculaneum, visitors were able to experience daily life as it was two thousand years ago. Like the eighteenth- and nineteenth-century Neapolitan poor, whom authors would have seen living in the streets and only going home at night, Pompeian citizens are portrayed as *fannulloni* who enjoy life in an Eden-like climate. They stroll through the forum or down shaded streets, chat with friends, and do little or nothing; houses are but nightly shelters. Interestingly, the supposedly carefree eighteenth- and nineteenth-century Neapolitan *joie de vivre*, supplemented by the climatic and agricultural wealth of the Bay of Naples, contrasted with the solemn northern European societies of many visitors in which, as we have seen, a large number of these intimations were written. Romantic readers of Pompeii novels were briefly transported to the Eden they might have experienced during a visit to the South.

Due to the impression authors had of Pompeii and Herculaneum as provincial towns, they are rarely portrayed in fiction as the birthplaces of famous Greeks or Romans, and in fact, citizens of Pompeii or Herculaneum rarely would have attained high political or military positions in the Roman Empire. To the contrary, Pompeian and Herculanean works of art were relatively modest and often nothing more than mere interior design elements, but are often portrayed as expensive and high-level creations in fiction. Of course, any actual Pompeian artists alive in A.D. 79 would have faced the same fate as those featuring in Pompeii novels, and the same goes for the artwork, which in fiction is usually desperately lost or plundered after the eruption.

Over the course of time, even if the suggestion of luxury constantly crept into works of fiction, the ideal that a reader was supposed to be easily able to identify him- or herself with the ancients has become commonplace. The persistent publication of Pompeii novels through the present (including the amazing increase in such novels in the past two decades) is a clear sign that intimating Pompeii appeals to as many people today as it did in the days of the first excavations.

In his novel, Bulwer-Lytton merely inserted contemporary upper-class English people into an ancient environment, so as to be easily recognizable by his readership. Slavery, poverty and misery are either simply invisible or concern groups of people far from the protagonists' orbits. Bulwer-Lytton and other authors relied on ancient texts, which were written by elite members of Roman society and therefore do little to correct the elitist and highly idealized image of "pure" Greeks and "noble" Romans. The examples of contemporary Neapolitan turmoil found in Bulwer-Lytton and others, which stemmed from their own experiences or were sampled from travel books, serve as an ideal backdrop that gives the ancient world more color. Comparisons between ancient and modern societies, especially between ancient Pompeii and Bourbon Naples, feature prominently in Bulwer-Lytton and other novels, but gradually disappeared as ongoing excavations in Pompeii rendered it a sufficient source of material for fiction. If over the last thirty years, this traditional image of high society has given way to a greater concentration on lower class people or, better, a more nuanced image of how complicated society Rome was, modern society is responsible. Slavery has become a hot topic in novels, with noble Romans setting their slaves free, and cruel Romans treating theirs badly. The presence of foreigners is explained more explicitly in more recent novels; they are often found as slaves in Roman households, or serve as rowers on galleys, where they try to survive the harsh conditions of forced labor. In recent works, both gladiators and Christians are being portrayed in more historically accurate ways. Gladiators, often seen in earlier novels as noble savages, have been "demoted" to the dejected wrecks they mostly were in Roman society. Similarly, Christians, seen in earlier books as the "pure" and "noble" ones, voluntarily become fodder for animals in the amphitheaters in nineteenth-century books, and begin to act as gladiators in twentieth-century intimations.

In addition to the many alterations to Roman social norms and customs authors have made in their fiction to suit the tastes of their contemporary readers, Pompeii fiction also attempts to answer a plethora of questions about what caused the disaster that destroyed it and Herculaneum. Were the gods angry? Had they not received their customary offerings? Did the ancients' immoral and decadent life cause an almighty God's wrath, which led to their total destruction? Did mankind somehow damage nature by abusing its natural resources, or was mankind simply unable to escape nature's infinite and inexplicable power? Starting in the twentieth century, authors make comparisons to man-made disasters. World Wars I and II have been examined through the lens of Pompeii, as have more recent tragedies like September 11, 2011.

As we have seen, the ruins that are the consequence of the eruption of Vesuvius in AD 79 have formed the basis of an extremely rich corpus of fictional and poetic expressions, in which each author creates his or her own personalized version of Pompeii or Herculaneum, which often has little to do with reality. The consequence of a seemingly never-ending series of accidents, Pompeii and Herculaneum – ruins created by Vesuvius and subsequently discovered and further ruined by centuries of tourism and careless reconstruction – have stimulated untold authors, poets and directors to produce countless novels, poems, performances and visual works. These works have further stimulated scientists, archaeologists, and ancient historians to re-assess the evidence gleaned from the excavations and to recreate the history and archaeology of the ancient sites.

We all create a version of Pompeii or Herculaneum that suits us. My goal with this book has not necessarily been to eternize all of the recreations herein, but merely to present the wide array of responses to Pompeii and Herculaneum, which makes clear that there are still original texts to be written which in turn will evoke a side of the Vesuvian towns not yet highlighted in earlier works. These works are not tombstones of dead towns, but monuments that illustrate how very much alive they still are.

Appendix: Works of fiction discussed in this book

Dr: drama; Fi: film; Mu: music; Po: poetry; Pr: prose

1341–1342 Boccaccio, G., *Ameto* Pr
1358, Petrarca, F., *Itinerario in Terra Santa* Pr
1500 Sannazaro, J., *Ecologa Piscatoria* Po
1504 Sannazaro, J., *Arcadia* Pr
1633 Opitz, M., *Vesuvius* Po
1635 Bidermann, J., *Campanum seu Vesuvius flagrans* Po
1728 Mallet, D., *The Excursion* Po
1749 *Some Account of the Roman History of Fabius Pictor* Pr
1753 De Bressay, C.A., *Lettres de Julie à Ovide* Pr
1755 Bettinelli, S., *Al Signor Abate Benaglio* Po
1758 *A Fragment of the Chronicles of Nathan Ben Saddi* Pr
1769 Cavalli, A., *Il Vesuvio* Po
1771 *Democritus: Or the Laughing Philosopher* Pr
1772 Cazotte, J., *Le diable amoureux* Pr
1777 Gisborne, Th., *Herculaneum* Po
1788 Barthélemy, J., *Voyage du jeune Anacharsis en Grèce* Pr
1791, Mozart, W.A., *La clemenza di Tito* Mu
1795 Lantier, E.-F., *Voyages d'Anténor en Grèce et en Asie* Pr
1797 Sade, D.A.F. de, *Histoire de Juliette* Pr
1797 Monti, V., *La Musogonia* Po
1797 Schiller, F., *Pompeji und Herculaneum* Po
1800 Delille, J., *L'homme des Champs* Po
1803 Böttiger, C.A., *Sabina* Pr
1803 Jean Paul, *Titan* Pr
1803 Romanelli, L., *Il trionfo di Vitellio Massimino* Mu
1807 De Staël, A.L.G., *Corinne ou l'Italie* Pr
1808 Edgeworth, M., *The Little Merchants* Pr
1810 Brun, F., *Pompeji* Po
1810 Della Valle, C., *Il Vesuvio* Po
1811 Hayter, J., *A Report upon the Herculaneum Manuscripts* Po/Pr
1811 Hughes, J., *Herculaneum* Po
1818 Nicolai, C., *Das Grab am Vesuv* Pr
1819 Mazois, F., *Le palais de Scaurus* Pr
1819 Wordsworth, W., *September 1819* Po

1821 Atherstone, E., *The Last Days of Herculaneum* Po
1822 Wright, F., *A few days in Athens* Pr
1825 Pacini, G./Tottola, A.L., *Gli ultimi giorni di Pompei* Mu
1826 Grillparzer, F., *Schreiben des jungen Tomes Dikson* Pr
1827 [?] D'Azeglio, M. Tapparelli, *I miei ricordi* Pr
1827 De Pixerécourt, R.-Ch.G., *La tête de mort* Mu
1828 D'Urso, M., *I nuovi scavi d'Ercolano* Po
1828 Room, C., *Herculaneum* Po
1829 De Latouche H., *Fragoletta* Pr
1830 *The Vestal, or A Tale of Pompeii* Pr
1831, Gray, D., *Le dernier jour de Pompéi* Pr
1832 Fairfield, S.L., *The Last Night of Pompeii* Po
1833 Bianco, G., *Una notte sulle rovine di Pompei* Pr
1833 Gisborne, Th./N.L. Torre, *Herculaneum* Po
1834 Bulwer-Lytton, E., *The Last Days of Pompeii* Pr
1834 Méry, J., *Herculanum ou l'Orgie romaine* Po
1835 Grün, A., *Cincinnatus* Po
1835, Medina, L.H., *The Last Days of Pompeii* Dr
1836 Croly, G., *The Young Enchanter* Pr
1837 Maizony de Lauréal, J.-S.-F., *L'Hércaléade* Po
1837 Albini, G., *Jone e Glauco ossia Gli ultimi giorni di Pompei* Mu
1838 Becker, W., *Gallus* Pr
1841 Lemercier, A., *Les derniers jours de Pompéi* Pr
1842 Keogh, M., *Herculaneum & Pompeii* Po
1842 Leopardi, G., *Paralipomeni* Po
1843 Dumas, A., *Le corricolo* Pr
1846 Baudelaire, C., *Le jeune enchanteur* Pr
1846 Dezobry, Ch., *Rome au siècle d'Auguste* Pr
1849 Körber, Ph.W., *Diomedes und Clodius* Pr
1850 Nieritz, G., *Pompeji's letzte Tage* Pr
1850 [ca.] Cellarius, J., *Die Isispriester in den letzten Tagen von Pompeji* Dr

1850 Bresciani, A., *L'Ebreo di Verona* Pr
1851 De Lamartine, A., *Graziella* Pr
1851 Pabst, A., *Die letzten Tage von Pompeji* Mu
1852 Gautier,Th., *Arria Marcella* Pr
1854 Nerval, G. de, *Isis* Pr
1854 Nerval, G. de, *Octavie* Pr
1856 Gautier, Th., *Jettatura* Pr
1857 Dickens, C., *Little Dorrit* Pr
1857 Medina, L.H., *The Last Days of Pompeii* Dr
1858 Abbott, J., *Rollo in Naples* Pr
1858 Gregorovius, F., *Euphorion* Po
1858 Petrella, E., *Jone* Mu
1858 Vitrioli, D., *Veglie pompeiane* Pr
1859 David, F., *Herculanum* Mu
1861 *Homardiana* Po
1863 Imbriani, V., *Pompei notturna* Pr
1863 Norwid, C., *Pompeja* Po
1863 Von Arnold, J., *Die Nazarener in Pompeji* Mu
1864 Vecchi, C.A., *Pompei* Pr
1868 Meuris, E., *Glaucus et Arbaces* Pr
1869 Hequet, C., *Une habitation romaine à Pompéi* Pr
1869 Joncières, V., *Le dernier jour de Pompéi* Mu
1871 Mansell, Wm. L., *Ione* Dr
1872 Alberti, E., *Marcus Charinus* Pr
1872 Reece, R., *The Very Last days of Pompeii!* Dr
1872 Offenbach, J./Sardou, V., *Le roi carotte* Mu
1874 De Graaff, M.H., *De ondergang van Pompeji* Pr
1875 Collins, W., *The Law and the Lady* Pr
1876 Griffa, L., *The Last Days of Pompeii* Dr
1877 Toudouze, G., *Le Cécube de l'an 79* Pr
1878 Toudouze, G., *La Coupe d'Hercule* Pr
1878 Vischer, F.Th., *Auch Einer* Pr
1879 De Lamothe, A., *Le fou du Vésuve* Pr
1880 [ca.] Bassanville, Contesse de, *Nouvelles cosmopolites* Pr
1883 Clark, H.H., *Lost in Pompeii* Pr
1883 Lingg, H., *Clytia* Dr
1883 Pothey, A., *Un vieux lapin* Pr
1885 Boker, G.H., *Glaucus* Dr
1885 Boker, G.H., *Nydia* Dr
1886 Holt, E.S., *The Slave Girl of Pompeii* Pr
1887 Muck, J., *Die Nazarener in Pompeji* Mu
1888 Barallat y Felguera, C., *Ione* Dr

1888 Conforti, L., *Pompei* Po
1888 Conrad, M.G., *Was die Isar rauscht* Pr
1888 Rochester, J.-W., *Herculanum* Pr
1889 Höcker, O., *Die letzten Tage von Pompeji* Pr
1890 [ca.] Hogo-Hunt, J.W./Sunavill, J.F., *The Last Daze of Pompeii* Dr
1890 Bory, P., *Mémoires d'un Romain* Pr
1892 Fox, G., *Nydia, the blind girl of Pompeii* Mu
1892 Kaden, W., *Pompejanische Novellen* Pr
1892 Espantaleón, J., *Pompeya* Dr
1892 Moritz, P., *Die letzten Tage von Pompeji* Pr
1893 Sousa, J.P. *The Last Days of Pompeii* Mu
1894 Rebell, H., *Chants de la Pluie et du Soleil* Po
1896 Morton, M.W., *Scenes from The Last Days of Pompeii* Dr
1897 Kulczycki, L., *Pompei* Po
1899 Bertheroy, J., *La danseuse de Pompéi* Pr
1899 Carrozzari, R., *Leo gladiator* Po
1900 Müller, G.A., *Römische Liebesopfer* Pr
1901 Douglas, N., *Nerinda* Pr
1903 Jensen, W., *Gradiva* Pr
1903 Von Montowt, R.K.S., *Die letzten Tage von Pompeji* Mu
1907 Behrend, O., *Der Bildhauer* Pr
1907 Hollander, B., *Pompeii* Mu
1907 Schuré, E., *La prêtresse d'Isis* Pr
1908 Toudouze, G.G., *La sorcière du Vésuve (1808)* Pr
1908 Maggi, L., *Gli ultimi giorni di Pompei* Fi
1910 Müller, G.A., *Das sterbende Pompeji* Pr
1911 Visser, P., *De beeldhouwer van Pompeji* Pr
1912 Augustin-Thierry, G., *La fresque de Pompéi* Pr
1912 Nouguès, J., *La Danseuse de Pompéi* Mu
1912 Perosi, M., *Pompeji* Mu
1913 Rodolfi, E., *Gli ultimi giorni di Pompei* Fi
1913 Vidali, G.E., *Ione o gli ultimi giorni di Pompei* Fi
1914 Formont, M., *Visions antiques* Pr
1917 Montfort, N., *Nydia* Po
1921 Giordano, U., *Giove a Pompei* Mu
1922 Maynial, E., *Les Robinsons de Pompéi* Pr
1926 Gallone, C./A. Palermi, *Gli ultimi giorni di Pompei* Fi
1927 Proust, M., *Le temps retrouvé* Pr

Appendix: Works of fiction discussed in this book — 427

1928 Maurois, A., *Les derniers jours de Pompéi* Pr
1930 [ca.] Eichhorn, O., *Maddalena* Pr
1930 Debout, J., *Le chanoine Brousillard à Herculanum* Pr
1931 Daudet, L., *Les bacchantes* Pr
1934 Golding, L., *The Doomington Wanderer* Pr
1935 Cooper, M./Schoedsack, E.B., *The Last Days of Pompeii* Fi
1936 Gusman, P., *Elskée* Pr
1936 Milanesi, G., *Sancta Maria* Pr
1937 Von Horváth, Ö., *Pompeji* Dr
1941 Achterberg, G, *Herculaneum* Po
1942 Garro, E., *Pompeiana juventus* Pr
1945 Hartlaub, F., *Kriegsaufzeichnungen* Pr
1950 L'Herbier, M./Moffa, P., *Sins of Pompeii* Fi
1952 Peyrefitte, R., *Du Vésuve à l'Etna* Pr
1952 Reed, H., *The Streets of Pompeii* Dr
1954 Rossellini, R., *Viaggio in Italia* Fi
1955 Brod, M., *Armer Cicero* Pr
1955 Getty, J.P., *A Journey from Corinth* Pr
1955 Llewellyn, R., *The Flame of Hercules* Pr
1956 Bachmann, I., *Unterrichtet in der Liebe* Po
1959 Bonnard, M., *Last Days* Fi
1960 Aafjes, B., *Dag van gramschap in Pompeji* Pr
1960 Bunce, P., *Last Days of Pompeii* Pr
1961 Lowry, M., *The real estate of Pompeii* Pr
1961 Roblès, E., *Le Vésuve* Pr
1961 De Meuse, J., *Flaviana* Pr
1962 Parolini, G., *Les derniers jours d'Herculaneum* Fi
1965 Bassett, R., *The Pompeians* Pr
1965 Fuller, L.H., *Fire in the Sky* Pr
1966 Saul, M., *The Last Nights of Pompeii* Pr
1968 Lerme-Walter, M., *Les enfants de Pompéi* Pr
1969 Fellini, F., *Satyricon* Fi
1969 Reggiani, R., *Carla degli scavi* Pr
1970 Albertazzi, G., *Gradiva* Fi
1970 Rosoni, O., *Amore e morte a Pompei* Pr
1970 Howerd, F., *Up Pompeii* Fi
1972 Fellini, F., *Roma* Fi
1972 Maben, A., *Pink Floyd in Pompeii* Mu/Fi
1973 Lins, O., *Avalovara* Pr
1974 Melton, W., *Nine Lives to Pompeii* Pr
1975 La Tourette, J., *The Pompeii Scroll* Pr
1978 Dillon, E., *The Shadow of Vesuvius* Pr

1979, Bruin, P.G., *Es geschah vor 1900 Jahren* Pr
1979 Grönemeier, H., *Pompeji* Mu
1980 Újhelyi, J., *Pompeji vörös* Pr
1982 De Corcelles, L., *Portrait de la poétesse* Pr
1984 Stöver, H.D., *Attentat in Pompeji* Pr
1984 Janovic, V., *O mašince Žofince (The house of the Tragic Poet)* Po
1984 Rouland, N., *Les lauriers de cendre* Pr
1984, Levi, P., *Plinio; La bambina di Pompei* Po
1984 Hunt, P., *The Last Days of Pompeii* Fi
1986 Bastet, F.L., *Resten ven een dagboek* Pr
1986 Vandenberg, Ph., *Der Pompejaner* Pr
1989 Blauer, J.M./McManigal, R., *Pompeii* Dr
1990 Davis, L., *Shadows in Bronze* Pr
1990 Bisel, S., *The Secrets of Vesuvius* Pr
1992 Marino, N., *Le rouge de Pompéi* Pr
1992 Sontag, S., *The Volcano Lover* Pr
1993 Federspiel, J., *Eine Halbtagsstelle in Pompeji* Pr
1994 Cioffi, V.A., *Pompei. Magia di rose* Pr
1996 Manfredi, V.M., *La torre della solitudine* Pr
1996 Nothomb, A., *Péplum* Pr
1996 Peri, C., *Avventura a Pompei* Pr
1997 Rhodes, X., *A volcanic affair* Pr
1999 Hopkins, K., *A World Full of Gods* Pr
1999 Mielke, G., *Die verflixten Fälle aus Pompeji* Pr
2000 Slot, P., *Blauwbaard* Pr
2001 De La Rochefoucauld, S., *Le mystère de Pompéi* Pr
2001 Lawrence, C., *The Secrets of Vesuvius* Pr
2001 Lundgren, M., *Pompeji* Pr
2001 Shults, S., *Games of Vesuvius* Pr
2001 Helleberg, M., *Børnere fra Pompeji* Pr
2002 Ohnheiser, D., *Voyage à Naples* Pr
2002 Citino, D., *The News and other poems* Po
2002 Lawrence, C., *The Pirates of Pompeii* Pr
2002 Lenk, F., *Anschlag auf Pompeji* Pr
2002 Robbe-Grillet, A., *C'est Gradiva qui vous appelle* Pr
2003 East, R., *A.D 62: Pompeii* Pr
2003 Harris, R., *Pompeii* Pr
2003 Pagliara, G., *Giallo pompeiano* Pr
2003 Saylor, S., *Something Fishy in Pompeii* Pr
2003 Japin, A., *Een schitterend gebrek* Pr
2003 Nichelson, P., *Pompeii, the Last Day* Fi

2004 Krausser, H., *Die wilden Hunde von Pompeji* Pr
2004 Pellegrino, C., *Ghosts of Vesuvius* Pr
2005 Butterwort, A./Laurence R., *Pompeii the Living City* Pr
2005 Comastri Montanari, D., *Ars moriendi* Pr
2005 Castellano, A., *La lucerna sotto il Vesuvio* Pr
2005 Cirillo, A., *Vita e morte di un uomo fortunato* Pr
2006 Crane, A., *I veleni di Pompei* Pr
2006 Robbe-Grillet, A., *C'est Gradiva qui vous appelle* Fi
2007 Ascione, M., *La Villa dei Papiri* Pr
2007 Krohn, B., *Was im Dunkeln bleibt* Pr
2007 Lasky, K., The *Last Girls of Pompeii* Pr
2007 Patanè, S., *Nel cuore e nell'anima di POMPEI* Pr
2007 Rice, D., *The Pompeii Syndrome* Pr
2007 Roberts, J.M., *Under Vesuvius* Pr
2008 Goodman, C., *The Night Villa* Pr
2008 Le Ninèze, A., *Sator* Pr
2008 Rodríguez, C., *Les mystères de Pompéi* Pr
2008 Russell, G., *La congiura di Pompei* Pr
2008 Moran, J., *The Fires of Pompeii* Fi
2008 Messika, N., *Adamah Shehora* Pr
2011 Pohl, F., *All the Lives He Led* Pr
2011 Menduni de' Rossi, S., *Il prodigio del sistro* Pr
2012 Covito, C., *Le ragazze di Pompei* Pr
2013 Covito, C., *Il processo di Giusta* Pr
2014 Anderson, P., *Pompeii* Fi

Bibliography

Aafjes, B. 1960, *Dag van gramschap in Pompeji*, Amsterdam.
Abbott, J. 1858, *Rollo in Naples*, Boston.
Achterberg, G. 1980, *Verzamelde gedichten*, Amsterdam.
Acosta-Hughes, B./C. Cusset (eds) 2012, *Euphorion. Oeuvre poétique et autres fragments*, Paris.
Acton, H. 1956, *The Bourbons of Naples 1734–1825*, London.
Adamo Muscettola, S. 1982, Nuove letture borboniche: I Nonii Balbi ed il Foro di Ercolano, *Prospettiva* 28, 2–16.
Adler, J.G.C. 1783, *Reisebemerkungen auf einer Reise nach Rom. Aus seinem Tagebuche herausgegeben von seinem Bruder Johann Christoph Georg Adler*, Altona.
A.G. n.y., *Continuazione di riflessioni in risposta alla Continuazione delle novelle letterarie per una lettera scritta da Catanzaro sulla spiegazione delle due parole SEXS. & GRATIS nell'Iscrizione trovata sul Tempio d'ISIDE di là dalla Torre dell'Annunziata*, n.p.
Alberti, E. 1872, *Marcus Charinus, der junge Christ in Pompeji. Eine Erzählung aus dem Römischen Alterthum für die Jugend*, Leipzig.
Alberti, F.L. 1568, *Descrittione di tutta Italia*, third edition, Venice (reprint Bergamo 2003).
Alföldi, G. 1995, Eine Bauinschrift aus dem Colosseum, *Zeitschrift für Papyrologie und Epigraphik* 109, 195–226.
Alfonsetti, A./N. Bellucci (eds) 2010, *Corinne e l'Italia di Mme de Staël*, Rome (Studi (e testi) italiani 25).
Aliquò-Lenzi, L. 1933, *Diego Vitrioli*, Reggio di Calabria.
Allen, S.H. 1999, *Finding the Walls of Troy*, Berkeley/Los Angeles/London.
Allroggen-Bedel, A. 1983a, Piranesi e l'archeologia nel reame di Napoli, in *Piranesi e la cultura antiquaria. Gli antecedenti e il contesto*, Rome, 281–286.
Allroggen-Bedel 1983b, Dokumente des 18. Jahrhunderts zur Topographie von Herculaneum, *Cronache Ercolanesi* 13, 139–158.
Allroggen-Bedel, A. 1986, Tanucci e la cultura antiquaria del suo tempo, in *Tanucci* 1986, 519–536.
Allroggen-Bedel, A. 1990, Winckelmann und die Archäologie im Königreich Neapel, in *Johann Joachim Winckelmann, neue Forschungen*, Stendal, 27–46.
Allroggen-Bedel, A. 1996, Archäologie und Politik: Heculaneum und Pompeji im 18. Jahrhundert, *Hephaistos* 14, 217–252.
Alroggen-Bedel, A. 2000, Gli scavi borbonici nella villa San Marco: pitture antiche e gusto settecentesco, in G. Bonifacio/A.M. Sodo (eds), *Stabiae. Storia e Architettura. 250° Anniversario degli Scavi di Stabia*, Rome, 101–107.
Allroggen-Bedel, A. 2010, A proposito dei Balbi: note archivistiche alla topografia di Ercolano, in C. Gasparri et al. (eds), *Dall'immagine alla storia. Studi per ricordare Stefania Adamo Muscettola*, Pozzuoli, 353–373.
Allroggen-Bedel, A./H. Kammerer-Grothaus 1980, Das Museo Ercolanese in Portici, *Cronache Ercolanesi* 10, 175–218 (= Il Museo Ercolanese di Portici, in *La Villa dei Papiri*, Cronache Ercolanesi Supplement 2, Naples 1983, 83–128).
Alma Tadema 2007: E. Querci/S. De Caro (eds), *Alma Tadema e la nostalgia dell'antico*, Milan.
Alonso Rodrígez, M.C. 2003, La colleccíon de antigüedades comprada por Camillo Paderni en Roma para el rey Carlos III, in J. Beltrán Fortes et al. (eds), *Illuminismo e illustración. Le antichità e i loro protagonisti in Spagna e in Italia nel XVIII secolo*, Rome, 29–45.
Andreae, B. 1977, *Das Alexandermosaik aus Pompeji*, Recklinghausen.

Andreae, B. (ed.) 1995, *Bildkatalog der Skulpturen des Vatikanischen Museums* I. *Museo Chiaramonti* I–III, Berlin/New York.
Andreasen, Ø. (ed.) 1937, *Aus den Tagebüchern Friedrich Münters. Wander- und Lehrjahren eines dänischen Gelehrten*, Copenhagen/Leipzig.
Andrés, J. 2004, *Cartas familares (Viaje de Italia)* I, Madrid.
Antoine, Ph. 1997, *Les récits de voyage de Chateaubriand*, Paris.
Antoni, A. 2002, L'officina dei papiri dans la description de Vivant Denon, *Cronache Ercolanesi* 32, 313–330.
Appleton, T.G. 1872, *Mother Goose's melodies. The only pure edition containing all that have even come to light of her memorable writings together with those which have been discovered among the manuscripts of Herculaneum*, Boston (published anonymously).
Arbillaga, I. 2005, *Estética y teoría del libro de viaje. El 'viaje a Italia' en España*, Málaga.
Armstrong, R.H. 2005, *A Compulsion for Antiquity: Freud and the Ancient World*, Ithaca, NY.
Ascione, M. 2007, *La Villa dei Papiri*, Imperia.
Aßkamp, R. et al. (eds) 2008, *Luxus und Dekadenz. Römisches Leben am Golf von Neapel*, Mainz.
Assmann, J. 2005, *Die Zauberflöte Oper und Mysterium*, Munich.
Astarita, T. 2013, *A Companion to Early Modern Naples*, Leiden/Boston.
Atherstone, E. 1821, *The Last Days of Herculaneum; and Abradates and Panthea: Poems*, London.
Aubaude, C. 1997, *Nerval et le mythe d'Isis*, Paris.
Audano, S. 2009, Un ambiguo esempio di 'sfortuna' dell'Antico: *I miei ricordi* di Massimo D'Azeglio, in S. Audano (ed.), *Aspetti della Fortuna dell'Antico nella Cultura Europea: atti della quinta giornata di studi, Sestri Levante, 7 marzo 2008*, Pisa, 31–53.
Audot, L.-E. 1835, *L'Italie, la Sicile, les Iles éoliennes, l'Ile d'Elbe…. Royaume de Naples par MM. C.-D. De La Chavanne, D.-D. Farjasse et P***, … recueillis et publiés par Audot Père*, Paris.
Augustin-Thierry, G. 1912, *La fresque de Pompéi. La madone qui pleure*, Paris.
Avvisati, C. 2010, *Una camicia rossa a Pompei*, Rome.
Aziza, C. 1992, *Pompéi. Le rêve sous les ruines*, Paris.
Aziza, C. 2009, *Le péplum un mauvais genre*, Paris.
B. 1886, *Panorama van de verwoesting van Pompeii door de uitbarsting van den Vesuvius*, Amsterdam.
Bachmann, I. 1978, *Werke* I, Munich.
Balderston, K.C. (ed.) 1951, *Thraliana. The Diary of Mrs. Hester Lynch Thrale (the late Mrs. Piozzi) 1776–1809*, second edition, Oxford.
Baldi, A. 1964, *La Pompei giudaico-cristiana*, Cava dei Tirreni.
Barallat y Felguera, C. 1888, *Ione*, Barcelona.
Barbanera, M. 1998, *L'archeologia degli Italiani*, Rome.
Barbet, A./P. Miniero (eds) 1999, *La villa San Marco a Stabia*, Naples.
Barbet, A./A. Verbanck-Piérard 2013, *La villa romaine de Boscoreate et ses fresques*, Paris.
Baretti, G. 1768, *Account of the Manners and Customs of Italy*, London.
Barré, L. 1872, *Herculanum et Pompéi. Recueil général* (etc.) VIII. *Musée secret*, Paris (= García y García/Jacobelli 2001). First edition, Paris 1840.
Bartels, J.H. 1791, *Briefe über Kalabrien und Sizilien* I. *Reise von Neapel bis Reggio in Kalabrien*, second edition, Göttingen.
Barthélemy, J.-J. 1788, *Voyage du jeune Anacharsis en Grèce*, Paris.
Bartsch, K. 2000, *Ödön von Horváth*, Stuttgart/Weimar.
Barüske, H. 1980, *Aus Andersens Tagebüchern* 1, Frankfurt am Main.

Bassanville, Contesse de n.y., *Nouvelles cosmopolites. Moeurs, coutumes de divers peuples de l'Europe*, Paris.
Bassett, R. 1965, *The Pompeians*, London.
Basso, A. 2006, *I Mozart in Italia*, Rome.
Bastet, F.L. 1986a, Mozart in Pompeji, Mitteilungen der Internationalen Stiftung Mozarteum 34, 50–59.
Bastet, F.L. 1986b, *Lobster cocktail en andere verhalen*, Utrecht.
Baudelaire, C. 1975, *Oeuvres complètes* I (Bibliothèque de la Pléiade), Paris.
Baudelaire, C. 1980, *Oeuvres complètes*, Paris.
Baudrand, M.A. 1682, *Geographia ordine litterarum disposita*, Paris.
Baudy, G.J. 1991, *Die Brände Roms. Ein apokalyptisches Motiv in der antiken Historiographie*, Hildesheim/Zürich/New York.
Baudy, W.T. 1950, Baudelaire et Croly. La vérité sur *Le jeune enchanteur*, Mercure de France 308, 233–247.
Baumann, P. 2003, *Ödön von Horváth: "Jugend ohne Gott," Autor mit Gott?: Analyse der Religionsthematik anhand ausgewählter Werke*, Bern.
Bayardi, O.A. 1752, *Prodromo delle antichità d'Ercolano* I–V, Naples.
Bayardi, O.A. 1755, *Catalogo degli antichi monumenti dissotterrati dalla discoperta città di Ercolano per ordine della Maestà di Carlo Re delle Due Sicilie*, Naples.
Bayman, L. 2011, *Directory of World Cinema: Italy*, Bristol.
Beard, M. 2008, *Pompeii. The Life of a Roman Town*, London.
Beck, H./U. Walter 2001, *Die frühen römischen Historiker* I. *Von Fabius Pictor bis Cn. Gellius*, Darmstadt.
Becker, W. 1849, *Gallus*, second enlarged edition curated by W. Rhein, Leipzig (first edition, Leipzig 1838).
Beckford, W. 1971, *Dreams, Waking Thoughts and Incidents*, edited by R.J. Gennett, Rutherford/Madison/Teaneck (first edition, London 1783).
Beebel, Th.O. 2002, Ways of Seeing Italy: Landscapes of Nation in Goethe's *Italienische Reise* and its Counter-Narratives, Monatshefte für deutschsprachige Literatur und Kultur 94, 322–345.
Behlmann, L. 2007, The Sentinel of Pompeii: An Exemplum for the Nineteenth Century, in Gardner Coates/Seydl 2007, 157–170.
Behrend, O. 1907, *Der Bildhauer. Künstlerroman aus Pompeji*, Berlin.
Beldam, J. 1851, *Recollections of Scenes and Institutions in Italy and the East*, London.
Bellemin-Noël, J. 1983, *Gradiva au pied de lettre*, Paris.
Bendixen, A./J. Hamera (eds), *The Cambridge Companion to American Travel Writing*, Cambridge.
Benjamin, W. 1980, Neapel, in *Denkbilder = Gesammelte Schriften* IV.1, Frankfurt am Main, 307–316.
Benkowitz, C.F. 1806, *Reisen von Neapel in die umliegenden Gegenden*, Berlin.
Berger-Fix, A. 1988, *Auch einer. Friedrich Theodor Vischer zum 100. Todestage*, Ludwigsburg.
Bergeret de Grancourt, P.-J.O. 1895, *Journal inédit d'un voyage en Italie 1772–1774*, edited by M.A. Tornézy, Paris.
Bernard, C. 1996, *Le Passé recomposé. Le roman historique français du dix-neuvième siècle*, Paris.
Berry, P. 1995, *The Christian Inscriptions at Pompeii*, Lewiston/Queenston/Lampeter.
Bertheroy, J. 1899, *La danseuse de Pompéi*, Paris.
Bertrand, G. 2008, *Le Grand Tour revisité. Pour une archéologie du tourisme: le voyage des Français en Italie (milieu XVIIIe siecle – début XIXe siècle)*, Rome.
Bertrand, G./M.T. Pichetto (eds) 2001, *Le vie delle Alpi: il reale e l'immaginario*, Aosta.

Beschorner, A. 1992, *Untersuchungen zu Dares Phrygius*, Tübingen.
Besterman, Th. 1976, *Voltaire*, third edition, Oxford.
Bettinelli, S. 1755, 1969, *Al Signor Abate Benaglio*, Milan = E. Bonora (ed.), *Illuministi italiani* II. *Opere di Francesco Algarotti e Saverio Bettinelli*, Milan/Naples 1969, 616–627.
Betzer, S. 2010, Afterimage of the Eruption: An Archaeology of Chassériau's *Tepidarium* (1853), *Art History* 33, 466–489.
Beucker Andreae J.H. 1856, *Herinneringen aan Italië*, Leeuwarden.
Bianchini, F. 1697, 1747, *La Istoria universale provata con monumenti e figurata con simboli degli antichi*, first and second editions, Rome.
Bianco, G. 1833, *Una notte sulle rovine di Pompei. Romanzo storico*, Naples.
Bidermann, J. 1637, *Campanum seu Vesuvius flagrans*, in *Silvulae Hendecasyllaborum*, second edition, Antwerp (first edition 1635).
Bierbaum, J.O. n.y., Eine empfindsame Reise im Automobil von Berlin nach Sorrent und zurück an den Rhein, in *Gesammelte Werke 7*, Munich, 233–449 (first edition 1903).
Bilinski, B. 1982, Viaggiatori illuministi polacchi sul Vesuvio e nelle città vesuviane, in *Regione* 1982, 41–88.
Biondo, F. 2010, *Italia illustrata*, text, translation, and commentary by C.J. Castner, II, Binghamton N.Y.
Bisel, S. 1990, *The Secrets of Vesuvius*, Toronto/New York.
Björnståhl, J.J. 1777, *Briefe auf Reisen durch Frankreich.... Erster Band, der die Reisen durch Frankreich und Unter-Italien enthält*, Stralsund.
Black, J. 1988, The eruption of Vesuvius in Pacini's L'ultimo giorno di Pompei, *The Donizetti Society Journal* 6, 95–104.
Black, J. 1999, *The Grand Tour in the Eighteenth Century*, Phoenix Mill etc.
Blackburne, F. 1780, *A memoir of Thomas Hollis Esq. F.R. and A.S.S.*, London (published anonymously).
Blank, D. 1999, Reflections on Re-Reading Piaggio and the Early History of the Herculaneum Papyri, *Cronache Ercolanesi* 29, 55–82.
Blasco Ibáñez, V. 1980, *En el pais del arte*, Bacelona.
Blauer, J.M./R. McManigal 1989, *Pompeii*, San Francisco.
Blessington, M.G. Power, Countess of 1839, *The Idler in Italy*, Paris (also editions in London and Philadelphia).
Blix, G. 2009, *From Paris to Pompeii. French Romanticism and the Cultural Politics of Archaeology*, Philadelphia.
Bloedow, E.F. 2001, Heinrich Schliemann in Italy in 1868: tourist or archaeologist, *Quaderni Urbinati di Cultura Classica* 69.3, 115–129.
Bloom, E.A./L.D. Bloom (eds) 1989, *The Piozzi Letters. Correspondence of Hester Lynch Piozzi, 1784–1821 (formerly Mrs. Thrale)* I. *1784–1791*, Newark/London/Toronto.
Boadella, A. 2006, *Ubú president, o, Los últimos días de Pompeya; La increíble historia del Dr. Floit & Mr. Pla; Daaalí*, edited by M. Sánchez Arnosi, Madrid.
Boccaccio, G. 1964, *Tutte le opere di Giovanni Boccaccio* 2, edited by V. Branca, Milan.
Böttiger, C.A. 1803, 1806 *Sabina oder Morgenszenen im Putzzimmer einer reichen Römerin*, first and second editions, Leipzig.
Böttiger, C.A. 1837–1838, *Kleine Schriften archäologischen und antiquarischen Inhalts 1–3*, Dresden/Leipzig.
Boker, G.H. 1929, *Nydia. A Tragic Play*, edited by E.S. Bradley, Philadelphia.
Boker, G.H. 1940, *Glaucus & Other Plays*, edited by E.S. Bradley, Princeton NJ.

Bologna, F. 1979, Le scoperte di Ercolano e Pompei nella cultura europea del XVIII secolo, *Parola del Passato* 188–189, 377–404.
Bonajuto, A. 2000, I papiri ercolanesi nelle memorie dei viaggiatori inglesi del Settecento, *Cronache Ercolanesi* 30, 243–244.
Bondanella, P. 2009, *A History of Italian Cinema*, New York/London.
Bonucci, C. 1827, *Pompei descritta*, third edition, Naples.
Bonucci, C. 1828, 1830, *Pompéi décrite par Charles Bonucci; ou précis historique des excavations depuis l'année 1748 jusqu'à nos jours*, first and second editions, Naples.
Borrelli, G. 1992, Le delizie in villa a Portici e un "giallo archeologico", *Napoli Nobilissima* 31.1–2, 33–67.
Borriello, M.R. 2008, Note per l'indirizzario di Pompei, *Rivista di Studi Pompeiani* 19, 63–68.
Bory, P. 1890, *Mémoires d'un Romain. Vie privée de l'ancienne Rome*, Tours.
Boswell, J. 1955, *Boswell on the Grand Tour*, London/New York.
Boulton, J.T./T.O. McLoughlin (eds) 2012, *News from Abroad. Letters Written by British Travellers on the Grand Tour, 1728–71*, Liverpool.
Bowersock, G.S. 1978, The rediscovery of Herculaneum and Pompeii, *The American Scholar* 47, 461–470.
Bowersock, G.W. 2009, *From Gibbon to Auden. Essays on the Classical Tradition*, Oxford/New York [including Bowersock 1978 at pp. 66–76].
Bowker, G. 1995, *Pursued by furies: a life of Malcolm Lowry*, New York.
Boyle, N. 1991, *Goethe. The Poet and the Age* I. *The Poetry of Desire (1749–1790)*, Oxford/New York.
Bracco, V. 1982, Leopardi e le antichità napoletane, in *Leopardi e il mondo antico. Atti del V Convegno Internazionale di studi leopardini* (Recanati 1980), Florence, 301–319.
Bracco, V. 1983, *L'archeologia del regime*, Rome.
Bramsen, M. 1818, *Promenade d'un voyageur prussien en diverses parties de l'Europe, de l'Asie et de l'Afrique, en 1813, 1814 et 1815, en forme de lettres*, Paris.
Brango, J.-C./V. Giroud 2008, *Figures de l'Antiquité dans l'opéra français: des Troyens de Berlioz à Œdipe d'Enesco*, Saint-Étienne.
Bresciani, A. 1872, *L'Ebreo di Verona, romanzo storico dall'anno 1846 al 1849*, Milan (first edition published anonymously, Turin 1850).
Breton, E. 1855, 1869, *Pompéia décrite et dessinée*, first/second and third editions, Paris.
Breton, E. 1862, *Athènes*, Paris.
Brett-Smith, H.F.B. (ed.) 1909, *Peacock's Memoirs of Shelley, with Shelley's Letters to Peacock*, London.
Brilli, A. 1991, *Il Grand Tour dell'Europa in automobile*, Milan.
Brilli, A. 1992, *Arte del viaggiare. Il viaggio materiale dal XVI al XIX secolo*, Milan.
Brilli, A. 1995, *Quando viaggiare era un'arte. Il romanzo del Grand Tour*, Bologna.
Brilli, A. 2003, *Un paese di romantici briganti. Gli italiani nell'immaginario del Grand Tour*, Bologna.
Brilli, A. 2006, *Il viaggio in Italia. Storia di una grande tradizione culturale*, Bologna.
Brod, M. 1955, *Armer Cicero. Roman*, Berlin.
Brok, M.F.A. 1995, *L. Annaeus Seneca Naturales Quaestiones*, Darmstadt.
Brooks, R. Van Wyck 1958, The *Dream of Arcadia. American Writers and Artists in Italy 1760–1915*, New York.
Bruggiss, Ph. 2009, Numa Pompilius et la Rome sacrée. Regards croisés d'Augustin et de Thémistios, *Revue des études augustiniennes* 55, 3–22.
Bruin, P. 1979, *Es geschah vor 1900 Jahren. Die Anfänge des Christentums in Pompeji und Herculaneum*, Luzern/Stuttgart.

Brussel, P. 1768, *Promenade utile et récréative de deux Parisiens en cent soixante cinq jours*, Avignon.
Bulwer-Lytton, E. 1834, *The Last Days of Pompeii*, London (published anonymously).
Bulwer-Lytton, R. 2008, *The Collected Letters of Rosina Bulwer Lytton*, London.
Bunce, P. 1960, *Last Days of Pompeii*, New York.
Buonajuto, A. 2000, I papiri ercolanesi nelle memorie dei viaggiatori inglesi del Settecento, *Cronache Ercolanesi* 30, 243–244.
Burckhardt, J. 1869, *Cicerone*, second edition, Leipzig.
Burgin, V. 2006, *Voyage to Italy*, Cologne.
Burgin, V. 2009, Monument and Melancholia, in U. Staiger et al. (eds), *Memory Culture and the Contemporary City*, New York, 17–31
Burgon, J.W. 1862, *Letters from Rome to Friends in England*, London.
Burlot, D. 2011, The *Disegni intagliati*. A forgotten book illustrating the first discoveries in Herculaneum, *Journal of the History of Collections* 23, 15–28.
Busken Huet, C. 1877, *Van Napels naar Amsterdam. Italiaansche Reis-Aanteekeningen*, Amsterdam.
Butterworth, A./R Laurence 2005, *Pompeii the Living City*, London.
Caccia, J. 1817, *Nouveau guide du voyageur en Italie*, Paris.
Cacciapuoti, F. (ed.) 1998, *Giacomo Leopardi da Recanati a Napoli*, Naples.
Cafasso G. (ed.) 1998, *Il Vesuvio e le città vesuviane 1730–1860*, Naples.
Cain, H.U./A. Haug/Y. Asisi (eds) 2011, *Das antike Rom und sein Bild*, Berlin/Boston.
Calder III, W.M./R. Schlesier (eds) 1998, *Zwischen Rationalismus und Romantik. Karl Otfried Müller und die antike Kultur*, Hildesheim.
Camardo, D. 2013, Herculaneum from the 79 Eruption to the Medieval Period, *Papers of the British School at Rome* 81, 303–340.
Cammilleri, R. 1999, *Il quadrato magico: un mistero che dura da duemila anni*, Milan.
Campbell, J.L. 1986, *Edward Bulwer-Lytton*, Boston.
Cantilena, R./A. Porzio 2008, *Herculanense Museum. Laboratorio sull'antico nella Reggia di Portici*, Naples.
Capacius, I.C. 1607, *Neapolitana historia*, Naples.
Capasso, L. 2001, *I fuggiaschi di Ercolano*, Rome.
Capasso, M. 1983, *Storia fotografica dell'Officina dei papiri ercolanesi*, Naples.
Capasso, M. et al. 1986, *Monumenti della storia degli studi classici fra Ottocento e Novecento*, Naples.
Capasso, M. 1994, John Hayter, l'Officina dei Papiri Ercolanesi e il Carme *De Bello Actiaco* in una sconosciuta testimonianza di un viaggiatore ottocentesco, in M. Capasso/E. Puglia (eds), *Scritti di varia umanità in memoria di Benito Iezzi*, Naples, 273–287.
Capasso, M. (ed.) 1997, *Bicentenario della morte di Antonio Piaggio*, Galatina.
Capasso, M. 2000, *Come tele di ragno sgualcite. D.-V. Denon et J.-F. Champollion nell'Officina dei Papiri Ercolanesi*, Naples.
Capuano, G. 1999, *Viaggiatori britannici a Napoli nel '700, la città del Sole*, Naples.
Carcopino, J. 1953, Le christianisme secret du "carré magique", in J. Carcopino, *Etudes d'histoire chrétienne*, Paris, 9–91.
Carotenuto, M. 1980, *Ercolano attraverso i secoli*, Naples.
Carotenuto, S. 1932, *Herculaneum. Storia dell'antica città di Ercolano e dei suoi scavi*, Naples.
Carrington, R.C. 1936, *Pompeii*, Oxford.
Carrozzari, R. 1899, *Leo gladiator seu Pompei Vesuvii montis conflagratione obruti*, Amsterdam.
Casale, A. 1985, *Salvatore di Giacomo e le ville romane di Boscoreale*, Boscoreale.

Casillo, R. 2006, *The Empire of Stereotype. Germaine de Staël and the Idea of Italy*, New York/Houndmills.
Cassini, J.D. Comte de 1778, *Manuel de l'étranger qui voyage en Italie*, Paris (published anonymously).
Castaldi, G. 1840, *Della regale Accademia Ercolanese ...*, Naples.
Castellan, A.-L. 1819, *Lettres sur l'Italie, faisant suite aux Lettres sur la Morée, l'Hellespont et Constantinople*, Paris.
Castiglione Morelli, V. 2008, Di alcune riviste che accompagnarono le scoperte pompeiane, in A. Garzya (ed.), *Le riviste a Napoli dal XVIII secolo al primo Novecento* (Quaderni dell'Accademia Pontaniana 53), Naples, 519–550.
Castrén, P. 1975, *Ordo populusque pompeianus. Polity and Society in Roman Pompeii*, Rome.
Castrucci, G. 1858, *Tesoro letterario di Ercolano ossia la reale officina dei papiri ercolanesi*, Naples (re-edited by L. García y García and L. Santoro in 1999).
Cavalli, A. 1769, *Il Vesuvio, poemetto storico-fisico con annotazioni*, Milan.
Caylus, A.C.P. de I–VII: *Recueil d'Antiquités égyptiennes, étrusques, grecques et romaines*, Paris 1752–1767.
Cazotte, J. 1772, *Le diable amoureux. Nouvelle espagnole*, Paris.
Cellarius, J. n.y., *Die Isispriester in den letzten Tagen von Pompeji*, Leipzig.
Cerasuolo, S. 1987, Gli studi classici a Napoli nell'Ottocento, in *Momenti della storia degli studi classici fra ottocento e novecento*, Naples, 7–67.
Cerasuolo, S 2005, *Tra papirologia e archeologia ercolanesi. I carteggi Comparetti-De Petra*, Messina.
Chabaud, G. et al. 2000, *Les guides imprimés du XVe au XXe siècle. Villes, paysages, voyages*, Paris.
Champollion, J.-F. 1909, *Lettres de Champollion le Jeune, recueillies et annotées par H. Hartleben I. Lettres écrites d'Italie*, Paris 1909.
Chaney, E. 1998, *The Evolution of the Grand Tour. Anglo-Italian Cultural Relations since the Renaissance*, London/Portland.
Chapman, A./J. Stabler (eds) 2003, *Unfolding the South. Nineteenth-century British women writers and artists in Italy*, Manchester/New York.
Chard, C. 2007, Picnic at Pompeii: Hyperbole and Digression in the Warm South, in Gardner Coates/Seydl 2007, 115–132.
Chateaubriand, R. de 1968, *Voyage en Italie*, edited by J.-M. Gautier, Geneva.
Chateaubriand, R. de 1969, *Œuvres romanesques et voyages* II (Bibliothèque de la Pléiade), Paris.
Chatterton, G. (ed.) 1861, *Memorials, personal and historical of Admiral Lord Gambier, G.C.B.*, London.
Chevallier, E. 1977, Les peintures découvertes à Herculanum, Pompéi et Stabies vues par les voyageurs du XVIIIe siècle, *Gazette des Beaux-Arts* 90, 177–188.
Chevallier, E. 1980 (ed.), *Les Tableaux d'Italie de Friedrich Johann Lorenz Meyer*, Naples.
Chevallier, E./R. Chevallier 1984, *Iter italicum. Les voyageurs français à la découverte de l'Italie ancienne*, Geneva.
Christensen, A.C. (ed.) 2004, *The subverting vision of Bulwer Lytton: bicentenary reflections*, New York.
Christmas, J. 2009, *Incontinent on the Continent. My Mother, Her Walker and Our Grand Tour to Italy*, Vancouver/Toronto/Berkeley.
Ciarallo, A./E. De Carolis 1998, La data dell'eruzione, *Rivista di Studi Pompeiani* 9, 63–73.

Cichocka, M. 2007, *Entre la nouvelle histoire et le nouveau roman historique*, Paris.
CIL: Corpus Inscriptionum Latinarum IV, X Berlin 1871 etc.
Cioffi, V.A. 1994, *Pompei. Magia di rose*, Naples/Rome.
Ciprotti, P. 1975, Ancora poche parole sugli indizi di cristianesimo in Pompei, in B. Andreae/H. Kyrieleis (eds), *Neue Forschungen in Pompeji*, Recklinghausen, 277–278.
Citino, D. 2002, *The News and other poems*, Notre Dame, Indiana.
Civiltà 1979: *Civiltà del Settecento a Napoli* I–II, Florence.
Clarac, F. Comte de 1813, *Fouille faite à Pompei en présence de S.M. la Reine des Deux Siciles le 18 mars 1813*, Paris.
Clark, H.H. 1883, *Lost in Pompeii*, Boston.
Clarke, J.R. 1998, *Looking at Lovemaking. Constructions of Sexuality in Roman Art 100 B.C. – A.D. 250*, Berkeley/Los Angeles/London.
Clarke, W.B. 1832, 1847, *Pompeii: its destruction and re-discovery*, fourth edition / new edition, London (published anonymously).
Classens de Jongste, C.A. 1841, *Souvenirs d'une promenade au mont Vésuve*, Naples.
Clay, E. 1976, *Sir William Gell in Italy. Letters to the Society of Dilettanti, 1831–1835*, London.
Clay, E. 1979, *Lady Blessington at Naples*, London.
Clébert, J.-P. 1988, *Les Daudet, une famille bien française, 1840–1940*, Paris.
Cochin, C.-N. 1751, *Lettre sur les peintures d'Herculanum, aujourd'hui à Portici*, Brussels.
Cochin, C.-N./J.-C. Bellicard 1754, 1757, 1996, *Observations sur les antiquités d'Herculanum avec Quelques Réflexions sur la Peinture & la Sculpture des Anciens; & une courte description de quelques Antiquités des environs de Naples*, first and second editions, Paris (new edition with introduction and notes by E. Flamarion and C. Volpilhac-Auger, Saint-Étienne 1996).
Coleman, K.M. 1990, Fatal Charades: Roman Executions Staged as Mythological Enactments, *Journal of Roman Studies* 80, 44–73.
Colet, L. 1861, *Naples sous Garibaldi: souvenirs de la guerre de l'indépendance*, Paris.
Colet, L. 1862, *L'Italie des Italiens. Le libérateur*, Paris.
Colligan, M. 2002, *Canvas Documentaries. Panoramic Entertainments in Nineteenth-Century Australia and New-Zealand*, Melbourne.
Collins, W. 1998, *The Law and the Lady*, Harmondworth.
Comastri Montanari, D. 2005, *Ars moriendi. Indagine a Pompei*, Cinisello Balsamo.
Contributi 1980: *Contributi alla storia della Officina dei Papiri Ercolanesi*, Rome.
Comparetti, D./G. De Petra 1883, *La Villa ercolanese dei Pisoni, i suoi monumenti e la sua biblioteca*, Turin (facsimile: Naples 1972).
Conforti, L. 1888, *Pompei. Scene*, Naples.
Conrad, M. G. 1888, *Was die Isar rauscht. Münchener Roman* I, Leipzig.
Constantine, D. 2001, *Fields of Fire. A Life of Sir William Hamilton*, London.
Conti, A. 1907, *Sul fiume del tempo*, Naples.
Cooley, A.E./M.G.L. Cooley 2004, *Pompeii: a sourcebook*, London/New York.
Cooper, J.F. 1981, *Italy*, edited by J. Conron and C.A. Denne, Albany.
Corti, E.C. 1940, *Untergang und Auferstehung von Pompeji und Herculaneum*, Munich.
Costa, M. 1996, *Sentimento del sublime e strategie del simbolico: il Vesuvio nella letteratura francese*, Salerno.
Cotugno, A./A. Lucignano 2009, *Il fondo bibliografico di Amedeo Maiuri. Libri, carteggi e cimeli di un grande archeologo*, Naples.
Covito, C. 2012, *Le ragazze di Pompei*, Siena.
Covito, C. 2013, *Il processo di Giusta*, Siena.

Coxe, H. (John Millard) 1825, *A Picture of Italy Being a Guide to the Antiquities and Curiosities of that Classical and Interesting Country*, second edition, London.
Coyer, G.F. 1775, *Voyage d'Italie et de Hollande, par M. l'abbé Coyer, des Académies de Nancy, de Rome & de Londres*, Paris.
Cramme, S. 2004, 2009, Morde am Vesuv und anderswo: Städte und Regionen des römischen Reiches im Kriminalroman, in K. Brodersen (ed.), *Crimina. Die Antike im modernen Kriminalroman*, first and second editions, Frankfurt am Main, 109–124.
Craven, K. 1821, *A Tour through the Southern Provinces of the Kingdom of Naples*, London.
Craven, K. 1837, *Excursions in the Abruzzi and Northern Provinces of Naples*, London.
Cremante, R. 2008, Gli ultimi giorni di Pompei in un dimenticato poema di Luigi Conforti, in Cremante et al. 2008, 113–134.
Cremante, R. et al. (eds) 2008, *I misteri di Pompei. Antichità pompeiane nell'immaginario della modernità. Atti della giornata di studio, Pavia, Collegio Ghislieri, 1 marzo 2007*, Pompei.
Creuzé de Lesser, A.F. 1806, *Voyage en Italie et en Sicile, fait en MDCCCI et MDCCCII*, Paris.
Croly, G. 1836, *The Young Enchanter – From a Papyrus of Herculaneum*, in *Forget me not. A Christmas, New Year's and Birthday present, for 1836*, London, 9–38.
Crombet, P. 1941, *Les souvenirs d'Italie de Paul Crombet, officier belge de la marine royale des Pays-Bas (1817–1826)*, edited by C. Terlinden, Brussels/Rome.
Cross, J. 1860, *The American Pastor in Europe*, London.
Curti, P.A. 1872–1874, *Pompei e le sue rovine*, Milan/Naples, I–III.
Cusk, R. 2009, *The Last Supper. A Summer in Italy*, London/New York.
D'Achille, A.M. et al. 2011 (eds), *Aubin-Louis Millin (1759–1818) entre France et Italie*, Rome.
Daehner, J. (ed.) 2007, *The Herculaneum Women. History, Context, Identities*, Los Angeles.
Dahl, C. 1956, Recreations of Pompeii, *Archaeology* 9, 182–191.
Dalcastagnè, R. 2000, *A garganta das coisas: movimentos de Avalovara de Osman Lins*, Brasilia.
D'Alconzo, P. 2002, *Picturae excisae. Conservazione e restauro dei dipinti ercolanesi e pompeiani fra XVIII e XIX secolo*, Rome.
Dale, C. 1973, Pater's Marius and Historical Novels on Early Christian Times, *Nineteenth-Century Fiction* 28, 1–24.
D'Aloë, S. 1857, *Die Ruinen von Pompeji, übersetzt von Eduard von Lossow*, second edition, Berlin
D'Ambrosio, A. 1998 (ed.), *Alla scoperta di Pompei. Itinerari di visita in occasione del 250º anniversario dell'inizio degli scavi*, Milan.
D'Ambrosio, A./S. De Caro 1983, *Un Impegno per Pompei: Fotopiano e documentazione della Necropoli di Porta Nocera*, Milan.
D'Amelio, P. 1888, *Dipinti murali di Pompei*, Naples.
Damiani, R. 1998, *Leopardi e Napoli, 1833–1837*, Naples.
D'Ancora, G. 1803, *Prospetto storico-fisico degli scavi di Ercolano e di Pompei e dell'antico e presente stato del Vesuvio per guida de' Forestieri*, Naples.
D'Arthenay, P.-F. 1748, *Mémoire historique et critique sur la Ville souterraine*, Avignon (published anonymously).
Daudet, L. 1931, *Les bacchantes, roman contemporain*, Paris.
D'Augerot, A. 1877, *Le Vésuve. Description du volcan et de ses environs*, Limoges.
David, M.-F. 2001, *Antiquité latine et Décadence*, Paris.
David-de Palacio, M.-F. 2005, *Reviviscences romaines. La latinité au miroir de l'esprit fin-de-siècle*, Bern etc.
Davis, L. 1990, *Shadows in Bronze. A Marcus Didius Falco novel*, London.
D'Azeglio, M. Tapparelli 1867, *I miei ricordi*, Florence.

De Alarcón, P.A. 1943, *Obras completas*. Con un comento preliminar, por Luis Martínez Kleiser, Madrid.
De Beauvoir, S. 1960, *La force de l'âge*, Paris.
De Bourke, E. 1823, *Notice sur les ruines le plus remarquables de Naples et de ses environs*, Paris.
De Bressay, C.A. marquise de Lezay de Marnésia 1753, 1766, *Lettres de Julie à Ovide*, Geneva.
De Brosses, C. 1991, *Lettres familières. Texte établi par Giuseppina Cafasso, Introduction, notes et bibliographie par Letizia Norci Cagiano de Azevedo*, Naples.
De Caro, S. (ed.) 2000, *Il gabinetto segreto del Museo Archeologico Nazionale*, Naples.
De Caro, S. 2013, La riscoperta delle città vesuviane, in Guzzo/Tagliamonte/Lucchetti 2013, 14–25.
De Caro S./P.G. Guzzo (eds) 1999, *A Giuseppe Fiorelli nel primo centenario della morte*, Naples.
De Carolis, E./G. Patricelli/A. Ciarallo 1998, Ritrovamenti di corpi nell'area urbana di Pompei, *Rivista di Studi Pompeiani* 9, 75–123.
De Corcelles, L. 1982, *Portrait de la poétesse*, Paris.
De Feis, L. 1906, *Alcune memorie bibliche scoperte a Pompei*, Florence.
De Faria, Z./E. Ferreira (eds) 2009, *Osman Lins, 85 anos: a harmonia de imponderáveis*, Recife.
De Franciscis, A. 1963, *Il Museo Nazionale di Napoli*, Cava dei Tirreni/Naples.
De Franciscis, A. 1975, L'esperienza napoletana del Winckelmann, *Cronache Pompeiane* 1, 7–24.
De Franciscis, A. et al. 1990, *Amedeo Maiuri nel centenario della nascita* (Memorie dell'Istituto italiano per gli studi filosofici 21), Naples.
De Gonzague, Princess 1797, *Lettres de Madame la Princesse De Gonzague sur l'Italie, la France, l'Allemagne et les beaux-arts*, second enlarged edition, Hamburg.
De Graaff, M.H. 1874, De ondergang van Pompeji, in *Aurora. Letterkundige almanak*, Amsterdam, 9–60.
De Haan, N. 2010, *Römische Privatbäder*, Frankfurt am Main etc.
De Haan, N. 2014a, "Abbracciare in una le gloriose memorie antiche e moderne." Gli scavi di Pompei tra patrimonio universale, ambiente internazionale e identità italiana, forthcoming.
De Haan, N. 2014b, Archeologia classica in Campania nel ventennio fascista: un chiaroscuro continuo, forthcoming.
De Jong, S. 2010, *Rediscovering Architecture. Paestum in Eighteenth-Century Architectural Experience and Theory*, PhD Leiden (edition forthcoming Yale University Press, Winter 2014).
De Jorio, A. 1825, *Officina de' papiri*, Naples (re-edited by M. Capasso in 1998).
De Jorio, A. 1832, *La mimica degli antichi investigata nel gestire napoletano*, Naples (see Kendon 2000).
De Joucy, E. 1824–1825, *L'Hermite en Italie ou Observations sur les moeurs et les usages des Italiens au commencement du XIX siècle, faisant suite à la collection des moeurs françaises de M. de Joucy*, Paris.
De la Condamine, C.M. 1762, Extrait d'un journal de voyage en Italie, *Histoire de l'Académie royale des sciences*, 336–410.
De la Roche, M. 1783, *Voyage d'un amateur des arts en Flandre, dans les Pays-Bas, en Hollande, en France, en Savoye, en Italie, en Suisse, fait dans les Années 1775-76-77-78*, Amsterdam.
De la Rochefoucauld, S. 2008, *Le mystère de Pompéi*, Paris.
De Lalande, J. 1769, 1786, *Voyage en Italie* I–VIII, first and second editions, Paris.
De Latouche H. 1829, *Fragoletta. Naples et Paris en 1799*, Paris.
De Lamartine, A. 1867, *Graziella*, Paris (first edition, Paris 1851).
De Lamothe, A. 1881, *Le fou du Vésuve*, seventh edition, Paris (first edition, Paris 1879).

De Maria, S. 1988, *Gli archi onorari di Roma e dell'Italia romana*, Rome.
De Meuse, J. 1967, *Flaviana (la mitica eroina di Stabia)*, translation L. D'Orsi, Castellammare di Stabia (first edition 1961).
De Musset, P.-E. 1865, *Voyage pittoresque en Italie, partie méridionale et en Sicile*, Paris (first edition, Paris 1855–1856).
De Pixerécourt, R.-Ch.G. 1827, *La tête de mort, ou, Les ruïnes de Pompeïa: mélodrame en trois actes*, Paris.
De Séranon, J. 1877, *La Campanie. Pompéï-Herculanum. Étude sur les mœurs romaines*, second edition, Paris.
De Seta, C. 1981, *Architettura, ambiente e società a Napoli nel '700*, Turin.
De Seta, C. (ed.) 1982, *Arti e civiltà del Settecento a Napoli*, Bari.
De Seta, C. 1988, *Napoli* (Le città nella storia d'Italia), fourth edition, Bari.
De Seta, C. 1992, *L'Italia del Grand Tour. Da Montaigne a Goethe*, Naples.
De Singlande, R.P. 1765, *Mémoires & voyages*, Paris.
De Sivry, L. 1843, *Rome et l'Italie méridionale. Promenades et pélérinages suivis d'une description sommaire de la Sicile*, Paris.
De Staël, A.L.G. Necker 1841, *Corinne ou l'Italie*, Paris (first edition, Paris 1807).
De Staël, A.L.G. Necker 1930, *Correspondance générale* V. 2, Paris.
De Staël, A.L.G. Necker 1971, *Les carnets de voyage de Madame de Staël. Contributions à la genèse de ses œuvres*, edited by S. Balayé, Geneva.
De Unamuno, M. 1951, Pompeya. Divagaciones, in *Notas de un viaje a Italia*, in *Obras completas* I. *Paisaje*, Madrid, 835–840.
De Waele, J.A.K.E. 2001, *Il tempio dorico del Foro triangolare di Pompei*, Rome.
Debout, J. 1930, *Le chanoine Brousillard à Herculanum. Aux Assassins comme il faut. Le péché des hommes*, Paris.
Del Litto, V. /E. Kanceff (eds) 1986, *Le Journal de voyage et Stendhal*, Geneva.
Delatttre D. 2006, *La Villa des Papyrus et les rouleaux d'Herculanum. La Biblothèque de Philodème*, Liège.
Delille, J. 1800, *L'homme des Champs, ou les Géorgiques françoises*, Strasburg.
Della Corte, M. 1924, *IVVENTVS. Un nuovo aspetto della vita pubblica di Pompei finora inesplorato*, Arpinio.
Della Corte, M. 1926, 1965, *Case ed abitanti di Pompei*, first and third editions, Naples.
Della Valle, C. 1810, *Il Vesuvio. Poema in ottava rima*, Naples.
Democritus 1771: (anon.), *Democritus: Or the Laughing Philosopher. A collection of merry stories, jests, epigrams, riddles, repartees, epitaphs, &c. taken from a manuscript found at HERCULANEUM, an ancient Roman city, in the year 1770*, Berwick.
Demont, L. 1821, *Voyages and Travels of Her Majesty, Caroline, Queen of Great Britain, ..., by one of Her Majesty's Suite*, London (published anonymously).
Denon, V. 1997, *Voyage au royaume de Naples*, Paris.
Denon, V. 2009 *Les itinéraires de Vivant-Denon. Naples et Pompéi*, Paris.
Derrida, J. 1980, *La carte postale: de Socrate à Freud et au-delà*, Paris.
Derrida, J. 1995, *Mal d'archive. Une impression freudienne*, Paris.
Dezobry, Ch. 1846–1847, *Rome au siècle d'Auguste ou Voyage d'un Gaulois à Rome à l'époque du règne d'Auguste et pendant une partie du règne de Tibère, précédé d'une description de Rome aux époques d'Auguste et de Tibère*, nouvelle édition, Paris.
Dickens, C. 1998, *Pictures from Italy*, Harmondsworth (first edition, London 1847).
Dickens, C. 1991, *Little Dorrit*, Oxford (first edition, London 1857).

Diderot, D. 1875–1877, *Œuvres complètes*, edited by J. Assézat and M. Torneaux, Paris.
Diderot, D. 1963, *Les Salons* III. *1767*, edited by J. Seznec and J. Adhémer, Oxford.
Diderot, D. 1969, 1970, 1971, *Œuvres complètes* I, VII, VIII, Paris.
Diderot, D. 1984, *Œuvres complètes* XIII. *Arts et lettres (1767–1770). Critique* II. Édition critique et annoté par J. Schlobach et Jeanne Carniat, Paris.
Dillon, E. 1978, *The Shadow of Vesuvius*, London/Boston.
Dix, W.G. 1848, *Pompeii and other Poems*, Boston.
Dobai, J. 1975, *Die Kunstliteratur des Klassizismus und der Romantik in England* II. *1750–1790*, Berne.
Donaldson, Th.L. 1827, *Pompeii, Illustrated with Picturesque Views engraved by W.B. Cooke from the original drawings of Lieut. Col. Cockburn, of the Royal Artillery*, London.
Donatone, G. 2000, *William Hamilton. Diario segreto napoletano (1764–1789)*, Naples.
D'Onofri, P. 1789, *Elogio estemporaneo per la gloriosa memoria di Carlo III monarca delle Spagne e delle Indie. Dedicato alla maestà di Ferdinando III re delle Due Sicilie suo amatissimo figlio*, Naples.
Doolittle, Hilda > H.D.
D'Orsi, L. 1996, *Gli scavi di Stabia. Giornali di scavo*, edited by A. Carosella, Rome.
Douglas, N. 1929, *Nerinda*, New York.
Doyle, W. 1985, Dupaty (1746–1788): a career in the late Enlightenment, in *Studies on Voltaire and the eighteenth century* 230, Oxford, 1–125.
Dronia, M. 2006, Der Vesuvausbruch von 1631. Rezeption antiker Literatur im Barockgedicht eines süddeutschen Jesuiten, in Richter/Wamser 2006, 30–39.
Drummond, W./R. Walpole 1810, *Herculanensia; or Archaeological and Philological Dissertations, containing a Manuscript Found Among the Ruins of Herculaneum*, London (published anonymously).
Du Bocage, A.-M. Lepage 1771, *Lettres contenant ses voyages en France, en Angleterre, en Hollande et en Italie pendant les années 1750, 1757 et 1758*, Dresden.
Du Bocage, J.D. Barbié 1788, 1790, *Recueil de cartes géographiques, plans, vues et médailles de l'ancienne Grèce, relatifs au voyage du jeune Anacharsis; précédé d'une analyse critique des cartes*, first and third editions, Paris.
Duclos, C.P. n.y., *Le Voyage en Italie, ou Considérations sur l'Italie*, in *Œuvres complètes*, Paris.
Ducos, B. 1829, *Itinéraire et souvenirs d'un voyage en Italie en 1819 et 1820*, Paris.
Dumas, A. 2001, *Le corricolo*, Paris (first edition, Paris 1842).
Dumont, H. 2009, *L'Antiquité au cinéma: vérités, légendes et manipulations*, Paris/Lausanne.
Dupaty, C.-M.J.-B. Mercier 1789, *Lettres sur l'Italie en 1785 par feu M. Dupaty*, Rome/Paris.
Durrani, O./J. Preece (eds) 2001, *Travellers in Time and Space. The German Historical Novel*, Amsterdam/New York.
D'Urso, M. 1828, *I nuovi scavi d'Ercolano*, Naples.
Dwight, Th. 1824, *A Journal of a Tour in Italy in the Year 1821 with a Description of Gibraltar, Accompanied by Several Engravings, By an American*, New York (published anonymously).
Dwyer, E. 2007, Science or Morbid Curiosity? The Casts of Giuseppe Fiorelli and the Last Days of Romantic Pompeii, in Gardner Coates/Seydl 2007, 171–188.
Dwyer, E. 2010, *Pompeii's Living Statues: Ancient Roman Lives Stolen from Death*, Ann Arbor.
Dyer, Th.H. 1868, *Pompeii. Its History, Buildings and Antiquities*, second edition, London.
Dyson, M.E. 2006, *Come Hell or High Water. Katrina and the Color of Disaster*, New York.
East, R. 2003, *A.D 62: Pompeii*, New York/Lincoln/Shanghai.
Eco, U. 2006, *Sator arepo eccetera*, Rome.

Edele eenvoud 1989: *Edele eenvoud. Neo-classicisme in Nederland 1765–1800*, exhibition catalogue Haarlem, Den Bosch, Zwolle.
Edgeworth, M. 1808, *The Little Merchants, or Homely and Known Contrast*, New Haven.
Eichhorn, O. n.y., *Maddalena*, Konstanz.
Eliot, G. 1977, *The George Eliot Letters edited by G.S. Haight* 3. *1859–1861*, New Haven/London.
Encyclopédie: Encyclopédie ou Dictionnaire raisonné des sciences, des arts et des métiers 1–17, 1751–1772, edited by D'Alembert and Diderot, Paris.
Engelbach, L. 1815, *Naples and the Campagna Felice. In a Series of Letters Addressed to a Friend in England in 1802*, London (published anonymously).
Ercolano 2008: M.P. Guidobaldi (ed.), *Ercolano tre secoli di scoperte*, Naples.
Eristov, H. 2005, Décors méconnus de la villa de Diomède, in Th. Ganschow/M. Steinhart (eds), *Otium. Festschrift für Volker Michael Strocka*, Remshalden, 75–86.
Erll, A./A. Nünning (eds) 2010, *A Companion to Cultural Memory*, Berlin/New York.
Ernst, W. 1992, *Historismus im Verzug. Museale Antike(n)rezeption im britischen Neoklassizismus (und jenseits)*, Hagen.
Erskine Clement Waters, C. 1894, *Naples, the city of Parthenope and its Environs*, London/Boston.
Espantaleón, J. 1892, *Pompeya. Drama histórico de espectaculo en cuatro actos, divididos en quince quadros*, Madrid.
Esposito, M. 2008, Garibaldi, Pompei e il Museo di Napoli, *Rivista di Studi Pompeiani* 19, 69–76.
Eustace, J.C. 1817, *A Classical Tour through Italy An. MDCCCII*, fourth edition, London.
Everist, M. 2002, *Music Drama at the Paris Odéon 1824–1828*, Berkeley/Los Angeles/London.
Fairfield, J. 1847, *The Life of Sumner Lincoln Fairfield Esq.*, New York.
Fairfield, S.L. 1832, *The Last Night of Pompeii; A Poem: and Lays and Legends*, New York.
Fairfield, S.L. 1835, The Last Night of Pompeii versus The Last Days of Pompeii, *The North American Magazine* 5, no. 27, January 1835, 193–201 (published anonymously).
Falanga, L. 1981, *La croce di Ercolano. Cronistoria di una scoperta*, Naples.
Fallowell, D. 1989, *To Noto or from London to Sicily in a Ford*, London.
Faris, A. 1980, *Jacques Offenbach*, London/Boston.
Fasulo, M. 1938, *Il "Golfo di Napoli" nelle descrizioni di Italiani e Stranieri*, Sorrento.
Federspiel, J. 1993, *Eine Halbtagsstelle in Pompeji. Erzählungen*, Frankfurt am Main.
Ferber, J.J. 1773, *Briefe aus Wälschland über natürliche Merkwürdigkeiten dieses Landes*, Prague.
Fernández Murga, F. 1965, Pompeya en la literatura española, *Annali dell'Istituto Universitario Orientale. Sezione Romanza* VII.
Fernández Murga, F. 1986, Tanucci, Alcubierre e gli scavi di antichità, in *Tanucci 1986*, 479–491.
Fernández Murga, F. 1989, *Carlos III y el descubrimiento de Herculano, Pompeya y Estabia*, Salamanca.
Ficcadenti, B. 1981, *Figure del Risorgimento. Candido e C. Augusto Vecchi*, Urbino.
Fierz-David., L. 1989, *Women's Dionysian Initiation. The Villa of the Mysteries in Pompeii*, Dallas.
Fiorelli, G. 1858, *Sulle regioni pompeiane e della loro antica distribuzione. Programma pubblicato in ricorrenza dell'onomastico di Sua Altezza Reale il Conte di Siracusa*, Naples.
Fiorelli, G. 1873, *Gli scavi di Pompei dal 1862 al 1872. Relazione al Ministro della Istruzione Pubblica*, Naples.
Fiorelli, G. 1875, *La descrizione di Pompei*, Naples (= re-edition, Naples 2001).
Fiorelli, G. 1994, *Appunti autobiografici*, Sorrento/Naples.
Fisk, W. 1838, *Travels on the Continent of Europe*, New York.
Fitzon, Th. 2002a, Pompeji/Literatur und Film, in *Der neue Pauly* 15/2, 490–496.

Fitzon, Th. 2002b, Pompejanische Schatten. Die Rezeption Pompejis in der Literatur um 1900, in A. Aurenhammer/Th. Pittrof (eds), *"Mehr Dionysos als Apoll." Antiklassizistische Antike-Rezeption um 1900*, Frankfurt am Main, 299–331.
Fitzon, Th. 2004, *Reisen in das befremdliche Pompeji. Antiklassizistische Antikenwahrnehmung deutscher Italienreisender 1750–1870*, Berlin/New York.
Fitzon, Th. 2012, Ausgrabungssituationen und lyrische Reflexion. Ein Modell archäologischer Lyrik erprobt an Pompeji-Gedichten des 19. Jahrhundert, in J. Broch/J. Lang (eds), *Literatur der Archäologie. Materialität und Rhetorik im 18. und 19. Jahrhundert*, Paderborn, 131–154.
Florack-Kröll, C. 1986, Vom Erlebnis "Italien" zur Veröffentlichung der 'Italienischen Reise', in *Goethe in Italien*, Mainz am Rhein, 126–132
Forcellino, M. 1993, La formazione e il metodo di Camillo Paderni, *Eutopia* 2.2, 49–64.
Forcellino, M. 1999, *Camillo Paderni Romano e l'immagine storica degli scavi di Pompei, Ercolano e Stabia*, Rome.
Formont, M. 1914, *Visions antiques. La Danseuse. Roman*, Paris.
Forsyth, J. 1813, 2001, *Remarks on Antiquities, Arts, and Letters during an Excursion in Italy in the Years 1802 and 1803*, London; reprint edited by K. Crook, Cranbury NY/London/Mississauge Ont.
Foster, H.B. 1955, *Dio's Roman History* 8, London/Cambridge Mass. (Loeb Classical Library).
Fougeroux de Bondaroy, A.D. 1770, *Recherches sur les ruines d'Herculanum; et sur les lumières qui peuvent en résulter, relativement à l'état présent des Sciences & des Arts*, Paris.
Fox, G. 1892, *Nydia, the blind girl of Pompeii. Grand opera in V acts, adapted from Bulwer Lyttons's novel "The Last Days of Pompeii"*, London.
Fragment 1758: *A Fragment of the Chronicles of Nathan Ben Saddi; A Rabbi of the Jews Lately Discovered in the Ruins of Herculaneum; and Translated from the Original, into the Italian Language. By the Command of the King of the Two-Sicilies and now first publish'd in English*, Constantinople: printed in the year of the Vulgar Era 5707 (= Philadelphia 1758).
Franchi dell'Orto, L. (ed.) 1993, *Ercolano 1738–1988: 250 anni di recerca archeologica*, Rome.
Francis, J.G. 1847, *Notes from a Journal Kept in Italy and Sicily During the Years 1844, 1845, and 1846*, London.
Frank-van Westrienen, A. 1983, *De Groote Tour. Tekening van de educatiereis der Nederlanders in de zeventiende eeuw*, Amsterdam.
Franklin, J.C. 2001, *Pompeiis difficile est: Studies in the Political Life of Imperial Pompeii*, Ann Arbor.
Freud, S. 1989, *Studienausgabe* X, Frankfurt am Main.
Freud, S. 2002, *Unser Herz zeigt nach dem Süden. Reisebriefe 1895–1923*, Berlin.
Friedländer, H. 1819, *Ansichten von Italien, während einer Reise in den Jahren 1815 und 1816*, Leipzig.
Fröhlig, Th. 2008, The Study of the Lombards and the Ostrogoths at the German Archaeological Institute of Rome, 1937–1943, *Fragmenta* 2, 183–213.
Frye, W.E. 1908, *After Waterloo. Reminiscences of European Travel 1815–1819*, London.
Fucini, R. 1997, *Napoli a occhio nudo*, edited by T. Iermano, Venosa.
Fuller, L.H. 1965, *Fire in the Sky. Story of a Boy of Pompeii*, New York/Nashville.
Furchheim, F. 1891, *Bibliografia di Pompei, Ercolano e Stabia*, Naples.
Fussell, P. 1980, *Abroad: British Literary Traveling Between the Wars*, New York/Oxford.
Gadille, J. 1995, Les îles britanniques, in J. Gadille/J.-M. Mayeur (eds), *Histoire du Christianisme des origines à nos jours* XI. *Libéralisme, industrisalisation, expansion européenne (1830–1914)*, Paris, 225–243

Gäumann, H. 1977, *David Mallet: The Excursion. Mit einem Überblick über das dichterische Gesamtwerk*, PhD Zürich.
Galanti, G.M. 1792, *Napoli e contorni*, Naples.
Galanti, L. 1832, *Napoli e contorni*, Naples.
Galiani, B. 1765, *Considerazioni sopra la lettera dell'abate Winkelmann*, Naples (published anonymously = Winckelmann 2001b, 151–155).
Galiffe, J.A. 1820, *Italy and its Inhabitants; an Account of a Tour in that Country in 1816 and 1817*, London.
Galignani 1819: *Galignani's Traveller's Guide through Italy ... carefully composed from the Works of Coxe, Eustace, Forsyth, Reichard etc.*, Paris.
Gamper, G. 1915, *Rom und Reise. Mit einigen Reproduktionen nach Holzschnitten, Aquarellen und Zeichnungen des Verfassers*, Zürich/Leipzig.
García y García, L. 1998, *Nova bibliotheca pompeiana. 250 anni di bibliografia archeologica*, Rome.
García y García. L. 2006, *Danni di guerra a Pompei. Una dolorosa vicenda quasi dimenticata*, Rome.
García y García, L. 2012, *Nova bibliotheca pompeiana. 1º supplemento (1999–2011)*, Rome.
García y García, L. /L. Jacobelli 2001, facsimile edition of Barré 1877, with extensive commentary, Pompeii.
Gardner Coates, V.C./K. Lapatin/J.L. Seydl (eds) 2012, *The Last Days of Pompeii. Decadence Apocalypse Resurrection*, Los Angeles.
Gardner Coates, V.C./J.L. Seydl (eds) 2007, *Antiquity Recovered. The Legacy of Pompeii and Herculaneum*, Los Angeles.
Garibaldi, G. 1874, *I mille*, Turin.
Garrard, G. 2004, *Ecocriticism*, London/New York.
Garro, E. 1942, *Pompeiana juventus*, Torino.
Garrucci, R. 1853, *Questioni pompeiane*, Napels.
Gasparini, P./S. Musella 1991, *Un viaggio al Vesuvio. Il Vesuvio visto attraverso diari, lettere e resoconti di viaggi*, Naples.
Gasparri, C. (ed.) 2007, *Le sculture Farnese. Storia e documenti*, Naples.
Gautier, Th. 1970, *Poésies complètes* III, edited by R. Jasinski, Paris.
Gautier, Th. 1997, *Italia. Voyage en Italie, présenté et annoté par Marie-Hélène Girard*, Paris.
Gautier, Th. 2002, *Romans, contes et nouvelles* II (Bibliothèque de la Pléiade), Paris.
Gazda, E. 2000, *The Villa of the Mysteries in Pompeii: ancient ritual, modern muse*, Ann Arbor.
Gell, W. 1832, *Pompeiana. The Topography, Edifices, and Ornaments of Pompeii, the Result of Excavations since 1819* I–II, London.
Gell, W. 1957, *Reminiscences of Sir Walter Scott's Residence in Italy 1832*, edited by J.C. Corson, London.
Gell, W. 1976, *Sir William Gell in Italy: letters to the Society of Dilettanti, 1831–1835*, edited by Edith Clay in collaboration with Martin Frederiksen, London.
Gell, W./J.P. Gandy 1852, *Pompeiana. The Topography, Edifices, and Ornaments of Pompeii*, third edition, London (first edition, 1819).
Gengembre, G. 2006, *Le roman historique*, Paris.
Genovese, R.A. 1992, *Giuseppe Fiorelli e la tutela dei beni culturali dopo l'Unità d'Italia*, Naples.
Gere, C. 2009, *Knossos and the Prophets of Modernism*, Chicago/London.
Gerning, J.I. 1802, *Reise durch Oestreich und Italien*, Frankfurt am Main.
Getty, J.P. 1955, A Journey from Corinth, in E. Le Vaine/J.P. Getty, *Collector's Choice. The Chronicle of an Artistic Odyssey Through Europe*, London, 286–329.
Giannettasio, N.P. 1704, *Ver Herculaneum*, Naples.

Giannettasio, N.P. 1722, *Annus eruditus in partes quatuor seu stata tempora distributus*, Naples.
Gibbon, E. 1956, *Letters* I, edited by J.E. Norton, London.
Gibbon, E. 1984, *Memoirs of My Life*, Harmondsworth.
Gigante, M. 1979, *Civiltà delle forme letterarie nell'antica Pompei*, Naples.
Gigante, M. 1981, Carlo Borbone e i papiri ercolanesi, *Cronache Ercolanesi* 11, 7–18.
Gigante, M. 1982, Il Catalogo dei Papiri Ercolanesi quale contributo alla storia della Filologia Classica, in *Regione* 1982, 383–404.
Gigante, M. (ed.) 1986, *Contributi alla storia della Officina dei Papiri Ercolanesi*, Rome.
Gigante, M. (ed.) 1987, *La cultura classica a Napoli nell'Ottocento* I–II, Naples.
Gigante, M. 2003, *Leopardi e l'antico*, Bologna.
Giordani, C./I. Kahn 1965, Gli Ebrei in Pompei, in *Ercolano e le città della Campania Felix*, Pompei, 31–101
Giordani, C./I. Kahn 1974, Gli Ebrei a Pompei, *Rendiconti dell'Accademia di Archeologia Napoli* 49, 167–174
Giordani, C./I. Kahn 2001, *The Jews in Pompeii, Herculaneum, Stabiae and in the Cities of Campania Felix*, third edition, Rome 2001.
Gisborne, Th. 1833, Herculaneum, in *Translations of the Oxford and Cambridge Latin prize poems*, second series, London, 61–71.
Giudizio 1765: *Giudizio dell'opera dell'abbate Winckelmann intorno alle scoverte di Ercolano contenuto in una lettera ad un'amico*, Naples (published anonymously = Winckelmann 2001b, 139–151).
Giustiniani, V.R. 1979, *Neulateinische Dichtung in Italien 1850–1950*, Tübingen.
Glücklich, H.-J. 2008, *Pompeji lebt. 2000 Jahre Texte, Bilder, Opern und Filme*, Göttingen.
Göbel, W. 1993, *Edward Bulwer-Lytton. Systemreferenz, Funktion, literarischer Wert in seinem Erzählwerk*, Heidelberg.
Goethe in Italien 1986, exhibition catalogue, Mainz am Rhein.
Goethe, A. von 1999, *Auf einer Reise nach Süden*, edited by A. Beyer and G. Radecke, Munich/Vienna.
Goethe, J.C. 1932, *Viaggio in Italia* I–II, edited by A. Farinelli, Rome.
Goethe, J.C. 1986, 1988, *Reise durch Italien in 1740*, translated and edited by A. Meier, first and second editions, Munich.
Goethe, J.W. von 1988, *Italienische Reise*, 'Hamburger Ausgabe', Munich.
Gogol, N.V. 1982, *Arabesques*, translated by A. Tulloch, Ann Arbor, Mi.
Golden Age 1981: *The Golden Age of Naples. Art and Civilization Under the Bourbons 1734–1805*, Chicago.
Goldhill, S. 2011, *Victorian Culture and Classical Antiquity*, Princeton/Oxford.
Golding, L. 1934, *The Doomington Wanderer. A Book of Tales*, London.
Goldstein, L. 1979, The Impact of Pompeii on the Literary Imagination, *Centennial Review* 23, 227–241.
Goodman, C. 2008, *The Night Villa*, New York.
Gorden, A.R. 1990, Jérome-Charles Bellicard's Italian Notebook of 1750–51: The Discoveries at Herculaneum and Observations on Ancient and Modern Architecture, *Metropolitan Museum Journal* 25, 49–142.
Gori, A.F. 1748, *Notizie del memorabile scoprimento dell'antica città Ercolano vicino a Napoli, del suo famoso teatro*, Florence.
Grand Tour 1997: A. Wilton/I. Bignamini (eds), *Grand Tour. Il fascino dell'Italia nel XVIII secolo*, Milan (= *Grand Tour. The Lure of Italy in the Eighteenth Century*, London 1996).

Gray, D. 1829, *Le dernier jour de Pompéi, Poème, suivie de poésies diverses*, Paris.
Gray, Th. 1890, Notes of travel. France, Italy, Scotland, in D.C. Tovey, *Gray and His Friends*, Cambridge, 201–265.
Gray, Th. 1935, *Correspondence of Thomas Gray* I, edited by P. Toynbee and L.W. Libley, Oxford.
Gregorovius, F. 1872. *Euphorion. Eine Dichtung aus Pompeji in vier Gesängen*. Illustrirte Prachtausgabe mit Original-Compositionen von Theodor Grosse, Leipzig (first edition, Leipzig 1858).
Gregorovius, F. 1953, *Wanderjahren in Italien*, Cologne.
Gregorovius, F. 1991. *Römische Tagebücher 1852–1889*, edited by H.-W. Kruft and M. Völkel, Munich.
Grell, C. 1983, *Herculanum et Pompéi dans les récits des voyageurs français du XVIIIe siècle*, Naples.
Grell, C. 1995, *Le Dix-huitième siècle et l'antiquité en France 1680–1789*, Oxford.
Griener, P. 1992, *Le Antichità Etrusche Greche e Romane 1766–1776 di Pierre Hugues d'Hancarville*, Rome.
Griffa, L. 1876, *The Last Days of Pompeii, by Sir Edward Bulwer Lytton, bart. Dramatized*, Oswego N.Y.
Grillparzer, F. 1930, Schreiben des jungen *Tomes Dikson* an seinen Vater in Philadelphia, in *Sämtliche Werke, Erste Abteilung, Dreizehnter Band: Prosaschriften* 1. *Erzählungen, Satiren in Prosa, Aufsätze sur Zeitgeschichte und Politik*, Vienna, 105–106.
Grillparzer, F. n.y., *Grillparzers Werke in sechs Bänden* 5. *Novellen/Selbstbiographie/Aus den Tagebüchern*, Leipzig.
Grosley, P.J. 1769, *New Observations on Italy and its Inhabitants written in French by two Swedish Gentlemen translated into English by Thomas Nugent*, London.
Gross, N. 1989, *Senecas Naturales Quaestiones. Kompostion, naturphilosophische Aussagen und ihre Quellen*, Stuttgart.
Grün, A. 1849, Cincinnatus, in *Schutt. Dichtungen von Anastasius Grün*, ninth edition, Leipzig (first edition, Vienna 1835).
Grumach, E. 1949, *Goethe und die Antike. Eine Sammlung*, Berlin.
Guarducci, M. 1965, Il misterioso "quadrato magico": l'interpretazione di Jérôme Carecopino, e documenti nuovi, *Archeologia Classica* 17, 219–270
Guarducci, M. 1967, Le reliquie di Pietro sotto la Confessione della Basilica vaticana: una messa a punto, *Archeologia Classica* 19, 1–97, 144–145.
Guerrieri, G. 1982, Breve nota in margine alla scoperta di Ercolano, in *Regione* 1982, 99–102.
Güthenke, C. 2008, *Placing Modern Greece. The Dynamics of Romantic Hellenism, 1770–1840*, Oxford.
Gusman, P. 1899, *Pompéi. La ville – les mœurs – les arts*, Paris.
Gusman, P. 1900, *Pompei: The City, its Life and Art*, London.
Gusman, P. 1936, *Elskée. Au jardin de Vénus (Souvenirs de Pompéi). Hexaméron polychrome*, Paris.
Guzzo, P.G. (ed.) 2001, *Pompei. Scienza e società*, Naples.
Guzzo, P.G. 2003a, *Pompei 1998–2003. L'esperimento dell'autonomia*, Milan.
Guzzo, P.G. (ed.) 2003b, *Storie da un'eruzione. Pompei Ercolano Oplontis*, exhibition catalogue Naples etc., Milan (also in English, German, French and Dutch editions).
Guzzo, P.G. 2004, *Antico e archeologia*, second edition, Bologna.
Guzzo, P.G. 2007, Prefazioni, proposte e prassi pompeiane, *Archeologia Classica* 58, 571–575.
Guzzo, P.G. 2008, Intorno all'"esquisse" di Latapie, *Rivista di Studi Pompeiani* 19, 9–12.
Guzzo, P.G. 2010, Un discorso di Amedeio Maiuri alla Reale Accademia d'Italia, *Clio. Rivista trimestrale di studi storici* 46, 499–505.

Guzzo, P.G. 2011, *Pompei, tra la polvere degli scavi. Essere soprintendente a Pompei: memorie*, Naples.
Guzzo, P.G./V. Scarano Ussani 2011, Casti amanti? *Pistrina, triclinia, halicariae* a Pompei. *Vesuviana* 3, 53–66.
Guzzo, P.G./G. Tagliamonte/L. Lucchetti (eds) 2013, *Città vesuviane. Antichità e fortuna. Il suburbio e l'agro di Pompei, Ercolano, Oplontis e Stabiae*, Rome.
Hale, J.R. 1956, *The Italian Journal of Samuel Rogers, edited with an account of Roger's life and of travel in Italy in 1814–1821*, London.
Hales, S./J. Paul (eds) 2011, *Pompeii in the Public Imagination from its Discovery to Today*, Oxford.
Hall, N. 1988, *Those Women*, Dallas.
Hamilton, W. 1776, *Campi Phlegraei. Observations on the Volcanos of the Two Sicilies*, Naples.
Hamilton, W. 1777, Account of the Discoveries at Pompeii, *Archaeologia: or Miscellaneous Tracts Relating to Antiquity* 4, 160–175.
Hannestad, N. 1999, The accessibility of information in Classical Archaeology, in R.F. Docter/E.M. Moormann (eds), *Proceedings of the XVth International Congress of Classical Archaeology*, Amsterdam, 189–194.
Harder, H. 1981, *Le Président de Brosses et le Voyage en Italie au dix-huitième siècle*, Geneva.
Harris, J. 2007, *Pompeii Awakened. A Story of Rediscovery*, London/New York.
Harris, R. 2003, *Pompeii*, London.
Harrison, F. 1890, A Pompeii for the Twenty-Ninth Century, *The Eclectic Magazine of Foreign Literature, Science, and Art* n.s. 52, July-December, 599–606.
Hartlaub, F. 1955, *Das Gesamtwerk. Dichtungen. Tagebücher*, Frankfurt am Main.
Hartlaub, F. 2002, *In den eigenen Umkreis gebannt*, edited by G.L. Ewenz, Frankfurt am Main.
Haskell, F./N. Penny 1982, *Taste and the Antique*, second edition, New Haven/London.
Hayter, J. 1811, *A Report upon the Herculaneum Manuscripts, in a Second Letter, Addressed by Permission, to His Royal Highness the Prince Regent*, London.
H.D. (Hilda Doolittle) 1998, *Trilogy*. Introduction and Readers' Notes by A. Barnstone, New York.
Headley, J.T. 1845, *Letters from Italy*, London.
Heine, H. 1956, *Reisebilder. Italien*, in *Werke in einem Band ausgewählt und eingeleitet von Walther Vontin*, Hamburg, 255–380.
Hentschel, U. 1991, Die Reiseliteratur am Ausgang des 18. Jahrhunderts. Vom gelehrten Bericht zur literarischen Beschreibung, *Internationales Archiv für Sozialgeschichte der deutschen Literatur* 16, 51–83.
Helbig, W. 1868, *Wandgemälde der vom Vesuv verschütteten Städte Campaniens*, Leipzig.
Helbig, W. 1873, *Untersuchungen über die campanische Malerei*, Leipzig.
Hequet, Ch. 1869, *Une habitation romaine à Pompéï. La maison dite de Marcus-Arrius Diomèdes. Fragments et notes*, Nancy.
Herbig, R. 1956, review of Spinazzola 1953, *Göttingische Gelehrte Anzeigen* 210, 169–180.
Herbig, R. 1960, Don Carlos von Bourbon als Ausgräber von Herculaneum und Pompeji, *Madrider Mitteilungen* 1, 11–19.
Herman, J./F. Hallyn (eds) 1999, *Le topos du manuscrit trouvé. Hommages à Christian Angelet. Actes du colloque international, Louvain – Gand, 22-23-24 mai 1997*, Louvain / Paris.
Hersant, Y. 1988, *Italies. Anthologie des voyageurs français aux dix-huitième et dix-neuvième siècle*, Paris.
Hervey, C. 1785, *Letters from Portugal, Spain, Italy and Germany, in the years 1759, 1760, and 1761*, London.

Herzen, A. 1995, *Letters from France and Italy, 1847–1851*, edited and translated by Judith E. Zimmerman, Pittsburgh/London.
Heydenreich, T. 1996, Noch Einer. Theodor Friedrich Vischers Versuche (1839/1840) mit Italien, in F.-R. Hausmann (ed.), *"Italien in Germanien." Deutsche Italien-Rezeption 1750–1850*, Tübingen, 84–95.
Hirsch, J. 2007, Odysseys of Life and Death in the Bay of Naples: Roberto Rossellini's *Voyage in Italy* and Jean-Luc Godard's *Contempt*, in Gardner Coates/Seydl 2007, 271–289.
Hobden, F. 2009, History Meets Fiction in Doctor Who, 'The Fires of Pompeii': A BBC Reception of Ancient Rome on Screen and Online, Greece and Rome 56 147–163.
Höcker, O. 1889, *Die letzten Tage von Pompeji. Kulturhistorische Erzählung aus dem Jahr 79 nach Christo*, third edition, Berlin.
Hoffer, W. 1982, *Volcano. The Search for Vesuvius*, New York.
Hoffmeister, G. (ed.) 1988, *Goethe in Italy, 1786–1986: A Bi-Centennial Symposium November 14–16, 1986, University of California, Santa Barbara*, Amsterdam.
Hog, R. 1824, *Tour on the Continent in France, Switzerland, and Italy, in the years 1817 and 1818*, London.
Hogg, Th.J. 1827, *Two hundred and nine days; or, the Journal of a traveller on the continent*, London.
Hogo-Hunt, J.W./J.F. Sunavill [1870]: *The Last Daze of Pompeii: An Antiquarian Muddle*, London.
Hollander, B. 1907, *Pompeii, a dramatic Vocal and Symphonic Poem in four parts for Soli, Chorus, Orchestra and Organ. The Libretto after Bulwer Lytton's novel "The last days of Pompeii" by George H.R. Dabbs, M.D.*, London.
Hollmer, H. (ed.) 1999, *Anna Amalia von Sachsen-Weimar-Eisenach. Briefe über Italien*, St. Ingbert.
Holstenius, L. 1666, *Annotationes in Geographiam Sacram Car. a Paolo* (etc.), Rome.
Holt, E.S. 1886, *The Slave Girl of Pompeii*, London (no year indicated).
Homardiana 1861, *Homardiana, poème héroï-comique en plusieurs chants et presque en vers. Fragments attribués à Moïse lors de son ascension au Mont-Blanc, quelques jours après le passage de la Mer-Rouge, trouvés dans les ruines d'Herculanum ou de Pompéi*, Montpellier.
Hopkins, K. 1999, *A World Full of Gods. Pagans, Jews and Christians in the Roman Empire*, London.
Howells, W.D. 1988, *Italian Journeys*, Marlboro, Vermont (first edition, New York 1867).
Hufschmid, Th. 2009, *Amphitheatrum in provincia et Italia. Architektur und Nutzung römischer Amphitheater von Augusta Raurica bis Puteoli*, Augst.
Hughes, J. 1811, *Herculaneum: carmen latinum, in Theatro Sheldoniano recitatum MDCCCXI*, Oxford.
Hunink, V. 2014, *Oh Happy Place! Pompeii in 1000 Graffiti*, Rome.
Iannelli, N. 2009, *Sator: epigrafe del culto delle sacre origini di Roma*, Foggia.
Iezzi, B. 1986, Viaggiatori stranieri nell'officina dei papiri ercolanesi, in Gigante 1986, 157–188.
Illica, L. 1921, *Giove a Pompei*, Rome.
Imbriani, V. 1992, Pompei notturna. A Matteo dei principi Sturza in Miclauscheni (Romania), in F. Pusterla (ed.), *V. Imbriani, Racconti e prose (1863–1876)*, Parma, 3–21.
Imbroglia, G. (ed.) 2000, *Naples in the Eighteenth Century*, Cambridge.
Indelli, G. 1980, John Hayter e i papiri ercolanesi, *Quaderni della Biblioteca Nazionale di Napoli* serie V.2, 451–466.
Ingamells, J. 1997, *A Dictionary of British and Irish Travellers in Italy 1701–1800*, New Haven/London.
Ippel, A. 1924, *Pompeji*, Leipzig.

Iside 1992: *Alla ricerca di Iside*, exhibition catalogue, Naples.
Ittershagen, U. 1999, *Lady Hamiltons Attitüden*, Mainz am Rhein.
Jacobelli, L. (ed.) 2008, *Pompei. La costruzione di un mito. Arte, letteratura, aneddotica di un'icona turistica*, Rome.
Jacobelli, L. 2009, Pompei ricostruita nelle scenografie del melodramma L'ultimo giorno di Pompei, *Rivista di Studi Pompeiani* 20, 49–60.
Jacobelli, L. 2011, *Pompei nell'Unità d'Italia*, Pompei.
Jacobs, J. 2004, *Wiedergeburt in Rom: Goethes 'Italienische Reise' als Teil seiner Autobiographie*, Paderborn.
Jaffé, A. (ed.) 1971, *Erinnerungen, Träume, Gedanken von C.G. Jung*, Olten/Freiburg im Breisgau.
James, H. 1993, *Collected Travel Writings: The Continent. A Little Tour in France. Italian Hours. Other Travels (Works* VII), New York.
James, H. 2006, *The Complete Letters of Henry James, 1855–1873*, edited by P.A. Walker and G.W. Zacharias, Lincoln/London, II.
Jameson, Mrs. 1826 (= Anna Brownell Murphey), *Diary of an Ennuyée*, London.
Janin, F. (ed.) 2007, *Négocier sur un volcan: Dominique Vivant Denon et sa correspondence de Naples avec le comte de Vergennes (1782–1785)*, Paris etc.
Japin, A. 2003, *Een schitterend gebrek*, Amsterdam (= *Through Lucia's Eyes*, London 2005).
Janovic, V. 1988, *The house of the Tragic Poet*. Translated by Ewald Osers, Newcastle upon Tyne (Czech original *O mašince Žofince*, Prague 1984).
Jaton, A.M. 1988, *Le Vésuve et la Sirène: le mythe de Naples de Madame de Staël à Nerval*, Pisa.
Jean Paul (Richter) 1933, *Sämtliche Werke*, Erste Abteilung, Band 8–9, *Titan*, Weimar.
Jean Paul (Richter) 1961, *Werke* III, Munich.
Jenkins, I./K. Sloan (eds) 1996, *Vases & Volcanoes. Sir William Hamilton and his Collection*, London.
Johnston, P.A. 2005, Volcanoes in Classical Mythology, in M.S. Balmuth et al. (eds), *Cultural Responses to the Volcanic Landscape. The Mediterranean and Beyond*, Boston, Mass., 296–310.
Joncières, V. 1869, *Le dernier jour de Pompéi*, Paris.
Jones, J.l. 2006, *Renegades, Showmen & Angles. A Theatrical History of Fort Worth from 1873–2001*, Fort Worth.
Kaden, W. 1892, *Pompejanische Novellen und andere*, Stuttgart.
Kahn, R.A. (ed.) 1974, *Theodor Gomperz. Ein Gelehrtenleben im Bürgertum der Franz-Josefs-Zeit*, Vienna.
Kalinowka, M. 2011, The Myth of Sparta in Julius Słowacki and Cyprian Norwid's Dramas: Romantic Reinterpretation of Greek Heritage – the Polish Variant, in G. Klaniczai/M. Werner/O. Gecser (eds), *Multiple Antiquities Multiple Modernities. Ancient Histories in Nineteenth Century Europen Cultures*, Frankfurt/New York, 547–562.
Kammerer-Grothaus, H. 1981, Die erste Aufstellung der Antiken aus den Vesuvstädten in Portici, in H. Beck et al. (eds), *Antikensammlungen im 18. Jahrhundert*, Berlin, 11–20.
Kammerer-Grothaus, H. (ed.) 1998, *›Voyage d'Italie‹ (1755). Markgräfin Wilhelmine von Bayreuth im Königreich Neapel*, Stendal.
Kanceff, E. (ed.) 2003, *Stendhal, L'Italie, le voyage. Mélanges offerts à V. Del Litto*, Moncalieri.
Kanceff, E./R. Lewanski (eds) 1988, *Viaggiatori polacchi in Italia*, Geneva.
Kanceff, E./R. Rampone (eds) 1992, *"Viaggio nel sud"* II. *Verso la Calabria*, Geneva.
Kassies, W. 1989, *En Alexander is een schim in mij. Stukjes antiek bij Gerrit Achterberg*, Leiden.
Keerl, J.H. 1791, *Ueber die Ruinen Herkulanums und Pompeji. Nebst einer kurzen Beschreibung von den Schauspielen der alten Römer und Griechen*, Gotha.

Kendon, A. 2000 (translation of), *Andrea de Jorio, Gesture in Naples and Gesture in Classical Antiquity*, Bloomington/Indianapolis (see De Jorio 1832).
Keogh, M. 1842, *Herculaneum & Pompeii, and other poems*, London.
Kephalides, A.W. 1822, *Reise durch Italien und Sicilien*, second edition, Leipzig (first edition, Leipzig 1818).
Kidwell, C. 1993, *Sannazaro and Arcadia*, London.
Kimball, F. 1953, The Reception of the Art of Herculaneum in France, in *Studies Presented to D.M. Robinson*, Washington/S. Louis Miss., II, 1254–1256.
Kimbell, D. 1991, *Italian opera*, Cambridge.
King, M.F./E. Engel 1981, The Emerging Carlylean Hero in Bulwer's Novels of the 1830s, *Nineteenth-Century Fiction* 36, 277–295.
Kinnard, R./T. Davis 1992, *Divine Images. A History of Jesus on the Screen*, New York.
Kneale, J.D. 2010, Italy Visited and Revisited; Wordsworth's 'Magnificent Debt', in C. Bode/J. Labbe (eds), *Romantic Localities. Europe Writes Places*, London, 185–196.
Knight, C. 1979, William Robinson ufficiale dei marines britannici 'scopritore' di Oplontis, *Cronache Pompeiane* 5, 156–173.
Knight, C. 1995, *Sulle orme del Grand Tour. Uomini, luoghi, società del Regno di Napoli*, Naples.
Knight, C. 2002, Canguri e papiri, *Cronache Ercolanesi* 32, 305–320.
Knight, C. 2003, *Hamilton a Napoli. Cultura, svaghi, civiltà di una grande capitale europea*, Naples.
Kockel, V. 1983, *Die Grabbauten vor dem Herkulaner Tor in Pompeji*, Mainz am Rhein.
Kockel, V. 1993, Das Haus des Sallust in Pompeji. Eine dreidimensionale Dokumentation aus dem 19. Jahrhundert, in W. Helmberger/V. Kockel (eds), *Rom über die Alpen tragen. Fürsten sammeln antike Architektur: Die Aschaffenburger Korkmodelle*, Landshut/Ergolding, 119–134, 345–347.
Kockel, V. 2000, Archäologie und Politik. Francesco Piranesi und seine drei Pompeji-Pläne, *Rivista di Studi Pompeiani* 11, 33–46.
Kockel, V. 2002, Pompeji, in *Der neue Pauly* 15/2, 472–490.
Kockel, V. 2006, *Pompei 360⁰. I due Panorami di Carl Georg Enslen del 1836/ Pompeji 360⁰. Die zwei Panoramen Carl Georg Enslens aus dem Jahre 1836*, Milan.
Körber, Ph.W. 1848, *Diomedes und Clodius: Erzählung aus den letzten Tagen von Pompeji*, Nürnberg.
Kopp, D. 2010, *"Goethe Pater". Johann Caspar Goethe (1710–1782)*, Frankfurt am Main.
Kovacs, C.L. 2013, Pompeii and its material reproductions: the rise of a tourist site in the nineteenth century, *Journal of Tourism History* 5, 25–49.
Krausser, H. 2004, *Die wilden Hunde von Pompeii*, Reinbek bei Hamburg.
Krebs, C.B. 2011, *A Most Dangerous Book. Tacitus's* Germania *from the Roman Empire to the Third Reich*, New York/London.
Krohn, B. 2007, *Was im Dunkeln bleibt. Ein Neapel-Krimi*, Munich.
Kulczycki, L. 1897, *Il Palazzo di Nerone, Elegia antica, Isella*, Rome.
La Rocca, E./M. and A. de Vos 1976, *Guida archeologica di Pompei*, Milan.
La Rochefoucauld, S. 2001, *Le mystère de Pompéi*, n.p.
La Rosa, L.A. 2010, *Vesuvio. Il Grand Tour dell'Accademia Ercolanese dal passato al futuro*, Naples 2010.
La Tourette, J. 1975, *The Pompeii Scroll*, New York.
Lacerenza, G. 2001, Per un riesame della presenza ebraica a Pompei, *Materia giudaica. Rivista dell'Associazione italiana per lo studio del giudaismo* 6, 99–103.

Lacerenza, G. 2004, La realtà documentaria e il mito romantico della presenza giudaica a Pompei, in F. Senatore (ed.), *Pompei, Capri e la Penisola Sorrentina*, Capri, 245–271.

Lagrèze, G.-B. de 1887, *Une visite à Pompéi*, Paris.

Lagrèze, G.-B. de 1889, *Pompéi, Les catacombes, L'Alhambra. Étude à l'aide des monuments de la vie païenne à son déclin, de la vie chrétienne à son aurore, de la vie musulmane à son apogée*, third edition, Paris (first edition, Paris 1872).

Lamers, P. 1995, *Il viaggio nel Sud dell'Abbé de Saint-Non : il Voyage pittoresque à Naples et en Sicile : la genesi, i disegni preparatori, le incisioni*, Naples.

Lampe, P. 2003, *From Paul to Valentinus. Christians in Rome in the First Two Centuries*, Minneapolis.

Lantier, E.-F. 1795, 1798, *Voyages d'Anténor en Grèce et en Asie*, first and second editions, Paris.

Lasky, K. 2007, The *Last Girls of Pompeii*, New York.

Lazer, E. 2009, *Resurrecting Pompeii*, London/New York.

Latapie, F. de Paule 1953, Description des fouilles de Pompéii, edited by P. Barrière and A. Maiuri, *Rendiconti dell'Accademia di Archeologia Napoli* 28, 223–248.

Lawrence, C. 2001, *The Roman Mysteries. The Secrets of Vesuvius*, London.

Lawrence, C. 2002, *The Roman Mysteries. The Pirates of Pompeii*, London.

Le Ninèze, A. 2008, *Sator. L'énigme du carré magique. Roman historique*, Arles.

Le R(iche), J.M. 1820, *Antiquités des environs de Naples, et dissertations qui y sont relatives*, Naples.

Leander Touati, A.-M. (ed.) forthcoming, Returns to Pompeii. Interior space and decoration documented and revived. 18th to 20th century, Opuscula Romana.

Lefevre, E. 2006, Die sentimentale Erinnerung der Humanisten an antiken Stätten und Sannazaros Cumae-Elegie, in E. Schäfer (ed.), *Sannazaro und die Augusteische Dichtung*, Tübingen, 49–68.

Leibetseder, M. 2004, *Die Kavalierstour. Adelige Erziehungsreisen im 17. und 18. Jahrhundert*, Cologne.

Lemercier, A. 1841, *Les derniers jours de Pompéi*, Tours.

Lemercier de Longpré, C. Baron d'Haussez 1835, *Voyage d'un exilé de Londres à Naples et en Sicile*, Paris.

Lenk, F. 2002, *Anschlag auf Pompeji. Ein Ratekrimi aus der Römerzeit*, Bindlach.

Leontyev, G. 1996, *Karl Briullov, Artist of Russian Romanticism*, Burnemouth/St. Petersburg.

Leopardi, G. 1987, *Poesie e prose*, edited by R. Damiani and M.A. Rigon, Milan.

Leopardi, G. 1991, *Zibaldone dei pensieri*, edited by G. Pacella, Milan.

Lepelley, C. 2000, Les chrétiens et l'empire romain, in L. Petri (ed.), *Histoire du Christianisme des origines à nos jours* I. *Le nouveau peuple (Des origines à 250)*, Paris, 227–266.

Leppmann, W. 1966, *Pompeji. Eine Stadt in Literatur und Leben*, Munich (= *Pompeii in Fact and Fiction*, London 1968).

Lerme-Walter, M. 1968, *Les enfants de Pompéi ou Le Jeu du roi*, Paris/Verona.

Leroy, I. 2009, *Le panorama de la bataille de Waterloo*, Waterloo.

Leroy du Lardonnoy, É. 2012, Le voyage de Grillparzer à Rome en 1819 ou les affaires d'un épigone, in J.C. D'Amico et al. (eds), *Le mythe de Rome en Europe*, Caen, 197–209.

Levi, P. 1984, *Ad ora incerta. Poesie*, Milan.

Lipinsky, A. 1983, Goethe und Schiller erleben Pompeji und Herculaneum, *Pompeii Herculaneum Stabiae* 1, 289–296.

Lewald, F. 1847, *Italienisches Bilderbuch*, Berlin.

Lingg, H. 1883, *Clytia. Eine Szene aus Pompeji*, Munich.

Lins, O. 1980, *Avalovara*, translated from the Portuguese by Gregory Rabassa, New York (original edition, São Paulo 1973).
Llewellyn, R. 1955, *The Flame of Hercules. The Story of a Fugitive Galley Slave*, Garden City N.Y.
Lo Gatto, E. 1971, *Russi in Italia dal secolo XVII ad oggi*, Rome.
Lochman, T. et al. 2008, *Antike im Kino: auf dem Weg zu einer Kulturgeschichte des Antikenfilms*, Basel.
Loewenberg, A. 1978, *Annals of Opera 1597–1940*, Totowa NJ.
Longo Auricchio, F. 1986, La figura del P. Antonio Piaggio nel carteggio Martorelli-Vargas, in *I papiri ercolanesi* 4, Rome, 15–23.
Longo Auricchio, F. 1997, Le prime scoperte a Ercolano, *Cronache Ercolanesi* 27, 175–179.
Longo Auricchio, F. 2000, La Villa Ercolanese dei Papiri: storia delle scoperte e vita dell'Officina dal Museo di Portici al Palazzo Reale di Napoli, *Cronache Ercolanesi* 30, 11–20.
Longo Auricchio, F./M. Capasso 1980, Nuove accessioni al dossier Piaggio, in *Contributi* 1980, 17–59.
Longobardi, G. 2002, *Pompei sostenibile*, Rome.
López Martínez, M.P./A.M. Sabater Beltrá 2011, Los papiros de Herculano en la España de finales del siglo XVIII y comienzos del XIX, *Cronache Ercolanesi* 41, 261–271.
Lothane, Z. 2010, The Lessons of a Classic Revisited: Freud on Jensen's *Gradiva*, *Psychoanalytic Review* 97(5), 789–817.
Loubinoux, G. 1998, L'ultimo giorno di Pompei (Le dernier jour de Pompéï), opéra de Giovanni Pacini et Andrea Leone Tottola, in *Vesuvio* 1988, 497–508.
Lowry, M. 1961, *Hear us O Lord from heaven thy dwelling place*, London.
Lühning, H. 1983, Titus-*Vertonungen im 18. Jahrhundert. Untersuchungen zur Tradition der Opera Seria von Hasse bis Mozart*, Volkach.
Lukács, G. 1965, *Der historische Roman. Probleme des Realismus* III (*Werke* 6), Neuwied/Berlin (first, Hungarian edition, Budapest 1937).
Lullin de Chateauvieux, F. 1820, *Lettres écrites d'Italie en 1812 et 13, à M.r Charles Pictet*, second edition, Geneva/Paris.
Lumisden, A. 1797, *Remarks on the Antiquities of Rome and its Environs*, London.
Lundgren, M. 2001, *Pompeji*, Stockholm.
Lytton, V.A.G. R. Earl of 1913, *The Life of Edward Bulwer first Lord Lytton*, London.
Mączak, A. 2003, Gentlemen's Europe: Nineteenth-Century Handbooks for Travellers, *Annali d'italianistica* 26, 347–362.
Mafrici, M. (ed.) 2010, *All'ombra della Corte. Donne e potere nella Napoli borbonica (1734–1860)*, Naples.
Maiuri, A. 1931, *Pompei. I nuovi scavi e la Villa dei Misteri*, Rome.
Maiuri, A. 1950, Gli scavi di Pompei dal 1879 al 1948, in *Pompeiana*, Naples, 9–40.
Maiuri, A. 1998, *Pompei ed Ercolano fra case ed abitanti*, Naples (first edition, Naples 1958).
Maizony de Lauréal, J.-S.-F. 1837, *L'Héracléade ou Herculanum enseveli sous la lave du Vésuve, poëme de L.A. Florus*, Paris.
Malamud, M. 2009, *Ancient Rome and Modern America*, Chichester.
Malinowski, W.M. 1989, *Le roman historique en France après le romanticisme 1870–1914*, Poznán.
Mallet, D. 1728, *The Excursion. A Poem in Two Cantos*, London.
Mallet, D. 1759, *The Works of D. Mallet*, London.
Manacorda, D. 1982, Per un'indagine sull'archeologia italiana durante il ventennio fascista, *Archeologia medievale* 9, 443–470.

Manacorda, D./R. Tamassia 1985, *Il piccone del regime*, Rome.
Manfredi, V.M. 1996, *La torre della solitudine*, Milan (English translation, London 2006).
Mansell, Wm. L. 1871, *Ione; The Last Days of Pompeii*, London.
Márai, S. 2001, *Tagebücher 6. 1945-1957*, ausgewählt und aus dem Ungarischen übersetzt von Paul Kárpáti, Berlin.
Marose, M. 2005, *Unter der Tarnkappe. Felix Hartlaub. Eine Biographie*, Berlin.
Martin, F. 2002, *L'Antiquité au cinéma*, Paris.
Martin, R.K./L.S. Person (eds) 2002, *Roman Holidays. American Writers and Artists in Nineteenth-Century Italy*, Iowa City.
Martin, S. 1831, *Narrative of a Three Years' Residence in Italy, 1819-1822. With illustrations of the present state of religion in that country*, second edition, Dublin (first edition, 1828).
Martinet, M.-M. 1996, *Les voyages d'Italie dans les littératures européennes*, Paris.
Martínez, J. (ed.) 2011, *Fakes and Forgers of Classical Literature / Falsificaciones y falsarios de la Literatura Clásica*, Madrid.
Martini, G.H. 1779, *Das gleichsam auflebende Pompeji. Oder Versuch einer Geschichte dieser Stadt* [etc.], Leipzig.
Mattusch, C.C. 2005, *The Villa dei Papiri at Herculaneum. Life and Afterlife of a Sculpture Collection*, Los Angeles.
Mattusch, C.C. (ed.) 2008, *Pompeii and the Pompeian Villa*, Washington.
Mattusch, C.C. (ed.) 2013, *Rediscovering the Ancient World on the Bay of Naples, 1710-1890*, New Haven/London.
Mau, A. 1902, *Pompeii, Its Life and Art*, London.
Mau, A. 1908, *Pompeji in Leben und Kunst*, second edition, Leipzig.
Mauclair, C./J.-F. Bouchor 1928, *Naples et son golfe. Trente planches en couleurs d'après les tableaux du peintre*, Paris.
Maulucci Vivolo, F.P. 1990, *E l'acqua zampillerà dal deserto. Testimonianze giudaiche e cristiane a Pompei prima del 79*, Naples.
Maurois, A. 1928, *Les derniers jours de Pompéi*, Paris.
Maxwell, R./K. Trumpener (eds) 2008, *The Cambridge Companion to Fiction in the Romantic Period*, Cambridge.
Mayer, D. 1994, *Playing out the Empire. Ben Hur and other Toga Plays and Films, 1883-1908. A critical Anthology*, Oxford.
Mayer-Flaschberger, M. 1984, *Marie Eugenie delle Grazie (1864-1931). Eine Österreichische Dichterin der Jahrhundertwende. Studien zu ihrer mittleren Schaffensperiode*, Munich.
Maynial, E. 1922, *Les Robinsons de Pompéi*, Paris.
Mazois, F. 1819, 1822, *Le palais de Scaurus, ou description d'une maison romaine, fragment d'un voyage fait à Rome, vers la fin de la République, par Mérovir, prince des Suèves*, first and second editions, Paris.
Mazois, F. 1820, *Der Pallast des Scaurus oder Beschreibung eines römischen Stadthauses. Bruchstück aus dem Tagebuch Merovirs, eines suevischen Königssohns, über seine gegen das Ende der Republik nach Rom unternommene Reise*, edited and translated by K.Chr. and E.F.Wüstemann, Gotha/Erfurt.
Mazois, F. 1824, 1829, 1838, *Les ruines de Pompéi*, Paris, I-II, III, IV.
McIlwane, I.C. 1988, *Herculaneum. A Guide to Printed Sources*, Naples.
McIlwane, I.C. 2009, *Herculaneum. A Guide to Printed Sources, 1980-2007*, Naples.
Medina, L.H. 1857, *The Last Days of Pompeii*, New York.

Melini, R. 2007, Un illustre musicologo al Museo di Portici: Charles Burney e l'archeologia musicale del Settecento, *Rivista di Studi Pompeiani* 18, 87–94.
Meller, H./J.-A. Dickmann 2011, *Pompeji-Nola-Herculaneum. Katastrophen am Vesuv*, Munich.
Melton, W. 1974, *Nine Lives to Pompeii. A Novel of Suspense*, New York.
Menduni de' Rossi, S. 2011, *Il prodigio del sistro dalla Pompei sepolta*, Sorrento.
Menichelli, G. 1962, *Viaggiatori francesi nell'Italia dell'Ottocento*, Rome.
Mercier, A. 1980, *Edouard Schuré et le renouveau idéaliste en Europe*, Lille/Paris.
Merkle, G. 1989, *Die Ephemeris Belli Troiani des Diktys von Kreta*, Frankfurt am Main.
Méry, J. 1834, *Herculanum ou l'Orgie romaine*, Paris.
Méry, J. 1837, *Scènes de la vie italienne* Paris.
Méry, J./T. Hadot 1859, *Herculanum, grand opéra en quatre actes par M.M. Méry et Hadot. Musique de M. Félicien David*, Paris.
Messika, N. 2008, *Adamah Shehora*, Rosh Pina.
Metastasio, P. 1892, *Drammi scelti*, Milan.
Meuris, E. 1868, *Glaucus et Arbaces ou le dernier jour de Pompeïa*, Limoges/Paris.
Meyer, F.J.L. 1792, *Darstellungen aus Italien*, Berlin.
Michel, Ch. 1984, Les peintures d'Herculanum et la Querelle des Anciens et des Modernes (1740–1760), *Bulletin de la Société de l'Histoire de l'Art français*, 105–117.
Michel, Ch. 1991, *Le voyage d'Italie de Charles Nicolas Cochin (1758)*, Rome.
Michel, Ch. 1993, *Charles Nicolas Cochin et l'art des Lumières*, Rome.
Micheletti, P. 1846, *Storia dei monumenti del Reame delle Due Sicilie*, Naples.
Mielke, G. 1999, *Die verflixten Fälle aus Pompeji*, Gaggenau.
Migliacci, D. 1765, *Riflessioni Sopra al Tempio d'ISIDE, nuovamente cavato nel corrente anno 1765. di là della Torre dell'Annunziata nel luogo detta* la Taverna del Rapillo, *nella città che si crede di* Pompei, *atterrata di ceneri, e sabbione dalla primiera eruttazione del Vesuvio sotto l'Imperadore* Tito Vespasiano *nell'anno 81. dell'Era corrente*, Naples.
Mikocki, T. 1988, *A la recherche de l'art antique. Les voyageurs polonais en Italie dans les années 1750–1830*, Wroclaw.
Milanesi, G. 1944, *Sancta Maria*, twelfth edition, Milan (first edition, Milan 1936).
Miller, A. 1776, *Letters from Italy, describing the Manners, Customs, Antiquities, Paintings, &c. of that Country, in the years MDCCLXX and MDCCLXXI, to a Friend Residing in France*, London (published anonymously).
Millin de Grandmaison, A.L. 1813, *Description des tombeaux qui ont été découvertes à Pompeï dans l'année 1812*, Naples.
Miltoun, F. 1909, *Italian Highways and Byways from a Motor Car*, Boston.
Mirabelli, A. 1879, *Versi in occasione del XVIII Centenario dalla destruzione di Pompei recitati da' due academici Mirabelli e Guanciali nella tornata de' IX di settembre MDCCCLXXIX*, Naples.
Mitchell, J. 1845, *Notes from Over Sea: Consisting of Observations made in Europe in the Years 1843 and 1844: Adressed to a Brother*, New York.
Mitchell, L. 2003, *Bulwer Lytton. The Rise and Fall of a Victorian Man of Letters*, London/New York.
Miziołek, J. 2010, *Muse, Baccanti e Centauri. I capolavori della pittura pompeiana e la loro fortuna in Polonia*, Warsaw.
Moe, N. 2002, *The View from Vesuvius. Italian Culture and the Southern Question*, Berkeley/Los Angeles/London.
Mols, S.T.A.M. 1999a, *Wooden Furniture in Herculaneum. Form, Technique and Function*, Amsterdam.

Mols, S.T.A.M. 1999b, Ricerche archeologiche olandesi nell'area vesuviana (1841–1999), in F. Senatore (ed.), *Pompei, il Vesuvio e la Penisola Sorrentina*, Rome, 69–89.
Mols, S.T.A.M./E.M. Moormann 2005 (eds), *Omni pede stare. Saggi architettonici e vesuviani in memoriam Jos de Waele*, Naples.
Monnier, M. 1865, *Pompéi et les Pompéiens*, second edition, Paris.
Monod, J. n.y., *La cité antique de Pompéi. Histoire – fouilles – monuments – rues – maisons – mœurs – vie intime – inscriptions*, Paris.
Monteix, N. 2010, *Les lieux de métier. Boutiques et ateliers d'Herculanum*, Rome.
Montfort, N. 1917, *Nydia and other poems*, Kansas City Missoury.
Monti, V. 1797, *La Musogonia. Canto unico*, Venice.
Monti, V. 1998, *Poesie (1797–1803)*, edited by L. Frassineti, Ravenna.
Moormann, E.M. 1991, Destruction and Restoration of Campanian Mural Paintings in the 18th and 19th Centuries, in S. Cather (ed.), *The Conservation of Wall Paintings*, Malibu, 87–101
Moormann, E.M. 2001, Una città mummificata: qualche aspetto della fortuna di Pompei nella letteratura europea ed americana, in Guzzo 2001, 9–18.
Moormann, E.M. 2003a, Guides in the Vesuvius Area Eternalised in Travelogues and Fiction, *Rivista di Studi Pompeiani* 14, 31–48.
Moormann, E.M. 2003b, *Pompéi à la grecque*: A Roman City with a Greek Mask, in M. Haagsma et al. (eds), *The Impact of Classical Greece on European and National Identities. Proceedings of an international colloquium, held at the Netherlands Institute at Athens, 2–4 October 2000*, Amsterdam, 241–265.
Moormann, E.M. 2003c, Evocazioni letterarie dell'antica Pompei, in Guzzo 2003b, 15–33.
Moormann, E.M. 2005, The Sense of Time in Early Studies on Pompeii, in Mols/Moormann 2005, 335–342.
Moormann, E.M. 2006, Jews and Christians at Pompeii in Fiction and Faction, in S. Mucznik (ed.), *Kalathos. Studies in Honour of Asher Ovadiah*, Tel Aviv, 53–76.
Moormann, E.M. 2007, Questa rovina viva; Pompei nella letteratura del secondo Ottocento, in *Alma Tadema* 2007, 123–137.
Moormann, E.M. 2008, Pompéi et Herculanum éternisées dans des romans historiques français, in F. Galtier/Y. Perrin (eds), *Ars pictoris, ars scriptoris. Peinture, littérature, histoire. Mélanges offerts à Jean-Michel Croisille*, Clermont-Ferrand, 377–391.
Moormann, E.M. 2010, Fictitious Manuscripts from Herculaneum, Pompeii and Antiquity, *Cronache Ercolanesi* 40, 239–250.
Moormann, E.M. 2011a, Christians and Jews at Pompeii in Late Nineteenth-Century Fiction, in Hales/Paul 2011, 171–184.
Moormann, E.M. 2011b, Three Generations of Goethes at Herculaneum and Pompeii, in A.J.P. Raat/W.R.E. Velema/C. Baar-de Weerd (eds), *De Oudheid in de Achttiende Eeuw; Classical antiquity in the Eighteenth Century* (Congresreeks Werkgroep 18e Eeuw nummer 1), Utrecht, 127–138.
Moormann, E.M. 2013, Pompeii in Neo-Latin Poetry from Nineteenth-Century Italy, in *Interpretando l'antico. Scritti di archeologia offerti a Maria Bonghi Jovino* (Quadern di ACME 134), Milan, II, 821–847.
Morgan, S.O. 1821, *Italy*, Paris.
Moritz, K.Ph. 1997, *Reisen eines Deutschen in Italien*, in H. Hollmer/A. Meier (eds), *Werke in zwei Bänden*, Frankfurt am Main, II (first edition, Berlin 1792–1793).
Moritz, P. 1892, *Die letzten Tage von Pompeji: eine Erzählung für die Jugend*, Stuttgart.
Morris, C. 1992, *Fanny Wright. Rebel in America*, Urbana/Chicago.

Morton, M.W. 1896, *Scenes from The Last Days of Pompeii*, Philadelphia.
Motekat, H. 1986, Der bronzene Kandelaber. Ferdinand Gregorovius und sein Versepos "Euphorion", in F. Kienecker/P. Wolfersdorf (eds), *Dichtung Wissenschaft Unterricht. Rüdiger Frommholz zum 60. Geburtstag*, Paderborn, 215–227.
Mouritsen, H. 1988, *Elections, Magistrates and Municipal Élite. Studies in Pompeian Epigraphy*, Rome.
Moussinot 1748 > D'Arthenay 1748.
Mozart, W.A. 1962, *Mozart. Briefe und Aufzeichnungen* I. *1755–1776*, edited by W.A. Bauer and O.E. Deutz, Kassel.
Mozzillo, A. 1992, *La frontiera del Grand Tour. Viaggi e viaggiatori nel Mezzogiorno borbonico*, Naples.
Muck, J. 1887, *Die Nazarener in Pompeji*. Große romantische Oper in vier Akten, frei nach Bulwer, von C. Gollmick und L. Bauer, Darmstadt.
Mühlenbrock, J./D. Richter 2005 (eds), *Verschüttet vom Vesuv. Die letzten Stunden von Herculaneum*, Mainz am Rhein.
Müllenbrock, H.-J. 1980, *Der historische Roman*, Heidelberg.
Müllenbrock, H.-J. 2003, *Der historische Roman. Aufsätze*, Heidelberg.
Müller, A. 2012, *Sehnsucht nach Wissen. Friederike Brun, Elisa von der Recke und die Altertumskunde um 1800*, Berlin.
Müller, C.O. 1908, *Lebensbild in Briefen an seine Eltern mit dem Tagebuch seiner italienisch-griechischen Reise*, edited by O. and E. Kern, Berlin.
Müller, G.A. 1900, *Römische Liebesopfer. Drei realistische Novellen*, Berlin, n.y.
Müller, G.A. 1910, *Das sterbende Pompeji. Ein Roman aus Pompejis letzten Tagen*, Leipzig.
Müller, K. 2011, *Die Ehrenbogen in Pompeji*, Wiesbaden.
Mullen, R./J. Munson 2009, *The Smell of the Continent. The British Discover Europe 1814–1914*, London.
Mullett, C.F. 1957, Englishmen discover Herculaneum and Pompeii, *Archaeology* 10, 31–38.
Murray, J. 1873, 1883, *A Handbook for Travellers in Southern Italy*, seventh and eighth editions, London.
Museo Borbonico: Real Museo Borbonico, I–XVI, Naples 1824 (1829)–1867.
Nerval, G. de 1989, 1993, *Oeuvres complètes* I, III (Bibliothèque de la Pléiade), Paris.
Neumann, F.-W. 1993, *Der englische historische Roman im 20. Jahrhundert*, Heidelberg.
Neutsch, B. 1975, Pompeiana in Weimar, in *Neue Forschungen in Pompeji*, Recklinghausen, 317–330.
New Grove: The New Grove dictionary of music and musicians, London 1980–.
Niccolini, F. and F. 1854–1896, *Le case ed i monumenti di Pompei disegnati e descritti* I–IV, Naples.
Niccolini, F. and F. 1997, *Le case ed i monumenti di Pompei nell'opera di Fausto e Felice Niccolini*, Novara (also in other languages).
Nicolai, C. 1818, *Das Grab am Vesuv*, Quedlinburg/Leipzig.
Nicolai, G. 1835, *Italien wie es wirklich ist* I–II, second edition, Leipzig.
Nieritz, G. 1850, *Pompeji's letzte Tage*, Berlin.
Nietzsche, F. 1975–2004, *Briefwechsel* I–XX, Berlin/New York.
Nietzsche, F. 1988, *Kritische Gesamtausgabe*, I–XV, Berlin/New York.
Nippel, W. 2003, Der Apostel Paulus – ein Jude als römischer Bürger, in K.-J. Hölkeskamp et al. (eds), *Sinn (in) der Antike. Orientierungssysteme, Leitbilder und Wertkonzepte im Altertum*, Mainz am Rhein, 357–374.
Nisard, C. (ed.) 1877, *Correspondance inédite du Comte de Caylus avec le P. Paciaudi Théatin (1757–1765) suivi de celles de l'Abbé Barthélemy e de P. Mariette avec le même*, Paris.

Norwid, C.K. 1968, *Pisma wybrane 2. Poematy*, edited by J.W. Gomulicki, Warsaw.
Norwid, C.K. 1974, *Wybór poezji – Choix de poèmes*, traduits par Feliks Kanoplia, Cracow.
Northall, J. 1766, *Travels through Italy*, London.
Nothomb, A. 1996, *Péplum*, Paris.
Nouguès, J. 1912, *La Danseuse de Pompéi*. Opéra-ballet en cinq actes et huit tableaux d'après le roman de Jean Bertheroy, Paris.
Oettel, A. 1996, *Fundkontexte römischer Vesuvvillen im Gebiet um Pompeji*, Mainz am Rhein.
Oleksijczuk, D.B. 2011, *The First Panoramas. Visions of British Imperialism*, Minneapolis/London.
Olmos Romera, R. 1993a, La arqueologia soñada. Los últimos días de Pompeya de E. Bulwer-Lytton, *Revista de Arqueología* 14, no. 141, 52–58.
Olmos Romera, R. 1993b, La arqueologia soñada. La Isis de Gerardo de Nerval, *Revista de Arqueología* 14, no. 146, 46–53.
Olmos Romera, R. 1993c, La arqueologia soñada. Arria Marcella de Théophile Gautier, *Revista de Arqueología* 14, no. 147, 50–57.
Opitz, M. 1644, *Weltliche Poemata* I, Frankfurt am Main (= facsimile, Tübingen 1967).
Orel, H. 1995, *The Historical Novel from Scott to Sabatini*, Houndmills/London.
Orloff, G. 1819–1821, *Mémoires historiques, politiques et littéraires sur le Royaume de Naples*, Paris.
Orrells, D. 2010, Derrida's Impressions of *Gradiva: Archive Fever* and Antiquity, in M. Leonard (ed.), *Derrida and Antiquity*, Oxford, 159–184.
Ossanna Cavadini, N. (ed.) 1995, *Pietro Bianchi (1787–1849) architetto e archeologo*, exhibition catalogue, Rancate/Milan.
Osterkamp. E. 1993, Vom Ideal der "mäßigen Form". Ferdinand Gregorovius als Dichter, in A. Esch/J. Petersen (eds), *Ferdinand Gregorovius und Italien. Eine kritische Würdigung*, Tübingen, 185–202.
Overbeck, J. 1856, 1866, 1875, *Pompeji in seinen Gebäuden, Alterthümern und Kunstwerken für Kunst- und Alterthumsfreunde*, first, second, third editions, Leipzig.
Overbeck, J./A. Mau 1884, *Pompeji in seinen Gebäuden, Alterthümern und Kunstwerken*, fourth edition, Leipzig.
Pabst, A. 1851, *Die letzten Tage von Pompeji*. Große Oper in vier Akten, Dresden.
Pace, S. 2000, *Ercolano e la cultura europea tra Settecento e Novecento*, Naples.
Pacini, G. 1865, *Le mie memorie artistiche*, Florence.
Paderni, C. 2000, *Monumenti antichi rinvenuti nei reali scavi di Ercolano e Pompej & delineati e spiegati da D Camillo Paderni Romano*, edited by U. Pannuti, Naples.
Pagano, M. 1993, Il teatro di Ercolano, *Cronache Ercolanesi* 13, 121–151.
Pagano, M. 1997a, *I diari di scavo di Pompei, Ercolano e Stabia di Francesco e Pietro La Vega*, Rome.
Pagano, M. 1997b, Ercolano e il padre Piaggio nel viaggio a Napoli di Tommaso Puccini (1783), *Cronache Ercolanesi* 27, 169–174.
Pagano, M. (ed.) 2000, *Gli antichi Ercolanesi. Antropologia, società, economia*, Naples.
PAH I–III: I. Fiorelli, *Pompeianarum antiquitatum historia* I–III, Naples 1860–1864.
Pagliara, G. 2003, *Giallo pompeiano*, Castel Maggiore.
Palermo, S. 1792, 1969, *Notizie del bello, dell'antico, e del curioso che contengono le reali ville di Portici, Resina, lo scavamento di Pompejano, Capodimonte Cardito, Caserta, e S. Leucio che servono di continuazione all'opera del canonico Carlo Celano*, first edition and reprint, Naples (published anonymously).
Pannuti, U. 1983, Il 'Giornale degli scavi' di Ercolano (1738–1756), *Memorie dell'Accademia dei Lincei* Serie 8, Vol. 26, Fasc. 3, 159–410.

Pannuti, U. 2000, Incisori e disegnatori della stamperia reale di Napoli nel secolo XVIII. La pubblicazione delle *Antichità di Ercolano, Xenia Antiqua* 9, 151–178.
Paoletta, E. 1989, *Svelato il mistero della Pompeiana Villa dei Misteri. Il dramma di Ottavia e il trionfo di Poppea nella trama di Aniceto e nelle pitture di Glicone attraverso un filo di Arianna epigrafico e una scabrosa sequenza di epigrafi e figurazioni minori*, Naples.
Papaccio, V. 1992, Il progetto di Ferdinando Fuga per il Museo Ercolanese di Portici. Con un carteggio inedito, *Cronache Ercolanesi* 22, 197–202.
Papaccio, V. 1995, *Marmi ercolanesi in Francia. Storia di alcune distrazioni del principe E.M. d'Elbeuf*, Naples.
Parisi, C. 2000, *Ercolano: profili e figure*, Naples.
Parker Willis, N. 1835, *Pencillings by the Way*, London.
Parslow, C.C. 1995, *Rediscovering Antiquity. Karl Weber and the Excavation of Herculaneum, Pompeii, and Stabiae*, Cambridge.
Pascolini, R. 2006, *Il Vangelo di Pompei: il messaggio scritto da Gesù nel Quadrato magico. Un mistero svelato dopo duemila anni*, Vicenza.
Passio 2008: *Passio Perpetuae et Felicitatis*, edited by M. Formigano, Milan.
Patanè, S. 2007, *Nel cuore e nell'anima di POMPEI*, Naples.
Patterson, M.A. 1932, *Sumner Lincoln Fairfield 1803–1844*, PhD Yale.
Pellegrino, C. 2004, *Ghosts of Vesuvius. A new look on the last days of Pompeii, how towns fall, and other strange connections*, New York.
Pemble, J. 1987, *The Mediterranean Passion. Victorians and Edwardians to the South*, London.
Peri, C. 1996, *Avventura a Pompei*, Milan.
Pernice, E. 1926, *Pompeji*, Leipzig.
Perosi, M. 1912, *Pompeji*. Oper in vier Aufzügen, Dichtung frei nach Bulwer, von Karl Schreder und Robert Maria Prosl, Vienna.
Perotti, N. 1994, *Cornu copiae, seu, Linguae latinae commentarii* IV, edited by M. Pade and J. Ramminger, Sassoferrato.
Pesando, F./M.P. Guidobaldi 2006, *Pompei, Oplontis, Ercolano, Stabiae*, Rome/Bari.
Peters, W.J.Th. 1993, *La casa di Marcus Lucretius Fronto a Pompei e le sue pitture*, Amsterdam.
Petrarca, F. 1990, *Itinerario in Terra Santa 1358*, edited by F. Lo Monaco, Begamo.
Petrella, E. 1858, *Jone o l'ultimo giorno di Pompei*, Milan.
Peyrefitte, R. 1976, *Du Vésuve à l'Etna*, Paris (first edition, Paris 1952).
Pfister, M. (ed.) 1996, *The Fatal Gift of Beauty: The Italies of British Travellers. An Annotated Anthology*, Amsterdam/Atlanta.
Phillips, J. 1869, *Vesuvius*, Oxford.
PdE: Pitture de' Ercolano I–V, Naples 1756–1779.
Piccioli, C. (ed.) 1998, *Identità di Portici e qualità della vita*, Naples.
Pint, K. 2010, *The Perverse Art of Reading. On the phantasmatic semiology in Roland Barthes' Cours au Collège de France*, Amsterdam/New York.
Pio IX 1987: *Pio IX a Pompei. Memorie e testimonianze di un viaggio*, exhibition catalogue, Naples.
Piovene, G. 1957, *Viaggio in Italia*, Milan.
Piozzi, H.L. 1789, *Observations and Reflections Made in the Course of a Journey through France, Italy, and Germany*, London.
Piranesi, F. 1804, 1804, 1807, *Antiquités de la Grande Grèce* I–III, Paris.
Pitou, S. 1990, *The Paris Opéra. An Encyclopedia of Operas, Ballets, Composers, and Performers. Growth and Grandeur, 1815–1914* I, New York.

Platen, A. von 1896, *Die Tagebücher* I–II, Stuttgart.
Platt, D.F. 1908, *Through Italy with Car and Camera*, New York/London.
Pohl, F. 2011, *All the Lives He Led*, New York.
Pompei 1748–1980: Pompei 1748–1980. I tempi della documentazione, Rome 1981.
Pompei. L'informatica al servizio di una città antica, Rome 1988.
Pompéi. Travaux et envois des architectes français au XIXe siècle, Paris/Naples 1981 (= *Pompei e gli architetti francesi*).
Pompeji 79–1979: Pompeji 79–1979. Beiträge zum Vesuvausbruch und seiner Nachwirkung, Stendal 1982.
Pothey, A. 1883, *La Muette (quarante contes nouveaux)*, Paris.
Potthast, B./A. Red (eds) 2011, *Friedrich Theodor Vischer. Leben – Werk – Wirkung*, Heidelberg.
Power, Mrs. 1846, *Hand-Book or New Guide of Naples*, Rome.
PPM: Pompei Pitture e Mosaici I–X, Rome 1990–2003.
PPM Disegnatori: Pompei Pitture e Mosaici. La documentazione nell'opera di disegnatori e pittori dei secoli XVIII e XIX, Rome 1995.
Praz, M. 1979, Le antichità di Ercolano, in *Civiltà* 1979, I, 35–39.
Prein, Ph. 2005, *Bürgerliches Reisen im 19. Jahrhundert: Freizeit, Kommunikation und soziale Grenzen*, Münster.
Presuhn, E. 1877, *Die pompejanischen Wanddecorationen. Für Künstler und Kunstgewerbeschulen, sowie Freunde des Alterthums*, Leipzig.
Presuhn, E. 1878, *Pompeji. Die neuesten Ausgrabungen von 1874 bis 1878. Für Kunst- und Alterthumsfreunde illustrirt herausgegeben*, Leipzig.
Presuhn, E. 1882, *Pompeji. Die neuesten Ausgrabungen von 1878 bis 1881. Für Kunst- und Alterthumsfreunde illustrirt herausgegeben*, Leipzig.
Preuß, J.D.E. (ed.) 1846–1856, *Oeuvres de Frédéric le Grand* I–XXXI, Berlin.
Proffer, C.R. (ed.) 1967, *Letters of Nikolai Gogol*, Ann Arbor.
Proust, M. 1954, *A la recherche du temps perdu* I–III, edited by P. Clarac and A. Ferré (Bibliothèque de la Pléiade), Paris.
Proust, M. 1987, 1988, 1989, *A la recherche du temps perdu* I, II–III, IV, edited by J.-Y. Tadié (Bibliothèque de la Pléiade), Paris
Pucci, G. 1989, Scavo e cultura materiale tra '700 e '800, *Annali della Facoltà di Lettere e Filosofia Università di Siena* 10, 45–57.
Pucci, G. 1993, *Il passato prossimo. La scienza dell'antichità alle origini della cultura moderna*, Rome.
Pucci, G. 2012, Cadaveri eccellenti: le vittime di Pompei nell'immaginario moderno, *Mare Internum* 4, 71–88.
Pucci, G. 2014a, Salviamo Pompei (almeno al cinema!), *Dionysus ex machina*, rivista on line di studi sul teatro antico (http://dionysusexmachina.it/?cmd=news&id=139).
Pucci, G. 2014b, Splendori e miserie di Scipione l'Africano nel cinema, in W. Geerts et al. (eds), *Scipione l'Africano. Un eroe tra Rinascimento e Barocco*. Atti del convegno di studi, Roma, Academia Belgica, 24–25 maggio 2012, Milan, 299–310.
Pullo, D. 1792, *Notizie del bello, dell'antico e del curioso che contengono le reali ville di Portici, Resina, lo scavamento di Pompejano, Capodimonte, Cardito, Caserta, e S. Leucio, che servono di continuazione all'opera del canonico Carlo Celano*, Naples.
Ramage, N.H. 1990, Sir William Hamilton as Collector, Exporter, and Dealer: The Acquisition and Dispersion of His Collections, *American Journal of Archaeology* 94, 469–480.

Ramage, N.H. 1992, Goods, Graves and scholars: 18th-Century Archaeologists in Britain and Italy, *American Journal of Archaeology* 96, 653–661.
Raspi Serra, J. 1986, *La fortuna di Paestum e la memoria moderna del dorico (1750–1830)*, Florence.
Raspi Serra, J. 1990, *Paestum. Idea e immagine. Antologia di testi critici e di immagini di Paestum 1750–1836*, Modena.
Raspi Serra, J. 1993, La Roma di Winckelmann e dei *pensionnaires*, *Eutopia* 2.2, 79–132.
RE: *Realencyclopädie der Classischen Altertumswissenschaft* 1–83; Suppl. 1–15, 1894–1978.
Rebell, H. 1894, *Chants de la Pluie et du Soleil*, Paris (reprint Paris 1977).
Redford, B. 2008, *Dilettanti. The Antic and the Antique in Eighteenth-Century England*, Los Angeles.
Redi, R. (ed.) 1994, *Gli ultimi giorni di Pompei*, Naples.
Reece, R. 1872, *The Very Last Days of Pompeii!*, London.
Reed, H. 1970, *The Streets of Pompeii and other plays for radio*, London.
Reggiani, R. 1969, *Carla degli scavi*, third edition, Milan (first edition, Milan 1968).
Regione 1982: *La regione sotterrata dal Vesuvio. Studi e prospettive*, Naples.
Reimers, T. 2012, Archäologisches Wissen in Edward Bulwer-Lyttons *The Last Days of Pompeii* und Robert Hamerlings *Aspasia*, in J. Broch/J. Lang (eds), *Literatur der Archäologie. Materialität und Rhetorik im 18. und 19. Jahrhundert*, Paderborn, 176–196.
Reinhold, M. 1984, *Classica Americana. The Greek and Roman Heritage in the United States*, Detroit.
Reinsberg, C./F. Meynersen (eds) 2012, *Jenseits von Pompeji. Faszination und Rezeption*, Darmstadt/Mainz.
Reischert, A. 2001, *Kompendium der musikalischen Sujets*, Kassel.
Reisel, W. 1992, *Heimwee. Vier toneelstukken*, Amsterdam.
Represa Fernández, M.R. 1988, *El Real Museo de Portici (Nápoles): 1750–1825*, Valladolid.
Reynolds, M. (ed.) 2000, *The Sappho Companion*, London.
Rice, D. 2007, *The Pompeii Syndrome*, Douglas Village, Cork.
Richard, J.G. 1769, *Description historique et critique de l'Italie ou Nouveaux mémoires sur l'état actuel de son gouvernement, des sciences, des arts, du commerce, de la population & de l'histoire naturelle* IV, Paris.
Richter, D. 2005a, *Pompeji und Herculaneum. Ein Reisebericht*, Frankfurt am Main/Leipzig.
Richter, D. 2005b, *Neapel. Biographie einer Stadt*, Berlin.
Richter, D. 2007, *Der Vesuv. Geschichte eines Berges*, Berlin.
Richter, D./L. Wamser 2006, *Vorbild Herculaneum. Römisches Bayern und Antikenrezeption im Norden*, Munich.
Ridley, R.T. 1983, Dumas Père, Director of Excavations, *Pompeii Herculaneum Stabiae* 1, 259–288.
Ridley, R.T. 1992, A pioneer art-historian ... Caylus, *Storia dell'arte* 76, 362–375.
Riikonen, H. 1978, *Die Antike im historischen Roman des 19. Jahrhunderts. Eine literatur- und kulturgeschichtliche Untersuchung*, Helsinki.
Risaliti, R. 1996, *Gli Slavi in Italia. Viaggi e rapporti dal Quattrocento al Novecento*, Moncalieri.
Risi, C. 2004, *Auf dem Weg zu einem italienischen Musikdrama. Konzeption, Inszenierung und Rezeption des melodramma vor 1850 bei Saverio Mercadante und Giovanni Pacini*, Tutzing.
Robbe-Grillet, A. 2002, *C'est Gradiva qui vous appelle*, Paris.
Robert-Boissier, B. 2011, *Pompéi. Les doubles vies de la cité du Vésuve*, Paris.
Roberts, J.M. 2007, *Under Vesuvius. A Mystery*, New York, N.Y. (SPQR XI).
Roblès, E. 1986, *Le Vésuve*, Paris (first edition, Paris 1961).
Robotti, C. 1987, *Immagini di Ercolano e Pompei. Disegni, rilievi, vedute dei secoli XVIII e XIX*, Naples.

Rocchi, S. 2006–2007, Gialli storici ambientati a Pompei, *Delitti di carta. Quaderni gialli di racconti, studi, storie e cronistorie* 708, 50–63.
Rocchi, S. 2008, Gialli storici ambientati a Pompei, in Cremante et al. 2008, 163–174.
Rochester, J.-W. 1888, *Herculanum. Dessin médianimique obtenu au groupe qu'inspire J.-W. Rochester*, Paris.
Rodríguez, C. 2008, *Les mystères de Pompéi*, Paris.
Rohrwasser, M. et al. (eds) 1996, *Freuds Pompejanische Muse: Beiträge zu Wilhelm Jensens Novella Gradiva*, Vienna.
Rohrwasser, M. 2005, *Freuds Lektüren. Von Arthur Conan Doyle bis zu Arthur Schnitzler*, Giessen.
Roland de La Platière, J.-M. 1780, *Lettres écrites de Suisse, d'Italie, de Sicile et de Malthe ... en 1776, 1777 & 1778*, Amsterdam (published anonymously).
Romanelli, D. 1811, *Viaggio a Pompei, a Pesto e di ritorno ad Ercolano*, Naples.
Romanelli, L. 1803, *Il trionfo di Vitellio Massimino e la Distruzione di Pompejano*. Ballo eroico in cinque atti composto espressamente per il Teatro alla Scala nell'autunno del 1803, Anno II, Milan.
Romanelli, L. 1807, *Castore e Polluce, melodramma serio in due atti. Poesia del Sig. Luigi Romanelli, Musica del Sig. Maestro Vincenzo Federici*, La Fenice, Carnival 1807, Venice.
Romero Recio, M. 2012, *Ecos de un descubrimiento. Viajeros españoles en Pompeya (1748–1936)*, Madrid.
Room, C. 1828, *Herculaneum and other poems*, London.
Ropers, M.A. 2012, *Der Dialog in den späten Dramen Ödön von Horváths*, Frankfurt am Main.
Rosoni, O. 1970, *Amore e morte a Pompei*, Padova.
Rossignani, M.P. 1967, *Saggio sui restauri settecenteschi ai dipinti di Ercolano e Pompei*, Milan.
Rothemann, S. 1996, Als baute der Mensch im Hinblick auf die Ruinen. Pompeji als literarisches Motiv, in C. Hilmes/D. Mathy (eds), *Protomoderne: Künstlerische Formen überlieferter Gegenwart*, Bielefeld, 71–86.
Rouland, N. 1984 *Les lauriers de cendre*, Paris.
Roux, H./L. Barré, *Herculanum et Pompéi. Recueil général des peintures, bronzes, mosaïques etc.* I–VIII, Paris 1870.
Rowland, I.D. 2014, *From Pompeii: The Afterlife of a Roman Town*, Cambridge, MA/London.
Royo, M. 1999, *Domus imperatoriae*, Rome.
Ruggiero, M. 1885, *Storia degli scavi di Ercolano ricomposta su' documenti superstiti*, Naples.
Russel, J. 1750, *Letters from a young painter abroad to his friends in England*, London.
Russel, J. 1972, *Nelson and the Hamiltons*, second edition, Harmondsworth.
Russell, G. 2008, *La congiura di Pompei*, Casale Monferrato.
Russo, D. 1991, *Il tempio di Giove Meilichio a Pompei*, Naples.
Rutenfranz, M. 2004, 2009, Caius und die Detektive. Detektivegeschichten aus dem alten Rom für Kinder und Jugendliche auf dem Buchmarkt, in K. Brodersen (ed.), *Crimina. Die Antike im modernen Kriminalroman*, first and second editions, Frankfurt am Main, 31–46.
Sacchetti, R. 1979, *Il forno della marchesa e altri racconti*, Florence.
Sade, D.A.F. Marquis de 1998, *Oeuvres* III, edited by M. Delon (Bibliothèque de la Pléiade), Paris.
Sade, D.A.F. Marquis de 2008, *Voyage à Naples*, Paris.
Saint-Non, J.-C.R. 1782, *Voyage Pittoresque ou Description des Royaumes de Naples et de Sicile. Seconde Partie du Premier Volume, Contenant une Description des Antiquités d'Herculanum, des Plans & des Détails de son Théâtre, avec une Notice abrégée des différens Spectacles des Anciens. Les Antiquités de Pompéïi. La Description des Champs Phlégréens, & enfin celle de la Campanie & des Villes des Environs de Naples*, Paris.

Salaberry, Ch.M. d'Irumberry 1798, *Voyage à Constantinople, en Italie, et aux îles de l'archipel, par l'Allemagne et la Hongrie*, Paris.
Sampaolo, V. 2013, Le acquisizioni delle antichità vesuviane nel Museo Archeologico Nazionale di Napoli, in Guzzo/Tagliamonte/Lucchetti 2013, 26–33.
Sanders, A. 1979, *Victorian Historical Novel 1840–1880*, New York.
Sannazaro, A.S. 1689, *Opera latina omnia & integra*, Amsterdam.
Sannazaro, I, 1961, *Opere volgari*, edited by A. Mauro, Bari.
Sannazaro, I. 1966, *Arcadia, and Piscatorial Eclogues*, translated by Ralph Nash, Detroit.
Sannazaro, I. 1990, *Arcadia*, edited by F. Erspamer, Milan.
Sannazaro, I. 2004, *Arcadia – Arcadie*, edited by F. Erspamer, translated into French by G. Marino, Paris.
Sannazaro, J. 2009, *Latin Poetry*, translated by M.C.J. Putnam, Cambridge, Mass./London.
Sansom, J. 1805, *Letters from Europe, during a Tour through Switzerland and Italy in the years 1802 and 1803, written by a native of Pennsylvania*, Philadelphia (published anonymously).
Santo-Domingo, J.-H. 1829, *Tablettes napolitaines, deuxième édition revue et considérablement augmentée*, Brussels.
Sardou, V./J. Offenbach 1872, *Le Roi Carotte. Opéra-Bouffe-Féerie en 4 Actes, 18 Tableaux*, Paris.
Sarnelli Cerqua, C. 1993, La macchina del Piaggio nella descrizione di un ambasciatore marocchino, *Cronache Ercolanesi* 23, 107–108.
Sartre, J.-P. 1981, *Œuvres romanesques* (Bibliothèque de la Pléiade), Paris.
Sass, H. 1818, *A Journey to Rome and Naples, Performed in 1817; Giving an Account of the Present State of Society in Italy; and Containing Observations on the Fine Arts*, London.
Saul, M. 1966, *The Last Nights of Pompeii*, Toronto.
Sauron, G. 1998, *La grande fresque de la Villa des Mystères à Pompéi*, Paris.
Savarese, N. 1991, *Cose d'Italia*, edited by S.A. Nigro, Palermo (first edition, Florence 1940).
Saviano, R. 2007, *A Personal Journey into the Violent International Empire of Naples' Organized Crime System*, New York (first Italian edition, Milan 2006).
Saylor, S. 2005, *A Gladiator Dies Only Once. The Further Investigations of Gordianus the Finder*, New York.
Scarth, A. 2009, *Vesuvius. A Biography*, Princeton/Oxford.
Scatozza Höricht, L.A. 1982, Restauri alle collezioni del Museo Ercolanese di Portici alla luce di documenti inediti, *Atti dell'Accademia Pontiana* 31, 495–540.
Schaller, H.-W. 1992, *Der frühe historische Roman in Amerika. Eine literaturgeschichtliche und typologische Darstellung*, Heidelberg.
Scheurmann, K./U. Bongaerts-Schomer 1997, *"…endlich in dieser Hauptstadt der Welt angelangt!" Goethe in Rom* I–II, Frankfurt am Main.
Schiller, F. 1943: *Schillers Werke. Nationalausgabe* I. *Gedichte in der Reihenfolge ihres Erscheinens*, Weimar.
Schiller, F. 1991, *Schillers Werke. Nationalausgabe*, Zweiter Band, Teil IIA, edited by G. Kurscheidt and N. Oellers, Weimar.
Schinkel, K.F. 1979, *Reisen nach Italien. Tagebücher, Briefe, Zeichnungen, Aquarelle*, Berlin.
Schleimer, U. 2004, *Die Opera Nazionale Balilla bzw. Gioventù Italiana del Littorio und die Hitlerjugend – eine vergleichende Darstellung*, Munich.
Schnabel, E.J. 2002, *Die urchristliche Mission*, Wuppertal.
Schnapp, A. 1996, *Discovery of the Past. The Origins of Archaeology*, London (= *La conquête du passé*, Paris 1993).

Schnurbusch, D. 2011, *Convivium. Form und Bedeutung aristokratischer Geselligkeit in der römischen Antike*, Stuttgart.
Scholes, A. (ed.) 1959, *An Eighteenth-Century Musical Tour in France and Italy Being Dr. Charles Burney's Account of his Musical Experiences etc.*, London.
Schramm, R. 1890, *Italienische Skizzen. Wanderungen durch Rom und Neapel*, second enlarged edition, Leipzig (first edition, Leipzig 1881).
Schubert, C. 2010, *Anacharsis der Weise. Nomade, Skythe, Grieche*, Tübingen.
Schuchhardt, C. (ed.) 1925, *Robert Koldewey. Heitere und ernste Briefe aus einem Archäologenleben*, Berlin.
Schuerewegen, F. 1991, Volcans: Mme De Staël, Gobineau, Gautier, *Les lettres romaines* 45, 319–328.
Schulze, S. (ed.) 1994, *Goethe und die Kunst*, exhibition catalogue, Ostfildern.
Schuré, E. 1907, *La prêtresse d'Isis. Légende de Pompéï*, Paris.
Schwegman, M. 2008, Giuseppe Garibaldi, Alexandre Dumas and Giuseppe Fiorelli in Naples, *Fragmenta* 2, 7–18.
Scott, W. 1885, *Fragmenta Herculanensia. A Descriptive Catalogue of the Oxford Copies of the Herculanean Rolls*, Oxford.
Scott, W. 1890, *The Journal of Sir Walter Scott*, Edinburgh.
Sedgwick, C.M. 1841, *Letters from Abroad to Kindred at Home, by the author of 'Hope Leslie'*, New York (published anonymously).
Sehsucht 1993: *Sehsucht. Das Panorama als Massenunterhaltung des 19. Jahrhunderts*, Frankfurt am Main.
Seigneux de Correvon, G. 1770, *Lettres sur la découverte de l'ancienne ville d'Herculane et de ses principales antiquités*, Yverdon.
Sergejenko, M.J. 1953, *Pompeji*, Leipzig (first, Russian edition, Moscow 1948).
Sérieys. A. (ed.) 1801, *Voyage en Italie de M. l'Abbé Barthélemy de l'Académie Française, de celle des inscriptions et belles-lettres, et auteur du voyage d'Anacharsis, imprimé sur ses lettres originales écrites au comte de Caylus*, Paris.
Seume, J.G. 1879, *Spaziergang nach Syrakus im Jahre 1802*, in *Prosaische und poetische Werke* III, Berlin (first edition, Brunswick/Leipzig/Berlin 1803).
Seznec, J. 1949, Herculaneum and Pompeii in French Literature of the Eighteenth Century, *Archaeology* 2, 150–158.
Sharp, S. 1766, *Letters from Italy, Describing the Customs and Manners of the Country, in the Years 1765, and 1766*, London.
Sheldon, R.M. 2003, *Espionage in the ancient world: an annotated bibliography of books and articles in Western languages*, Jefferson N.C.
Shelley, P.B. 1964, *The Letters of Percy Bysshe Shelley* II. *Shelley in Italy*, edited by F.L. Jones, Oxford.
Sider, D. 2005, *The Library of the Villa dei Papiri at Herculaneum*, Los Angeles.
Silliman, B. 1853, *A visit to Europe in 1851*, New York.
Simas, R. 1993, *Circularity and Vision of the New World in William Faulkner, Gabriel García Márquez, and Osman Lins*, Levinston NY/Queenston, Ontario.
Simmons, J.C. 1969, Bulwer and Vesuvius: The Topicality of The Last Days of Pompeii, *Nineteenth-Century Fiction* 24, 103–105.
Simond, L. 1828, *A Tour in Italy and Sicily*, London.
Siotto, E. 2007, Tecniche di stacco, trasporto, foderatura ed incassatura dei "quadretti" parietali dei siti vesuviani nell'Ottocento alla luce di documenti inediti, *Rendiconti dell'Accademia dei Lincei* serie IX, 18, 119–154.

Skene, J. 1937, *Italian Journey Being Excerpts from the Pre-Victorian Diary of James Skene of Rubislaw*, London.
Slot, P. 2000, *Blauwbaard*, Amsterdam.
Slugocki, L. 1977, Hic habitat felicitas. Stendhal à Pompéi en 'touriste', *Micromégas. Rivista di studi e confronti italiani e francesi* 4.1–2, 11–23.
Smith, G.A. 2004, *Epic Films*, second edition, Jefferson North Carolina/London.
Smith, N.E. 1996 Androgyny and the Refusal of Classicism: Rereading Fragoletta, *Romance Quarterly* 43, 81–92.
Smolenaars, J.J.L. 2005, Earthquakes and Volcanic Eruptions in Latin Literature: Reflections and Emotional Responses, in M.S. Balmuth et al. (eds), *Cultural Responses to the Volcanic Landscape. The Mediterranean and Beyond*, Boston, Mass., 311–329.
Sogliano, A. 1888, *Pompei nella letteratura*, Naples.
Solomon, J. 1978, 2001, *The Ancient World in the Cinema*, first and second editions, South Brunswick/New York/London.
Some Account 1749: *Some Account of the Roman History of Fabius Pictor; From a Manuscript lately discover'd in Herculaneum; the Underground City near Naples: In a Letter from an English Gentleman residing at Naples to his Friend at London*, London.
Sontag, S. 1992, *The Volcano Lover. A Romance*, New York.
Soprintendenti 2012: *Dizionario biografico dei Soprintendenti Archeologici (1904–1974)*, Bologna.
Spence, J. 1975, *Letters from the Grand Tour*, edited by S. Klima, Montreal/London.
Spengler, O. 1932, *Der Mensch und die Technik. Beitrag zu einer Philosophie des Lebens*, Munich.
Spinazzola, V. 1953, *Pompei alla luce degli scavi nuovi di Via dell'Abbondanza (1910–1923)*, Rome.
Staats Evers J.W. 1872, *Honderd dagen in Italië en Midden Europa*, Arnhem.
Stähli, A. 1999, *Die Verweigerung der Lüste. Erotische Gruppen in der antiken Plastik*, Berlin.
Stamer, W.J.A. 1878, *Dolce Napoli. Naples: Its streets, people, fêtes, pilgrimages, environs, &c., &c.*, London.
Stanley, A.P. 1844, 1904, *Life of Thomas Arnold, D.D. Head-Master of Rugby*, first and second editions, London.
Stansgård, E. 1935, *H.C. Andersen i Italien*, Milan.
Starke, M. 1802, *Travels in Italy between the Years 1792 and 1798*, London.
Starke, M. 1828, *Travels in Europe between the years 1824 and 1828 adapted to the use of travellers comprising an historical account of Sicily*, sixth edition, London.
St Clair, W./A. Bautz 2012, Imperial Decadence: The Making of the Myths in Edward Bulwer-Lytton's *The Last Days of Pompeii*, *Victorian Literature and Culture* 40, 359–396.
Stefani, G. 2010, *One at a Time. The Casts*, Naples.
Stein- Hölkeskamp, E./K.-J. Hölkeskamp (eds) 2006, *Erinnerungsorte der Antike*, Munich.
Stendhal 1962, *Correspondence* I, edited by V. del Litto (Bibliothèque de la Pléiade), Paris.
Stendhal 1973, *Voyages en Italie*, edited by V. del Litto (Bibliothèque de la Pléiade), Paris.
Stendhal 1981, *Œuvres intimes* I, edited by V. del Litto (Bibliothèque de la Pléiade), Paris.
Sterne, L. 1930, *Letters of Laurence Sterne*, edited by L.P. Curtis, Oxford.
Stöver, H.D. 1984, *Attentat in Pompeji. C.V.T. im Dienste der Cäsaren* 6, Munich.
Stolberg, F.L. 1822, *Reise in Deutschland, der Schweiz, Italien und Sicilien in den Jahren 1791–92*, III (*Gesammelte Werke* VIII), Hamburg (= *Gesammelte Werke* IV, Hildesheim/New York 1974).
Strazzullo, F. 1980, Documenti per l'Ing. Rocco Alcubierre scopritore di Ercolano, *Atti della Accademia Pontiana* N.S. 29, 263–296.
Strazzullo, F. 1982, I primi anni dello scavo di Ercolano nel diario dell'ingegnere militare Rocco Gioacchino d'Alcubierre, in *Regione* 1982, 103–182.

Strazzullo, F. 1997, Il "curriculum" dell'ing. Rocco Gioacchino d'Alcubierre dal 1733 al 1757, *Cronache Ercolanesi* 27, 159–168.
Swan, Ch. 1826, *Journal of a Voyage up the Mediterranean*, London.
Swinburne, A. 1905, *The Poems*, London.
Swinburne, H. 1783, 1790, *Travels in the Two Sicilies in the Years 1778, 1779, and 1780*, first and second editions, London.
Syme, A.M. 2004, Love among the Ruins: David Cannon Dashiell's "Queer Mysteries", *Art Journal* 63.4, 80–95.
Szmurlo, K. (ed.) 2011, *Germaine de Staël: forging a politics of Mediterranean*, Oxford (SVEC 2011: 12).
Taine, H. 1910, *Voyage en Italie*, fourteenth edition, Paris (first edition, Paris 1866).
Tammisto, A. 2000, Nova bibliotheca pompeiana I–II – Corrigenda ed addenda con una bibliografia pompeiana fennica, *Arctos* 24, 211–232.
Tammisto, A. 2002, Loistavan Armfeltin "pompejilainen uurna"- Vesuviuksen alueen varhaisten kaivausten tuntemus Suomessa ja uusklassismi, in P. Janne/J. Eero, *Antiquitas borea – Antiikin kulttuurin pohjoinen ulottuvuus*, Oulu, 191–253 (with English summary, pp. 266–268).
Tanucci I–XX: Bernardo Tanucci, *Epistolario* I–XX, Rome/Naples 1980–2007 (vols. VI–VIII and XIX not yet edited).
Tanucci 1986: R. Ajello/M. D'Addio (eds), *Bernardo Tanucci Statista Letterato Giurista. Atti del Convegno internazionale di studi per il secondo centenario, 1783–1983*, Naples.
Ternite, W. 1839–1856, *Wandgemälde aus Pompeji und Herculaneum nach den Zeichnungen und Nachbildungen in Farben*, Berlin.
Thédenat, H. 1928, *Pompéi*, third edition, Paris (first edition, Paris 1906).
Thomas, S. 2010, The Location of Vacancy: Pompeii and the Panorama, in C. Bode/J. Labbe (eds), *Romanic Localities. Europe Writes Places*, London, 169–184.
Tice, P./R. Karson/K. Corsey 1997, *Pompeii as Source and Inspiration: Reflection in Eighteenth and Nineteenth Century Art*, exhibition catalogue, Ann Arbor.
Tomei, M.A. 1995, Domus oppure lupanar? I materiali dello scavo Boni della 'Casa repubblicana' a ovest dell'Arco di Tito, *Melanges de l'Ecole Française de Rome. Antiquité* 107, 547–619.
Tottola, A.L. 1825, *Gli ultimi giorni di Pompei*. Opera by G. Pacini, Naples.
Toudouze, G. 1877, *Le Cécube de l'an 79*, Paris.
Toudouze, G. 1878, *La Coupe d'Hercule (Papyrus pompéien)*, Paris.
Toudouze, G.G. 1908, *La sorcière du Vésuve (1808)*, Paris
Toynbee, A. 1948, *Civilization on trial*, Oxford.
Trevelyan, R. 1976, *The Shadow of Vesuvius. Pompeii AD 79*, London.
Trollope, E. 1854, *Illustrations of Ancient Art, Selected from Objects Discovered at Pompeii and Herculaneum*, London.
Trombetta, V. 1984, L'edizione di *Le antichità di Ercolano esposte*, *Rendiconti dell'Accademia di Archeologia, Lettere e Belle Arti Napoli* 59, 151–172.
Tsingarida, A./D. Kurtz (eds) 2002, *Appropriating Antiquity. Saisir l'Antique. Collections et collectionneurs d'antiques en Belgique et en Grande-Bretagne au XIXe siècle*, Brussels.
Twain, M., 1869, 1984, *The Innocents Abroad*, New York (facsimile New York/Oxford 1993).
Urban, B./J. Cremerius (eds) 1973, *S. Freud, Der Wahn und die Träume in W. Jensens "Gradiva"*, Frankfurt am Main.
Valéry, M. 1838, *Voyages historiques, littéraires et artistiques en Italie. Guide raisonné et complet du voyageur et de l'artiste*, second edition, Paris (first edition, Paris 1828).
Vallejo, A. 2002, *La rambla paralela*, Bogotà.

Vance, W.L. 1989, *America's Rome* I–II, New Haven.
Vandenberg, Ph. 1989, *Der Pompejaner*, Bergisch Gladbach (first edition 1986).
Varone, A. 1979, *Presenze giudaiche e cristiane a Pompei*, Naples.
Vatré, E. 1987, *Léon Daudet ou le libre réactionnaire*, Paris.
Vautier, D. 2007, *Tous les chemins mènent à Rome. Voyages d'artistes du 16ième au 19ième siècle*, exhibition catalogue, Ixelles.
Vecchi, C.A. 1864, 1868, *Pompei*, first and second editions, Turin/Florence.
Venuti, M.N. de 1748, *Descrizione delle prime scoperte dell'antica città d'Ercolano ritrovata vicino a Portici, villa della Maestà del Re delle Due Sicilie*, Rome.
Versluys, M.J. 2002, *Aegyptiaca Romana. Nilotic Scenes and the Roman Views of Egypt*, Leiden.
Vestal 1830: *The Vestal, or A Tale of Pompeii*, Boston.
Vesuvio 1998: *Il Vesuvio e le città vesuviane 1730–1860. In ricordo di George Vallet*, Naples.
Viardot, L. 1842, *Les musées d'Italie. Guide et memento de l'artiste et du voyageur, précédé d'une dissertation sur les origines traditionnelles de la peinture moderne*, Paris.
Villiers de l'Isle-Adam, A. 1986, *Œuvres complètes* (Bibliothèque de la Pléiade), Paris.
Vinci, G. 1827, 1831, *Descrizione delle ruine di Pompei*, first and second editions, Naples.
Visa-Ondarçuhu, V. 2008, Parler et penser grec: les Scythes Anacharsis et Toxaris et l'expérience rhétorique de Lucien, *Revue d'Études Anciennes* 110, 175–194.
Vischer, F.Th. 1907, *Briefe aus Italien*, edited by R. Vischer, Munich.
Vischer, F.Th. 1918, *Auch Einer. Eine Reisebekanntschaft*, Stuttgart/Berlin.
Visser, P. 1911, *De beeldhouwer van Pompeji*, Amsterdam.
Vitale, F. 2000, *Astronomia ed esoterismo nell'antica Pompei*, Padova.
Vitrioli, D. 1930, *Opere scelte*, Messina.
Vitrioli, D. 1998, *Xyphias. Epigrammata. Elegiae*. A cura e con un'introduzione di Antonio Zumbo, Reggio di Calabria.
Voci, A.M. 2007, *Wolfgang Helbig a Napoli 1863–1865: archeologia e politica dopo l'annessione*, Naples.
Völker, W. 1992, *Der Sohn. August von Goethe*, Frankfurt am Main/Leipzig.
Volkmann, J.J. 1771, 1777–1778, *Historisch-kritische Nachrichten von Italien, welche eine Beschreibung dieses Landes, der Sitten, Regierungsform, Handlung, des Zustandes der Wissenschaften und insonderheit der Werke der Kunst enthalten*, first and second editions, Dresden.
Volney, C.-F. 1791, *Les Ruines ou Méditations sur les révolutions des empires*, Geneva.
Voltaire 1970, *Les œuvres complètes de Voltaire* 2. Edition critique par O.R. Taylor, second edition, Geneva.
Von Agyagfalva, L.G. 1825, *Wanderungen durch Pompeji*, Vienna.
Von Albrecht, M. 1997, *A History of Roman Literature. From Livius Andronicus to Boethius*, Leiden/New York/Cologne.
Von Archenholz, J.W. 1990, *Rom und Neapel*, edited by F. Maier-Solgk, Heidelberg (first and second editions, 1785, 1787).
Von Archenholz, J.W. 1993, *England und Italien* II. *Italien*, edited by M. Maurer, Heidelberg.
Von Arnold, J. 1863, *Die Nazarener in Pompeji. Musikdrama in drei Aufzügen*, Leipzig (n.d.).
Von Charpentier, T. 1820, *Bemerkungen auf einer Reise von Breslau ... im Jahre 1813*, II, Leipzig.
Von der Hagen, F.H. 1818–1819, *Briefe in die Heimat aus Deutschland, der Schweiz und Italien*, Breslau.
Von der Recke, E. 1815, *Tagebuch einer Reise durch ein Theil Deutschlands und durch Italien in den Jahren 1804 bis 1806 von Elisa von der Recke, gebornen Reichsgräfin von Medem, herausgegeben vom Hofrath Böttiger*, Berlin.

Von der Thüsen, J. 1999, "Auch ich war in Arkadien" – Goethes *Italienische Reise*, in J. Enklaar/H. Ester (eds), *Von Goethe war die Rede*, Amsterdam/Atlanta, GA, 129–140.
Von der Thüsen, J. 2008, *Schönheit und Schrecken der Vulkane. Zur Kulturgeschichte des Vulkanismus*, Darmstadt.
Von Hase, K. 1891, *Erinnerungen an Italien in Briefen an die künftige Geliebte*, second edition, Leipzig.
Von Horváth, Ö. 1972, *Gesammelte Werke II. Komödien*, second edition, Frankfurt am Main.
Von Kotzebue, A. 1805, *Erinnerungen von einer Reise aus Liefland nach Rom und Neapel*, Berlin.
Von Montowt, R.K.S. 1903, *Die letzten Tage von Pompeji Oper in fünf Akten unter teilweiser Benutzung des gleichnamigen Romans von Bulwer*, Magdeburg.
Von Pilar, U. 1995, *Studenten-, Künstler- und Bohemefiguren im Erzählwerk Otto Julius Bierbaums*, Mainz.
Von Prochwitz, G. 1986, *Gustav III par ses lettres*, Stockholm/Paris.
Von Rochau, A.L. 1852, *Italienisches Wanderbuch. 1850–1851*, Leipzig.
Von Roda, B. 1988, *Schloß Aschaffenburg und Pompejanum*, Munich.
Von Sacher-Masoch, L. 2003, *Venus im Pelz. Ausgabe letzter Hand (1869/1878)*, edited by P. Weibel, Munich (first edition in *Die Vermachtniß Kains. Novellen. Erster Theil. Die Liebe*, Stuttgart 1870, Band 2, 121–368; here after third edition of the same work, Leipzig 1878, 121–390).
Von Wilamowiz-Moellendorff, U. 1928, *Erinnerungen 1848–1914*, Leipzig.
Vottero, D. 1989, *Questioni naturali di Lucio Anneo Seneca*, Turin.
Wackernagel, W. 1849, *Pompeji. Oeffentlicher Vortag gehalten zu Basel im Namen der Antiquarischen Gesellschaft 27 Oct. 1847*, Basel.
Wagner, C. 1976–1977, *Die Tagebücher*, edited by M. Gregor-Dellin and D. Mack, I–II, Munich/Zürich.
Waldie, J. 1820, *Sketches descriptive of Italy in the years 1816 and 1817*, London.
Waldstein, C./L. Shoobridge 1908, *Herculaneum Past Present & Future*, London.
Wallace-Hadrill, A. 2011, *Herculaneum Past and Future*, London.
Wallat, K. 2000, Seneca und Tacitus. Zwei Daten für ein Erdbeben in Pompeji?, in Th. Ganschow/M. Steinhart (eds), *Otium. Festchrift für Volker Michael Strocka*, Remshalden, 413–420.
Wallisch, F. 1957, *Egon Conte Corti. Die Wahrheit spricht den Urteil*, Graz/Vienna.
Walpole, H. 1948, *The Yale Edition of Horace Walpole's Correspondence 13. Horace Walpole's Correspondence with Thomas Gray, Richard West and Thomas Ashton 1*, edited by W.S. Lewis, New Haven.
Wanderer, R. 1859, *Der pompejanische Bau bei Aschaffenburg*, Heidelberg.
Watkins, Th. 1792, *Travels through Switserland, Italy, Sicily, The Greek Islands to Constantinople through part of Greece, Ragusa, and the Dalmatian Isles; in a Series of Letters to Pennoyre Watkins Esq.*, London.
Weed, Th. 1866, *Letters from Europe and the West Indies 1843–1852*, Albany.
Wegerhoff, E. 2012, *Das Kolosseum. Bewundert, bewohnt, ramponiert*, Berlin.
Werner, P. 1970, *Pompeji und die Wanddekoration der Goethezeit*, Munich.
Werr, S. 1999, *Die Opern von Errico Petrella: Rezeptionsgeschichte, Interpretationen und Dokumente*, Vienna.
Wesseling, E. 1991, *Writing History as a Prophet. Postmodernist Innovations of the Historical Novel*, Amsterdam/Philadelphia.
Wickert, L. 1964, *Theodor Mommsen. Eine Biographie II*, Frankfurt am Main.
Wilkening, W.H. 1977, *Otto Julius Bierbaum: The Tragedy of a Poet*, Stuttgart.
Williams, P. 1847, *Recollections of Malta, Sicily and the Continent*, Edinburgh.

Williams, R. 2008, *Notes on the Underground. An Essay on Technology, Society, and the Imagination*, second edition, Cambridge Mass./London.
Willis, I. 2007, "She Who Steps Along": Gradiva, Telecommunication, History, *Helios* 34.2, 223–242.
Wilson, W.R. 1835, *Records of a Route through France and Italy; with Sketches of Catholicism*, London.
Winckelmann, J.J. 1762, 2001a, *Anmerkungen über die Baukunst der Alten*, first edition, Leipzig; = *Schriften und Nachlaß* 3, edited by M. Gross, Mainz am Rhein.
Winckelmann, J.J. 1762, 1997a, *Sendschreiben von den Herculanischen Entdeckungen*, first edition, Dresden; = *Schriften und Nachlaß* 2.1, edited by S.G. Bruer and M. Kunze, Mainz am Rhein.
Winckelmann, J.J. 1764, 1997b, *Nachrichten von den neuesten Herculanischen Entdeckungen*, first edition, Dresden = *Schriften und Nachlaß* 2.2, edited by S.G. Bruer and M. Kunze, Mainz am Rhein.
Winckelmann, J.J. 1952–1957, *Briefe, in Verbindung mit Hans Diepolder herausgegeben von Walther Rehm* I–IV, Berlin.
Winckelmann, J.J., 2001b: *Briefe, Entwürfe und Rezensionen zu den herculanischen Schriften*, = Schriften und Nachlaß 2.3, edited by M. Gross and M. Kunze, Mainz am Rhein.
Wordsworth, W. 1908, *The Poems of William Wordsworth* II, edited by H.C. Smith, London.
Wordsworth, W. 1977, *The Poems*, edited by J.O. Hayden, New Haven/London.
Woś, J.W. 2006, *"Florenza bella tutto il vulgo canta" Testimonianze di viaggiatori polacchi*, Trento.
Wright, F. 1822, *A few days in Athens, being the translation of a Greek manuscript discovered in Herculaneum*, London.
Wright, N. 1965, *American Novelists in Italy. The Discoverers: Allston to James*, Philadelphia.
Wyke, M. 1997, *Projecting the Past. Ancient Rome, Cinema and History*, New York/London.
Yablon, N. 2007, "A Picture Painted in Fire": Pain's Reenactments of *The Last Days of Pompeii*, 1879–1914, in Gardner Coates/Seydl 2007, 189–205.
Yon, J.-C. 2000, *Jacques Offenbach*, Paris.
Young, W.R. 2002, *Around the World With Captain Grant*, edited by M. Fellmann, Baltimore.
Zander, H. 2007, *Anthroposophie in Deutschland*, 2 vols, Göttingen.
Zani, N. 1993, Lettere di Camillo Paderni ad Allen Ramsay: 1739–1740, *Eutopia* 2.2, 65–78.
Zarmakoupi M. (ed.) 2010, *The Villa of the Papyri at Herculaneum. Archaeology, Reception, and Digital Reconstruction*, Berlin/New York.
Zevi, F. 1979, Gli scavi di Ercolano, in *Civiltà* 1979, II, 58–68.
Zimmerman, V. 2008, *Excavating Victorians*, Albany, NY.
Zintzen, C. 1998, *Von Pompeji nach Troja. Archäologische Literatur und Öffentlichkeit*, Vienna.

Index of Names, Places, and Subjects

A.G. 144
Aafjes, Bertus (1914–1993) 162, 172
Abbott, Jacob (1803–1879) 131, 187n691
Academia Herculanensis 373
Academia Pontiana 343
Accademia di Cortona 22
Accademia Ercolanese 35, 37, 44, 141
Achilles Tatius (2nd century A.D.) 341
Achilles 45n181, 113
Achterberg, Gerrit (1905–1962) 410
Acton, John (1736–1811) 30n95
Adamo Muscettola, Stefania (1945–2004) 24
Adler, Jakob Georg Christian (1756–1834) 116
Aegina 206, 386
Aegle 200n762, 235
Aeneas 222, 303, 346
Aeschylus (5th century B.C.) 60, 310–312
Aetna 344
Agrigento/-um 62, 158, 264
Agrippa Postumus, Marcus Vipsanius (12 B.C.–A.D. 14) 8
Agrippa, Marcus Vipsanius (63–12 B.C.) 8, 347
Ahasver/us 221, 244, 246, 247
Albertazzi, Giorgio (*1923) 268
Alberti, Eduard (1827–1898) 241, 242
Albini, Girolamo (175?, 183?) 367n1362
Alcaeus (6th century B.C.) 403
Alcubierre, Roque Joaquín de (1702–1780) 19, 20, 32n105, 44, 45, 283n1090
Aleppo 353
Alexander I Pavlovitch (1775–1825) 183
Alexander the Great (356–323) 51, 124, 155
Alexandria 348
Algarotti, Francesco (1712–1764) 123
Allroggen-Bedel, Agnes 31, 113
Alma-Tadema, Laurence (1836–1912) 349
Alps 95, 145, 272
Althaus, Friedrich (1829–1897) 205n781
Amalfi 62n243
Amenta, Niccolò (1659–1719) 13n28, 17
Amphitheater 109, 174, 202, 208, 210, 211, 216, 251n973, 252, 253n982, 255, 383n1426, 414, 415, 424
Ampliatus 26n76, 48n189

Amsterdam 211n806, 380n1414, 381
Anacharsis 189–190
Anchises 222
Ancona 145
Andersen, Hans Christian (1805–1875) 151, 152, 181n667, 231
Anderson, Paul William Scott (*1965) 385
Andrés y Morell, Juan (1740–1817) 21
Angiolini, Pietro (c. 1760–after 1836) 362n1342
Anna Amalia of Sachsen-Weimar-Eisenach (1739–1807) 150, 297n1142
Antenor 340
Antichità d'Ercolano 23n66, 31n102, 33, 35–38, 40, 92, 361
Antiochia 286n1101
Apelles (4th century B.C.) 112, 114
Aphrodite 314n1196, 320, 325
Aphrodite → Venus
Apollo 176, 207, 209
Appleton, Thomas Gold (1812–1884) 354
Apuleius, Lucius (123/5–170/80) 142, 262n1012
Arditi, Michele (1746–1838) 48n183, 49, 50
Argos 84, 405
Argus 405
Arnold, Thomas (1795–1842) 74, 136
Artaude 55
Artorius Primus, Marcus 29
Ascanius 222
Aschaffenburg, Pompeianum 115
Ascione, Michela (*1972) 349, 350
Asellina 198n755, 249
Aspasia (5th century B.C.) 97n358
Assisi 145
Athens 69, 73, 80, 114, 176, 190, 265, 342, 384, 402, 419
Atherstone, Edwin (1788–1872) 404–405
Auber, Daniel-François-Esprit (1782–1871) 363n1349
Augustin-Thierry, Gilbert (1843–1915) 324–325
Augustine, St. (354–430) 338
Augustus, Emperor (63 B.C.–A.D. 14) 8, 65, 67, 191, 347

Aurigemma, Salvatore (1885–1969) 83, 88n344
Austria 10, 73, 119, 145, 369, 378
Avellino, Francesco Maria (1788–1850) 54, 75
Aziza, Claude 5
Bacchus → Dionysus
Bachmann, Ingeborg (1926–1973) 411
Baiae 10, 73, 103n383, 117, 174n639, 196n744, 208, 398n1470
Barallat y Felguera, Celestino 377n1403
Barbaia, Domenico (1777–1841) 363
Bardet de Villeneuve, Pierre (*1680) 20, 21
Barlow, Catherine (†1783) 46n172, 277
Barrett, Lawrence (1838–1891) 374
Bartels, Johann Heinrich (1761–1850) 117
Barthélemy, Jean-Jacques (1716–1795) 24n71, 35n121, 189–190, 339
Baschi, Antonio 332n1256
Bassanville, Thérèse Anaïs Rigo Lebrun, Countess of (1806–1884) 247, 253
Bassett, Ronald Leslie (*1924) 198
Bastet, Frédéric Louis (1926–2008) 279, 280, 361
Baths/ing 57, 59, 71, 140, 174, 183, 192, 201, 207, 209, 212, 216, 241, 242, 315, 422
Battaglia, Dario → Russell, Gordon
Baudelaire, Charles (1821–1867) 341, 356
Baudouin, Pierre-Antoine (1723–1769) 119n436
Baudy, W.T. 341
Bauer, L. 338n1366
Bay of Naples 149n568, 163, 208, 215, 270, 271, 369, 399, 423
Bayardi, Ottavio Antonio (1694–1764) 19n52, 34, 35, 36, 44, 71, 103n383, 336
Beard, Winifred Mary (*1955) 122n449, 123n453, 178
Beaumont, Alexandre (1827–1909) 368n1365
Becker, Wilhelm Adolph (1796–1846) 190, 191
Beckford, William (1760–1844) 122, 228, 277
Behrend, Otto (*1857) 206
Beldam, Joseph (1795–1866) 135
Bellicard, Charles (1726–1786) 39, 40, 44, 63, 71, 113, 190
Belloli, Luigi (1770–1817) 362
Benaglio, Francesco (1708–1759) 399
Benjamin, Walter (1892–1940) 159
Benkowitz, Carl Friedrich (1764–1807) 124, 125, 294

Bergeret de Grancourt, Pierre-Jacques-Onésyme (1715–1785) 121n444, 134n509
Bergman, Ingrid (1915–1982) 387
Berkeley, Elisabeth 56n216
Berry, Paul (*1931) 236, 240, 263, 272, 371, 389
Bertheroy, Jean (1868–1927) 5, 172, 173fig9, 176, 177, 207, 208
Berthier, Philippe 127
Bettinelli, Saverio (1718–1808) 394, 399
Beucker Andreae, Johan Hendrik (1811–1865) 155
Beyle, Henri → Stendhal
Bianchi, Pietro (1787–1849) 51
Bianchini, Francesco (1662–1729) 12
Bianco, Giacinto (1812–1885) 263, 264
Bidermann, Jakob (1578–1639) 391, 392, 393
Bierbaum, Gemma 156
Bierbaum, Otto Julius (1865–1910) 156, 157
Bilderdijk, Willem (1756–1831) 407n1497
Biondo, Flavio (1392–1463) 10, 11n20
Bisel, Sara C. (1932–1996) 178
Björnståhl, Jacob Jonas (1731–1779) 37, 65, 114, 121
Blauer, John M. 379, 383
Blavatsky, Helena P. (1831–1891) 210
Blessington, Marguerite (1789–1848) 66n262, 115n426, 125, 186, 230
Blewitt, Octavian (1810–1884) 129n483
Blix, Göran 5, 207
Blockley, John (1800–1882) 370
Bluebeard 269
Boadella, Albert (*1943) 377
Bobin 381
Boccaccio, Giovanni (1313–1375) 9–10, 169
Böttiger, Carl August (1760–1835) 66, 190, 191, 209, 263n1012
Boker, Georg Henry (1823–1890) 373, 374, 375
Bologna 145
Bonaparte, Caroline (1782–1839) 48, 55
Bonaparte, Joseph-Napoléon (1768–1844) 48
Bonnard, Mario (1889–1965) 383, 386
Bonucci, Antonio 50
Bonucci, Carlo (1799–1870) 50, 57, 64, 69, 75, 81, 153, 218
Borrelli, Gennaro 13, 16

Bory, Paul (*1837) 199, 323, 332f14,
    348–349, 356
Boscoreale 82, 89, 270n1047, 1047, 277n1072
Boscotrecase 8
Boston 217
Boswell, James (1740–1795) 101n378
Bouchor, Joseph-Félix (1853–1937) 158
Boudicca (†60/61) 192n717
Bowman, David A. 380
Bracco, Vittorio (1929–2012) 53n203, 248n960
Bradley, Edward S. 374
Brebrix 200
Brenta 161
Bresciani Borsa, Antonio (1797–1862)
    242, 243
Breton, Ernest (1812–1875) 13n28, 57, 59,
    65, 67, 68, 69, 70, 79n312, 81n320, 187,
    323, 398fig14
Briullov, Aleksandr (1798–1877) 221n848
Briullov, Karl Pavlovitsj (1799–1852)
    221–224, 256
Brizio, Eduardo (1846–1907) 79n312, 80
Brod, Max (1884–1968) 172, 193, 194, 209
Brothel/s 51, 58, 91n350, 140–141, 159,
    160n609, 161, 162, 199n756, 200, 213,
    236, 249, 280, 285–286, 302, 303, 304,
    305, 330, 420
Brothel → Pompeii, *Lupanar*
Bruin, Paul Georg (1914–2007) 239
Brulloff, Alexander Pavlovich (1798–1877) 50
Brun, Sophie Christiane Friederike
    (1765–1835) 310
Brussel, Pierre 107
Buff, Charlotte (1753–1828) 155
Bulwer-Lytton, Edward George (1803–1873)
    2, 5, 144, 169, 176, 187, 196, 199, 200,
    203, 210, 213, 215, 216, 220, 224–234,
    243, 246, 247, 248, 249, 253, 255,
    310, 316, 328, 341, 359, 360, 367–370,
    372–377, 378, 379, 380, 382, 383, 384,
    389, 390, 416, 418, 420, 421, 423
Bulwer-Lytton, Edward Robert (1831–1891) 224
Bunce, Lou P. 231n888
Burckhardt, Jacob (1818–1897) 192, 205n781
Burford, Robert (1792–1861) 380
Burgin, Victor (*1941) 266n1032
Burgon, John William (1813–1888) 235n905

Burlot, Delphine 34
Burney, Charles (1726–1814) 113, 117
Busken Huet, Conrad (1826–1886) 232–233,
    246
Butterworth, Alex (*1969) 172
Byron, George Gordon (1788–1824) 205, 206
Caecilius Jucundus/Secundus, Gaius
    312n1187, 384, 386
Cain, Henri (1859–1937) 371, 389
Calabria 18, 145, 282
Caligula, Emperor (12–41) 66n263, 195, 255
Calpurnius Piso 8, 270, 352n1324
Calvert, Frank (1828–1908) 373
Calvino, Italo (1923–1985) 350
Campania 10, 12, 72, 73, 84, 97, 98, 100, 116,
    117, 120, 130, 137, 149, 234, 240, 259,
    262, 270, 296, 341, 346, 401, 402
Campbell, Joseph (1904–1987) 233
Campi Flegrei 40
Camuccini, Vincenzo (1771–1844) 111
Canart, Joseph/Giuseppe (c. 1738–1790)
    22n64, 26, 32, 111, 117, 119n437, 120n440
Canova, Antonio (1757–1822) 48n185
Capaccio, Giulio Cesare (c. 1555–1634) 11
Capri 211, 241, 272, 280n1080
Carcopino, Jérôme (1881–1970) 237
Carducci, Giosuè (1835–1907) 212
Carlo/Carlos → Charles
Carroll, Lewis (1832–1898) 354n1331
Carrozzari, Raphaelis (*1855) 211
Carthage 199, 252, 406
Cartoni, Filippo 292
Casanova, Giacomo Girolamo (1729–1798)
    19n52, 402n1475
Casanova, Giovanni Battista (c. 1735–c. 1810)
    38, 142n542
Caserta 17, 90, 99, 361n1340
Cassandra 278
Castellammare di Stabia → Stabiae
Castellani, Charles-Jules (1838–1904)
    381n1417
Castellano 360n1335
Castori, Filippo 111
Catacombs 32, 138, 217, 253, 254, 286
Catel, Ludwig Friedrich (1776–1819) 49
Cava dei Tirreni 99
Cavalli, Atanasio (c. 1717–c. 1798) 394–395

Caylus, Philippe Claude Anne de Thubières Comte de (1692–1765) 14n38, 31, 38, 40, 41, 44, 47, 113n415, 190
Cazotte, Jacques (1719–1792) 398–399
Cellarius, J. 378
Cerrinius Restitutus, Marcus 154fig5, 185, 186n685, 244
Cerulli Irelli, Maria Giuseppina (*1935) 89, 90
Championnet, Jean-Etienne (1762–1800) 48
Charcot, Jean-Martin (1825–1893) 276
Charikleia 264n1020
Charles, King of Naples (1716–1788) 16, 17, 21, 29, 51, 104, 111, 380, 381, 383, 394, 399, 400, 412, 415, 424
Chassériau, Théodore (1819–1856) 184, 212n812, 313n1190
Chateaubriand, François-René de (1768–1848) 178n650, 181, 215, 252, 274n1057
Chernobyl 278
Chevallier, Elisabeth 6, 258
Chevallier, Raymond (1929–2004) 6
Chopin, Frédéric (1810–1849) 279n1079
Christians 2, 169, 200n476, 210, 215–256, 301, 306, 325, 348, 351, 364, 365, 367, 368, 369, 373, 377
Ciccone, Michelangelo (1751–1800) 395n1456
Cicero, Marcus Tullius (106–43 B.C.) 7, 16, 28, 65n255, 67, 70n172, 172, 193, 194, 209, 243, 263, 265, 322, 414
Cicerone/i 78, 124, 183n674, 291, 293n1126, 295, 299, 361n1340
Cicolano 74
Cilea, Francesco (1866–1950) 360n1335
Cinquantaquattro, Teresa Elena (*1964) 91
Ciprotti, Pio (1914–1993) 234n903, 236n911
Citino, David (*1947) 355, 357
Civita 11, 25
Clarac, Charles Othon Frédéric de (1777–1847) 48n185
Clark, Henry Howard (*1845) 281
Clarke, William Barnard 57
Classens de Jongste, E.A. 187
Claudia (Vestal) 16
Claudius Claudianus (c. 370–404) 344
Claudius, Emperor (10 B.C.–A.D. 54) 195, 196, 209

Claudius Pulcher, Appius (97–49) 16n41
Cleanthes (330–232) 342
Clement of Rome (c. A.D. 100) 215n818, 252n974
Clésinger, Auguste (1814–1883) 317
Cochin, Nicolas (1715–1790) 39, 40, 44, 63, 71, 112, 113, 114, 189, 190
Cola di Rienzo (1313–1354) 224
Colet, Louise (1810–1876) 74n300, 187
Collins, Wilkie (1824–1889) 352
Comastri Montanari, Danila (*1948) 196, 197, 203
Como 145
Conforti, Luigi (1854–1907) 211–212
Conrad, Michael Georg (1846–1927) 52n198
Constance 145
Constanța 347
Constantinople 336
Conti, Angelo (1860–1930) 158
Conticello, Baldassare (1932–2011) 90, 91n350
Cook, Thomas (1808–1892) 98, 157
Cooper, Mary 336n1264
Cooper, Merian C. (1894–1973) 379, 383
Corinna (6th century B.C.) 260n1000
Corti, Egon Caesar (1886–1952) 4
Couperus, Louis (1863–1923) 279n1079
Covito, Carmen (*1948) 174, 209, 250n969, 351
Coyer, Gabriel François (1707–1782) 97
Cozzi, Salvatore (1849–1933) 81n318
Craven, Elizabeth Berkeley (1750–1828) 56n216
Craven, Richard Keppel (1779–1851) 56
Cremante, Renzo 212
Creuzé de Lesser, Augustin (1771–1839) 142, 181
Croce, Benedetto (1866–1952) 62n244, 83n324
Croly, George (1780–1860) 221n846, 340–341, 356
Crombet, Paul (1786–1851) 183, 187, 291, 364
Cumae 10, 63, 85, 103n383, 401n1476
Cuoco, Domenico 27
Cusk, Rachel (*1967) 163, 412
Cybele 341, 346, 369
Daehner, Jens 14
Dahl, Curtis 4, 218
D'Aloë, Stanislao (1814–1888) 133, 318fig13

D'Amelio, Pasquale 61
D'Ancrevil, M. 123
Dante Alighieri (1265–1321) 263, 344, 396
Dares 338, 339
Darius III (c. 380–330) 51, 124n454, 155
D'Arthenay, Guillaume Marie 24, 39
Dashiell, David Cannon (1952–1993) 276n1066
Daudet, Alphonse (1840–1897) 275
Daudet, Léon (1867–1942) 158n601, 177, 275–276
D'Augerot, Alphonse 64
D'Aumale, Claude (1563–1591) 346n1300
David, Félicien César (1810–1876) 220, 360, 364, 365
David, Marie-France (*1969) 5
Davis, Lindsey (*1949) 196–197, 203, 212
D'Azeglio, Massimo Tapparelli (1798–1866) 166, 169, 172
De Alarcón, Pedro Antonio (1833–1891) 133, 139
De Amicis, Edmondo (1846–1908) 211n808
De Angelis, Vanna → Russell, Gordon
De Beauvoir, Simone (1908–1986) 160, 161
De Bourke, Edmond (1761–1821) 238
De Bressay, Charlotte-Antoinette marquise de Lezay de Marnésia (1710–1785) 347
De Brosses, Charles (1709–1777) 16, 107, 113, 127
De Caro, Stefano (*1950) 51n193, 89, 90
De Corcelles, Louis 211
De Franciscis, Alfonso (1915–1989) 51n193, 89, 275n1077
De Graaff, Martinus Hendrik (1813–1887) 221, 247
De Jaucourt, Louis (1704–1779) 292
De Jorio, Andrea (1769–1851) 293
De l'Hôpital, Marquis 24n68
De La Condamine, Charles-Marie (1701–1774) 35n118, 115
De la Roche 140
De La Rochefoucauld, Stéphanie 195
De Lagrèze, Gustave-Bascle (1811–1891) 59
De Lalande, Joseph-Jérôme (1732–1807) 13n30, 127, 293n1125
De Lamartine, Alphonse (1790–1869) 260, 271
De Lamothe, Alexandre (1823–1897) 300–301
De Latouche, Henri (1785–1851) 258, 271
De Meuse, Jean 283n1090, 320n1213

De Petra, Giulio (1841–1925) 80, 81, 82, 157
De Pixerécourt, René-Charles Guilbert (1773–1844) 371, 390
De Prisco, Vincenzo (1855–1921) 82
De Rothschild, Edmond Benjamin James (1845–1934) 82
De Simone, Antonio 91n352
De Singlande, R.P. Caprais (1706–c. 1775) 106n388
De Sivry, Louis Poinsinet (1733–1804) 295
De Staël-Holstein, Germaine (1766–1817) 169, 236, 258–260, 262, 345, 395
De Unamuno, Miguel (1869–1936) 136
Debout, Jacques (1872–1939) 251
Decius, Emperor (190/201–251) 252n974
Del Litto, Vittorio (1911–2004) 126
Delacroix, Eugène (1798–1863) 268
D'Elbeuf → Elbeuf
Delille, Jacques (1738–1813) 407–408
Della Corte, Matteo (1875–1962) 88n344, 140, 162, 172, 234n903, 237, 248, 278n1074
Della Sambucca, Giuseppe Beccadelli (1726–1813) 51n192
Della Valle, Cesare (1777–1860) 396
Delphi 189
DeMille, Cecil B. (1881–1959) 373n1387, 383n1426
Demont, Louise 70
Denon, Dominique-Vivant (1747–1825) 32n103, 47, 140, 142, 180, 181, 292
Derrida, Jacques (1930–2004) 266n1032
Desprez, Louis-Jean (1743–1804) 47n179, 51n192
Dezobry, Louis Charles (1798–1871) 190
Di Castelbarco, Cesare Pompeo (1782–1860) 221n848
Di Giacomo, Salvatore (1860–1934) 101
Dickens, Charles (1812–1870) 98, 128n477, 131–132, 230n884
Dictys 339
Diderot, Denys (1713–1784) 4, 32, 38n133, 42, 73, 118–119
Dillon, Eilís (1920–1994) 203
Dilthey, Karl (1839–1907) 80n315
Dinner (parties) 60n235, 125, 130, 141, 147, 174, 201, 209, 211, 212, 216, 241, 312n1187, 321n1216, 354, 365, 371, 414

Dino, Francesco Salvatore 79n312, 80
Dio Cassius, Lucius (c. 155–after 229)
    8, 63n245, 109, 129n480, 192n717, 201,
    289n1112, 344, 381, 393, 416
Diocletian, Emperor (244–311) 215, 252n947
Diomedes (Arrius) 171, 176, 182, 301, 378
Diomedes (hero) 339
Diomedes, Gaius Pompeius 172
Dionysius of Halicarnassus (60 B.C.–A.D. 7)
    63, 336n1263
Dionysus 57, 190n706, 275, 277n1068,
    381, 397
Disraeli, Benjamin (1804–1881) 228
Dörpfeld, Wilhelm (1853–1940) 84n329
Domitian, Emperor (51–96) 190, 215n818, 218
Donaldson, Thomas Leverton (1795–1885)
    56, 57, 64, 186, 381n1415
Donizetti, Gaetano (1797–1848) 372
D'Onofri, Pietro (1740–1813) 21, 22n63–64
Doolittle, Hilda (1886–1961) 276
Dorat, Claude-Joseph (1734–1780) 374n1303
D'Orsi, Libero (1888–1977) 29, 162n615,
    282–283
Douglas, Norman (1868–1952) 267, 317–320
Dresden 16, 17, 267n1032
Dronia, Michael 392, 393
Drummond, William (c. 1770–1828) 129n479
Drusus, Nero Claudius (13 B.C.–A.D. 23)
    66n263
Du Bocage, Anne-Marie Lepage (1710–1802)
    110
Duclos, Charler Pinot (1704–117) 127
Dumas, Alexandre (1802–1870) 51n195,
    58n223, 74, 123, 127, 143, 262n1010,
    298, 299
Dunford, Katherine → Fetherstonhaugh,
    Katherine
Dupaty, Charles-Mercier (1748–1788) 37, 181
D'Urso, Michele (*1800) 405–406, 408
Dyer, Thomas Henry (1804–1888) 74n300,
    185, 188n699
East, Rebecca 109, 326–327
Ebenhöh, Horst (*1930) 379n1412
Eckermann, Johann Peter (1792–1854) 152
Eco, Umberto (*1932) 239
Ecocriticism 201, 211, 290, 279n1078
Edgeworth, Mary (1767–1849) 281

Eichhorn, Otto (*1884) 271
Elbeuf, Emmanuel-Maurice de Lorraine d'
    (1677–1763) 13, 14, 16, 18, 19, 40n146
Elia, Olga (1902–1977) 89
Eliot, George (1819–1880) 130n484, 265n1025
Encyclopédie 14n37, 26n76, 40, 42, 73, 292
Engelbach, Lewis 296
Enslen, Carl Georg (1792–1866) 381
Epicurus (341–270 B.C.) 32n106, 342
Eridanus 301, 303
Ertel, Jean Paul (1865–1933) 360n1335
Espantaleón, Juan 377
Ethiopia 383
Etna 8n9, 10, 343, 381
Eugene, Prince of Savoy (1663–1736) 16
Euphorion 205, 315n1199
Eustace, John Chetwode (1762–1815) 128,
    129, 143
Fabius Pictor 335, 336n1263, 353, 356, 357
Fairfield, Jane Frazee (*1810) 219
Fairfield, Sumner Lincoln (1803–1844) 218,
    219, 229, 230, 252, 253
Fallowell, Duncan (*1948) 162
Federici, Vincenzo (1764–1826) 362n1342
Federspiel, Jürg (1931–2007) 268–269
Fellini, Federico (1920–1993) 386
Fénelon, François de Salignac de la Mothe
    (1651–1715) 190n705
Ferber, Johann Jacob (1743–1790) 3
Ferdinand I, King of Naples (1751–1825) 29,
    48, 49, 50, 55, 101n378, 119, 142n542,
    340, 400
Ferdinand II, King of Naples (1810–1850) 75
Ferdinand VI, King of Spain (1713–1759) 29
Ferrare, Henry 371, 389
Fetherstonhaugh, Katherine 106
Fetherstonhaugh, Utrick (1717/8–1788)
    106n387
Fierz-David, Linda (1891–1955) 276
Fiore, Domenico 126
Fiorelli, Giuseppe (1823–1896) 19n51, 58, 60,
    74–81, 82, 84, 87, 88, 93, 164, 179, 188,
    192, 193, 205n783, 236, 240, 281, 296,
    299, 300, 301, 331, 421
Fisk, Wilbur (1792–1839) 141n540
Flaubert, Gustave (1821–1880) 316
Flavius Josephus (37–100) 210, 242

Flaxman, John (1755–1826) 349
Florence 16, 126, 131, 145, 308
Florus, Annius 343, 344
Florus, L. Annaeus 345n1295
Florus, P. Annius 345n1295
Fondi 131n494
Fontana, Domenico (1543–1607) 11
Formont, Maxime (*1864) 208
Forster, Josef (1859–1951) 368n1366
Forsyth, Joseph (1763–1815) 71n287, 128
Fort Worth 382
Fougeroux de Bondaroy, August Denis (1732–1789) 31, 41fig2, 42, 119n436
Fox, George (1854?–1902) 360n1334, 370
Fragonard, Jean-Honoré (1732–1806) 121n444
Franc, César (1822–1890) 324n1228
Franchetti, Alberto (1860–1942) 371, 390
Francis, John George 132n496, 184n678
Frank, Anne (1929–1945) 288, 289
Frankfurt 148, 155
Frederick the Great (1712–1786) 106, 123
Frederick III of Bayreuth (1711–1761) 106
Frederick Augustus II (1696–1763) 16
Frederick Christian, Prince of Poland, Elector of Saxonia (1722–1763) 23
Freedman/men 80, 144n550, 172, 174, 176, 202, 255, 420
Freud, Sigmund (1856–1939) 266, 267n1036, 269, 306, 323n1226
Friedländer, Ludwig Hermann (1790–1851) 141, 175n642
Fucini, Renato (1843–1921) 62
Fuller, Lois Hamilton 202
Fuller/y/ies 195n78, 200n764, 202, 203n774, 330
Funeral 174, 216, 308, 348, 414
Furius Camillus, Marcus 335n1262, 336
Galanti, Giuseppe Maria (1743–1806) 186
Galiani, Berardo (1724–1774) 45n171, 118n436
Galiani, Fernando (1728–1783) 37, 38, 45n168
Galiffe, James Augustus (1776–1853) 183
Gallone, Carmine (1886–1973) 383n1424, 387
Gallus, Gaius Cornelius (70–26 B.C.) 191
Galway 278
Gandy, John Peter (1771–1850) 55
Ganymedes 372
Gardner Coates, Victoria C. 5

Garibaldi, Giuseppe (1807–1882) 74, 75, 187, 192
Garro, Emilio 188, 189n702, 214fig10, 248–249, 252
Garrucci, Raffaele (1812–1885) 234
Gau, François-Charles (1790–1854) 55
Gautier, Théophile (1811–1872) 5, 127, 169, 191n716, 263, 267, 268, 295, 296n1137, 313–317, 319, 322, 331, 366
Gazda, Elaine K. 277n1068
Gell, William (1777–1836) 55, 56, 57, 58, 65, 66, 67, 68, 69, 124n454, 125, 186, 224, 225n857, 226
Gellius, Aulus (130–after 180) 252, 264
Genoa 131, 145, 152
George IV (1762–1830) 401
Germanicus Caesar (15 B.C.–A.D. 19) 66n263
Gerning, Johann Isaac (1767–1837) 186n656
Gérôme, Jean-Léon (1824–1904) 349
Geryoneus 63n245
Getty, J. Paul (1892–1976) 269–270
Giannettasio, Niccolò Partenio (1648–1715) 12
Giants 201, 343, 344, 396, 412, 416
Gibbon, Edward (1737–1794) 101n378, 245n949
Gigante, Marcello (1923–2001) 91, 304n1167, 333n1254, 334n1256
Gilmore, Patrick S. (1829–1892) 382
Giordano, Umberto (1867–1948) 371, 390
Gisborne, Thomas (1758–1846) 400
Gladiator/s 200, 202, 211, 212, 228, 249, 253, 268, 290n119, 379, 385, 420, 424
Gladiator shows/games 26n76, 29, 174n639, 175, 199, 218, 330, 393
Glinka, Mikhail (1807–1854) 221n847
Godfrey, Herbert Alberlkin 360n1335
Goethe, August von (1789–1830) 144, 145, 152–155
Goethe, Johann Caspar (1710–1782) 11n19, 101n373, 144, 145–147, 155, 397n1465
Goethe, Johann Wolfgang von (1749–1832) 46n173, 51, 97n360, 99, 101, 106n388, 108n398, 114n422, 121, 124n453, 144, 145, 148–152, 176, 205, 206, 270n1047, 277, 315, 355
Gogol, Nikolai Vasilievich (1809–1852) 221n846, 222

Golding, Louis (1895–1958) 327–328, 329n1245
Goldoni, Carlo (1707–1793) 161
Gollmick, Carl (1796–1866) 368n1366
Gomorrah → Sodom
Gompertz, Heinrich (1873–1942) 80n314
Gomperz, Theodor (1832–1912) 79
Gonzague, Élisabeth Rangoni, princesse de (†1832) 181n670
Goodman, Carol 350–351, 357
Gori, Antonio Francesco (1691–1757) 23, 35n119, 102
Grand Tour 47, 95, 96, 97, 98, 99, 259
Grant, Ulysses (1822–1885) 281
Grassal, George-Joseph (1867–1905) 228n874
Gray, Thomas (1716–1771) 103, 218n834
Gray, Thomas (1803–1849) 218
Gregorovius, Ferdinand (1821–1891) 11n17, 204–206, 209, 270, 310n1181, 315n1199
Grell, Chantal 6
Griffa, Lewis (†1891) 373
Grillparzer, Franz (1791–1872) 283–284
Grönemeyer, Herbert (*1956) 389n1441
Gros, Camille 365n1356
Grosley, Pierre Jean (1718–1785) 106
Grün, Athanasius (1806–1876) 334
Guarducci, Margherita (1902–1999) 236, 238
Gubbins, Henrietta G. 370
Guide/s 3, 39, 56, 76fig3, 78, 96, 105, 111, 129, 131n480, 136, 140, 141, 145, 159, 177, 183, 185, 186, 211, 247, 248, 262, 268, 272, 291–305, 306, 309, 310, 312, 396, 398fig14
Guidebook/s 39, 55–61, 81, 86, 97, 101, 103, 108, 124, 128, 130n484, 131, 156, 176, 179, 184, 254, 334n1256, 399, 403, 412
Guidobaldi, Maria Paola (*1961) 91
Gusman, Pierre (1863–1941) 272, 273fig11, 280
Gustav III, King of Sweden (1746–1792) 22
Guzzo, Pietro Giovanni (*1944) 91, 337
Gynoeceum 191
Gypsum cast 77, 99, 203, 212, 274, 280, 288, 289, 308, 314fig12, 317, 320, 387n1436
Gypsum cast → Plaster cast
Hackert, Georg (1755–1805) 149n570
Hackert, Jakob Philipp (1737–1807) 149n570, 150
Hadot, T. 364n1353

Hadrian, Emperor (76–138) 270n1046
Hakewill, James (1778–1843) 128n477
Hales, Shelley (*1971) 5, 200n767
Hall, Eleanor I. (1947) 276
Hamilton, William (1730–1803) 43n161, 46, 48, 56, 101n378, 110n403, 117n432, 123, 142n542, 150, 180, 258, 277, 281
Hamlet 134
Hannibal (247–182) 240
Harris, Robert (*1957) 169, 199–201, 202, 211, 212
Harrison, Frederic 82
Harrison, Jane (1850–1928) 276
Hart, Emma (1765–1815) 46n172, 150, 277
Hartlaub, Felix (1913–1945?) 286–287
Hayter, John (1756–1818) 128, 342n1285, 401
Headley, Joel Tyler (1813–1897) 184
Hebbel, Christian Friedrich (1813–1863) 79n313
Heggie, Jake (*1961) 372
Heine, Heinrich (1797–1856) 102
Helbig, Wolfgang (1839–1915) 79
Heliodorus 264n1020
Henri IV, King of France (1553–1610) 346
Hensen, Johann Heinrich Wilhelm (1816–1887) 79n313
Hequet, Charles 185n682
Heracles → Hercules
Herbig, Reinhard (1898–1961) 88n344
Herculaneum (with number on plan, fig. 8)
– "Basilica" (2) 19n52, 24, 39, 113, 114, 153, 402
– House of Argus (6) 52, 139, 398fig14, 405
– House of Aristides (5) 52
– House of Skeleton (3) 52
– Public Baths (4) 54
– Suburban Baths 351n1319
– Theater (1) 15fig1, 16, 19, 20, 32, 76, 84, 109, 132, 138, 153, 190, 395, 409
– Villa of the Papyri (7) 3, 8, 20, 21, 23, 25, 32n106, 51n193, 91, 117, 118fig4, 120, 269, 270, 333, 334n1256, 335, 347, 348, 349, 350, 352n1324, 357, 399, 403, 412, 421
Hercules 6, 16, 30n96, 36, 63, 64, 71, 93, 153, 170, 229, 236, 264, 285, 343, 344, 346, 391n1442, 395, 401, 402, 405
Hercules, Pillars of 327

Hermes 303, 304, 306, 320, 346, 391n1442, 395, 401, 402
Herodotus 190n705
Hervey, Christopher (1696–1764) 109
Herzen, Aleksandr (1812–1870) 234
Hesiod (8th/7th century B.C.) 395
Heyne, Christian Gottlob (1729–1812) 43
Heyse, Paul Johann Ludwig von (1830–1914) 206
Hill, Anne 389n1441
Hippocrates (c. 460–370) 351
Hiroshima 267n1032, 288, 289
Höcker, O. 231n888
Hogg, Thomas Jefferson (1792–1862) 141, 142, 182, 292, 293, 381n1415
Hogo-Hunt, J.W. → Houghton, John William
Holconius Priscus, M. 308, 312n1187
Holconius Rufus 313, 386
Hollander, Benoit (1853–1942) 370
Hollis, Thomas (1720–1774) 33, 36
Holocaust 194
Holstenius, Lucas (1596–1661) 11, 393n1449
Holt, Emily Sarah (1836–1893) 242
Homer (8th century B.C.) 71n287, 191, 222, 338, 340n1277
Hopkins, Keith (1934–2004) 306, 326
Horace Flaccus, Quintus (65–8) 159n604, 400, 403, 404
Houghton, John William 376
Howells, William Dean (1837–1920) 131, 297
Howerd, Frankie (1917–1992) 384
Hughes, John (1790–1857) 401–403
Hugo, Victor Marie (1802–1885) 123n453, 165, 316
Hunt, Peter (1925–2002 384n1430
Icarus 202, 270
Illica, Luigi (1857–1919) 371
Imbriani, Vittorio (1840–1886) 265, 267
Imperato, Minico 14n40
Ingres, Jean-Auguste-Dominique (1780–1867) 342
Irace, Filippo 27
Isidorus from Sevilla 63n245
Isis 69n279, 141, 179n661, 193, 196, 210, 217n825, 225, 243, 244, 247, 250, 256, 262, 263, 277, 322, 323, 324, 368, 369, 374, 375, 378, 386, 421

Jacobelli, Luciana 397
James II (1633–1701) 336
James, Henry (1843–1916) 123n452, 135, 136
Jameson, Anna Brownell Murphy (1794–1860) 125, 294
Janovic, Vladimír (*1935) 310–312
Japin, Arthur (*1956) 19n52, 402n1479
Jashemski, Wilhelmina Feemster (1910–2007) 350n1317
Jean Paul Richter (1763–1825) 76, 160, 261, 262
Jensen, Wilhelm (1837–1911) 169, 177, 265–268, 323
Jerusalem 204, 209n797, 210, 216, 217 252n971, 254, 364, 365
Jesus Christ (†33) 235, 238, 244n945, 246, 247, 254, 379
Jew/s 102, 194, 196n739, 210, 216, 219n840, 220, 221, 234, 235, 236n912, 237, 240, 241, 243, 244, 246, 248, 249, 253, 254, 255, 256, 365, 415
Jewelry 133, 141, 180, 203, 222, 226n859, 324
Johnson, Samuel (1709–1784) 95
Joncières, Victorin, Félix-Ludger Rossignol (1839–1903) 368
Jones, Jan L. (*1947) 382
Joseph (Old Testament) 379
Joseph II, Emperor of Austria (1741–1790) 22, 26n76, 27n83, 30, 122, 133
Juan of Austria (1547–1578) 11n17
Julia Agrippina, Vipsania (19 B.C.–A.D. 28) 347
Julia Caesaris (39 B.C.-A.D. 14) 8, 347
Julia Felix 201, 326, 327
Julius Proculus, Gaius 172
Jung, Carl Gustav (1875–1961) 159, 276
Jupiter 343, 346, 372, 380
Juvenal, Decimus Junius (c. 55–c. 130) 174, 191, 218n830, 420
Juventus 248
Kaden, Woldemar (1838–1907) 11n17, 211n808, 243–245, 246, 268, 270–271
Kafka, Franz (1883–1924) 193
Kammerer-Grothaus, Helke 31
Kaunitz-Rietberg, Wenzel Anton (1711–1794) 123
Keerl, Johann Heinrich (†1810) 111, 112n412
Keogh, Margareth 408–409

Kerinthos 264n1020
Kessel, Franz 368n1366
Kestner, Christian August (1777–1853) 155
Kiessling, Alfred 236n908
Knapton, George (1698–1778) 104
Kneip, Gustav (1905–1992) 360n1335
Körber, Philipp W. 231n888
Kopácsi, Sándor (1922–2001) 189
Kotzebue, August Friedrich Ferdinand von (1761–1819) 70
Krausser, Helmut (*1964) 290
Krohn, Barbara (*1957) 280
Kryzhanovskaia, Vera Ivanova (1861–1924) 247
Kulczycki, Władysław (1834–1895) 284
La Platière, Jean-Marie Roland de (1734–1793) 140
La Spezia 145, 152
La Tourette, Jacqueline (*1926) 280, 352
La Vega, Francesco (1737–1804) 22n61, 24, 26n76, 29, 32n103, 48n183, 49, 122n450, 123, 180
La Vega, Francesco (c. 1715–c. 1766) 27, 185, 188
La Vega, Pietro (1738–1814) 49
Lacan, Jacques (1901–1981) 266n1028
Lacerenza, Giancarlo 234
Lachner, Franz (1803–1890) 368n1366
Lacryma Christi 100n368, 146
Lamers, Petra 47
Lantier, Etienne-François (1734–1826) 339, 340n1276, 341
Lasena, Pietro (1590–1636) 24n75
Lasky, Kathryn 203
Latapie, François-de-Paule (1739–1823) 43, 84
Laurence, Ray (*1963) 172
Lawrence, Caroline 203–204
Layard, Austen Henry (1817–1894) 135n511
Lazzarone/i 53–54, 99, 163, 183, 294, 298, 299
Le Ninèze, Alain 238, 352n1323
Le Riche, Jean M. 298
Lee, Sebastian (1805–1887) 364n1353
Leghorn 145, 152
Lehmann-Hartleben, Karl (1894–1960) 87n343
Leiden 269n1042
Lemercier, Adrien 271

Lenk, Fabian (*1963) 201, 202
Lentulus 322–323, 348–349
Leopardi, Giacomo (1798–1837) 5, 45n169, 53–54, 132n497, 136, 345, 366, 409
Leopold, prince of Salerno (1790–1851) 75
Leopold II (1747–1792) 361
Leppmann, Wolfgang (1922–2002) 5, 106n387, 168n623, 224n854, 233, 260, 266, 316, 398n1469, 403n1482
Lerme-Walter, Marcelle 202, 203
Lettice, John (1737–1832) 38
Levi, Primo (1919–1987) 177n649, 288–289, 303n1164, 306
Lewald-Mendelssohn Bartholdy, Fanny (1811–1889) 138
L'Herbier, Marcel (1888–1979) 383n1425
Libya 372, 383
Lingg, Hermann (1820–1905) 206, 377–378, 390
Lins, Osman (1924–1978) 238–239
Linus, Pope 249n961
Liverpool 302
Livineius Regulus, Lucius 8
Livy, Titus (64/59 B.C.–A.D. 12/17) 64n249, 66, 334n1258, 336n1263, 337, 338, 345n1295, 349n1310
Llewellyn, Richard (1906–1983) 5, 250–251
Lollobrigida, Gina (*1927) 162
London 56, 125, 131, 132, 162, 182, 225, 227, 231, 380, 384, 414
Longo Auricchio, Francesca 14, 16n42
Longo, Bartolo (1841–1926) 5
Loreius Tiburtinus 202, 278n1074
Loren, Sofia (*1934) 162
Loreto 145, 146n558
Lotringer, Sylvère (*1938) 266n10128
Loubinoux, Gérard 363
Louis XII, King of France (1462–1515) 346
Louis XIV, King of France (1638–1715) 13n27, 286n1101
Lowry, Malcolm (1909–1957) 88n345, 177, 287–288, 296n1137, 301–304
Lucian (c. 117–c. 180) 190n705
Lucretius, Publius 336n1263
Ludwig I of Bavaria (1786–1868) 115
Lumisden, Andrew (1720–1801) 24, 107–108, 114

Lundgren, Marja (*1965) 207n792, 235n907, 249–250
Maben, Adrian 388
Macchioro, Vittorio (1880–1958) 276n1062
Maffei, Francesco Scipione (1675–1755) 14n40
Maiuri, Amedeo (1886–1963) 26, 81, 84–88, 89, 93, 139, 180n664, 203, 213, 251, 387
Maizony de Lauréal, Joseph- François-Stanislas 342–346, 357, 391, 386n1461
Malamud, Margaret 229n875, 231n891, 373, 383n1426
Malaparte, Curzio (1898–1957) 302n1157
Malibu 269, 270
Mallet, David (1705–1765) 393–394
Mamia/Mammia 33n111, 150, 154fig5, 308, 310n1181
Mandelli, Giovanni 169
Manfredi, Valerio Massimiano 353
Mann, Thomas (1875–1955) 267, 279
Mansell, William L. 375
Márai, Sándor (1900–1989) 161
Marcus Aurelius, Emperor (121–180) 9n9, 24
Margherita, Queen of Italy (1851–1926) 80
Maria 200n762, 239, 246, 249–250
Maria Amalia Christina, Queen of Naples (1724–1760) 17
Maria Carolina, Queen of Naples (1752–1814) 30
Maria Isabella, Queen of Naples (1789–1848) 362
Maria Theresia, Empress of Austria (1706–1780) 30
Marquardt, Karl Joachim (1812–1882) 175n642
Martha 200n762, 235, 246
Martial, Marcus Valerius (c. 40–c. 104) 8, 10n16, 174, 391n1442, 402, 420
Martin, Selina 229
Martorelli, Giacomo (1699–1777) 23n65, 34, 44, 45
Martyn, Thomas (1735–1825) 38
Martyr/s/dom 250, 251, 252, 253, 255, 415
Mary, St. 250, 324
Mathé, Edouard 360n1335
Matzner, Ilna (1900–1986) 161
Mau, August (1840–1909) 58, 61, 79, 80, 85, 87n341, 157
Mauclair, Camille (1872–1945) 158

Maurois, André (1885–1967) 224n852
Maynial, Edouard (*1879) 282
Mazois, Charles François (1783–1826) 49, 55, 57, 58, 65, 66, 67, 68, 69, 177, 184, 186, 187, 190, 191–192, 193, 239, 241n931, 352, 356
Mazzini, Giuseppe (1805–1872) 192, 243
Mazzocchi, Alessio Simmaco (1684–1771) 30n96, 34, 44, 45, 49
Mazzolà, Caterino (1745–1806) 361
McCarthy, Justin Huntly (1859–1936) 370n137
McManigal, Rod 379, 383
McNally, Terrence 372
Medina, Louisa H. (1814/5–1838) 372–373
Melandro, Luigi (1892–1955) 214f10
Melton, William 279, 330n1246
Menander (342/341–292/291 B.C.) 28n91
Menduni de' Rossi, Stefania 191n710, 250, 324
Merli, Vincenzo 38n135
Méry, Joseph (1798–1865) 220–221, 364n1753
Messika, Natalie 255n985
Metastasio, Pietro (1698–1782) 361
Metempsychosis 247, 313
Meuris, Eugène 231
Meyer, Friedrich Johann Lorenz (1760–1844) 6, 99, 100, 110
Michel, Christian 112, 113n415
Michelangelo Buonarroti (1475–1564) 117n431, 222
Mielke, Germund (*1953) 202
Migliacci, Domenico 143
Milan 145, 152, 221, 234, 283, 367
Milanesi, Guido (1875–1956) 278
Miller, Anna (1741–1781) 31, 110, 294
Miller, John 110
Millin, Aubin-Louis (1759–1818) 49
Miltoun, Francis (*1871) 157
Minervini, Giulio (1819–1891) 74n300
Minucius Felix (2nd/3rd century A.D.) 301
Miot de Mélito, André-François (1762–1841) 48n183
Misenum 199, 201, 221, 395
Mitchell, John (1794–1870) 184
Mock manuscript 174, 217, 218, 238, 308, 323, 343–357, 416
Modestino, Carmine 193n724

Moffa, Paolo (1915–2004) 383n1425
Mommsen, Theodor (1817–1903) 61, 79, 80
Monnet, Charles (1732–after 1808) 47n179
Monnier, Marc (1827–1885) 57, 58, 76fig3, 316
Monod, Jules 60n238
Monte Cassino 88
Monte Somma 7, 170
Montfaucon, Bernard de (1655–1741) 34
Montfort, Nannie 232
Monti, Vincenzo (1754–1828) 259n992, 395
Moran, James (1972) 384
Morelli, Ercole Luigi 371n1382
Morelli, Francesco (1768–1832) 38
Morghen, Raffaello (1758–1833) 37, 142n542
Moriconi, Stefano 26n79
Moritz, Karl Philipp (1757–1793) 115–116
Moritz, P. 231n888
Morton, Marguerite W. 374
Moschino, Ettore (1867–1941) 360n1335
Moussinot → D'Arthenay
Mozart, Leopold (1719–1789) 360–362
Mozart, Wolfgang Amadeus (1756–1791) 122n447, 326, 360–362, 372
Muck, Joseph 368
Müllenbrock, Heinz-Joachim 165n620
Müller, Carl Ottfried (1797–1840) 54n204
Müller, Gustav Adolf (1866–1928) 209, 221, 244–246, 253
Müller, Peter (1791–1877) 368n1366
Münter, Friedrich Christian (1761–1830) 38n135
Munich 397
Murat née Bonaparte, Caroline (1782–1839) 48, 55, 291n1117
Murat, Joaquino/Joachim (1767–1815) 48, 50, 55, 295
Murecine 209n798
Murray II, John (1778–1843) 129
Murray III, John (1808–1892) 129, 130, 186n686
Muses 16, 73, 209, 395, 403, 409
Mussolini, Benito (1883–1945) 86, 158n601
Mycenae 69
Naevoleia Tyche 49n188, 314n1195, 321–322
Naples
– Albergo dei Poveri 17
– Capodimonte 17, 19, 361n1340
– Catacombs S. Gennaro 13n30, 159

– Museo Borbonico 51, 61n240, 75
– National Museum 52, 75, 90, 120n436, 235n95
– Palazzo Caramarico 151
– Royal Palace 17
– San Carlo Theater 17, 362, 364
– San Gregorio degli Armeni 18
– Santa Chiara 18
– Studi (palazzo degli) 50, 182n671, 205n783, 226n859, 236n859, 314n1196
Napoleon Bonaparte (1769–1827) 48, 129, 142, 295
Napoleon III (1808–1873) 364n1353, 366, 367
Nazarenes 206, 241, 300n1153, 348, 368, 377
Nazarenes → Christians
Nepos, Cornelius (100–25 B.C.) 338, 339
Nero, Emperor (37–68) 66n263, 89, 209, 211, 215, 239n927, 243, 254, 255, 327, 339
Nerval, Gérard de (1808–1855) 127, 209, 262–263, 313n1192, 319
New York 289, 372, 373, 382, 416
Niccolini, Antonio (1772–1850) 61n239, 363
Niccolini, Antonio (active 1865–1900) 61
Niccolini, Fausto (1816–1886) 61
Niccolini, Felice (1812–before 1886) 61, 74n301
Nichelson, Peter 384n1430
Nicholson, A. 375
Nicolai, Carl 217, 219, 230
Nicolas I Pavlovitch (1796–1855) 221n847
Nicolas, Felice 49
Niebuhr, Barthold (1776–1831) 52
Niemann, Walter (1876–1953) 360n1335
Nieritz, Karl Gustav (1795–1876) 231n888
Nietzsche, Friedrich (1844–1900) 137–138
Nîmes, Maison Carrée 58
Nissen, Heinrich (1839–1912) 79, 85, 87n341
Noack, Friedrich (1869–1930) 87n342
Nocera → Nuceria
Nonius Balbus, Marcus 24, 351n1319
Norbanus 172
Northall, John (1723–1759) 105
Norwid, Cyprian Kamil (1821–1883) 150n573, 308–310
Nossis 351
Nothomb, Amélie (*1967) 328–329
Noto 162

Toudouze, Gustave (1837–1904) 177, 267, 314n1195, 321–323
Toudouze, Gustave-Georges (1877–1972) 277–278, 371
Toxaris 190n705
Toynbee, Arnold Joseph (1889–1975) 303
Troy 80, 222, 338, 340n1277, 373, 396, 406
Troyes 106
Tullius, Marcus 67, 326–327
Turin 79n312, 101n376, 145
Tuscia 240
Twain, Mark (1835–1910) 98, 135, 187
Typhon 401
Tyrus 406
Ululitremulus 202
Umberto I (1844–1900) 80
Umbricius Scaurus 48n185, 49n188, 246
Urban, Julius 368n1366
Válek, Jiří (1923–2005) 360n1335
Valerius Maximus (1st century A.D.) 16, 338
Vallejo, Fernando (*1942) 286n1101
Van Limburg Stirum, family 399
Vandenberg, Philipp (*1941) 195
Vandières, Abel-François de 39
Varro, Marcus Terentius (116–27 B.C.) 112, 338
Vecchi, Candido Augusto (1813–1869) 172, 192–193, 209, 213, 270n1047
Venereum 50, 140, 177, 191, 340n1279
Venice 14n40, 96, 132, 135n515, 139, 145, 152, 236, 274, 276
Venus 60, 73, 116, 117, 196, 197, 207, 245, 249, 250n967, 272, 312n1187, 320n1214, 325, 341, 381, 391n1442
Venuti, Domenico (1715–after 1799) 149n570
Venuti, Marcello Niccolò de (1700–1755) 19, 23, 24n67, 40n144, 71, 102, 107, 109, 112
Venuti, Ridolfino (1703–1763) 19n52
Verdi, Giuseppe (1813–1901) 220, 364n1353, 373
Verona 102, 383
Versailles 286n1101
Vespasian, Emperor (7–79) 25n76, 195, 196, 208, 217, 248, 249n962, 255
Vesta 217, 291
Vestal/s 16, 216, 217–218, 291, 363n1345
Vésuviennes 345
Vesuvius 1, 2, 3, 7, 10, 12, 16n45, 19n52, 21, 30, 46, 51, 72, 73, 96, 99, 103n383, 107, 110, 115, 124, 128n475, 131n489, 132, 136, 141, 146, 149, 153, 157, 169, 170–171, 177, 178, 183, 197n748, 201, 203, 204, 206, 208, 211, 213, 215, 216, 217, 218, 219, 220, 221, 225, 227, 229, 233, 234, 236, 237, 240, 243, 244, 250, 251, 252, 253, 255, 259–260, 261, 262, 266, 278–279, 280n1080, 282, 283, 284, 285, 289, 290, 291, 293, 296n1140, 301, 311, 312, 328, 330, 333, 343, 345, 350n1317, 353, 354n1329, 355, 359, 361n1340, 362, 363, 364, 365, 366, 368, 369, 372, 373, 376, 380, 381, 384, 385, 389, 390, 391–397, 399, 401, 404, 407, 409, 411, 412, 413, 415, 418, 421, 424
– Eruption of 472 12n23, 88
– of 1631 12n23, 363n1345, 391–393, 411, 416
– of 1769 395
– of 1779 99
– of 1787 149
– of 1822 381n1415
– of 1830 153
– of 1834 226n861, 231
– of 1872 281
– hermit 127, 128n475, 131n489, 215n816, 259n946, 261n1007, 407
Victor Emanuel III (1869–1947) 84
Vienna 9n12, 145, 284, 367n1361, 369
Viereck, I.C. 370
Villiers de l'Isle Adam, Auguste (1838–1898) 365n1356
Vinci, Gaspare (1780–c. 1855) 57
Virgil (70–19) 36n125, 66, 159n604, 170, 242n935, 263, 303, 344, 346n1300, 396, 400, 403, 407
Virginius Rufus, Titus (consul A.D. 63) 8
Vischer, Friedrich Theodor (1807–1887) 272–274
Visser, P. (1887–1929) 206–207
Vitrioli, Diego (1819–1898) 263, 264–265, 333n1251
Vitruvius (1st century B.C.) 66, 190, 200n766
Volkmann, Johann Joachim (1732–1803) 21, 35–36 72, 107n389, 108, 111, 116, 117, 121, 142, 176

Volney, Constantin de Chasseboeuf, comte de (1757–1820) 303
Voltaire, François-Marie Arouet (1694–1778) 267n1036, 345–346
Volterra 63
Von Agyagfalva, Ludwig Goro (1786–1843) 57n220
Von Archenholz, Johann Wilhelm (1743–1812) 108
Von Arnold, Yourij Karlovich (1811–1898) 368–369
Von Brieg, Johann Christian (1591–1639) 391n1444
Von Charpentier, Johann (1786–1855) 182n671
Von Creutz, Gustav Philip (1716–1785) 22
Von der Hagen, Friedrich Heinrich (1780–1856) 151–152, 182n672
Von der Recke, Elisa (1754–1833) 182
Von Hase, Karl August (1800–1891) 178n652
Von Horváth, Ödön (1901–1938) 378–379, 390
Von Meysenbug, Malwida (1816–1903) 137
Von Montowt, Reinhold Karl Sylvius (1842–1925) 360n1334, 369
Von Platen, August Graf (1796–1835) 261n1006
Von Pogwisch, Ottilie (1796–1872) 152
Von Sacher-Masoch, Leopold (1838–1895) 215–316
Von Stein, Charlotte (1742–1827) 148n566, 149n569
Von Wilamowitz-Möllendorf, Ulrich (1845–1931) 80
Vulcan/us 204, 346n1301, 392n1448, 393
Vulci 240
Vulpius, Christiane (1765–1816) 152
Wagner, Cosima (1837–1930) 137
Wagner, Richard (1813–1883) 137, 316n1201, 368, 388n1439
Waldie, Jane (1793–1826) 126n462, 295
Waldstein, Charles (1856–1927) 84, 86n339
Wallace, Lew (1827–1905) 215, 373n1387
Wallace-Hadrill, Andrew (*1951) 12, 13, 91
Wallat, Kurt (*1960) 6n7, 62
Walpole, Horace (1717–1797) 103–104, 218n834, 228

Walters, William T. (1819–1894) 253n982
Wandering Jew → Ahasverus
Weber, Karl (1712–1764) 20, 21, 27, 35n118, 44, 283n1090
Wedding 174, 212, 216, 242, 414
Weed, Thurlow (1797–1882) 296
Weimar 51, 145, 148, 150, 152
Werre, Sebastian 368
West, Richard 103
Wheeler, Rosina Doyle (1802–1882) 224
Wilde, Oscar (1854–1900) 206
Wilhelmine, margravine of Bayreuth (1709–1758) 106
Wilkes, John (1725–1797) 101n378
Williams, Penny (1802–1885) 295
Willis, Ika 2, 66, 275n1061
Wilson, William Rae (1772–1849) 138
Winckelmann, Johann Joachim (1717–1768) 11n19, 31–32, 37, 42, 43, 44–45, 59, 64, 72, 100n368, 101, 117n431, 119n436, 138, 185, 206, 422
Winnemore, Anthony Fannen (1801–1851) 370
Wiseman, Nicholas Patrick Stephen (1802–1865) 215
Wollstonecraft Shelley, Mary (1797–1851) 228
Wollstonecraft, Mary (1759–1797) 129
Wordsworth, William (1770–1850) 403
Wordsworth, William (1835–1917) 403n1482
World War I 248, 282, 284, 287, 306, 329, 385, 416, 424
World War II 83, 286, 287, 288, 301, 303, 304, 306, 325, 382, 424
Wright d'Arusmont, Frances (1795–1852) 341–342
Zahn, Wilhelm Johann Karl (1800–1871) 50, 54n204, 58, 150, 151, 152, 153, 155
Zangemeister, Karl (1837–1902) 61, 236
Zarilli/o, Mattia (1729–1804) 45
Zeno (335–262 B.C.) 342
Zeno, Apostolo (1669–1750) 14n40
Zeuxis (c. 430–c. 390 B.C.) 112, 177, 400
Zevi, Fausto (*1938) 89
Zimmerman, Virginia 5, 26n78, 52
Zintzen, Christiane (*1966) 5, 233, 267, 317
Zmyrina 200n762, 235
Zurich 274n1058

Index of Names, Places, and Subjects —— **481**

Nouguès, Jean-Charles (1875–1932) 359, 371, 389
Nuceria 10, 11n20, 243
Nuittier, Charles 368n1365
Numa Pompilius (c. 700 B.C.) 337–338
Numerius 312n1187
Octavia 262n1010
Odysseus 190n705, 366
Offenbach, Jacques (1819–1880) 365–366
Officina dei Papiri 333n1254, 334n1256
Olmos Romera, Ricardo (*1946) 317, 377n1403
Olympia 189, 365
Olympus 335, 340, 380
Opitz, Martin (1597–1639) 391–392
Oplontis 8, 89, 197, 207, 208n794
Oracula Sibyllina 8
Orloff, Grégoire (1777–1826) 103
Orpheus 207, 329, 410
Osanna, Massimo (*1963) 91
Oscan/s 10, 63, 64, 66, 68, 69, 72
Osterkamp, Ernst 206
Ostia 162, 235
Ottaviano 262n1010
Ottawa 119n436
Overbeck, Johannes (1826–1895) 58–59, 73, 154fig5, 179n661, 187, 188
Ovid Naso, Publius (43 B.C.–17 A.D.) 148, 347, 351, 356, 393n1451
Oxford 105, 401
Oxford Movement 229
Pabst, August (1811–1885) 368, 369
Pabst, Julius 368n1367
Paciaudi, Paolo Maria (1710–1785) 38, 40
Pacini, Giovanni (1796–1867) 61n240, 359, 360, 362–364, 367, 406n1491
Paderni, Camillo (c. 1715–1781) 19n49, 22n63, 26, 27, 29, 32, 33, 38n135, 112, 115n426
Padua 56
Paestum 48, 64, 99, 135n515, 158, 189
Pagliara, Giuseppe (*1949) 175
Pain, James 382
Pais, Ettore (1856–1939) 83
Palermi, Amleto (1889–1941) 383n1424
Palermo 48, 128, 145, 258, 395
Palmyra 353
Pan 117, 118fig4, 119
Panorama 380, 381, 416

Pansa, Cuspius 171, 172, 176, 219, 220, 227, 308, 312n1187
Paoletta, Erminio 276–277
Papyrus/i 3, 24, 31, 41fig2, 48, 79, 91, 115, 128, 237, 280, 308, 322, 333–357 (mock), 399, 400, 401, 409, 416
Paquius Proculus 202, 213, 237, 282, 312n1187
Paris (myth) 153
Paris (town) 82, 96, 100, 107, 129, 145, 190, 226, 276, 285–287, 321, 322, 340, 364, 367, 368, 378,
Pâris, Pierre-Adrien (1745–1819) 47n179, 361n1339
Parrhasius (5th century B.C.) 177, 400
Parslow, Christopher Charles (*1958) 20, 117n432
Passio Perpetuae et Felicitatis 252
Pastrone, Giovanni (1883–1959) 386
Patanè, Sebastiano (*1950) 172
Paul, Joanne 5
Paul, St. (†64) 194, 215, 219, 239, 243, 248, 249, 250, 255, 379
Peisistratus (†528/527) 329
Pelasgi 10, 71, 292
Pellegrino, Charles R. 259n925, 289
Perec, Georges (1936–1982) 239n923
Peri, Cesare 323
Pericles (495–429) 97n358
Pernice, Erich (1864–1945) 87n342
Perosi, Marziano (1875–1959) 369–370
Perotti, Niccolò (1430–1480) 10
Peruzzini, Giovanni (1816–1869) 367n1363
Pesando, Fabrizio (*1958) 200n767, 201
Peter, St. (†64) 215, 236, 248, 250
Petra 353
Petrarca, Francesco (1304–1374) 169
Petrella, Errico (1813–1877) 360, 367–368
Petronius Arbiter (†66) 51, 172, 174, 175n643, 178, 228, 351, 420
Peyrefitte, Roger (1907–2000) 88n745, 304–305
Phallus 27n82, 31, 34n117, 73, 79n314, 80n314, 113n416, 116, 140, 141, 163, 177, 196, 197, 280, 302n1161, 307
Philadelphia 231, 284n1091, 337
Phillips, John (1800–1874) 71

Philodemus (c. 110–c. 40/35) 334
Piaggio, Antonio (1713–1796) 31, 38n135, 41, 44, 333, 334n1256
Picchetti, Francesco Antonio (1619–1694) 12
Piccini, Louis Alexandre (1779–1830) 371
Piccini, Nicolò (1728–1800) 371
Pilatus, Pontius (1st century A.D.) 379, 380
Pimentel Fonseca, Eleonora (1752–1799) 258
Pindar (522–443 B.C.) 64, 260n1000
Pink Floyd 388–389
Piovene, Guido (1907–1975) 161–162
Piozzi, Hester Lynch (1741–1821) 96, 121, 181
Piranesi, Francesco (1756/8–1810) 30, 31, 43
Piso → Calpurnius Piso
Pitt, William (1759–1806) 106n387
Pius IX, Pope (1792–1878) 133, 243
Plaster cast 2, 7, 60, 78, 178, 179, 181n670, 288, 289, 331, 355, 356, 385, 414, 421
Plaster cast → Gypsum cast
Platt, Dan Fellows (1873–1938) 157
Plautus, Titus Maccius (c. 254–184 B.C.) 60, 66, 139, 379
Pliny the Younger (c. 62–c. 113) 5, 7, 8, 9n11, 25, 70, 114n421, 169, 199, 201, 222, 226, 278, 329, 343, 345, 381, 393, 404n1483, 421
Pliny the Elder (23–79) 10, 40, 112n412, 170, 177, 191n715, 201, 204, 210, 215, 262, 263, 264, 338, 395, 396, 406
Podalirius 393
Poe, Edgar Allan (1809–1849) 316
Poggioreale 132
Pohl, Frederick (1919–2013) 330
Polyclitus (5th century B.C.) 29n93
Pompadour, Jeannette Antoinette Poisson, Madame de (1721–1764) 39
Pompei (modern town)
– Hotel Sole 80, 157n600, 162, 179
– Hotel Diomede 157n600
– Hotel Suisse 157n600
– St Mary's Basilica 250, 324
Pompeii (plus number on plan, fig. 7)
– Amphitheater (29) 25, 29, 54, 55, 58, 59n230, 60, 63, 140, 172, 175, 211, 218, 219, 225, 228, 241n931, 252, 255, 273fig11, 300, 301, 318, 330, 367, 368, 373, 376, 377, 380, 381, 383, 385, 388, 422

– Antiquarium → Museum
– Bar of Elephant/Sittius (46) 159, 249, 376n1401, 420
– Bar of Fortunata (13) 160fig6, 298n1144
– Bar of Nympherois (9) 297n1142, 298
– Bar/Brothel of Asellina 166fig7, 249
– Basilica (19) 68, 198, 389
– Barracks of Gladiators 46, 125, 130, 178n650, 187n693
– Castellum Aquae (70) 200
– Doric Temple (22) 64–65, 66, 71, 85, 229
– Eumachia Building (40) 153
– Forum (41) 49, 50, 55, 57n221, 65, 66, 67, 85, 124n454, 140, 153, 157, 179n661, 197, 198, 205n781, 207, 212, 218, 227, 228n868, 244, 279, 300, 363, 366, 373, 380, 381, 388, 389, 422
– Forum Baths (63) 50, 65n260, 89, 183n675, 201, 213, 263
– Forum/o triangulare 29, 64, 65, 66, 71, 180n661, 229, 254
– Fullery of Stephanus (36) 202
– Herculanean Gate (8) 2, 27, 28, 49, 50, 140, 154fig5, 180, 185–189, 218, 222, 254, 264, 298n1146, 308, 363, 381
– Houses
  – I 9, 3 202
  – II 5, 1 (30) 236
  – VII 11, 11 (44) 236
  – IX 1, 26 (50) 236
  – Bacchus (61) 166
  – Baker (59) 389
  – Caecilius Iucundus (67) 385, 386
  – Ceii (35) 166
  – Centenary (49) 80n314, 235
  – Chaste Lovers (52) 90, 140n
  – Cither Player (38) 386
  – Cornelius Tages (32) 83
  – Cryptoporticus (37) 83, 289
  – Docter 235n905
  – Ephebe → Cornelius Tages
  – Faun (66) 51, 52, 124, 126, 154, 155
  – Gilded Cupids (69) 158, 386
  – Holconius Rufus (39) 386
  – Loreius Tiburtinus 278n1074
  – Marcus Lucretius (55) 133
  – Marcus Lucretius Fronto (56) 269

Index of Names, Places, and Subjects — 483

- Meleager (73) 57, 153, 177
- the Menander (25) 203, 213, 271n1050
- Octavius Quartio 278n1074
- Pansa (14) 51, 57, 127, 239, 318fig13, 321
- Paquius Proculus (34) 213, 237, 282
- Regina Carolina (21) 57, 201n1117
- Restaurant (57) 80n314
- Sacerdos Amandus (33) 162, 202, 213
- Sallustius (12) 48n184–185, 50
- Sarnus Lararium (26) 166, 386
- Silver Wedding (68) 80
- Siricus (47) 77
- Skeletons (58) 78
- Small Bull 76fig3
- Surgeon (11) 28
- Tragic Poet (64) 51
- Vestals (10) 217, 291, 363n1345
- Vettii (72) 61, 80, 158, 159n605, 162, 172, 176, 203, 208, 211, 213, 244, 246, 282, 302, 386
- *Lupanar* (45) 134n508, 209, 280, 305, 420
- Macellum (43) 20, 57, 26
- Mercury Street 69
- Museum (17) 77, 88, 217, 314fig12, 320, 322
- Nocera Gate (27) 166
- Nolan Gate (53) 68, 69
- *Pagus Augustus Felix* 28
- Pantheon → Macellum
- Palaestra (28) 237
- Palaestra, Samnite 29, 248n960
- Porta Marina (16) 50, 77, 88
- *Praedia* of Julia Felix (31) 20n57, 26, 31n101, 50n189, 117, 186n690, 228n868, 319
- Sarno Baths (20) 166
- *Schola* of Mamia (6) 150, 154fig5, 308, 310n1181, 33n111
- Stabian Baths (48) 155, 213
- Suburban Baths 351n1319
- Temple of Apollo (15) 50, 66, 67, 85, 177, 381
- Temple of Genius Augusti (62) 67
- Temple of Isis (24) 29, 38, 47n177, 47n179, 51n193, 57n221, 58, 59n230, 65, 121, 126, 129n480, 130n484, 140, 141, 142, 143n548, 144, 195, 197, 209, 211, 218, 226, 244, 248n960, 262, 278, 285n1092, 294, 312n1187, 323, 361, 368, 377
- Temple of Jupiter (42) 50, 56n214, 66, 67, 187, 381, 404
- Temple of Venus (18) 50, 66, 381
- Theater/s (23) 8, 29, 55, 60, 65, 66, 67, 140, 153, 179, 218, 244, 294, 308, 381, 389
- Thermopolium IX 11, 2 (51) 235
- Tomb/s/Street of 28, 49, 55, 57, 122, 134, 180, 242, 264, 296n1146, 308, 310, 322, 363, 377, 419
- Tomb of Ampliatus (3) 48n185
- Tomb of Calventius Quietus 49n88
- Tomb of Cerrinius Restitutus (7) 154fig5, 185, 186n689
- Tomb of Naevoleia Tyche 314n1195
- Tomb of Umbricius Scaurus (4) 48n185, 49n188
- Vesuvian Gate (71) 69
- Villa of Cicero (5) 38n133, 47n179
- Villa of Diomedes (2) 43, 47n179, 57, 58n226, 77n307, 78n309, 122, 129, 130, 132, 140, 149, 153, 176, 180, 181n669, 183, 205, 221n847, 225, 226, 247, 295, 300, 313, 316n1203–1204, 363, 378
- Villa of Mysteries (1) 161, 177, 275–276, 277, 386, 389, 421

Pontine Marshes 145
Popidius Celsinus, Numerius 65, 143, 295, 312n1187
Poppaea Sabina (30–65) 8, 89, 209, 276, 277
Porcius, Marcus 29
Portici 2, 13n28, 17, 18, 20, 21, 22, 23, 24, 25, 30–33, 37n128, 39, 44, 48, 51, 63, 72n292, 73, 99, 101, 103, 104, 108, 109n399, 110–120, 127, 128, 130, 142, 147, 150, 180, 261, 291, 293, 333, 339, 361, 363n1349, 398, 399, 414, 419
Pothey, Alexandre 320–321
Pozzi Paolini, Enrica (†2010) 90
Pozzuoli 99
Praeneste 69
Praxiteles 386
Presuhn, Emil (1844–1881) 61
Priapus 34n117, 116, 117n432, 118n436, 140n534, 141, 280, 302, 325
Prosl, Robert Maria (1873–1957) 369
Proust, Marcel (1871–1922) 257n986, 276, 284–286

Publicola, Publius Valerius (†501 B.C.) 336n1262
Pucci, Giuseppe (*1948) 12, 289, 317
Pujol i Soley, Jordi (*1930) 377
Purcell, Henry (c. 1659–1695) 370n1373
Pushkin, Aleksandr (1799–1837) 221n847, 222n850
Pygmalion 206, 316, 317
Pyrodram 380, 381–382
Pythagoras (c. 572–500 B.C.) 210n802, 238, 338, 350
Quatremère de Quincy, Antoine-Chrysostome (1755–1849) 55n212
Queneau, Raymond (1903–1976) 239n923
Quinctius Valgus, Gaius 29
Raida, Carl Alexander 360n1335
Ramsey, Allan (1713–1784) 32
Ranieri, Antonio (1806–1888) 53n201
Raphael Sanzio (1483–1520) 114, 222
Ravello 137
Rebell, Hugues → Grassal
Rée, Paul (1849–1901) 137
Reece, Robert (1838–1891) 252n979, 375–376
Reed, Henry (1914–1986) 387–388, 390
Regensburg 145, 151n581
Reggiani, Renée 282–283
Reggio di Calabria 264
Regulus (consul A.D. 63) 8
Reimers, Timm 233
Reisel, Wanda (*1955) 54n203
Renan, Ernest (1823–1892) 260n1005
Renard, Jean-Augustin (1744–1807) 47n179
Resina 13, 14n40, 16n45, 17, 18, 20, 23n65, 25, 26, 32n106, 53n202, 54, 84, 92, 104, 109, 147, 153, 260, 293, 396, 409n1501
Rice, David (*1964) 278–279, 289
Richard, Jérôme Gabriel (1720–1795) 108, 111, 114n420
Richter, Jean Paul → Jean Paul
Riikonen, Hannu (*1945) 165, 233
Rimini 145
Robbe-Grillet, Alain (1922–2008) 268
Robert, Hubert (1733–1808) 47
Robert-Boissier, Béatrice 5, 221n847
Roberts, John Maddox (*1947) 174n639
Roblès, Emmanuel (1914–1995) 302n1157
Rocchi, Stefano 5

Rochester, John Wilmot (1647–1680) 247
Rodríguez, Cristina 195
Rodwell, George Herbert Bonaparte (1800–1852) 358fig16, 360n1334, 370
Rogers, Samuel (1763–1855) 298
Rogers, William Randolph (1825–1892) 231
Rohde, Erwin (1845–1898) 80n315
Roland de la Platière, Jean-Marie (1734–1793) 140
Romagnoli, Ettore (1871–1938) 271
Romanelli, Domenico (1756–1819) 291
Romanelli, Luigi (1751–1839) 362
Rome
– Caelius 192n718
– Capitol 245n949, 336n1264
– Cinecittà 386
– Colosseum 132, 249n962, 251–252, 386, 422
– Golden House 209n798
– Pantheon 58
– Pyramid Cestius 155, 261
– Servian Wall 69
– St Peter's 236
– Temple of Ceres 112
– Theater of Pompey 67
Room, Charles 406–407
Rose, M. 367
Rosén, Johan Magnus (1806–1885) 360n1335
Rosini, Carlo Maria (1748–1836) 9n11
Rosoni, Oscar (*1900) 249
Rossellini, Roberto (1906–1977) 387
Rossini, Gioacchino (1792–1868) 362, 363, 406
Rotterdam 288, 302
Rouland, Norbert 194, 209
Ruggiero, Michele (1875–1893) 20n54, 81, 82
Russel, James (c. 1720–1763) 109
Russell, Gordon 198–199, 212
Sacchetti, Roberto (1847–1881) 79n312, 101n376
Sacheverell, Henry (1674?–1724) 336
Sade, Donatien Alphonse François de (1740–1814) 28, 119–120, 277, 396, 397n1464
Saint-Non, Jean-Claude Richard de (1727–1791) 47–48, 51n192, 112n412, 116n430, 117, 180, 292

Saint-Simonistes 365
Salerno 99
Sallust Crispus, Gaius (86–34 B.C.) 171, 215n818, 338, 339
Sallustius 171
Salsa, Princess of 13n27
Sambuca, Giuseppe Beccadelli di Bologna, Marchese della (1726–1813) 51n192
Samnites 10, 194, 196n739
Sand, Georges (1804–1876) 279n1079
Sanders, George (1906–1972) 387
Sannazaro, Iacopo (1456–1530) 5, 53, 170–171, 344
Sansom, Joseph (1765/6–1826) 186n686
Santo-Domingo, Joseph Hippolyte (1785–1832) 184, 408n1459
Sappho (6th century B.C.) 334n1259, 403
Sardou, Victorien (1831–1908) 365–366
Sarno 25n74, 171, 201
Sartre, Jean-Paul (1905–1980) 160–161
Sass, Henri (1788–1844) 63
SATOR 237–239, 352n1323
Satyr/s/ism 31, 32n106, 34n117, 46n179, 51, 117, 119n438, 120, 186n690, 391n1442
Saul, Martin 210–211
Savarese, Nino (1882–1945) 159
Saviano, Roberto (*1979) 289
Saylor, Steven (*1956) 197
Scafati 11n18, 11n20, 12
Scaurus 191–192
Schefold, Karl (1905–1999) 87n340
Schikaneder, Emanuel (1751–1812) 361, 362
Schiller, Friedrich (1759–1805) 310n1181, 359
Schinkel, Karl Friedrich (1781–1841) 125n459
Schleuning, Peter (*1941) 365
Schliemann, Heinrich (1822–1890) 5, 80, 373
Schoedsack, Ernest B. (1893–1979) 383
Schöne, Richard (1840–1922) 87n341
Schopin, Frédéric Henri (1804–1880) 221n847
Schramm, Rudolph Karl (1837–1890) 188, 296
Schreder, Karl 369
Schuerewegen, Franc (*1959) 257
Schuré, Édouard (1841–1929) 73, 209–210, 325
Schwaiger, Ernst 368n1366
Scipio Maior, Publius Cornelius (253–183) 65n260

Scognamiglio, Pasquale 46n183
Scott, Ridley (*1937) 385n1432
Scott, Walter (1771–1832) 56n215, 124, 136, 165, 224, 225, 231, 307, 359
Sebeto river 170–171
Seed, Lancelot 185n684
Selinus 264
Seneca, Lucius Annaeus (c. 4 B.C.–A.D. 65) 8, 9, 65n260, 169, 170, 201, 202, 243, 249n964, 255, 344, 396
Sergejenko, Maria J. (*1892) 88n344
Settembrini, Luigi (1813–1876) 78
Seume, Johann Gottfried (1763–1810) 125–126
Seydl, Jon L. (*1969) 5
Sharp, Samuel (1700–1778) 97n359, 334
Shelley, Mary → Wollstonecraft, Mary
Shelley, Percy Bysshe (1792–1822) 71, 72, 182
Shoobridge, Leonard (1858–1935) 84
Sicily 10, 74, 145, 148, 149
Sickler, Friedrich C.L. (1773–1836) 342n1285
Siena 145
Sienkiewicz, Henryk Adam Aleksander Pius Oszyk (1846–1916) 215, 371n1381
Simond, Louis (1767–1831) 183
Simonides (c. 556–468 B.C.) 403
Siren/s 170, 285, 286, 324–325, 395
Sittius 249n966
Skeleton/s 2, 8n8, 22n61, 28, 29, 46, 47, 50, 62, 78, 132, 141, 162, 163, 178–189, 192, 195, 218, 222, 225, 247, 250, 256, 268, 285n1097, 286, 300, 321, 322, 323, 337, 388, 414, 419
Skene, James (1775–1864) 307
Skövde 250n967
Slave/s/ry 18n49, 29, 106, 120, 134, 172, 178, 191, 195, 197, 198, 199, 200, 201, 202, 203, 204, 206, 209, 210, 211, 212, 213, 225, 235, 236, 238, 239, 241, 242, 247, 251, 254, 255, 268, 300, 301, 315, 323, 326–327, 348, 350, 351n1320, 367, 374, 378, 379, 385, 416, 420, 423, 424
Slot, Pauline (*1960) 269
Slugocki, Leslek (*1924) 126
Smith, Alabama 389n1441
Smith, Michael 389n1441
Smith, William (1727–1803) 337
Smith-Masters, Anthony 387

Sodom 58, 74, 229, 245n948, 250, 255, 285, 286
Sogliano, Antonio (1854–1945) 4, 168n623, 211n808, 260, 316
Sojnikow, Alexander 360n1335
Solfatara 99, 389
Solimena, Francesco (1657–1747) 113
Sontag, Susan (1933–2004) 46n172, 277
Sophocles (497/6–406/5 B.C.) 310
Sorrento 10, 62n244, 129, 137, 161, 266n1028
Sousa, John Philip (1854–1932) 370
Spartacus (†71 B.C.) 263
Spence, Joseph (1699–1768) 105
Spengler, Oswald (1880–1936) 188
Spinazzola, Vittorio (1863–1943) 81, 83–84, 88, 93, 213
Spinelli, Domenico Maria Odoardo (1788–1863) 74n300, 75, 77n307
Staats Evers, Jan Willem (1828–1894) 299–300
Stabia/ae 1, 7, 10, 11n17, 11n19, 21n59, 25, 29, 32n105–106, 36, 56, 89, 90, 109, 113n415, 151, 162n615, 171, 196, 204, 241n934, 244, 282–283, 320, 386
Stamer, William John Alexander 308
Starke, Mariana (1762–1838) 31, 68, 128, 129, 130, 138, 142–143, 186, 292, 297
Statius, Publius Papinius (c. 40–96) 345
Stendardo, Giuseppe 14n37, 404n40, 17
Stendhal (1783–1842) 11n17, 186–188
Stephanus 202
Sterne, Laurence (1713–1768) 101n378
St. Malo 302, 303
Stockholm 250n967
Stolberg, Friedrich Leopold Graf zu (1750–1819) 64, 182n670
St. Petersburg 221, 223fig10
Strabo (c. 64 B.C.–A.D. 23) 14n40, 63n245, 201
Strasbourg 145
Striano, Enzo (1927–1987) 258n989
Strocka, Volker Michael (*1940) 90n348
Stromboli 8n9
Stuart, Charles Edward (1720–1788) 336
Successus 202
Suetonius Tranquillus, Gaius (c. 69–c. 122) 195n738, 199, 207n792, 347n1304, 349, 361n1336, 420

Sulla, Lucius Cornelius (138–78) 63, 65, 66, 69, 276n1064
Sullivan, James Frank (1853–1936) 376–377
Sunavill, J.F. → Sullivan, James Frank
Swan, Charles (†1838) 183
Swinburne, Algernon Charles (1837–1909) 258n990
Swinburne, Henry (1752–1803) 73, 114, 142
Sybaris 221
Syracuse 62
Tabula Peutineriana 9n12
Tacitus, Publius Cornelius (56–117) 7, 8, 70, 192n717, 199, 207n792, 215n818, 252, 345, 347n1304, 349
Taine, Hippolyte (1828–1893) 100, 133–134, 260n1005, 282
Tanucci, Bernardo (1698–1783) 19, 21, 23n65, 29, 30, 32n105, 34, 35, 36n125, 37, 38n135, 40n144, 44, 110n403 120n440, 142
Tarquinius Superbus (6th century B.C.) 336
Telemachus 190n705
Telephus 47n181, 153
Terence Afer, Publius (190–159) 139
Ternite, Wilhelm (1786–1871) 153
Tertullianus, Quintus Septimius Florens (c. 160–c. 220) 240
Theagenes 264n1020
Thédenat, Henri (1844–1916) 59, 60
Theocritus (3rd century B.C.) 64
Thorvaldsen, Bertel (1770–1844) 155
Thrale, Henry (1724/1730?–1781) 96n357
Thrale, Hester → Piozzi, Hester Lynch
Thusci 10
Tiberius, Emperor (42 B.C.–A.D. 37) 66n263, 195, 324, 347
Tieck, Ludwig (1773–1853) 152n581
Tischbein, Johann Heinrich Wilhelm (1751–1829) 149, 150
Titus, Emperor (39–81) 30n96, 70, 103n383, 204, 208, 209n797, 210, 211, 217, 255, 360, 361, 364n1354, 399
Tivoli, Hadrian's Villa 270
Torre Annunziata 8, 10, 10n20, 25
Torre del Greco 10, 11n20, 128n475, 296n1140
Torre, Nicholas Lee (*1795) 400
Tottola, Andrea Leone (†1831) 362–363